The Pathway to Glory

This is the story of Jesus of Nazareth, mankind's greatest benefactor, whose teaching and example is destined to free humanity from every form of evil when understood in its true light, and put into practice.

His story is told by combining the complete text of the four Gospels: Matthew, Mark, Luke and John in chronological order. Combining the Gospels in order allows events to be seen in their proper context and not as isolated incidents. The result is a clearer picture of what took place and a deeper insight into the wisdom and practical value of what Jesus taught and lived.

There are two versions of the combined Gospels. Both are arranged in identical chapters and sub-chapters to highlight the subject matter under discussion. The first version presents the four Gospels combined in chronological order without any notes. The second version is the identical except that notes have been added .

The Introduction explains more fully how the Gospels were organized and why the King James Version of 1611 was selected as the source. It is recommended that you read Appendixes 1 and 3 before reading the Gospels as they will make reading this book, and the entire Bible itself, better understood and more enjoyable.

The goal of this book is to enable the reader to experience the Light that Jesus brought for *all* mankind, the Light that enlightens every man, woman, and child "that cometh into the world," brighter than before.

"And thine ears shall hear a word behind thee, saying, This *is* the way, walk ye in it, when ye turn to the right hand, and when ye turn to the left." - Isaiah

The Pathway to Glory

presented in

The Combined Gospels

of

(Matthew, Mark, Luke, and John)

arranged in chronological order compiled from

The Authorized King James Version of the Bible

in two parts

Part I. The Gospels combined and arranged in chronological order *without* notes.

Part II. The Gospels combined and arranged in chronological order *with* notes.

Compiled by

William D. Saunders

First edition, first issue, September, 2020
Printed in the United States and other countries.

ISBN: 978-1-68007-076-7
First Trade paperback edition

Library of Congress Control Number: 2020915086

Website: www.ThePathwayToGlory.com

Email Address: info@thepathwaytoglory.com

My words fly up, my thoughts remain below:
Words without thoughts never to heaven go. - Shakespeare

How think ye?
When ye pray, use not vain repetitions, as the heathen do: *for they think that they shall be heard for their much speaking. Be not ye therefore like unto them: for your Father knoweth what things ye have need of, before ye ask him.*
But what think ye? - Christ Jesus

If we are not secretly yearning and openly striving for the accomplishment of all we ask, our prayers are "vain repetitions" such as the heathen use. If our petitions are sincere, we labor for what we ask; and our Father, who seeth in secret, will reward us openly. – Mary Baker Eddy

Jesus said, "I took my place in the midst of the world, and I appeared to them in flesh. I found all of them intoxicated; I found none of them thirsty. And my soul became afflicted for the sons of men, because they are blind in their hearts and do not have sight; for empty they came into the world, and empty too they seek to leave the world. But for the moment they are intoxicated. When they shake off their wine, then they will repent." – The Coptic Gospel of Thomas

Awake thou that sleepest, and arise from the dead, and Christ shall give thee light.
- St. Paul

These things have I spoken unto you, that in me ye might have peace. In the world ye shall have tribulation: but be of good cheer; I have overcome the world. – Christ Jesus

Behold, the LORD *hath proclaimed unto the end of the world, Say ye to the daughter of Zion, Behold, thy salvation cometh; behold, his reward* is *with him, and his work is before him.* - Isaiah

To understand God strengthens hope, enthrones faith in Truth, and verifies Jesus' word: "Lo, I am with you alway, even unto the end of the world." – Mary Baker Eddy

See Appendix 6 for the source of these quotations

LIST OF ABBREVIATIONS

'01	*Message to the Mother Church 1901* by Mary Baker Eddy
CGT	*The Coptic Gospel of Thomas*
Col	*The Epistle to the Colossians*
Eph	*The Epistle to the Ephesians*
Ex	*Exodus*
Gen	*Genesis*
GOE	*The Gospel of the Ebionites*
GON	*The Gospel of the Nazareans*
GOP	*The Gospel of Peter*
Hea	*Christian Healing* by Mary Baker Eddy
II Cor	*The Second Epistle to the Corinthians*
I Pet	*The First Epistle of Peter*
Isa	*Isaiah*
Jn	*The Gospel of John*
Lk	*The Gospel of Luke*
MBE	Mary Baker Eddy
Mk	*The Gospel of Mark*
Matt	*The Gospel of Matthew*
Mt	*The Gospel of Matthew*
Mis	*Miscellaneous Writings* by Mary Baker Eddy
NIS	*Number in Scripture* by Rev. E.W. Bullinger
Num	*Numbers*
OMOSN	*Original Meaning of Scriptural Names* by Lucy Bates
Ret	*Retrospection and Introspection* by Mary Baker Eddy
S&H	*Science and Health with Key to the Scriptures* by Mary Baker Eddy
TCB	*The Companion Bible*
Un	*Unity of Good* by Mary Baker Eddy
UNG	*Papyrus Egerton 2: The Unknown Gospel*

TABLE OF CONTENTS

PASSOVER NISAN 15TH, FRIDAY NISAN 16TH AND THE WEEKLY SABBATH NISAN 17TH

The lonely precincts of the tomb gave Jesus a refuge from his foes, a place in which to solve the great problem of being. His three days' work in the sepulchre set the seal of eternity on time. He proved Life to be deathless and Love to be the master of hate. He met and mastered on the basis of Christian Science, the power of Mind over matter, all the claims of medicine, surgery, and hygiene.

His disciples believed Jesus to be dead while he was hidden in the sepulchre, whereas he was alive, demonstrating within the narrow tomb the power of Spirit to overrule mortal, material sense. There were rock-ribbed walls in the way, and a great stone must be rolled from the cave's mouth; but Jesus vanquished every material obstacle, overcame every law of matter, and stepped forth from his gloomy resting-place, crowned with the glory of a sublime success, an everlasting victory.

Our Master fully and finally demonstrated divine Science in his victory over death and the grave. Jesus' deed was for the enlightenment of men and for the salvation of the whole world from sin, sickness, and death. Paul writes: "For if, when we were enemies, we were reconciled to God by the [seeming] death of His Son, much more, being reconciled, we shall be saved by his life." Three days after his bodily burial he talked with his disciples. The persecutors had failed to hide immortal Truth and Love in a sepulchre. – Mary Baker Eddy

PASSOVER – 15TH DAY OF NISAN THE GENTILE THURSDAY - A HIGH SABBATH

THE THIRD DAY AFTER PASSOVER – 18TH DAY OF NISAN THE GENTILE SUNDAY

THE DAYS PRECEDING THE ASCENSION

APPENDIXES

Introduction

How the Combined Gospels Came to be Compiled

The compiler was given his first Bible on his tenth birthday, and thus began the quest to understand its message. The Bible is more than a book. It is the Word of God, i.e. God speaking directly to humanity through many wonderful witnesses. The highpoint is the coming of Jesus Christ, the Son God told in four books of the New Testament called the Gospels. Because they differ from each other, sometimes greatly, it is difficult to formulate a complete picture reading them separately. In order to understand what transpired from beginning to end in chronological order, the compiler attempted to read all four simultaneously by going back and forth between them. He finally came to realize that the solution was to create a single written document. This required preparing the complete text of each Gospel in an editable form. Text was then extracted from each of these documents and placed in chronological order in a single document. This constituted the first draft. The combined text was then arranged in chapters to highlight major events. Several proof-readings and revisions were done to ensure that no text was left out, that there were no misspellings or omissions, and that the text was accurately referenced and presented in an easy to read format.

Why the King James Version of 1611

The reader may ask why the Authorized King James Version of 1611 was used, and not a more modern translation. First, the KJV is a very precise translation of the Gospels into English. Next, the revisers alert the reader to any words not in the original texts that were added. Finally, the KJV has more resources available for study than any other translation.

The translation of the King James Bible from the original languages was more a labor of love than a *commercial* endeavor. The goal of that remarkable group of scholars was to accurately translate the original texts into the best English of the time. Their dedication resulted in a book of remarkable accuracy.

The King James Version of 1611 is in Elizabethan English, the English of Shakespeare. Many love this classic style of writing and find it uplifting. Its lyrical form of communicating ideas lends verses and whole chapters to memorization. For these readers going back to its pages for inspiration, insight, and comfort is deeply satisfying. Others consider it strange and overly formal. They want something more aligned to present day English, something more familiar and *easier* to read. Caution: Let us not forget that we are seeking Truth.

Every discipline has developed a specialized vocabulary to facilitate accurate communication between teacher, learner, and among practitioners. To master any subject a student must become familiar with its specialized vocabulary. If a student neglects the vocabulary by using words with imprecise meaning the result will be confusion and greater difficulty in mastering the subject. Why imagine that the Bible is written with any less need for precision than textbooks on mathematics, chemistry, physics, art, or music? Students of the Bible who are unable to read Hebrew or Greek need to find an accurate rendition of the original texts in English. What many readers don't realize is how much the funny sounding pronouns in the KJV contribute to making it a clear and accurate translation. Appendix 1 discusses the meaning and value of these pronouns.

The Authorized King James Version of 1611 has numerous resources to aid its study. *Strong's Exhaustive Concordance to the Bible* enables the student to look up words in English and find the original Hebrew or Greek word and it's meaning as defined by theologians. You have free access to this resource at *www.Eliyah.com. The Interpreter's Bible* presents the KJV and *Revised Standard Version* of the Bible side by side and includes exegesis and exposition written by scholastic theologians. *The Companion Bible in the Authorized Version of 1611* is a valuable resource that gives the original Hebrew or Greek word and its best meaning in the verse being read. It also includes enlightening Appendixes that provide valuable background information. Books by the Reverend E.W. Bullinger are excellent sources of information for the serious Bible student. While there are many translations and resources available to aid one's study, "but one thing is needful,"[1] and that is an earnest and open-minded study of the Bible itself. This compilation is intended to aid the reader to that end.

Jesus the Master Teacher

Nicodemus acknowledged the divine origin of Jesus' teaching when he said: "we know that thou art a teacher (*Gr.* διδάσκαλος; *didaskalos*) come from God."[2] When Jesus appeared to Mary Magdalene after the resurrection she addressed him: "Rabboni; which is to say, Master." [3] The Greek word translated *Master* is *didaskalos*, the identical word used by Nicodemus translated *teacher*. Thus, Mary was addressing Jesus as the supreme, ultimate or Master teacher. This aligns with what Jesus declared, for he said: "I have not spoken of myself; but the Father which sent me, he gave me a commandment, what I should say, and what I should speak." [4] In other words, God told him *what* to teach and *how* to teach it.

A good teacher strives to meet the individual needs of students. To this end the teacher often repeats ideas, facts and explanations. The teacher may vary the words and illustrations to maintain interest so the quick learner doesn't get bored and the slow learner finally grasps the point being made. A good teacher works with students to overcome individual obstacles to learning. Most important, a good teacher has pupils put into practice what they are learning. Jesus did all of these things! So why should it be thought strange that Jesus varied his words to make a point? Why should it be thought strange that he reinforced a point being made by repeating it over and over again? Why question or doubt that the healing of the same disease or malady occurred more than once? Note how many times the scriptures inform us that what Jesus said was not understood! No wonder Jesus repeated what he said and did many times. Recall what John the Beloved Disciple wrote: "And there are also many other things which Jesus did, the which, if they should be written every one, I suppose the world itself could not contain the books that should be written." [5]

What this Compilation Includes

This compilation was completed without adding, deleting or changing a single word in the KJV texts. Italicized words have been left in italics. Appendix 3 discusses the significance of italicized words.

Two fonts are used to distinguish KJV Bible text from added material. Bible text and verse numbers that were added by the translators to facilitate referencing and are printed in a Roman font. Everything else is printed in Arial.

There are two combined Gospels. *The Combined Gospels* is 167 pages arranged in 179 chapters. Bible text is in 12-point Roman. Verse numbers are in 9-point Roman. Chapter number and title are in 9-point Arial. The heading: "According to the Gospel of . . ." that precedes any event included in two or more Gospels is in 9-point Arial. Book, chapter, and verse number are placed in parenthesis and printed in 8-point Arial.

The Combined Gospels with Notes is 200 pages in length with the same chapter designations as the version without notes. This makes it identical to *The Combined Gospels* except for the addition of notes. Notes are printed in 8-point Arial to distinguish them from the Bible text and make them easy to skip over by the reader. Notes serve various purposes: to date an event; to amplify the meaning of a word; to share a non-canonical scripture that reinforces or illuminates the canonical version; to provide spiritual insight; to present useful background information, etc. Appendix 6 is a list of quotations.

Appendix 5 is a list of "Check Point Events." The fact that some events are recorded in more than one Gospel is useful in combining the text in proper order because anything that precedes an event in one Gospel must necessarily precede that event in the other Gospels as well.

Whenever an event is presented in more than one Gospel each occurrence is introduced by the phrase "According to the Gospel of . . . ". While it may seem advantageous to use only one version of an event to avoid repetition, there are reasons for rejecting that approach. It is a known fact that several witnesses to an event may report it differently. This does not mean that witnesses are leaving out or distorting facts. One observer may see details overlooked by another. Seldom do witnesses use the same words when repeating what they heard another person say. For these reasons placing all versions of the same event together may provide a more complete picture of what happened or was said.

Appendix 8 is a Verse Locator prepared in four tables in the order: Matthew, Mark, Luke, and John. The Appendix was compiled so that anyone reading another translation can easily look up the King James Version and compare. The following will illustrate how to use Appendix 8. Assume you have just read John 1:14 in the *Revised English Bible*: "So the Word became flesh; he made his home among us, and we saw his glory, such glory as befits the Father's only Son, full of grace and truth." To compare this translation to the KJV open the Verse Locator for the Gospel of John. It begins on page 437. In the column headed "Chapter/Verse(s)" read down until you reach 1:14. Reading across you see it is located on page 177 in the chapter titled: *Mary Conceives Christ Jesus*. Opening *The Combined Gospels with Notes* to this page you read: And the Word was made flesh, and dwelt among us, (and we beheld his glory, the glory as of the only begotten of the Father,) full of grace and truth. (John 1:14)

Establishing Unity Among Christians

The life of Jesus was an unparalleled demonstration of overcoming all forms of limitation, even death, through universal and timeless spiritual laws.

Consequently, his words are not as "sounding brass, or a tinkling cymbal"[6] like those of so many professors, who "declare or admit in words or appearances only."[7] Jesus was a Master who proved his teaching practical by what are called miracles. These demonstrations are often denied as having ever happened, or ridiculed as exaggerations, because they are contrary to what mankind today considers possible. Jesus cautioned against such an attitude in his *first* beatitude: "Blessed *are* the poor in spirit: for theirs is the kingdom of heaven."[8] He did not say "the poor." He said "the poor in spirit!" Here the word "spirit" refers to an inclination to exercise self-will, a tendency toward the *conceit* and *arrogance* that often accompanies academic achievement, or the attainment of positions of authority in organizations or institutions. To be "poor in spirit" is to have renounced elitism, the feeling of being superior to others while harboring the inclination to rule over them.

Jesus established no organized religion. From the minute he proclaimed his mission in Nazareth at the age of thirty, until he was brutally murdered in Jerusalem a little over three years later, he was constantly harassed by the religious authorities of his time. And for what was he persecuted? Most often for healing on the Sabbath! Today that seems ridiculous. What hospital operated by either Jews or Christians would refuse to treat the sick or injured on the Sabbath [Saturday for the Jew or Sunday for a Christian] in this day and age? Not one!

We know that on two occasions Jesus warned his disciples NOT to establish a religious hierarchy. The second warning took place the evening of the "Last Supper" *AFTER* he had washed the feet of his disciples. Why? Because he found them *again* arguing about who should be the greatest. Jesus was soon to be crucified, and here they were quarreling over who would become the top dog when he was no longer with them. Do we think it was only among his followers that such thinking and behavior is possible, or is it an ugly characteristic of the human mind that tends to be manifested in all forms of organization?

Today there are thousands of Christian denominations. Unfortunately they tend to claim to be right and that the others are wrong. Many profess to love, and even to worship Jesus, while at the same time they condemn anyone who holds a different view from theirs. Frankly, most of these doctrinal differences have nothing to do with LIVING what Jesus taught. It is recorded that when there were doctrinal disagreements, John the Beloved Disciple would stand up saying, "Little children, love one another." Apparently, this priceless advice from the one disciple found worthy to receive the Revelation has been thrown to the winds.

The fact is everyone must eventually come to realize that the most relevant and practical understanding of what Jesus taught comes not from men, but from listening to the "still small voice."[9] The reason for reading the Bible and pondering the words and deeds of Jesus in the context in which they occurred is to help us make that connection. What Jesus expected is that we would then put into practice what has unfolded to us. Contradictory human opinions are worse than useless. So, why not trust the all-loving God to unfold the Truth directly to you?

Perhaps the time has come for mankind to consider what Jesus taught and demonstrated in a broader context. Organized religion and politics were no friend to Jesus. Two days before he was executed for the purpose of silencing forever his message to mankind, he spoke these words: "Heaven and earth shall pass away, but my words shall not pass away."[10] They have not, and they never will, even if they cease to exist in printed form. Whatever theologians may say, the real reason for the brutal crucifixion of Jesus was envy. Jesus' success in reaching the people through healing and teaching was seen as a threat by the established religious and political authorities. The last straw for the ecclesiastics was when Jesus restored Lazarus to life. The Gospel of John records: "from that day forth they took counsel together for to put him to death."[11] Just days later, when the people cheered his entry into Jerusalem the ecclesiastics "said among themselves, Perceive ye how ye prevail nothing? behold, the world is gone after him."[12] The night of the sham trial Jesus was sent from Pilate (the Roman Governor) to Herod Antipas (tetrarch of Galilee appointed by Caesar) and back to Pilate. "The same day Pilate and Herod were made friends together: for before they were at enmity between themselves."[13] Roman soldiers crucified Jesus because the ecclesiastics blackmailed Pilate to do their dirty work. How else can the following words be understood: "And from thenceforth Pilate sought to release him: but the Jews cried out, saying, If thou let this man go, thou art not Caesar's friend: whosoever maketh himself a king speaketh against Caesar."[14]

In the Bible this relatively small but powerful group of envious, greedy, self-seeking, deceptive, dishonest, hateful, and cruel men is referred to as "the Jews." It is only in reference to this specific group of men that plotted for and insisted upon the crucifixion of Jesus that the term "Jews" is used in the Gospels. Even within the Sanhedrin there were honorable Jewish men, such as Joseph of Arimathæa and Nicodemus, who were opposed to the execution of Jesus. Among the common folk there was no animosity toward Jesus. The common people were manipulated by the ecclesiastical and political elites to demand that Pilate crucify Jesus. Yet despite the persecution, torture, and crucifixion Jesus prevailed. His refusal to hate his betrayer and those that persecuted him has implications for all mankind far beyond any merely religious considerations.

It has been nearly one hundred and fifty years since the following words were written: "Jesus of Nazareth was the most scientific man that ever trod the globe. He plunged beneath the material surface and found the spiritual cause."[15] "Jesus of Nazareth was a natural and divine Scientist. He was so before the material world saw him."[16] The author of those words was an amazing healer and follower of Jesus' because she understood and put into practice what he taught.

Perhaps we are not asking the right questions and therefore are not finding the answers that would lift humanity far above and beyond the claims of mortality. One question to consider is: how can science and religion work together instead of remaining in isolated compartments of human experience where they operate from such apparently irreconcilable standpoints?

Religion, when dealing with inexplicable phenomena resorts to tradition sometimes, coupled with fear, to perpetuate a doctrine. The doctrine itself may have been formulated in the past by a respected individual, or developed by a committee and then ratified by vote. From that point forward it became a matter of orthodox belief and any doubting or questioning was viewed as infidelity. For that reason, many today refuse to consider any form of religious affiliation simply because this dogmatic and manipulative approach stifles free thought and honest investigation. To gain advancing insights into *any* subject requires an open and inquisitive mind. Unfortunately, organized religion often does not promote such an attitude toward those with a different point of view. It is unfortunate how narrow minded and self-righteous are some, claiming to be Christians, toward those of other denominations, or no denomination at all, who see things in a different light.

What is called science can be equally dogmatic. How can that be? Science begins its quest for answers under the assumption that only evidence obtained through the physical senses is worthy of consideration. In short, it limits its investigation to matter. What would happen if our scientists did as Jesus of Nazareth and began to plunge beneath the material surface of things to find the spiritual cause? In other words, what if scientists would open thought to a "fourth dimension of Spirit,"[17] while at the same time, religionists accepted the idea that there are logical answers to unexplained phenomena, and teach that *understanding* and *doing* as Jesus taught, not merely believing in him, is the way to find reasonable and practical approaches in both religion and science?

"If God, the All-in-all, be the creator of the universe, including man, then everything entitled to a classification as truth or Science, must be comprised in a knowledge or understanding of God, for there can be nothing beyond illimitable divinity."[18] This understanding brings science and religion together. Can you see how such an approach, by breaking down the walls of prejudice, bigotry, conceit, and rivalry would open the door to amazing advances in healthcare, personal freedom, and solutions to complex social issues such as poverty, crime, hatred, addiction, racism, etc., thereby creating a much brighter future for all mankind?

May the reading of this unified presentation of the four Gospels open to you, and through you, greater possibilities for everyone here on earth, bless you as it has me, and may "we all come in the unity of the faith, and of the knowledge of the Son of God, unto a perfect man, unto the measure of the stature of the fulness of Christ."[19]

God Bless us one and all,

William D. Saunders
July 4, 2020

[1]Lk. 10:42. [2]Jn. 3:2.3Jn. 20:16. [4]Jn. 13:1. [5]Jn. 21:25. [6]I Cor. 13:1. [7]Webster. [8]Matt. 5:3. [9]I Ki. 19:12. [10]Matt. 24:35; Mk. 13:31 & Lk. 21:33. [11]Jn. 11:53. [12]Jn. 12:19. [13]Lk. 23:12. [14]Jn. 19:12. [15]S&H. 313:23-26. [16]Ret. 26:17-18. [17]Mis. 22:12. [18]S&H 127:4-8. [19]Eph. 4:13.

Part I

THE COMBINED GOSPELS

of

(Matthew, Mark, Luke, and John)

compiled from

The King James Bible of 1611

and

arranged in chronological order

without notes

THE COMBINED GOSPELS
(MATTHEW, MARK, LUKE AND JOHN)
COMPILED FROM
THE AUTHORIZED KING JAMES VERSION OF THE BIBLE
IN
CHRONOLOGICAL ORDER

1 - THE ETERNAL ORDER OF BEING

1 In the beginning was the Word, and the Word was with God, and the Word was God.
2 The same was in the beginning with God.
3 All things were made by him; and without him was not any thing made that was
made.
4 In him was life; and the life was the light of men.
5 And the light shineth in darkness; and the darkness comprehended it not. (John 1:1-5)

2 – THE PURPOSE OF THE GOSPELS

1 Forasmuch as many have taken in hand to set forth in order a declaration of those
things which are most surely believed among us,
2 Even as they delivered them unto us, which from the beginning were eyewitnesses,
and ministers of the word;
3 It seemed good to me also, having had perfect understanding of all things from the
very first, to write unto thee in order, most excellent Theophilus,
4 That thou mightest know the certainty of those things, wherein thou hast been
instructed. (Luke 1:1-4)

3 - THE MISSION OF JOHN THE BAPTIST

6 ¶ There was a man sent from God, whose name *was* John.
7 The same came for a witness, to bear witness of the Light, that all *men* through him
might believe.
8 He was not that Light, but *was sent* to bear witness of that Light.
9 *That* was the true Light, which lighteth every man that cometh into the world.
10 He was in the world, and the world was made by him, and the world knew him not.
11 He came unto his own, and his own received him not.
12 But as many as received him, to them gave he power to become the sons of God,
even to them that believe on his name:
13 Which were born, not of blood, nor of the will of the flesh, nor of the will of man,
but of God. (John 1:6-13)

4 - ELISABETH CONCEIVES JOHN THE BAPTIST

5 ¶ There was in the days of Herod, the king of Judæa, a certain priest named
Zacharias, of the course of Abia: and his wife *was* of the daughters of Aaron, and her
name *was* Elisabeth.
6 And they were both righteous before God, walking in all the commandments and
ordinances of the Lord blameless.
7 And they had no child, because that Elisabeth was barren, and they both were *now*
well stricken in years.
8 And it came to pass, that while he executed the priest's office before God in the order
of his course,
9 According to the custom of the priest's office, his lot was to burn incense when he
went into the temple of the Lord.
10 And the whole multitude of the people were praying without at the time of incense.
11 And there appeared unto him an angel of the Lord standing on the right side of the
altar of incense.
12 And when Zacharias saw *him*, he was troubled, and fear fell upon him.
13 But the angel said unto him, Fear not, Zacharias: for thy prayer is heard; and thy
wife Elisabeth shall bear thee a son, and thou shalt call his name John.
14 And thou shalt have joy and gladness; and many shall rejoice at his birth.
15 For he shall be great in the sight of the Lord, and shall drink neither wine nor strong
drink; and he shall be filled with the Holy Ghost, even from his mother's womb.
16 And many of the children of Israel shall he turn to the Lord their God.
17 And he shall go before him in the spirit and power of Elias, to turn the hearts of the
fathers to the children, and the disobedient to the wisdom of the just; to make ready a
people prepared for the Lord.
18 And Zacharias said unto the angel, Whereby shall I know this? for I am an old man,
and my wife well stricken in years.
19 And the angel answering said unto him, I am Gabriel, that stand in the presence of
God; and am sent to speak unto thee, and to shew thee these glad tidings.
20 And, behold, thou shalt be dumb, and not able to speak, until the day that these
things shall be performed, because thou believest not my words, which shall be fulfilled
in their season.
21 And the people waited for Zacharias, and marvelled that he tarried so long in the
temple.
22 And when he came out, he could not speak unto them: and they perceived that he
had seen a vision in the temple: for he beckoned unto them, and remained speechless.
23 And it came to pass, that, as soon as the days of his ministration were accomplished,
he departed to his own house.
24 And after those days his wife Elisabeth conceived, and hid herself five months,
saying,
25 Thus hath the Lord dealt with me in the days wherein he looked on *me*, to take away
my reproach among men. (Luke 1:5-25)

5 - MARY CONCEIVES CHRIST JESUS

26 And in the sixth month the angel Gabriel was sent from God unto a city of Galilee,
named Nazareth,
27 To a virgin espoused to a man whose name was Joseph, of the house of David; and

the virgin's name *was* Mary.
28 And the angel came in unto her, and said, Hail, *thou that art* highly favoured, the
Lord *is* with thee: blessed *art* thou among women.
29 And when she saw *him*, she was troubled at his saying, and cast in her mind what
manner of salutation this should be.
30 And the angel said unto her, Fear not, Mary: for thou hast found favour with God.
31 And, behold, thou shalt conceive in thy womb, and bring forth a son, and shalt call
his name JESUS.
32 He shall be great, and shall be called the Son of the Highest: and the Lord God shall
give unto him the throne of his father David:
33 And he shall reign over the house of Jacob for ever; and of his kingdom there shall
be no end.
34 Then said Mary unto the angel, How shall this be, seeing I know not a man?
35 And the angel answered and said unto her, The Holy Ghost shall come upon thee,
and the power of the Highest shall overshadow thee: therefore also that holy thing
which shall be born of thee shall be called the Son of God.
36 And, behold, thy cousin Elisabeth, she hath also conceived a son in her old age: and
this is the sixth month with her, who was called barren.
37 For with God nothing shall be impossible.
38 And Mary said, Behold the handmaid of the Lord; be it unto me according to thy
word. And the angel departed from her. (Luke 1:26-38)
14 And the Word was made flesh, and dwelt among us, (and we beheld his glory, the
glory as of the only begotten of the Father,) full of grace and truth. (John 1:14)

6 - THE LEGAL & ROYAL GENEALOGY OF JESUS

1 The book of the generation of Jesus Christ, the son of David, the son of Abraham.
2 Abraham begat Isaac; and Isaac begat Jacob; and Jacob begat Judas and his brethren;
3 And Judas begat Phares and Zara of Thamar; and Phares begat Esrom; and Esrom
begat Aram;
4 And Aram begat Aminadab; and Aminadab begat Naasson; and Naasson begat
Salmon;
5 And Salmon begat Booz of Rachab; and Booz begat Obed of Ruth; and Obed begat
Jesse;
6 And Jesse begat David the king; and David the king begat Solomon of her *that had
been the wife* of Urias;
7 And Solomon begat Roboam; and Roboam begat Abia; and Abia begat Asa;
8 And Asa begat Josaphat; and Josaphat begat Joram; and Joram begat Ozias;
9 And Ozias begat Joatham; and Joatham begat Achaz; and Achaz begat Ezekias;
10 And Ezekias begat Manasses; and Manasses begat Amon; and Amon begat Josias;
11 And Josias begat Jechonias and his brethren, about the time they were carried away
to Babylon:
12 And after they were brought to Babylon, Jechonias begat Salathiel; and Salathiel
begat Zorobabel;
13 And Zorobabel begat Abiud; and Abiud begat Eliakim; and Eliakim begat Azor;
14 And Azor begat Sadoc; and Sadoc begat Achim; and Achim begat Eliud;
15 And Eliud begat Eleazar; and Eleazar begat Matthan; and Matthan begat Jacob;

16 And Jacob begat Joseph the husband of Mary, of whom was born Jesus, who is
called Christ.
17 So all the generations from Abraham to David *are* fourteen generations; and from
David until the carrying away into Babylon *are* fourteen generations; and from the
carrying away into Babylon unto Christ *are* fourteen generations. (Matt. 1:1-17)

7 - MARY VISITS ELISABETH

39 And Mary arose in those days, and went into the hill country with haste, into a city
of Juda;
40 And entered into the house of Zacharias, and saluted Elisabeth.
41 And it came to pass, that, when Elisabeth heard the salutation of Mary, the babe
leaped in her womb; and Elisabeth was filled with the Holy Ghost:
42 And she spake out with a loud voice, and said, Blessed *art* thou among women, and
blessed *is* the fruit of thy womb.
43 And whence *is* this to me, that the mother of my Lord should come to me?
44 For, lo, as soon as the voice of thy salutation sounded in mine ears, the babe leaped
in my womb for joy.
45 And blessed *is* she that believed: for there shall be a performance of those things
which were told her from the Lord.
46 And Mary said, My soul doth magnify the Lord,
47 And my spirit hath rejoiced in God my Saviour.
48 For he hath regarded the low estate of his handmaiden: for, behold, from henceforth
all generations shall call me blessed.
49 For he that is mighty hath done to me great things; and holy *is* his name.
50 And his mercy *is* on them that fear him from generation to generation.
51 He hath shewed strength with his arm; he hath scattered the proud in the imagination
of their hearts.
52 He hath put down the mighty from *their* seats, and exalted them of low degree.
53 He hath filled the hungry with good things; and the rich he hath sent empty away.
54 He hath holpen his servant Israel, in remembrance of *his* mercy;
55 As he spake to our fathers, to Abraham, and to his seed for ever.
56 And Mary abode with her about three months, and returned to her own house. (Luke
1:39-56)

8 - THE BIRTH AND PROPHECY OF JOHN THE BAPTIST

57 Now Elisabeth's full time came that she should be delivered; and she brought forth a
son.
58 And her neighbours and her cousins heard how the Lord had shewed great mercy
upon her; and they rejoiced with her.
59 And it came to pass, that on the eighth day they came to circumcise the child; and
they called him Zacharias, after the name of his father.
60 And his mother answered and said, Not *so*; but he shall be called John.
61 And they said unto her, There is none of thy kindred that is called by this name.
62 And they made signs to his father, how he would have him called.
63 And he asked for a writing table, and wrote, saying, His name is John. And they
marvelled all.
64 And his mouth was opened immediately, and his tongue *loosed*, and he spake, and
praised God.

65 And fear came on all that dwelt round about them: and all these sayings were noised
abroad throughout all the hill country of Judæa.
66 And all they that heard *them* laid *them* up in their hearts, saying, What manner of
child shall this be! And the hand of the Lord was with him.
67 And his father Zacharias was filled with the Holy Ghost, and prophesied, saying,
68 Blessed *be* the Lord God of Israel; for he hath visited and redeemed his people,
69 And hath raised up an horn of salvation for us in the house of his servant David;
70 As he spake by the mouth of his holy prophets, which have been since the world
began:
71 That we should be saved from our enemies, and from the hand of all that hate us;
72 To perform the mercy *promised* to our fathers, and to remember his holy covenant;
73 The oath which he sware to our father Abraham,
74 That he would grant unto us, that we being delivered out of the hand of our enemies
might serve him without fear,
75 In holiness and righteousness before him, all the days of our life.
76 And thou, child, shalt be called the prophet of the Highest: for thou shalt go before
the face of the Lord to prepare his ways;
77 To give knowledge of salvation unto his people by the remission of their sins,
78 Through the tender mercy of our God; whereby the dayspring from on high hath
visited us,
79 To give light to them that sit in darkness and *in* the shadow of death, to guide our
feet into the way of peace.
80 And the child grew, and waxed strong in spirit, and was in the deserts till the day of
his shewing unto Israel. (Luke 1:57-80)

9 – THE IMMACULATE CONCEPTION REVEALED TO JOSEPH

18 ¶ Now the birth of Jesus Christ was on this wise: When as his mother Mary was
espoused to Joseph, before they came together, she was found with child of the Holy
Ghost.
19 Then Joseph her husband, being a just *man*, and not willing to make her a public
example, was minded to put her away privily.
20 But while he thought on these things, behold, the angel of the Lord appeared unto
him in a dream, saying, Joseph, thou son of David, fear not to take unto thee Mary thy
wife: for that which is conceived in her is of the Holy Ghost.
21 And she shall bring forth a son, and thou shalt call his name JESUS: for he shall
save his people from their sins.
22 Now all this was done, that it might be fulfilled which was spoken of the Lord by the
prophet, saying,
23 Behold, a virgin shall be with child, and shall bring forth a son, and they shall call
his name Emmanuel, which being interpreted is, God with us.
24 Then Joseph being raised from sleep did as the angel of the Lord had bidden him,
and took unto him his wife:
25 And knew her not till she had brought forth her firstborn son: and he called his name
JESUS. (Matt.1:18-25)

10- BETHLEHEM AND THE BIRTH OF JESUS

1 And it came to pass in those days, that there went out a decree from Cæsar Augustus,

that all the world should be taxed.
2 (*And* this taxing was first made when Cyrenius was governor of Syria.)
3 And all went to be taxed, every one into his own city.
4 And Joseph also went up from Galilee, out of the city of Nazareth, into Judæa, unto
the city of David, which is called Bethlehem; (because he was of the house and lineage
of David:)
5 To be taxed with Mary his espoused wife, being great with child.
6 And so it was, that, while they were there, the days were accomplished that she
should be delivered.
7 And she brought forth her firstborn son, and wrapped him in swaddling clothes, and
laid him in a manger; because there was no room for them in the inn.
8 And there were in the same country shepherds abiding in the field, keeping watch
over their flock by night.
9 And, lo, the angel of the Lord came upon them, and the glory of the Lord shone
round about them: and they were sore afraid.
10 And the angel said unto them, Fear not: for, behold, I bring you good tidings of great
joy, which shall be to all people.
11 For unto you is born this day in the city of David a Saviour, which is Christ the
Lord.
12 And this *shall be* a sign unto you; Ye shall find the babe wrapped in swaddling
clothes, lying in a manger.
13 And suddenly there was with the angel a multitude of the heavenly host praising
God, and saying,
14 Glory to God in the highest, and on earth peace, good will toward men.
15 And it came to pass, as the angels were gone away from them into heaven, the
shepherds said one to another, Let us now go even unto Bethlehem, and see this thing
which is come to pass, which the Lord hath made known unto us.
16 And they came with haste, and found Mary, and Joseph, and the babe lying in a
manger.
17 And when they had seen *it*, they made known abroad the saying which was told
them concerning this child.
18 And all they that heard *it* wondered at those things which were told them by the
shepherds.
19 But Mary kept all these things, and pondered *them* in her heart.
20 And the shepherds returned, glorifying and praising God for all the things that they
had heard and seen, as it was told unto them. (Luke 2:1-20)

11 - SIMEON AND ANNA TESTIFY CONCERNING JESUS

21 And when eight days were accomplished for the circumcising of the child, his name
was called JESUS, which was so named of the angel before he was conceived in the
womb.
22 And when the days of her purification according to the law of Moses were
accomplished, they brought him to Jerusalem, to present *him* to the Lord;
23 (As it is written in the law of the Lord, Every male that openeth the womb shall be
called holy to the Lord;)
24 And to offer a sacrifice according to that which is said in the law of the Lord, A pair
of turtledoves, or two young pigeons.

25 And, behold, there was a man in Jerusalem, whose name *was* Simeon; and the same
man *was* just and devout, waiting for the consolation of Israel: and the Holy Ghost was
upon him.
26 And it was revealed unto him by the Holy Ghost, that he should not see death,
before he had seen the Lord's Christ.
27 And he came by the Spirit into the temple: and when the parents brought in the child
Jesus, to do for him after the custom of the law,
28 Then took he him up in his arms, and blessed God, and said,
29 Lord, now lettest thou thy servant depart in peace, according to thy word:
30 For mine eyes have seen thy salvation,
31 Which thou hast prepared before the face of all people;
32 A light to lighten the Gentiles, and the glory of thy people Israel.
33 And Joseph and his mother marvelled at those things which were spoken of him.
34 And Simeon blessed them, and said unto Mary his mother, Behold, this *child* is set
for the fall and rising again of many in Israel; and for a sign which shall be spoken
against;
35 (Yea, a sword shall pierce through thy own soul also,) that the thoughts of many
hearts may be revealed.
36 And there was one Anna, a prophetess, the daughter of Phanuel, of the tribe of Aser:
she was of a great age, and had lived with an husband seven years from her virginity;
37 And she *was* a widow of about fourscore and four years, which departed not from
the temple, but served *God* with fastings and prayers night and day.
38 And she coming in that instant gave thanks likewise unto the Lord, and spake of him
to all them that looked for redemption in Jerusalem.
39 And when they had performed all things according to the law of the Lord, they
returned into Galilee, to their own city Nazareth. (Luke 2:21-39)

12 - THE EARLY YEARS

1 Now when Jesus was born in Bethlehem of Judæa in the days of Herod the king,
behold, there came wise men from the east to Jerusalem,
2 Saying, Where is he that is born King of the Jews? for we have seen his star in the
east, and are come to worship him.
3 When Herod the king had heard *these things*, he was troubled, and all Jerusalem with
him.
4 And when he had gathered all the chief priests and scribes of the people together, he
demanded of them where Christ should be born.
5 And they said unto him, In Bethlehem of Judæa: for thus it is written by the prophet,
6 And thou Bethlehem, *in* the land of Juda, art not the least among the princes of Juda:
for out of thee shall come a Governor, that shall rule my people Israel.
7 Then Herod, when he had privily called the wise men, inquired of them diligently
what time the star appeared.
8 And he sent them to Bethlehem, and said, Go and search diligently for the young
child; and when ye have found *him*, bring me word again, that I may come and worship
him also.
9 When they had heard the king, they departed; and, lo, the star, which they saw in the
east, went before them, till it came and stood over where the young child was.
10 When they saw the star, they rejoiced with exceeding great joy.

11 ¶ And when they were come into the house, they saw the young child with Mary his
mother, and fell down, and worshipped him: and when they had opened their treasures,
they presented unto him gifts; gold, and frankincense, and myrrh.
12 And being warned of God in a dream that they should not return to Herod, they
departed into their own country another way.
13 And when they were departed, behold, the angel of the Lord appeareth to Joseph in a
dream, saying, Arise, and take the young child and his mother, and flee into Egypt, and
be thou there until I bring thee word: for Herod will seek the young child to destroy
him.
14 When he arose, he took the young child and his mother by night, and departed into
Egypt:
15 And was there until the death of Herod: that it might be fulfilled which was spoken
of the Lord by the prophet, saying, Out of Egypt have I called my son.
16 ¶ Then Herod, when he saw that he was mocked of the wise men, was exceeding
wroth, and sent forth, and slew all the children that were in Bethlehem, and in all the
coasts thereof, from two years old and under, according to the time which he had
diligently inquired of the wise men.
17 Then was fulfilled that which was spoken by Jeremy the prophet, saying,
18 In Rama was there a voice heard, lamentation, and weeping, and great mourning,
Rachel weeping *for* her children, and would not be comforted, because they are not.
19 ¶ But when Herod was dead, behold, an angel of the Lord appeareth in a dream to
Joseph in Egypt,
20 Saying, Arise, and take the young child and his mother, and go into the land of
Israel: for they are dead which sought the young child's life.
21 And he arose, and took the young child and his mother, and came into the land of
Israel.
22 But when he heard that Archelaus did reign in Judæa in the room of his father
Herod, he was afraid to go thither: notwithstanding, being warned of God in a dream,
he turned aside into the parts of Galilee:
23 And he came and dwelt in a city called Nazareth: that it might be fulfilled which was
spoken by the prophets, He shall be called a Nazarene. (Matt. 2:1-23)
40 And the child grew, and waxed strong in spirit, filled with wisdom: and the grace of
God was upon him. (Luke 2:40)

13 - JESUS VISITS JERUSALEM AT THE AGE OF TWELVE

41 Now his parents went to Jerusalem every year at the feast of the passover.
42 And when he was twelve years old, they went up to Jerusalem after the custom of
the feast.
43 And when they had fulfilled the days, as they returned, the child Jesus tarried behind
in Jerusalem; and Joseph and his mother knew not *of it*.
44 But they, supposing him to have been in the company, went a day's journey; and
they sought him among *their* kinsfolk and acquaintance.
45 And when they found him not, they turned back again to Jerusalem, seeking him.
46 And it came to pass, that after three days they found him in the temple, sitting in the
midst of the doctors, both hearing them, and asking them questions.
47 And all that heard him were astonished at his understanding and answers.
48 And when they saw him, they were amazed: and his mother said unto him, Son, why

hast thou thus dealt with us? behold, thy father and I have sought thee sorrowing.
49 And he said unto them, How is it that ye sought me? wist ye not that I must be about
my Father's business?
50 And they understood not the saying which he spake unto them.
51 And he went down with them, and came to Nazareth, and was subject unto them: but
his mother kept all these sayings in her heart.
52 And Jesus increased in wisdom and stature, and in favour with God and man. (Luke
2:41-52)

14 - JOHN THE BAPTIST PREPARING THE WAY

According to the Gospel of Mark

1 The beginning of the gospel of Jesus Christ, the Son of God;
2 As it is written in the prophets, Behold, I send my messenger before thy face, which
shall prepare thy way before thee.
3 The voice of one crying in the wilderness, Prepare ye the way of the Lord, make his
paths straight.
4 John did baptize in the wilderness, and preach the baptism of repentance for the
remission of sins.
5 And there went out unto him all the land of Judæa, and they of Jerusalem, and were
all baptized of him in the river of Jordan, confessing their sins.
6 And John was clothed with camel's hair, and with a girdle of a skin about his loins;
and he did eat locusts and wild honey;
7 And preached, saying, There cometh one mightier than I after me, the latchet of
whose shoes I am not worthy to stoop down and unloose.
8 I indeed have baptized you with water: but he shall baptize you with the Holy Ghost.
(Mark 1:1-8)

According to the Gospel of Matthew

1 In those days came John the Baptist, preaching in the wilderness of Judæa,
2 And saying, Repent ye: for the kingdom of heaven is at hand.
3 For this is he that was spoken of by the prophet Esaias, saying, The voice of one
crying in the wilderness, Prepare ye the way of the Lord, make his paths straight
4 And the same John had his raiment of camel's hair, and a leathern girdle about his
loins; and his meat was locusts and wild honey.
5 Then went out to him Jerusalem, and all Judæa, and all the region round about
Jordan,
6 And were baptized of him in Jordan, confessing their sins.
7 ¶ But when he saw many of the Pharisees and Sadducees come to his baptism, he said
unto them, O generation of vipers, who hath warned you to flee from the wrath to
come?
8 Bring forth therefore fruits meet for repentance:
9 And think not to say within yourselves, We have Abraham to *our* father: for I say
unto you, that God is able of these stones to raise up children unto Abraham.
10 And now also the axe is laid unto the root of the trees: therefore every tree which
bringeth not forth good fruit is hewn down, and cast into the fire.
11 I indeed baptize you with water unto repentance: but he that cometh after me is
mightier than I, whose shoes I am not worthy to bear: he shall baptize you with the
Holy Ghost, and *with* fire:

12 Whose fan *is* in his hand, and he will throughly purge his floor, and gather his wheat
into the garner; but he will burn up the chaff with unquenchable fire. (Matt 3:1-12)

According to the Gospel of Luke

1 Now in the fifteenth year of the reign of Tiberius Cæsar, Pontius Pilate being
governor of Judæa, and Herod being tetrarch of Galilee, and his brother Philip tetrarch
of Ituræa and of the region of Trachonitis, and Lysanias the tetrarch of Abilene,
2 Annas and Caiaphas being the high priests, the word of God came unto John the son
of Zacharias in the wilderness.
3 And he came into all the country about Jordan, preaching the baptism of repentance
for the remission of sins;
4 As it is written in the book of the words of Esaias the prophet, saying, The voice of
one crying in the wilderness, Prepare ye the way of the Lord, make his paths straight.
5 Every valley shall be filled, and every mountain and hill shall be brought low; and the
crooked shall be made straight, and the rough ways *shall be* made smooth;
6 And all flesh shall see the salvation of God.
7 Then said he to the multitude that came forth to be baptized of him, O generation of
vipers, who hath warned you to flee from the wrath to come?
8 Bring forth therefore fruits worthy of repentance, and begin not to say within
yourselves, We have Abraham to *our* father: for I say unto you, That God is able of
these stones to raise up children unto Abraham.
9 And now also the axe is laid unto the root of the trees: every tree therefore which
bringeth not forth good fruit is hewn down, and cast into the fire.
10 And the people asked him, saying, What shall we do then?
11 He answereth and saith unto them, He that hath two coats, let him impart to him that
hath none; and he that hath meat, let him do likewise.
12 Then came also publicans to be baptized, and said unto him, Master, what shall we
do?
13 And he said unto them, Exact no more than that which is appointed you.
14 And the soldiers likewise demanded of him, saying, And what shall we do? And he
said unto them, Do violence to no man, neither accuse *any* falsely; and be content with
your wages.
15 And as the people were in expectation, and all men mused in their hearts of John,
whether he were the Christ, or not;
16 John answered, saying unto *them* all, I indeed baptize you with water; but one
mightier than I cometh, the latchet of whose shoes I am not worthy to unloose: he shall
baptize you with the Holy Ghost and with fire:
17 Whose fan *is* in his hand, and he will throughly purge his floor, and will gather the
wheat into his garner; but the chaff he will burn with fire unquenchable.
18 And many other things in his exhortation preached he unto the people.
19 But Herod the tetrarch, being reproved by him for Herodias his brother Philip's wife,
and for all the evils which Herod had done,
20 Added yet this above all, that he shut up John in prison. (Luke 3:1-20)

15 - THE BAPTISM OF JESUS THE CHRIST

According to the Gospel of Matthew

13 ¶ Then cometh Jesus from Galilee to Jordan unto John, to be baptized of him.
14 But John forbad him, saying, I have need to be baptized of thee, and comest thou to

me?
15 And Jesus answering said unto him, Suffer *it to be so* now: for thus it becometh us
to fulfil all righteousness. Then he suffered him.
16 And Jesus, when he was baptized, went up straightway out of the water: and, lo, the
heavens were opened unto him, and he saw the Spirit of God descending like a dove,
and lighting upon him:
17 And lo a voice from heaven, saying, This is my beloved Son, in whom I am well
pleased. (Matt 3:13-17)

According to the Gospel of Mark

9 And it came to pass in those days, that Jesus came from Nazareth of Galilee, and was
baptized of John in Jordan.
10 And straightway coming up out of the water, he saw the heavens opened, and the
Spirit like a dove descending upon him:
11 And there came a voice from heaven, *saying*, Thou art my beloved Son, in whom I
am well pleased. (Mark 1:9-11)

According to the Gospel of John

15 ¶ John bare witness of him, and cried, saying, This was he of whom I spake, He that
cometh after me is preferred before me: for he was before me.
16 And of his fulness have all we received, and grace for grace.
17 For the law was given by Moses, *but* grace and truth came by Jesus Christ.
18 No man hath seen God at any time; the only begotten Son, which is in the bosom of
the Father, he hath declared *him*.
19 ¶ And this is the record of John, when the Jews sent priests and Levites from
Jerusalem to ask him, Who art thou?
20 And he confessed, and denied not; but confessed, I am not the Christ.
21 And they asked him, What then? Art thou Elias? And he saith, I am not. Art thou
that prophet? And he answered, No.
22 Then said they unto him, Who art thou? that we may give an answer to them that
sent us. What sayest thou of thyself?
23 He said, I *am* the voice of one crying in the wilderness, Make straight the way of the
Lord, as said the prophet Esaias.
24 And they which were sent were of the Pharisees.
25 And they asked him, and said unto him, Why baptizest thou then, if thou be not that
Christ, nor Elias, neither that prophet?
26 John answered them, saying, I baptize with water: but there standeth one among you,
whom ye know not;
27 He it is, who coming after me is preferred before me, whose shoe's latchet I am not
worthy to unloose.
28 These things were done in Bethabara beyond Jordan, where John was baptizing. (John
1:15-28)

According to the Gospel of Luke

21 Now when all the people were baptized, it came to pass, that Jesus also being
baptized, and praying, the heaven was opened,
22 And the Holy Ghost descended in a bodily shape like a dove upon him, and a voice
came from heaven, which said, Thou art my beloved Son; in thee I am well pleased.
(Luke 3:21-22)

16 - THE NATURAL GENEALOGY OF JESUS – THE SON OF MAN

23 And Jesus himself began to be about thirty years of age, being (as was supposed) the
son of Joseph, which was *the son* of Heli,
24 Which was *the son* of Matthat, which was *the son* of Levi, which was *the son* of
Melchi, which was *the son* of Janna, which was *the son* of Joseph,
25 Which was *the son* of Mattathias, which was *the son* of Amos, which was *the son* of
Naum, which was *the son* of Esli, which was *the son* of Nagge,
26 Which was *the son* of Maath, which was *the son* of Mattathias, which was *the son* of
Semei, which was *the son* of Joseph, which was *the son* of Juda,
27 Which was *the son* of Joanna, which was *the son* of Rhesa, which was *the son* of
Zorobabel, which was *the son* of Salathiel, which was *the son* of Neri,
28 Which was *the son* of Melchi, which was *the son* of Addi, which was *the son* of
Cosam, which was *the son* of Elmodam, which was *the son* of Er,
29 Which was *the son* of Jose, which was *the son* of Eliezer, which was *the son* of
Jorim, which was *the son* of Matthat, which was *the son* of Levi,
30 Which was *the son* of Simeon, which was *the son* of Juda, which was *the son* of
Joseph, which was *the son* of Jonan, which was *the son* of Eliakim,
31 Which was *the son* of Melea, which was *the son* of Menan, which was *the son* of
Mattatha, which was *the son* of Nathan, which was *the son* of David,
32 Which was *the son* of Jesse, which was *the son* of Obed, which was *the son* of Booz,
which was *the son* of Salmon, which was *the son* of Naasson,
33 Which was *the son* of Aminadab, which was *the son* of Aram, which was *the son* of
Esrom, which was *the son* of Phares, which was *the son* of Juda,
34 Which was *the son* of Jacob, which was *the son* of Isaac, which was *the son* of
Abraham, which was *the son* of Thara, which was *the son* of Nachor,
35 Which was *the son* of Saruch, which was *the son* of Ragau, which was *the son* of
Phalec, which was *the son* of Heber, which was *the son* of Sala,
36 Which was *the son* of Cainan, which was *the son* of Arphaxad, which was *the son* of
Sem, which was *the son* of Noe, which was *the son* of Lamech,
37 Which was *the son* of Mathusala, which was *the son* of Enoch, which was *the son* of
Jared, which was *the son* of Maleleel, which was *the son* of Cainan,
38 Which was *the son* of Enos, which was *the son* of Seth, which was *the son* of Adam,
which was *the son* of God. (Luke 3:23-38)

17 – JESUS AND HIS FIRST SIX DISCIPLES

29 ¶ The next day John seeth Jesus coming unto him, and saith, Behold the Lamb of
God, which taketh away the sin of the world.
30 This is he of whom I said, After me cometh a man which is preferred before me: for
he was before me.
31 And I knew him not: but that he should be made manifest to Israel, therefore am I
come baptizing with water.
32 And John bare record, saying, I saw the Spirit descending from heaven like a dove,
and it abode upon him.
33 And I knew him not: but he that sent me to baptize with water, the same said unto
me, Upon whom thou shalt see the Spirit descending, and remaining on him, the same
is he which baptizeth with the Holy Ghost.

34 And I saw, and bare record that this is the Son of God.
35 ¶ Again the next day after John stood, and two of his disciples;
36 And looking upon Jesus as he walked, he saith, Behold the Lamb of God!
37 And the two disciples heard him speak, and they followed Jesus.
38 Then Jesus turned, and saw them following, and saith unto them, What seek ye?
They said unto him, Rabbi, (which is to say, being interpreted, Master,) where dwellest
thou?
39 He saith unto them, Come and see. They came and saw where he dwelt, and abode
with him that day: for it was about the tenth hour.
40 One of the two which heard John *speak*, and followed him, was Andrew, Simon
Peter's brother.
41 He first findeth his own brother Simon, and saith unto him, We have found the
Messias, which is, being interpreted, the Christ.
42 And he brought him to Jesus.
42 And when Jesus beheld him, he said, Thou art Simon the son of Jona: thou shalt be
called Cephas, which is by interpretation, A stone.
43 ¶ The day following Jesus would go forth into Galilee, and findeth Philip, and saith
unto him, Follow me.
44 Now Philip was of Bethsaida, the city of Andrew and Peter.
45 Philip findeth Nathanael, and saith unto him, We have found him, of whom Moses
in the law, and the prophets, did write, Jesus of Nazareth, the son of Joseph.
46 And Nathanael said unto him, Can there any good thing come out of Nazareth?
Philip saith unto him, Come and see.
47 Jesus saw Nathanael coming to him, and saith of him, Behold an Israelite indeed, in
whom is no guile!
48 Nathanael saith unto him, Whence knowest thou me? Jesus answered and said unto
him, Before that Philip called thee, when thou wast under the fig tree, I saw thee.
49 Nathanael answered and saith unto him, Rabbi, thou art the Son of God; thou art the
King of Israel.
50 Jesus answered and said unto him, Because I said unto thee, I saw thee under the fig
tree, believest thou? thou shalt see greater things than these.
51 And he saith unto him, Verily, verily, I say unto you, Hereafter ye shall see heaven
open, and the angels of God ascending and descending upon the Son of man. (John 1:29-51)

18 - WATER INTO WINE

1 And the third day there was a marriage in Cana of Galilee; and the mother of Jesus
was there:
2 And both Jesus was called, and his disciples, to the marriage.
3 And when they wanted wine, the mother of Jesus saith unto him, They have no wine.
4 Jesus saith unto her, Woman, what have I to do with thee? mine hour is not yet come.
5 His mother saith unto the servants, Whatsoever he saith unto you, do *it*.
6 And there were set there six waterpots of stone, after the manner of the purifying of
the Jews, containing two or three firkins apiece.
7 Jesus saith unto them, Fill the waterpots with water. And they filled them up to the
brim.
8 And he saith unto them, Draw out now, and bear unto the governor of the feast. And
they bare *it*.

9 When the ruler of the feast had tasted the water that was made wine, and knew not
whence it was: (but the servants which drew the water knew;) the governor of the feast
called the bridegroom,
10 And saith unto him, Every man at the beginning doth set forth good wine; and when
men have well drunk, then that which is worse; *but* thou hast kept the good wine until
now.
11 This beginning of miracles did Jesus in Cana of Galilee, and manifested forth his
glory; and his disciples believed on him.
12 ¶ After this he went down to Capernaum, he, and his mother, and his brethren, and
his disciples: and they continued there not many days. (John 2:1-12)

19 - THE FIRST TEMPLE CLEANSING

13 ¶ And the Jews' passover was at hand, and Jesus went up to Jerusalem,
14 And found in the temple those that sold oxen and sheep and doves, and the changers
of money sitting:
15 And when he had made a scourge of small cords, he drove them all out of the
temple, and the sheep, and the oxen; and poured out the changers' money, and
overthrew the tables;
16 And said unto them that sold doves, Take these things hence; make not my Father's
house an house of merchandise.
17 And his disciples remembered that it was written, The zeal of thine house hath eaten
me up.
18 ¶ Then answered the Jews and said unto him, What sign shewest thou unto us,
seeing that thou doest these things?
19 Jesus answered and said unto them, Destroy this temple, and in three days I will
raise it up.
20 Then said the Jews, Forty and six years was this temple in building, and wilt thou
rear it up in three days?
21 But he spake of the temple of his body.
22 When therefore he was risen from the dead, his disciples remembered that he had
said this unto them; and they believed the scripture, and the word which Jesus had said.
23 ¶ Now when he was in Jerusalem at the passover, in the feast *day*, many believed in
his name, when they saw the miracles which he did.
24 But Jesus did not commit himself unto them, because he knew all *men*,
25 And needed not that any should testify of man: for he knew what was in man. (John
2:13-25)

20 - THE NEED FOR SPIRITUAL REBIRTH

1 There was a man of the Pharisees, named Nicodemus, a ruler of the Jews:
2 The same came to Jesus by night, and said unto him, Rabbi, we know that thou art a
teacher come from God: for no man can do these miracles that thou doest, except God
be with him.
3 Jesus answered and said unto him, Verily, verily, I say unto thee, Except a man be
born again, he cannot see the kingdom of God.
4 Nicodemus saith unto him, How can a man be born when he is old? can he enter the
second time into his mother's womb, and be born?
5 Jesus answered, Verily, verily, I say unto thee, Except a man be born of water and *of*

the Spirit, he cannot enter into the kingdom of God.
6 That which is born of the flesh is flesh; and that which is born of the Spirit is spirit.
7 Marvel not that I said unto thee, Ye must be born again.
8 The wind bloweth where it listeth, and thou hearest the sound thereof, but canst not
tell whence it cometh, and whither it goeth: so is every one that is born of the Spirit.
9 Nicodemus answered and said unto him, How can these things be?
10 Jesus answered and said unto him, Art thou a master of Israel, and knowest not these
things?
11 Verily, verily, I say unto thee, We speak that we do know, and testify that we have
seen; and ye receive not our witness.
12 If I have told you earthly things, and ye believe not, how shall ye believe, if I tell
you *of* heavenly things?
13 And no man hath ascended up to heaven, but he that came down from heaven, *even*
the Son of man which is in heaven.
14 ¶ And as Moses lifted up the serpent in the wilderness, even so must the Son of man
be lifted up:
15 That whosoever believeth in him should not perish, but have eternal life.
16 ¶ For God so loved the world, that he gave his only begotten Son, that whosoever
believeth in him should not perish, but have everlasting life.
17 For God sent not his Son into the world to condemn the world; but that the world
through him might be saved.
18 ¶ He that believeth on him is not condemned: but he that believeth not is condemned
already, because he hath not believed in the name of the only begotten Son of God.
19 And this is the condemnation, that light is come into the world, and men loved
darkness rather than light, because their deeds were evil.
20 For every one that doeth evil hateth the light, neither cometh to the light, lest his
deeds should be reproved.
21 But he that doeth truth cometh to the light, that his deeds may be made manifest, that
they are wrought in God. (John 3:1-21)

21 - TEMPTATION - REJECTION - VICTORY - DOMINION

1 And Jesus being full of the Holy Ghost returned from Jordan, and was led by the
Spirit into the wilderness,
2 Being forty days tempted of the devil. And in those days he did eat nothing: and
when they were ended, he afterward hungered.
3 And the devil said unto him, If thou be the Son of God, command this stone that it be
made bread.
4 And Jesus answered him, saying, It is written, That man shall not live by bread alone,
but by every word of God.
5 And the devil, taking him up into an high mountain, shewed unto him all the
kingdoms of the world in a moment of time.
6 And the devil said unto him, All this power will I give thee, and the glory of them:
for that is delivered unto me; and to whomsoever I will I give it.
7 If thou therefore wilt worship me, all shall be thine.
8 And Jesus answered and said unto him, Get thee behind me, Satan: for it is written,
Thou shalt worship the Lord thy God, and him only shalt thou serve.
9 And he brought him to Jerusalem, and set him on a pinnacle of the temple, and said

unto him, If thou be the Son of God, cast thyself down from hence:
10 For it is written, He shall give his angels charge over thee, to keep thee:
11 And in *their* hands they shall bear thee up, lest at any time thou dash thy foot against
a stone.
12 And Jesus answering said unto him, It is said, Thou shalt not tempt the Lord thy
God.
13 And when the devil had ended all the temptation, he departed from him for a season.
14 ¶ And Jesus returned in the power of the Spirit into Galilee: and there went out a
fame of him through all the region round about.
15 And he taught in their synagogues, being glorified of all.
16 ¶ And he came to Nazareth, where he had been brought up: and, as his custom was,
he went into the synagogue on the sabbath day, and stood up for to read.
17 And there was delivered unto him the book of the prophet Esaias. And when he had
opened the book, he found the place where it was written,
18 The Spirit of the Lord *is* upon me, because he hath anointed me to preach the gospel
to the poor; he hath sent me to heal the brokenhearted, to preach deliverance to the
captives, and recovering of sight to the blind, to set at liberty them that are bruised,
19 To preach the acceptable year of the Lord.
20 And he closed the book, and he gave *it* again to the minister, and sat down. And the
eyes of all them that were in the synagogue were fastened on him.
21 And he began to say unto them, This day is this scripture fulfilled in your ears.
22 And all bare him witness, and wondered at the gracious words which proceeded out
of his mouth. And they said, Is not this Joseph's son?
23 And he said unto them, Ye will surely say unto me this proverb, Physician, heal
thyself: whatsoever we have heard done in Capernaum, do also here in thy country.
24 And he said, Verily I say unto you, No prophet is accepted in his own country.
25 But I tell you of a truth, many widows were in Israel in the days of Elias, when the
heaven was shut up three years and six months, when great famine was throughout all
the land;
26 But unto none of them was Elias sent, save unto Sarepta, *a city* of Sidon, unto a
woman *that was* a widow.
27 And many lepers were in Israel in the time of Eliseus the prophet; and none of them
was cleansed, saving Naaman the Syrian.
28 And all they in the synagogue, when they heard these things, were filled with wrath,
29 And rose up, and thrust him out of the city, and led him unto the brow of the hill
whereon their city was built, that they might cast him down headlong.
30 But he passing through the midst of them went his way, (Luke 4:1-30)
12 And immediately the spirit driveth him into the wilderness.
13 And he was there in the wilderness forty days, tempted of Satan; and was with the
wild beasts; and the angels ministered unto him. (Mark 1:12-13)
1 Then was Jesus led up of the Spirit into the wilderness to be tempted of the devil.
2 And when he had fasted forty days and forty nights, he was afterward an hungered.
3 And when the tempter came to him, he said, If thou be the Son of God, command that
these stones be made bread.
4 But he answered and said, It is written, Man shall not live by bread alone, but by
every word that proceedeth out of the mouth of God.

5 Then the devil taketh him up into the holy city, and setteth him on a pinnacle of the
temple,
6 And saith unto him, If thou be the Son of God, cast thyself down: for it is written, He
shall give his angels charge concerning thee: and in *their* hands they shall bear thee up,
lest at any time thou dash thy foot against a stone.
7 Jesus said unto him, It is written again, Thou shalt not tempt the Lord thy God.
8 Again, the devil taketh him up into an exceeding high mountain, and sheweth him all
the kingdoms of the world, and the glory of them;
9 And saith unto him, All these things will I give thee, if thou wilt fall down and
worship me.
10 Then saith Jesus unto him, Get thee hence, Satan: for it is written, Thou shalt
worship the Lord thy God, and him only shalt thou serve.
11 Then the devil leaveth him, and, behold, angels came and ministered unto him. (Matt.
4:1-11)

22 - QUESTIONS ABOUT BAPTISM

22 ¶ After these things came Jesus and his disciples into the land of Judæa; and there he
tarried with them, and baptized.
23 ¶ And John also was baptizing in Aenon near to Salim, because there was much
water there: and they came, and were baptized.
24 For John was not yet cast into prison.
25 ¶ Then there arose a question between *some* of John's disciples and the Jews about
purifying.
26 And they came unto John, and said unto him, Rabbi, he that was with thee beyond
Jordan, to whom thou barest witness, behold, the same baptizeth, and all *men* come to
him.
27 John answered and said, A man can receive nothing, except it be given him from
heaven.
28 Ye yourselves bear me witness, that I said, I am not the Christ, but that I am sent
before him.
29 He that hath the bride is the bridegroom: but the friend of the bridegroom, which
standeth and heareth him, rejoiceth greatly because of the bridegroom's voice: this my
joy therefore is fulfilled.
30 He must increase, but I *must* decrease.
31 He that cometh from above is above all: he that is of the earth is earthly, and
speaketh of the earth: he that cometh from heaven is above all.
32 And what he hath seen and heard, that he testifieth; and no man receiveth his
testimony.
33 He that hath received his testimony hath set to his seal that God is true.
34 For he whom God hath sent speaketh the words of God: for God giveth not the Spirit
by measure *unto him*.
35 The Father loveth the Son, and hath given all things into his hand.
36 He that believeth on the Son hath everlasting life: and he that believeth not the Son
shall not see life; but the wrath of God abideth on him. (John 3:22-36)
1 When therefore the Lord knew how the Pharisees had heard that Jesus made and
baptized more disciples than John,
2 (Though Jesus himself baptized not, but his disciples,)

3 He left Judæa, and departed again into Galilee.
4 And he must needs go through Samaria. (John 4:1-4)

23 – THE TRUE GOD AND THE TRUE WORSHIP

5 Then cometh he to a city of Samaria, which is called Sychar, near to the parcel of
ground that Jacob gave to his son Joseph.
6 Now Jacob's well was there. Jesus therefore, being wearied with *his* journey, sat thus
on the well: *and* it was about the sixth hour.
7 There cometh a woman of Samaria to draw water: Jesus saith unto her, Give me to
drink.
8 (For his disciples were gone away unto the city to buy meat.)
9 Then saith the woman of Samaria unto him, How is it that thou, being a Jew, askest
drink of me, which am a woman of Samaria?
9 for the Jews have no dealings with the Samaritans.
10 Jesus answered and said unto her, If thou knewest the gift of God, and who it is that
saith to thee, Give me to drink; thou wouldest have asked of him, and he would have
given thee living water.
11 The woman saith unto him, Sir, thou hast nothing to draw with, and the well is deep:
from whence then hast thou that living water?
12 Art thou greater than our father Jacob, which gave us the well, and drank thereof
himself, and his children, and his cattle?
13 Jesus answered and said unto her, Whosoever drinketh of this water shall thirst
again:
14 But whosoever drinketh of the water that I shall give him shall never thirst; but the
water that I shall give him shall be in him a well of water springing up into everlasting
life.
15 The woman saith unto him, Sir, give me this water, that I thirst not, neither come
hither to draw.
16 Jesus saith unto her, Go, call thy husband, and come hither.
17 The woman answered and said, I have no husband. Jesus said unto her, Thou hast
well said, I have no husband:
18 For thou hast had five husbands; and he whom thou now hast is not thy husband: in
that saidst thou truly.
19 The woman saith unto him, Sir, I perceive that thou art a prophet.
20 Our fathers worshipped in this mountain; and ye say, that in Jerusalem is the place
where men ought to worship
21 Jesus saith unto her, Woman, believe me, the hour cometh, when ye shall neither in
this mountain, nor yet at Jerusalem, worship the Father
22 Ye worship ye know not what: we know what we worship: for salvation is of the
Jews.
23 But the hour cometh, and now is, when the true worshippers shall worship the Father
in spirit and in truth: for the Father seeketh such to worship him.
24 God *is* a Spirit: and they that worship him must worship *him* in spirit and in truth.
25 The woman saith unto him, I know that Messias cometh, which is called Christ:
when he is come, he will tell us all things.
26 Jesus saith unto her, I that speak unto thee am *he*.
27 ¶ And upon this came his disciples, and marvelled that he talked with the woman:

yet no man said, What seekest thou? or, Why talkest thou with her?
28 The woman then left her waterpot, and went her way into the city, and saith to the
men,
29 Come, see a man, which told me all things that ever I did: is not this the Christ
30 Then they went out of the city, and came unto him.
31 In the mean while his disciples prayed him, saying, Master, eat.
32 But he said unto them, I have meat to eat that ye know not of.
33 Therefore said the disciples one to another, Hath any man brought him *ought* to eat?
34 Jesus saith unto them, My meat is to do the will of him that sent me, and to finish his
work.
35 Say not ye, There are yet four months, and *then* cometh harvest? behold, I say unto
you, Lift up your eyes, and look on the fields; for they are white already to harvest.
36 And he that reapeth receiveth wages, and gathereth fruit unto life eternal: that both
he that soweth and he that reapeth may rejoice together.
37 And herein is that saying true, One soweth, and another reapeth.
38 I sent you to reap that whereon ye bestowed no labour: other men laboured, and ye
are entered into their labours.
39 ¶ And many of the Samaritans of that city believed on him for the saying of the
woman, which testified, He told me all that ever I did.
40 So when the Samaritans were come unto him, they besought him that he would tarry
with them: and he abode there two days.
41 And many more believed because of his own word;
42 And said unto the woman, Now we believe, not because of thy saying: for we have
heard *him* ourselves, and know that this is indeed the Christ, the Saviour of the world.

Two days later Jesus departed Samaria for Galilee rather than to return to Nazareth

43 ¶ Now after two days he departed thence, and went into Galilee.
44 For Jesus himself testified, that a prophet hath no honour in his own country. (John 4:5-44)

24 - JOHN THE BAPTIST IS CAST INTO PRISON

According to the Gospel of Matthew

12 ¶ Now when Jesus had heard that John was cast into prison, he departed into Galilee; (Matt 4:12)

According to the Gospel of Mark

14 Now after that John was put in prison, Jesus came into Galilee, preaching the gospel
of the kingdom of God,
15 And saying, The time is fulfilled, and the kingdom of God is at hand: repent ye, and
believe the gospel. (Mark 1:14-15)

25 - JESUS DEPARTS NAZARETH TO DWELL IN CAPERNAUM

According to the Gospel of Matthew

13 And leaving Nazareth, he came and dwelt in Capernaum, which is upon the sea
coast, in the borders of Zabulon and Nephthalim:
14 That it might be fulfilled which was spoken by Esaias the prophet, saying,
15 The land of Zabulon, and the land of Nephthalim, *by* the way of the sea, beyond
Jordan, Galilee of the Gentiles;
16 The people which sat in darkness saw great light; and to them which sat in the region
and shadow of death light is sprung up.
17 ¶ From that time Jesus began to preach, and to say, Repent: for the kingdom of

heaven is at hand. (Matt. 4:13-17)

According to the Gospel of John

45 Then when he was come into Galilee, the Galilæans received him, having seen all
the things that he did at Jerusalem at the feast: for they also went unto the feast.
46 So Jesus came again into Cana of Galilee, where he made the water wine. And there
was a certain nobleman, whose son was sick at Capernaum.
47 When he heard that Jesus was come out of Judæa into Galilee, he went unto him,
and besought him that he would come down, and heal his son: for he was at the point of
death.
48 Then said Jesus unto him, Except ye see signs and wonders, ye will not believe.
49 The nobleman saith unto him, Sir, come down ere my child die.
50 Jesus saith unto him, Go thy way; thy son liveth. And the man believed the word
that Jesus had spoken unto him, and he went his way.
51 And as he was now going down, his servants met him, and told *him*, saying, Thy son
liveth.
52 Then inquired he of them the hour when he began to amend. And they said unto
him, Yesterday at the seventh hour the fever left him.
53 So the father knew that *it was* at the same hour, in the which Jesus said unto him,
Thy son liveth: and himself believed, and his whole house.
54 This *is* again the second miracle *that* Jesus did, when he was come out of Judæa into
Galilee. (John 4:45-54)

26 - THE FIRST CALLING OF PETER & ANDREW, JAMES & JOHN

According to the Gospel of Mark

16 Now as he walked by the sea of Galilee, he saw Simon and Andrew his brother
casting a net into the sea: for they were fishers.
17 And Jesus said unto them, Come ye after me, and I will make you to become fishers
of men.
18 And straightway they forsook their nets, and followed him.
19 And when he had gone a little further thence, he saw James the *son* of Zebedee, and
John his brother, who also were in the ship mending their nets.
20 And straightway he called them: and they left their father Zebedee in the ship with
the hired servants, and went after him. (Mark 1:16-20)

According to the Gospel of Matthew

18 ¶ And Jesus, walking by the sea of Galilee, saw two brethren, Simon called Peter,
and Andrew his brother, casting a net into the sea: for they were fishers.
19 And he saith unto them, Follow me, and I will make you fishers of men.
20 And they straightway left *their* nets, and followed him.
21 And going on from thence, he saw other two brethren, James *the son* of Zebedee,
and John his brother, in a ship with Zebedee their father, mending their nets; and he
called them.
22 And they immediately left the ship and their father, and followed him. (Matt 4:18-22)

27 - AN EXTENSIVE MINISTRY IN AND BEYOND GALILEE

23 ¶ And Jesus went about all Galilee, teaching in their synagogues, and preaching the
gospel of the kingdom, and healing all manner of sickness and all manner of disease
among the people.

24 And his fame went throughout all Syria: and they brought unto him all sick people
that were taken with divers diseases and torments, and those which were possessed with
devils, and those which were lunatic, and those that had the palsy; and he healed them.
25 And there followed him great multitudes of people from Galilee, and *from*
Decapolis, and *from* Jerusalem, and *from* Judæa, and *from* beyond Jordan. (Matt 4:23-25)

28 - THE SERMON ON THE MOUNT

1 And seeing the multitudes, he went up into a mountain: and when he was set, his
disciples came unto him:
2 And he opened his mouth, and taught them, saying,
3 Blessed *are* the poor in spirit: for theirs is the kingdom of heaven.
4 Blessed *are* they that mourn: for they shall be comforted.
5 Blessed *are* the meek: for they shall inherit the earth.
6 Blessed *are* they which do hunger and thirst after righteousness: for they shall be
filled.
7 Blessed *are* the merciful: for they shall obtain mercy.
8 Blessed *are* the pure in heart: for they shall see God.
9 Blessed *are* the peacemakers: for they shall be called the children of God.
10 Blessed *are* they which are persecuted for righteousness' sake: for theirs is the
kingdom of heaven.
11 Blessed are ye, when *men* shall revile you, and persecute *you*, and shall say all
manner of evil against you falsely, for my sake.
12 Rejoice, and be exceeding glad: for great *is* your reward in heaven: for so persecuted
they the prophets which were before you.
13 ¶ Ye are the salt of the earth: but if the salt have lost his savour, wherewith shall it
be salted? it is thenceforth good for nothing, but to be cast out, and to be trodden under
foot of men.
14 Ye are the light of the world. A city that is set on an hill cannot be hid.
15 Neither do men light a candle, and put it under a bushel, but on a candlestick; and it
giveth light unto all that are in the house.
16 Let your light so shine before men, that they may see your good works, and glorify
your Father which is in heaven.
17 ¶ Think not that I am come to destroy the law, or the prophets: I am not come to
destroy, but to fulfil.
18 For verily I say unto you, Till heaven and earth pass, one jot or one tittle shall in no
wise pass from the law, till all be fulfilled.
19 Whosoever therefore shall break one of these least commandments, and shall teach
men so, he shall be called the least in the kingdom of heaven: but whosoever shall do
and teach *them*, the same shall be called great in the kingdom of heaven.
20 For I say unto you, That except your righteousness shall exceed *the righteousness* of
the scribes and Pharisees, ye shall in no case enter into the kingdom of heaven.
21 ¶ Ye have heard that it was said by them of old time, Thou shalt not kill; and
whosoever shall kill shall be in danger of the judgment:
22 But I say unto you, That whosoever is angry with his brother without a cause shall
be in danger of the judgment: and whosoever shall say to his brother, Raca, shall be in
danger of the council: but whosoever shall say, Thou fool, shall be in danger of hell
fire.

23 Therefore if thou bring thy gift to the altar, and there rememberest that thy brother
hath aught against thee;
24 Leave there thy gift before the altar, and go thy way; first be reconciled to thy
brother, and then come and offer thy gift.
25 Agree with thine adversary quickly, whiles thou art in the way with him; lest at any
time the adversary deliver thee to the judge, and the judge deliver thee to the officer,
and thou be cast into prison.
26 Verily I say unto thee, Thou shalt by no means come out thence, till thou hast paid
the uttermost farthing.
27 ¶ Ye have heard that it was said by them of old time, Thou shalt not commit
adultery:
28 But I say unto you, That whosoever looketh on a woman to lust after her hath
committed adultery with her already in his heart.
29 And if thy right eye offend thee, pluck it out, and cast *it* from thee: for it is profitable
for thee that one of thy members should perish, and not *that* thy whole body should be
cast into hell.
30 And if thy right hand offend thee, cut it off, and cast *it* from thee: for it is profitable
for thee that one of thy members should perish, and not *that* thy whole body should be
cast into hell.
31 It hath been said, Whosoever shall put away his wife, let him give her a writing of
divorcement:
32 But I say unto you, That whosoever shall put away his wife, saving for the cause of
fornication, causeth her to commit adultery: and whosoever shall marry her that is
divorced committeth adultery.
33 ¶ Again, ye have heard that it hath been said by them of old time, Thou shalt not
forswear thyself, but shalt perform unto the Lord thine oaths:
34 But I say unto you, Swear not at all; neither by heaven; for it is God's throne:
35 Nor by the earth; for it is his footstool: neither by Jerusalem; for it is the city of the
great King.
36 Neither shalt thou swear by thy head, because thou canst not make one hair white or
black.
37 But let your communication be, Yea, yea; Nay, nay: for whatsoever is more than
these cometh of evil.
38 ¶ Ye have heard that it hath been said, An eye for an eye, and a tooth for a tooth:
39 But I say unto you, That ye resist not evil: but whosoever shall smite thee on thy
right cheek, turn to him the other also.
40 And if any man will sue thee at the law, and take away thy coat, let him have *thy*
cloak also.
41 And whosoever shall compel thee to go a mile, go with him twain.
42 Give to him that asketh thee, and from him that would borrow of thee turn not thou
away.
43 ¶ Ye have heard that it hath been said, Thou shalt love thy neighbour, and hate thine
enemy.
44 But I say unto you, Love your enemies, bless them that curse you, do good to them
that hate you, and pray for them which despitefully use you, and persecute you;
45 That ye may be the children of your Father which is in heaven: for he maketh his

sun to rise on the evil and on the good, and sendeth rain on the just and on the unjust.
46 For if ye love them which love you, what reward have ye? do not even the publicans
the same?
47 And if ye salute your brethren only, what do ye more *than others*? do not even the
publicans so?
48 Be ye therefore perfect, even as your Father which is in heaven is perfect. (Matt. 5:1-48)
1 Take heed that ye do not your alms before men, to be seen of them: otherwise ye have
no reward of your Father which is in heaven.
2 Therefore when thou doest *thine* alms, do not sound a trumpet before thee, as the
hypocrites do in the synagogues and in the streets, that they may have glory of men.
Verily I say unto you, They have their reward.
3 But when thou doest alms, let not thy left hand know what thy right hand doeth:
4 That thine alms may be in secret: and thy Father which seeth in secret himself shall
reward thee openly.
5 ¶ And when thou prayest, thou shalt not be as the hypocrites *are:* for they love to
pray standing in the synagogues and in the corners of the streets, that they may be seen
of men. Verily I say unto you, They have their reward.
6 But thou, when thou prayest, enter into thy closet, and when thou hast shut thy door,
pray to thy Father which is in secret; and thy Father which seeth in secret shall reward
thee openly.
7 But when ye pray, use not vain repetitions, as the heathen *do:* for they think that they
shall be heard for their much speaking.
8 Be not ye therefore like unto them: for your Father knoweth what things ye have need
of, before ye ask him.
9 After this manner therefore pray ye: Our Father which art in heaven, Hallowed be thy
name.
10 Thy kingdom come. Thy will be done in earth, as *it is* in heaven.
11 Give us this day our daily bread.
12 And forgive us our debts, as we forgive our debtors.
13 And lead us not into temptation, but deliver us from evil: For thine is the kingdom,
and the power, and the glory, for ever. Amen.
14 For if ye forgive men their trespasses, your heavenly Father will also forgive you:
15 But if ye forgive not men their trespasses, neither will your Father forgive your
trespasses.
16 ¶ Moreover when ye fast, be not, as the hypocrites, of a sad countenance: for they
disfigure their faces, that they may appear unto men to fast. Verily I say unto you,
They have their reward.
17 But thou, when thou fastest, anoint thine head, and wash thy face;
18 That thou appear not unto men to fast, but unto thy Father which is in secret: and thy
Father, which seeth in secret, shall reward thee openly.
19 ¶ Lay not up for yourselves treasures upon earth, where moth and rust doth corrupt,
and where thieves break through and steal:
20 But lay up for yourselves treasures in heaven, where neither moth nor rust doth
corrupt, and where thieves do not break through nor steal:
21 For where your treasure is, there will your heart be also.
22 The light of the body is the eye: if therefore thine eye be single, thy whole body

shall be full of light.
23 But if thine eye be evil, thy whole body shall be full of darkness. If therefore the
light that is in thee be darkness, how great *is* that darkness!
24 ¶ No man can serve two masters: for either he will hate the one, and love the other;
or else he will hold to the one, and despise the other. Ye cannot serve God and
mammon.
25 Therefore I say unto you, Take no thought for your life, what ye shall eat, or what ye
shall drink; nor yet for your body, what ye shall put on. Is not the life more than meat,
and the body than raiment?
26 Behold the fowls of the air: for they sow not, neither do they reap, nor gather into
barns; yet your heavenly Father feedeth them. Are ye not much better than they?
27 Which of you by taking thought can add one cubit unto his stature?
28 And why take ye thought for raiment? Consider the lilies of the field, how they
grow; they toil not, neither do they spin:
29 And yet I say unto you, That even Solomon in all his glory was not arrayed like one
of these.
30 Wherefore, if God so clothe the grass of the field, which to-day is, and to-morrow is
cast into the oven, *shall he* not much more *clothe* you, O ye of little faith?
31 Therefore take no thought, saying, What shall we eat? or, What shall we drink? or,
Wherewithal shall we be clothed?
32 (For after all these things do the Gentiles seek:) for your heavenly Father knoweth
that ye have need of all these things.
33 But seek ye first the kingdom of God, and his righteousness; and all these things
shall be added unto you.
34 Take therefore no thought for the morrow: for the morrow shall take thought for the
things of itself. Sufficient unto the day *is* the evil thereof. (Matt. 6:1-34)
1 Judge not, that ye be not judged.
2 For with what judgment ye judge, ye shall be judged: and with what measure ye
mete, it shall be measured to you again.
3 And why beholdest thou the mote that is in thy brother's eye, but considerest not the
beam that is in thine own eye?
4 Or how wilt thou say to thy brother, Let me pull out the mote out of thine eye; and,
behold, a beam *is* in thine own eye?
5 Thou hypocrite, first cast out the beam out of thine own eye; and then shalt thou see
clearly to cast out the mote out of thy brother's eye.
6 ¶ Give not that which is holy unto the dogs, neither cast ye your pearls before swine,
lest they trample them under their feet, and turn again and rend you.
7 ¶ Ask, and it shall be given you; seek, and ye shall find; knock, and it shall be opened
unto you:
8 For every one that asketh receiveth; and he that seeketh findeth; and to him that
knocketh it shall be opened.
9 Or what man is there of you, whom if his son ask bread, will he give him a stone?
10 Or if he ask a fish, will he give him a serpent?
11 If ye then, being evil, know how to give good gifts unto your children, how much
more shall your Father which is in heaven give good things to them that ask him?
12 Therefore all things whatsoever ye would that men should do to you, do ye even so

to them: for this is the law and the prophets.
13 ¶ Enter ye in at the strait gate: for wide *is* the gate, and broad *is* the way, that leadeth
to destruction, and many there be which go in thereat:
14 Because strait *is* the gate, and narrow *is* the way, which leadeth unto life, and few
there be that find it.
15 ¶ Beware of false prophets, which come to you in sheep's clothing, but inwardly
they are ravening wolves.
16 Ye shall know them by their fruits. Do men gather grapes of thorns, or figs of
thistles?
17 Even so every good tree bringeth forth good fruit; but a corrupt tree bringeth forth
evil fruit.
18 A good tree cannot bring forth evil fruit, neither *can* a corrupt tree bring forth good
fruit.
19 Every tree that bringeth not forth good fruit is hewn down, and cast into the fire.
20 Wherefore by their fruits ye shall know them.
21 ¶ Not every one that saith unto me, Lord, Lord, shall enter into the kingdom of
heaven; but he that doeth the will of my Father which is in heaven.
22 Many will say to me in that day, Lord, Lord, have we not prophesied in thy name?
and in thy name have cast out devils? and in thy name done many wonderful works?
23 And then will I profess unto them, I never knew you: depart from me, ye that work
iniquity.
24 ¶ Therefore whosoever heareth these sayings of mine, and doeth them, I will liken
him unto a wise man, which built his house upon a rock:
25 And the rain descended, and the floods came, and the winds blew, and beat upon
that house; and it fell not: for it was founded upon a rock.
26 And every one that heareth these sayings of mine, and doeth them not, shall be
likened unto a foolish man, which built his house upon the sand:
27 And the rain descended, and the floods came, and the winds blew, and beat upon that
house; and it fell: and great was the fall of it.
28 And it came to pass, when Jesus had ended these sayings, the people were
astonished at his doctrine:
29 For he taught them as *one* having authority, and not as the scribes. (Matt 7:1-29)

29 – JESUS PROVES HIS TEACHING PRACTICAL

1 When he was come down from the mountain, great multitudes followed him.
2 And, behold, there came a leper and worshipped him, saying, Lord, if thou wilt, thou
canst make me clean.
3 And Jesus put forth *his* hand, and touched him, saying, I will; be thou clean. And
immediately his leprosy was cleansed.
4 And Jesus saith unto him, See thou tell no man; but go thy way, shew thyself to the
priest, and offer the gift that Moses commanded, for a testimony unto them. (Matt 8:1-4)

30 - MORE HEALING IN CAPERNAUM

According to the Gospel of Matthew

5 ¶ And when Jesus was entered into Capernaum, there came unto him a centurion,
beseeching him,
6 And saying, Lord, my servant lieth at home sick of the palsy, grievously tormented.

7 And Jesus saith unto him, I will come and heal him.
8 The centurion answered and said, Lord, I am not worthy that thou shouldest come
under my roof: but speak the word only, and my servant shall be healed.
9 For I am a man under authority, having soldiers under me: and I say to this *man*, Go,
and he goeth; and to another, Come, and he cometh; and to my servant, Do this, and he
doeth *it*.
10 When Jesus heard *it*, he marvelled, and said to them that followed, Verily I say unto
you, I have not found so great faith, no, not in Israel.
11 And I say unto you, That many shall come from the east and west, and shall sit down
with Abraham, and Isaac, and Jacob, in the kingdom of heaven.
12 But the children of the kingdom shall be cast out into outer darkness: there shall be
weeping and gnashing of teeth.
13 And Jesus said unto the centurion, Go thy way; and as thou hast believed, *so* be it
done unto thee. And his servant was healed in the selfsame hour.
14 ¶ And when Jesus was come into Peter's house, he saw his wife's mother laid, and
sick of a fever.
15 And he touched her hand, and the fever left her: and she arose, and ministered unto
them.
16 ¶ When the even was come, they brought unto him many that were possessed with
devils: and he cast out the spirits with *his* word, and healed all that were sick:
17 That it might be fulfilled which was spoken by Esaias the prophet, saying, Himself
took our infirmities, and bare *our* sicknesses. (Matt 8:5-17)

According to the Gospel of Mark

21 And they went into Capernaum; and straightway on the sabbath day he entered into
the synagogue, and taught.
22 And they were astonished at his doctrine: for he taught them as one that had
authority, and not as the scribes.
23 And there was in their synagogue a man with an unclean spirit; and he cried out,
24 Saying, Let *us* alone; what have we to do with thee, thou Jesus of Nazareth? art thou
come to destroy us? I know thee who thou art, the Holy One of God.
25 And Jesus rebuked him, saying, Hold thy peace, and come out of him.
26 And when the unclean spirit had torn him, and cried with a loud voice, he came out
of him.
27 And they were all amazed, insomuch that they questioned among themselves,
saying, What thing is this? what new doctrine *is* this? for with authority commandeth he
even the unclean spirits, and they do obey him.
28 And immediately his fame spread abroad throughout all the region round about
Galilee.
29 And forthwith, when they were come out of the synagogue, they entered into the
house of Simon and Andrew, with James and John.
30 But Simon's wife's mother lay sick of a fever, and anon they tell him of her.
31 And he came and took her by the hand, and lifted her up; and immediately the fever
left her, and she ministered unto them.
32 And at even, when the sun did set, they brought unto him all that were diseased, and
them that were possessed with devils.
33 And all the city was gathered together at the door.

34 And he healed many that were sick of divers diseases, and cast out many devils; and
suffered not the devils to speak, because they knew him. (Mark 1:21-34)

According to the Gospel of Luke

31 And came down to Capernaum, a city of Galilee, and taught them on the sabbath
days.
32 And they were astonished at his doctrine: for his word was with power.
33 ¶ And in the synagogue there was a man, which had a spirit of an unclean devil, and
cried out with a loud voice,
34 Saying, Let *us* alone; what have we to do with thee, *thou* Jesus of Nazareth? art thou
come to destroy us? I know thee who thou art; the Holy One of God.
35 And Jesus rebuked him, saying, Hold thy peace, and come out of him. And when
the devil had thrown him in the midst, he came out of him, and hurt him not.
36 And they were all amazed, and spake among themselves, saying, What a word *is*
this! for with authority and power he commandeth the unclean spirits, and they come
out.
37 And the fame of him went out into every place of the country round about.
38 ¶ And he arose out of the synagogue, and entered into Simon's house. And Simon's
wife's mother was taken with a great fever; and they besought him for her.
39 And he stood over her, and rebuked the fever; and it left her: and immediately she
arose and ministered unto them. (Luke 4:38-39)
40 ¶ Now when the sun was setting, all they that had any sick with divers diseases
brought them unto him; and he laid his hands on every one of them, and healed them.
41 And devils also came out of many, crying out, and saying, Thou art Christ the Son
of God. And he rebuking *them* suffered them not to speak: for they knew that he was
Christ. (Luke 4:31-41)

31 - PRAYER & PREACHING

According to the Gospel of Mark

35 And in the morning, rising up a great while before day, he went out, and departed
into a solitary place, and there prayed.
36 And Simon and they that were with him followed after him.
37 And when they had found him, they said unto him, All *men* seek for thee.
38 And he said unto them, Let us go into the next towns, that I may preach there also:
for therefore came I forth.
39 And he preached in their synagogues throughout all Galilee, and cast out devils. (Mark
1:35-39)

According to the Gospel of Luke

42 And when it was day, he departed and went into a desert place: and the people
sought him, and came unto him, and stayed him, that he should not depart from them.
43 And he said unto them, I must preach the kingdom of God to other cities also: for
therefore am I sent.
44 And he preached in the synagogues of Galilee. (Luke 4:42-44)

32 - THE FIRST GREAT CATCH OF FISHES

1 And it came to pass, that, as the people pressed upon him to hear the word of God, he
stood by the lake of Gennesaret,

2 And saw two ships standing by the lake: but the fishermen were gone out of them,
and were washing *their* nets.
3 And he entered into one of the ships, which was Simon's, and prayed him that he
would thrust out a little from the land. And he sat down, and taught the people out of
the ship.
4 Now when he had left speaking, he said unto Simon, Launch out into the deep, and
let down your nets for a draught.
5 And Simon answering said unto him, Master, we have toiled all the night, and have
taken nothing: nevertheless at thy word I will let down the net.
6 And when they had this done, they enclosed a great multitude of fishes: and their net
brake.
7 And they beckoned unto *their* partners, which were in the other ship, that they should
come and help them. And they came, and filled both the ships, so that they began to
sink.
8 When Simon Peter saw *it*, he fell down at Jesus' knees, saying, Depart from me; for I
am a sinful man, O Lord.
9 For he was astonished, and all that were with him, at the draught of the fishes which
they had taken:
10 And so *was* also James, and John, the sons of Zebedee, which were partners with
Simon. And Jesus said unto Simon, Fear not; from henceforth thou shalt catch men.
11 And when they had brought their ships to land, they forsook all, and followed him.
(Luke 5:1-11)

33 – A LEPER'S BETRAYAL

According to the Gospel of Mark

40 And there came a leper to him, beseeching him, and kneeling down to him, and
saying unto him, If thou wilt, thou canst make me clean.
41 And Jesus, moved with compassion, put forth *his* hand, and touched him, and saith
unto him, I will; be thou clean.
42 And as soon as he had spoken, immediately the leprosy departed from him, and he
was cleansed.
43 And he straitly charged him, and forthwith sent him away;
44 And saith unto him, See thou say nothing to any man: but go thy way, shew thyself
to the priest, and offer for thy cleansing those things which Moses commanded, for a
testimony unto them.
45 But he went out, and began to publish *it* much, and to blaze abroad the matter,
insomuch that Jesus could no more openly enter into the city, but was without in desert
places: and they came to him from every quarter. (Mark 1:40-45)

According to the Gospel of Luke

12 ¶ And it came to pass, when he was in a certain city, behold a man full of leprosy:
who seeing Jesus fell on *his* face, and besought him, saying, Lord, if thou wilt, thou
canst make me clean.
13 And he put forth *his* hand, and touched him, saying, I will: be thou clean. And
immediately the leprosy departed from him.
14 And he charged him to tell no man: but go, and shew thyself to the priest, and offer
for thy cleansing, according as Moses commanded, for a testimony unto them.
15 But so much the more went there a fame abroad of him: and great multitudes came

together to hear, and to be healed by him of their infirmities.
16 ¶ And he withdrew himself into the wilderness, and prayed. (Luke 5:12-16)

34 - A TSUNAMI IS STILLED

18 ¶ Now when Jesus saw great multitudes about him, he gave commandment to depart
unto the other side.
19 And a certain scribe came, and said unto him, Master, I will follow thee
whithersoever thou goest.
20 And Jesus saith unto him, The foxes have holes, and the birds of the air *have* nests;
but the Son of man hath not where to lay *his* head.
21 And another of his disciples said unto him, Lord, suffer me first to go and bury my
father.
22 But Jesus said unto him, Follow me; and let the dead bury their dead.
23 ¶ And when he was entered into a ship, his disciples followed him.
24 And, behold, there arose a great tempest in the sea, insomuch that the ship was
covered with the waves: but he was asleep.
25 And his disciples came to *him*, and awoke him, saying, Lord, save us: we perish.
26 And he saith unto them, Why are ye fearful, O ye of little faith? Then he arose, and
rebuked the winds and the sea; and there was a great calm.
27 But the men marvelled, saying, What manner of man is this, that even the winds and
the sea obey him! (Matt 8:18-27)

35 – THE HEALING OF TWO DEMONIACS IN GERGESA

28 ¶ And when he was come to the other side into the country of the Gergesenes, there
met him two possessed with devils, coming out of the tombs, exceeding fierce, so that
no man might pass by that way.
29 And, behold, they cried out, saying, What have we to do with thee, Jesus, thou Son
of God? art thou come hither to torment us before the time?
30 And there was a good way off from them an herd of many swine feeding. (Matt 8:30)
31 So the devils besought him, saying, If thou cast us out, suffer us to go away into the
herd of swine.
32 And he said unto them, Go. And when they were come out, they went into the herd
of swine: and, behold, the whole herd of swine ran violently down a steep place into the
sea, and perished in the waters.
33 And they that kept them fled, and went their ways into the city, and told every thing,
and what was befallen to the possessed of the devils.
34 And, behold, the whole city came out to meet Jesus: and when they saw him, they
besought *him* that he would depart out of their coasts. (Matt. 8:28-34)
1 And he entered into a ship, and passed over, and came into his own city. (Matt 9:1)

36 - A MAN IN CAPERNAUM IS HEALED OF THE PALSY

According to the Gospel of Mark

1 And again he entered into Capernaum after *some* days; and it was noised that he was
in the house.
2 And straightway many were gathered together, insomuch that there was no room to
receive *them*, no, not so much as about the door: and he preached the word unto them.
3 And they come unto him, bringing one sick of the palsy, which was borne of four.

4 And when they could not come nigh unto him for the press, they uncovered the roof
where he was: and when they had broken *it* up, they let down the bed wherein the sick
of the palsy lay.
5 When Jesus saw their faith, he said unto the sick of the palsy, Son, thy sins be
forgiven thee.
6 But there were certain of the scribes sitting there, and reasoning in their hearts,
7 Why doth this *man* thus speak blasphemies? who can forgive sins but God only?
8 And immediately when Jesus perceived in his spirit that they so reasoned within
themselves, he said unto them, Why reason ye these things in your hearts?
9 Whether is it easier to say to the sick of the palsy, *Thy* sins be forgiven thee; or to
say, Arise, and take up thy bed, and walk?
10 But that ye may know that the Son of man hath power on earth to forgive sins, (he
saith to the sick of the palsy,)
11 I say unto thee, Arise, and take up thy bed, and go thy way into thine house.
12 And immediately he arose, took up the bed, and went forth before them all;
insomuch that they were all amazed, and glorified God, saying, We never saw it on this
fashion.
13 And he went forth again by the sea side; and all the multitude resorted unto him, and
he taught them. (Mark 2:1-13)

According to the Gospel of Matthew

2 And, behold, they brought to him a man sick of the palsy, lying on a bed: and Jesus
seeing their faith said unto the sick of the palsy; Son, be of good cheer; thy sins be
forgiven thee.
3 And, behold, certain of the scribes said within themselves, This *man* blasphemeth.
4 And Jesus knowing their thoughts said, Wherefore think ye evil in your hearts?
5 For whether is easier, to say, *Thy* sins be forgiven thee; or to say, Arise, and walk?
6 But that ye may know that the Son of man hath power on earth to forgive sins, (then
saith he to the sick of the palsy,) Arise, take up thy bed, and go unto thine house.
7 And he arose, and departed to his house.
8 But when the multitudes saw *it*, they marvelled, and glorified God, which had given
such power unto men. (Matt 9:2-8)

According to the Gospel of Luke

17 And it came to pass on a certain day, as he was teaching, that there were Pharisees
and doctors of the law sitting by, which were come out of every town of Galilee, and
Judæa, and Jerusalem: and the power of the Lord was *present* to heal them.
18 ¶ And, behold, men brought in a bed a man which was taken with a palsy: and they
sought *means* to bring him in, and to lay *him* before him.
19 And when they could not find by what *way* they might bring him in because of the
multitude, they went upon the housetop, and let him down through the tiling with *his*
couch into the midst before Jesus.
20 And when he saw their faith, he said unto him, Man, thy sins are forgiven thee.
21 And the scribes and the Pharisees began to reason, saying, Who is this which
speaketh blasphemies? Who can forgive sins, but God alone?
22 But when Jesus perceived their thoughts, he answering said unto them, What reason
ye in your hearts?
23 Whether is easier, to say, Thy sins be forgiven thee; or to say, Rise up and walk?

24 But that ye may know that the Son of man hath power upon earth to forgive sins, (he
said unto the sick of the palsy,) I say unto thee, Arise, and take up thy couch, and go
into thine house.
25 And immediately he rose up before them, and took up that whereon he lay, and
departed to his own house, glorifying God.
26 And they were all amazed, and they glorified God, and were filled with fear, saying,
We have seen strange things to-day. (Luke 5:17-26)

37 - THE CALLING OF MATTHEW (LEVI)

According to the Gospel of Mark

14 And as he passed by, he saw Levi the *son* of Alphæus sitting at the receipt of
custom, and said unto him, Follow me. And he arose and followed him. (Mark 2:14)

According to the Gospel of Matthew

9 ¶ And as Jesus passed forth from thence, he saw a man, named Matthew, sitting at the
receipt of custom: and he saith unto him, Follow me. And he arose, and followed him.
(Matt 9:9)

According to the Gospel of Luke

27 ¶ And after these things he went forth, and saw a publican, named Levi, sitting at the
receipt of custom: and he said unto him, Follow me.
28 And he left all, rose up, and followed him. (Luke 5:27-28)

38 – JESUS DECLARES THE PURPOSE OF HIS MISSION

According to the Gospel of Luke

29 And Levi made him a great feast in his own house: and there was a great company
of publicans and of others that sat down with them.
30 But their scribes and Pharisees murmured against his disciples, saying, Why do ye
eat and drink with publicans and sinners?
31 And Jesus answering said unto them, They that are whole need not a physician; but
they that are sick.
32 I came not to call the righteous, but sinners to repentance. (Luke 5:29-32)

According to the Gospel of Matthew

10 ¶ And it came to pass, as Jesus sat at meat in the house, behold, many publicans and
sinners came and sat down with him and his disciples.
11 And when the Pharisees saw *it*, they said unto his disciples, Why eateth your Master
with publicans and sinners?
12 But when Jesus heard *that*, he said unto them, They that be whole need not a
physician, but they that are sick. (Matt 9:10-12)
13 But go ye and learn what *that* meaneth, I will have mercy, and not sacrifice: for I am
not come to call the righteous, but sinners to repentance. (Matt 9:10-13)

According to the Gospel of Mark

15 And it came to pass, that, as Jesus sat at meat in his house, many publicans and
sinners sat also together with Jesus and his disciples: for there were many, and they
followed him.
16 And when the scribes and Pharisees saw him eat with publicans and sinners, they
said unto his disciples, How is it that he eateth and drinketh with publicans and sinners?

17 When Jesus heard *it*, he saith unto them, They that are whole have no need of the
physician, but they that are sick: I came not to call the righteous, but sinners to
repentance. (Mark 2:15-17)

39 - NO MIXING ALLOWED

According to the Gospel of Mark

18 And the disciples of John and of the Pharisees used to fast: and they come and say
unto him, Why do the disciples of John and of the Pharisees fast, but thy disciples fast
not?
19 And Jesus said unto them, Can the children of the bridechamber fast, while the
bridegroom is with them? as long as they have the bridegroom with them, they cannot
fast.
20 But the days will come, when the bridegroom shall be taken away from them, and
then shall they fast in those days.
21 No man also seweth a piece of new cloth on an old garment: else the new piece that
filled it up taketh away from the old, and the rent is made worse.
22 And no man putteth new wine into old bottles: else the new wine doth burst the
bottles, and the wine is spilled, and the bottles will be marred: but new wine must be
put into new bottles. (Mark 2:18-22)

According to the Gospel of Luke

33 ¶ And they said unto him, Why do the disciples of John fast often, and make
prayers, and likewise *the disciples* of the Pharisees; but thine eat and drink?
34 And he said unto them, Can ye make the children of the bridechamber fast, while the
bridegroom is with them?
35 But the days will come, when the bridegroom shall be taken away from them, and
then shall they fast in those days.
36 ¶ And he spake also a parable unto them; No man putteth a piece of a new garment
upon an old; if otherwise, then both the new maketh a rent, and the piece that was *taken*
out of the new agreeth not with the old.
37 And no man putteth new wine into old bottles; else the new wine will burst the
bottles, and be spilled, and the bottles shall perish.
38 But new wine must be put into new bottles; and both are preserved.
39 No man also having drunk old *wine* straightway desireth new: for he saith, The old
is better. (Luke 5:33-39)

According to the Gospel of Matthew

14 ¶ Then came to him the disciples of John, saying, Why do we and the Pharisees fast
oft, but thy disciples fast not?
15 And Jesus said unto them, Can the children of the bridechamber mourn, as long as
the bridegroom is with them? but the days will come, when the bridegroom shall be
taken from them, and then shall they fast.
16 No man putteth a piece of new cloth unto an old garment, for that which is put in to
fill it up taketh from the garment, and the rent is made worse.
17 Neither do men put new wine into old bottles: else the bottles break, and the wine
runneth out, and the bottles perish: but they put new wine into new bottles, and both are
preserved. (Matt 9:14-17)

40 - DEATH OVERCOME AND HEMORRHAGING HEALED

18 ¶ While he spake these things unto them, behold, there came a certain ruler, and
worshipped him, saying, My daughter is even now dead: but come and lay thy hand
upon her, and she shall live.
19 And Jesus arose, and followed him, and *so did* his disciples.
20 ¶ And, behold, a woman, which was diseased with an issue of blood twelve years,
came behind *him*, and touched the hem of his garment:
21 For she said within herself, If I may but touch his garment, I shall be whole.
22 But Jesus turned him about, and when he saw her, he said, Daughter, be of good
comfort; thy faith hath made thee whole. And the woman was made whole from that
hour.
23 And when Jesus came into the ruler's house, and saw the minstrels and the people
making a noise,
24 He said unto them, Give place: for the maid is not dead, but sleepeth. And they
laughed him to scorn.
25 But when the people were put forth, he went in, and took her by the hand, and the
maid arose.
26 And the fame hereof went abroad into all that land. (Matt 9:18-26)

41 - HEALING AND MOCKERY

27 ¶ And when Jesus departed thence, two blind men followed him, crying, and saying,
Thou Son of David, have mercy on us.
28 And when he was come into the house, the blind men came to him: and Jesus saith
unto them, Believe ye that I am able to do this? They said unto him, Yea, Lord.
29 Then touched he their eyes, saying, According to your faith be it unto you.
30 And their eyes were opened; and Jesus straitly charged them, saying, See *that* no
man know *it*.
31 But they, when they were departed, spread abroad his fame in all that country.
32 ¶ As they went out, behold, they brought to him a dumb man possessed with a devil.
33 And when the devil was cast out, the dumb spake:
33 and the multitudes marvelled, saying, It was never so seen in Israel.
34 But the Pharisees said, He casteth out devils through the prince of the devils.
35 And Jesus went about all the cities and villages, teaching in their synagogues, and
preaching the gospel of the kingdom, and healing every sickness and every disease
among the people.
36 ¶ But when he saw the multitudes, he was moved with compassion on them, because
they fainted, and were scattered abroad, as sheep having no shepherd.
37 Then saith he unto his disciples, The harvest truly *is* plenteous, but the labourers *are*
few;
38 Pray ye therefore the Lord of the harvest, that he will send forth labourers into his
harvest. (Matt 9:27-38)

42 - THE DISCIPLES ARE TAUGHT TO HEAL

1 And when he had called unto *him* his twelve disciples, he gave them power *against*
unclean spirits, to cast them out, and to heal all manner of sickness and all manner of
disease.
2 Now the names of the twelve apostles are these; The first, Simon, who is called Peter,

and Andrew his brother; James *the son* of Zebedee, and John his brother;
3 Philip, and Bartholomew; Thomas, and Matthew the publican; James *the son* of
Alphæus, and Lebbæus, whose surname was Thaddæus;
4 Simon the Canaanite, and Judas Iscariot, who also betrayed him.
5 These twelve Jesus sent forth, and commanded them, saying,
5 Go not into the way of the Gentiles, and into *any* city of the Samaritans enter ye not:
6 But go rather to the lost sheep of the house of Israel.
7 And as ye go, preach, saying, The kingdom of heaven is at hand.
8 Heal the sick, cleanse the lepers, raise the dead, cast out devils: freely ye have
received, freely give.
9 Provide neither gold, nor silver, nor brass in your purses,
10 Nor scrip for *your* journey, neither two coats, neither shoes, nor yet staves: for the
workman is worthy of his meat.
11 And into whatsoever city or town ye shall enter, inquire who in it is worthy; and
there abide till ye go thence.
12 And when ye come into an house, salute it.
13 And if the house be worthy, let your peace come upon it:
13 but if it be not worthy, let your peace return to you.
14 And whosoever shall not receive you, nor hear your words, when ye depart out of
that house or city, shake off the dust of your feet.
15 Verily I say unto you, It shall be more tolerable for the land of Sodom and
Gomorrha in the day of judgment, than for that city.
16 ¶ Behold, I send you forth as sheep in the midst of wolves: be ye therefore wise as
serpents, and harmless as doves.
17 But beware of men: for they will deliver you up to the councils, and they will
scourge you in their synagogues;
18 And ye shall be brought before governors and kings for my sake, for a testimony
against them and the Gentiles.
19 But when they deliver you up, take no thought how or what ye shall speak: for it
shall be given you in that same hour what ye shall speak.
20 For it is not ye that speak, but the Spirit of your Father which speaketh in you.
21 And the brother shall deliver up the brother to death, and the father the child: and the
children shall rise up against *their* parents, and cause them to be put to death.
22 And ye shall be hated of all *men* for my name's sake: but he that endureth to the end
shall be saved.
23 But when they persecute you in this city, flee ye into another: for verily I say unto
you, Ye shall not have gone over the cities of Israel, till the Son of man be come.
24 The disciple is not above *his* master, nor the servant above his lord.
25 It is enough for the disciple that he be as his master, and the servant as his lord. If
they have called the master of the house Beelzebub, how much more *shall they call*
them of his household?
26 Fear them not therefore: for there is nothing covered, that shall not be revealed; and
hid, that shall not be known.
27 What I tell you in darkness, *that* speak ye in light: and what ye hear in the ear, *that*
preach ye upon the housetops.
28 And fear not them which kill the body, but are not able to kill the soul: but rather

fear him which is able to destroy both soul and body in hell.
29 Are not two sparrows sold for a farthing? and one of them shall not fall on the
ground without your Father.
30 But the very hairs of your head are all numbered.
31 Fear ye not therefore, ye are of more value than many sparrows.
32 Whosoever therefore shall confess me before men, him will I confess also before my
Father which is in heaven.
33 But whosoever shall deny me before men, him will I also deny before my Father
which is in heaven.
34 Think not that I am come to send peace on earth: I came not to send peace, but a
sword.
35 For I am come to set a man at variance against his father, and the daughter against
her mother, and the daughter in law against her mother in law.
36 And a man's foes *shall be* they of his own household.
37 He that loveth father or mother more than me is not worthy of me: and he that loveth
son or daughter more than me is not worthy of me.
38 And he that taketh not his cross, and followeth after me, is not worthy of me.
39 He that findeth his life shall lose it: and he that loseth his life for my sake shall find
it.
40 ¶ He that receiveth you receiveth me, and he that receiveth me receiveth him that
sent me.
41 He that receiveth a prophet in the name of a prophet shall receive a prophet's reward;
and he that receiveth a righteous man in the name of a righteous man shall receive a
righteous man's reward.
42 And whosoever shall give to drink unto one of these little ones a cup of cold *water*
only in the name of a disciple, verily I say unto you, he shall in no wise lose his reward.
(Matt 10:1-42)

43 - UNBELIEF, CALLOUSNESS, AND INGRATITUDE REBUKED

1 And it came to pass, when Jesus had made an end of commanding his twelve
disciples, he departed thence to teach and to preach in their cities.
2 Now when John had heard in the prison the works of Christ, he sent two of his
disciples,
3 And said unto him, Art thou he that should come, or do we look for another?
4 Jesus answered and said unto them, Go and shew John again those things which ye
do hear and see:
5 The blind receive their sight, and the lame walk, the lepers are cleansed, and the deaf
hear, the dead are raised up, and the poor have the gospel preached to them.
6 And blessed is *he*, whosoever shall not be offended in me.
7 ¶ And as they departed, Jesus began to say unto the multitudes concerning John,
What went ye out into the wilderness to see? A reed shaken with the wind?
8 But what went ye out for to see? A man clothed in soft raiment? behold, they that
wear soft *clothing* are in kings' houses.
9 But what went ye out for to see? A prophet? yea, I say unto you, and more than a
prophet.
10 For this is *he*, of whom it is written, Behold, I send my messenger before thy face,
which shall prepare thy way before thee.

11 Verily I say unto you, Among them that are born of women there hath not risen a
greater than John the Baptist: notwithstanding he that is least in the kingdom of heaven
is greater than he.
12 And from the days of John the Baptist until now the kingdom of heaven suffereth
violence, and the violent take it by force.
13 For all the prophets and the law prophesied until John.
14 And if ye will receive *it*, this is Elias, which was for to come.
15 He that hath ears to hear, let him hear.
16 ¶ But whereunto shall I liken this generation? It is like unto children sitting in the
markets, and calling unto their fellows,
17 And saying, We have piped unto you, and ye have not danced; we have mourned
unto you, and ye have not lamented.
18 For John came neither eating nor drinking, and they say, He hath a devil.
19 The Son of man came eating and drinking, and they say, Behold a man gluttonous,
and a winebibber, a friend of publicans and sinners. But wisdom is justified of her
children.
20 ¶ Then began he to upbraid the cities wherein most of his mighty works were done,
because they repented not:
21 Woe unto thee, Chorazin! woe unto thee, Bethsaida! for if the mighty works, which
were done in you, had been done in Tyre and Sidon, they would have repented long ago
in sackcloth and ashes.
22 But I say unto you, It shall be more tolerable for Tyre and Sidon at the day of
judgment, than for you.
23 And thou, Capernaum, which art exalted unto heaven, shalt be brought down to hell:
for if the mighty works, which have been done in thee, had been done in Sodom, it
would have remained until this day.
24 But I say unto you, That it shall be more tolerable for the land of Sodom in the day
of judgment, than for thee.
25 ¶ At that time Jesus answered and said, I thank thee, O Father, Lord of heaven and
earth, because thou hast hid these things from the wise and prudent, and hast revealed
them unto babes.
26 Even so, Father: for so it seemed good in thy sight.
27 All things are delivered unto me of my Father: and no man knoweth the Son, but the
Father; neither knoweth any man the Father, save the Son, and *he* to whomsoever the
Son will reveal *him*.
28 ¶ Come unto me, all *ye* that labour and are heavy laden, and I will give you rest.
29 Take my yoke upon you, and learn of me; for I am meek and lowly in heart: and ye
shall find rest unto your souls.
30 For my yoke *is* easy, and my burden is light. (Matt 11:1-30)

44 – PARALYSIS HEALED AT THE POOL OF BETHESDA

1 After this there was a feast of the Jews; and Jesus went up to Jerusalem.
2 Now there is at Jerusalem by the sheep *market* a pool, which is called in the Hebrew
tongue Bethesda, having five porches.
3 In these lay a great multitude of impotent folk, of blind, halt, withered, waiting for
the moving of the water.
4 For an angel went down at a certain season into the pool, and troubled the water:

whosoever then first after the troubling of the water stepped in was made whole of
whatsoever disease he had.
5 And a certain man was there, which had an infirmity thirty and eight years.
6 When Jesus saw him lie, and knew that he had been now a long time *in that case*, he
saith unto him, Wilt thou be made whole?
7 The impotent man answered him, Sir, I have no man, when the water is troubled, to
put me into the pool: but while I am coming, another steppeth down before me.
8 Jesus saith unto him, Rise, take up thy bed, and walk.
9 And immediately the man was made whole, and took up his bed, and walked: and on
the same day was the sabbath.
10 ¶ The Jews therefore said unto him that was cured, It is the sabbath day: it is not
lawful for thee to carry *thy* bed.
11 He answered them, He that made me whole, the same said unto me, Take up thy
bed, and walk.
12 Then asked they him, What man is that which said unto thee, Take up thy bed, and
walk?
13 And he that was healed wist not who it was: for Jesus had conveyed himself away, a
multitude being in *that* place.
14 Afterward Jesus findeth him in the temple, and said unto him, Behold, thou art made
whole: sin no more, lest a worse thing come unto thee.
15 The man departed, and told the Jews that it was Jesus, which had made him whole.
16 And therefore did the Jews persecute Jesus, and sought to slay him, because he had
done these things on the sabbath day.
17 ¶ But Jesus answered them, My Father worketh hitherto, and I work.
18 Therefore the Jews sought the more to kill him, because he not only had broken the
sabbath, but said also that God was his Father, making himself equal with God.
19 Then answered Jesus and said unto them, Verily, verily, I say unto you, The Son can
do nothing of himself, but what he seeth the Father do: for what things soever he doeth,
these also doeth the Son likewise.
20 For the Father loveth the Son, and sheweth him all things that himself doeth: and he
will shew him greater works than these, that ye may marvel.
21 For as the Father raiseth up the dead, and quickeneth *them*; even so the Son
quickeneth whom he will.
22 For the Father judgeth no man, but hath committed all judgment unto the Son:
23 That all *men* should honour the Son, even as they honour the Father. He that
honoureth not the Son honoureth not the Father which hath sent him.
24 Verily, verily, I say unto you, He that heareth my word, and believeth on him that
sent me, hath everlasting life, and shall not come into condemnation; but is passed from
death unto life.
25 Verily, verily, I say unto you, The hour is coming, and now is, when the dead shall
hear the voice of the Son of God: and they that hear shall live.
26 For as the Father hath life in himself; so hath he given to the Son to have life in
himself;
27 And hath given him authority to execute judgment also, because he is the Son of
man.
28 Marvel not at this: for the hour is coming, in the which all that are in the graves shall

hear his voice,
29 And shall come forth; they that have done good, unto the resurrection of life; and they that have done evil, unto the resurrection of damnation.
30 I can of mine own self do nothing: as I hear, I judge: and my judgment is just; because I seek not mine own will, but the will of the Father which hath sent me.
31 If I bear witness of myself, my witness is not true.
32 ¶ There is another that beareth witness of me; and I know that the witness which he witnesseth of me is true.
33 Ye sent unto John, and he bare witness unto the truth.
34 But I receive not testimony from man: but these things I say, that ye might be saved.
35 He was a burning and a shining light: and ye were willing for a season to rejoice in his light.
36 ¶ But I have greater witness than *that* of John: for the works which the Father hath given me to finish, the same works that I do, bear witness of me, that the Father hath sent me.
37 And the Father himself, which hath sent me, hath borne witness of me. Ye have neither heard his voice at any time, nor seen his shape.
38 And ye have not his word abiding in you: for whom he hath sent, him ye believe not.
39 ¶ Search the scriptures; for in them ye think ye have eternal life: and they are they which testify of me.
40 And ye will not come to me, that ye might have life.
41 I receive not honour from men.
42 But I know you, that ye have not the love of God in you.
43 I am come in my Father's name, and ye receive me not: if another shall come in his own name, him ye will receive.
44 How can ye believe, which receive honour one of another, and seek not the honour that *cometh* from God only?
45 Do not think that I will accuse you to the Father: there is *one* that accuseth you, *even* Moses, in whom ye trust.
46 For had ye believed Moses, ye would have believed me: for he wrote of me.
47 But if ye believe not his writings, how shall ye believe my words? (John 5:1-47

45 - DISPUTES CONCERNING THE SABBATH

According to the Gospel of Mark

23 And it came to pass, that he went through the corn fields on the sabbath day; and his disciples began, as they went, to pluck the ears of corn.
24 And the Pharisees said unto him, Behold, why do they on the sabbath day that which is not lawful?
25 And he said unto them, Have ye never read what David did, when he had need, and was an hungered, he, and they that were with him?
26 How he went into the house of God in the days of Abiathar the high priest, and did eat the shewbread, which is not lawful to eat but for the priests, and gave also to them which were with him?
27 And he said unto them, The sabbath was made for man, and not man for the sabbath:
28 Therefore the Son of man is Lord also of the sabbath. (Mark 2:23-28)

According to the Gospel of Luke

1 And it came to pass on the second sabbath after the first, that he went through the
corn fields; and his disciples plucked the ears of corn, and did eat, rubbing *them* in *their*
hands.
2 And certain of the Pharisees said unto them, Why do ye that which is not lawful to do
on the sabbath days?
3 And Jesus answering them said, Have ye not read so much as this, what David did,
when himself was an hungered, and they which were with him;
4 How he went into the house of God, and did take and eat the shewbread, and gave
also to them that were with him; which it is not lawful to eat but for the priests alone?
5 And he said unto them, That the Son of man is Lord also of the sabbath. (Luke 6:1-5)

According to the Gospel of Matthew

1 At that time Jesus went on the sabbath day through the corn; and his disciples were
an hungered, and began to pluck the ears of corn, and to eat.
2 But when the Pharisees saw *it*, they said unto him, Behold, thy disciples do that
which is not lawful to do upon the sabbath day.
3 But he said unto them, Have ye not read what David did, when he was an hungered,
and they that were with him;
4 How he entered into the house of God, and did eat the shewbread, which was not
lawful for him to eat, neither for them which were with him, but only for the priests?
5 Or have ye not read in the law, how that on the sabbath days the priests in the temple
profane the sabbath, and are blameless?
6 But I say unto you, That in this place is *one* greater than the temple.
7 But if ye had known what *this* meaneth, I will have mercy, and not sacrifice, ye
would not have condemned the guiltless.
8 For the Son of man is Lord even of the sabbath day. (Matt 12:1-8)

46 - IT IS LAWFUL TO HEAL ON THE SABBATH DAYS!

According to the Gospel of Matthew

9 And when he was departed thence, he went into their synagogue:
10 ¶ And, behold, there was a man which had *his* hand withered. And they asked him,
saying, Is it lawful to heal on the sabbath days? that they might accuse him.
11 And he said unto them, What man shall there be among you, that shall have one
sheep, and if it fall into a pit on the sabbath day, will he not lay hold on it, and lift *it*
out?
12 How much then is a man better than a sheep? Wherefore it is lawful to do well on
the sabbath days.
13 Then saith he to the man, Stretch forth thine hand. And he stretched *it* forth; and it
was restored whole, like as the other.
14 ¶ Then the Pharisees went out, and held a council against him, how they might
destroy him.
15 But when Jesus knew *it*, he withdrew himself from thence: (Matt 12:9-15 to :)

According to the Gospel of Luke

6 And it came to pass also on another sabbath, that he entered into the synagogue and
taught: and there was a man whose right hand was withered.

7 And the scribes and Pharisees watched him, whether he would heal on the sabbath
day; that they might find an accusation against him.
8 But he knew their thoughts, and said to the man which had the withered hand, Rise
up, and stand forth in the midst. And he arose and stood forth.
9 Then said Jesus unto them, I will ask you one thing; Is it lawful on the sabbath days
to do good, or to do evil? to save life, or to destroy *it*?
10 And looking round about upon them all, he said unto the man, Stretch forth thy
hand. And he did so: and his hand was restored whole as the other.
11 And they were filled with madness; and communed one with another what they
might do to Jesus. (Luke 6:6-11)

According to the Gospel of Mark

1 And he entered again into the synagogue; and there was a man there which had a
withered hand.
2 And they watched him, whether he would heal him on the sabbath day; that they
might accuse him.
3 And he saith unto the man which had the withered hand, Stand forth.
4 And he saith unto them, Is it lawful to do good on the sabbath days, or to do evil? to
save life, or to kill? But they held their peace.
5 And when he had looked round about on them with anger, being grieved for the
hardness of their hearts, he saith unto the man, Stretch forth thine hand. And he
stretched *it* out: and his hand was restored whole as the other.
6 And the Pharisees went forth, and straightway took counsel with the Herodians
against him, how they might destroy him.
7 But Jesus withdrew himself with his disciples to the sea: (Mark 3:1-7 to :)

47 - MULTITUDES SEEK HEALING

According to the Gospel of Mark

7 and a great multitude from Galilee followed him, and from Judæa,
8 And from Jerusalem, and from Idumæa, and *from* beyond Jordan; and they about
Tyre and Sidon, a great multitude, when they had heard what great things he did, came
unto him.
9 And he spake to his disciples, that a small ship should wait on him because of the
multitude, lest they should throng him.
10 For he had healed many; insomuch that they pressed upon him for to touch him, as
many as had plagues.
11 And unclean spirits, when they saw him, fell down before him, and cried, saying,
Thou art the Son of God.
12 And he straitly charged them that they should not make him known. (Mark 3:7-12 *and*)

According to the Gospel of Matthew

15 and great multitudes followed him, and he healed them all;
16 And charged them that they should not make him known:
17 That it might be fulfilled which was spoken by Esaias the prophet, saying,
18 Behold my servant, whom I have chosen; my beloved, in whom my soul is well
pleased: I will put my spirit upon him, and he shall shew judgment to the Gentiles.
19 He shall not strive, nor cry; neither shall any man hear his voice in the streets.
20 A bruised reed shall he not break, and smoking flax shall he not quench, till he send

forth judgment unto victory.
21 And in his name shall the Gentiles trust. (Matt 12:15-21 *and*)

48 - MORE PREPARATION TO PREACH AND HEAL

According to the Gospel of Mark

13 And he goeth up into a mountain, and calleth *unto him* whom he would: and they
came unto him.
14 And he ordained twelve, that they should be with him, and that he might send them
forth to preach,
15 And to have power to heal sicknesses, and to cast out devils:
16 And Simon he surnamed Peter;
17 And James the *son* of Zebedee, and John the brother of James; and he surnamed
them Boanerges, which is, The sons of thunder:
18 And Andrew, and Philip, and Bartholomew, and Matthew, and Thomas, and James
the *son* of Alphæus, and Thaddæus, and Simon the Canaanite,
19 And Judas Iscariot, which also betrayed him: (Mark 3:13-19 to :)

According to the Gospel of Luke

12 And it came to pass in those days, that he went out into a mountain to pray, and
continued all night in prayer to God.
13 ¶ And when it was day, he called *unto him* his disciples: and of them he chose
twelve, whom also he named apostles;
14 Simon, (whom he also named Peter,) and Andrew his brother, James and John,
Philip and Bartholomew,
15 Matthew and Thomas, James the *son* of Alphæus, and Simon called Zelotes,
16 And Judas *the brother* of James, and Judas Iscariot, which also was the traitor.
17 ¶ And he came down with them, and stood in the plain, and the company of his
disciples, and a great multitude of people out of all Judæa and Jerusalem, and from the
sea coast of Tyre and Sidon, which came to hear him, and to be healed of their diseases;
18 And they that were vexed with unclean spirits: and they were healed.
19 And the whole multitude sought to touch him: for there went virtue out of him, and
healed *them* all. (Luke 6:12-19)

49 - THE SERMON ON THE PLAIN

20 ¶ And he lifted up his eyes on his disciples, and said, Blessed *be ye* poor: for yours
is the kingdom of God.
21 Blessed *are ye* that hunger now: for ye shall be filled. Blessed *are ye* that weep
now: for ye shall laugh.
22 Blessed are ye, when men shall hate you, and when they shall separate you *from
their company*, and shall reproach *you*, and cast out your name as evil, for the Son of
man's sake.
23 Rejoice ye in that day, and leap for joy: for, behold, your reward *is* great in heaven:
for in the like manner did their fathers unto the prophets.
24 But woe unto you that are rich! for ye have received your consolation.
25 Woe unto you that are full! for ye shall hunger. Woe unto you that laugh now! for
ye shall mourn and weep.
26 Woe unto you, when all men shall speak well of you! for so did their fathers to the

false prophets.
27 ¶ But I say unto you which hear, Love your enemies, do good to them which hate
you,
28 Bless them that curse you, and pray for them which despitefully use you.
29 And unto him that smiteth thee on the *one* cheek offer also the other; and him that
taketh away thy cloak forbid not *to take thy* coat also.
30 Give to every man that asketh of thee; and of him that taketh away thy goods ask
them not again.
31 And as ye would that men should do to you, do ye also to them likewise.
32 For if ye love them which love you, what thank have ye? for sinners also love those
that love them.
33 And if ye do good to them which do good to you, what thank have ye? for sinners
also do even the same.
34 And if ye lend *to them* of whom ye hope to receive, what thank have ye? for sinners
also lend to sinners, to receive as much again.
35 But love ye your enemies, and do good, and lend, hoping for nothing again; and
your reward shall be great, and ye shall be the children of the Highest: for he is kind
unto the unthankful and *to* the evil.
36 Be ye therefore merciful, as your Father also is merciful.
37 Judge not, and ye shall not be judged: condemn not, and ye shall not be condemned:
forgive, and ye shall be forgiven:
38 Give, and it shall be given unto you; good measure, pressed down, and shaken
together, and running over, shall men give into your bosom. For with the same
measure that ye mete withal it shall be measured to you again.
39 And he spake a parable unto them, Can the blind lead the blind? shall they not both
fall into the ditch?
40 The disciple is not above his master: but every one that is perfect shall be as his
master.
41 And why beholdest thou the mote that is in thy brother's eye, but perceivest not the
beam that is in thine own eye?
42 Either how canst thou say to thy brother, Brother, let me pull out the mote that is in
thine eye, when thou thyself beholdest not the beam that is in thine own eye? Thou
hypocrite, cast out first the beam out of thine own eye, and then shalt thou see clearly to
pull out the mote that is in thy brother's eye.
43 For a good tree bringeth not forth corrupt fruit; neither doth a corrupt tree bring forth
good fruit.
44 For every tree is known by his own fruit. For of thorns men do not gather figs, nor
of a bramble bush gather they grapes.
45 A good man out of the good treasure of his heart bringeth forth that which is good;
and an evil man out of the evil treasure of his heart bringeth forth that which is evil: for
of the abundance of the heart his mouth speaketh.
46 ¶ And why call ye me, Lord, Lord, and do not the things which I say?
47 Whosoever cometh to me, and heareth my sayings, and doeth them, I will shew you
to whom he is like:
48 He is like a man which built an house, and digged deep, and laid the foundation on a
rock: and when the flood arose, the stream beat vehemently upon that house, and could

not shake it: for it was founded upon a rock.
49 But he that heareth, and doeth not, is like a man that without a foundation built an
house upon the earth; against which the stream did beat vehemently, and immediately it
fell; and the ruin of that house was great. (Luke 6:20-49)

50 - THE CENTURION'S SERVANT IS HEALED

1 Now when he had ended all his sayings in the audience of the people, he entered into
Capernaum.
2 And a certain centurion's servant, who was dear unto him, was sick, and ready to die.
3 And when he heard of Jesus, he sent unto him the elders of the Jews, beseeching him
that he would come and heal his servant.
4 And when they came to Jesus, they besought him instantly, saying, That he was
worthy for whom he should do this:
5 For he loveth our nation, and he hath built us a synagogue.
6 Then Jesus went with them. And when he was now not far from the house, the
centurion sent friends to him, saying unto him, Lord, trouble not thyself: for I am not
worthy that thou shouldest enter under my roof:
7 Wherefore neither thought I myself worthy to come unto thee: but say in a word, and
my servant shall be healed.
8 For I also am a man set under authority, having under me soldiers, and I say unto
one, Go, and he goeth; and to another, Come, and he cometh; and to my servant, Do
this, and he doeth *it*.
9 When Jesus heard these things, he marvelled at him, and turned him about, and said
unto the people that followed him, I say unto you, I have not found so great faith, no,
not in Israel.
10 And they that were sent, returning to the house, found the servant whole that had
been sick. (Luke 7:1-10)

51 - A WIDOW'S SON IS RAISED TO LIFE

11 ¶ And it came to pass the day after, that he went into a city called Nain; and many of
his disciples went with him, and much people.
12 Now when he came nigh to the gate of the city, behold, there was a dead man
carried out, the only son of his mother, and she was a widow: and much people of the
city was with her.
13 And when the Lord saw her, he had compassion on her, and said unto her, Weep not.
14 And he came and touched the bier: and they that bare *him* stood still. And he said,
Young man, I say unto thee, Arise.
15 And he that was dead sat up, and began to speak. And he delivered him to his
mother.
16 And there came a fear on all: and they glorified God, saying, That a great prophet is
risen up among us; and, That God hath visited his people.
17 And this rumour of him went forth throughout all Judæa, and throughout all the
region round about.
18 And the disciples of John shewed him of all these things. (Luke 7:11-18)

52 - JESUS TESTIFIES CONCERNING JOHN THE BAPTIST

19 ¶ And John calling *unto him* two of his disciples sent *them* to Jesus, saying, Art thou
he that should come? or look we for another?
20 When the men were come unto him, they said, John Baptist hath sent us unto thee,
saying, Art thou he that should come? or look we for another?
21 And in that same hour he cured many of *their* infirmities and plagues, and of evil
spirits; and unto many *that were* blind he gave sight.
22 Then Jesus answering said unto them, Go your way, and tell John what things ye
have seen and heard; how that the blind see, the lame walk, the lepers are cleansed, the
deaf hear, the dead are raised, to the poor the gospel is preached.
23 And blessed is *he*, whosoever shall not be offended in me.
24 ¶ And when the messengers of John were departed, he began to speak unto the
people concerning John, What went ye out into the wilderness for to see? A reed
shaken with the wind?
25 But what went ye out for to see? A man clothed in soft raiment? Behold, they which
are gorgeously apparelled, and live delicately, are in kings' courts.
26 But what went ye out for to see? A prophet? Yea, I say unto you, and much more
than a prophet.
27 This is *he*, of whom it is written, Behold, I send my messenger before thy face,
which shall prepare thy way before thee.
28 For I say unto you, Among those that are born of women there is not a greater
prophet than John the Baptist:
28 but he that is least in the kingdom of God is greater than he. (Luke 7:19-28)

53 - PHARISEES REBUKED FOR REJECTING JOHN AND JESUS

29 And all the people that heard *him*, and the publicans, justified God, being baptized
with the baptism of John.
30 But the Pharisees and lawyers rejected the counsel of God against themselves, being
not baptized of him.
31 ¶ And the Lord said, Whereunto then shall I liken the men of this generation? and to
what are they like?
32 They are like unto children sitting in the marketplace, and calling one to another,
and saying, We have piped unto you, and ye have not danced; we have mourned to you,
and ye have not wept.
33 For John the Baptist came neither eating bread nor drinking wine; and ye say, He
hath a devil.
34 The Son of man is come eating and drinking; and ye say, Behold a gluttonous man,
and a winebibber, a friend of publicans and sinners!
35 But wisdom is justified of all her children. (Luke 7:29-35)

54 - A LESSON IN LOVE

36 ¶ And one of the Pharisees desired him that he would eat with him. And he went
into the Pharisee's house, and sat down to meat.
37 And, behold, a woman in the city, which was a sinner, when she knew that *Jesus* sat
at meat in the Pharisee's house, brought an alabaster box of ointment,
38 And stood at his feet behind *him* weeping, and began to wash his feet with tears, and

did wipe *them* with the hairs of her head, and kissed his feet, and anointed *them* with
the ointment.
39 Now when the Pharisee which had bidden him saw *it*, he spake within himself,
saying, This man, if he were a prophet, would have known who and what manner of
woman *this is* that toucheth him: for she is a sinner.
40 And Jesus answering said unto him, Simon, I have somewhat to say unto thee. And
he saith, Master, say on.
41 There was a certain creditor which had two debtors: the one owed five hundred
pence, and the other fifty.
42 And when they had nothing to pay, he frankly forgave them both. Tell me therefore,
which of them will love him most?
43 Simon answered and said, I suppose that *he*, to whom he forgave most. And he said
unto him, Thou hast rightly judged.
44 And he turned to the woman, and said unto Simon, Seest thou this woman? I
entered into thine house, thou gavest me no water for my feet: but she hath washed my
feet with tears, and wiped *them* with the hairs of her head.
45 Thou gavest me no kiss: but this woman since the time I came in hath not ceased to
kiss my feet.
46 My head with oil thou didst not anoint: but this woman hath anointed my feet with
ointment.
47 Wherefore I say unto thee, Her sins, which are many, are forgiven; for she loved
much: but to whom little is forgiven, *the same* loveth little
48 And he said unto her, Thy sins are forgiven.
49 And they that sat at meat with him began to say within themselves, Who is this that
forgiveth sins also?
50 And he said to the woman, Thy faith hath saved thee; go in peace. (Luke 7:36-50)

55 - SOME QUALITIES NEEDED TO BE A SUCCESSFUL DISCIPLE

1 And it came to pass afterward, that he went throughout every city and village,
preaching and shewing the glad tidings of the kingdom of God: and the twelve *were*
with him,
2 And certain women, which had been healed of evil spirits and infirmities, Mary
called Magdalene, out of whom went seven devils,
3 And Joanna the wife of Chuza Herod's steward, and Susanna, and many others,
which ministered unto him of their substance.
4 ¶ And when much people were gathered together, and were come to him out of every
city, he spake by a parable:
5 A sower went out to sow his seed: and as he sowed, some fell by the way side; and it
was trodden down, and the fowls of the air devoured it.
6 And some fell upon a rock; and as soon as it was sprung up, it withered away,
because it lacked moisture.
7 And some fell among thorns; and the thorns sprang up with it, and choked it.
8 And other fell on good ground, and sprang up, and bare fruit an hundredfold. And
when he had said these things, he cried, He that hath ears to hear, let him hear.
9 ¶ And his disciples asked him, saying, What might this parable be?
10 And he said, Unto you it is given to know the mysteries of the kingdom of God: but

to others in parables; that seeing they might not see, and hearing they might not
understand.
11 Now the parable is this: The seed is the word of God.
12 Those by the way side are they that hear; then cometh the devil, and taketh away the
word out of their hearts, lest they should believe and be saved.
13 They on the rock *are they*, which, when they hear, receive the word with joy; and
these have no root, which for a while believe, and in time of temptation fall away.
14 And that which fell among thorns are they, which, when they have heard, go forth,
and are choked with cares and riches and pleasures of *this* life, and bring no fruit to
perfection.
15 But that on the good ground are they, which in an honest and good heart, having
heard the word, keep *it*, and bring forth fruit with patience.
16 ¶ No man, when he hath lighted a candle, covereth it with a vessel, or putteth *it*
under a bed; but setteth *it* on a candlestick, that they which enter in may see the light.
17 For nothing is secret, that shall not be made manifest; neither *any thing* hid, that
shall not be known and come abroad.
18 Take heed therefore how ye hear: for whosoever hath, to him shall be given; and
whosoever hath not, from him shall be taken even that which he seemeth to have. (Luke
8:1-18)

56 – DECLARED INSANE BY HIS FAMIILY

19 and they went into an house.
20 And the multitude cometh together again, so that they could not so much as eat
bread.
21 And when his friends heard *of it*, they went out to lay hold on him: for they said, He
is beside himself. (Mark 3:19-21 *and*)

57 – ACCUSED OF HEALING THROUGH BEELZEBUB

22 ¶ And the scribes which came down from Jerusalem said, He hath Beelzebub, and
by the prince of the devils casteth he out devils.
23 And he called them *unto him*, and said unto them in parables, How can Satan cast
out Satan?
24 And if a kingdom be divided against itself, that kingdom cannot stand.
25 And if a house be divided against itself, that house cannot stand.
26 And if Satan rise up against himself, and be divided, he cannot stand, but hath an
end.
27 No man can enter into a strong man's house, and spoil his goods, except he will first
bind the strong man; and then he will spoil his house.
28 Verily I say unto you, All sins shall be forgiven unto the sons of men, and
blasphemies wherewith soever they shall blaspheme:
29 But he that shall blaspheme against the Holy Ghost hath never forgiveness, but is in
danger of eternal damnation
30 Because they said, He hath an unclean spirit. (Mark 3:22-30)
22 ¶ Then was brought unto him one possessed with a devil, blind, and dumb: and he
healed him, insomuch that the blind and dumb both spake and saw.
23 And all the people were amazed, and said, Is not this the son of David?
24 But when the Pharisees heard *it*, they said, This *fellow* doth not cast out devils, but

by Beelzebub the prince of the devils.
25 And Jesus knew their thoughts, and said unto them, Every kingdom divided against
itself is brought to desolation; and every city or house divided against itself shall not
stand:
26 And if Satan cast out Satan, he is divided against himself; how shall then his
kingdom stand?
27 And if I by Beelzebub cast out devils, by whom do your children cast *them* out?
therefore they shall be your judges.
28 But if I cast out devils by the Spirit of God, then the kingdom of God is come unto
you.
29 Or else how can one enter into a strong man's house, and spoil his goods, except he
first bind the strong man? and then he will spoil his house.
30 He that is not with me is against me; and he that gathereth not with me scattereth
abroad.
31 ¶ Wherefore I say unto you, All manner of sin and blasphemy shall be forgiven unto
men: but the blasphemy *against* the *Holy* Ghost shall not be forgiven unto men.
32 And whosoever speaketh a word against the Son of man, it shall be forgiven him:
but whosoever speaketh against the Holy Ghost, it shall not be forgiven him, neither in
this world, neither in the *world* to come.
33 Either make the tree good, and his fruit good; or else make the tree corrupt, and his
fruit corrupt: for the tree is known by *his* fruit.
34 O generation of vipers, how can ye, being evil, speak good things? for out of the
abundance of the heart the mouth speaketh.
35 A good man out of the good treasure of the heart bringeth forth good things: and an
evil man out of the evil treasure bringeth forth evil things.
36 But I say unto you, That every idle word that men shall speak, they shall give
account thereof in the day of judgment.
37 For by thy words thou shalt be justified, and by thy words thou shalt be condemned.
38 ¶ Then certain of the scribes and of the Pharisees answered, saying, Master, we
would see a sign from thee.
39 But he answered and said unto them, An evil and adulterous generation seeketh after
a sign; and there shall no sign be given to it, but the sign of the prophet Jonas:
40 For as Jonas was three days and three nights in the whale's belly; so shall the Son of
man be three days and three nights in the heart of the earth.
41 The men of Nineveh shall rise in judgment with this generation, and shall condemn
it: because they repented at the preaching of Jonas; and, behold, a greater than Jonas *is*
here.
42 The queen of the south shall rise up in the judgment with this generation, and shall
condemn it: for she came from the uttermost parts of the earth to hear the wisdom of
Solomon; and, behold, a greater than Solomon *is* here.
43 When the unclean spirit is gone out of a man, he walketh through dry places,
seeking rest, and findeth none.
44 Then he saith, I will return into my house from whence I came out; and when he is
come, he findeth *it* empty, swept, and garnished.
45 Then goeth he, and taketh with himself seven other spirits more wicked than
himself, and they enter in and dwell there: and the last *state* of that man is worse than

the first. Even so shall it be also unto this wicked generation. (Matt 12:22-45)

58 – GOD'S FAMILY ARE THOSE WHO DO HIS WILL

According to the Gospel of Mark

31 ¶ There came then his brethren and his mother, and, standing without, sent unto him,
calling him.
32 And the multitude sat about him, and they said unto him, Behold, thy mother and thy
brethren without seek for thee.
33 And he answered them, saying, Who is my mother, or my brethren?
34 And he looked round about on them which sat about him, and said, Behold my
mother and my brethren!
35 For whosoever shall do the will of God, the same is my brother, and my sister, and
mother. (Mark 3:31-35)

According to the Gospel of Luke

19 ¶ Then came to him *his* mother and his brethren, and could not come at him for the
press.
20 And it was told him *by certain* which said, Thy mother and thy brethren stand
without, desiring to see thee.
21 And he answered and said unto them, My mother and my brethren are these which
hear the word of God, and do it. (Luke 8:19-21)

According to the Gospel of Matthew

46 ¶ While he yet talked to the people, behold, *his* mother and his brethren stood
without, desiring to speak with him.
47 Then one said unto him, Behold, thy mother and thy brethren stand without, desiring
to speak with thee.
48 But he answered and said unto him that told him, Who is my mother? and who are
my brethren?
49 And he stretched forth his hand toward his disciples, and said, Behold my mother
and my brethren!
50 For whosoever shall do the will of my Father which is in heaven, the same is my
brother, and sister, and mother. (Matt 12:46-50)

59 – CHRISTIANITY IN PARABLES

1 The same day went Jesus out of the house, and sat by the sea side.
2 And great multitudes were gathered together unto him, so that he went into a ship,
and sat; and the whole multitude stood on the shore.
3 And he spake many things unto them in parables, saying,
3 Behold, a sower went forth to sow;
4 And when he sowed, some *seeds* fell by the way side, and the fowls came and
devoured them up:
5 Some fell upon stony places, where they had not much earth: and forthwith they
sprung up, because they had no deepness of earth:
6 And when the sun was up, they were scorched; and because they had no root, they
withered away.
7 And some fell among thorns; and the thorns sprung up, and choked them:

8 But other fell into good ground, and brought forth fruit, some an hundredfold, some
sixtyfold, some thirtyfold.
9 Who hath ears to hear, let him hear.
10 And the disciples came, and said unto him, Why speakest thou unto them in
parables?
11 He answered and said unto them, Because it is given unto you to know the mysteries
of the kingdom of heaven, but to them it is not given.
12 For whosoever hath, to him shall be given, and he shall have more abundance: but
whosoever hath not, from him shall be taken away even that he hath.
13 Therefore speak I to them in parables: because they seeing see not; and hearing they
hear not, neither do they understand.
14 And in them is fulfilled the prophecy of Esaias, which saith, By hearing ye shall
hear, and shall not understand; and seeing ye shall see, and shall not perceive:
15 For this people's heart is waxed gross, and *their* ears are dull of hearing, and their
eyes they have closed; lest at any time they should see with *their* eyes, and hear with
their ears, and should understand with *their* heart, and should be converted, and I
should heal them.
16 But blessed *are* your eyes, for they see: and your ears, for they hear.
17 For verily I say unto you, That many prophets and righteous *men* have desired to see
those things which ye see, and have not seen *them*; and to hear *those things* which ye
hear, and have not heard *them*.
18 ¶ Hear ye therefore the parable of the sower.
19 When any one heareth the word of the kingdom, and understandeth *it* not, then
cometh the wicked *one*, and catcheth away that which was sown in his heart. This is he
which received seed by the way side.
20 But he that received the seed into stony places, the same is he that heareth the word,
and anon with joy receiveth it;
21 Yet hath he not root in himself, but dureth for a while: for when tribulation or
persecution ariseth because of the word, by and by he is offended.
22 He also that received seed among the thorns is he that heareth the word; and the care
of this world, and the deceitfulness of riches, choke the word, and he becometh
unfruitful
23 But he that received seed into the good ground is he that heareth the word, and
understandeth *it*; which also beareth fruit, and bringeth forth, some an hundredfold,
some sixty, some thirty.
24 ¶ Another parable put he forth unto them, saying, The kingdom of heaven is likened
unto a man which sowed good seed in his field:
25 But while men slept, his enemy came and sowed tares among the wheat, and went
his way.
26 But when the blade was sprung up, and brought forth fruit, then appeared the tares
also.
27 So the servants of the householder came and said unto him, Sir, didst not thou sow
good seed in thy field? from whence then hath it tares?
28 He said unto them, An enemy hath done this. The servants said unto him, Wilt thou
then that we go and gather them up?
29 But he said, Nay; lest while ye gather up the tares, ye root up also the wheat with

them.
30 Let both grow together until the harvest: and in the time of harvest I will say to the
reapers, Gather ye together first the tares, and bind them in bundles to burn them: but
gather the wheat into my barn.
31 ¶ Another parable put he forth unto them, saying, The kingdom of heaven is like to a
grain of mustard seed, which a man took, and sowed in his field:
32 Which indeed is the least of all seeds: but when it is grown, it is the greatest among
herbs, and becometh a tree, so that the birds of the air come and lodge in the branches
thereof.
33 ¶ Another parable spake he unto them; The kingdom of heaven is like unto leaven,
which a woman took, and hid in three measures of meal, till the whole was leavened.
34 All these things spake Jesus unto the multitude in parables; and without a parable
spake he not unto them:
35 That it might be fulfilled which was spoken by the prophet, saying, I will open my
mouth in parables; I will utter things which have been kept secret from the foundation
of the world.
36 Then Jesus sent the multitude away, and went into the house: and his disciples came
unto him, saying, Declare unto us the parable of the tares of the field.
37 He answered and said unto them, He that soweth the good seed is the Son of man;
38 The field is the world; the good seed are the children of the kingdom; but the tares
are the children of the wicked *one*;
39 The enemy that sowed them is the devil; the harvest is the end of the world; and the
reapers are the angels.
40 As therefore the tares are gathered and burned in the fire; so shall it be in the end of
this world.
41 The Son of man shall send forth his angels, and they shall gather out of his kingdom
all things that offend, and them which do iniquity;
42 And shall cast them into a furnace of fire: there shall be wailing and gnashing of
teeth.
43 Then shall the righteous shine forth as the sun in the kingdom of their Father.
43 Who hath ears to hear, let him hear.
44 ¶ Again, the kingdom of heaven is like unto treasure hid in a field; the which when a
man hath found, he hideth, and for joy thereof goeth and selleth all that he hath, and
buyeth that field.
45 ¶ Again, the kingdom of heaven is like unto a merchant man, seeking goodly pearls:
46 Who, when he had found one pearl of great price, went and sold all that he had, and
bought it.
47 ¶ Again, the kingdom of heaven is like unto a net, that was cast into the sea, and
gathered of every kind:
48 Which, when it was full, they drew to shore, and sat down, and gathered the good
into vessels, but cast the bad away.
49 So shall it be at the end of the world: the angels shall come forth, and sever the
wicked from among the just,
50 And shall cast them into the furnace of fire: there shall be wailing and gnashing of
teeth.
51 Jesus saith unto them, Have ye understood all these things? They say unto him,

Yea, Lord.
52 Then said he unto them, Therefore every scribe *which is* instructed unto the kingdom
of heaven is like unto a man *that is* an householder, which bringeth forth out of his
treasure *things* new and old. (Matt 13:1-52)

60 - THE NEXT DAY: REVIEW AND DEPARTURE

1 And he began again to teach by the sea side: and there was gathered unto him a great
multitude, so that he entered into a ship, and sat in the sea; and the whole multitude was
by the sea on the land.
2 And he taught them many things by parables, and said unto them in his doctrine,
3 Hearken; Behold, there went out a sower to sow:
4 And it came to pass, as he sowed, some fell by the way side, and the fowls of the air
came and devoured it up.
5 And some fell on stony ground, where it had not much earth; and immediately it
sprang up, because it had no depth of earth:
6 But when the sun was up, it was scorched; and because it had no root, it withered
away.
7 And some fell among thorns, and the thorns grew up, and choked it, and it yielded no
fruit.
8 And other fell on good ground, and did yield fruit that sprang up and increased; and
brought forth, some thirty, and some sixty, and some an hundred.
9 And he said unto them, He that hath ears to hear, let him hear.
10 And when he was alone, they that were about him with the twelve asked of him the
parable.
11 And he said unto them, Unto you it is given to know the mystery of the kingdom of
God: but unto them that are without, all *these* things are done in parables:
12 That seeing they may see, and not perceive; and hearing they may hear, and not
understand; lest at any time they should be converted, and *their* sins should be forgiven
them.
13 And he said unto them, Know ye not this parable? and how then will ye know all
parables?
14 ¶ The sower soweth the word.
15 And these are they by the way side, where the word is sown; but when they have
heard, Satan cometh immediately, and taketh away the word that was sown in their
hearts.
16 And these are they likewise which are sown on stony ground; who, when they have
heard the word, immediately receive it with gladness;
17 And have no root in themselves, and so endure but for a time: afterward, when
affliction or persecution ariseth for the word's sake, immediately they are offended.
18 And these are they which are sown among thorns; such as hear the word,
19 And the cares of this world, and the deceitfulness of riches, and the lusts of other
things entering in, choke the word, and it becometh unfruitful.
20 And these are they which are sown on good ground; such as hear the word, and
receive *it*, and bring forth fruit, some thirtyfold, some sixty, and some an hundred.
21 ¶ And he said unto them, Is a candle brought to be put under a bushel, or under a
bed? and not to be set on a candlestick?

22 For there is nothing hid, which shall not be manifested; neither was any thing kept
secret, but that it should come abroad.
23 If any man have ears to hear, let him hear.
24 And he said unto them, Take heed what ye hear: with what measure ye mete, it shall
be measured to you: and unto you that hear shall more be given.
25 For he that hath, to him shall be given: and he that hath not, from him shall be taken
even that which he hath.
26 ¶ And he said, So is the kingdom of God, as if a man should cast seed into the
ground;
27 And should sleep, and rise night and day, and the seed should spring and grow up,
he knoweth not how.
28 For the earth bringeth forth fruit of herself; first the blade, then the ear, after that the
full corn in the ear.
29 But when the fruit is brought forth, immediately he putteth in the sickle, because the
harvest is come.
30 ¶ And he said, Whereunto shall we liken the kingdom of God? or with what
comparison shall we compare it?
31 *It is* like a grain of mustard seed, which, when it is sown in the earth, is less than all
the seeds that be in the earth:
32 But when it is sown, it groweth up, and becometh greater than all herbs, and
shooteth out great branches; so that the fowls of the air may lodge under the shadow of
it.
33 And with many such parables spake he the word unto them, as they were able to
hear *it*.
34 But without a parable spake he not unto them:
34 and when they were alone, he expounded all things to his disciples.
35 And the same day, when the even was come, he saith unto them, Let us pass over
unto the other side. (Mark 4:1-35)
53 ¶ And it came to pass, *that* when Jesus had finished these parables, he departed
thence. (Matt 13:53)

61 - A TEMPEST IS STILLED

According to the Gospel of Mark

36 And when they had sent away the multitude, they took him even as he was in the
ship. And there were also with him other little ships.
37 And there arose a great storm of wind, and the waves beat into the ship, so that it
was now full.
38 And he was in the hinder part of the ship, asleep on a pillow: and they awake him,
and say unto him, Master, carest thou not that we perish?
39 And he arose, and rebuked the wind, and said unto the sea, Peace, be still. And the
wind ceased, and there was a great calm.
40 And he said unto them, Why are ye so fearful? how is it that ye have no faith?
41 And they feared exceedingly, and said one to another, What manner of man is this,
that even the wind and the sea obey him? (Mark 4:36-41)

According to the Gospel of Luke

22 ¶ Now it came to pass on a certain day, that he went into a ship with his disciples:
and he said unto them, Let us go over unto the other side of the lake. And they

launched forth.
23 But as they sailed he fell asleep: and there came down a storm of wind on the lake;
and they were filled *with water*, and were in jeopardy.
24 And they came to him, and awoke him, saying, Master, master, we perish. Then he
arose, and rebuked the wind and the raging of the water: and they ceased, and there was
a calm.
25 And he said unto them, Where is your faith? And they being afraid wondered,
saying one to another, What manner of man is this! for he commandeth even the winds
and water, and they obey him. (Luke 8:22-25)

62 – HEALING THE DEMONIAC IN GADARA

According to the Gospel of Luke

26 ¶ And they arrived at the country of the Gadarenes, which is over against Galilee.
27 And when he went forth to land, there met him out of the city a certain man, which
had devils long time, and ware no clothes, neither abode in *any* house, but in the tombs.
28 When he saw Jesus, he cried out, and fell down before him, and with a loud voice
said, What have I to do with thee, Jesus, *thou* Son of God most high? I beseech thee,
torment me not.
29 (For he had commanded the unclean spirit to come out of the man. For oftentimes it
had caught him: and he was kept bound with chains and in fetters; and he brake the
bands, and was driven of the devil into the wilderness.)
30 And Jesus asked him, saying, What is thy name? And he said, Legion: because
many devils were entered into him.
31 And they besought him that he would not command them to go out into the deep.
32 And there was there an herd of many swine feeding on the mountain: and they
besought him that he would suffer them to enter into them. And he suffered them.
33 Then went the devils out of the man, and entered into the swine: and the herd ran
violently down a steep place into the lake, and were choked.
34 When they that fed *them* saw what was done, they fled, and went and told *it* in the
city and in the country.
35 Then they went out to see what was done; and came to Jesus, and found the man, out
of whom the devils were departed, sitting at the feet of Jesus, clothed, and in his right
mind: and they were afraid.
36 They also which saw *it* told them by what means he that was possessed of the devils
was healed.
37 ¶ Then the whole multitude of the country of the Gadarenes round about besought
him to depart from them; for they were taken with great fear: and he went up into the
ship, and returned back again.
38 Now the man out of whom the devils were departed besought him that he might be
with him: but Jesus sent him away, saying,
39 Return to thine own house, and shew how great things God hath done unto thee.
And he went his way and published throughout the whole city how great things Jesus
had done unto him. (Luke 8:26-39)

According to the Gospel of Mark

1 And they came over unto the other side of the sea, into the country of the Gadarenes.
2 And when he was come out of the ship, immediately there met him out of the tombs a

man with an unclean spirit,
3 Who had *his* dwelling among the tombs; and no man could bind him, no, not with
chains:
4 Because that he had been often bound with fetters and chains, and the chains had
been plucked asunder by him, and the fetters broken in pieces: neither could any *man*
tame him.
5 And always, night and day, he was in the mountains, and in the tombs, crying, and
cutting himself with stones.
6 But when he saw Jesus afar off, he ran and worshipped him,
7 And cried with a loud voice, and said, What have I to do with thee, Jesus, *thou* Son of
the most high God? I adjure thee by God, that thou torment me not.
8 For he said unto him, Come out of the man, *thou* unclean spirit.
9 And he asked him, What *is* thy name? And he answered, saying, My name *is* Legion:
for we are many.
10 And he besought him much that he would not send them away out of the country.
11 Now there was there nigh unto the mountains a great herd of swine feeding.
12 And all the devils besought him, saying, Send us into the swine, that we may enter
into them.
13 And forthwith Jesus gave them leave. And the unclean spirits went out, and entered
into the swine: and the herd ran violently down a steep place into the sea, (they were
about two thousand;) and were choked in the sea.
14 And they that fed the swine fled, and told *it* in the city, and in the country. And they
went out to see what it was that was done.
15 And they come to Jesus, and see him that was possessed with the devil, and had the
legion, sitting, and clothed, and in his right mind: and they were afraid.
16 And they that saw *it* told them how it befell to him that was possessed with the devil,
and *also* concerning the swine.
17 And they began to pray him to depart out of their coasts.
18 And when he was come into the ship, he that had been possessed with the devil
prayed him that he might be with him.
19 Howbeit Jesus suffered him not, but saith unto him, Go home to thy friends, and tell
them how great things the Lord hath done for thee, and hath had compassion on thee.
20 And he departed, and began to publish in Decapolis how great things Jesus had done
for him: and all *men* did marvel. (Mark 5:1-20)

63 - BACK IN CAPERNAUM AND MORE HEALING

According to the Gospel of Luke

40 And it came to pass, that, when Jesus was returned, the people *gladly* received him:
for they were all waiting for him.
41 ¶ And, behold, there came a man named Jairus, and he was a ruler of the synagogue:
and he fell down at Jesus' feet, and besought him that he would come into his house:
42 For he had one only daughter, about twelve years of age, and she lay a-dying. But
as he went the people thronged him.
43 ¶ And a woman having an issue of blood twelve years, which had spent all her living
upon physicians, neither could be healed of any,
44 Came behind *him*, and touched the border of his garment: and immediately her issue
of blood stanched.

45 And Jesus said, Who touched me? When all denied, Peter and they that were with
him said, Master, the multitude throng thee and press *thee*, and sayest thou, Who
touched me?
46 And Jesus said, Somebody hath touched me: for I perceive that virtue is gone out of
me.
47 And when the woman saw that she was not hid, she came trembling, and falling
down before him, she declared unto him before all the people for what cause she had
touched him, and how she was healed immediately.
48 And he said unto her, Daughter, be of good comfort: thy faith hath made thee whole;
go in peace.
49 ¶ While he yet spake, there cometh one from the ruler of the synagogue's *house*,
saying to him, Thy daughter is dead; trouble not the Master.
50 But when Jesus heard *it*, he answered him, saying, Fear not: believe only, and she
shall be made whole.
51 And when he came into the house, he suffered no man to go in, save Peter, and
James, and John, and the father and the mother of the maiden.
52 And all wept, and bewailed her: but he said, Weep not; she is not dead, but sleepeth.
53 And they laughed him to scorn, knowing that she was dead.
54 And he put them all out, and took her by the hand, and called, saying, Maid, arise.
55 And her spirit came again, and she arose straightway: and he commanded to give her
meat.
56 And her parents were astonished: but he charged them that they should tell no man
what was done. (Luke 8:40-56)

According to the Gospel of Mark

21 And when Jesus was passed over again by ship unto the other side, much people
gathered unto him: and he was nigh unto the sea
22 And, behold, there cometh one of the rulers of the synagogue, Jairus by name; and
when he saw him, he fell at his feet,
23 And besought him greatly, saying, My little daughter lieth at the point of death: *I
pray thee*, come and lay thy hands on her, that she may be healed; and she shall live.
24 And *Jesus* went with him; and much people followed him, and thronged him.
25 And a certain woman, which had an issue of blood twelve years,
26 And had suffered many things of many physicians, and had spent all that she had,
and was nothing bettered, but rather grew worse,
27 When she had heard of Jesus, came in the press behind, and touched his garment.
28 For she said, If I may touch but his clothes, I shall be whole.
29 And straightway the fountain of her blood was dried up; and she felt in *her* body that
she was healed of that plague.
30 And Jesus, immediately knowing in himself that virtue had gone out of him, turned
him about in the press, and said, Who touched my clothes?
31 And his disciples said unto him, Thou seest the multitude thronging thee, and sayest
thou, Who touched me?
32 And he looked round about to see her that had done this thing.
33 But the woman fearing and trembling, knowing what was done in her, came and fell
down before him, and told him all the truth.

34 And he said unto her, Daughter, thy faith hath made thee whole; go in peace, and be
whole of thy plague.
35 While he yet spake, there came from the ruler of the synagogue's *house certain*
which said, Thy daughter is dead: why troublest thou the Master any further?
36 As soon as Jesus heard the word that was spoken, he saith unto the ruler of the
synagogue, Be not afraid, only believe.
37 And he suffered no man to follow him, save Peter, and James, and John the brother
of James.
38 And he cometh to the house of the ruler of the synagogue, and seeth the tumult, and
them that wept and wailed greatly.
39 And when he was come in, he saith unto them, Why make ye this ado, and weep?
the damsel is not dead, but sleepeth.
40 And they laughed him to scorn. But when he had put them all out, he taketh the
father and the mother of the damsel, and them that were with him, and entereth in
where the damsel was lying.
41 And he took the damsel by the hand, and said unto her, Talitha cumi; which is, being
interpreted, Damsel, I say unto thee, arise.
42 And straightway the damsel arose, and walked; for she was *of the age* of twelve
years. And they were astonished with a great astonishment.
43 And he charged them straitly that no man should know it; and commanded that
something should be given her to eat. (Mark 5:21-43)

64 - HEALING IN NAZARETH FORESTALLED BY UNBELIEF

According to the Gospel of Matthew

54 And when he was come into his own country, he taught them in their synagogue,
insomuch that they were astonished, and said, Whence hath this *man* this wisdom, and
these mighty works?
55 Is not this the carpenter's son? is not his mother called Mary? and his brethren,
James, and Joses, and Simon, and Judas?
56 And his sisters, are they not all with us? Whence then hath this *man* all these
things?
57 And they were offended in him. But Jesus said unto them, A prophet is not without
honour, save in his own country, and in his own house.
58 And he did not many mighty works there because of their unbelief. (Matt 13:54-58)

According to the Gospel of Mark

1 And he went out from thence, and came into his own country; and his disciples
follow him.
2 And when the sabbath day was come, he began to teach in the synagogue: and many
hearing *him* were astonished, saying, From whence hath this *man* these things? and
what wisdom *is* this which is given unto him, that even such mighty works are wrought
by his hands?
3 Is not this the carpenter, the son of Mary, the brother of James, and Joses, and of
Juda, and Simon? and are not his sisters here with us? And they were offended at him.
4 But Jesus said unto them, A prophet is not without honour, but in his own country,
and among his own kin, and in his own house.

5 And he could there do no mighty work, save that he laid his hands upon a few sick
folk, and healed *them.*
6 And he marvelled because of their unbelief. And he went round about the villages,
teaching. (Mark 6:1-6)

65 - THE APOSTLES ARE SENT AGAIN TO PREACH AND TO HEAL

According to the Gospel of Mark

7 ¶ And he called *unto him* the twelve, and began to send them forth by two and two;
and gave them power over unclean spirits;
8 And commanded them that they should take nothing for *their* journey, save a staff
only; no scrip, no bread, no money in *their* purse:
9 But *be* shod with sandals; and not put on two coats.
10 And he said unto them, In what place soever ye enter into an house, there abide till
ye depart from that place.
11 And whosoever shall not receive you, nor hear you, when ye depart thence, shake
off the dust under your feet for a testimony against them. Verily I say unto you, It shall
be more tolerable for Sodom and Gomorrha in the day of judgment, than for that city.
12 And they went out, and preached that men should repent.
13 And they cast out many devils, and anointed with oil many that were sick, and
healed *them.* (Mark 6:7-13)

According to the Gospel of Luke

1 Then he called his twelve disciples together, and gave them power and authority over
all devils, and to cure diseases.
2 And he sent them to preach the kingdom of God, and to heal the sick.
3 And he said unto them, Take nothing for *your* journey, neither staves, nor scrip,
neither bread, neither money; neither have two coats apiece.
4 And whatsoever house ye enter into, there abide, and thence depart.
5 And whosoever will not receive you, when ye go out of that city, shake off the very
dust from your feet for a testimony against them.
6 And they departed, and went through the towns, preaching the gospel, and healing
every where. (Luke 9:1-6)

66 - ACCOUNTS OF JOHN THE BAPTIST'S BEHEADING

According to the Gospel of Luke (A summary statement)

7 ¶ Now Herod the tetrarch heard of all that was done by him: and he was perplexed,
because that it was said of some, that John was risen from the dead;
8 And of some, that Elias had appeared; and of others, that one of the old prophets was
risen again.
9 And Herod said, John have I beheaded: but who is this, of whom I hear such things?
And he desired to see him. (Luke 9:7-9)

According to the Gospel of Matthew (A more detailed account)

1 At that time Herod the tetrarch heard of the fame of Jesus,
2 And said unto his servants, This is John the Baptist; he is risen from the dead; and
therefore mighty works do shew forth themselves in him.
3 ¶ For Herod had laid hold on John, and bound him, and put *him* in prison for
Herodias' sake, his brother Philip's wife.
4 For John said unto him, It is not lawful for thee to have her.

5 And when he would have put him to death, he feared the multitude, because they
counted him as a prophet.
6 But when Herod's birthday was kept, the daughter of Herodias danced before them,
and pleased Herod.
7 Whereupon he promised with an oath to give her whatsoever she would ask.
8 And she, being before instructed of her mother, said, Give me here John Baptist's
head in a charger.
9 And the king was sorry: nevertheless for the oath's sake, and them which sat with him
at meat, he commanded *it* to be given *her*.
10 And he sent, and beheaded John in the prison.
11 And his head was brought in a charger, and given to the damsel: and she brought *it*
to her mother.
12 And his disciples came, and took up the body, and buried it, and went and told Jesus.
13 ¶ When Jesus heard *of it*, he departed thence by ship into a desert place apart: and
when the people had heard *thereof*, they followed him on foot out of the cities.
14 And Jesus went forth, and saw a great multitude, and was moved with compassion
toward them, and he healed their sick. (Matt 14:1-14)

According to the Gospel of Mark (The most complete account)

14 And king Herod heard *of him*; (for his name was spread abroad:) and he said, That
John the Baptist was risen from the dead, and therefore mighty works do shew forth
themselves in him.
15 Others said, That it is Elias. And others said, That it is a prophet, or as one of the
prophets.
16 But when Herod heard *thereof*, he said, It is John, whom I beheaded: he is risen
from the dead.
17 For Herod himself had sent forth and laid hold upon John, and bound him in prison
for Herodias' sake, his brother Philip's wife: for he had married her.
18 For John had said unto Herod, It is not lawful for thee to have thy brother's wife.
19 Therefore Herodias had a quarrel against him, and would have killed him; but she
could not:
20 For Herod feared John, knowing that he was a just man and an holy, and observed
him; and when he heard him, he did many things, and heard him gladly.
21 And when a convenient day was come, that Herod on his birthday made a supper to
his lords, high captains, and chief *estates* of Galilee;
22 And when the daughter of the said Herodias came in, and danced, and pleased Herod
and them that sat with him, the king said unto the damsel, Ask of me whatsoever thou
wilt, and I will give *it* thee.
23 And he sware unto her, Whatsoever thou shalt ask of me, I will give *it* thee, unto the
half of my kingdom.
24 And she went forth, and said unto her mother, What shall I ask? And she said, The
head of John the Baptist.
25 And she came in straightway with haste unto the king, and asked, saying, I will that
thou give me by and by in a charger the head of John the Baptist.
26 And the king was exceeding sorry; *yet* for his oath's sake, and for their sakes which
sat with him, he would not reject her.

27 And immediately the king sent an executioner, and commanded his head to be
brought: and he went and beheaded him in the prison.
28 And brought his head in a charger, and gave it to the damsel: and the damsel gave it
to her mother.
29 And when his disciples heard *of it*, they came and took up his corpse, and laid it in a
tomb. (Mark 6:14-29)

67 - THE LOAVES AND FISHES MULTIPLIED (1ST OCCASION)

(5,000 men plus women and children)

According to the Gospel of Mark

30 And the apostles gathered themselves together unto Jesus, and told him all things,
both what they had done, and what they had taught.
31 And he said unto them, Come ye yourselves apart into a desert place, and rest a
while: for there were many coming and going, and they had no leisure so much as to
eat.
32 And they departed into a desert place by ship privately.
33 And the people saw them departing, and many knew him, and ran afoot thither out
of all cities, and outwent them, and came together unto him.
34 And Jesus, when he came out, saw much people, and was moved with compassion
toward them, because they were as sheep not having a shepherd: and he began to teach
them many things.
35 And when the day was now far spent, his disciples came unto him, and said, This is
a desert place, and now the time *is* far passed:
36 Send them away, that they may go into the country round about, and into the
villages, and buy themselves bread: for they have nothing to eat.
37 He answered and said unto them, Give ye them to eat. And they say unto him, Shall
we go and buy two hundred pennyworth of bread, and give them to eat?
38 He saith unto them, How many loaves have ye? go and see. And when they knew,
they say, Five, and two fishes.
39 And he commanded them to make all sit down by companies upon the green grass.
40 And they sat down in ranks, by hundreds, and by fifties.
41 And when he had taken the five loaves and the two fishes, he looked up to heaven,
and blessed, and brake the loaves, and gave *them* to his disciples to set before them; and
the two fishes divided he among them all.
42 And they did all eat, and were filled.
43 And they took up twelve baskets full of the fragments, and of the fishes.
44 And they that did eat of the loaves were about five thousand men. (Mark 6:30-44)

According to the Gospel of Luke

10 ¶ And the apostles, when they were returned, told him all that they had done. And
he took them, and went aside privately into a desert place belonging to the city called
Bethsaida.
11 And the people, when they knew *it*, followed him: and he received them, and spake
unto them of the kingdom of God, and healed them that had need of healing.
12 And when the day began to wear away, then came the twelve, and said unto him,
Send the multitude away, that they may go into the towns and country round about, and
lodge, and get victuals: for we are here in a desert place.

13 But he said unto them, Give ye them to eat. And they said, We have no more but
five loaves and two fishes; except we should go and buy meat for all this people.
14 For they were about five thousand men. And he said to his disciples, Make them sit
down by fifties in a company.
15 And they did so, and made them all sit down.
16 Then he took the five loaves and the two fishes, and looking up to heaven, he
blessed them, and brake, and gave to the disciples to set before the multitude.
17 And they did eat, and were all filled: and there was taken up of fragments that
remained to them twelve baskets. (Luke 9:10-17)

According to the Gospel of Matthew

15 ¶ And when it was evening, his disciples came to him, saying, This is a desert place,
and the time is now past; send the multitude away, that they may go into the villages,
and buy themselves victuals.
16 But Jesus said unto them, They need not depart; give ye them to eat.
17 And they say unto him, We have here but five loaves, and two fishes.
18 He said, Bring them hither to me.
19 And he commanded the multitude to sit down on the grass, and took the five loaves,
and the two fishes, and looking up to heaven, he blessed, and brake, and gave the
loaves to *his* disciples, and the disciples to the multitude.
20 And they did all eat, and were filled: and they took up of the fragments that
remained twelve baskets full.
21 And they that had eaten were about five thousand men, beside women and children.
(Matt 14:15-21)

According to the Gospel of John

1 After these things Jesus went over the sea of Galilee, which is *the sea* of Tiberias.
2 And a great multitude followed him, because they saw his miracles which he did on
them that were diseased.
3 And Jesus went up into a mountain, and there he sat with his disciples.
4 And the passover, a feast of the Jews, was nigh.
5 ¶ When Jesus then lifted up *his* eyes, and saw a great company come unto him, he
saith unto Philip, Whence shall we buy bread, that these may eat?
6 And this he said to prove him: for he himself knew what he would do.
7 Philip answered him, Two hundred pennyworth of bread is not sufficient for them,
that every one of them may take a little.
8 One of his disciples, Andrew, Simon Peter's brother, saith unto him,
9 There is a lad here, which hath five barley loaves, and two small fishes: but what are
they among so many?
10 And Jesus said, Make the men sit down. Now there was much grass in the place. So
the men sat down, in number about five thousand.
11 And Jesus took the loaves; and when he had given thanks, he distributed to the
disciples, and the disciples to them that were set down; and likewise of the fishes as
much as they would.
12 When they were filled, he said unto his disciples, Gather up the fragments that
remain, that nothing be lost.
13 Therefore they gathered *them* together, and filled twelve baskets with the fragments
of the five barley loaves, which remained over and above unto them that had eaten. (John
6:1-13)

68 - JESUS ESCAPES BEING MADE A KING

14 Then those men, when they had seen the miracle that Jesus did, said, This is of a
truth that prophet that should come into the world.
15 ¶ When Jesus therefore perceived that they would come and take him by force, to
make him a king, he departed again into a mountain himself alone. (John 6:14-15)

69 – LAWS OF NATURE AND PHYSICS NULLIFIED

According to the Gospel of John

16 And when even was *now* come, his disciples went down unto the sea,
17 And entered into a ship, and went over the sea toward Capernaum. And it was now
dark, and Jesus was not come to them.
18 And the sea arose by reason of a great wind that blew.
19 So when they had rowed about five and twenty or thirty furlongs, they see Jesus
walking on the sea, and drawing nigh unto the ship: and they were afraid.
20 But he saith unto them, It is I; be not afraid.
21 Then they willingly received him into the ship: and immediately the ship was at the
land whither they went. (John 6:16-21)

According to the Gospel of Mark

45 And straightway he constrained his disciples to get into the ship, and to go to the
other side before unto Bethsaida, while he sent away the people.
46 And when he had sent them away, he departed into a mountain to pray.
47 And when even was come, the ship was in the midst of the sea, and he alone on the
land.
48 And he saw them toiling in rowing; for the wind was contrary unto them: and about
the fourth watch of the night he cometh unto them, walking upon the sea, and would
have passed by them.
49 But when they saw him walking upon the sea, they supposed it had been a spirit, and
cried out:
50 For they all saw him, and were troubled. And immediately he talked with them, and
saith unto them, Be of good cheer: it is I; be not afraid.
51 And he went up unto them into the ship; and the wind ceased: and they were sore
amazed in themselves beyond measure, and wondered.
52 For they considered not *the miracle* of the loaves: for their heart was hardened.
53 And when they had passed over, they came into the land of Gennesaret, and drew to
the shore. (Mark 6:45-53)

According to the Gospel of Matthew

22 ¶ And straightway Jesus constrained his disciples to get into a ship, and to go before
him unto the other side, while he sent the multitudes away.
23 And when he had sent the multitudes away, he went up into a mountain apart to
pray: and when the evening was come, he was there alone.
24 But the ship was now in the midst of the sea, tossed with waves: for the wind was
contrary.
25 And in the fourth watch of the night Jesus went unto them, walking on the sea.
26 And when the disciples saw him walking on the sea, they were troubled, saying, It is
a spirit; and they cried out for fear.

27 But straightway Jesus spake unto them, saying, Be of good cheer; it is I; be not
afraid.
28 And Peter answered him and said, Lord, if it be thou, bid me come unto thee on the
water.
29 And he said, Come. And when Peter was come down out of the ship, he walked on
the water, to go to Jesus.
30 But when he saw the wind boisterous, he was afraid; and beginning to sink, he cried,
saying, Lord, save me.
31 And immediately Jesus stretched forth *his* hand, and caught him, and said unto him,
O thou of little faith, wherefore didst thou doubt?
32 And when they were come into the ship, the wind ceased.
33 Then they that were in the ship came and worshipped him, saying, Of a truth thou art
the Son of God.
34 ¶ And when they were gone over, they came into the land of Gennesaret. (Matt 14:22-34)

70 - EVENTS IN GENNESARET

According to the Gospel of Matthew

35 And when the men of that place had knowledge of him, they sent out into all that
country round about, and brought unto him all that were diseased;
36 And besought him that they might only touch the hem of his garment: and as many
as touched were made perfectly whole. (Matt 14:35-36)

According to the Gospel of Mark

54 And when they were come out of the ship, straightway they knew him,
55 And ran through that whole region round about, and began to carry about in beds
those that were sick, where they heard he was.
56 And whithersoever he entered, into villages, or cities, or country, they laid the sick
in the streets, and besought him that they might touch if it were but the border of his
garment: and as many as touched him were made whole. (Mark 6:54-56)

71 - SPIRITUAL TEACHING REJECTED BY MANY

22 ¶ The day following, when the people which stood on the other side of the sea saw
that there was none other boat there, save that one whereinto his disciples were entered,
and that Jesus went not with his disciples into the boat, but *that* his disciples were gone
away alone;
23 (Howbeit there came other boats from Tiberias nigh unto the place where they did
eat bread, after that the Lord had given thanks:)
24 When the people therefore saw that Jesus was not there, neither his disciples, they
also took shipping, and came to Capernaum, seeking for Jesus.
25 And when they had found him on the other side of the sea, they said unto him,
Rabbi, when camest thou hither?
26 Jesus answered them and said, Verily, verily, I say unto you, Ye seek me, not
because ye saw the miracles, but because ye did eat of the loaves, and were filled.
27 Labour not for the meat which perisheth, but for that meat which endureth unto
everlasting life, which the Son of man shall give unto you: for him hath God the Father
sealed.
28 Then said they unto him, What shall we do, that we might work the works of God?

29 Jesus answered and said unto them, This is the work of God, that ye believe on him
whom he hath sent.
30 They said therefore unto him, What sign shewest thou then, that we may see, and
believe thee? what dost thou work?
31 Our fathers did eat manna in the desert; as it is written, He gave them bread from
heaven to eat.
32 Then Jesus said unto them, Verily, verily, I say unto you, Moses gave you not that
bread from heaven;
32 but my Father giveth you the true bread from heaven.
33 For the bread of God is he which cometh down from heaven, and giveth life unto the
world.
34 Then said they unto him, Lord, evermore give us this bread.
35 And Jesus said unto them, I am the bread of life: he that cometh to me shall never
hunger; and he that believeth on me shall never thirst.
36 But I said unto you, That ye also have seen me, and believe not.
37 All that the Father giveth me shall come to me; and him that cometh to me I will in
no wise cast out.
38 For I came down from heaven, not to do mine own will, but the will of him that sent
me.
39 And this is the Father's will which hath sent me, that of all which he hath given me I
should lose nothing, but should raise it up again at the last day.
40 And this is the will of him that sent me, that every one which seeth the Son, and
believeth on him, may have everlasting life: and I will raise him up at the last day.
41 The Jews then murmured at him, because he said, I am the bread which came down
from heaven.
42 And they said, Is not this Jesus, the son of Joseph, whose father and mother we
know? how is it then that he saith, I came down from heaven?
43 Jesus therefore answered and said unto them, Murmur not among yourselves.
44 No man can come to me, except the Father which hath sent me draw him: and I will
raise him up at the last day.
45 It is written in the prophets, And they shall be all taught of God. Every man
therefore that hath heard, and hath learned of the Father, cometh unto me.
46 Not that any man hath seen the Father, save he which is of God, he hath seen the
Father.
47 Verily, verily, I say unto you, He that believeth on me hath everlasting life.
48 I am that bread of life.
49 Your fathers did eat manna in the wilderness, and are dead.
50 This is the bread which cometh down from heaven, that a man may eat thereof, and
not die.
51 I am the living bread which came down from heaven: if any man eat of this bread,
he shall live for ever: and the bread that I will give is my flesh, which I will give for the
life of the world.
52 The Jews therefore strove among themselves, saying, How can this man give us *his*
flesh to eat?
53 Then Jesus said unto them, Verily, verily, I say unto you, Except ye eat the flesh of
the Son of man, and drink his blood, ye have no life in you.

54 Whoso eateth my flesh, and drinketh my blood, hath eternal life; and I will raise him
up at the last day.
55 For my flesh is meat indeed, and my blood is drink indeed.
56 He that eateth my flesh, and drinketh my blood, dwelleth in me, and I in him.
57 As the living Father hath sent me, and I live by the Father: so he that eateth me, even
he shall live by me.
58 This is that bread which came down from heaven: not as your fathers did eat manna,
and are dead: he that eateth of this bread shall live for ever.
59 These things said he in the synagogue, as he taught in Capernaum.
60 Many therefore of his disciples, when they had heard *this*, said, This is an hard
saying; who can hear it?
61 When Jesus knew in himself that his disciples murmured at it, he said unto them,
Doth this offend you?
62 *What* and if ye shall see the Son of man ascend up where he was before?
63 It is the spirit that quickeneth; the flesh profiteth nothing: the words that I speak unto
you, *they* are spirit, and *they* are life.
64 But there are some of you that believe not. For Jesus knew from the beginning who
they were that believed not, and who should betray him.
65 And he said, Therefore said I unto you, that no man can come unto me, except it
were given unto him of my Father.
66 ¶ From that *time* many of his disciples went back, and walked no more with him.
67 Then said Jesus unto the twelve, Will ye also go away?
68 Then Simon Peter answered him, Lord, to whom shall we go? thou hast the words of
eternal life.
69 And we believe and are sure that thou art that Christ, the Son of the living God.
70 Jesus answered them, Have not I chosen you twelve, and one of you is a devil?
71 He spake of Judas Iscariot *the son* of Simon: for he it was that should betray him,
being one of the twelve. (John 6:22-71)

72 – GOD'S COMMANDMENTS MOCKED BY MEN'S TRADITIONS

According to the Gospel of Mark

1 Then came together unto him the Pharisees, and certain of the scribes, which came
from Jerusalem.
2 And when they saw some of his disciples eat bread with defiled, that is to say, with
unwashen, hands, they found fault.
3 For the Pharisees, and all the Jews, except they wash *their* hands oft, eat not, holding
the tradition of the elders.
4 And *when they come* from the market, except they wash, they eat not. And many
other things there be, which they have received to hold, *as* the washing of cups, and
pots, brasen vessels, and of tables.
5 Then the Pharisees and scribes asked him, Why walk not thy disciples according to
the tradition of the elders, but eat bread with unwashen hands?
6 He answered and said unto them, Well hath Esaias prophesied of you hypocrites, as it
is written, This people honoureth me with *their* lips, but their heart is far from me.
7 Howbeit in vain do they worship me, teaching *for* doctrines the commandments of
men.

8 For laying aside the commandment of God, ye hold the tradition of men, *as* the
washing of pots and cups: and many other such like things ye do.
9 And he said unto them, Full well ye reject the commandment of God, that ye may
keep your own tradition.
10 For Moses said, Honour thy father and thy mother; and, Whoso curseth father or
mother, let him die the death:
11 But ye say, If a man shall say to his father or mother, *It is* Corban, that is to say, a
gift, by whatsoever thou mightest be profited by me; *he shall be free*.
12 And ye suffer him no more to do ought for his father or his mother;
13 Making the word of God of none effect through your tradition, which ye have
delivered: and many such like things do ye.
14 ¶ And when he had called all the people *unto him*, he said unto them, Hearken unto
me every one *of you*, and understand:
15 There is nothing from without a man, that entering into him can defile him: but the
things which come out of him, those are they that defile the man.
16 If any man have ears to hear, let him hear.
17 And when he was entered into the house from the people, his disciples asked him
concerning the parable.
18 And he saith unto them, Are ye so without understanding also? Do ye not perceive,
that whatsoever thing from without entereth into the man, *it* cannot defile him;
19 Because it entereth not into his heart, but into the belly, and goeth out into the
draught, purging all meats?
20 And he said, That which cometh out of the man, that defileth the man.
21 For from within, out of the heart of men, proceed evil thoughts, adulteries,
fornications, murders,
22 Thefts, covetousness, wickedness, deceit, lasciviousness, an evil eye, blasphemy,
pride, foolishness:
23 All these evil things come from within, and defile the man. (Mark 7:1-23)

According to the Gospel of Matthew

1 Then came to Jesus scribes and Pharisees, which were of Jerusalem, saying,
2 Why do thy disciples transgress the tradition of the elders? for they wash not their
hands when they eat bread.
3 But he answered and said unto them, Why do ye also transgress the commandment of
God by your tradition?
4 For God commanded, saying, Honour thy father and mother: and, He that curseth
father or mother, let him die the death.
5 But ye say, Whosoever shall say to *his* father or *his* mother, *It is* a gift, by whatsoever
thou mightest be profited by me;
6 And honour not his father or his mother, *he shall be free*. Thus have ye made the
commandment of God of none effect by your tradition.
7 *Ye* hypocrites, well did Esaias prophesy of you, saying,
8 This people draweth nigh unto me with their mouth, and honoureth me with *their*
lips; but their heart is far from me.
9 But in vain they do worship me, teaching *for* doctrines the commandments of men.
10 ¶ And he called the multitude, and said unto them, Hear, and understand:
11 Not that which goeth into the mouth defileth a man; but that which cometh out of the

mouth, this defileth a man.
12 Then came his disciples, and said unto him, Knowest thou that the Pharisees were
offended, after they heard this saying?
13 But he answered and said, Every plant, which my heavenly Father hath not planted,
shall be rooted up.
14 Let them alone: they be blind leaders of the blind. And if the blind lead the blind,
both shall fall into the ditch
15 Then answered Peter and said unto him, Declare unto us this parable.
16 And Jesus said, Are ye also yet without understanding?
17 Do not ye yet understand, that whatsoever entereth in at the mouth goeth into the
belly, and is cast out into the draught?
18 But those things which proceed out of the mouth come forth from the heart; and they
defile the man.
19 For out of the heart proceed evil thoughts, murders, adulteries, fornications, thefts,
false witness, blasphemies:
20 These are *the things* which defile a man: but to eat with unwashen hands defileth not
a man. (Matt 15:1-20)

73 - A CANAANITE CHILD HEALED

According to the Gospel of Matthew

21 ¶ Then Jesus went thence, and departed into the coasts of Tyre and Sidon.
22 And, behold, a woman of Canaan came out of the same coasts, and cried unto him,
saying, Have mercy on me, O Lord, *thou* son of David; my daughter is grievously
vexed with a devil.
23 But he answered her not a word. And his disciples came and besought him, saying,
Send her away; for she crieth after us.
24 But he answered and said, I am not sent but unto the lost sheep of the house of
Israel.
25 Then came she and worshipped him, saying, Lord, help me.
26 But he answered and said, It is not meet to take the children's bread, and to cast *it* to
dogs.
27 And she said, Truth, Lord: yet the dogs eat of the crumbs which fall from their
masters' table.
28 Then Jesus answered and said unto her, O woman, great *is* thy faith: be it unto thee
even as thou wilt. And her daughter was made whole from that very hour.
29 And Jesus departed from thence, and came nigh unto the sea of Galilee; and went up
into a mountain, and sat down there. (Matt 15:21-29)

According to the Gospel of Mark

24 ¶ And from thence he arose, and went into the borders of Tyre and Sidon, and
entered into an house, and would have no man know *it*: but he could not be hid.
25 For a *certain* woman, whose young daughter had an unclean spirit, heard of him,
and came and fell at his feet:
26 The woman was a Greek, a Syrophenician by nation; and she besought him that he
would cast forth the devil out of her daughter.
27 But Jesus said unto her, Let the children first be filled: for it is not meet to take the
children's bread, and to cast *it* unto the dogs.

28 And she answered and said unto him, Yes, Lord: yet the dogs under the table eat of
the children's crumbs.
29 And he said unto her, For this saying go thy way; the devil is gone out of thy
daughter.
30 And when she was come to her house, she found the devil gone out, and her
daughter laid upon the bed.
31 ¶ And again, departing from the coasts of Tyre and Sidon, he came unto the sea of
Galilee, through the midst of the coasts of Decapolis. (Mark 7:24-31)

74 - HEALING IN THE REGION OF DECAPOLIS

32 And they bring unto him one that was deaf, and had an impediment in his speech;
and they beseech him to put his hand upon him.
33 And he took him aside from the multitude, and put his fingers into his ears, and he
spit, and touched his tongue;
34 And looking up to heaven, he sighed, and saith unto him, Ephphatha, that is, Be
opened.
35 And straightway his ears were opened, and the string of his tongue was loosed, and
he spake plain.
36 And he charged them that they should tell no man: but the more he charged them, so
much the more a great deal they published *it*;
37 And were beyond measure astonished, saying, He hath done all things well:
he maketh both the deaf to hear, and the dumb to speak. (Mark 7:32-37)
30 And great multitudes came unto him, having with them *those that were* lame, blind,
dumb, maimed, and many others, and cast them down at Jesus' feet; and he healed
them:
31 Insomuch that the multitude wondered, when they saw the dumb to speak, the
maimed to be whole, the lame to walk, and the blind to see: and they glorified the God
of Israel. (Matt 15:30-31)

75 - THE LOAVES AND FISHES ARE MULTIPLIED (2ND OCCASION)

According to the Gospel of Matthew

32 ¶ Then Jesus called his disciples *unto him*, and said, I have compassion on the
multitude, because they continue with me now three days, and have nothing to eat: and
I will not send them away fasting, lest they faint in the way.
33 And his disciples say unto him, Whence should we have so much bread in the
wilderness, as to fill so great a multitude?
34 And Jesus saith unto them, How many loaves have ye? And they said, Seven, and a
few little fishes.
35 And he commanded the multitude to sit down on the ground.
36 And he took the seven loaves and the fishes, and gave thanks, and brake *them*, and
gave to his disciples, and the disciples to the multitude.
37 And they did all eat, and were filled:
37 and they took up of the broken *meat* that was left seven baskets full.
38 And they that did eat were four thousand men, beside women and children.
39 And he sent away the multitude, and took ship, and came into the coasts of Magdala.
(Matt 15:32-39)

1 In those days the multitude being very great, and having nothing to eat, Jesus called
his disciples *unto him*, and saith unto them,
2 I have compassion on the multitude, because they have now been with me three days,
and have nothing to eat:
3 And if I send them away fasting to their own houses, they will faint by the way: for
divers of them came from far.
4 And his disciples answered him, From whence can a man satisfy these *men* with
bread here in the wilderness?
5 And he asked them, How many loaves have ye? And they said, Seven.
6 And he commanded the people to sit down on the ground: and he took the seven
loaves, and gave thanks, and brake, and gave to his disciples to set before *them*; and
they did set *them* before the people.
7 And they had a few small fishes: and he blessed, and commanded to set them also
before *them*.
8 So they did eat, and were filled: and they took up of the broken *meat* that was left
seven baskets.
9 And they that had eaten were about four thousand: and he sent them away. (Mark 8:1-9)

76 - BEWARE OF EVIL DOCTRINES

10 ¶ And straightway he entered into a ship with his disciples, and came into the parts
of Dalmanutha.
11 And the Pharisees came forth, and began to question with him, seeking of him a sign
from heaven, tempting him.
12 And he sighed deeply in his spirit, and saith, Why doth this generation seek after a
sign? verily I say unto you, There shall no sign be given unto this generation.
13 And he left them, and entering into the ship again departed to the other side.
14 ¶ Now *the disciples* had forgotten to take bread, neither had they in the ship with
them more than one loaf.
15 And he charged them, saying, Take heed, beware of the leaven of the Pharisees, and
of the leaven of Herod.
16 And they reasoned among themselves, saying, *It is* because we have no bread.
17 And when Jesus knew *it*, he saith unto them, Why reason ye, because ye have no
bread? perceive ye not yet, neither understand? have ye your heart yet hardened?
18 Having eyes, see ye not? and having ears, hear ye not? and do ye not remember?
19 When I brake the five loaves among five thousand, how many baskets full of
fragments took ye up? They say unto him, Twelve.
20 And when the seven among four thousand, how many baskets full of fragments took
ye up? And they said, Seven.
21 And he said unto them, How is it that ye do not understand? (Mark 8:10-21)
1 The Pharisees also with the Sadducees came, and tempting desired him that he would
shew them a sign from heaven.
2 He answered and said unto them, When it is evening, ye say, *It will be* fair weather:
for the sky is red.
3 And in the morning, *It will be* foul weather to-day: for the sky is red and lowering. O
ye hypocrites, ye can discern the face of the sky; but can ye not *discern* the signs of the
times?

4 A wicked and adulterous generation seeketh after a sign; and there shall no sign be
given unto it, but the sign of the prophet Jonas. And he left them, and departed.
5 And when his disciples were come to the other side, they had forgotten to take bread.
6 ¶ Then Jesus said unto them, Take heed and beware of the leaven of the Pharisees
and of the Sadducees.
7 And they reasoned among themselves, saying, *It is* because we have taken no bread.
8 *Which* when Jesus perceived, he said unto them, O ye of little faith, why reason ye
among yourselves, because ye have brought no bread?
9 Do ye not yet understand, neither remember the five loaves of the five thousand, and
how many baskets ye took up?
10 Neither the seven loaves of the four thousand, and how many baskets ye took up?
11 How is it that ye do not understand that I spake *it* not to you concerning bread, that
ye should beware of the leaven of the Pharisees and of the Sadducees?
12 Then understood they how that he bade *them* not beware of the leaven of bread, but
of the doctrine of the Pharisees and of the Sadducees. (Matt 16:1-12)

77 - A MAN IN BETHSAIDA HEALED OF BLINDNESS

22 ¶ And he cometh to Bethsaida; and they bring a blind man unto him, and besought
him to touch him.
23 And he took the blind man by the hand, and led him out of the town; and when he
had spit on his eyes, and put his hands upon him, he asked him if he saw ought.
24 And he looked up, and said, I see men as trees, walking.
25 After that he put *his* hands again upon his eyes, and made him look up: and he was
restored, and saw every man clearly.
26 And he sent him away to his house, saying, Neither go into the town, nor tell *it* to
any in the town. (Mark 8:22-26)

78 – PETER'S REALIZATION THAT JESUS IS THE CHRIST

According to the Gospel of Mark

27 ¶ And Jesus went out, and his disciples, into the towns of Cæsarea Philippi: and by
the way he asked his disciples, saying unto them, Whom do men say that I am?
28 And they answered, John the Baptist: but some *say*, Elias; and others, One of the
prophets.
29 And he saith unto them, But whom say ye that I am? And Peter answereth and saith
unto him, Thou art the Christ.
30 And he charged them that they should tell no man of him. (Mark 8:27-30)

According to the Gospel of Matthew

13 ¶ When Jesus came into the coasts of Cæsarea Philippi, he asked his disciples,
saying, Whom do men say that I the Son of man am?
14 And they said, Some *say that thou art* John the Baptist: some, Elias; and others,
Jeremias, or one of the prophets.
15 He saith unto them, But whom say ye that I am? (
16 And Simon Peter answered and said, Thou art the Christ, the Son of the living God.
17 And Jesus answered and said unto him, Blessed art thou, Simon Bar-jona: for flesh
and blood hath not revealed *it* unto thee, but my Father which is in heaven.

18 And I say also unto thee, That thou art Peter, and upon this rock I will build my
church; and the gates of hell shall not prevail against it.
19 And I will give unto thee the keys of the kingdom of heaven: and whatsoever thou
shalt bind on earth shall be bound in heaven: and whatsoever thou shalt loose on earth
shall be loosed in heaven.
20 Then charged he his disciples that they should tell no man that he was Jesus the
Christ. (Matt 16:13-20)

According to the Gospel of Luke

18 ¶ And it came to pass, as he was alone praying, his disciples were with him: and he
asked them, saying, Whom say the people that I am?
19 They answering said, John the Baptist; but some *say*, Elias; and others *say*, that one
of the old prophets is risen again.
20 He said unto them, But whom say ye that I am? Peter answering said, The Christ of
God
21 And he straitly charged them, and commanded *them* to tell no man that thing; (Luke
9:18-21)

79 - THE 1ST ANNOUNCEMENT OF SUFFERINGS

According to the Gospel of Luke

22 Saying, The Son of man must suffer many things, and be rejected of the elders and
chief priests and scribes, and be slain, and be raised the third day.
23 ¶ And he said to *them* all, If any *man* will come after me, let him deny himself, and
take up his cross daily, and follow me.
24 For whosoever will save his life shall lose it: but whosoever will lose his life for my
sake, the same shall save it.
25 For what is a man advantaged, if he gain the whole world, and lose himself, or be
cast away?
26 For whosoever shall be ashamed of me and of my words, of him shall the Son of
man be ashamed, when he shall come in his own glory, and *in his* Father's, and of the
holy angels. (Luke 9:22-26)

According to the Gospel of Matthew

21 ¶ From that time forth began Jesus to shew unto his disciples, how that he must go
unto Jerusalem, and suffer many things of the elders and chief priests and scribes, and
be killed, and be raised again the third day.
22 Then Peter took him, and began to rebuke him, saying, Be it far from thee, Lord: this
shall not be unto thee.
23 But he turned, and said unto Peter, Get thee behind me, Satan: thou art an offence
unto me: for thou savourest not the things that be of God, but those that be of men.
24 ¶ Then said Jesus unto his disciples, If any *man* will come after me, let him deny
himself, and take up his cross, and follow me.
25 For whosoever will save his life shall lose it: and whosoever will lose his life for my
sake shall find it.
26 For what is a man profited, if he shall gain the whole world, and lose his own soul?
or what shall a man give in exchange for his soul?
27 For the Son of man shall come in the glory of his Father with his angels; and then he
shall reward every man according to his works. (Matt 16:21-27)

31 And he began to teach them, that the Son of man must suffer many things, and be
rejected of the elders, and *of* the chief priests, and scribes, and be killed, and after three
days rise again.
32 And he spake that saying openly. And Peter took him, and began to rebuke him.
33 But when he had turned about and looked on his disciples, he rebuked Peter, saying,
Get thee behind me, Satan: for thou savourest not the things that be of God, but the
things that be of men.
34 ¶ And when he had called the people *unto him* with his disciples also, he said unto
them, Whosoever will come after me, let him deny himself, and take up his cross, and
follow me.
35 For whosoever will save his life shall lose it; but whosoever shall lose his life for my
sake and the gospel's, the same shall save it.
36 For what shall it profit a man, if he shall gain the whole world, and lose his own
soul?
37 Or what shall a man give in exchange for his soul?
38 Whosoever therefore shall be ashamed of me and of my words in this adulterous and
sinful generation; of him also shall the Son of man be ashamed, when he cometh in the
glory of his Father with the holy angels. (Mark 8:31-38)

80 - A PROPHECY CONCERNING THE KINGDOM OF GOD

According to the Gospel of Mark

1 And he said unto them, Verily I say unto you, That there be some of them that stand
here, which shall not taste of death, till they have seen the kingdom of God come with
power. (Mark 9:1)

According to the Gospel of Matthew

28 Verily I say unto you, There be some standing here, which shall not taste of death,
till they see the Son of man coming in his kingdom. (Matt 16:28)

According to the Gospel of Luke

27 But I tell you of a truth, there be some standing here, which shall not taste of death,
till they see the kingdom of God. (Luke 9:27)

81 - TRANSFIGURATION – THE FIRST RESURRECTION

According to the Gospel of Luke

28 ¶ And it came to pass about an eight days after these sayings, he took Peter and John
and James, and went up into a mountain to pray.
29 And as he prayed, the fashion of his countenance was altered, and his raiment *was*
white *and* glistering.
30 And, behold, there talked with him two men, which were Moses and Elias:
31 Who appeared in glory, and spake of his decease which he should accomplish at
Jerusalem.
32 But Peter and they that were with him were heavy with sleep: and when they were
awake, they saw his glory, and the two men that stood with him.
33 And it came to pass, as they departed from him, Peter said unto Jesus, Master, it is
good for us to be here: and let us make three tabernacles; one for thee, and one for
Moses, and one for Elias: not knowing what he said.

34 While he thus spake, there came a cloud, and overshadowed them: and they feared
as they entered into the cloud.
35 And there came a voice out of the cloud, saying, This is my beloved Son: hear him.
36 And when the voice was past, Jesus was found alone. And they kept *it* close, and
told no man in those days any of those things which they had seen. (Luke 9:28-36)

According to the Gospel of Matthew

1 And after six days Jesus taketh Peter, James, and John his brother, and bringeth them
up into an high mountain apart,
2 And was transfigured before them: and his face did shine as the sun, and his raiment
was white as the light.
3 And, behold, there appeared unto them Moses and Elias talking with him.
4 Then answered Peter, and said unto Jesus, Lord, it is good for us to be here: if thou
wilt, let us make here three tabernacles; one for thee, and one for Moses, and one for
Elias.
5 While he yet spake, behold, a bright cloud overshadowed them: and behold a voice
out of the cloud, which said, This is my beloved Son, in whom I am well pleased; hear
ye him.
6 And when the disciples heard *it*, they fell on their face, and were sore afraid.
7 And Jesus came and touched them, and said, Arise, and be not afraid.
8 And when they had lifted up their eyes, they saw no man, save Jesus only.
9 And as they came down from the mountain, Jesus charged them, saying, Tell the
vision to no man, until the Son of man be risen again from the dead. (Matt 17:1-9)

According to the Gospel of Mark

2 ¶ And after six days Jesus taketh *with him* Peter, and James, and John, and leadeth
them up into an high mountain apart by themselves: and he was transfigured before
them.
3 And his raiment became shining, exceeding white as snow; so as no fuller on earth
can white them.
4 And there appeared unto them Elias with Moses: and they were talking with Jesus.
5 And Peter answered and said to Jesus, Master, it is good for us to be here: and let us
make three tabernacles; one for thee, and one for Moses, and one for Elias.
6 For he wist not what to say; for they were sore afraid.
7 And there was a cloud that overshadowed them: and a voice came out of the cloud,
saying, This is my beloved Son: hear him.
8 And suddenly, when they had looked round about, they saw no man any more, save
Jesus only with themselves.
9 And as they came down from the mountain, he charged them that they should tell no
man what things they had seen, till the Son of man were risen from the dead.
10 And they kept that saying with themselves, questioning one with another what the
rising from the dead should mean. (Mark 9:2-10)

82 - THE 2ND ANNOUNCEMENT OF SUFFERINGS

According to the Gospel of Mark

11 ¶ And they asked him, saying, Why say the scribes that Elias must first come?
12 And he answered and told them, Elias verily cometh first, and restoreth all things;
and how it is written of the Son of man, that he must suffer many things, and be set at

nought.
13 But I say unto you, That Elias is indeed come, and they have done unto him
whatsoever they listed, as it is written of him. (Mark 9:11-13)

According to the Gospel of Matthew

10 And his disciples asked him, saying, Why then say the scribes that Elias must first
come?
11 And Jesus answered and said unto them, Elias truly shall first come, and restore all
things.
12 But I say unto you, That Elias is come already, and they knew him not, but have
done unto him whatsoever they listed. Likewise shall also the Son of man suffer of
them.
13 Then the disciples understood that he spake unto them of John the Baptist. (Matt 17:10-13)

83 - THREE CASES OF OVERCOMING UNBELIEF

14 ¶ And when they were come to the multitude, there came to him a *certain* man,
kneeling down to him, and saying,
15 Lord, have mercy on my son: for he is lunatic, and sore vexed: for ofttimes he falleth
into the fire, and oft into the water.
16 And I brought him to thy disciples, and they could not cure him.
17 Then Jesus answered and said, O faithless and perverse generation, how long shall I
be with you? how long shall I suffer you? bring him hither to me.
18 And Jesus rebuked the devil; and he departed out of him: and the child was cured
from that very hour.
19 Then came the disciples to Jesus apart, and said, Why could not we cast him out?
20 And Jesus said unto them, Because of your unbelief: for verily I say unto you, If ye
have faith as a grain of mustard seed, ye shall say unto this mountain, Remove hence to
yonder place; and it shall remove; and nothing shall be impossible unto you.
21 Howbeit this kind goeth not out but by prayer and fasting. (Matt 17:14-21)
14 ¶ And when he came to *his* disciples, he saw a great multitude about them, and the
scribes questioning with them.
15 And straightway all the people, when they beheld him, were greatly amazed, and
running to *him* saluted him.
16 And he asked the scribes, What question ye with them?
17 And one of the multitude answered and said, Master, I have brought unto thee my
son, which hath a dumb spirit;
18 And wheresoever he taketh him, he teareth him: and he foameth, and gnasheth with
his teeth, and pineth away: and I spake to thy disciples that they should cast him out;
and they could not.
19 He answereth him, and saith, O faithless generation, how long shall I be with you?
how long shall I suffer you? bring him unto me.
20 And they brought him unto him: and when he saw him, straightway the spirit tare
him; and he fell on the ground, and wallowed foaming.
21 And he asked his father, How long is it ago since this came unto him? And he said,
Of a child.
22 And ofttimes it hath cast him into the fire, and into the waters, to destroy him: but if
thou canst do any thing, have compassion on us, and help us.

23 Jesus said unto him, If thou canst believe, all things *are* possible to him that
believeth.
24 And straightway the father of the child cried out, and said with tears, Lord, I believe;
help thou mine unbelief.
25 When Jesus saw that the people came running together, he rebuked the foul spirit,
saying unto him, *Thou* dumb and deaf spirit, I charge thee, come out of him, and enter
no more into him.
26 And *the spirit* cried, and rent him sore, and came out of him: and he was as one
dead; insomuch that many said, He is dead.
27 But Jesus took him by the hand, and lifted him up; and he arose.
28 And when he was come into the house, his disciples asked him privately, Why could
not we cast him out?
29 And he said unto them, This kind can come forth by nothing, but by prayer and
fasting. (Mark 9:14-29)
37 ¶ And it came to pass, that on the next day, when they were come down from the
hill, much people met him.
38 And, behold, a man of the company cried out, saying, Master, I beseech thee, look
upon my son: for he is mine only child.
39 And, lo, a spirit taketh him, and he suddenly crieth out; and it teareth him that he
foameth again, and bruising him hardly departeth from him.
40 And I besought thy disciples to cast him out; and they could not.
41 And Jesus answering said, O faithless and perverse generation, how long shall I be
with you, and suffer you? Bring thy son hither.
42 And as he was yet a-coming, the devil threw him down, and tare *him*. And Jesus
rebuked the unclean spirit, and healed the child, and delivered him again to his father.
(Luke 9:37-42)

84 - THE 3RD ANNOUNCEMENT OF SUFFERINGS

According to the Gospel of Luke

43 ¶ And they were all amazed at the mighty power of God. But while they wondered
every one at all things which Jesus did, he said unto his disciples,
44 Let these sayings sink down into your ears: for the Son of man shall be delivered
into the hands of men.
45 But they understood not this saying, and it was hid from them, that they perceived it
not: and they feared to ask him of that saying. (Luke 9:43-45)

According to the Gospel of Mark

30 ¶ And they departed thence, and passed through Galilee; and he would not that any
man should know *it*.
31 For he taught his disciples, and said unto them, The Son of man is delivered into the
hands of men, and they shall kill him; and after that he is killed, he shall rise the third
day.
32 But they understood not that saying, and were afraid to ask him. (Mark 9:30-32)

According to the Gospel of Matthew

22 ¶ And while they abode in Galilee, Jesus said unto them, The Son of man shall be
betrayed into the hands of men:
23 And they shall kill him, and the third day he shall be raised again. And they were
exceeding sorry. (Matt 17:22-23)

85 - MONEY FOR THE TAXES

24 ¶ And when they were come to Capernaum, they that received tribute *money* came
to Peter, and said, Doth not your master pay tribute?
25 He saith, Yes. And when he was come into the house, Jesus prevented him, saying,
What thinkest thou, Simon? of whom do the kings of the earth take custom or tribute?
of their own children, or of strangers?
26 Peter saith unto him, Of strangers. Jesus saith unto him, Then are the children free.
27 Notwithstanding, lest we should offend them, go thou to the sea, and cast an hook,
and take up the fish that first cometh up; and when thou hast opened his mouth, thou
shalt find a piece of money: that take, and give unto them for me and thee. (Matt 17:24-27)

86 - WHO SHALL BE THE GREATEST?

According to the Gospel of Mark

33 ¶ And he came to Capernaum: and being in the house he asked them, What was it
that ye disputed among yourselves by the way?
34 But they held their peace: for by the way they had disputed among themselves, who
should be the greatest.
35 And he sat down, and called the twelve, and saith unto them, If any man desire to be
first, *the same* shall be last of all, and servant of all.
36 And he took a child, and set him in the midst of them: and when he had taken him in
his arms, he said unto them,
37 Whosoever shall receive one of such children in my name, receiveth me: and
whosoever shall receive me, receiveth not me, but him that sent me. (Mark 9:33-37)

According to the Gospel of Matthew

1 At the same time came the disciples unto Jesus, saying, Who is the greatest in the
kingdom of heaven?
2 And Jesus called a little child unto him, and set him in the midst of them,
3 And said, Verily I say unto you, Except ye be converted, and become as little
children, ye shall not enter into the kingdom of heaven.
4 Whosoever therefore shall humble himself as this little child, the same is greatest in
the kingdom of heaven.
5 And whoso shall receive one such little child in my name receiveth me. (Matt 18:1-5)

According to the Gospel of Luke

46 ¶ Then there arose a reasoning among them, which of them should be greatest.
47 And Jesus, perceiving the thought of their heart, took a child, and set him by him,
48 And said unto them, Whosoever shall receive this child in my name receiveth me:
and whosoever shall receive me receiveth him that sent me: for he that is least among
you all, the same shall be great. (Luke 9:46-48)

87 - EXCLUSIVENESS AND ENVY MUST BE UNSELFED

According to the Gospel of Luke

49 ¶ And John answered and said, Master, we saw one casting out devils in thy name;
and we forbad him, because he followeth not with us.
50 And Jesus said unto him, Forbid *him* not: for he that is not against us is for us. (Luke
59:49-50)

38 ¶ And John answered him, saying, Master, we saw one casting out devils in thy
name, and he followeth not us: and we forbad him, because he followeth not us.
39 But Jesus said, Forbid him not: for there is no man which shall do a miracle in my
name, that can lightly speak evil of me.
40 For he that is not against us is on our part.
41 For whosoever shall give you a cup of water to drink in my name, because ye belong
to Christ, verily I say unto you, he shall not lose his reward. (Mark 9:38-41)

88 - AVOID OFFENSES

According to the Gospel of Mark

42 And whosoever shall offend one of *these* little ones that believe in me, it is better for
him that a millstone were hanged about his neck, and he were cast into the sea.
43 And if thy hand offend thee, cut if off: it is better for thee to enter into life maimed,
than having two hands to go into hell, into the fire that never shall be quenched:
44 Where their worm dieth not, and the fire is not quenched.
45 And if thy foot offend thee, cut it off: it is better for thee to enter halt into life, than
having two feet to be cast into hell, into the fire that never shall be quenched:
46 Where their worm dieth not, and the fire is not quenched.
47 And if thine eye offend thee, pluck it out: it is better for thee to enter into the
kingdom of God with one eye, than having two eyes to be cast into hell fire:
48 Where their worm dieth not, and the fire is not quenched.
49 For every one shall be salted with fire, and every sacrifice shall be salted with salt.
50 Salt *is* good: but if the salt have lost his saltness, wherewith will ye season it? Have
salt in yourselves, and have peace one with another. (Mark 9:42-50)

According to the Gospel of Matthew

6 But whoso shall offend one of these little ones which believe in me, it were better for
him that a millstone were hanged about his neck, and *that* he were drowned in the depth
of the sea.
7 ¶ Woe unto the world because of offences! for it must needs be that offences come;
but woe to that man by whom the offence cometh!
8 Wherefore if thy hand or thy foot offend thee, cut them off, and cast *them* from thee:
it is better for thee to enter into life halt or maimed, rather than having two hands or two
feet to be cast into everlasting fire.
9 And if thine eye offend thee, pluck it out, and cast *it* from thee: it is better for thee to
enter into life with one eye, rather than having two eyes to be cast into hell fire.
10 Take heed that ye despise not one of these little ones; for I say unto you, That in
heaven their angels do always behold the face of my Father which is in heaven.
11 For the Son of man is come to save that which was lost.
12 How think ye? if a man have an hundred sheep, and one of them be gone astray,
doth he not leave the ninety and nine, and goeth into the mountains, and seeketh that
which is gone astray?
13 And if so be that he find it, verily I say unto you, he rejoiceth more of that *sheep*,
than of the ninety and nine which went not astray.
14 Even so it is not the will of your Father which is in heaven, that one of these little
ones should perish. (Matt 18:6-14)

89 - LOVE ENOUGH TO SEEK RECONCILIATION

15 ¶ Moreover if thy brother shall trespass against thee, go and tell him his fault
between thee and him alone: if he shall hear thee, thou hast gained thy brother.
16 But if he will not hear *thee, then* take with thee one or two more, that in the mouth
of two or three witnesses every word may be established.
17 And if he shall neglect to hear them, tell *it* unto the church: but if he neglect to hear
the church, let him be unto thee as an heathen man and a publican.
18 Verily I say unto you, Whatsoever ye shall bind on earth shall be bound in heaven:
and whatsoever ye shall loose on earth shall be loosed in heaven.
19 Again I say unto you, That if two of you shall agree on earth as touching any thing
that they shall ask, it shall be done for them of my Father which is in heaven.
20 For where two or three are gathered together in my name, there am I in the midst of
them.
21 ¶ Then came Peter to him, and said, Lord, how oft shall my brother sin against me,
and I forgive him? till seven times?
22 Jesus saith unto him, I say not unto thee, Until seven times: but, Until seventy times
seven.
23 ¶ Therefore is the kingdom of heaven likened unto a certain king, which would take
account of his servants.
24 And when he had begun to reckon, one was brought unto him, which owed him ten
thousand talents.
25 But forasmuch as he had not to pay, his lord commanded him to be sold, and his
wife, and children, and all that he had, and payment to be made.
26 The servant therefore fell down, and worshipped him, saying, Lord, have patience
with me, and I will pay thee all.
27 Then the lord of that servant was moved with compassion, and loosed him, and
forgave him the debt.
28 But the same servant went out, and found one of his fellowservants, which owed
him an hundred pence: and he laid hands on him, and took *him* by the throat, saying,
Pay me that thou owest.
29 And his fellowservant fell down at his feet, and besought him, saying, Have patience
with me, and I will pay thee all.
30 And he would not: but went and cast him into prison, till he should pay the debt.
31 So when his fellowservants saw what was done, they were very sorry, and came and
told unto their lord all that was done.
32 Then his lord, after that he had called him, said unto him, O thou wicked servant, I
forgave thee all that debt, because thou desiredst me:
33 Shouldest not thou also have had compassion on thy fellowservant, even as I had
pity on thee?
34 And his lord was wroth, and delivered him to the tormentors, till he should pay all
that was due unto him.
35 So likewise shall my heavenly Father do also unto you, if ye from your hearts
forgive not every one his brother their trespasses. (Matt 18:15-35)

90 – TREACHEROUS ADVICE REJECTED

1 After these things Jesus walked in Galilee: for he would not walk in Jewry, because
the Jews sought to kill him.

2 Now the Jews' feast of tabernacles was at hand.
3 His brethren therefore said unto him, Depart hence, and go into Judæa, that thy
disciples also may see the works that thou doest.
4 For *there is* no man *that* doeth any thing in secret, and he himself seeketh to be
known openly. If thou do these things, shew thyself to the world.
5 For neither did his brethren believe in him.
6 Then Jesus said unto them, My time is not yet come: but your time is alway ready.
7 The world cannot hate you; but me it hateth, because I testify of it, that the works
thereof are evil.
8 Go ye up unto this feast: I go not up yet unto this feast; for my time is not yet full
come.
9 When he had said these words unto them, he abode *still* in Galilee.
10 ¶ But when his brethren were gone up, then went he also up unto the feast, not
openly, but as it were in secret. (John 7:1-10)
1 And it came to pass, *that* when Jesus had finished these sayings, he departed from
Galilee, (Matt 19:1 to 3rd,)

91 - FROM GALILEE THROUGH SAMARIA TOWARD JUDÆA

51 ¶ And it came to pass, when the time was come that he should be received up, he
stedfastly set his face to go to Jerusalem,
52 And sent messengers before his face: and they went, and entered into a village of the
Samaritans, to make ready for him.
53 And they did not receive him, because his face was as though he would go to
Jerusalem.
54 And when his disciples James and John saw *this*, they said, Lord, wilt thou that we
command fire to come down from heaven, and consume them, even as Elias did?
55 But he turned, and rebuked them, and said, Ye know not what manner of spirit ye
are of.
56 For the Son of man is not come to destroy men's lives, but to save *them*. And they
went to another village. (Luke 9:51-56)

92 - EXCUSES - EXCUSES - EXCUSES

57 ¶ And it came to pass, that, as they went in the way, a certain *man* said unto him,
Lord, I will follow thee whithersoever thou goest.
58 And Jesus said unto him, Foxes have holes, and birds of the air *have* nests; but the
Son of man hath not where to lay *his* head.
59 And he said unto another, Follow me. But he said, Lord, suffer me first to go and
bury my father.
60 Jesus said unto him, Let the dead bury their dead: but go thou and preach the
kingdom of God.
61 And another also said, Lord, I will follow thee; but let me first go bid them farewell,
which are at home at my house.
62 And Jesus said unto him, No man, having put his hand to the plough, and looking
back, is fit for the kingdom of God. (Luke 9:57-62)

93 - SEVENTY MORE DISCIPLES APPOINTED

1 After these things the Lord appointed other seventy also, and sent them two and two
before his face into every city and place, whither he himself would come.

2 Therefore said he unto them, The harvest truly *is* great, but the labourers *are* few:
pray ye therefore the Lord of the harvest, that he would send forth labourers into his
harvest.
3 Go your ways: behold, I send you forth as lambs among wolves.
4 Carry neither purse, nor scrip, nor shoes: and salute no man by the way.
5 And into whatsoever house ye enter, first say, Peace *be* to this house.
6 And if the son of peace be there, your peace shall rest upon it: if not, it shall turn to
you again.
7 And in the same house remain, eating and drinking such things as they give: for the
labourer is worthy of his hire. Go not from house to house.
8 And into whatsoever city ye enter, and they receive you, eat such things as are set
before you:
9 And heal the sick that are therein, and say unto them, The kingdom of God is come
nigh unto you.
10 But into whatsoever city ye enter, and they receive you not, go your ways out into
the streets of the same, and say,
11 Even the very dust of your city, which cleaveth on us, we do wipe off against you:
notwithstanding be ye sure of this, that the kingdom of God is come nigh unto you.
12 But I say unto you, that it shall be more tolerable in that day for Sodom, than for that
city.
13 Woe unto thee, Chorazin! woe unto thee, Bethsaida! for if the mighty works had
been done in Tyre and Sidon, which have been done in you, they had a great while ago
repented, sitting in sackcloth and ashes.
14 But it shall be more tolerable for Tyre and Sidon at the judgment, than for you.
15 And thou, Capernaum, which art exalted to heaven, shalt be thrust down to hell.
16 He that heareth you heareth me; and he that despiseth you despiseth me; and he that
despiseth me despiseth him that sent me.
17 ¶ And the seventy returned again with joy, saying, Lord, even the devils are subject
unto us through thy name.
18 And he said unto them, I beheld Satan as lightning fall from heaven.
19 Behold, I give unto you power to tread on serpents and scorpions, and over all the
power of the enemy: and nothing shall by any means hurt you.
20 Notwithstanding in this rejoice not, that the spirits are subject unto you; but rather
rejoice, because your names are written in heaven.
21 In that hour Jesus rejoiced in spirit, and said, I thank thee, O Father, Lord of heaven
and earth, that thou hast hid these things from the wise and prudent, and hast revealed
them unto babes: even so, Father; for so it seemed good in thy sight.
22 All things are delivered to me of my Father: and no man knoweth who the Son is,
but the Father; and who the Father is, but the Son, and *he* to whom the Son will reveal
him.
23 ¶ And he turned him unto *his* disciples, and said privately, Blessed *are* the eyes
which see the things that ye see:
24 For I tell you, that many prophets and kings have desired to see those things which
ye see, and have not seen *them*; and to hear those things which ye hear, and have not
heard *them*. (Luke 10:1-24)

94 - ETERNAL LIFE IS NOT FOR SALE

25 ¶ And, behold, a certain lawyer stood up, and tempted him, saying, Master, what
shall I do to inherit eternal life?
26 He said unto him, What is written in the law? how readest thou?
27 And he answering said, Thou shalt love the Lord thy God with all thy heart, and
with all thy soul, and with all thy strength, and with all thy mind; and thy neighbour as
thyself.
28 And he said unto him, Thou hast answered right: this do, and thou shalt live.
29 But he, willing to justify himself, said unto Jesus, And who is my neighbour?
30 And Jesus answering said, A certain *man* went down from Jerusalem to Jericho, and
fell among thieves, which stripped him of his raiment, and wounded *him*, and departed,
leaving *him* half dead.
31 And by chance there came down a certain priest that way: and when he saw him, he
passed by on the other side.
32 And likewise a Levite, when he was at the place, came and looked *on him*, and
passed by on the other side.
33 But a certain Samaritan, as he journeyed, came where he was: and when he saw him,
he had compassion *on him*,
34 And went to *him*, and bound up his wounds, pouring in oil and wine, and set him on
his own beast, and brought him to an inn, and took care of him.
35 And on the morrow when he departed, he took out two pence, and gave *them* to the
host, and said unto him, Take care of him; and whatsoever thou spendest more, when I
come again, I will repay thee.
36 Which now of these three, thinkest thou, was neighbour unto him that fell among the
thieves?
37 And he said, He that shewed mercy on him. Then said Jesus unto him, Go, and do
thou likewise. (Luke 10:25-37)

95 - ARRIVAL IN THE REGION OF JUDÆA

According to the Gospel of Matthew

1 and came into the coasts of Judæa beyond Jordan;
2 And great multitudes followed him; and he healed them there. (Matt 19:1-2 2nd *and*)

According to the Gospel of Mark

1 And he arose from thence, and cometh into the coasts of Judæa by the farther side of
Jordan: and the people resort unto him again; and, as he was wont, he taught them
again. (Mark 10:1)

96 - THE ONE THING NEEDFUL

38 ¶ Now it came to pass, as they went, that he entered into a certain village: and a
certain woman named Martha received him into her house.
39 And she had a sister called Mary, which also sat at Jesus' feet, and heard his word.
40 But Martha was cumbered about much serving, and came to him, and said, Lord,
dost thou not care that my sister hath left me to serve alone? bid her therefore that she
help me.
41 And Jesus answered and said unto her, Martha, Martha, thou art careful and troubled
about many things:
42 But one thing is needful: and Mary hath chosen that good part, which shall not be

taken away from her. (Luke 10:38-42)

97 - JESUS AT THE FEAST OF TABERNACLES

11 Then the Jews sought him at the feast, and said, Where is he?
12 And there was much murmuring among the people concerning him: for some said,
He is a good man: others said, Nay; but he deceiveth the people.
13 Howbeit no man spake openly of him for fear of the Jews.
14 ¶ Now about the midst of the feast Jesus went up into the temple, and taught
15 And the Jews marvelled, saying, How knoweth this man letters, having never
learned?
16 Jesus answered them, and said, My doctrine is not mine, but his that sent me.
17 If any man will do his will, he shall know of the doctrine, whether it be of God, or
whether I speak of myself.
18 He that speaketh of himself seeketh his own glory: but he that seeketh his glory that
sent him, the same is true, and no unrighteousness is in him.
19 Did not Moses give you the law, and *yet* none of you keepeth the law? Why go ye
about to kill me?
20 The people answered and said, Thou hast a devil: who goeth about to kill thee?
21 Jesus answered and said unto them, I have done one work, and ye all marvel
22 Moses therefore gave unto you circumcision; (not because it is of Moses, but of the
fathers;) and ye on the sabbath day circumcise a man.
23 If a man on the sabbath day receive circumcision, that the law of Moses should not
be broken; are ye angry at me, because I have made a man every whit whole on the
sabbath day?
24 Judge not according to the appearance, but judge righteous judgment.
25 Then said some of them of Jerusalem, Is not this he, whom they seek to kill?
26 But, lo, he speaketh boldly, and they say nothing unto him. Do the rulers know
indeed that this is the very Christ?
27 Howbeit we know this man whence he is: but when Christ cometh, no man knoweth
whence he is.
28 Then cried Jesus in the temple as he taught, saying, Ye both know me, and ye know
whence I am: and I am not come of myself, but he that sent me is true, whom ye know
not.
29 But I know him: for I am from him, and he hath sent me.
30 Then they sought to take him: but no man laid hands on him, because his hour was
not yet come.
31 And many of the people believed on him, and said, When Christ cometh, will he do
more miracles than these which this *man* hath done?
32 ¶ The Pharisees heard that the people murmured such things concerning him; and
the Pharisees and the chief priests sent officers to take him.
33 Then said Jesus unto them, Yet a little while am I with you, and *then* I go unto him
that sent me.
34 Ye shall seek me, and shall not find *me*: and where I am, *thither* ye cannot come.
35 Then said the Jews among themselves, Whither will he go, that we shall not find
him? will he go unto the dispersed among the Gentiles, and teach the Gentiles?
36 What *manner of* saying is this that he said, Ye shall seek me, and shall not find *me*:
and where I am, *thither* ye cannot come?

37 In the last day, that great *day* of the feast, Jesus stood and cried, saying, If any man
thirst, let him come unto me, and drink.
38 He that believeth on me, as the scripture hath said, out of his belly shall flow rivers
of living water.
39 (But this spake he of the Spirit, which they that believe on him should receive: for
the Holy Ghost was not yet *given*; because that Jesus was not yet glorified.)
40 ¶ Many of the people therefore, when they heard this saying, said, Of a truth this is
the Prophet.
41 Others said, This is the Christ. But some said, Shall Christ come out of Galilee?
42 Hath not the scripture said, That Christ cometh of the seed of David, and out of the
town of Bethlehem, where David was?
43 So there was a division among the people because of him.
44 And some of them would have taken him; but no man laid hands on him.
45 ¶ Then came the officers to the chief priests and Pharisees; and they said unto them,
Why have ye not brought him?
46 The officers answered, Never man spake like this man.
47 Then answered them the Pharisees, Are ye also deceived?
48 Have any of the rulers or of the Pharisees believed on him?
49 But this people who knoweth not the law are cursed.
50 Nicodemus saith unto them, (he that came to Jesus by night, being one of them,)
51 Doth our law judge *any* man, before it hear him, and know what he doeth?
52 They answered and said unto him, Art thou also of Galilee? Search, and look: for
out of Galilee ariseth no prophet.
53 And every man went unto his own house. (John 7:11-53)
1 Jesus went unto the mount of Olives. (John 8:1)

98 - A CRUEL AND HEARTLESS PLAN TO ENTRAP JESUS

2 And early in the morning he came again into the temple, and all the people came unto
him; and he sat down, and taught them.
3 And the scribes and Pharisees brought unto him a woman taken in adultery; and when
they had set her in the midst,
4 They say unto him, Master, this woman was taken in adultery, in the very act.
5 Now Moses in the law commanded us, that such should be stoned: but what sayest
thou?
6 This they said, tempting him, that they might have to accuse him. But Jesus stooped
down, and with *his* finger wrote on the ground, *as though he heard them not*.
7 So when they continued asking him, he lifted up himself, and said unto them, He that
is without sin among you, let him first cast a stone at her.
8 And again he stooped down, and wrote on the ground.
9 And they which heard *it*, being convicted by *their own* conscience, went out one by
one, beginning at the eldest, *even* unto the last: and Jesus was left alone, and the woman
standing in the midst.
10 When Jesus had lifted up himself, and saw none but the woman, he said unto her,
Woman, where are those thine accusers? hath no man condemned thee?
11 She said, No man, Lord. And Jesus said unto her, Neither do I condemn thee: go,
and sin no more. (John 8:2-11)

99 - THE LIGHT OF THE WORLD

12 ¶ Then spake Jesus again unto them, saying, I am the light of the world: he that
followeth me shall not walk in darkness, but shall have the light of life.
13 The Pharisees therefore said unto him, Thou bearest record of thyself; thy record is
not true.
14 Jesus answered and said unto them, Though I bear record of myself, *yet* my record is
true; for I know whence I came, and whither I go; but ye cannot tell whence I come,
and whither I go.
15 Ye judge after the flesh; I judge no man.
16 And yet if I judge, my judgment is true: for I am not alone, but I and the Father that
sent me.
17 It is also written in your law, that the testimony of two men is true.
18 I am one that bear witness of myself, and the Father that sent me beareth witness of
me.
19 Then said they unto him, Where is thy Father? Jesus answered, Ye neither know
me, nor my Father: if ye had known me, ye should have known my Father also.
20 These words spake Jesus in the treasury, as he taught in the temple: and no man laid
hands on him; for his hour was not yet come.
21 Then said Jesus again unto them, I go my way, and ye shall seek me, and shall die in
your sins: whither I go, ye cannot come.
22 Then said the Jews, Will he kill himself? because he saith, Whither I go, ye cannot
come.
23 And he said unto them, Ye are from beneath; I am from above: ye are of this world;
I am not of this world.
24 I said therefore unto you, that ye shall die in your sins: for if ye believe not that I am
he, ye shall die in your sins.
25 Then said they unto him, Who art thou? And Jesus saith unto them, Even *the same*
that I said unto you from the beginning.
26 I have many things to say and to judge of you: but he that sent me is true; and I
speak to the world those things which I have heard of him.
27 They understood not that he spake to them of the Father.
28 Then said Jesus unto them, When ye have lifted up the Son of man, then shall ye
know that I am *he*, and *that* I do nothing of myself; but as my Father hath taught me, I
speak these things.
29 And he that sent me is with me: the Father hath not left me alone; for I do always
those things that please him.
30 As he spake these words, many believed on him. (John 8:12-30)

100 - JESUS CONFUTES THE HOSTILE DISCIPLES AT JERUSALEM

31 Then said Jesus to those Jews which believed on him, If ye continue in my word,
then are ye my disciples indeed;
32 And ye shall know the truth, and the truth shall make you free
33 ¶ They answered him, We be Abraham's seed, and were never in bondage to any
man: how sayest thou, Ye shall be made free?
34 Jesus answered them, Verily, verily, I say unto you, Whosoever committeth sin is
the servant of sin.
35 And the servant abideth not in the house for ever: *but* the Son abideth ever.

36 If the Son therefore shall make you free, ye shall be free indeed.
37 I know that ye are Abraham's seed; but ye seek to kill me, because my word hath no
place in you.
38 I speak that which I have seen with my Father: and ye do that which ye have seen
with your father.
39 They answered and said unto him, Abraham is our father.
39 Jesus saith unto them, If ye were Abraham's children, ye would do the works of
Abraham.
40 But now ye seek to kill me, a man that hath told you the truth, which I have heard of
God: this did not Abraham.
41 Ye do the deeds of your father. Then said they to him, We be not born of
fornication; we have one Father, *even* God.
42 Jesus said unto them, If God were your Father, ye would love me: for I proceeded
forth and came from God; neither came I of myself, but he sent me.
43 Why do ye not understand my speech? *even* because ye cannot hear my word.
44 Ye are of *your* father the devil, and the lusts of your father ye will do. He was a
murderer from the beginning, and abode not in the truth, because there is no truth in
him. When he speaketh a lie, he speaketh of his own: for he is a liar, and the father of
it.
45 And because I tell *you* the truth, ye believe me not.
46 Which of you convinceth me of sin? And if I say the truth, why do ye not believe
me?
47 He that is of God heareth God's words: ye therefore hear *them* not, because ye are
not of God.
48 Then answered the Jews, and said unto him, Say we not well that thou art a
Samaritan, and hast a devil?
49 Jesus answered, I have not a devil; but I honour my Father, and ye do dishonour me.
50 And I seek not mine own glory: there is one that seeketh and judgeth.
51 Verily, verily, I say unto you, If a man keep my saying, he shall never see death.
52 Then said the Jews unto him, Now we know that thou hast a devil. Abraham is dead,
and the prophets; and thou sayest, If a man keep my saying, he shall never taste of
death.
53 Art thou greater than our father Abraham, which is dead? and the prophets are dead:
whom makest thou thyself?
54 Jesus answered, If I honour myself, my honour is nothing: it is my Father that
honoureth me; of whom ye say, that he is your God:
55 Yet ye have not known him; but I know him: and if I should say, I know him not, I
shall be a liar like unto you: but I know him, and keep his saying.
56 Your father Abraham rejoiced to see my day: and he saw *it*, and was glad.
57 Then said the Jews unto him, Thou art not yet fifty years old, and hast thou seen
Abraham?
58 Jesus said unto them, Verily, verily, I say unto you, Before Abraham was, I am.
59 Then took they up stones to cast at him: but Jesus hid himself, and went out of the
temple, going through the midst of them, and so passed by. (John 8:31-59)

101 - HEALING A MAN BORN BLIND

1 And as *Jesus* passed by, he saw a man which was blind from *his* birth.

2 And his disciples asked him, saying, Master, who did sin, this man, or his parents,
that he was born blind?
3 Jesus answered, Neither hath this man sinned, nor his parents: but that the works of
God should be made manifest in him.
4 I must work the works of him that sent me, while it is day: the night cometh, when no
man can work.
5 As long as I am in the world, I am the light of the world.
6 When he had thus spoken, he spat on the ground, and made clay of the spittle, and he
anointed the eyes of the blind man with the clay,
7 And said unto him, Go, wash in the pool of Siloam, (which is by interpretation, Sent.)
He went his way therefore, and washed, and came seeing.
8 ¶ The neighbours therefore, and they which before had seen him that he was blind,
said, Is not this he that sat and begged?
9 Some said, This is he: others *said*, He is like him: *but* he said, I am *he*.
10 Therefore said they unto him, How were thine eyes opened?
11 He answered and said, A man that is called Jesus made clay, and anointed mine
eyes, and said unto me, Go to the pool of Siloam, and wash: and I went and washed,
and I received sight.
12 Then said they unto him, Where is he? He said, I know not.
13 ¶ They brought to the Pharisees him that aforetime was blind.
14 And it was the sabbath day when Jesus made the clay, and opened his eyes.
15 Then again the Pharisees also asked him how he had received his sight. He said
unto them, He put clay upon mine eyes, and I washed, and do see.
16 Therefore said some of the Pharisees, This man is not of God, because he keepeth
not the sabbath day. Others said, How can a man that is a sinner do such miracles?
And there was a division among them.
17 They say unto the blind man again, What sayest thou of him, that he hath opened
thine eyes? He said, He is a prophet.
18 But the Jews did not believe concerning him, that he had been blind, and received
his sight, until they called the parents of him that had received his sight.
19 And they asked them, saying, Is this your son, who ye say was born blind? how then
doth he now see?
20 His parents answered them and said, We know that this is our son, and that he was
born blind:
21 But by what means he now seeth, we know not; or who hath opened his eyes, we
know not: he is of age; ask him: he shall speak for himself.
22 These *words* spake his parents, because they feared the Jews: for the Jews had
agreed already, that if any man did confess that he was Christ, he should be put out of
the synagogue.
23 Therefore said his parents, He is of age; ask him.
24 Then again called they the man that was blind, and said unto him, Give God the
praise: we know that this man is a sinner.
25 He answered and said, Whether he be a sinner *or no*, I know not: one thing I know,
that, whereas I was blind, now I see.
26 Then said they to him again, What did he to thee? how opened he thine eyes?
27 He answered them, I have told you already, and ye did not hear: wherefore would ye

hear *it* again? will ye also be his disciples?
28 Then they reviled him, and said, Thou art his disciple; but we are Moses' disciples.
29 We know that God spake unto Moses: *as for* this *fellow*, we know not from whence
he is.
30 The man answered and said unto them, Why herein is a marvellous thing, that ye
know not from whence he is, and *yet* he hath opened mine eyes.
31 Now we know that God heareth not sinners: but if any man be a worshipper of God,
and doeth his will, him he heareth.
32 Since the world began was it not heard that any man opened the eyes of one that was
born blind.
33 If this man were not of God, he could do nothing.
34 They answered and said unto him, Thou wast altogether born in sins, and dost thou
teach us? And they cast him out.
35 Jesus heard that they had cast him out; and when he had found him, he said unto
him, Dost thou believe on the Son of God?
36 He answered and said, Who is he, Lord, that I might believe on him?
37 And Jesus said unto him, Thou hast both seen him, and it is he that talketh with thee.
38 And he said, Lord, I believe. And he worshipped him.
39 ¶ And Jesus said, For judgment I am come into this world, that they which see not
might see; and that they which see might be made blind.
40 And *some* of the Pharisees which were with him heard these words, and said unto
him, Are we blind also?
41 Jesus said unto them, If ye were blind, ye should have no sin: but now ye say, We
see; therefore your sin remaineth. (John 9:1-41)
1 Verily, verily, I say unto you, He that entereth not by the door into the sheepfold, but
climbeth up some other way, the same is a thief and a robber.
2 But he that entereth in by the door is the shepherd of the sheep.
3 To him the porter openeth; and the sheep hear his voice: and he calleth his own sheep
by name, and leadeth them out.
4 And when he putteth forth his own sheep, he goeth before them, and the sheep follow
him: for they know his voice.
5 And a stranger will they not follow, but will flee from him: for they know not the
voice of strangers.
6 This parable spake Jesus unto them: but they understood not what things they were
which he spake unto them.
7 Then said Jesus unto them again, Verily, verily, I say unto you, I am the door of the
sheep.
8 All that ever came before me are thieves and robbers: but the sheep did not hear
them.
9 I am the door: by me if any man enter in, he shall be saved, and shall go in and out,
and find pasture.
10 The thief cometh not, but for to steal, and to kill, and to destroy: I am come that they
might have life, and that they might have *it* more abundantly.
11 I am the good shepherd: the good shepherd giveth his life for the sheep.
12 But he that is an hireling, and not the shepherd, whose own the sheep are not, seeth
the wolf coming, and leaveth the sheep, and fleeth: and the wolf catcheth them, and

scattereth the sheep.
13 The hireling fleeth, because he is an hireling, and careth not for the sheep.
14 I am the good shepherd, and know my *sheep*, and am known of mine.
15 As the Father knoweth me, even so know I the Father: and I lay down my life for the
sheep.
16 And other sheep I have, which are not of this fold: them also I must bring, and they
shall hear my voice; and there shall be one fold, *and* one shepherd.
17 Therefore doth my Father love me, because I lay down my life, that I might take it
again.
18 No man taketh it from me, but I lay it down of myself. I have power to lay it down,
and I have power to take it again. This commandment have I received of my Father.
19 ¶ There was a division therefore again among the Jews for these sayings.
20 And many of them said, He hath a devil, and is mad; why hear ye him?
21 Others said, These are not the words of him that hath a devil. Can a devil open the
eyes of the blind? (John 10:1-21)

102 - MORE INSTRUCTION ON PRAYER

1 And it came to pass, that, as he was praying in a certain place, when he ceased, one
of his disciples said unto him, Lord, teach us to pray, as John also taught his disciples.
2 And he said unto them, When ye pray, say, Our Father which art in heaven, Hallowed
be thy name. Thy kingdom come. Thy will be done, as in heaven, so in earth.
3 Give us day by day our daily bread.
4 And forgive us our sins; for we also forgive every one that is indebted to us. And
lead us not into temptation; but deliver us from evil.
5 And he said unto them, Which of you shall have a friend, and shall go unto him at
midnight, and say unto him, Friend, lend me three loaves;
6 For a friend of mine in his journey is come to me, and I have nothing to set before
him?
7 And he from within shall answer and say, Trouble me not: the door is now shut, and
my children are with me in bed; I cannot rise and give thee.
8 I say unto you, Though he will not rise and give him, because he is his friend, yet
because of his importunity he will rise and give him as many as he needeth.
9 And I say unto you, Ask, and it shall be given you; seek, and ye shall find; knock,
and it shall be opened unto you.
10 For every one that asketh receiveth; and he that seeketh findeth; and to him that
knocketh it shall be opened.
11 If a son shall ask bread of any of you that is a father, will he give him a stone? or if
he ask a fish, will he for a fish give him a serpent?
12 Or if he shall ask an egg, will he offer him a scorpion?
13 If ye then, being evil, know how to give good gifts unto your children: how much
more shall *your* heavenly Father give the Holy Spirit to them that ask him? (Luke 11:1-13)

103 – CHRIST-HEALING OPPOSED TO DEMONOLOGY

14 ¶ And he was casting out a devil, and it was dumb. And it came to pass, when the
devil was gone out, the dumb spake; and the people wondered.
15 But some of them said, He casteth out devils through Beelzebub the chief of the
devils.

16 And others, tempting *him*, sought of him a sign from heaven.
17 But he, knowing their thoughts, said unto them, Every kingdom divided against
itself is brought to desolation; and a house *divided* against a house falleth.
18 If Satan also be divided against himself, how shall his kingdom stand? because ye
say that I cast out devils through Beelzebub.
19 And if I by Beelzebub cast out devils, by whom do your sons cast *them* out?
therefore shall they be your judges.
20 But if I with the finger of God cast out devils, no doubt the kingdom of God is come
upon you.
21 When a strong man armed keepeth his palace, his goods are in peace:
22 But when a stronger than he shall come upon him, and overcome him, he taketh
from him all his armour wherein he trusted, and divideth his spoils.
23 He that is not with me is against me: and he that gathereth not with me scattereth.
24 When the unclean spirit is gone out of a man, he walketh through dry places,
seeking rest; and finding none, he saith, I will return unto my house whence I came out.
25 And when he cometh, he findeth *it* swept and garnished.
26 Then goeth he, and taketh *to him* seven other spirits more wicked than himself; and
they enter in, and dwell there: and the last *state* of that man is worse than the first.
27 ¶ And it came to pass, as he spake these things, a certain woman of the company
lifted up her voice, and said unto him, Blessed *is* the womb that bare thee, and the paps
which thou hast sucked.
28 But he said, Yea rather, blessed *are* they that hear the word of God, and keep it. (Luke
11:14-28)

104 - QUESTIONS CONCERNING DIVORCE AND CELIBACY

2 ¶ And the Pharisees came to him, and asked him, Is it lawful for a man to put away
his wife? tempting him.
3 And he answered and said unto them, What did Moses command you?
4 And they said, Moses suffered to write a bill of divorcement, and to put *her* away.
5 And Jesus answered and said unto them, For the hardness of your heart he wrote you
this precept.
6 But from the beginning of the creation God made them male and female.
7 For this cause shall a man leave his father and mother, and cleave to his wife;
8 And they twain shall be one flesh: so then they are no more twain, but one flesh.
9 What therefore God hath joined together, let not man put asunder.
10 And in the house his disciples asked him again of the same *matter*.
11 And he saith unto them, Whosoever shall put away his wife, and marry another,
committeth adultery against her.
12 And if a woman shall put away her husband, and be married to another, she
committeth adultery. (Mark 10:2-12)
3 ¶ The Pharisees also came unto him, tempting him, and saying unto him, Is it lawful
for a man to put away his wife for every cause?
4 And he answered and said unto them, Have ye not read, that he which made *them* at
the beginning made them male and female,
5 And said, For this cause shall a man leave father and mother, and shall cleave to his
wife: and they twain shall be one flesh?
6 Wherefore they are no more twain, but one flesh. What therefore God hath joined

together, let not man put asunder.
7 They say unto him, Why did Moses then command to give a writing of divorcement,
and to put her away?
8 He saith unto them, Moses because of the hardness of your hearts suffered you to put
away your wives: but from the beginning it was not so.
9 And I say unto you, Whosoever shall put away his wife, except *it be* for fornication,
and shall marry another, committeth adultery: and whoso marrieth her which is put
away doth commit adultery.
10 ¶ His disciples say unto him, If the case of the man be so with *his* wife, it is not good
to marry.
11 But he said unto them, All *men* cannot receive this saying, save *they* to whom it is
given.
12 For there are some eunuchs, which were so born from *their* mother's womb: and
there are some eunuchs, which were made eunuchs of men and there be eunuchs, which
have made themselves eunuchs for the kingdom of heaven's sake. He that is able to
receive *It*, let him receive *it*. (Matt 19:3-12)

105 - THE "EVIL GENERATION" CONFRONTED

29 ¶ And when the people were gathered thick together, he began to say, This is an evil
generation: they seek a sign; and there shall no sign be given it, but the sign of Jonas
the prophet.
30 For as Jonas was a sign unto the Ninevites, so shall also the Son of man be to this
generation.
31 The queen of the south shall rise up in the judgment with the men of this generation,
and condemn them: for she came from the utmost parts of the earth to hear the wisdom
of Solomon; and, behold, a greater than Solomon *is* here.
32 The men of Nineve shall rise up in the judgment with this generation, and shall
condemn it: for they repented at the preaching of Jonas; and, behold, a greater than
Jonas *is* here.
33 No man, when he hath lighted a candle, putteth *it* in a secret place, neither under a
bushel, but on a candlestick, that they which come in may see the light.
34 The light of the body is the eye: therefore when thine eye is single, thy whole body
also is full of light; but when *thine eye* is evil, thy body also *is* full of darkness.
35 Take heed therefore that the light which is in thee be not darkness.
36 If thy whole body therefore *be* full of light, having no part dark, the whole shall be
full of light, as when the bright shining of a candle doth give thee light. (Luke 11:29-36)

106 - AN UNPLEASANT DINNER IN THE HOME OF A PHARISEE

37 ¶ And as he spake, a certain Pharisee besought him to dine with him: and he went in,
and sat down to meat.
38 And when the Pharisee saw *it*, he marvelled that he had not first washed before
dinner.
39 And the Lord said unto him, Now do ye Pharisees make clean the outside of the cup
and the platter; but your inward part is full of ravening and wickedness.
40 *Ye* fools, did not he that made that which is without make that which is within also?
41 But rather give alms of such things as ye have; and, behold, all things are clean unto
you.

42 But woe unto you, Pharisees! for ye tithe mint and rue and all manner of herbs, and
pass over judgment and the love of God: these ought ye to have done, and not to leave
the other undone.
43 Woe unto you, Pharisees! for ye love the uppermost seats in the synagogues, and
greetings in the markets.
44 Woe unto you, scribes and Pharisees, hypocrites! for ye are as graves which appear
not, and the men that walk over *them* are not aware *of them*.
45 ¶ Then answered one of the lawyers, and said unto him, Master, thus saying thou
reproachest us also.
46 And he said, Woe unto you also, *ye* lawyers! for ye lade men with burdens grievous
to be borne, and ye yourselves touch not the burdens with one of your fingers.
47 Woe unto you! for ye build the sepulchres of the prophets, and your fathers killed
them.
48 Truly ye bear witness that ye allow the deeds of your fathers: for they indeed killed
them, and ye build their sepulchres.
49 Therefore also said the wisdom of God, I will send them prophets and apostles, and
some of them they shall slay and persecute:
50 That the blood of all the prophets, which was shed from the foundation of the world,
may be required of this generation;
51 From the blood of Abel unto the blood of Zacharias, which perished between the
altar and the temple: verily I say unto you, It shall be required of this generation.
52 Woe unto you, lawyers! for ye have taken away the key of knowledge: ye entered
not in yourselves, and them that were entering in ye hindered.
53 And as he said these things unto them, the scribes and the Pharisees began to urge
him vehemently, and to provoke him to speak of many things:
54 Laying wait for him, and seeking to catch something out of his mouth, that they
might accuse him. (Luke 11:37-54)

107 - WARNINGS

1 In the mean time, when there were gathered together an innumerable multitude of
people, insomuch that they trode one upon another, he began to say unto his disciples
first of all, Beware ye of the leaven of the Pharisees, which is hypocrisy.
2 For there is nothing covered, that shall not be revealed; neither hid, that shall not be
known.
3 Therefore whatsoever ye have spoken in darkness shall be heard in the light; and that
which ye have spoken in the ear in closets shall be proclaimed upon the housetops.
4 And I say unto you my friends, Be not afraid of them that kill the body, and after that
have no more that they can do.
5 But I will forewarn you whom ye shall fear: Fear him, which after he hath killed hath
power to cast into hell; yea, I say unto you, Fear him.
6 Are not five sparrows sold for two farthings, and not one of them is forgotten before
God?
7 But even the very hairs of your head are all numbered. Fear not therefore: ye are of
more value than many sparrows.
8 Also I say unto you, Whosoever shall confess me before men, him shall the Son of
man also confess before the angels of God:
9 But he that denieth me before men shall be denied before the angels of God.

10 And whosoever shall speak a word against the Son of man, it shall be forgiven him:
but unto him that blasphemeth against the Holy Ghost it shall not be forgiven.
11 And when they bring you unto the synagogues, and *unto* magistrates, and powers,
take ye no thought how or what thing ye shall answer, or what ye shall say:
12 For the Holy Ghost shall teach you in the same hour what ye ought to say.
13 ¶ And one of the company said unto him, Master, speak to my brother, that he divide
the inheritance with me.
14 And he said unto him, Man, who made me a judge or a divider over you?
15 And he said unto them, Take heed, and beware of covetousness: for a man's life
consisteth not in the abundance of the things which he possesseth.
16 And he spake a parable unto them, saying, The ground of a certain rich man brought
forth plentifully:
17 And he thought within himself, saying, What shall I do, because I have no room
where to bestow my fruits?
18 And he said, This will I do: I will pull down my barns, and build greater; and there
will I bestow all my fruits and my goods.
19 And I will say to my soul, Soul, thou hast much goods laid up for many years; take
thine ease, eat, drink, *and* be merry.
20 But God said unto him, *Thou* fool, this night thy soul shall be required of thee: then
whose shall those things be, which thou hast provided?
21 So *is* he that layeth up treasure for himself, and is not rich toward God.
22 ¶ And he said unto his disciples, Therefore I say unto you, Take no thought for your
life, what ye shall eat; neither for the body, what ye shall put on.
23 The life is more than meat, and the body *is more* than raiment.
24 Consider the ravens: for they neither sow nor reap; which neither have storehouse
nor barn; and God feedeth them: how much more are ye better than the fowls?
25 And which of you with taking thought can add to his stature one cubit?
26 If ye then be not able to do that thing which is least, why take ye thought for the
rest?
27 Consider the lilies how they grow: they toil not, they spin not; and yet I say unto
you, that Solomon in all his glory was not arrayed like one of these.
28 If then God so clothe the grass, which is to-day in the field, and to-morrow is cast
into the oven; how much more *will he clothe* you, O ye of little faith?
29 And seek not ye what ye shall eat, or what ye shall drink, neither be ye of doubtful
mind.
30 For all these things do the nations of the world seek after: and your Father knoweth
that ye have need of these things.
31 ¶ But rather seek ye the kingdom of God; and all these things shall be added unto
you.
32 Fear not, little flock; for it is your Father's good pleasure to give you the kingdom.
33 Sell that ye have, and give alms; provide yourselves bags which wax not old, a
treasure in the heavens that faileth not, where no thief approacheth, neither moth
corrupteth.
34 For where your treasure is, there will your heart be also.
35 Let your loins be girded about, and *your* lights burning;
36 And ye yourselves like unto men that wait for their lord, when he will return from

the wedding; that when he cometh and knocketh, they may open unto him immediately.
37 Blessed *are* those servants, whom the lord when he cometh shall find watching:
verily I say unto you, that he shall gird himself, and make them to sit down to meat, and
will come forth and serve them.
38 And if he shall come in the second watch, or come in the third watch, and find *them*
so, blessed are those servants.
39 And this know, that if the goodman of the house had known what hour the thief
would come, he would have watched, and not have suffered his house to be broken
through.
40 Be ye therefore ready also: for the Son of man cometh at an hour when ye think not.
41 ¶ Then Peter said unto him, Lord, speakest thou this parable unto us, or even to all?
42 And the Lord said, Who then is that faithful and wise steward, whom his lord shall
make ruler over his household, to give *them their* portion of meat in due season?
43 Blessed is that servant, whom his lord when he cometh shall find so doing.
44 Of a truth I say unto you, that he will make him ruler over all that he hath.
45 But and if that servant say in his heart, My lord delayeth his coming; and shall begin
to beat the menservants and maidens, and to eat and drink, and to be drunken;
46 The lord of that servant will come in a day when he looketh not for *him*, and at an
hour when he is not aware, and will cut him in sunder, and will appoint him his portion
with the unbelievers.
47 And that servant, which knew his lord's will, and prepared not *himself*, neither did
according to his will, shall be beaten with many *stripes*.
48 But he that knew not, and did commit things worthy of stripes, shall be beaten with
few *stripes*.
48 For unto whomsoever much is given, of him shall be much required: and to whom
men have committed much, of him they will ask the more.
49 I am come to send fire on the earth; and what will I, if it be already kindled?
50 But I have a baptism to be baptized with; and how am I straitened till it be
accomplished!
51 Suppose ye that I am come to give peace on earth? I tell you, Nay; but rather
division:
52 For from henceforth there shall be five in one house divided, three against two, and
two against three.
53 The father shall be divided against the son, and the son against the father; the mother
against the daughter, and the daughter against the mother; the mother in law against her
daughter in law, and the daughter in law against her mother in law.
54 ¶ And he said also to the people, When ye see a cloud rise out of the west,
straightway ye say, There cometh a shower; and so it is.
55 And when *ye see* the south wind blow, ye say, There will be heat; and it cometh to
pass.
56 *Ye* hypocrites, ye can discern the face of the sky and of the earth; but how is it that
ye do not discern this time?
57 Yea, and why even of yourselves judge ye not what is right?
58 ¶ When thou goest with thine adversary to the magistrate, *as thou art* in the way,
give diligence that thou mayest be delivered from him; lest he hale thee to the judge,
and the judge deliver thee to the officer, and the officer cast thee into prison.

59 I tell thee, thou shalt not depart thence, till thou hast paid the very last mite. (Luke 12:1-
59)

108 - TOTAL REPENTANCE REQUIRED

1 There were present at that season some that told him of the Galilæans, whose blood
Pilate had mingled with their sacrifices.
2 And Jesus answering said unto them, Suppose ye that these Galilæans were sinners
above all the Galilæans, because they suffered such things?
3 I tell you, Nay: but, except ye repent, ye shall all likewise perish.
4 Or those eighteen, upon whom the tower in Siloam fell, and slew them, think ye that
they were sinners above all men that dwelt in Jerusalem?
5 I tell you, Nay: but, except ye repent, ye shall all likewise perish.
6 ¶ He spake also this parable; A certain *man* had a fig tree planted in his vineyard; and
he came and sought fruit thereon, and found none.
7 Then said he unto the dresser of his vineyard, Behold, these three years I come
seeking fruit on this fig tree, and find none: cut it down; why cumbereth it the ground?
8 And he answering said unto him, Lord, let it alone this year also, till I shall dig about
it, and dung *it*:
9 And if it bear fruit, *well*: and if not, *then* after that thou shalt cut it down.
10 And he was teaching in one of the synagogues on the sabbath.
eighteen years, and was bowed together, and could in no wise lift up *herself*.
12 And when Jesus saw her, he called *her* to *him*, and said unto her, Woman, thou art
loosed from thine infirmity.
13 And he laid *his* hands on her: and immediately she was made straight, and glorified
God.
14 And the ruler of the synagogue answered with indignation, because that Jesus had
healed on the sabbath day, and said unto the people, There are six days in which men
ought to work: in them therefore come and be healed, and not on the sabbath day.
15 The Lord then answered him, and said, *Thou* hypocrite, doth not each one of you on
the sabbath loose his ox or *his* ass from the stall, and lead *him* away to watering?
16 And ought not this woman, being a daughter of Abraham, whom Satan hath bound,
lo, these eighteen years, be loosed from this bond on the sabbath day?
17 And when he had said these things, all his adversaries were ashamed: and all the
people rejoiced for all the glorious things that were done by him.
18 ¶ Then said he, Unto what is the kingdom of God like? and whereunto shall I
resemble it?
19 It is like a grain of mustard seed, which a man took, and cast into his garden; and it
grew, and waxed a great tree; and the fowls of the air lodged in the branches of it.
20 And again he said, Whereunto shall I liken the kingdom of God?
21 It is like leaven, which a woman took and hid in three measures of meal, till the
whole was leavened.
22 And he went through the cities and villages, teaching, and journeying toward
Jerusalem. (Luke 13:1-22)

109 - IN JERSUALEM AT THE FEAST OF DEDICATION

22 ¶ And it was at Jerusalem the feast of the dedication, and it was winter.
23 And Jesus walked in the temple in Solomon's porch.

24 Then came the Jews round about him, and said unto him, How long dost thou make
us to doubt? If thou be the Christ, tell us plainly.
25 Jesus answered them, I told you, and ye believed not: the works that I do in my
Father's name, they bear witness of me.
26 But ye believe not, because ye are not of my sheep, as I said unto you.
27 My sheep hear my voice, and I know them, and they follow me:
28 And I give unto them eternal life; and they shall never perish, neither shall any *man*
pluck them out of my hand.
29 My Father, which gave *them* me, is greater than all; and no *man* is able to pluck
them out of my Father's hand.
30 I and *my* Father are one.
31 Then the Jews took up stones again to stone him.
32 Jesus answered them, Many good works have I shewed you from my Father; for
which of those works do ye stone me?
33 The Jews answered him, saying, For a good work we stone thee not; but for
blasphemy; and because that thou, being a man, makest thyself God.
34 Jesus answered them, Is it not written in your law, I said, Ye are gods?
35 If he called them gods, unto whom the word of God came, and the scripture cannot
be broken;
36 Say ye of him, whom the Father hath sanctified, and sent into the world, Thou
blasphemest; because I said, I am the Son of God?
37 If I do not the works of my Father, believe me not.
38 But if I do, though ye believe not me, believe the works: that ye may know, and
believe, that the Father *is* in me, and I in him.
39 Therefore they sought again to take him: but he escaped out of their hand, (John 10:22-
39)

110 - TEACHNG IN RETREAT BEYOND JORDAN

40 And went away again beyond Jordan into the place where John at first baptized; and
there he abode.
41 And many resorted unto him, and said, John did no miracle: but all things that John
spake of this man were true.
42 And many believed on him there. (John 10:40-42)
23 Then said one unto him, Lord, are there few that be saved? And he said unto them,
24 ¶ Strive to enter in at the strait gate: for many, I say unto you, will seek to enter in,
and shall not be able.
25 When once the master of the house is risen up, and hath shut to the door, and ye
begin to stand without, and to knock at the door, saying, Lord, Lord, open unto us; and
he shall answer and say unto you, I know you not whence ye are:
26 Then shall ye begin to say, We have eaten and drunk in thy presence, and thou hast
taught in our streets.
27 But he shall say, I tell you, I know you not whence ye are; depart from me, all *ye*
workers of iniquity.
28 There shall be weeping and gnashing of teeth, when ye shall see Abraham, and
Isaac, and Jacob, and all the prophets, in the kingdom of God, and you *yourselves* thrust
out.
29 And they shall come from the east, and *from* the west, and from the north, and *from*

the south, and shall sit down in the kingdom of God.
30 And, behold, there are last which shall be first, and there are first which shall be last.
(Luke 13:23-30)

111 – JESUS REPLIES TO HEROD'S THREATS

31 ¶ The same day there came certain of the Pharisees, saying unto him, Get thee out,
and depart hence: for Herod will kill thee.
32 And he said unto them, Go ye, and tell that fox, Behold, I cast out devils, and I do
cures to-day and to-morrow, and the third *day* I shall be perfected.
33 Nevertheless I must walk to-day, and to-morrow, and the *day* following: for it
cannot be that a prophet perish out of Jerusalem.
34 O Jerusalem, Jerusalem, which killest the prophets, and stonest them that are sent
unto thee;
34 how often would I have gathered thy children together, as a hen *doth gather* her
brood under *her* wings, and ye would not!
35 Behold, your house is left unto you desolate: and verily I say unto you, Ye shall not
see me, until *the time* come when ye shall say, Blessed *is* he that cometh in the name of
the Lord. (Luke 13:31-35)

112 - DINING WITH A CHIEF PHARISEE

1 And it came to pass, as he went into the house of one of the chief Pharisees to eat
bread on the sabbath day, that they watched him.
2 And, behold, there was a certain man before him which had the dropsy.
3 And Jesus answering spake unto the lawyers and Pharisees, saying, Is it lawful to
heal on the sabbath day?
4 And they held their peace. And he took *him*, and healed him, and let him go;
5 And answered them, saying, Which of you shall have an ass or an ox fallen into a pit,
and will not straightway pull him out on the sabbath day?
6 And they could not answer him again to these things
7 ¶ And he put forth a parable to those which were bidden, when he marked how they
chose out the chief rooms; saying unto them,
8 When thou art bidden of any *man* to a wedding, sit not down in the highest room; lest
a more honourable man than thou be bidden of him;
9 And he that bade thee and him come and say to thee, Give this man place; and thou
begin with shame to take the lowest room.
10 But when thou art bidden, go and sit down in the lowest room; that when he that
bade thee cometh, he may say unto thee, Friend, go up higher: then shalt thou have
worship in the presence of them that sit at meat with thee.
11 For whosoever exalteth himself shall be abased; and he that humbleth himself shall
be exalted.
12 ¶ Then said he also to him that bade him, When thou makest a dinner or a supper,
call not thy friends, nor thy brethren, neither thy kinsmen, nor *thy* rich neighbours; lest
they also bid thee again, and a recompence be made thee.
13 But when thou makest a feast, call the poor, the maimed, the lame, the blind:
14 And thou shalt be blessed; for they cannot recompense thee: for thou shalt be
recompensed at the resurrection of the just.
15 ¶ And when one of them that sat at meat with him heard these things, he said unto

him, Blessed *is* he that shall eat bread in the kingdom of God.
16 Then said he unto him, A certain man made a great supper, and bade many:
17 And sent his servant at supper time to say to them that were bidden, Come; for all
things are now ready.
18 And they all with one *consent* began to make excuse. The first said unto him, I have
bought a piece of ground, and I must needs go and see it: I pray thee have me excused.
19 And another said, I have bought five yoke of oxen, and I go to prove them: I pray
thee have me excused.
20 And another said, I have married a wife, and therefore I cannot come.
21 So that servant came, and shewed his lord these things. Then the master of the
house being angry said to his servant, Go out quickly into the streets and lanes of the
city, and bring in hither the poor, and the maimed, and the halt, and the blind.
22 And the servant said, Lord, it is done as thou hast commanded, and yet there is
room.
23 And the lord said unto the servant, Go out into the highways and hedges, and
compel *them* to come in, that my house may be filled.
24 For I say unto you, That none of those men which were bidden shall taste of my
supper. (Luke 14:1-24)

113 - THE COST OF DISCIPLESHIP

25 ¶ And there went great multitudes with him: and he turned, and said unto them,
26 If any *man* come to me, and hate not his father, and mother, and wife, and children,
and brethren, and sisters, yea, and his own life also, he cannot be my disciple.
27 And whosoever doth not bear his cross, and come after me, cannot be my disciple.
28 For which of you, intending to build a tower, sitteth not down first, and counteth the
cost, whether he have *sufficient* to finish *it*?
29 Lest haply, after he hath laid the foundation, and is not able to finish *it*, all that
behold *it* begin to mock him,
30 Saying, This man began to build, and was not able to finish.
31 Or what king, going to make war against another king, sitteth not down first, and
consulteth whether he be able with ten thousand to meet him that cometh against him
with twenty thousand?
32 Or else, while the other is yet a great way off, he sendeth an ambassage, and desireth
conditions of peace.
33 So likewise, whosoever he be of you that forsaketh not all that he hath, he cannot be
my disciple.
34 ¶ Salt *is* good: but if the salt have lost his savour, wherewith shall it be seasoned?
35 It is neither fit for the land, nor yet for the dunghill; *but* men cast it out. He that hath
ears to hear, let him hear. (Luke 14:25-35)

114 - SALVATION COMES THROUGH GRACE NOT PRIVILEGE

1 Then drew near unto him all the publicans and sinners for to hear him.
2 And the Pharisees and scribes murmured, saying, This man receiveth sinners, and
eateth with them.
3 ¶ And he spake this parable unto them, saying,
4 What man of you, having an hundred sheep, if he lose one of them, doth not leave the
ninety and nine in the wilderness, and go after that which is lost, until he find it?

5 And when he hath found *it*, he layeth *it* on his shoulders, rejoicing.
6 And when he cometh home, he calleth together *his* friends and neighbours, saying
unto them, Rejoice with me; for I have found my sheep which was lost.
7 I say unto you, that likewise joy shall be in heaven over one sinner that repenteth,
more than over ninety and nine just persons, which need no repentance.
8 ¶ Either what woman having ten pieces of silver, if she lose one piece, doth not light
a candle, and sweep the house, and seek diligently till she find *it*?
9 And when she hath found *it*, she calleth *her* friends and *her* neighbours together,
saying, Rejoice with me; for I have found the piece which I had lost.
10 Likewise, I say unto you, there is joy in the presence of the angels of God over one
sinner that repenteth.
12 And the younger of them said to *his* father, Father, give me the portion of goods that
falleth *to me*. And he divided unto them *his* living.
13 And not many days after the younger son gathered all together, and took his journey
into a far country, and there wasted his substance with riotous living.
14 And when he had spent all, there arose a mighty famine in that land; and he began to
be in want.
15 And he went and joined himself to a citizen of that country; and he sent him into his
fields to feed swine.
16 And he would fain have filled his belly with the husks that the swine did eat: and no
man gave unto him.
17 And when he came to himself, he said, How many hired servants of my father's have
bread enough and to spare, and I perish with hunger!
18 I will arise and go to my father, and will say unto him, Father, I have sinned against
heaven, and before thee,
19 And am no more worthy to be called thy son: make me as one of thy hired servants.
20 And he arose, and came to his father.
20 But when he was yet a great way off, his father saw him, and had compassion, and
ran, and fell on his neck, and kissed him.
21 And the son said unto him, Father, I have sinned against heaven, and in thy sight,
and am no more worthy to be called thy son.
22 But the father said to his servants, Bring forth the best robe, and put *it* on him; and
put a ring on his hand, and shoes on *his* feet:
23 And bring hither the fatted calf, and kill *it*; and let us eat, and be merry:
24 For this my son was dead, and is alive again; he was lost, and is found. And they
began to be merry.
25 Now his elder son was in the field: and as he came and drew nigh to the house, he
heard music and dancing.
26 And he called one of the servants, and asked what these things meant.
27 And he said unto him, Thy brother is come; and thy father hath killed the fatted calf,
because he hath received him safe and sound.
28 And he was angry, and would not go in: therefore came his father out, and entreated
him.
29 And he answering said to *his* father, Lo, these many years do I serve thee, neither
transgressed I at any time thy commandment: and yet thou never gavest me a kid, that I
might make merry with my friends:

30 But as soon as this thy son was come, which hath devoured thy living with harlots,
thou hast killed for him the fatted calf.
31 And he said unto him, Son, thou art ever with me, and all that I have is thine.
32 It was meet that we should make merry, and be glad: for this thy brother was dead,
and is alive again; and was lost, and is found. (Luke 15:1-32)

115 - INTEGRITY AND THE FIRST COMMANDMENT

1 And he said also unto his disciples, There was a certain rich man, which had a
steward; and the same was accused unto him that he had wasted his goods.
2 And he called him, and said unto him, How is it that I hear this of thee? give an
account of thy stewardship; for thou mayest be no longer steward.
3 Then the steward said within himself, What shall I do? for my lord taketh away from
me the stewardship: I cannot dig; to beg I am ashamed.
4 I am resolved what to do, that, when I am put out of the stewardship, they may
receive me into their houses.
5 So he called every one of his lord's debtors *unto him*, and said unto the first, How
much owest thou unto my lord?
6 And he said, An hundred measures of oil. And he said unto him, Take thy bill, and
sit down quickly, and write fifty.
7 Then said he to another, And how much owest thou? And he said, An hundred
measures of wheat. And he said unto him, Take thy bill, and write fourscore.
8 And the lord commended the unjust steward, because he had done wisely: for the
children of this world are in their generation wiser than the children of light.
9 And I say unto you, Make to yourselves friends of the mammon of unrighteousness;
that, when ye fail, they may receive you into everlasting habitations.
10 He that is faithful in that which is least is faithful also in much: and he that is unjust
in the least is unjust also in much.
11 If therefore ye have not been faithful in the unrighteous mammon, who will commit
to your trust the true *riches*?
12 And if ye have not been faithful in that which is another man's, who shall give you
that which is your own?
13 ¶ No servant can serve two masters: for either he will hate the one, and love the
other; or else he will hold to the one, and despise the other. Ye cannot serve God and
mammon. (Luke 16:1-13)

116 - COVETOUSNESS REBUKED

14 And the Pharisees also, who were covetous, heard all these things: and they derided
him.
15 And he said unto them, Ye are they which justify yourselves before men; but God
knoweth your hearts: for that which is highly esteemed among men is abomination in
the sight of God.
16 The law and the prophets *were* until John: since that time the kingdom of God is
preached, and every man presseth into it.
17 And it is easier for heaven and earth to pass, than one tittle of the law to fail.
18 Whosoever putteth away his wife, and marrieth another, committeth adultery: and
whosoever marrieth her that is put away from *her* husband committeth adultery.
19 ¶ There was a certain rich man, which was clothed in purple and fine linen, and
fared sumptuously every day:

20 And there was a certain beggar named Lazarus, which was laid at his gate, full of
sores,
21 And desiring to be fed with the crumbs which fell from the rich man's table:
moreover the dogs came and licked his sores.
22 And it came to pass, that the beggar died, and was carried by the angels into
Abraham's bosom: the rich man also died, and was buried;
23 And in hell he lift up his eyes, being in torments, and seeth Abraham afar off, and
Lazarus in his bosom.
24 And he cried and said, Father Abraham, have mercy on me, and send Lazarus, that
he may dip the tip of his finger in water, and cool my tongue; for I am tormented in this
flame.
25 But Abraham said, Son, remember that thou in thy lifetime receivedst thy good
things, and likewise Lazarus evil things: but now he is comforted, and thou art
tormented.
26 And beside all this, between us and you there is a great gulf fixed: so that they which
would pass from hence to you cannot; neither can they pass to us, that *would come* from
thence.
27 Then he said, I pray thee therefore, father, that thou wouldest send him to my
father's house:
28 For I have five brethren; that he may testify unto them, lest they also come into this
place of torment.
29 Abraham saith unto him, They have Moses and the prophets; let them hear them.
30 And he said, Nay, father Abraham: but if one went unto them from the dead, they
will repent.
31 And he said unto him, If they hear not Moses and the prophets, neither will they be
persuaded, though one rose from the dead. (Luke 16:14-31)

117 – DOING "THAT WHICH IS OUR DUTY TO DO"

1 Then said he unto the disciples, It is impossible but that offences will come: but woe
unto him, through whom they come!
2 It were better for him that a millstone were hanged about his neck, and he cast into
the sea, than that he should offend one of these little ones.
3 ¶ Take heed to yourselves: If thy brother trespass against thee, rebuke him; and if he
repent, forgive him.
4 And if he trespass against thee seven times in a day, and seven times in a day turn
again to thee, saying, I repent: thou shalt forgive him.
5 And the apostles said unto the Lord, Increase our faith.
6 And the Lord said, If ye had faith as a grain of mustard seed, ye might say unto this
sycamine tree, Be thou plucked up by the root, and be thou planted in the sea; and it
should obey you.
7 But which of you, having a servant plowing or feeding cattle, will say unto him by
and by, when he is come from the field, Go and sit down to meat?
8 And will not rather say unto him, Make ready wherewith I may sup, and gird thyself,
and serve me, till I have eaten and drunken; and afterward thou shalt eat and drink?
9 Doth he thank that servant because he did the things that were commanded him? I
trow not.
10 So likewise ye, when ye shall have done all those things which are commanded you,

say, We are unprofitable servants: we have done that which was our duty to do. (Luke 17:1-10)

118 - "BUT WHERE ARE THE NINE?"

11 ¶ And it came to pass, as he went to Jerusalem, that he passed through the midst of
Samaria and Galilee.
12 And as he entered into a certain village, there met him ten men that were lepers,
which stood afar off:
13 And they lifted up *their* voices, and said, Jesus, Master, have mercy on us.
14 And when he saw *them*, he said unto them, Go shew yourselves unto the priests.
And it came to pass, that, as they went, they were cleansed.
15 And one of them, when he saw that he was healed, turned back, and with a loud
voice glorified God,
16 And fell down on *his* face at his feet, giving him thanks: and he was a Samaritan.
17 And Jesus answering said, Were there not ten cleansed? but where *are* the nine?
18 There are not found that returned to give glory to God, save this stranger.
19 And he said unto him, Arise, go thy way: thy faith hath made thee whole. (Luke 17:11-19)

119 - WHEN THE KINGDOM OF GOD WILL COME

20 ¶ And when he was demanded of the Pharisees, when the kingdom of God should
come, he answered them and said, The kingdom of God cometh not with observation:
21 Neither shall they say, Lo here! or, lo there! for, behold, the kingdom of God is
within you. (Luke 17:20-21)

120 - END OF THE WORLD ORDER

22 And he said unto the disciples, The days will come, when ye shall desire to see one
of the days of the Son of man, and ye shall not see *it*.
23 And they shall say to you, See here; or, see there: go not after *them*, nor follow *them*.
24 For as the lightning, that lighteneth out of the one *part* under heaven, shineth unto
the other *part* under heaven; so shall also the Son of man be in his day.
25 But first must he suffer many things, and be rejected of this generation.
26 And as it was in the days of Noe, so shall it be also in the days of the Son of man.
27 They did eat, they drank, they married wives, they were given in marriage, until the
day that Noe entered into the ark, and the flood came, and destroyed them all.
28 Likewise also as it was in the days of Lot; they did eat, they drank, they bought, they
sold, they planted, they builded;
29 But the same day that Lot went out of Sodom it rained fire and brimstone from
heaven, and destroyed *them* all.
30 Even thus shall it be in the day when the Son of man is revealed.
31 In that day, he which shall be upon the housetop, and his stuff in the house, let him
not come down to take it away: and he that is in the field, let him likewise not return
back.
32 Remember Lot's wife.
33 Whosoever shall seek to save his life shall lose it; and whosoever shall lose his life
shall preserve it.
34 I tell you, in that night there shall be two *men* in one bed; the one shall be taken, and
the other shall be left.
35 Two *women* shall be grinding together; the one shall be taken, and the other left.

36 Two *men* shall be in the field; the one shall be taken, and the other left.
37 And they answered and said unto him, Where, Lord?
37 And he said unto them, Wheresoever the body *is*, thither will the eagles be gathered together. (Luke 17:22-37)

121 – EVEN MORE INSTRUCTION ON PRAYER

1 And he spake a parable unto them *to this end*, that men ought always to pray, and not to faint;
2 Saying, There was in a city a judge, which feared not God, neither regarded man:
3 And there was a widow in that city; and she came unto him, saying, Avenge me of mine adversary.
4 And he would not for a while: but afterward he said within himself, Though I fear not God, nor regard man;
5 Yet because this widow troubleth me, I will avenge her, lest by her continual coming she weary me.
6 And the Lord said, Hear what the unjust judge saith.
7 And shall not God avenge his own elect, which cry day and night unto him, though he bear long with them?
8 I tell you that he will avenge them speedily. Nevertheless when the Son of man cometh, shall he find faith on the earth?
9 And he spake this parable unto certain which trusted in themselves that they were righteous, and despised others:
10 Two men went up into the temple to pray; the one a Pharisee, and the other a publican
11 The Pharisee stood and prayed thus with himself, God, I thank thee, that I am not as other men *are*, extortioners, unjust, adulterers, or even as this publican.
12 I fast twice in the week, I give tithes of all that I possess.
13 And the publican, standing afar off, would not lift up so much as *his* eyes unto heaven, but smote upon his breast, saying, God be merciful to me a sinner.
14 I tell you, this man went down to his house justified *rather* than the other: for every one that exalteth himself shall be abased; and he that humbleth himself shall be exalted. (Luke 18:1-14)

122 – THE RESURRECTION OF LAZARUS

1 Now a certain *man* was sick, *named* Lazarus, of Bethany, the town of Mary and her sister Martha.
2 (It was *that* Mary which anointed the Lord with ointment, and wiped his feet with her hair, whose brother Lazarus was sick.)
3 Therefore his sisters sent unto him, saying, Lord, behold, he whom thou lovest is sick.
4 When Jesus heard *that*, he said, This sickness is not unto death, but for the glory of God, that the Son of God might be glorified thereby.
5 Now Jesus loved Martha, and her sister, and Lazarus.
6 When he had heard therefore that he was sick, he abode two days still in the same place where he was.
7 Then after that saith he to *his* disciples, Let us go into Judæa again.
8 *His* disciples say unto him, Master, the Jews of late sought to stone thee; and goest thou thither again?

9 Jesus answered, Are there not twelve hours in the day? If any man walk in the day,
he stumbleth not, because he seeth the light of this world.
10 But if a man walk in the night, he stumbleth, because there is no light in him.
11 These things said he: and after that he saith unto them, Our friend Lazarus sleepeth;
but I go, that I may awake him out of sleep
12 Then said his disciples, Lord, if he sleep, he shall do well.
13 Howbeit Jesus spake of his death: but they thought that he had spoken of taking of
rest in sleep.
14 Then said Jesus unto them plainly, Lazarus is dead.
15 And I am glad for your sakes that I was not there, to the intent ye may believe;
nevertheless let us go unto him.
16 Then said Thomas, which is called Didymus, unto his fellow-disciples, Let us also
go, that we may die with him.
17 Then when Jesus came, he found that he had *lain* in the grave four days already.
18 Now Bethany was nigh unto Jerusalem, about fifteen furlongs off:
19 And many of the Jews came to Martha and Mary, to comfort them concerning their
brother.
20 Then Martha, as soon as she heard that Jesus was coming, went and met him: but
Mary sat *still* in the house.
21 Then said Martha unto Jesus, Lord, if thou hadst been here, my brother had not died.
22 But I know, that even now, whatsoever thou wilt ask of God, God will give *it* thee.
23 Jesus saith unto her, Thy brother shall rise again.
24 Martha saith unto him, I know that he shall rise again in the resurrection at the last
day.
25 Jesus said unto her, I am the resurrection, and the life: he that believeth in me,
though he were dead, yet shall he live:
26 And whosoever liveth and believeth in me shall never die. Believest thou this?
27 She saith unto him, Yea, Lord: I believe that thou art the Christ, the Son of God,
which should come into the world.
28 And when she had so said, she went her way, and called Mary her sister secretly,
saying, The Master is come, and calleth for thee.
29 As soon as she heard *that*, she arose quickly, and came unto him.
30 Now Jesus was not yet come into the town, but was in that place where Martha met
him.
31 The Jews then which were with her in the house, and comforted her, when they saw
Mary, that she rose up hastily and went out, followed her, saying, She goeth unto the
grave to weep there.
32 Then when Mary was come where Jesus was, and saw him, she fell down at his feet,
saying unto him, Lord, if thou hadst been here, my brother had not died.
33 When Jesus therefore saw her weeping, and the Jews also weeping which came with
her, he groaned in the spirit, and was troubled,
34 And said, Where have ye laid him? They said unto him, Lord, come and see.
35 Jesus wept.
36 Then said the Jews, Behold how he loved him!
37 And some of them said, Could not this man, which opened the eyes of the blind,
have caused that even this man should not have died?

38 Jesus therefore again groaning in himself cometh to the grave. It was a cave, and a
stone lay upon it.
39 Jesus said, Take ye away the stone. Martha, the sister of him that was dead, saith
unto him, Lord, by this time he stinketh: for he hath been *dead* four days.
40 Jesus saith unto her, Said I not unto thee, that, if thou wouldest believe, thou
shouldest see the glory of God?
41 Then they took away the stone *from the place* where the dead was laid. And Jesus
lifted up *his* eyes, and said, Father, I thank thee that thou hast heard me.
42 And I knew that thou hearest me always: but because of the people which stand by I
said *it*, that they may believe that thou hast sent me.
43 And when he thus had spoken, he cried with a loud voice, Lazarus, come forth.
44 And he that was dead came forth, bound hand and foot with graveclothes: and his
face was bound about with a napkin. Jesus saith unto them, Loose him, and let him go.
(John 11:1-44)

123 - OPPOSING REACTIONS TO RAISING LAZARUS

45 Then many of the Jews which came to Mary, and had seen the things which Jesus
did, believed on him.
46 But some of them went their ways to the Pharisees, and told them what things Jesus
had done.
47 ¶ Then gathered the chief priests and the Pharisees a council, and said, What do we?
for this man doeth many miracles.
48 If we let him thus alone, all *men* will believe on him: and the Romans shall come
and take away both our place and nation.
49 And one of them, *named* Caiaphas, being the high priest that same year, said unto
them, Ye know nothing at all,
50 Nor consider that it is expedient for us, that one man should die for the people, and
that the whole nation perish not.
51 And this spake he not of himself: but being high priest that year, he prophesied that
Jesus should die for that nation;
52 And not for that nation only, but that also he should gather together in one the
children of God that were scattered abroad.
53 Then from that day forth they took counsel together for to put him to death.
54 Jesus therefore walked no more openly among the Jews; but went thence unto a
country near to the wilderness, into a city called Ephraim, and there continued with his
disciples. (John 11:45-54)

124 - TWO REQUIREMENTS TO ENTER THE KINGDOM

According to the Gospel of Mark

13 ¶ And they brought young children to him, that he should touch them: and *his*
disciples rebuked those that brought *them*.
14 But when Jesus saw *it*, he was much displeased, and said unto them, Suffer the little
children to come unto me, and forbid them not: for of such is the kingdom of God.
15 Verily I say unto you, Whosoever shall not receive the kingdom of God as a little
child, he shall not enter therein.
16 And he took them up in his arms, put *his* hands upon them, and blessed them.
17 ¶ And when he was gone forth into the way, there came one running, and kneeled to

him, and asked him, Good Master, what shall I do that I may inherit eternal life?
18 And Jesus said unto him, Why callest thou me good? *there is* none good but one,
that is, God.
19 Thou knowest the commandments, Do not commit adultery, Do not kill, Do not
steal, Do not bear false witness, Defraud not, Honour thy father and mother.
20 And he answered and said unto him, Master, all these have I observed from my
youth.
21 Then Jesus beholding him loved him, and said unto him, One thing thou lackest: go
thy way, sell whatsoever thou hast, and give to the poor, and thou shalt have treasure in
heaven: and come, take up the cross, and follow me.
22 And he was sad at that saying, and went away grieved: for he had great possessions.
23 ¶ And Jesus looked round about, and saith unto his disciples, How hardly shall they
that have riches enter into the kingdom of God!
24 And the disciples were astonished at his words. But Jesus answereth again, and saith
unto them, Children, how hard is it for them that trust in riches to enter into the
kingdom of God!
25 It is easier for a camel to go through the eye of a needle, than for a rich man to enter
into the kingdom of God.
26 And they were astonished out of measure, saying among themselves, Who then can
be saved?
27 And Jesus looking upon them saith, With men *it is* impossible, but not with God: for
with God all things are possible. (Mark 10:13-27)

According to the Gospel of Matthew

13 ¶ Then were there brought unto him little children, that he should put *his* hands on
them, and pray: and the disciples rebuked them.
14 But Jesus said, Suffer little children, and forbid them not, to come unto me: for of
such is the kingdom of heaven.
15 And he laid *his* hands on them, and departed thence.
16 ¶ And, behold, one came and said unto him, Good Master, what good thing shall I
do, that I may have eternal life?
17 And he said unto him, Why callest thou me good? *there is* none good but one, *that
is*, God: but if thou wilt enter into life, keep the commandments.
18 He saith unto him, Which? Jesus said, Thou shalt do no murder, Thou shalt not
commit adultery, Thou shalt not steal, Thou shalt not bear false witness,
19 Honour thy father and *thy* mother: and, Thou shalt love thy neighbour as thyself.
20 The young man saith unto him, All these things have I kept from my youth up: what
lack I yet?
21 Jesus said unto him, If thou wilt be perfect, go *and* sell that thou hast, and give to the
poor, and thou shalt have treasure in heaven: and come *and* follow me.
22 But when the young man heard that saying, he went away sorrowful: for he had
great possessions.
23 ¶ Then said Jesus unto his disciples, Verily I say unto you, That a rich man shall
hardly enter into the kingdom of heaven.
24 And again I say unto you, It is easier for a camel to go through the eye of a needle,
than for a rich man to enter into the kingdom of God.

25 When his disciples heard *it*, they were exceedingly amazed, saying, Who then can be
saved?
26 But Jesus beheld *them*, and said unto them, With men this is impossible; but with
God all things are possible. (Matt 19:13--26)

According to the Gospel of Luke

15 And they brought unto him also infants, that he would touch them: but when *his*
disciples saw *it*, they rebuked them.
16 But Jesus called them *unto him*, and said, Suffer little children to come unto me, and
forbid them not: for of such is the kingdom of God.
17 Verily I say unto you, Whosoever shall not receive the kingdom of God as a little
child shall in no wise enter therein.
18 And a certain ruler asked him, saying, Good Master, what shall I do to inherit eternal
life?
19 And Jesus said unto him, Why callest thou me good? none *is* good, save one, *that is*,
God.
20 Thou knowest the commandments, Do not commit adultery, Do not kill, Do not
steal, Do not bear false witness, Honour thy father and thy mother.
21 And he said, All these have I kept from my youth up.
22 Now when Jesus heard these things, he said unto him, Yet lackest thou one thing:
sell all that thou hast, and distribute unto the poor, and thou shalt have treasure in
heaven: and come, follow me
23 And when he heard this, he was very sorrowful: for he was very rich.
24 And when Jesus saw that he was very sorrowful, he said, How hardly shall they that
have riches enter into the kingdom of God!
25 For it is easier for a camel to go through a needle's eye, than for a rich man to enter
into the kingdom of God.
26 And they that heard *it* said, Who then can be saved?
27 And he said, The things which are impossible with men are possible with God. (Luke
18:15-27)

125 - WHAT'S IN IT FOR ME?

According to the Gospel of Luke

28 Then Peter said, Lo, we have left all, and followed thee,
29 And he said unto them, Verily I say unto you, There is no man that hath left house,
or parents, or brethren, or wife, or children, for the kingdom of God's sake,
30 Who shall not receive manifold more in this present time, and in the world to come
life everlasting. (Luke 18:28-30)

According to the Gospel of Mark

28 ¶ Then Peter began to say unto him, Lo, we have left all, and have followed thee.
29 And Jesus answered and said, Verily I say unto you, There is no man that hath left
house, or brethren, or sisters, or father, or mother, or wife, or children, or lands, for my
sake, and the gospel's,
30 But he shall receive an hundredfold now in this time, houses, and brethren, and
sisters, and mothers, and children, and lands, with persecutions; and in the world to
come eternal life.

31 But many *that are* first shall be last; and the last first. (Mark 10:28-31)

According to the Gospel of Matthew

27 ¶ Then answered Peter and said unto him, Behold, we have forsaken all, and
followed thee; what shall we have therefore?
28 And Jesus said unto them, Verily I say unto you, That ye which have followed me,
in the regeneration when the Son of man shall sit in the throne of his glory, ye also shall
sit upon twelve thrones, judging the twelve tribes of Israel.
29 And every one that hath forsaken houses, or brethren, or sisters, or father, or mother,
or wife, or children, or lands, for my name's sake, shall receive an hundredfold, and
shall inherit everlasting life.
30 But many *that are* first shall be last; and the last *shall be* first. (Matt 19:27-30)
1 For the kingdom of heaven is like unto a man *that is* an householder, which went out
early in the morning to hire labourers into his vineyard.
2 And when he had agreed with the labourers for a penny a day, he sent them into his
vineyard.
3 And he went out about the third hour, and saw others standing idle in the
marketplace,
4 And said unto them; Go ye also into the vineyard, and whatsoever is right I will give
you. And they went their way.
5 Again he went out about the sixth and ninth hour, and did likewise.
6 And about the eleventh hour he went out, and found others standing idle, and saith
unto them, Why stand ye here all the day idle?
7 They say unto him, Because no man hath hired us. He saith unto them, Go ye also
into the vineyard; and whatsoever is right, *that* shall ye receive.
8 So when even was come, the lord of the vineyard saith unto his steward, Call the
labourers, and give them *their* hire, beginning from the last unto the first.
9 And when they came that *were hired* about the eleventh hour, they received every
man a penny.
10 But when the first came, they supposed that they should have received more; and
they likewise received every man a penny.
11 And when they had received *it*, they murmured against the goodman of the house,
12 Saying, These last have wrought *but* one hour, and thou hast made them equal unto
us, which have borne the burden and heat of the day.
13 But he answered one of them, and said, Friend, I do thee no wrong: didst not thou
agree with me for a penny?
14 Take *that* thine *is*, and go thy way: I will give unto this last, even as unto thee.
15 Is it not lawful for me to do what I will with mine own? Is thine eye evil, because I
am good?
16 So the last shall be first, and the first last: for many be called, but few chosen. (Matt
20:1-16)

126 - THE 5TH ANNOUNCEMENT OF SUFFERINGS

According to the Gospel of Mark

32 ¶ And they were in the way going up to Jerusalem; and Jesus went before them: and
they were amazed; and as they followed, they were afraid. And he took again the
twelve, and began to tell them what things should happen unto him,

33 *Saying*, Behold, we go up to Jerusalem; and the Son of man shall be delivered unto
the chief priests, and unto the scribes; and they shall condemn him to death, and shall
deliver him to the Gentiles:
34 And they shall mock him, and shall scourge him, and shall spit upon him, and shall
kill him: and the third day he shall rise again. (Mark 10:32-34)

According to the Gospel of Matthew

17 ¶ And Jesus going up to Jerusalem took the twelve disciples apart in the way, and
said unto them,
18 Behold, we go up to Jerusalem; and the Son of man shall be betrayed unto the chief
priests and unto the scribes, and they shall condemn him to death,
19 And shall deliver him to the Gentiles to mock, and to scourge, and to crucify *him*:
and the third day he shall rise again. (Matt 20:17-19)

According to the Gospel of Luke

31 ¶ Then he took *unto him* the twelve, and said unto them, Behold, we go up to
Jerusalem, and all things that are written by the prophets concerning the Son of man
shall be accomplished.
32 For he shall be delivered unto the Gentiles, and shall be mocked, and spitefully
entreated, and spitted on:
33 And they shall scourge *him*, and put him to death: and the third day he shall rise
again.
34 And they understood none of these things: and this saying was hid from them,
neither knew they the things which were spoken. (Luke 18:31-34)

127 - PETITIONING FOR POSITIONS OF AUTHORITY

35 ¶ And James and John, the sons of Zebedee, come unto him, saying, Master, we
would that thou shouldest do for us whatsoever we shall desire.
36 And he said unto them, What would ye that I should do for you?
37 They said unto him, Grant unto us that we may sit, one on thy right hand, and the
other on thy left hand, in thy glory.
38 But Jesus said unto them, Ye know not what ye ask: can ye drink of the cup that I
drink of? and be baptized with the baptism that I am baptized with?
39 And they said unto him, We can. And Jesus said unto them, Ye shall indeed drink
of the cup that I drink of; and with the baptism that I am baptized withal shall ye be
baptized:
40 But to sit on my right hand and on my left hand is not mine to give; but *it shall be
given to them* for whom it is prepared.
41 And when the ten heard *it*, they began to be much displeased with James and John.
(Mark 10:35-41)
20 ¶ Then came to him the mother of Zebedee's children with her sons, worshipping
him, and desiring a certain thing of him.
21 And he said unto her, What wilt thou? She saith unto him, Grant that these my two
sons may sit, the one on thy right hand, and the other on the left, in thy kingdom.
22 But Jesus answered and said, Ye know not what ye ask. Are ye able to drink of the
cup that I shall drink of, and to be baptized with the baptism that I am baptized with?
They say unto him, We are able.

23 And he saith unto them, Ye shall drink indeed of my cup, and be baptized with the
baptism that I am baptized with: but to sit on my right hand, and on my left, is not mine
to give, but *it shall be given to them* for whom it is prepared of my Father.
24 And when the ten heard *it*, they were moved with indignation against the two
brethren. (Matt 20:20-24)

128 - JESUS ADVISES AGAINST A HIERARCHY

According to the Gospel of Mark

42 But Jesus called them *to him*, and saith unto them, Ye know that they which are
accounted to rule over the Gentiles exercise lordship over them; and their great ones
exercise authority upon them.
43 But so shall it not be among you: but whosoever will be great among you, shall be
your minister:
44 And whosoever of you will be the chiefest, shall be servant of all.
45 For even the Son of man came not to be ministered unto, but to minister, and to give
his life a ransom for many. (Mark 10:42-45)

According to the Gospel of Matthew

25 But Jesus called them *unto him*, and said, Ye know that the princes of the Gentiles
exercise dominion over them, and they that are great exercise authority upon them.
26 But it shall not be so among you: but whosoever will be great among you, let him be
your minister;
27 And whosoever will be chief among you, let him be your servant:
28 Even as the Son of man came not to be ministered unto, but to minister, and to give
his life a ransom for many. (Matt 20:25-28)

129 - APPROACHING JERICHO "A CERTAIN" BLIND MAN IS HEALED

35 ¶ And it came to pass, that as he was come nigh unto Jericho, a certain blind man sat
by the way side begging:
36 And hearing the multitude pass by, he asked what it meant.
37 And they told him, that Jesus of Nazareth passeth by.
38 And he cried, saying, Jesus, *thou* son of David, have mercy on me.
39 And they which went before rebuked him, that he should hold his peace: but he cried
so much the more, *Thou* son of David, have mercy on me.
40 And Jesus stood, and commanded him to be brought unto him: and when he was
come near, he asked him,
41 Saying, What wilt thou that I shall do unto thee? And he said, Lord, that I may
receive my sight.
42 And Jesus said unto him, Receive thy sight: thy faith hath saved thee.
43 And immediately he received his sight, and followed him, glorifying God: and all
the people, when they saw *it*, gave praise unto God. (Luke 18:35-43)
46 ¶ And they came to Jericho: (Mark 10:46 to :)

130 - JESUS AND ZACCHÆUS

1 And *Jesus* entered and passed through Jericho.
2 And, behold, *there was* a man named Zacchæus, which was the chief among the
publicans, and he was rich.

3 And he sought to see Jesus who he was; and could not for the press, because he was
little of stature.
4 And he ran before, and climbed up into a sycomore tree to see him: for he was to pass
that *way*.
5 And when Jesus came to the place, he looked up, and saw him, and said unto him,
Zacchæus, make haste, and come down; for to-day I must abide at thy house.
6 And he made haste, and came down, and received him joyfully.
7 And when they saw *it*, they all murmured, saying, That he was gone to be guest with
a man that is a sinner.
8 And Zacchæus stood, and said unto the Lord; Behold, Lord, the half of my goods I
give to the poor; and if I have taken any thing from any man by false accusation, I
restore *him* fourfold.
9 And Jesus said unto him, This day is salvation come to this house, forsomuch as he
also is a son of Abraham.
10 For the Son of man is come to seek and to save that which was lost. (Luke 19:1-10)

131 - BLINDNESS HEALED LEAVING AND DEPARTING JERICHO

46 and as he went out of Jericho with his disciples and a great number of people, blind
Bartimæus, the son of Timæus, sat by the highway side begging.
47 And when he heard that it was Jesus of Nazareth, he began to cry out, and say,
Jesus, *thou* son of David, have mercy on me.
48 And many charged him that he should hold his peace: but he cried the more a great
deal, *Thou* son of David, have mercy on me.
49 And Jesus stood still, and commanded him to be called. And they call the blind
man, saying unto him, Be of good comfort, rise; he calleth thee.
50 And he, casting away his garment, rose, and came to Jesus.
51 And Jesus answered and said unto him, What wilt thou that I should do unto thee?
The blind man said unto him, Lord, that I might receive my sight.
52 And Jesus said unto him, Go thy way; thy faith hath made thee whole. And
immediately he received his sight, and followed Jesus in the way. (Mark 10:46-52 *and*)
29 And as they departed from Jericho, a great multitude followed him.
30 ¶ And, behold, two blind men sitting by the way side, when they heard that Jesus
passed by, cried out, saying, Have mercy on us, O Lord, *thou* son of David.
31 And the multitude rebuked them, because they should hold their peace: but they
cried the more, saying, Have mercy on us, O Lord, *thou* son of David.
32 And Jesus stood still, and called them, and said, What will ye that I shall do unto
you?
33 They say unto him, Lord, that our eyes may be opened.
34 So Jesus had compassion *on them*, and touched their eyes: and immediately their
eyes received sight, and they followed him. (Matt 20:29-34)

132 - THE BRUTALITY OF WORLDLY RULERSHIP

11 And as they heard these things, he added and spake a parable, because he was nigh
to Jerusalem, and because they thought that the kingdom of God should immediately
appear.
12 He said therefore, A certain nobleman went into a far country to receive for himself
a kingdom, and to return.

13 And he called his ten servants, and delivered them ten pounds, and said unto them,
Occupy till I come.
14 But his citizens hated him, and sent a message after him, saying, We will not have
this *man* to reign over us.
15 And it came to pass, that when he was returned, having received the kingdom, then
he commanded these servants to be called unto him, to whom he had given the money,
that he might know how much every man had gained by trading.
16 Then came the first, saying, Lord, thy pound hath gained ten pounds.
17 And he said unto him, Well, thou good servant: because thou hast been faithful in a
very little, have thou authority over ten cities.
18 And the second came, saying, Lord, thy pound hath gained five pounds.
19 And he said likewise to him, Be thou also over five cities.
20 And another came, saying, Lord, behold, *here is* thy pound, which I have kept laid
up in a napkin:
21 For I feared thee, because thou art an austere man: thou takest up that thou layedst
not down, and reapest that thou didst not sow.
22 And he saith unto him, Out of thine own mouth will I judge thee, *thou* wicked
servant. Thou knewest that I was an austere man, taking up that I laid not down, and
reaping that I did not sow:
23 Wherefore then gavest not thou my money into the bank, that at my coming I might
have required mine own with usury?
24 And he said unto them that stood by, Take from him the pound, and give *it* to him
that hath ten pounds.
25 (And they said unto him, Lord, he hath ten pounds.)
26 For I say unto you, That unto every one which hath shall be given; and from him
that hath not, even that he hath shall be taken away from him.
27 But those mine enemies, which would not that I should reign over them, bring
hither, and slay *them* before me.
28 ¶ And when he had thus spoken he went before, ascending up to Jerusalem. (Luke
19:11-28)
55 ¶ And the Jews' passover was nigh at hand: and many went out of the country up to
Jerusalem before the passover, to purify themselves.
56 Then sought they for Jesus, and spake among themselves, as they stood in the
temple, What think ye, that he will not come to the feast?
57 Now both the chief priests and the Pharisees had given a commandment, that, if any
man knew where he were, he should shew *it*, that they might take him. (John 11:55-57)

133 – JESUS ON HIS FIRST ENTRY INTO JERUSALEM IS UNKNOWN

1 And when they drew nigh unto Jerusalem, and were come to Bethphage, unto the
mount of Olives, then sent Jesus two disciples,
2 Saying unto them, Go into the village over against you, and straightway ye shall find
an ass tied, and a colt with her: loose *them*, and bring *them* unto me.
3 And if any *man* say ought unto you, ye shall say, The Lord hath need of them; and
straightway he will send them.
4 All this was done, that it might be fulfilled which was spoken by the prophet, saying,
5 Tell ye the daughter of Sion, Behold, thy King cometh unto thee, meek, and sitting
upon an ass, and a colt the foal of an ass.

6 And the disciples went, and did as Jesus commanded them,
7 And brought the ass, and the colt, and put on them their clothes, and they set *him*
thereon.
8 And a very great multitude spread their garments in the way; others cut down
branches from the trees, and strawed *them* in the way.
9 And the multitudes that went before, and that followed, cried, saying, Hosanna to the
son of David: Blessed *is* he that cometh in the name of the Lord; Hosanna in the
highest.
10 And when he was come into Jerusalem, all the city was moved, saying, Who is this?
11 And the multitude said, This is Jesus the prophet of Nazareth of Galilee. (Matt 21:1-11)

134 - THE SECOND TEMPLE CLEANSING

12 ¶ And Jesus went into the temple of God, and cast out all them that sold and bought
in the temple, and overthrew the tables of the moneychangers, and the seats of them
that sold doves,
13 And said unto them, It is written, My house shall be called the house of prayer; but
ye have made it a den of thieves.
14 And the blind and the lame came to him in the temple; and he healed them.
15 And when the chief priests and scribes saw the wonderful things that he did, and the
children crying in the temple, and saying, Hosanna to the son of David; they were sore
displeased,
16 And said unto him, Hearest thou what these say? And Jesus saith unto them, Yea;
have ye never read, Out of the mouth of babes and sucklings thou hast perfected praise?
17 ¶ And he left them, and went out of the city into Bethany; and he lodged there. (Matt
21:12-17)
1 Then Jesus six days before the passover came to Bethany, where Lazarus was which
had been dead, whom he raised from the dead. (John 12:1)

135 - THE SECOND ANOINTING

2 There they made him a supper; and Martha served: but Lazarus was one of them that
sat at the table with him.
3 Then took Mary a pound of ointment of spikenard, very costly, and anointed the feet
of Jesus, and wiped his feet with her hair: and the house was filled with the odour of the
ointment.
4 Then saith one of his disciples, Judas Iscariot, Simon's *son*, which should betray him,
5 Why was not this ointment sold for three hundred pence, and given to the poor?
6 This he said, not that he cared for the poor; but because he was a thief, and had the
bag, and bare what was put therein.
7 Then said Jesus, Let her alone: against the day of my burying hath she kept this.
8 For the poor always ye have with you; but me ye have not always.
9 Much people of the Jews therefore knew that he was there: and they came not for
Jesus' sake only, but that they might see Lazarus also, whom he had raised from the
dead.
10 ¶ But the chief priests consulted that they might put Lazarus also to death;
11 Because that by reason of him many of the Jews went away, and believed on Jesus.
(John 12:2-11)

136 - THE SECOND OR TRIUMPHAL ENTRY INTO JERUSALEM

According to the Gospel of John

12 ¶ On the next day much people that were come to the feast, when they heard that
Jesus was coming to Jerusalem,
13 Took branches of palm trees, and went forth to meet him, and cried, Hosanna:
Blessed *is* the King of Israel that cometh in the name of the Lord.
14 And Jesus, when he had found a young ass, sat thereon; as it is written,
15 Fear not, daughter of Sion; behold, thy King cometh, sitting on an ass's colt.
16 These things understood not his disciples at the first: but when Jesus was glorified,
then remembered they that these things were written of him, and *that* they had done
these things unto him.
17 The people therefore that was with him when he called Lazarus out of his grave, and
raised him from the dead, bare record.
18 For this cause the people also met him, for that they heard that he had done this
miracle.
19 The Pharisees therefore said among themselves, Perceive ye how ye prevail
nothing? behold, the world is gone after him. (John 12:12-19)

According to the Gospel of Luke

29 And it came to pass, when he was come nigh to Bethphage and Bethany, at the
mount called *the mount* of Olives, he sent two of his disciples,
30 Saying, Go ye into the village over against *you*; in the which at your entering ye
shall find a colt tied, whereon yet never man sat: loose him, and bring *him hither*.
31 And if any man ask you, Why do ye loose *him*? thus shall ye say unto him, Because
the Lord hath need of him.
32 And they that were sent went their way, and found even as he had said unto them.
33 And as they were loosing the colt, the owners thereof said unto them, Why loose ye
the colt?
34 And they said, The Lord hath need of him.
35 And they brought him to Jesus: and they cast their garments upon the colt, and they
set Jesus thereon.
36 And as he went, they spread their clothes in the way.
37 And when he was come nigh, even now at the descent of the mount of Olives, the
whole multitude of the disciples began to rejoice and praise God with a loud voice for
all the mighty works that they had seen;
38 Saying, Blessed *be* the King that cometh in the name of the Lord: peace in heaven,
and glory in the highest.
39 And some of the Pharisees from among the multitude said unto him, Master, rebuke
thy disciples.
40 And he answered and said unto them, I tell you that, if these should hold their peace,
the stones would immediately cry out.
41 ¶ And when he was come near, he beheld the city, and wept over it,
42 Saying, If thou hadst known, even thou, at least in this thy day, the things *which
belong* unto thy peace! but now they are hid from thine eyes.
43 For the days shall come upon thee, that thine enemies shall cast a trench about thee,
and compass thee round, and keep thee in on every side,
44 And shall lay thee even with the ground, and thy children within thee; and they shall

not leave in thee one stone upon another; because thou knewest not the time of thy
visitation. (Luke 19:29-44)

According to the Gospel of Mark

1 And when they came nigh to Jerusalem, unto Bethphage and Bethany, at the mount
of Olives, he sendeth forth two of his disciples,
2 And saith unto them, Go your way into the village over against you: and as soon as
ye be entered into it, ye shall find a colt tied, whereon never man sat; loose him, and
bring *him.*
3 And if any man say unto you, Why do ye this? say ye that the Lord hath need of him;
and straightway he will send him hither.
4 And they went their way, and found the colt tied by the door without in a place where
two ways met; and they loose him.
5 And certain of them that stood there said unto them, What do ye, loosing the colt?
6 And they said unto them even as Jesus had commanded: and they let them go.
7 And they brought the colt to Jesus, and cast their garments on him; and he sat upon
him.
8 And many spread their garments in the way: and others cut down branches off the
trees, and strawed *them* in the way.
9 And they that went before, and they that followed, cried, saying, Hosanna; Blessed *is*
he that cometh in the name of the Lord:
10 Blessed *be* the kingdom of our father David, that cometh in the name of the Lord:
Hosanna in the highest.
11 And Jesus entered into Jerusalem, and into the temple: and when he had looked
round about upon all things, and now the eventide was come,
11 he went out unto Bethany with the twelve. (Mark 11:1-11)

137 - THE BARREN FIG TREE

According to the Gospel of Mark

12 ¶ And on the morrow, when they were come from Bethany, he was hungry:
13 And seeing a fig tree afar off having leaves, he came, if haply he might find
anything thereon: and when he came to it, he found nothing but leaves; for the time of
figs was not *yet.*
14 And Jesus answered and said unto it, No man eat fruit of thee hereafter for ever.
And his disciples heard *it.* (Mark 11:12-14)

According to the Gospel of Matthew

18 Now in the morning as he returned into the city, he hungered.
19 And when he saw a fig tree in the way, he came to it, and found nothing thereon, but
leaves only, and said unto it, Let no fruit grow on thee henceforward for ever. (Matt 21:18-19 to 1st.)

138 - THE THIRD TEMPLE CLEANSING

According to the Gospel of Mark

15 ¶ And they come to Jerusalem: and Jesus went into the temple, and began to cast out
them that sold and bought in the temple, and overthrew the tables of the
moneychangers, and the seats of them that sold doves;
16 And would not suffer that any man should carry *any* vessel through the temple.

17 And he taught, saying unto them, Is it not written, My house shall be called of all
nations the house of prayer? but ye have made it a den of thieves. (Mark 11:15-17)

According to the Gospel of Luke

45 And he went into the temple, and began to cast out them that sold therein, and them
that bought;
46 Saying unto them, It is written, My house is the house of prayer: but ye have made it
a den of thieves. (Luke 19:45-46)

139 - PREACHING IN THE TEMPLE GROUNDS

47 And he taught daily in the temple. (Luke 19:47 to 1st.)
20 ¶ And there were certain Greeks among them that came up to worship at the feast:
21 The same came therefore to Philip, which was of Bethsaida of Galilee, and desired
him, saying, Sir, we would see Jesus.
22 Philip cometh and telleth Andrew: and again Andrew and Philip tell Jesus.
23 ¶ And Jesus answered them, saying, The hour is come, that the Son of man should
be glorified.
24 Verily, verily, I say unto you, Except a corn of wheat fall into the ground and die, it
abideth alone: but if it die, it bringeth forth much fruit.
25 He that loveth his life shall lose it; and he that hateth his life in this world shall keep
it unto life eternal.
26 If any man serve me, let him follow me; and where I am, there shall also my servant
be: if any man serve me, him will *my* Father honour.
27 Now is my soul troubled; and what shall I say? Father, save me from this hour: but
for this cause came I unto this hour.
28 Father, glorify thy name. Then came there a voice from heaven, *saying*, I have both
glorified *it*, and will glorify *it* again.
29 The people therefore, that stood by, and heard *it*, said that it thundered: others said,
An angel spake to him.
30 Jesus answered and said, This voice came not because of me, but for your sakes.
31 Now is the judgment of this world: now shall the prince of this world be cast out.
32 And I, if I be lifted up from the earth, will draw all *men* unto me.
33 This he said, signifying what death he should die.
34 The people answered him, We have heard out of the law that Christ abideth for ever:
and how sayest thou, The Son of man must be lifted up? who is this Son of man?
35 Then Jesus said unto them, Yet a little while is the light with you. Walk while ye
have the light, lest darkness come upon you: for he that walketh in darkness knoweth
not whither he goeth.
36 While ye have light, believe in the light, that ye may be the children of light. These
things spake Jesus, and departed, and did hide himself from them.
37 ¶ But though he had done so many miracles before them, yet they believed not on
him:
38 That the saying of Esaias the prophet might be fulfilled, which he spake, Lord, who
hath believed our report? and to whom hath the arm of the Lord been revealed?
39 Therefore they could not believe, because that Esaias said again,
40 He hath blinded their eyes, and hardened their heart; that they should not see with
their eyes, nor understand with *their* heart, and be converted, and I should heal them.
41 These things said Esaias, when he saw his glory, and spake of him.

42 ¶ Nevertheless among the chief rulers also many believed on him; but because of the
Pharisees they did not confess *him*, lest they should be put out of the synagogue:
43 For they loved the praise of men more than the praise of God.
44 ¶ Jesus cried and said, He that believeth on me, believeth not on me, but on him that
sent me.
45 And he that seeth me seeth him that sent me.
46 I am come a light into the world, that whosoever believeth on me should not abide in
darkness.
47 And if any man hear my words, and believe not, I judge him not: for I came not to
judge the world, but to save the world.
48 He that rejecteth me, and receiveth not my words, hath one that judgeth him: the
word that I have spoken, the same shall judge him in the last day.
49 For I have not spoken of myself; but the Father which sent me, he gave me a
commandment, what I should say, and what I should speak.
50 And I know that his commandment is life everlasting: whatsoever I speak therefore,
even as the Father said unto me, so I speak. (John 12:20-50)

According to the Gospel of Luke

47 But the chief priests and the scribes and the chief of the people sought to destroy
him,
48 And could not find what they might do: for all the people were very attentive to hear
him. (Luke 19:47-48 *But*)

According to the Gospel of Mark

18 And the scribes and chief priests heard *it*, and sought how they might destroy him:
for they feared him, because all the people was astonished at his doctrine.
19 And when even was come, he went out of the city. (Mark 11:18-19)

140 - LESSONS FROM THE WITHERED FIG TREE

According to the Gospel of Matthew

19 And presently the fig tree withered away.
20 And when the disciples saw *it*, they marvelled, saying, How soon is the fig tree
withered away!
21 Jesus answered and said unto them, Verily I say unto you, If ye have faith, and
doubt not, ye shall not only do this *which is done* to the fig tree, but also if ye shall say
unto this mountain, Be thou removed, and be thou cast into the sea; it shall be done.
22 And all things, whatsoever ye shall ask in prayer, believing, ye shall receive. (Matt
21:19-22)

According to the Gospel of Mark

20 ¶ And in the morning, as they passed by, they saw the fig tree dried up from the
roots.
21 And Peter calling to remembrance saith unto him, Master, behold, the fig tree which
thou cursedst is withered away
22 And Jesus answering saith unto them, Have faith in God.
23 For verily I say unto you, That whosoever shall say unto this mountain, Be thou
removed, and be thou cast into the sea; and shall not doubt in his heart, but shall believe
that those things which he saith shall come to pass; he shall have whatsoever he saith.
24 Therefore I say unto you, What things soever ye desire, when ye pray, believe that

ye receive *them*, and ye shall have *them*.
25 And when ye stand praying, forgive, if ye have ought against any: that your Father
also which is in heaven may forgive you your trespasses.
26 But if ye do not forgive, neither will your Father which is in heaven forgive your
trespasses. (Mark 11:20-26)

141 - DISPUTING WITH THE PRIESTS, SCRIBES, AND ELDERS

According to the Gospel of Mark

27 ¶ And they come again to Jerusalem: and as he was walking in the temple, there
come to him the chief priests, and the scribes, and the elders,
28 And say unto him, By what authority doest thou these things? and who gave thee
this authority to do these things?
29 And Jesus answered and said unto them, I will also ask of you one question, and
answer me, and I will tell you by what authority I do these things.
30 The baptism of John, was *it* from heaven, or of men? answer me.
31 And they reasoned with themselves, saying, If we shall say, From heaven; he will
say, Why then did ye not believe him?
32 But if we shall say, Of men; they feared the people: for all *men* counted John, that he
was a prophet indeed.
33 And they answered and said unto Jesus, We cannot tell. And Jesus answering saith
unto them, Neither do I tell you by what authority I do these things. (Mark 11:27-33)
1 And he began to speak unto them by parables. A *certain* man planted a vineyard, and
set an hedge about *it*, and digged *a place for* the winefat, and built a tower, and let it out
to husbandmen, and went into a far country.
2 And at the season he sent to the husbandmen a servant, that he might receive from the
husbandmen of the fruit of the vineyard.
3 And they caught *him*, and beat him, and sent *him* away empty.
4 And again he sent unto them another servant; and at him they cast stones, and
wounded *him* in the head, and sent *him* away shamefully handled.
5 And again he sent another; and him they killed, and many others; beating some, and
killing some.
6 Having yet therefore one son, his wellbeloved, he sent him also last unto them,
saying, They will reverence my son.
7 But those husbandmen said among themselves, This is the heir; come, let us kill him,
and the inheritance shall be ours.
8 And they took him, and killed *him*, and cast *him* out of the vineyard.
9 What shall therefore the lord of the vineyard do? he will come and destroy the
husbandmen, and will give the vineyard unto others.
10 And have ye not read this scripture; The stone which the builders rejected is become
the head of the corner:
11 This was the Lord's doing, and it is marvellous in our eyes?
12 And they sought to lay hold on him, but feared the people: for they knew that he had
spoken the parable against them: and they left him, and went their way. (Mark 12:1-12)

According to the Gospel of Luke

1 And it came to pass, *that* on one of those days, as he taught the people in the temple,
and preached the gospel, the chief priests and the scribes came upon *him* with the

elders,
2 And spake unto him, saying, Tell us, by what authority doest thou these things? or
who is he that gave thee this authority?
3 And he answered and said unto them, I will also ask you one thing; and answer me:
4 The baptism of John, was it from heaven, or of men?
5 And they reasoned with themselves, saying, If we shall say, From heaven; he will
say, Why then believed ye him not?
6 But and if we say, Of men; all the people will stone us: for they be persuaded that
John was a prophet.
7 And they answered, that they could not tell whence *it was*.
8 And Jesus said unto them, Neither tell I you by what authority I do these things.
9 Then began he to speak to the people this parable; A certain man planted a vineyard,
and let it forth to husbandmen, and went into a far country for a long time.
10 And at the season he sent a servant to the husbandmen, that they should give him of
the fruit of the vineyard: but the husbandmen beat him, and sent *him* away empty.
11 And again he sent another servant: and they beat him also, and entreated *him*
shamefully, and sent *him* away empty.
12 And again he sent a third: and they wounded him also, and cast *him* out.
13 Then said the lord of the vineyard, What shall I do? I will send my beloved son: it
may be they will reverence *him* when they see him.
14 But when the husbandmen saw him, they reasoned among themselves, saying, This
is the heir: come, let us kill him, that the inheritance may be ours.
15 So they cast him out of the vineyard, and killed *him*. What therefore shall the lord
of the vineyard do unto them?
16 He shall come and destroy these husbandmen, and shall give the vineyard to others.
And when they heard *it*, they said, God forbid.
17 And he beheld them, and said, What is this then that is written, The stone which the
builders rejected, the same is become the head of the corner?
18 Whosoever shall fall upon that stone shall be broken; but on whomsoever it shall
fall, it will grind him to powder.
19 ¶ And the chief priests and the scribes the same hour sought to lay hands on him;
and they feared the people: for they perceived that he had spoken this parable against
them. (Luke 20:1-19)

According to the Gospel of Matthew

23 ¶ And when he was come into the temple, the chief priests and the elders of the
people came unto him as he was teaching, and said, By what authority doest thou these
things? and who gave thee this authority?
24 And Jesus answered and said unto them, I also will ask you one thing, which if ye
tell me, I in like wise will tell you by what authority I do these things.
25 The baptism of John, whence was it? from heaven, or of men? And they reasoned
with themselves, saying, If we shall say, From heaven; he will say unto us, Why did ye
not then believe him?
26 But if we shall say, Of men; we fear the people; for all hold John as a prophet.
27 And they answered Jesus, and said, We cannot tell. And he said unto them, Neither
tell I you by what authority I do these things.
28 ¶ But what think ye? A *certain* man had two sons; and he came to the first, and said,

Son, go work to-day in my vineyard.
29 He answered and said, I will not: but afterward he repented, and went.
30 And he came to the second, and said likewise. And he answered and said, I *go*, sir:
and went not.
31 Whether of them twain did the will of *his* father? They say unto him, The first.
Jesus saith unto them, Verily I say unto you, That the publicans and the harlots go into
the kingdom of God before you.
32 For John came unto you in the way of righteousness, and ye believed him not; but
the publicans and the harlots believed him: and ye, when ye had seen *it*, repented not
afterward, that ye might believe him.
33 ¶ Hear another parable: There was a certain householder, which planted a vineyard,
and hedged it round about, and digged a winepress in it, and built a tower, and let it out
to husbandmen, and went into a far country:
34 And when the time of the fruit drew near, he sent his servants to the husbandmen,
that they might receive the fruits of it.
35 And the husbandmen took his servants, and beat one, and killed another, and stoned
another.
36 Again, he sent other servants more than the first: and they did unto them likewise.
37 But last of all he sent unto them his son, saying, They will reverence my son.
38 But when the husbandmen saw the son, they said among themselves, This is the
heir; come, let us kill him, and let us seize on his inheritance.
39 And they caught him, and cast *him* out of the vineyard, and slew *him*.
40 When the lord therefore of the vineyard cometh, what will he do unto those
husbandmen?
41 They say unto him, He will miserably destroy those wicked men, and will let out *his*
vineyard unto other husbandmen, which shall render him the fruits in their seasons.
42 Jesus saith unto them, Did ye never read in the scriptures, The stone which the
builders rejected, the same is become the head of the corner: this is the Lord's doing,
and it is marvellous in our eyes?
43 Therefore say I unto you, The kingdom of God shall be taken from you, and given to
a nation bringing forth the fruits thereof.
44 And whosoever shall fall on this stone shall be broken: but on whomsoever it shall
fall, it will grind him to powder.
45 And when the chief priests and Pharisees had heard his parables, they perceived that
he spake of them.
46 But when they sought to lay hands on him, they feared the multitude, because they
took him for a prophet. (Matt 21:23-46)

142 - IMPOSTORS ARE TO BE CAST OUT

1 And Jesus answered and spake unto them again by parables, and said,
2 The kingdom of heaven is like unto a certain king, which made a marriage for his
son,
3 And sent forth his servants to call them that were bidden to the wedding: and they
would not come.
4 Again, he sent forth other servants, saying, Tell them which are bidden, Behold, I
have prepared my dinner: my oxen and *my* fatlings *are* killed, and all things *are* ready:
come unto the marriage.

5 But they made light of *it*, and went their ways, one to his farm, another to his
merchandise:
6 And the remnant took his servants, and entreated *them* spitefully, and slew *them*.
7 But when the king heard *thereof*, he was wroth: and he sent forth his armies, and
destroyed those murderers, and burned up their city.
8 Then saith he to his servants, The wedding is ready, but they which were bidden were
not worthy.
9 Go ye therefore into the highways, and as many as ye shall find, bid to the marriage.
10 So those servants went out into the highways, and gathered together all as many as
they found, both bad and good: and the wedding was furnished with guests.
11 ¶ And when the king came in to see the guests, he saw there a man which had not on
a wedding garment:
12 And he saith unto him, Friend, how camest thou in hither not having a wedding
garment?
12 And he was speechless.
13 Then said the king to the servants, Bind him hand and foot, and take him away, and
cast *him* into outer darkness; there shall be weeping and gnashing of teeth.
14 For many are called, but few *are* chosen. (Matt 22:1-14)

143 - FAILED ATTEMPTS TO ENTRAP JESUS

According to the Gospel of Luke

20 And they watched *him*, and sent forth spies, which should feign themselves just
men, that they might take hold of his words, that so they might deliver him unto the
power and authority of the governor.
21 And they asked him, saying, Master, we know that thou sayest and teachest rightly,
neither acceptest thou the person *of any*, but teachest the way of God truly:
22 Is it lawful for us to give tribute unto Cæsar, or no?
23 But he perceived their craftiness, and said unto them, Why tempt ye me?
24 Shew me a penny. Whose image and superscription hath it? They answered and
said, Cæsar's.
25 And he said unto them, Render therefore unto Cæsar the things which be Cæsar's,
and unto God the things which be God's.
26 And they could not take hold of his words before the people: and they marvelled at
his answer, and held their peace.
27 ¶ Then came to *him* certain of the Sadducees, which deny that there is any
resurrection; and they asked him,
28 Saying, Master, Moses wrote unto us, If any man's brother die, having a wife, and he
die without children, that his brother should take his wife, and raise up seed unto his
brother.
29 There were therefore seven brethren: and the first took a wife, and died without
children.
30 And the second took her to wife, and he died childless.
31 And the third took her; and in like manner the seven also: and they left no children,
and died.
32 Last of all the woman died also.
33 Therefore in the resurrection whose wife of them is she? for seven had her to wife.

34 And Jesus answering said unto them, The children of this world marry, and are
given in marriage:
35 But they which shall be accounted worthy to obtain that world, and the resurrection
from the dead, neither marry, nor are given in marriage:
36 Neither can they die any more: for they are equal unto the angels; and are the
children of God, being the children of the resurrection.
37 Now that the dead are raised, even Moses shewed at the bush, when he calleth the
Lord the God of Abraham, and the God of Isaac, and the God of Jacob.
38 For he is not a God of the dead, but of the living: for all live unto him.
39 ¶ Then certain of the scribes answering said, Master, thou hast well said.
40 And after that they durst not ask him any *question at all*. (Luke 20:20-40)

According to the Gospel of Matthew

15 ¶ Then went the Pharisees, and took counsel how they might entangle him in *his*
talk.
16 And they sent out unto him their disciples with the Herodians, saying, Master, we
know that thou art true, and teachest the way of God in truth, neither carest thou for any
man: for thou regardest not the person of men.
17 Tell us therefore, What thinkest thou? Is it lawful to give tribute unto Cæsar, or not?
18 But Jesus perceived their wickedness, and said, Why tempt ye me, *ye* hypocrites?
19 Shew me the tribute money. And they brought unto him a penny.
20 And he saith unto them, Whose *is* this image and superscription?
21 They say unto him, Cæsar's. Then saith he unto them, Render therefore unto Cæsar
the things which are Cæsar's; and unto God the things that are God's.
22 When they had heard *these words*, they marvelled, and left him, and went their way.
23 ¶ The same day came to him the Sadducees, which say that there is no resurrection,
and asked him,
24 Saying, Master, Moses said, If a man die, having no children, his brother shall marry
his wife, and raise up seed unto his brother.
25 Now there were with us seven brethren: and the first, when he had married a wife,
deceased, and, having no issue, left his wife unto his brother:
26 Likewise the second also, and the third, unto the seventh.
27 And last of all the woman died also.
28 Therefore in the resurrection whose wife shall she be of the seven? for they all had
her.
29 Jesus answered and said unto them, Ye do err, not knowing the scriptures, nor the
power of God.
30 For in the resurrection they neither marry, nor are given in marriage, but are as the
angels of God in heaven.
31 But as touching the resurrection of the dead, have ye not read that which was spoken
unto you by God, saying,
32 I am the God of Abraham, and the God of Isaac, and the God of Jacob? God is not
the God of the dead, but of the living.
33 And when the multitude heard *this*, they were astonished at his doctrine. (Matt 22:23-33)
34 ¶ But when the Pharisees had heard that he had put the Sadducees to silence, they
were gathered together.
35 Then one of them, *which was* a lawyer, asked *him a question*, tempting him, and

saying,
36 Master, which *is* the great commandment in the law?
37 Jesus said unto him, Thou shalt love the Lord thy God with all thy heart, and with all
thy soul, and with all thy mind.
38 This is the first and great commandment.
39 And the second *is* like unto it, Thou shalt love thy neighbour as thyself.
40 On these two commandments hang all the law and the prophets. (Matt 22:15-40)

According to the Gospel of Mark

13 ¶ And they send unto him certain of the Pharisees and of the Herodians, to catch him
in *his* words.
14 And when they were come, they say unto him, Master, we know that thou art true,
and carest for no man: for thou regardest not the person of men, but teachest the way of
God in truth: Is it lawful to give tribute to Cæsar, or not?
15 Shall we give, or shall we not give? But he, knowing their hypocrisy, said unto
them, Why tempt ye me? bring me a penny, that I may see *it*.
16 And they brought *it*. And he saith unto them, Whose *is* this image and
superscription? And they said unto him, Cæsar's.
17 And Jesus answering said unto them, Render to Cæsar the things that are Cæsar's,
and to God the things that are God's. And they marvelled at him.
18 ¶ Then come unto him the Sadducees, which say there is no resurrection; and they
asked him, saying,
19 Master, Moses wrote unto us, If a man's brother die, and leave *his* wife *behind him*,
and leave no children, that his brother should take his wife, and raise up seed unto his
brother.
20 Now there were seven brethren: and the first took a wife, and dying left no seed.
21 And the second took her, and died, neither left he any seed: and the third likewise.
22 And the seven had her, and left no seed: last of all the woman died also.
23 In the resurrection therefore, when they shall rise, whose wife shall she be of them?
for the seven had her to wife.
24 And Jesus answering said unto them, Do ye not therefore err, because ye know not
the scriptures, neither the power of God?
25 For when they shall rise from the dead, they neither marry, nor are given in
marriage; but are as the angels which are in heaven.
26 And as touching the dead, that they rise: have ye not read in the book of Moses, how
in the bush God spake unto him, saying, I *am* the God of Abraham, and the God of
Isaac, and the God of Jacob?
27 He is not the God of the dead, but the God of the living: ye therefore do greatly err.
28 ¶ And one of the scribes came, and having heard them reasoning together, and
perceiving that he had answered them well, asked him, Which is the first
commandment of all?
29 And Jesus answered him, The first of all the commandments *is*, Hear, O Israel; The
Lord our God is one Lord:
30 And thou shalt love the Lord thy God with all thy heart, and with all thy soul, and
with all thy mind, and with all thy strength: this *is* the first commandment.
31 And the second *is* like, *namely* this, Thou shalt love thy neighbour as thyself. There
is none other commandment greater than these.

32 And the scribe said unto him, Well, Master, thou hast said the truth: for there is one
God; and there is none other but he:
33 And to love him with all the heart and with all the understanding, and with all the
soul, and with all the strength, and to love *his* neighbour as himself, is more than all
whole burnt offerings and sacrifices.
34 And when Jesus saw that he answered discreetly, he said unto him, Thou art not far
from the kingdom of God.
34 And no man after that durst ask him *any question.* (Mark 12:13-34)

144 - THE DIVINITY OF THE CHRIST

According to the Gospel of Matthew

41 ¶ While the Pharisees were gathered together, Jesus asked them,
42 Saying, What think ye of Christ? whose son is he? They say unto him, *The Son* of
David.
43 He saith unto them, How then doth David in spirit call him Lord, saying,
44 The LORD said unto my Lord, Sit thou on my right hand, till I make thine enemies
thy footstool?
45 If David then call him Lord, how is he his son?
46 And no man was able to answer him a word, neither durst any *man* from that day
forth ask him any more *questions*. (Matt 22:41-46)

According to the Gospel of Mark

35 ¶ And Jesus answered and said, while he taught in the temple, How say the scribes
that Christ is the son of David?
36 For David himself said by the Holy Ghost, The LORD said to my Lord, Sit thou on
my right hand, till I make thine enemies thy footstool.
37 David therefore himself calleth him Lord; and whence is he *then* his son? And the
common people heard him gladly. (Mark 12:35-37)

According to the Gospel of Luke

41 And he said unto them, How say they that Christ is David's son?
42 And David himself saith in the book of Psalms, The LORD said unto my Lord, Sit
thou on my right hand,
43 Till I make thine enemies thy footstool.
44 David therefore calleth him Lord, how is he then his son? (Luke 20:41-44)

145 - BEWARE OF THE SCRIBES

According to the Gospel of Luke

45 ¶ Then in the audience of all the people he said unto his disciples,
46 Beware of the scribes, which desire to walk in long robes, and love greetings in the
markets, and the highest seats in the synagogues, and the chief rooms at feasts;
47 Which devour widows' houses, and for a shew make long prayers: the same shall
receive greater damnation. (Luke 20:45-47)

According to the Gospel of Mark

38 ¶ And he said unto them in his doctrine, Beware of the scribes, which love to go in
long clothing, and *love* salutations in the marketplaces,
39 And the chief seats in the synagogues, and the uppermost rooms at feasts:

40 Which devour widows' houses, and for a pretence make long prayers: these shall
receive greater damnation. (Mark 12:38-40)

146 - A CERTAIN POOR WIDOW A PROPHECY

According to the Gospel of Mark

41 ¶ And Jesus sat over against the treasury, and beheld how the people cast money into
the treasury: and many that were rich cast in much.
42 And there came a certain poor widow, and she threw in two mites, which make a
farthing.
43 And he called *unto him* his disciples, and saith unto them, Verily I say unto you,
That this poor widow hath cast more in, than all they which have cast into the treasury:
44 For all *they* did cast in of their abundance; but she of her want did cast in all that she
had, *even* all her living. (Mark 12:41-44)

According to the Gospel of Luke

1 And he looked up, and saw the rich men casting their gifts into the treasury.
2 And he saw also a certain poor widow casting in thither two mites.
3 And he said, Of a truth I say unto you, that this poor widow hath cast in more than
they all:
4 For all these have of their abundance cast in unto the offerings of God: but she of her
penury hath cast in all the living that she had. (Luke 21:1-4)

147 - PHARISEEISM (SELF-RIGHTEOUSNESS) CONDEMNED

1 Then spake Jesus to the multitude, and to his disciples,
2 Saying, The scribes and the Pharisees sit in Moses' seat:
3 All therefore whatsoever they bid you observe, *that* observe and do; but do not ye
after their works: for they say, and do not.
4 For they bind heavy burdens and grievous to be borne, and lay *them* on men's
shoulders; but they *themselves* will not move them with one of their fingers.
5 But all their works they do for to be seen of men: they make broad their phylacteries,
and enlarge the borders of their garments,
6 And love the uppermost rooms at feasts, and the chief seats in the synagogues,
7 And greetings in the markets, and to be called of men, Rabbi, Rabbi.
8 But be not ye called Rabbi: for one is your Master, *even* Christ; and all ye are
brethren.
9 And call no *man* your father upon the earth: for one is your Father, which is in
heaven.
10 Neither be ye called masters: for one is your Master, *even* Christ.
11 But he that is greatest among you shall be your servant.
12 And whosoever shall exalt himself shall be abased; and he that shall humble himself
shall be exalted.
13 ¶ But woe unto you, scribes and Pharisees, hypocrites! for ye shut up the kingdom of
heaven against men: for ye neither go in *yourselves*, neither suffer ye them that are
entering to go in.
14 Woe unto you, scribes and Pharisees, hypocrites! for ye devour widows' houses, and
for a pretence make long prayer: therefore ye shall receive the greater damnation.

15 Woe unto you, scribes and Pharisees, hypocrites! for ye compass sea and land to
make one proselyte, and when he is made, ye make him twofold more the child of hell
than yourselves.
16 Woe unto you, *ye* blind guides, which say, Whosoever shall swear by the temple, it
is nothing; but whosoever shall swear by the gold of the temple, he is a debtor!
17 *Ye* fools and blind: for whether is greater, the gold, or the temple that sanctifieth the
gold?
18 And, Whosoever shall swear by the altar, it is nothing; but whosoever sweareth by
the gift that is upon it, he is guilty.
19 *Ye* fools and blind: for whether *is* greater, the gift, or the altar that sanctifieth the
gift?
20 Whoso therefore shall swear by the altar, sweareth by it, and by all things thereon.
21 And whoso shall swear by the temple, sweareth by it, and by him that dwelleth
therein.
22 And he that shall swear by heaven, sweareth by the throne of God, and by him that
sitteth thereon.
23 Woe unto you, scribes and Pharisees, hypocrites! for ye pay tithe of mint and anise
and cummin, and have omitted the weightier *matters* of the law, judgment, mercy, and
faith: these ought ye to have done, and not to leave the other undone.
24 *Ye* blind guides, which strain at a gnat, and swallow a camel.
25 Woe unto you, scribes and Pharisees, hypocrites! for ye make clean the outside of
the cup and of the platter, but within they are full of extortion and excess.
26 *Thou* blind Pharisee, cleanse first that *which is* within the cup and platter, that the
outside of them may be clean also.
27 Woe unto you, scribes and Pharisees, hypocrites! for ye are like unto whited
sepulchres, which indeed appear beautiful outward, but are within full of dead *men's*
bones, and of all uncleanness.
28 Even so ye also outwardly appear righteous unto men, but within ye are full of
hypocrisy and iniquity.
29 Woe unto you, scribes and Pharisees, hypocrites! because ye build the tombs of the
prophets, and garnish the sepulchres of the righteous,
30 And say, If we had been in the days of our fathers, we would not have been
partakers with them in the blood of the prophets.
31 Wherefore ye be witnesses unto yourselves, that ye are the children of them which
killed the prophets.
32 Fill ye up then the measure of your fathers.
33 *Ye* serpents, *ye* generation of vipers, how can ye escape the damnation of hell?
34 ¶ Wherefore, behold, I send unto you prophets, and wise men, and scribes: and *some*
of them ye shall kill and crucify; and *some* of them shall ye scourge in your
synagogues, and persecute *them* from city to city:
35 That upon you may come all the righteous blood shed upon the earth, from the blood
of righteous Abel unto the blood of Zacharias son of Barachias, whom ye slew between
the temple and the altar.
36 Verily I say unto you, All these things shall come upon this generation.
37 O Jerusalem, Jerusalem, *thou* that killest the prophets, and stonest them which are
sent unto thee, how often would I have gathered thy children together, even as a hen

gathereth her chickens under *her* wings, and ye would not!
38 Behold, your house is left unto you desolate.
39 For I say unto you, Ye shall not see me henceforth, till ye shall say, Blessed *is* he
that cometh in the name of the Lord. (Matt 23:1-39)

148 - THE FIRST PORTION OF JESUS' PROPHECY

5 ¶ And as some spake of the temple, how it was adorned with goodly stones and gifts,
he said,
6 *As for* these things which ye behold, the days will come, in the which there shall not
be left one stone upon another, that shall not be thrown down.
7 And they asked him, saying, Master, but when shall these things be? and what sign
will there be when these things shall come to pass?
8 And he said, Take heed that ye be not deceived: for many shall come in my name,
saying, I am *Christ*; and the time draweth near: go ye not therefore after them.
9 But when ye shall hear of wars and commotions, be not terrified: for these things
must first come to pass; but the end *is* not by and by.
10 Then said he unto them, Nation shall rise against nation, and kingdom against
kingdom:
11 And great earthquakes shall be in divers places, and famines, and pestilences; and
fearful sights and great signs shall there be from heaven.
12 But before all these, they shall lay their hands on you, and persecute *you*, delivering
you up to the synagogues, and into prisons, being brought before kings and rulers for
my name's sake.
13 And it shall turn to you for a testimony.
14 Settle *it* therefore in your hearts, not to meditate before what ye shall answer:
15 For I will give you a mouth and wisdom, which all your adversaries shall not be able
to gainsay nor resist.
16 And ye shall be betrayed both by parents, and brethren, and kinsfolks, and friends;
and *some* of you shall they cause to be put to death.
17 And ye shall be hated of all *men* for my name's sake.
18 But there shall not an hair of your head perish.
19 In your patience possess ye your souls.
20 And when ye shall see Jerusalem compassed with armies, then know that the
desolation thereof is nigh.
21 Then let them which are in Judæa flee to the mountains; and let them which are in
the midst of it depart out; and let not them that are in the countries enter thereinto.
22 For these be the days of vengeance, that all things which are written may be
fulfilled.
23 But woe unto them that are with child, and to them that give suck, in those days! for
there shall be great distress in the land, and wrath upon this people.
24 And they shall fall by the edge of the sword, and shall be led away captive into all
nations: and Jerusalem shall be trodden down of the Gentiles, until the times of the
Gentiles be fulfilled.
25 ¶ And there shall be signs in the sun, and in the moon, and in the stars; and upon the
earth distress of nations, with perplexity; the sea and the waves roaring;
26 Men's hearts failing them for fear, and for looking after those things which are
coming on the earth: for the powers of heaven shall be shaken.

27 And then shall they see the Son of man coming in a cloud with power and great
glory.
28 And when these things begin to come to pass, then look up, and lift up your heads;
for your redemption draweth nigh.
29 And he spake to them a parable; Behold the fig tree, and all the trees;
30 When they now shoot forth, ye see and know of your own selves that summer is
now nigh at hand.
31 So likewise ye, when ye see these things come to pass, know ye that the kingdom of
God is nigh at hand.
32 Verily I say unto you, This generation shall not pass away, till all be fulfilled.
33 Heaven and earth shall pass away: but my words shall not pass away.
34 ¶ And take heed to yourselves, lest at any time your hearts be overcharged with
surfeiting, and drunkenness, and cares of this life, and *so* that day come upon you
unawares.
35 For as a snare shall it come on all them that dwell on the face of the whole earth.
36 Watch ye therefore, and pray always, that ye may be accounted worthy to escape all
these things that shall come to pass, and to stand before the Son of man.
37 And in the day time he was teaching in the temple; and at night he went out, and
abode in the mount that is called *the mount* of Olives.
38 And all the people came early in the morning to him in the temple, for to hear him.
(Luke 21:5-38)

149 - DEPARTURE FROM THE TEMPLE AREA

According to the Gospel of Matthew

1 And Jesus went out, and departed from the temple: and his disciples came to *him* for
to shew him the buildings of the temple.
2 And Jesus said unto them, See ye not all these things? verily I say unto you, There
shall not be left here one stone upon another, that shall not be thrown down. (Matt 24:1-2)

According to the Gospel of Mark

1 And as he went out of the temple, one of his disciples saith unto him, Master, see
what manner of stones and what buildings *are here!*
2 And Jesus answering said unto him, Seest thou these great buildings? there shall not
be left one stone upon another, that shall not be thrown down. (Mark 13:1-2)

150 - THE SECOND PORTION OF JESUS' PROPHECY

3 And as he sat upon the mount of Olives over against the temple, Peter and James and
John and Andrew asked him privately,
4 Tell us, when shall these things be? and what *shall be* the sign when all these things
shall be fulfilled?
5 And Jesus answering them began to say, Take heed lest any *man* deceive you:
6 For many shall come in my name, saying, I am *Christ*; and shall deceive many.
7 And when ye shall hear of wars and rumours of wars, be ye not troubled: for *such
things* must needs be; but the end *shall* not *be* yet.
8 For nation shall rise against nation, and kingdom against kingdom: and there shall be
earthquakes in divers places, and there shall be famines and troubles: these *are* the
beginnings of sorrows.

9 ¶ But take heed to yourselves: for they shall deliver you up to councils; and in the
synagogues ye shall be beaten: and ye shall be brought before rulers and kings for my
sake, for a testimony against them.
10 And the gospel must first be published among all nations.
11 But when they shall lead *you*, and deliver you up, take no thought beforehand what
ye shall speak, neither do ye premeditate: but whatsoever shall be given you in that
hour, that speak ye: for it is not ye that speak, but the Holy Ghost.
12 Now the brother shall betray the brother to death, and the father the son; and
children shall rise up against *their* parents, and shall cause them to be put to death.
13 And ye shall be hated of all *men* for my name's sake: but he that shall endure unto
the end, the same shall be saved.
14 ¶ But when ye shall see the abomination of desolation, spoken of by Daniel the
prophet, standing where it ought not, (let him that readeth understand,) then let them
that be in Judæa flee to the mountains:
15 And let him that is on the housetop not go down into the house, neither enter *therein*,
to take any thing out of his house:
16 And let him that is in the field not turn back again for to take up his garment.
17 But woe to them that are with child, and to them that give suck in those days!
18 And pray ye that your flight be not in the winter.
19 For *in* those days shall be affliction, such as was not from the beginning of the
creation which God created unto this time, neither shall be.
20 And except that the Lord had shortened those days, no flesh should be saved: but for
the elect's sake, whom he hath chosen, he hath shortened the days.
21 And then if any man shall say to you, Lo, here *is* Christ; or, lo, *he is* there; believe
him not:
22 For false Christs and false prophets shall rise, and shall shew signs and wonders, to
seduce, if *it were* possible, even the elect.
23 But take ye heed: behold, I have foretold you all things.
24 ¶ But in those days, after that tribulation, the sun shall be darkened, and the moon
shall not give her light,
25 And the stars of heaven shall fall, and the powers that are in heaven shall be shaken.
26 And then shall they see the Son of man coming in the clouds with great power and
glory.
27 And then shall he send his angels, and shall gather together his elect from the four
winds, from the uttermost part of the earth to the uttermost part of heaven.
28 Now learn a parable of the fig tree; When her branch is yet tender, and putteth forth
leaves, ye know that summer is near:
29 So ye in like manner, when ye shall see these things come to pass, know that it is
nigh, *even* at the doors.
30 Verily I say unto you, that this generation shall not pass, till all these things be done.
31 Heaven and earth shall pass away: but my words shall not pass away.
32 ¶ But of that day and *that* hour knoweth no man, no, not the angels which are in
heaven, neither the Son, but the Father.
33 Take ye heed, watch and pray: for ye know not when the time is.
34 *For the Son of man is* as a man taking a far journey, who left his house, and gave
authority to his servants, and to every man his work, and commanded the porter to

watch.
35 Watch ye therefore: for ye know not when the master of the house cometh, at even,
or at midnight, or at the cockcrowing, or in the morning:
36 Lest coming suddenly he find you sleeping.
37 And what I say unto you I say unto all, Watch. (Mark 13:3-37)
3 ¶ And as he sat upon the mount of Olives, the disciples came unto him privately,
saying, Tell us, when shall these things be? and what *shall be* the sign of thy coming,
and of the end of the world?
4 And Jesus answered and said unto them, Take heed that no man deceive you.
5 For many shall come in my name, saying, I am Christ; and shall deceive many.
6 And ye shall hear of wars and rumours of wars: see that ye be not troubled: for all
these things must come to pass, but the end is not yet.
7 For nation shall rise against nation, and kingdom against kingdom: and there shall be
famines, and pestilences, and earthquakes, in divers places.
8 All these *are* the beginning of sorrows.
9 Then shall they deliver you up to be afflicted, and shall kill you: and ye shall be hated
of all nations for my name's sake.
10 And then shall many be offended, and shall betray one another, and shall hate one
another.
11 And many false prophets shall rise, and shall deceive many.
12 And because iniquity shall abound, the love of many shall wax cold.
13 But he that shall endure unto the end, the same shall be saved.
14 And this gospel of the kingdom shall be preached in all the world for a witness unto
all nations; and then shall the end come.
15 When ye therefore shall see the abomination of desolation, spoken of by Daniel the
prophet, stand in the holy place, (whoso readeth, let him understand:)
16 Then let them which be in Judæa flee into the mountains:
17 Let him which is on the housetop not come down to take any thing out of his house:
18 Neither let him which is in the field return back to take his clothes.
19 And woe unto them that are with child, and to them that give suck in those days!
20 But pray ye that your flight be not in the winter, neither on the sabbath day:
21 For then shall be great tribulation, such as was not since the beginning of the world
to this time, no, nor ever shall be.
22 And except those days should be shortened, there should no flesh be saved: but for
the elect's sake those days shall be shortened.
23 Then if any man shall say unto you, Lo, here *is* Christ, or there; believe *it* not.
24 For there shall arise false Christs, and false prophets, and shall shew great signs and
wonders; insomuch that, if *it were* possible, they shall deceive the very elect.
25 Behold, I have told you before.
26 Wherefore if they shall say unto you, Behold, he is in the desert; go not forth:
behold, *he is* in the secret chambers; believe *it* not.
27 For as the lightning cometh out of the east, and shineth even unto the west; so shall
also the coming of the Son of man be.
28 For wheresoever the carcase is, there will the eagles be gathered together.
29 Immediately after the tribulation of those days shall the sun be darkened, and the
moon shall not give her light, and the stars shall fall from heaven, and the powers of the

heavens shall be shaken:
30 And then shall appear the sign of the Son of man in heaven: and then shall all the
tribes of the earth mourn, and they shall see the Son of man coming in the clouds of
heaven with power and great glory.
31 And he shall send his angels with a great sound of a trumpet, and they shall gather
together his elect from the four winds, from one end of heaven to the other.
32 Now learn a parable of the fig tree; When his branch is yet tender, and putteth forth
leaves, ye know that summer *is* nigh:
33 So likewise ye, when ye shall see all these things, know that it is near, *even* at the
doors.
34 Verily I say unto you, This generation shall not pass, till all these things be fulfilled.
35 Heaven and earth shall pass away, but my words shall not pass away.
36 ¶ But of that day and hour knoweth no *man*, no, not the angels of heaven, but my
Father only.
37 But as the days of Noe *were*, so shall also the coming of the Son of man be.
38 For as in the days that were before the flood they were eating and drinking, marrying
and giving in marriage, until the day that Noe entered into the ark,
39 And knew not until the flood came, and took them all away; so shall also the coming
of the Son of man be.
40 Then shall two be in the field; the one shall be taken, and the other left.
41 Two *women shall be* grinding at the mill; the one shall be taken, and the other left.
42 ¶ Watch therefore: for ye know not what hour your Lord doth come.
43 But know this, that if the goodman of the house had known in what watch the thief
would come, he would have watched, and would not have suffered his house to be
broken up.
44 Therefore be ye also ready: for in such an hour as ye think not the Son of man
cometh.
45 Who then is a faithful and wise servant, whom his lord hath made ruler over his
household, to give them meat in due season?
46 Blessed *is* that servant, whom his lord when he cometh shall find so doing.
47 Verily I say unto you, That he shall make him ruler over all his goods.
48 But and if that evil servant shall say in his heart, My lord delayeth his coming;
49 And shall begin to smite *his* fellowservants, and to eat and drink with the drunken;
50 The lord of that servant shall come in a day when he looketh not for *him*, and in an
hour that he is not aware of,
51 And shall cut him asunder, and appoint *him* his portion with the hypocrites: there
shall be weeping and gnashing of teeth. (Matt 24:3-51)
1 Then shall the kingdom of heaven be likened unto ten virgins, which took their
lamps, and went forth to meet the bridegroom.
2 And five of them were wise, and five *were* foolish.
3 They that *were* foolish took their lamps, and took no oil with them:
4 But the wise took oil in their vessels with their lamps.
5 While the bridegroom tarried, they all slumbered and slept.
6 And at midnight there was a cry made, Behold, the bridegroom cometh; go ye out to
meet him.
7 Then all those virgins arose, and trimmed their lamps.

8 And the foolish said unto the wise, Give us of your oil; for our lamps are gone out.
9 But the wise answered, saying, *Not so*; lest there be not enough for us and you: but go
ye rather to them that sell, and buy for yourselves.
10 And while they went to buy, the bridegroom came; and they that were ready went in
with him to the marriage: and the door was shut.
11 Afterward came also the other virgins, saying, Lord, Lord, open to us.
12 But he answered and said, Verily I say unto you, I know you not.
13 Watch therefore, for ye know neither the day nor the hour wherein the Son of man
cometh.
14 ¶ For *the kingdom of heaven is* as a man travelling into a far country, *who* called his
own servants, and delivered unto them his goods.
15 And unto one he gave five talents, to another two, and to another one; to every man
according to his several ability; and straightway took his journey.
16 Then he that had received the five talents went and traded with the same, and made
them other five talents.
17 And likewise he that *had received* two, he also gained other two.
18 But he that had received one went and digged in the earth, and hid his lord's money.
19 After a long time the lord of those servants cometh, and reckoneth with them.
20 And so he that had received five talents came and brought other five talents, saying,
Lord, thou deliveredst unto me five talents: behold, I have gained beside them five
talents more.
21 His lord said unto him, Well done, *thou* good and faithful servant: thou hast been
faithful over a few things, I will make thee ruler over many things: enter thou into the
joy of thy lord.
22 He also that had received two talents came and said, Lord, thou deliveredst unto me
two talents: behold, I have gained two other talents beside them.
23 His lord said unto him, Well done, good and faithful servant; thou hast been faithful
over a few things, I will make thee ruler over many things: enter thou into the joy of thy
lord.
24 Then he which had received the one talent came and said, Lord, I knew thee that
thou art an hard man, reaping where thou hast not sown, and gathering where thou hast
not strawed:
25 And I was afraid, and went and hid thy talent in the earth: lo, *there* thou hast *that is*
thine.
26 His lord answered and said unto him, *Thou* wicked and slothful servant, thou
knewest that I reap where I sowed not, and gather where I have not strawed:
27 Thou oughtest therefore to have put my money to the exchangers, and *then* at my
coming I should have received mine own with usury.
28 Take therefore the talent from him, and give *it* unto him which hath ten talents.
29 For unto every one that hath shall be given, and he shall have abundance: but from
him that hath not shall be taken away even that which he hath.
30 And cast ye the unprofitable servant into outer darkness: there shall be weeping and
gnashing of teeth.
31 ¶ When the Son of man shall come in his glory, and all the holy angels with him,
then shall he sit upon the throne of his glory:
32 And before him shall be gathered all nations: and he shall separate them one from

another, as a shepherd divideth *his* sheep from the goats:
33 And he shall set the sheep on his right hand, but the goats on the left.
34 Then shall the King say unto them on his right hand, Come, ye blessed of my Father,
inherit the kingdom prepared for you from the foundation of the world:
35 For I was an hungered, and ye gave me meat: I was thirsty, and ye gave me drink: I
was a stranger, and ye took me in:
36 Naked, and ye clothed me: I was sick, and ye visited me: I was in prison, and ye
came unto me.
37 Then shall the righteous answer him, saying, Lord, when saw we thee an hungered,
and fed *thee*? or thirsty, and gave *thee* drink?
38 When saw we thee a stranger, and took *thee* in? or naked, and clothed *thee*?
39 Or when saw we thee sick, or in prison, and came unto thee?
40 And the King shall answer and say unto them, Verily I say unto you, Inasmuch as ye
have done *it* unto one of the least of these my brethren, ye have done *it* unto me.
41 Then shall he say also unto them on the left hand, Depart from me, ye cursed, into
everlasting fire, prepared for the devil and his angels:
42 For I was an hungered, and ye gave me no meat: I was thirsty, and ye gave me no
drink:
43 I was a stranger, and ye took me not in: naked, and ye clothed me not: sick, and in
prison, and ye visited me not.
44 Then shall they also answer him, saying, Lord, when saw we thee an hungered, or
athirst, or a stranger, or naked, or sick, or in prison, and did not minister unto thee?
45 Then shall he answer them, saying, Verily I say unto you, Inasmuch as ye did *it* not
to one of the least of these, ye did *it* not to me.
46 And these shall go away into everlasting punishment: but the righteous into life
eternal. (Matt 25:1-46)

151 - THE 6TH ANNOUNCEMENT OF SUFFERINGS

1 And it came to pass, when Jesus had finished all these sayings, he said unto his
disciples,
2 Ye know that after two days is *the feast of* the passover, and the Son of man is
betrayed to be crucified. (Matt 26:1-2)

152 - PLOTTING TO KILL JESUS WITHOUT CREATING AN UPROAR

According to the Gospel of Luke

1 Now the feast of unleavened bread drew nigh, which is called the Passover.
2 And the chief priests and scribes sought how they might kill him; for they feared the
people. (Luke 22:1-2)

According to the Gospel of Mark

1 After two days was *the feast of* the passover, and of unleavened bread: and the chief
priests and the scribes sought how they might take him by craft, and put *him* to death.
2 But they said, Not on the feast *day*, lest there be an uproar of the people. (Mark 14:1-2)

According to the Gospel of Matthew

3 Then assembled together the chief priests, and the scribes, and the elders of the
people, unto the palace of the high priest, who was called Caiaphas,
4 And consulted that they might take Jesus by subtilty, and kill *him*.

5 But they said, Not on the feast *day*, lest there be an uproar among the people. (Matt 26:3-
5)

153 - THE THIRD ANOINTING

According to the Gospel of Matthew

6 ¶ Now when Jesus was in Bethany, in the house of Simon the leper,
7 There came unto him a woman having an alabaster box of very precious ointment,
and poured it on his head, as he sat *at meat*.
8 But when his disciples saw *it*, they had indignation, saying, To what purpose *is* this
waste?
9 For this ointment might have been sold for much, and given to the poor.
10 When Jesus understood *it*, he said unto them, Why trouble ye the woman? for she
hath wrought a good work upon me.
11 For ye have the poor always with you; but me ye have not always.
12 For in that she hath poured this ointment on my body, she did *it* for my burial.
13 Verily I say unto you, Wheresoever this gospel shall be preached in the whole
world, *there* shall also this, that this woman hath done, be told for a memorial of her.
(Matt 26:6-13)

According to the Gospel of Mark

3 ¶ And being in Bethany in the house of Simon the leper, as he sat at meat, there came
a woman having an alabaster box of ointment of spikenard very precious; and she brake
the box, and poured *it* on his head.
4 And there were some that had indignation within themselves, and said, Why was this
waste of the ointment made?
5 For it might have been sold for more than three hundred pence, and have been given
to the poor. And they murmured against her.
6 And Jesus said, Let her alone; why trouble ye her? she hath wrought a good work on
me.
7 For ye have the poor with you always, and whensoever ye will ye may do them good:
but me ye have not always.
8 She hath done what she could: she is come aforehand to anoint my body to the
burying.
9 Verily I say unto you, Wheresoever this gospel shall be preached throughout the
whole world, *this* also that she hath done shall be spoken of for a memorial of her. (Mark
14:3-9)

154 - JUDAS ARRANGES THE BETRAYAL OF JESUS

According to the Gospel of Mark

10 ¶ And Judas Iscariot, one of the twelve, went unto the chief priests, to betray him
unto them.
11 And when they heard *it*, they were glad, and promised to give him money. And he
sought how he might conveniently betray him. (Mark 14:10-11)

According to the Gospel of Luke

3 ¶ Then entered Satan into Judas surnamed Iscariot, being of the number of the
twelve.
4 And he went his way, and communed with the chief priests and captains, how he
might betray him unto them.
5 And they were glad, and covenanted to give him money.

6 And he promised, and sought opportunity to betray him unto them in the absence of
the multitude. (Luke 22:3-6)

According to the Gospel of Matthew

14 ¶ Then one of the twelve, called Judas Iscariot, went unto the chief priests,
15 And said *unto them*, What will ye give me, and I will deliver him unto you? And
they covenanted with him for thirty pieces of silver.
16 And from that time he sought opportunity to betray him. (Matt 26:14-16)

155 - PREPARATION FOR THE "LAST SUPPER"

According to the Gospel of Matthew

17 ¶ Now the first *day* of the *feast of* unleavened bread the disciples came to Jesus,
saying unto him, Where wilt thou that we prepare for thee to eat the passover?
18 And he said, Go into the city to such a man, and say unto him, The Master saith, My
time is at hand; I will keep the passover at thy house with my disciples.
19 And the disciples did as Jesus had appointed them; and they made ready the
passover. (Matt 26:17-19)

According to the Gospel of Mark

12 ¶ And the first day of unleavened bread, when they killed the passover, his disciples
said unto him, Where wilt thou that we go and prepare that thou mayest eat the
passover?
13 And he sendeth forth two of his disciples, and saith unto them, Go ye into the city,
and there shall meet you a man bearing a pitcher of water: follow him.
14 And wheresoever he shall go in, say ye to the goodman of the house, The Master
saith, Where is the guestchamber, where I shall eat the passover with my disciples?
15 And he will shew you a large upper room furnished *and* prepared: there make ready
for us.
16 And his disciples went forth, and came into the city, and found as he had said unto
them: and they made ready the passover. (Mark 14:12-16)

According to the Gospel of Luke

7 ¶ Then came the day of unleavened bread, when the passover must be killed.
8 And he sent Peter and John, saying, Go and prepare us the passover, that we may eat.
9 And they said unto him, Where wilt thou that we prepare?
10 And he said unto them, Behold, when ye are entered into the city, there shall a man
meet you, bearing a pitcher of water; follow him into the house where he entereth in.
11 And ye shall say unto the goodman of the house, The Master saith unto thee, Where
is the guestchamber, where I shall eat the passover with my disciples?
12 And he shall shew you a large upper room furnished: there make ready.
13 And they went, and found as he had said unto them: and they made ready the
passover. (Luke 22:7-13)

CHAPTER 156
SUPPER - FOOT WASHING - THE NEW TESTAMENT

The timing and reason for Jesus' "last supper" with his disciples

1 Now before the feast of the passover, when Jesus knew that his hour was come that
he should depart out of this world unto the Father, having loved his own which were in
the world, he loved them unto the end. (John 13:1)

The arrival of Jesus and the Apostles

According to the Gospel of Mark

17 And in the evening he cometh with the twelve. (Mark 14:17)

According to the Gospel of Matthew

20 Now when the even was come, he sat down with the twelve. (Matt 26:20)

According to the Gospel of Luke

14 And when the hour was come, he sat down, and the twelve apostles with him. (Luke 22:14)

During the meal Jesus announces that he will be betrayed

According to the Gospel of Luke

15 And he said unto them, With desire I have desired to eat this passover with you
before I suffer:
16 For I say unto you, I will not any more eat thereof, until it be fulfilled in the
kingdom of God.
17 And he took the cup, and gave thanks, and said, Take this, and divide *it* among
yourselves:
18 For I say unto you, I will not drink of the fruit of the vine, until the kingdom of God
shall come.
19 ¶ And he took bread, and gave thanks, and brake *it*, and gave unto them, saying,
This is my body which is given for you: this do in remembrance of me. (Luke 22:15-19)

According to the Gospel of Matthew

21 And as they did eat, he said, Verily I say unto you, that one of you shall betray me.
22 And they were exceeding sorrowful, and began every one of them to say unto him,
Lord, is it I?
23 And he answered and said, He that dippeth *his* hand with me in the dish, the same
shall betray me.
24 The Son of man goeth as it is written of him: but woe unto that man by whom the
Son of man is betrayed! it had been good for that man if he had not been born.
25 Then Judas, which betrayed him, answered and said, Master, is it I? He said unto
him, Thou hast said. (Matt 26:21-25)

According to the Gospel of Mark

18 And as they sat and did eat, Jesus said, Verily I say unto you, One of you which
eateth with me shall betray me.
19 And they began to be sorrowful, and to say unto him one by one, *Is* it I? and another
said, *Is* it I?
20 And he answered and said unto them, *It is* one of the twelve, that dippeth with me in
the dish.
21 The Son of man indeed goeth, as it is written of him: but woe to that man by whom
the Son of man is betrayed! good were it for that man if he had never been born. (Mark 14:18-21)

Washing the disciple's feet

2 And supper being ended, the devil having now put into the heart of Judas Iscariot,
Simon's *son*, to betray him;
3 Jesus knowing that the Father had given all things into his hands, and that he was
come from God, and went to God;

4 He riseth from supper, and laid aside his garments; and took a towel, and girded
himself.
5 After that he poureth water into a basin, and began to wash the disciples' feet, and to
wipe *them* with the towel wherewith he was girded.
6 Then cometh he to Simon Peter: and Peter saith unto him, Lord, dost thou wash my
feet?
7 Jesus answered and said unto him, What I do thou knowest not now; but thou shalt
know hereafter.
8 Peter saith unto him, Thou shalt never wash my feet. Jesus answered him, If I wash
thee not, thou hast no part with me.
9 Simon Peter saith unto him, Lord, not my feet only, but also *my* hands and *my* head.
10 Jesus saith to him, He that is washed needeth not save to wash *his* feet, but is clean
every whit: and ye are clean, but not all.
11 For he knew who should betray him; therefore said he, Ye are not all clean.
12 So after he had washed their feet, and had taken his garments, and was set down
again, he said unto them, Know ye what I have done to you?
13 Ye call me Master and Lord: and ye say well; for *so* I am.
14 If I then, *your* Lord and Master, have washed your feet; ye also ought to wash one
another's feet.
15 For I have given you an example, that ye should do as I have done to you.
16 Verily, verily, I say unto you, The servant is not greater than his lord; neither he that
is sent greater than he that sent him.
17 If ye know these things, happy are ye if ye do them. (John 13:1-17)

Jesus *again* announces that he will be betrayed, and that the betrayer would be an Apostle

According to the Gospel of John

18 I speak not of you all: I know whom I have chosen: but that the scripture may be
fulfilled, He that eateth bread with me hath lifted up his heel against me.
19 Now I tell you before it come, that, when it is come to pass, ye may believe that I am
he.
20 Verily, verily, I say unto you, He that receiveth whomsoever I send receiveth me;
and he that receiveth me receiveth him that sent me.
21 When Jesus had thus said, he was troubled in spirit, and testified, and said, Verily,
verily, I say unto you, that one of you shall betray me.
22 Then the disciples looked one on another, doubting of whom he spake. (John 1318-:22)

According to the Gospel of Luke

20 Likewise also the cup after supper, saying, This cup *is* the new testament in my
blood, which is shed for you.
21 ¶ But, behold, the hand of him that betrayeth me *is* with me on the table.
22 And truly the Son of man goeth, as it was determined: but woe unto that man by
whom he is betrayed!
23 And they began to inquire among themselves, which of them it was that should do
this thing. (Luke 22:20 -23)

Judas Iscariot leaves the others to carry out the betrayal

23 Now there was leaning on Jesus' bosom one of his disciples, whom Jesus loved.
24 Simon Peter therefore beckoned to him, that he should ask who it should be of

whom he spake.
25 He then lying on Jesus' breast saith unto him, Lord, who is it?
26 Jesus answered, He it is, to whom I shall give a sop, when I have dipped *it*. And
when he had dipped the sop, he gave *it* to Judas Iscariot, *the son* of Simon.
27 And after the sop Satan entered into him.
27 Then said Jesus unto him, That thou doest, do quickly.
28 Now no man at the table knew for what intent he spake this unto him.
29 For some *of them* thought, because Judas had the bag, that Jesus had said unto him,
Buy *those things* that we have need of against the feast; or, that he should give
something to the poor.
30 He then having received the sop went immediately out: and it was night. (John 13:27-30)

After eating and washing the disciples feet, the New Testament, *διαθήκη diathēkēis*, is announced

According to the Gospel of Mark

22 ¶ And as they did eat, Jesus took bread, and blessed, and brake *it*, and gave to them,
and said, Take, eat: this is my body.
23 And he took the cup, and when he had given thanks, he gave *it* to them: and they all
drank of it.
24 And he said unto them, This is my blood of the new testament, which is shed for
many.
25 Verily I say unto you, I will drink no more of the fruit of the vine, until that day that
I drink it new in the kingdom of God. (Mark 14:22-25)

According to the Gospel of Matthew

26 ¶ And as they were eating, Jesus took bread, and blessed *it*, and brake *it*, and gave *it*
to the disciples, and said, Take, eat; this is my body.
27 And he took the cup, and gave thanks, and gave *it* to them, saying, Drink ye all of it;
28 For this is my blood of the new testament, which is shed for many for the remission
of sins.
29 But I say unto you, I will not drink henceforth of this fruit of the vine, until that day
when I drink it new with you in my Father's kingdom. (Matt 26:26-29)

The "new" commandment (ἐντολή, entolē)

31 ¶ Therefore, when he was gone out, Jesus said, Now is the Son of man glorified, and
God is glorified in him.
32 If God be glorified in him, God shall also glorify him in himself, and shall
straightway glorify him.
33 Little children, yet a little while I am with you. Ye shall seek me: and as I said unto
the Jews, Whither I go, ye cannot come; so now I say to you.
34 A new commandment I give unto you, That ye love one another; as I have loved
you, that ye also love one another.
35 By this shall all *men* know that ye are my disciples, if ye have love one to another.
(John 13:31-35)

Peter's 1st profession of loyalty

36 ¶ Simon Peter said unto him, Lord, whither goest thou? Jesus answered him,
Whither I go, thou canst not follow me now; but thou shalt follow me afterwards.
37 Peter said unto him, Lord, why cannot I follow thee now? I will lay down my life
for thy sake. (John 13:36-37)

Jesus' 1st warning to Peter that he will deny him

38 Jesus answered him, Wilt thou lay down thy life for my sake? Verily, verily, I say
unto thee, The cock shall not crow, till thou hast denied me thrice. (John 13:38)

The disciples are again arguing "who should be the greatest" shortly *after* Jesus had washed their feet!

24 ¶ And there was also a strife among them, which of them should be accounted the
greatest.
25 And he said unto them, The kings of the Gentiles exercise lordship over them; and
they that exercise authority upon them are called benefactors.
26 But ye *shall* not *be* so: but he that is greatest among you, let him be as the younger;
and he that is chief, as he that doth serve.
27 For whether *is* greater, he that sitteth at meat, or he that serveth? *is* not he that sitteth
at meat? but I am among you as he that serveth.
28 Ye are they which have continued with me in my temptations.
29 And I appoint unto you a kingdom, as my Father hath appointed unto me;
30 That ye may eat and drink at my table in my kingdom, and sit on thrones judging the
twelve tribes of Israel. (Luke 22:24-30)

Peter is warned that he was at that very moment being tested

31 ¶ And the Lord said, Simon, Simon, behold, Satan hath desired *to have* you, that he
may sift *you* as wheat:
32 But I have prayed for thee, that thy faith fail not: and when thou art converted,
strengthen thy brethren. (Luke 22:31-32)

Peter's 2nd profession of loyalty

33 And he said unto him, Lord, I am ready to go with thee, both into prison, and to
death. (Luke 22:33)

Jesus' 2nd warning to Peter

34 And he said, I tell thee, Peter, the cock shall not crow this day, before that thou shalt
thrice deny that thou knowest me. (Luke 22:34)

157 - REVISED INSTRUCTIONS FOR CHANGED CONDITIONS

35 And he said unto them, When I sent you without purse, and scrip, and shoes, lacked
ye any thing? And they said, Nothing.
36 Then said he unto them, But now, he that hath a purse, let him take *it*, and likewise
his scrip: and he that hath no sword, let him sell his garment, and buy one.
37 For I say unto you, that this that is written must yet be accomplished in me, And he
was reckoned among the transgressors: for the things concerning me have an end.
38 And they said, Lord, behold, here *are* two swords. And he said unto them, It is
enough. (Luke 22:35-38)

158 - DISCOURSE ON THE COMFORTER

(During the Last Supper)

1 Let not your heart be troubled: ye believe in God, believe also in me.
2 In my Father's house are many mansions: if *it were* not *so*, I would have told you. I
go to prepare a place for you.
3 And if I go and prepare a place for you, I will come again, and receive you unto
myself; that where I am, *there* ye may be also.
4 And whither I go ye know, and the way ye know.

5 Thomas saith unto him, Lord, we know not whither thou goest; and how can we
know the way?
6 Jesus saith unto him, I am the way, the truth, and the life: no man cometh unto the
Father, but by me.
7 If ye had known me, ye should have known my Father also: and from henceforth ye
know him, and have seen him.
8 Philip saith unto him, Lord, shew us the Father, and it sufficeth us.
9 Jesus saith unto him, Have I been so long time with you, and yet hast thou not known
me, Philip? he that hath seen me hath seen the Father; and how sayest thou *then*, Shew
us the Father?
10 Believest thou not that I am in the Father, and the Father in me? the words that I
speak unto you I speak not of myself: but the Father that dwelleth in me, he doeth the
works.
11 Believe me that I *am* in the Father, and the Father in me: or else believe me for the
very works' sake.
12 Verily, verily, I say unto you, He that believeth on me, the works that I do shall he
do also; and greater *works* than these shall he do; because I go unto my Father.
13 And whatsoever ye shall ask in my name, that will I do, that the Father may be
glorified in the Son.
14 If ye shall ask any thing in my name, I will do *it*.
15 If ye love me, keep my commandments.
16 And I will pray the Father, and he shall give you another Comforter, that he may
abide with you for ever;
17 *Even* the Spirit of truth; whom the world cannot receive, because it seeth him not,
neither knoweth him: but ye know him; for he dwelleth with you, and shall be in you.
18 I will not leave you comfortless: I will come to you.
19 Yet a little while, and the world seeth me no more; but ye see me: because I live, ye
shall live also.
20 At that day ye shall know that I *am* in my Father, and ye in me, and I in you.
21 He that hath my commandments, and keepeth them, he it is that loveth me: and he
that loveth me shall be loved of my Father, and I will love him, and will manifest
myself to him.
22 Judas saith unto him, not Iscariot, Lord, how is it that thou wilt manifest thyself unto
us, and not unto the world?
23 Jesus answered and said unto him, If a man love me, he will keep my words: and my
Father will love him, and we will come unto him, and make our abode with him.
24 He that loveth me not keepeth not my sayings: and the word which ye hear is not
mine, but the Father's which sent me.
25 These things have I spoken unto you, being *yet* present with you.
26 But the Comforter, *which is* the Holy Ghost, whom the Father will send in my name,
he shall teach you all things, and bring all things to your remembrance, whatsoever I
have said unto you.
27 Peace I leave with you, my peace I give unto you: not as the world giveth, give I
unto you. Let not your heart be troubled, neither let it be afraid.
28 Ye have heard how I said unto you, I go away, and come *again* unto you. If ye
loved me, ye would rejoice, because I said, I go unto the Father: for my Father is

greater than I.
29 And now I have told you before it come to pass, that, when it is come to pass, ye
might believe.
30 Hereafter I will not talk much with you: for the prince of this world cometh, and
hath nothing in me.
31 But that the world may know that I love the Father; and as the Father gave me
commandment, even so I do. Arise, let us go hence. (John 14:1-31)

159 - DISCOURSE ON DEMONSTRATION

(During the Last Supper)

1 I am the true vine, and my Father is the husbandman.
2 Every branch in me that beareth not fruit he taketh away: and every *branch* that
beareth fruit, he purgeth it, that it may bring forth more fruit.
3 Now ye are clean through the word which I have spoken unto you.
4 Abide in me, and I in you. As the branch cannot bear fruit of itself, except it abide in
the vine; no more can ye, except ye abide in me.
5 I am the vine, ye *are* the branches: He that abideth in me, and I in him, the same
bringeth forth much fruit: for without me ye can do nothing.
6 If a man abide not in me, he is cast forth as a branch, and is withered; and men gather
them, and cast *them* into the fire, and they are burned.
7 If ye abide in me, and my words abide in you, ye shall ask what ye will, and it shall
be done unto you.
8 Herein is my Father glorified, that ye bear much fruit; so shall ye be my disciples.
9 As the Father hath loved me, so have I loved you: continue ye in my love.
10 If ye keep my commandments, ye shall abide in my love; even as I have kept my
Father's commandments, and abide in his love.
11 These things have I spoken unto you, that my joy might remain in you, and *that* your
joy might be full.
12 This is my commandment, That ye love one another, as I have loved you.
13 Greater love hath no man than this, that a man lay down his life for his friends.
14 Ye are my friends, if ye do whatsoever I command you.
15 Henceforth I call you not servants; for the servant knoweth not what his lord doeth:
but I have called you friends; for all things that I have heard of my Father I have made
known unto you.
16 Ye have not chosen me, but I have chosen you, and ordained you, that ye should go
and bring forth fruit, and *that* your fruit should remain: that whatsoever ye shall ask of
the Father in my name, he may give it you.
17 These things I command you, that ye love one another.
18 If the world hate you, ye know that it hated me before *it hated* you.
19 If ye were of the world, the world would love his own: but because ye are not of the
world, but I have chosen you out of the world, therefore the world hateth you.
20 Remember the word that I said unto you, The servant is not greater than his lord. If
they have persecuted me, they will also persecute you; if they have kept my saying,
they will keep yours also.
21 But all these things will they do unto you for my name's sake, because they know
not him that sent me.
22 If I had not come and spoken unto them, they had not had sin: but now they have no

cloak for their sin.
23 He that hateth me hateth my Father also.
24 If I had not done among them the works which none other man did, they had not had
sin: but now have they both seen and hated both me and my Father.
25 But *this cometh to pass*, that the word might be fulfilled that is written in their law,
They hated me without a cause.
26 But when the Comforter is come, whom I will send unto you from the Father, *even*
the Spirit of truth, which proceedeth from the Father, he shall testify of me:
27 And ye also shall bear witness, because ye have been with me from the beginning.
(John 15:1-27)

160 - THE LAST HOUR REMINDER: TAKE CARE NOT TO DESERT

(During the Last Supper)

1 These things have I spoken unto you, that ye should not be offended.
2 They shall put you out of the synagogues: yea, the time cometh, that whosoever
killeth you will think that he doeth God service.
3 And these things will they do unto you, because they have not known the Father, nor
me.
4 But these things have I told you, that when the time shall come, ye may remember
that I told you of them. And these things I said not unto you at the beginning, because I
was with you.
5 But now I go my way to him that sent me; and none of you asketh me, Whither goest
thou?
6 But because I have said these things unto you, sorrow hath filled your heart.
7 Nevertheless I tell you the truth; It is expedient for you that I go away: for if I go not
away, the Comforter will not come unto you; but if I depart, I will send him unto you.
8 And when he is come, he will reprove the world of sin, and of righteousness, and of
judgment:
9 Of sin, because they believe not on me;
10 Of righteousness, because I go to my Father, and ye see me no more;
11 Of judgment, because the prince of this world is judged.
12 I have yet many things to say unto you, but ye cannot bear them now.
13 Howbeit when he, the Spirit of truth, is come, he will guide you into all truth: for he
shall not speak of himself; but whatsoever he shall hear, *that* shall he speak: and he will
shew you things to come.
14 He shall glorify me: for he shall receive of mine, and shall shew *it* unto you.
15 All things that the Father hath are mine: therefore said I, that he shall take of mine,
and shall shew *it* unto you.
16 A little while, and ye shall not see me: and again, a little while, and ye shall see me,
because I go to the Father.
17 Then said *some* of his disciples among themselves, What is this that he saith unto us,
A little while, and ye shall not see me: and again, a little while, and ye shall see me:
and, Because I go to the Father?
18 They said therefore, What is this that he saith, A little while? we cannot tell what he
saith.
19 Now Jesus knew that they were desirous to ask him, and said unto them, Do ye
inquire among yourselves of that I said, A little while, and ye shall not see me: and

again, a little while, and ye shall see me?
20 Verily, verily, I say unto you, That ye shall weep and lament, but the world shall
rejoice: and ye shall be sorrowful, but your sorrow shall be turned into joy.
21 A woman when she is in travail hath sorrow, because her hour is come: but as soon
as she is delivered of the child, she remembereth no more the anguish, for joy that a
man is born into the world.
22 And ye now therefore have sorrow: but I will see you again, and your heart shall
rejoice, and your joy no man taketh from you.
23 And in that day ye shall ask me nothing. Verily, verily, I say unto you, Whatsoever
ye shall ask the Father in my name, he will give *it* you.
24 Hitherto have ye asked nothing in my name: ask, and ye shall receive, that your joy
may be full.
25 These things have I spoken unto you in proverbs: but the time cometh, when I shall
no more speak unto you in proverbs, but I shall shew you plainly of the Father
26 At that day ye shall ask in my name: and I say not unto you, that I will pray the
Father for you:
27 For the Father himself loveth you, because ye have loved me, and have believed that
I came out from God.
28 I came forth from the Father, and am come into the world: again, I leave the world,
and go to the Father.
29 His disciples said unto him, Lo, now speakest thou plainly, and speakest no proverb.
30 Now are we sure that thou knowest all things, and needest not that any man should
ask thee: by this we believe that thou camest forth from God.
31 Jesus answered them, Do ye now believe?
32 Behold, the hour cometh, yea, is now come, that ye shall be scattered, every man to
his own, and shall leave me alone: and yet I am not alone, because the Father is with
me.
33 These things I have spoken unto you, that in me ye might have peace. In the world
ye shall have tribulation: but be of good cheer; I have overcome the world. (John 16:1-33)

161 - THE FAREWELL DISCOURSE
(During the Last Supper)

1 These words spake Jesus, and lifted up his eyes to heaven, and said, Father, the hour
2 is come; glorify thy Son, that thy Son also may glorify thee:
2 As thou hast given him power over all flesh, that he should give eternal life to as
many as thou hast given him.
3 And this is life eternal, that they might know thee the only true God, and Jesus Christ,
whom thou hast sent.
4 I have glorified thee on the earth: I have finished the work which thou gavest me to
do.
5 And now, O Father, glorify thou me with thine own self with the glory which I had
with thee before the world was.
6 I have manifested thy name unto the men which thou gavest me out of the world:
thine they were, and thou gavest them me; and they have kept thy word.
7 Now they have known that all things whatsoever thou hast given me are of thee.
8 For I have given unto them the words which thou gavest me; and they have received
them, and have known surely that I came out from thee, and they have believed that

thou didst send me.
9 I pray for them: I pray not for the world, but for them which thou hast given me; for
they are thine.
10 And all mine are thine, and thine are mine; and I am glorified in them.
11 And now I am no more in the world, but these are in the world, and I come to thee.
Holy Father, keep through thine own name those whom thou hast given me, that they
may be one, as we *are*.
12 While I was with them in the world, I kept them in thy name: those that thou gavest
me I have kept, and none of them is lost, but the son of perdition; that the scripture
might be fulfilled.
13 And now come I to thee; and these things I speak in the world, that they might have
my joy fulfilled in themselves.
14 I have given them thy word; and the world hath hated them, because they are not of
the world, even as I am not of the world.
15 I pray not that thou shouldest take them out of the world, but that thou shouldest
keep them from the evil.
16 They are not of the world, even as I am not of the world.
17 Sanctify them through thy truth: thy word is truth.
18 As thou hast sent me into the world, even so have I also sent them into the world.
19 And for their sakes I sanctify myself, that they also might be sanctified through the
truth.
20 Neither pray I for these alone, but for them also which shall believe on me through
their word;
21 That they all may be one; as thou, Father, *art* in me, and I in thee, that they also may
be one in us: that the world may believe that thou hast sent me.
22 And the glory which thou gavest me I have given them; that they may be one, even
as we are one:
23 I in them, and thou in me, that they may be made perfect in one; and that the world
may know that thou hast sent me, and hast loved them, as thou hast loved me.
24 Father, I will that they also, whom thou hast given me, be with me where I am; that
they may behold my glory, which thou hast given me: for thou lovedst me before the
foundation of the world.
25 O righteous Father, the world hath not known thee: but I have known thee, and these
have known that thou hast sent me.
26 And I have declared unto them thy name, and will declare *it*: that the love wherewith
thou hast loved me may be in them, and I in them. (John 17:1-26)

162 - DEPARTURE TO THE MOUNT OF OLIVES

According to the Gospel of Mark

26 ¶ And when they had sung an hymn, they went out into the mount of Olives. (Mark 14:26)

According to the Gospel of Matthew

30 And when they had sung an hymn, they went out into the mount of Olives.
31 Then saith Jesus unto them, All ye shall be offended because of me this night: for it
is written, I will smite the shepherd, and the sheep of the flock shall be scattered
abroad.
32 But after I am risen again, I will go before you into Galilee. (Matt 26:30-32)

Peter's 3rd declaration of loyalty

33 Peter answered and said unto him, Though all *men* shall be offended because of
thee, *yet* will I never be offended. (Matt 26:33)

Jesus' 3rd warning to Peter that he would deny him, emphasizing with the words "this night"

34 Jesus said unto him, Verily I say unto thee, That this night, before the cock crow,
thou shalt deny me thrice. (Matt 26:34)

Peter's 4th and the disciples 1st declaration of loyalty, here adding: "even unto death"

35 Peter said unto him, Though I should die with thee, yet will I not deny thee.
Likewise also said all the disciples. (Matt 26:35)

According to the Gospel of John

1 When Jesus had spoken these words, he went forth with his disciples over the brook
Cedron, where was a garden, into the which he entered, and his disciples. (John 18:1)

163 - IN THE GARDEN

This first time Jesus prayed by himself. He withdrew "from them about a stone's cast"

39 ¶ And he came out, and went, as he was wont, to the mount of Olives; and his
disciples also followed him.
40 And when he was at the place, he said unto them, Pray that ye enter not into
temptation.
41 And he was withdrawn from them about a stone's cast, and kneeled down, and
prayed,
42 Saying, Father, if thou be willing, remove this cup from me: nevertheless not my
will, but thine, be done.
43 And there appeared an angel unto him from heaven, strengthening him.
44 And being in an agony he prayed more earnestly: and his sweat was as it were great
drops of blood falling down to the ground.
45 And when he rose up from prayer, and was come to his disciples, he found them
sleeping for sorrow,
46 And said unto them, Why sleep ye? rise and pray, lest ye enter into temptation. (Luke
22:39-46)
27 And Jesus saith unto them, All ye shall be offended because of me this night: for it is
written, I will smite the shepherd, and the sheep shall be scattered.
28 But after that I am risen, I will go before you into Galilee. (Mark 14:27-28)

Peter's 5th declaration of loyalty, this time adding, "even if all the others should desert"

29 But Peter said unto him, Although all shall be offended, yet *will* not I. (Mark 14:29)

Jesus' 4th warning to Peter that he will betray him, adding "this day, even in this night"

30 And Jesus saith unto him, Verily I say unto thee, That this day, *even* in this night,
before the cock crow twice, thou shalt deny me thrice. (Mark 14:30)

Peter's 6th and final declaration of loyalty, including the words, "if I should die with thee"

31 But he spake the more vehemently, If I should die with thee, I will not deny thee in
any wise. Likewise also said they all. (Mark 14:31)

This time Jesus takes Peter, James and John when he prays, while the others sit apart

According to the Gospel of Mark

32 And they came to a place which was named Gethsemane: and he saith to his
disciples, Sit ye here, while I shall pray.
33 And he taketh with him Peter and James and John, and began to be sore amazed, and
to be very heavy;
34 And saith unto them, My soul is exceeding sorrowful unto death: tarry ye here, and
watch.
35 And he went forward a little, and fell on the ground, and prayed that, if it were
possible, the hour might pass from him.
36 And he said, Abba, Father, all things *are* possible unto thee; take away this cup from
me: nevertheless not what I will, but what thou wilt.
37 And he cometh, and findeth them sleeping, and saith unto Peter, Simon, sleepest
thou? couldest not thou watch one hour?
38 Watch ye and pray, lest ye enter into temptation. The spirit truly *is* ready, but the
flesh *is* weak.
39 And again he went away, and prayed, and spake the same words.
40 And when he returned, he found them asleep again, (for their eyes were heavy,)
neither wist they what to answer him.
41 And he cometh the third time, and saith unto them, Sleep on now, and take *your* rest:
it is enough, the hour is come; behold, the Son of man is betrayed into the hands of
sinners.
42 Rise up, let us go; lo, he that betrayeth me is at hand. (Mark 14:32-42)

According to the Gospel of Matthew

36 ¶ Then cometh Jesus with them unto a place called Gethsemane, and saith unto the
disciples, Sit ye here, while I go and pray yonder.
37 And he took with him Peter and the two sons of Zebedee, and began to be sorrowful
and very heavy.
38 Then saith he unto them, My soul is exceeding sorrowful, even unto death: tarry ye
here, and watch with me.
39 And he went a little farther, and fell on his face, and prayed, saying, O my Father, if
it be possible, let this cup pass from me: nevertheless not as I will, but as thou *wilt*.
40 And he cometh unto the disciples, and findeth them asleep, and saith unto Peter,
What, could ye not watch with me one hour?
41 Watch and pray, that ye enter not into temptation: the spirit indeed *is* willing, but the
flesh *is* weak.
42 He went away again the second time, and prayed, saying, O my Father, if this cup
may not pass away from me, except I drink it, thy will be done.
43 And he came and found them asleep again: for their eyes were heavy.
44 And he left them, and went away again, and prayed the third time, saying the same
words.
45 Then cometh he to his disciples, and saith unto them, Sleep on now, and take *your*
rest: behold, the hour is at hand, and the Son of man is betrayed into the hands of
sinners.
46 Rise, let us be going: behold, he is at hand that doth betray me. (Matt 26:36-46)

164 - THE BETRAYAL AND ARREST

2 And Judas also, which betrayed him, knew the place: for Jesus ofttimes resorted
thither with his disciples.
3 Judas then, having received a band *of men* and officers from the chief priests and
Pharisees, cometh thither with lanterns and torches and weapons. (John 18:2-3)

Judas' signal to confirm the identity of Jesus

According to the Gospel of Matthew

47 ¶ And while he yet spake, lo, Judas, one of the twelve, came, and with him a great
multitude with swords and staves, from the chief priests and elders of the people.
48 Now he that betrayed him gave them a sign, saying, Whomsoever I shall kiss, that
same is he: hold him fast. (Matt 26:47-48)

According to the Gospel of Mark

43 ¶ And immediately, while he yet spake, cometh Judas, one of the twelve, and with
him a great multitude with swords and staves, from the chief priests and the scribes and
the elders.
44 And he that betrayed him had given them a token, saying, Whomsoever I shall kiss,
that same is he; take him, and lead *him* away safely. (Mark 14:43-44)

Jesus addresses the entourage

4 Jesus therefore, knowing all things that should come upon him, went forth, and said
unto them, Whom seek ye?
5 They answered him, Jesus of Nazareth. Jesus saith unto them, I am *he*. And Judas
also, which betrayed him, stood with them.
6 As soon then as he had said unto them, I am *he*, they went backward, and fell to the
ground.
7 Then asked he them again, Whom seek ye? And they said, Jesus of Nazareth.
8 Jesus answered, I have told you that I am *he*: if therefore ye seek me, let these go
their way:
9 That the saying might be fulfilled, which he spake, Of them which thou gavest me
have I lost none. (John 18:4-9)

According to the Gospel of Luke

47 ¶ And while he yet spake, behold a multitude, and he that was called Judas, one of
the twelve, went before them, and drew near unto Jesus to kiss him. (Luke 22:47)

The kiss of betrayal (kiss, *καταφιλέω kataphileō*, an ostentatious embrace

According to the Gospel of Luke

48 But Jesus said unto him, Judas, betrayest thou the Son of man with a kiss? (Luke 22:48)

According to the Gospel of Mark

45 And as soon as he was come, he goeth straightway to him, and saith, Master, master;
and kissed him. (Mark 14:45)

According to the Gospel of Matthew

49 And forthwith he came to Jesus, and said, Hail, master; and kissed him.
50 And Jesus said unto him, Friend, wherefore art thou come? (Matt 26:49-50 *to* ?)

The first effort to apprehend Jesus

According to the Gospel of Matthew

50 Then came they, and laid hands on Jesus, and took him. (Matt 26:50 *Then*)

According to the Gospel of Mark

46 ¶ And they laid their hands on him, and took him. (Mark 14:46)

Peter cuts off the right ear of the high priest's servant

According to the Gospel of Luke

49 When they which were about him saw what would follow, they said unto
him, Lord, shall we smite with the sword?
50 ¶ And one of them smote the servant of the high priest, and cut off his right ear. (Luke 22:49-50)

According to the Gospel of Mark

47 And one of them that stood by drew a sword, and smote a servant of the high priest, and cut off his ear. (Mark 14:47)

According to the Gospel of Matthew

51 And, behold, one of them which were with Jesus stretched out *his* hand, and drew his sword, and struck a servant of the high priest's, and smote off his ear. (Matt 26:51)

According to the Gospel of John

10 Then Simon Peter having a sword drew it, and smote the high priest's servant, and
cut off his right ear. The servant's name was Malchus.
11 Then said Jesus unto Peter, Put up thy sword into the sheath: the cup which my
Father hath given me, shall I not drink it? (John 18:10-11)

Jesus restores the ear of Malchus

51 And Jesus answered and said, Suffer ye thus far. And he touched his ear, and healed him. (Luke 22:51)

Jesus then rebuked the disciples for the use of physical force

52 Then said Jesus unto him, Put up again thy sword into his place: for all they that take
the sword shall perish with the sword.
53 Thinkest thou that I cannot now pray to my Father, and he shall presently give me
more than twelve legions of angels?
54 But how then shall the scriptures be fulfilled, that thus it must be? (Matt 26:52-54)

Jesus then addressed leaders of the mob

According to the Gospel of Luke

52 Then Jesus said unto the chief priests, and captains of the temple, and the elders,
which were come to him, Be ye come out, as against a thief, with swords and staves?
53 When I was daily with you in the temple, ye stretched forth no hands against me: but
this is your hour, and the power of darkness. (Luke 22:52-53)

According to the Gospel of Matthew

55 In that same hour said Jesus to the multitudes, Are ye come out as against a thief
with swords and staves for to take me? I sat daily with you teaching in the temple, and
ye laid no hold on me.
56 But all this was done, that the scriptures of the prophets might be fulfilled. (Matt 26:55-56 to 1st .)

According to the Gospel of Mark

48 And Jesus answered and said unto them, Are ye come out, as against a thief, with
swords and *with* staves to take me?
49 I was daily with you in the temple teaching, and ye took me not: but the scriptures
must be fulfilled. (Mark 14:48-49)

All of the disciples are "offended," meaning they all desert Jesus

According to the Gospel of Matthew

56 Then all the disciples forsook him, and fled. (Matt 26:56 *Then*)

According to the Gospel of Mark

50 And they all forsook him, and fled. (Mark 14:50)

A certain young man, very likely Lazarus, escapes arrest

51 And there followed him a certain young man, having a linen cloth cast about *his*
naked *body*; and the young men laid hold on him:
52 And he left the linen cloth, and fled from them naked. (Mark 14:51-52)

The arrest

12 Then the band and the captain and officers of the Jews took Jesus, and bound him,
(John 18:12)

165 - ECCLESIASTICAL TRIALS & PETER'S DENIALS

54 ¶ Then took they him, and led *him*, and brought him into the high priest's house.
And Peter followed afar off. (Luke 22:54)

Jesus was taken first to Annas for preliminary questioning

13 And led him away to Annas first; for he was father in law to Caiaphas, which was
the high priest that same year.
14 Now Caiaphas was he, which gave counsel to the Jews, that it was expedient that
one man should die for the people. (John 18:13-14)

Peter is granted admittance through "another disciple"

15 ¶ And Simon Peter followed Jesus, and *so did* another disciple: that disciple was
known unto the high priest, and went in with Jesus into the palace of the high priest.
16 But Peter stood at the door without. Then went out that other disciple, which was
known unto the high priest, and spake unto her that kept the door, and brought in Peter.
(John 18:15-16)

Peter's 1st denial is to a female doorkeeper

17 Then saith the damsel that kept the door unto Peter, Art not thou also *one* of this
man's disciples? He saith, I am not.
18 And the servants and officers stood there, who had made a fire of coals; for it was
cold: and they warmed themselves: and Peter stood with them, and warmed himself.
(John 18:17-18)

Preliminary questioning by Annas

19 ¶ The high priest then asked Jesus of his disciples, and of his doctrine.
20 Jesus answered him, I spake openly to the world; I ever taught in the synagogue, and
in the temple, whither the Jews always resort; and in secret have I said nothing.
21 Why askest thou me? ask them which heard me, what I have said unto them: behold,
they know what I said. (John 18:19-21)

The first physical assault on Jesus is by a temple guard

22 And when he had thus spoken, one of the officers which stood by struck Jesus with
the palm of his hand, saying, Answerest thou the high priest so?
23 Jesus answered him, If I have spoken evil, bear witness of the evil: but if well, why
smitest thou me? (John 18:22-23)

When the preliminary questioning was finished Jesus was taken to Caiaphas

24 Now Annas had sent him bound unto Caiaphas the high priest. (John 18:24)

The chief priests, scribes and elders were waiting with Caiaphas for Jesus to be brought in

According to the Gospel of Mark

53 ¶ And they led Jesus away to the high priest: and with him were assembled all the
chief priests and the elders and the scribes. (Mark 14:53)

According to the Gospel of Matthew

57 ¶ And they that had laid hold on Jesus led *him* away to Caiaphas the high priest,
where the scribes and the elders were assembled. (Matt 26:57)

Peter followed at a distance and then *sat* with others by a fire

According to the Gospel of Luke

55 And when they had kindled a fire in the midst of the hall, and were set down
together, Peter sat down among them. (Luke 22:55)

According to the Gospel of Mark

54 And Peter followed him afar off, even into the palace of the high priest: and he sat
with the servants, and warmed himself at the fire. (Mark 14:54)

According to the Gospel of Matthew

58 But Peter followed him afar off unto the high priest's palace, and went in, and sat
with the servants, to see the end. (Matt 26:58)

The strategy was to use false witnesses to establish that Jesus was guilty of blasphemy

59 Now the chief priests, and elders, and all the council, sought false witness against
Jesus, to put him to death;
60 But found none: yea, though many false witnesses came, *yet* found they none. (Matt
26:59-60 to 1st.)

No legitimate charges could not be established due to a lack of consistent blasphemy

55 And the chief priests and all the council sought for witness against Jesus to put him
to death; and found none.
56 For many bare false witness against him, but their witness agreed not together. (Mark
14:55-56)

The accusation that Jesus intended to destroy the temple could not be established

57 And there arose certain, and bare false witness against him, saying,
58 We heard him say, I will destroy this temple that is made with hands, and within
three days I will build another made without hands. (Mark 14:57-58)
60 At the last came two false witnesses,
61 And said, This *fellow* said, I am able to destroy the temple of God, and to build it in
three days. (Matt 26:60-61 *At*)

This accusation fails due to inconsistent testimony

59 But neither so did their witness agree together. (Mark 14:59)

Then the high priest demanded a reply from Jesus

According to the Gospel of Mark

60 And the high priest stood up in the midst, and asked Jesus, saying, Answerest thou
nothing? what *is it which* these witness against thee?
61 But he held his peace, and answered nothing. (Mark 14:60-61 to 1st.)

According to the Gospel of Matthew

62 And the high priest arose, and said unto him, Answerest thou nothing? what *is it*
which these witness against thee?
63 But Jesus held his peace. (Matt 26:62-63 to 1st.)

The next strategy was to trick Jesus into saying something chargeable as blasphemy

63 And the high priest answered and said unto him, I adjure thee by the living God, that
thou tell us whether thou be the Christ, the Son of God.
64 Jesus saith unto him, Thou hast said: nevertheless I say unto you, Hereafter shall ye
see the Son of man sitting on the right hand of power, and coming in the clouds of
heaven. (Matt 26:63-64 *And*)
61 Again the high priest asked him, and said unto him, Art thou the Christ, the Son of
the Blessed?
62 And Jesus said, I am: and ye shall see the Son of man sitting on the right hand of
power, and coming in the clouds of heaven. (Mark 14:61-62 *Again*)

The high priest orchestrates a demand for the death penalty for blasphemy

According to the Gospel of Mark

63 Then the high priest rent his clothes, and saith, What need we any further witnesses?
64 Ye have heard the blasphemy: what think ye? And they all condemned him to be
guilty of death.
65 And some began to spit on him, and to cover his face, and to buffet him, and to say
unto him, Prophesy: and the servants did strike him with the palms of their hands. (Mark 14:63-65)

According to the Gospel of Matthew

65 Then the high priest rent his clothes, saying, He hath spoken blasphemy; what
further need have we of witnesses? behold, now ye have heard his blasphemy.
66 What think ye? They answered and said, He is guilty of death.
67 Then did they spit in his face, and buffeted him; and others smote *him* with the
palms of their hands,
68 Saying, Prophesy unto us, thou Christ, Who is he that smote thee? (Matt 26:65-68)

Peter's 2rd denial is to a maid and a man while *sitting* by a fire

According to the Gospel of Luke

56 But a certain maid beheld him as he sat by the fire, and earnestly looked upon him,
and said, This man was also with him.
57 And he denied him, saying, Woman, I know him not. (Luke 22:56-57)

According to the Gospel of Matthew

69 ¶ Now Peter sat without in the palace: and a damsel came unto him, saying, Thou
also wast with Jesus of Galilee.
70 But he denied before *them* all, saying, I know not what thou sayest. (Matt 26:69-70)

According to the Gospel of Mark

66 ¶ And as Peter was beneath in the palace, there cometh one of the maids of the high
priest:
67 And when she saw Peter warming himself, she looked upon him, and said, And thou
also wast with Jesus of Nazareth.
68 But he denied, saying, I know not, neither understand I what thou sayest. (Mark 14:66-68
to 1st.)

Peter's 3rd denial is a little later, in the gateway or porch, while *standing* and warming himself with *others*

According to the Gospel of Luke

58 And after a little while another saw him, and said, Thou art also of them. And Peter
said, Man, I am not. (Luke 22:58)

According to the Gospel of Matthew

71 And when he was gone out into the porch, another *maid* saw him, and said unto
them that were there, This *fellow* was also with Jesus of Nazareth.
72 And again he denied with an oath, I do not know the man. (Matt 26:71-72)

According to the Gospel of John

25 And Simon Peter stood and warmed himself. They said therefore unto him, Art not
thou also *one* of his disciples? He denied *it*, and said, I am not.
26 One of the servants of the high priest, being *his* kinsman whose ear Peter cut off,
saith, Did not I see thee in the garden with him? (John 18:25-26)

When Peter denies for the 3rd time, a cock crows for the 1st time

According to the Gospel of John

27 Peter then denied again: and immediately the cock crew. (John 18:27)

According to the Gospel of Mark

68 And he went out into the porch; and the cock crew. (Mark 14:*68 And*)

Peter's 4th denial is a short time later while "beneath in the palace" to bystanders when questioned by a maid

According to the Gospel of Mark

69 And a maid saw him again, and began to say to them that stood by, This is *one* of
them.
70 And he denied it again. (Mark 14:69-70 to 1st.)

Peter's 5th denial is a little after when "they that stood by" noted his Galilæan accent

According to the Gospel of Mark

70 And a little after, they that stood by said again to Peter, Surely thou art *one* of them:
for thou art a Galilæan, and thy speech agreeth *thereto*.
71 But he began to curse and to swear, *saying*, I know not this man of whom ye speak.
(Mark 14:70-71 *And*)

According to the Gospel of Matthew

73 And after a while came unto *him* they that stood by, and said to Peter, Surely thou
also art *one* of them; for thy speech bewrayeth thee.
74 Then began he to curse and to swear, *saying*, I know not the man. (Matt 26:73-74 to 1st.)

Peter's 6th denial is an hour later in the midst of the hall to a group that again notes his Galilæan accent

According to the Gospel of Luke

59 And about the space of one hour after another confidently affirmed, saying, Of a

truth this *fellow* also was with him: for he is a Galilæan.
60 And Peter said, Man, I know not what thou sayest. (Luke 22:59-60 to 1st.)

A 2nd cock crow following the 2nd group of three denials

According to the Gospel of Mark

72 And the second time the cock crew. And Peter called to mind the word that Jesus
said unto him, Before the cock crow twice, thou shalt deny me thrice. (Mark 14:72 to 1st.)

According to the Gospel of Luke

60 And immediately, while he yet spake, the cock crew.
61 And the Lord turned, and looked upon Peter. And Peter remembered the word of
the Lord, how he had said unto him, Before the cock crow, thou shalt deny me thrice.
(Luke 22:60-61 Begin w/2nd *And*)

According to the Gospel of Matthew

74 And immediately the cock crew.
75 And Peter remembered the word of Jesus, which said unto him, Before the cock
crow, thou shalt deny me thrice. (Matt 26:74-75 *to* 1st.)

Peter weeps bitterly

According to the Gospel of Matthew

75 And he went out, and wept bitterly. (Matt 26:75 *And*)

According to the Gospel of Luke

62 And Peter went out, and wept bitterly. (Luke 22:62)

According to the Gospel of Mark

72 And when he thought thereon, he wept. (Mark 14:72 2nd *And*)

More mocking and abuse

63 ¶ And the men that held Jesus mocked him, and smote *him*.
64 And when they had blindfolded him, they struck him on the face, and asked him,
saying, Prophesy, who is it that smote thee?
65 And many other things blasphemously spake they against him. (Luke 22:63-65)

A political charge that Jesus claimed to be "the King of the Jews" is fabricated

66 ¶ And as soon as it was day, the elders of the people and the chief priests and the
scribes came together, and led him into their council, saying,
67 Art thou the Christ? tell us. And he said unto them, If I tell you, ye will not believe:
68 And if I also ask *you*, ye will not answer me, nor let *me* go.
69 Hereafter shall the Son of man sit on the right hand of the power of God.
70 Then said they all, Art thou then the Son of God? And he said unto them, Ye say
that I am.
71 And they said, What need we any further witness? for we ourselves have heard of
his own mouth. (Luke 22:66-71)

The plan of Caiaphas to have the Romans execute Jesus is put into play

According to the Gospel of Matthew

1 When the morning was come, all the chief priests and elders of the people took
counsel against Jesus to put him to death:
2 And when they had bound him, they led *him* away, and delivered him to Pontius

Pilate the governor. (Matt 27:1-2)

According to the Gospel of Mark

1 And straightway in the morning the chief priests held a consultation with the elders
and scribes and the whole council, and bound Jesus, and carried *him* away, and
delivered *him* to Pilate. (Mark 15:1)

According to the Gospel of Luke

1 And the whole multitude of them arose, and led him unto Pilate. (Luke 23:1)

166 – JUDAS ISACRIOT'S ACTIONS CONCURRENT WITH THE TRIALS

3 ¶ Then Judas, which had betrayed him, when he saw that he was condemned,
repented himself, and brought again the thirty pieces of silver to the chief priests and
elders, (Matt 27:3)

Judas Iscariot is the 1st to witness that Jesus was innocent

4 Saying, I have sinned in that I have betrayed the innocent blood. And they said, What
is that to us? see thou *to that.*
5 And he cast down the pieces of silver in the temple, and departed, and went and
hanged himself.
6 And the chief priests took the silver pieces, and said, It is not lawful for to put them
into the treasury, because it is the price of blood.
7 And they took counsel, and bought with them the potter's field, to bury strangers in.
8 Wherefore that field was called, The field of blood, unto this day.
9 Then was fulfilled that which was spoken by Jeremy the prophet, saying, And they
took the thirty pieces of silver, the price of him that was valued, whom they of the
children of Israel did value;
10 And gave them for the potter's field, as the Lord appointed me. (Matt 27:4-10)

167 - THE TRIAL BEFORE PILATE BEGINS

28 ¶ Then led they Jesus from Caiaphas unto the hall of judgment: and it was early; and
they themselves went not into the judgment hall, lest they should be defiled; but that
they might eat the passover.
29 Pilate then went out unto them, and said, What accusation bring ye against this man?
30 They answered and said unto him, If he were not a malefactor, we would not have
delivered him up unto thee. (John 18:28-30)

Three false charges are presented to Pilate

2 And they began to accuse him, saying, We found this *fellow* perverting the nation,
and forbidding to give tribute to Cæsar, saying that he himself is Christ a King. (Luke 23:2)

Jesus implies "Yes" to the question: Art thou the King of the Jews? meaning a spiritual, not an earthly dominion

According to the Gospel of Matthew

11 And Jesus stood before the governor: and the governor asked him, saying, Art thou
the King of the Jews? And Jesus said unto him, Thou sayest. (Matt 27:11)

According to the Gospel of Mark

2 And Pilate asked him, Art thou the King of the Jews? And he answering said unto
him, Thou sayest *it*. (Mark 15:2)

3 And Pilate asked him, saying, Art thou the King of the Jews? And he answered him
and said, Thou sayest *it*. (Luke 23:3)

Pilate is the 2nd to witness to Jesus' innocence, Judas having been the first

4 Then said Pilate to the chief priests and *to* the people, I find no fault in this man. (Luke 23:4)

Pilate's 1st plea to release Jesus is that he should be tried under ecclesiastical, and not Roman, law

31 Then said Pilate unto them, Take ye him, and judge him according to your law. (John 18:31 to 1st.)

The Jews lied. There were violations that called for death by stoning! Jesus was framed and Pilate trapped

31 The Jews therefore said unto him, It is not lawful for us to put any man to death:
32 That the saying of Jesus might be fulfilled, which he spake, signifying what death he
should die. (John 18:31-32 *The*)

More accusations - the chief priests and elders

12 And when he was accused of the chief priests and elders, he answered nothing.
13 Then said Pilate unto him, Hearest thou not how many things they witness against
thee?
14 And he answered him to never a word; insomuch that the governor marvelled
greatly. (Matt 27:12-14)

More accusations – The chief priests only

3 And the chief priests accused him of many things: but he answered nothing. (Mark 15:3)

Pilate asks Jesus *again* why he does not reply

4 And Pilate asked him again, saying, Answerest thou nothing? behold how many
things they witness against thee.
5 But Jesus yet answered nothing; so that Pilate marvelled. (Mark 15:4-5)

Pilate questions Jesus again as to the original charge

33 Then Pilate entered into the judgment hall again, and called Jesus, and said unto
him, Art thou the King of the Jews? (John 18:33)

Jesus asks Pilate why Pilate believes he is being tried: for a real crime or hearsay

34 Jesus answered him, Sayest thou this thing of thyself, or did others tell it thee of me?
35 Pilate answered, Am I a Jew? Thine own nation and the chief priests have delivered
thee unto me: what hast thou done? (John 18:34-35)

Jesus responds that he claims no earthly kingship, and is no enemy to Rome, Cæsar, or to him

36 Jesus answered, My kingdom is not of this world: if my kingdom were of this world,
then would my servants fight, that I should not be delivered to the Jews: but now is my
kingdom not from hence.
37 Pilate therefore said unto him, Art thou a king then? Jesus answered, Thou sayest
that I am a king. (John 18:36-37 to 1st.)

Jesus makes sure that Pilate understands that his mission is not political, but spiritual

37 To this end was I born, and for this cause came I into the world, that I should bear
witness unto the truth. Every one that is of the truth heareth my voice. (John 18:37 *To*)

Pilates evasive reply was a ruse

38 Pilate saith unto him, What is truth? (John 18:38 to ?)

Pilates 2nd is the 3rd witnessing to Jesus' innocence

38 And when he had said this, he went out again unto the Jews, and saith unto them, I
find in him no fault *at all*. (John 18:38 *And*)

Violent reaction and more false accusations

5 And they were the more fierce, saying, He stirreth up the people, teaching throughout
all Jewry, beginning from Galilee to this place. (Luke 23:5)

168 - THE MOCK TRIAL BEFORE HEROD

Pilate's first attempt to release Jesus

6 When Pilate heard of Galilee, he asked whether the man were a Galilæan.
7 And as soon as he knew that he belonged unto Herod's jurisdiction, he sent him to
Herod, who himself also was at Jerusalem at that time.
8 ¶ And when Herod saw Jesus, he was exceeding glad: for he was desirous to see him
of a long *season*, because he had heard many things of him; and he hoped to have seen
some miracle done by him.
9 Then he questioned with him in many words; but he answered him nothing.
10 And the chief priests and scribes stood and vehemently accused him.
11 And Herod with his men of war set him at nought, and mocked *him*, and arrayed him
in a gorgeous robe, and sent him again to Pilate.
12 ¶ And the same day Pilate and Herod were made friends together: for before they
were at enmity between themselves. (Luke 23:6-12)

169 - THE TRIAL BEFORE PILATE RESUMES

Pilates 3rd is the 4th witnessing to Jesus' innocence

13 ¶ And Pilate, when he had called together the chief priests and the rulers and the
people,
14 Said unto them, Ye have brought this man unto me, as one that perverteth the
people: and, behold, I, having examined *him* before you, have found no fault in this
man touching those things whereof ye accuse him: (Luke 23:13-14)

Herod provides the 5th witnessing to Jesus' innocence

15 No, nor yet Herod: for I sent you to him; and, lo, nothing worthy of death is done
unto him. (Luke 23:15)

The Passover tradition of the Roman Governor

According to the Gospel of Mark

6 Now at *that* feast he released unto them one prisoner, whomsoever they desired. (Mark 15:6)

According to the Gospel of Matthew

15 Now at *that* feast the governor was wont to release unto the people a prisoner, whom
they would. (Matt 27:15)

According to the Gospel of John

39 But ye have a custom, that I should release unto you one at the passover: (Jn. 18:39 to :)

According to the Gospel of Luke

16 I will therefore chastise him, and release *him*.
17 (For of necessity he must release one unto them at the feast.) (Luke 23:16-17)

The choice offered the mob: release Jesus who is innocent or Barabbas known for insurrection and murder

According to the Gospel of Matthew

16 And they had then a notable prisoner, called Barabbas.
17 Therefore when they were gathered together, Pilate said unto them, Whom will ye
that I release unto you? Barabbas, or Jesus which is called Christ?
18 For he knew that for envy they had delivered him. (Matt 27:16-18)

Pilate's wife provides the 6th witnessing to Jesus' innocence

19 ¶ When he was set down on the judgment seat, his wife sent unto him, saying, Have
thou nothing to do with that just man: for I have suffered many things this day in a
dream because of him.
20 But the chief priests and elders persuaded the multitude that they should ask
Barabbas, and destroy Jesus.
21 The governor answered and said unto them, Whether of the twain will ye that I
release unto you? They said, Barabbas. (Matt 27:16-21)

According to the Gospel of Mark

7 And there was *one* named Barabbas, *which lay* bound with them that had made
insurrection with him, who had committed murder in the insurrection.
8 And the multitude crying aloud began to desire *him to do* as he had ever done unto
them.
9 But Pilate answered them, saying, Will ye that I release unto you the King of the
Jews?
10 For he knew that the chief priests had delivered him for envy.
11 But the chief priests moved the people, that he should rather release Barabbas unto
them. (Mark 15:7-11)

According to the Gospel of Luke

18 And they cried out all at once, saying, Away with this *man*, and release unto us
Barabbas:
19 (Who for a certain sedition made in the city, and for murder, was cast into prison.)
20 Pilate therefore, willing to release Jesus, spake again to them.
21 But they cried, saying, Crucify *him*, crucify him. (Luke 23:18-21)

Pilate's 4th is the 7th witnessing to Jesus' innocence

22 And he said unto them the third time, Why, what evil hath he done? I have found no
cause of death in him: I will therefore chastise him, and let *him* go.
23 And they were instant with loud voices, requiring that he might be crucified. (Luke
23:22-23 to 1st.)

According to the Gospel of Mark

12 And Pilate answered and said again unto them, What will ye then that I shall do *unto*
him whom ye call the King of the Jews?
13 And they cried out again, Crucify him. (Mark 15:12-13)

Pilate's 4th is the 7th witnessing to Jesus' innocence

14 Then Pilate said unto them, Why, what evil hath he done? And they cried out the
more exceedingly, Crucify him. (Mark 15:14)

According to the Gospel of John

39 will ye therefore that I release unto you the King of the Jews?

40 Then cried they all again, saying, Not this man, but Barabbas. Now Barabbas was a robber. (John 18:39-40 *will*)

According to the Gospel of Matthew

22 Pilate saith unto them, What shall I do then with Jesus which is called Christ? *They* all say unto him, Let him be crucified. (Matt 27:22)

Pilate's 4th is the 7th witnessing to Jesus' innocence

23 And the governor said, Why, what evil hath he done? But they cried out the more, saying, Let him be crucified. (Matt. 27: 23)

170 - SENTENCING

According to the Gospel of Luke

23 And the voices of them and of the chief priests prevailed.
24 And Pilate gave sentence that it should be as they required.
25 And he released unto them him that for sedition and murder was cast into prison, whom they had desired; but he delivered Jesus to their will. (Luke 23:23-25 Begin 2nd *And*)

According to the Gospel of John

1 Then Pilate therefore took Jesus, and scourged *him*. (John 19:1)

According to the Gospel of Mark

15 ¶ And *so* Pilate, willing to content the people, released Barabbas unto them, and delivered Jesus, when he had scourged *him*, to be crucified. (Mark 15:15)

According to the Gospel of Matthew

Pilates' 5th is the 8th witnessing to Jesus' innocence. It occurs when Pilate washes his hands

24 ¶ When Pilate saw that he could prevail nothing, but *that* rather a tumult was made, he took water, and washed *his* hands before the multitude, saying, I am innocent of the blood of this just person: see ye *to it*.
25 Then answered all the people, and said, His blood *be* on us, and on our children.
26 ¶ Then released he Barabbas unto them: and when he had scourged Jesus, he delivered *him* to be crucified. (Matt 27:24-26)

171 - MALTREATMENT AFTER SENTENCING

According to the Gospel of Matthew

27 Then the soldiers of the governor took Jesus into the common hall, and gathered unto him the whole band *of soldiers*.
28 And they stripped him, and put on him a scarlet robe.
29 ¶ And when they had platted a crown of thorns, they put *it* upon his head, and a reed in his right hand: and they bowed the knee before him, and mocked him, saying, Hail, King of the Jews!
30 And they spit upon him, and took the reed, and smote him on the head. (Matt 27:27-30)

According to the Gospel of Mark

16 And the soldiers led him away into the hall, called Praetorium; and they call together the whole band.
17 And they clothed him with purple, and platted a crown of thorns, and put it about his *head*,

18 And began to salute him, Hail, King of the Jews!
19 And they smote him on the head with a reed, and did spit upon him, and bowing
their knees worshipped him. (Mark 15:16-19)

According to the Gospel of John

2 And the soldiers platted a crown of thorns, and put *it* on his head, and they put on
him a purple robe,
3 And said, Hail, King of the Jews! and they smote him with their hands. (John 19:2-3)

Pilates' 6th is the 9th witnessing to Jesus innocence

4 Pilate therefore went forth again, and saith unto them, Behold, I bring him forth to
you, that ye may know that I find no fault in him.
5 Then came Jesus forth, wearing the crown of thorns, and the purple robe. And *Pilate*
saith unto them, Behold the man!
6 When the chief priests therefore and officers saw him, they cried out, saying, Crucify
him, crucify *him*. (John 19:4-6 to 1st.)

Pilates 7th is the 10th witnessing to Jesus innocence

6 Pilate saith unto them, Take ye him, and crucify *him*: for I find no fault in him.
7 The Jews answered him, We have a law, and by our law he ought to die, because he
made himself the Son of God.
8 ¶ When Pilate therefore heard that saying, he was the more afraid;
9 And went again into the judgment hall, and saith unto Jesus, Whence art thou?
9 But Jesus gave him no answer.
10 Then saith Pilate unto him, Speakest thou not unto me? knowest thou not that I have
power to crucify thee, and have power to release thee?
11 Jesus answered, Thou couldest have no power *at all* against me, except it were given
thee from above: therefore he that delivered me unto thee hath the greater sin.
12 And from thenceforth Pilate sought to release him:
12 but the Jews cried out, saying, If thou let this man go, thou art not Cæsar's friend:
whosoever maketh himself a king speaketh against Cæsar.
13 ¶ When Pilate therefore heard that saying, he brought Jesus forth, and sat down in
the judgment seat in a place that is called the Pavement, but in the Hebrew, Gabbatha.
(John 19:6-13)

Jesus is presented "at about the 6th hour" of the trial. (Around 6:00 a.m. on Wednesday Morning)

14 And it was the preparation of the passover, and about the sixth hour: and he saith
unto the Jews, Behold your King!
15 But they cried out, Away with *him*, away with *him*, crucify him. Pilate saith unto
them, Shall I crucify your King?
15 The chief priests answered, We have no king but Cæsar. (John 19:14-15)

Not long after sunrise Jesus was led away to be crucified

According to the Gospel of Matthew

31 And after that they had mocked him, they took the robe off from him, and put his
own raiment on him, and led him away to crucify *him*. (Matt 27:31)

According to the Gospel of Mark

20 And when they had mocked him, they took off the purple from him, and put his own
clothes on him, and led him out to crucify him. (Mark 15:20)

According to the Gospel of John

16 Then delivered he him therefore unto them to be crucified. And they took Jesus, and
led *him away.* (John 19:16)

172 - THE WALK TO GOLGOTHA

17 And he bearing his cross went forth into a place called *the place* of a skull, which is
called in the Hebrew Golgotha:
18 Where they crucified him, and two other with him, on either side one, and Jesus in
the midst. (John 19:17-18)

The Jews protested the wording on the 1st sign that named the crime for which Jesus was being executed

19 ¶ And Pilate wrote a title, and put *it* on the cross. And the writing was, JESUS OF
NAZARETH THE KING OF THE JEWS.
20 This title then read many of the Jews: for the place where Jesus was crucified was
nigh to the city: and it was written in Hebrew, *and* Greek, *and* Latin.
21 Then said the chief priests of the Jews to Pilate, Write not, The King of the Jews; but
that he said, I am King of the Jews.
22 Pilate answered, What I have written I have written. (John 19:19-22)

Simon, a Cyrenian, is "compelled to bear the cross" beam

According to the Gospel of Matthew

32 And as they came out, they found a man of Cyrene, Simon by name: him they
compelled to bear his cross. (Matt 27:32)

According to the Gospel of Mark

21 And they compel one Simon a Cyrenian, who passed by, coming out of the country,
the father of Alexander and Rufus, to bear his cross. (Mark 15:21)

According to the Gospel of Luke

26 And as they led him away, they laid hold upon one Simon, a Cyrenian, coming out
of the country, and on him they laid the cross, that he might bear *it* after Jesus. (Luke 23:26)

Jesus addresses the women on the sorrows of child bearing

27 ¶ And there followed him a great company of people, and of women, which also
bewailed and lamented him.
28 But Jesus turning unto them said, Daughters of Jerusalem, weep not for me, but
weep for yourselves, and for your children.
29 For, behold, the days are coming, in the which they shall say, Blessed *are* the barren,
and the wombs that never bare, and the paps which never gave suck.
30 Then shall they begin to say to the mountains, Fall on us; and to the hills, Cover us.
31 For if they do these things in a green tree, what shall be done in the dry?
(Luke 23:27-31)

Jesus is accompanied by two malefactors, *κακοῦργος kakourgos*, evildoers. Their crimes are not stated

32 And there were also two other, malefactors, led with him to be put to death. (Luke 23:32)

On the way to Golgotha Jesus is offered a pain killer that he refuses to drink

22 And they bring him unto the place Golgotha, which is, being interpreted, The place
of a skull.
23 And they gave him to drink wine mingled with myrrh: but he received *it* not. (Mark 15:22-23)

CHAPTER 173 - THE CRUCIFIXION

At the site, before being crucified, Jesus refuses, for the second time, to drink a pain killer

33 And when they were come unto a place called Golgotha, that is to say, a place of a
skull,
34 ¶ They gave him vinegar to drink mingled with gall: and when he had tasted *thereof*,
he would not drink. (Matt 27:33-34)

The two *malefactors* led out with him are crucified at the same time as Jesus, one on each side

33 And when they were come to the place, which is called Calvary, there they crucified him, and the malefactors, one on the right hand, and the other on the left. (Luke 23:33)

Jesus prays for his executioners. (John 19:23 states there were four.)

34 ¶ Then said Jesus, Father, forgive them; for they know not what they do. (Luke 23:34 to 1st.)

Jesus is crucified

35 And they crucified him, (Matt 27:35 to 1st,)

The Roman soldiers parted, *διαμερίζω diamerizō,* divided up Jesus' garments and cast lots for his coat

According to the Gospel of Luke

34 And they parted his raiment, and cast lots. (Luke 23:34 *And*)

According to the Gospel of John

23 ¶ Then the soldiers, when they had crucified Jesus, took his garments, and made four parts, to every soldier a part; and also *his* coat: now the coat was without seam, woven from the top throughout.
24 They said therefore among themselves, Let us not rend it, but cast lots for it, whose it shall be: that the scripture might be fulfilled, which saith, They parted my raiment among them, and for my vesture they did cast lots. These things therefore the soldiers did. (John 19:23-24)

According to the Gospel of Mark

24 And when they had crucified him, they parted his garments, casting lots upon them, what every man should take.
25 And it was the third hour, and they crucified him.
26 And the superscription of his accusation was written over, THE KING OF THE JEWS. (Mark 15:24-26)

According to the Gospel of Matthew

35 and parted his garments, casting lots: that it might be fulfilled which was spoken by the prophet, They parted my garments among them, and upon my vesture did they cast lots.
36 And sitting down they watched him there; (Matt 27:35-36)

A 2rd sign with new wording arrives at the site and is used in place of the sign originally dictated by Pilate

37 And set up over his head his accusation written, THIS IS JESUS THE KING OF THE JEWS. (Matt 27:37)

Sometime later two *thieves, ληστής lēstēs*, robbers were brought out to be crucified

According to the Gospel of Matthew

38 Then were there two thieves crucified with him, one on the right hand, and another on the left. (Matt 27:38)

According to the Gospel of Mark

27 And with him they crucify two thieves; the one on his right hand, and the other on
his left.
28 And the scripture was fulfilled, which saith, And he was numbered with the
transgressors. (Mark 15:27-28)

The people and the rulers stood by mocking. A pain killer is offered and is again refused

35 And the people stood beholding. And the rulers also with them derided *him*, saying,
He saved others; let him save himself, if he be Christ, the chosen of God.
36 And the soldiers also mocked him, coming to him, and offering him vinegar,
37 And saying, If thou be the king of the Jews, save thyself. (Luke 23:35-37)

A final sign written in the order Greek, Latin, and Hebrew arrives and is hung in place

38 And a superscription also was written over him in letters of Greek, and Latin, and
Hebrew, THIS IS THE KING OF THE JEWS. (Luke 23:38)

The by-passers verbally abuse Jesus

According to the Gospel of Matthew

39 ¶ And they that passed by reviled him, wagging their heads,
40 And saying, Thou that destroyest the temple, and buildest *it* in three days, save
thyself. If thou be the Son of God, come down from the cross. (Matt 27:39-40)

According to the Gospel of Mark

29 And they that passed by railed on him, wagging their heads, and saying, Ah, thou
that destroyest the temple, and buildest *it* in three days,
30 Save thyself, and come down from the cross. (Mark 15:29-30)

The chief priests, scribes and elders are also there to mock Jesus

According to the Gospel of Matthew

41 Likewise also the chief priests mocking *him*, with the scribes and elders, said,
42 He saved others; himself he cannot save. If he be the King of Israel, let him now
come down from the cross, and we will believe him.
43 He trusted in God; let him deliver him now, if he will have him: for he said, I am the
Son of God. (Matt 27:41-43)

According to the Gospel of Mark

31 Likewise also the chief priests mocking said among themselves with the scribes, He
saved others; himself he cannot save.
32 Let Christ the King of Israel descend now from the cross, that we may see and
believe. (Mark 15:31-32 to 1st.)

Later the two thieves also rail on Jesus

According to the Gospel of Matthew

44 The thieves also, which were crucified with him, cast the same in his teeth. (Matt 27:44)

According to the Gospel of Mark

32 And they that were crucified with him reviled him. (Mark 15:32 *And*)

Jesus entrusts the care of his mother to John, the Beloved Disciple

25 ¶ Now there stood by the cross of Jesus his mother, and his mother's sister, Mary the
wife of Cleophas, and Mary Magdalene.

26 When Jesus therefore saw his mother, and the disciple standing by, whom he loved,
he saith unto his mother, Woman, behold thy son!
27 Then saith he to the disciple, Behold thy mother! And from that hour that disciple
took her unto his own *home*. (John 19:25-27)

One of the two malefactors then railed Jesus

39 ¶ And one of the malefactors which were hanged railed on him, saying, If thou be
Christ, save thyself and us.
40 But the other answering rebuked him, saying, Dost not thou fear God, seeing thou
art in the same condemnation? (Luke 23:39-40)

One of the malefactors testified to Jesus' innocence - the 11th witnessing to his innocence

41 And we indeed justly; for we receive the due reward of our deeds: but this man hath
done nothing amiss.
42 And he said unto Jesus, Lord, remember me when thou comest into thy kingdom.
43 And Jesus said unto him, Verily I say unto thee, To-day shalt thou be with me in
paradise. (Luke 23:41-43)

Next: Three hours of darkness from noon to 3:00 p.m.
(The ninth hour, 2:00 p.m. to 3:00 p.m. the same time when passover lambs were being slain)

According to the Gospel of Matthew

45 Now from the sixth hour there was darkness over all the land unto the ninth hour.
(Matt 27:45)

According to the Gospel of Mark

33 And when the sixth hour was come, there was darkness over the whole land until the
ninth hour. (Mark 15:33)

According to the Gospel of Luke

44 And it was about the sixth hour, and there was a darkness over all the earth until the
ninth hour.
45 And the sun was darkened, and the veil of the temple was rent in the midst. (Luke
23:44-45)

The cry of the Lord Jesus Christ. Pain killer offered and refused for the fourth time

According to the Gospel of Matthew

46 And about the ninth hour Jesus cried with a loud voice, saying, Eli, Eli, lama
sabachthani? that is to say, My God, my God, why hast thou forsaken me?
47 Some of them that stood there, when they heard *that*, said, This *man* calleth for
Elias.
48 And straightway one of them ran, and took a spunge, and filled *it* with vinegar, and
put *it* on a reed, and gave him to drink.
49 The rest said, Let be, let us see whether Elias will come to save him. (Matt 27:46-49)

According to the Gospel of Mark

34 And at the ninth hour Jesus cried with a loud voice, saying, Eloi, Eloi, lama
sabachthani? which is, being interpreted, My God, my God, why hast thou forsaken
me?
35 And some of them that stood by, when they heard *it*, said, Behold, he calleth Elias.
36 And one ran and filled a spunge full of vinegar, and put *it* on a reed, and gave him to
drink, saying, Let alone; let us see whether Elias will come to take him down. (Mark 15:34-
36)

Jesus requests something to drink

28 ¶ After this, Jesus knowing that all things were now accomplished, that the scripture might be fulfilled, saith, I thirst.
29 Now there was set a vessel full of vinegar: and they filled a spunge with vinegar, and put *it* upon hyssop, and put *it* to his mouth. (John 19:28-29)

"It is finished"

According to the Gospel of John

30 When Jesus therefore had received the vinegar, he said, It is finished: and he bowed his head, and gave up the ghost. (John 19:30)

According to the Gospel of Matthew

50 ¶ Jesus, when he had cried again with a loud voice, yielded up the ghost. (Matt 27:50)

According to the Gospel of Mark

37 And Jesus cried with a loud voice, and gave up the ghost. (Mark 15:37)

According to the Gospel of Luke

46 ¶ And when Jesus had cried with a loud voice, he said, Father, into thy hands I commend my spirit: and having said thus, he gave up the ghost. (Luke 23:46)

174 - EVENTS IMMEDIATELY FOLLOWING

The Veil of the Temple is Rent

According to the Gospel of Matthew

51 And, behold, the veil of the temple was rent in twain from the top to the bottom; and the earth did quake, and the rocks rent;
52 And the graves were opened; and many bodies of the saints which slept arose,
53 And came out of the graves after his resurrection, and went into the holy city, and appeared unto many.
54 Now when the centurion, and they that were with him, watching Jesus, saw the earthquake, and those things that were done, they feared greatly, saying, Truly this was the Son of God. (Matt 27:51-54)

According to the Gospel of Mark

38 And the veil of the temple was rent in twain from the top to the bottom.
39 ¶ And when the centurion, which stood over against him, saw that he so cried out, and gave up the ghost, he said, Truly this man was the Son of God. (Mark 15:38-39)

The centurion's testimony was the 12th witnessing to Jesus' innocence

47 Now when the centurion saw what was done, he glorified God, saying, Certainly this was a righteous man.
48 And all the people that came together to that sight, beholding the things which were done, smote their breasts, and returned. (Luke 23:47-48)

Confirmation that four others were crucified with Jesus (Two malefactors AND two thieves)

31 The Jews therefore, because it was the preparation, that the bodies should not remain upon the cross on the sabbath day, (for that sabbath day was an high day,) besought Pilate that their legs might be broken, and *that* they might be taken away.
32 Then came the soldiers, and brake the legs of the first, and of the other which was crucified with him.

33 But when they came to Jesus, and saw that he was dead already, they brake not his
legs:
34 But one of the soldiers with a spear pierced his side, and forthwith came there out
blood and water.
35 And he that saw *it* bare record, and his record is true: and he knoweth that he saith
true, that ye might believe
36 For these things were done, that the scripture should be fulfilled, A bone of him
shall not be broken.
37 And again another scripture saith, They shall look on him whom they pierced. (John
19:31-37)

The women followed Jesus and watched from a distance

According to the Gospel of Luke

49 And all his acquaintance, and the women that followed him from Galilee, stood afar
off, beholding these things. (Luke 23:49)

According to the Gospel of Matthew

55 And many women were there beholding afar off, which followed Jesus from Galilee,
ministering unto him:
56 Among which was Mary Magdalene, and Mary the mother of James and Joses, and
the mother of Zebedee's children. (Matt 27:55-56)

According to the Gospel of Mark

40 There were also women looking on afar off: among whom was Mary Magdalene,
and Mary the mother of James the less and of Joses, and Salome;
41 (Who also, when he was in Galilee, followed him, and ministered unto him;) and
many other women which came up with him unto Jerusalem. (Mark 15:40-41)

Joseph of Arimathæa

According to the Gospel of Mark

42 ¶ And now when the even was come, because it was the preparation, that is, the day
before the sabbath,
43 Joseph of Arimathæa, an honourable counsellor, which also waited for the kingdom
of God, came, and went in boldly unto Pilate, and craved the body of Jesus.
44 And Pilate marvelled if he were already dead: and calling *unto him* the centurion, he
asked him whether he had been any while dead.
45 And when he knew *it* of the centurion, he gave the body to Joseph.
46 And he bought fine linen, and took him down, and laid him in a sepulchre which
was hewn out of a rock,
46 and rolled a stone unto the door of the sepulchre.
47 And Mary Magdalene and Mary *the mother* of Joses beheld where he was laid. (Mark
15:42-47)

According to the Gospel of Luke

50 ¶ And, behold, *there was* a man named Joseph, a counsellor; *and he was* a good
man, and a just:
51 (The same had not consented to the counsel and deed of them;) *he was* of
Arimathæa, a city of the Jews: who also himself waited for the kingdom of God.
52 This *man* went unto Pilate, and begged the body of Jesus.
53 And he took it down, and wrapped it in linen, and laid it in a sepulchre that was

hewn in stone, wherein never man before was laid.
54 And that day was the preparation, and the sabbath drew on.
55 And the women also, which came with him from Galilee, followed after, and beheld
the sepulchre, and how his body was laid.
56 And they returned, and prepared spices and ointments; and rested the sabbath day
according to the commandment. (Luke 23:50-56)

According to the Gospel of Matthew

57 When the even was come, there came a rich man of Arimathæa, named Joseph, who
also himself was Jesus' disciple:
58 He went to Pilate, and begged the body of Jesus. Then Pilate commanded the body
to be delivered.
59 And when Joseph had taken the body, he wrapped it in a clean linen cloth,
60 And laid it in his own new tomb, which he had hewn out in the rock: and he rolled a
great stone to the door of the sepulchre, and departed.
61 And there was Mary Magdalene, and the other Mary, sitting over against the
sepulchre. (Matt 27:57-61)

According to the Gospel of John

38 ¶ And after this Joseph of Arimathæa, being a disciple of Jesus, but secretly for fear
of the Jews, besought Pilate that he might take away the body of Jesus: and Pilate gave
him leave. He came therefore, and took the body of Jesus.
39 And there came also Nicodemus, which at the first came to Jesus by night, and
brought a mixture of myrrh and aloes, about an hundred pound *weight*.
40 Then took they the body of Jesus, and wound it in linen clothes with the spices, as
the manner of the Jews is to bury.
41 Now in the place where he was crucified there was a garden; and in the garden a
new sepulchre, wherein was never man yet laid.
42 There laid they Jesus therefore because of the Jews' preparation *day*; for the
sepulchre was nigh at hand. (John 19:38-42)

175 – CONDUCTING BUSINESS IN VIOLATION OF A HIGH SABBATH

62 ¶ Now the next day, that followed the day of the preparation, the chief priests and
Pharisees came together unto Pilate,
63 Saying, Sir, we remember that that deceiver said, while he was yet alive, After three
days I will rise again.
64 Command therefore that the sepulchre be made sure until the third day, lest his
disciples come by night, and steal him away, and say unto the people, He is risen from
the dead: so the last error shall be worse than the first.
65 Pilate said unto them, Ye have a watch: go your way, make *it* as sure as ye can.
66 So they went, and made the sepulchre sure, sealing the stone, and setting a watch.
(Matt 27:62-66)

176 - RESURRECTION DAY

Before sunrise the women go to the sepulchre to anoint the body of Jesus

According to the Gospel of Matthew

1 In the end of the sabbath, as it began to dawn toward the first *day* of the week, came
Mary Magdalene and the other Mary to see the sepulchre. (Matt 28:1)

According to the Gospel of Luke

1 Now upon the first *day* of the week, very early in the morning, they came unto the
sepulchre, bringing the spices which they had prepared, and certain *others* with them.
(Luke 24:1)

According to the Gospel of Mark

1 And when the sabbath was past, Mary Magdalene, and Mary the *mother* of James,
and Salome, had bought sweet spices, that they might come and anoint him.
2 And very early in the morning the first *day* of the week, they came unto the sepulchre
at the rising of the sun. (Mark 16:1-2)

On their way to the tomb women discuss how the stone is to be rolled aside

3 And they said among themselves, Who shall roll us away the stone from the door of
the sepulchre? (Mark 16:3)

Unknown to the women the stone had already been rolled aside

2 And, behold, there was a great earthquake: for the angel of the Lord descended from
heaven, and came and rolled back the stone from the door, and sat upon it.
3 His countenance was like lightning, and his raiment white as snow: (Matt 28:2-3)

The watchmen pass out from shock

4 And for fear of him the keepers did shake, and became as dead *men*. (Matt 28:4)

Upon arriving the women see the stone already rolled aside

According to the Gospel of Mark

4 And when they looked, they saw that the stone was rolled away: for it was very great.
(Mark 16:4)

According to the Gospel of Luke

2 And they found the stone rolled away from the sepulchre. (Luke 24:2)

Although the other women were with her, John mentions only Mary Magdalene

1 The first *day* of the week cometh Mary Magdalene early, when it was yet dark, unto
the sepulchre, and seeth the stone taken away from the sepulchre. (John 20:1)

Seeing the stone rolled aside, Mary left the other women, and ran to tell Peter and John

2 Then she runneth, and cometh to Simon Peter, and to the other disciple, whom Jesus
loved, and saith unto them, They have taken away the Lord out of the sepulchre, and we
know not where they have laid him. (John 20:2)

Peter and John run to the sepulchre followed by Mary Magdalene

3 Peter therefore went forth, and that other disciple, and came to the sepulchre.
4 So they ran both together:
4 and the other disciple did outrun Peter, and came first to the sepulchre.
5 And he stooping down, *and looking in*, saw the linen clothes lying; yet went he not
in.
6 Then cometh Simon Peter following him, and went into the sepulchre, and seeth the
linen clothes lie,
7 And the napkin, that was about his head, not lying with the linen clothes, but
wrapped together in a place by itself.
8 Then went in also that other disciple, which came first to the sepulchre, and he saw,

and believed.
9 For as yet they knew not the scripture, that he must rise again from the dead.
10 Then the disciples went away again unto their own home. (John 20:3-10)

Peter and John didn't see the angel that rolled aside the stone, but the women did

5 And the angel answered and said unto the women, Fear not ye: for I know that ye seek Jesus, which was crucified.
6 He is not here: for he is risen, as he said. (Matt 28:5-6 to 1st .)

The women, including Mary Magdalene who has returned, are invited to enter the sepulchre

6 Come, see the place where the Lord lay. (Matt 28:6 *Come*)

The women, not believing what they hear, and not seeing a body, are confused

3 And they entered in, and found not the body of the Lord Jesus. (Luke 24:3)

Two "men" in shining garments stand by the women

4 And it came to pass, as they were much perplexed thereabout, behold, two men stood by them in shining garments: (Luke 24:4)

Mary Magdalene, standing outside weeping, looks into the sepulchre

11 ¶ But Mary stood without at the sepulchre weeping: and as she wept, she stooped down, *and looked* into the sepulchre,
12 And seeth two angels in white sitting, the one at the head, and the other at the feet, where the body of Jesus had lain
13 And they say unto her, Woman, why weepest thou? She saith unto them, Because they have taken away my Lord, and I know not where they have laid him.
14 And when she had thus said, she turned herself back, and saw Jesus standing, and knew not that it was Jesus.
15 Jesus saith unto her, Woman, why weepest thou? whom seekest thou? She, supposing him to be the gardener, saith unto him, Sir, if thou have borne him hence, tell me where thou hast laid him, and I will take him away.
16 Jesus saith unto her, Mary. She turned herself, and saith unto him, Rabboni; which is to say, Master.
17 Jesus saith unto her, Touch me not; for I am not yet ascended to my Father: (John 20:11-17 to :)

Concurrent with Mary encountering Jesus, the women inside were being addressed by one of the "young men"

5 And entering into the sepulchre, they saw a young man sitting on the right side, clothed in a long white garment; and they were affrighted.
6 And he saith unto them, Be not affrighted: Ye seek Jesus of Nazareth, which was crucified: he is risen; he is not here: behold the place where they laid him.
7 But go your way, tell his disciples and Peter that he goeth before you into Galilee: there shall ye see him, as he said unto you. (Mark 16:5-7)

Being perplexed the women react in fear as the "young men" speak to them

5 And as they were afraid, and bowed down *their* faces to the earth, they said unto them, Why seek ye the living among the dead?
6 He is not here, but is risen: remember how he spake unto you when he was yet in Galilee,
7 Saying, The Son of man must be delivered into the hands of sinful men, and be

crucified, and the third day rise again.
8 And they remembered his words, (Luke 24:5-8)

Mary Magdalene receives instruction from Jesus

17 but go to my brethren, and say unto them, I ascend unto my Father, and your Father;
and *to* my God, and your God. (John 20:17 *but*)

The other women, still in the tomb, receive instruction from the angel that had rolled aside the stone

7 And go quickly, and tell his disciples that he is risen from the dead; and, behold, he
goeth before you into Galilee; there shall ye see him: lo, I have told you. (Matt 28:7)

Mary Magdalene and the other women depart together, and as they are leaving, they encounter Jesus

8 And they departed quickly from the sepulchre with fear and great joy; and did run to
bring his disciples word.
9 ¶ And as they went to tell his disciples, behold, Jesus met them, saying, All hail. And
they came and held him by the feet, and worshipped him.
10 Then said Jesus unto them, Be not afraid: go tell my brethren that they go into
Galilee, and there shall they see me. (Matt 28:8-10)

After seeing Jesus they hurry to tell the disciples the good news

8 And they went out quickly, and fled from the sepulchre; for they trembled and were
amazed: neither said they any thing to any *man*; for they were afraid. (Mark 16:8)

Mary Magdalene tells the disciples that she has seen Jesus

18 Mary Magdalene came and told the disciples that she had seen the Lord, and *that* he
had spoken these things unto her. (John 20:18)

Mary Magdalene is not believed by the disciples

9 ¶ Now when *Jesus* was risen early the first *day* of the week, he appeared first to Mary
Magdalene, out of whom he had cast seven devils.
10 *And* she went and told them that had been with him, as they mourned and wept.
11 And they, when they had heard that he was alive, and had been seen of her, believed
not. (Mark 16:9-11)

The other women and Mary Magdalene tell *the rest of* the disciples, and they are not believed

9 And returned from the sepulchre, and told all these things unto the eleven, and to all
the rest.
10 It was Mary Magdalene, and Joanna, and Mary *the mother* of James, and other
women that were with them, which told these things unto the apostles.
11 And their words seemed to them as idle tales, and they believed them not. (Luke 24:9-11)

Peter, confused and unable to accept the resurrection, returns to the sepulchre by himself to look *again*

12 Then arose Peter, and ran unto the sepulchre; (Luke 24:12 to ;)

Peter, unlike John, sees only the physical evidence, and so he departs still confused and unbelieving

12 and stooping down, he beheld the linen clothes laid by themselves, and departed,
wondering in himself at that which was come to pass. (Luke 24:12 *and*)

In the meantime some of the watchmen report the empty tomb to the chief priests

11 ¶ Now when they were going, behold, some of the watch came into the city, and

shewed unto the chief priests all the things that were done.
12 And when they were assembled with the elders, and had taken counsel, they gave
large money unto the soldiers,
13 Saying, Say ye, His disciples came by night, and stole him *away* while we *slept.*
14 And if this come to the governor's ears, we will persuade him, and secure you.
15 So they took the money, and did as they were taught: and this saying is commonly
reported among the Jews until this day. (Matt 28:11-15)

The walk to Emmaus summarized

12 ¶ After that he appeared in another form unto two of them, as they walked, and went
into the country. (Mark 16:12)

A full account of the walk to Emmaus. (Three score furlongs is approximately 7½ miles)

13 ¶ And, behold, two of them went that same day to a village called Emmaus, which
was from Jerusalem *about* threescore furlongs.
14 And they talked together of all these things which had happened.
15 And it came to pass, that, while they communed *together* and reasoned, Jesus
himself drew near, and went with them.
16 But their eyes were holden that they should not know him.
17 And he said unto them, What manner of communications *are* these that ye have one
to another, as ye walk, and are sad?
18 And the one of them, whose name was Cleopas, answering said unto him, Art thou
only a stranger in Jerusalem, and hast not known the things which are come to pass
there in these days?
19 And he said unto them, What things? And they said unto him, Concerning Jesus of
Nazareth, which was a prophet mighty in deed and word before God and all the people:
20 And how the chief priests and our rulers delivered him to be condemned to death,
and have crucified him.
21 But we trusted that it had been he which should have redeemed Israel: and beside all
this, to-day is the third day since these things were done.
22 Yea, and certain women also of our company made us astonished, which were early
at the sepulchre;
23 And when they found not his body, they came, saying, that they had also seen a
vision of angels, which said that he was alive.
24 And certain of them which were with us went to the sepulchre, and found *it* even so
as the women had said: but him they saw not.
25 Then he said unto them, O fools, and slow of heart to believe all that the prophets
have spoken:
26 Ought not Christ to have suffered these things, and to enter into his glory?
27 And beginning at Moses and all the prophets, he expounded unto them in all the
scriptures the things concerning himself.
28 And they drew nigh unto the village, whither they went: and he made as though he
would have gone further.
29 But they constrained him, saying, Abide with us: for it is toward evening, and the
day is far spent. And he went in to tarry with them.
30 And it came to pass, as he sat at meat with them, he took bread, and blessed *it*, and
brake, and gave to them.

31 And their eyes were opened, and they knew him; and he vanished out of their sight.
32 And they said one to another, Did not our heart burn within us, while he talked with
us by the way, and while he opened to us the scriptures?
33 And they rose up the same hour, and returned to Jerusalem, and found the eleven
gathered together, and them that were with them,
34 Saying, The Lord is risen indeed, and hath appeared to Simon.
35 And they told what things *were done* in the way, and how he was known of them in
breaking of bread. (Luke 24:13-35)

Cleopas and his companion report their encounter of Jesus to other disciples, but they are *not* believed

13 And they went and told *it* unto the residue: neither believed they them. (Mark 16:13)

Jesus appears to all of the Apostles, except for Thomas, later that same day

According to the Gospel of Mark

14 ¶ Afterward he appeared unto the eleven as they sat at meat, and upbraided them
with their unbelief and hardness of heart, because they believed not them which had
seen him after he was risen. (Mark 16:14)

According to the Gospel of John

19 ¶ Then the same day at evening, being the first *day* of the week, when the doors
were shut where the disciples were assembled for fear of the Jews, came Jesus and
stood in the midst, and saith unto them, Peace *be* unto you.
20 And when he had so said, he shewed unto them *his* hands and his side. Then were
the disciples glad, when they saw the Lord.
21 Then said Jesus to them again, Peace *be* unto you: as *my* Father hath sent me, even
so send I you.
22 And when he had said this, he breathed on *them*, and saith unto them, Receive ye the
Holy Ghost:
23 Whose soever sins ye remit, they are remitted unto them; *and* whose soever *sins* ye
retain, they are retained.
24 ¶ But Thomas, one of the twelve, called Didymus, was not with them when Jesus
came.
25 The other disciples therefore said unto him, We have seen the Lord. But he said
unto them, Except I shall see in his hands the print of the nails, and put my finger into
the print of the nails, and thrust my hand into his side, I will not believe. (John 20:19-25)

According to the Gospel of Luke

36 ¶ And as they thus spake, Jesus himself stood in the midst of them, and saith unto
them, Peace *be* unto you.
37 But they were terrified and affrighted, and supposed that they had seen a spirit.
38 And he said unto them, Why are ye troubled? and why do thoughts arise in your
hearts?
39 Behold my hands and my feet, that it is I myself: handle me, and see; for a spirit
hath not flesh and bones, as ye see me have.
40 And when he had thus spoken, he shewed them *his* hands and *his* feet.
41 And while they yet believed not for joy, and wondered, he said unto them, Have ye
here any meat?
42 And they gave him a piece of a broiled fish, and of an honeycomb.

43 And he took *it*, and did eat before them.
44 And he said unto them, These are the words which I spake unto you, while I was yet
with you, that all things must be fulfilled, which were written in the law of Moses, and
in the prophets, and *in* the psalms, concerning me.
45 Then opened he their understanding, that they might understand the scriptures,
46 And said unto them, Thus it is written, and thus it behoved Christ to suffer, and to
rise from the dead the third day:
47 And that repentance and remission of sins should be preached in his name among all
nations, beginning at Jerusalem.
48 And ye are witnesses of these things.
49 ¶ And, behold, I send the promise of my Father upon you: but tarry ye in the city of
Jerusalem, until ye be endued with power from on high. (Luke 24:36-49)

177 – PREPARATION FOR DEPARTURE

26 ¶ And after eight days again his disciples were within, and Thomas with them: *then*
came Jesus, the doors being shut, and stood in the midst, and said, Peace *be* unto you.
27 Then saith he to Thomas, Reach hither thy finger, and behold my hands; and reach
hither thy hand, and thrust *it* into my side: and be not faithless, but believing.
28 And Thomas answered and said unto him, My Lord and my God.
29 Jesus saith unto him, Thomas, because thou hast seen me, thou hast believed:
blessed *are* they that have not seen, and *yet* have believed. (John 20:26-29)
15 And he said unto them, Go ye into all the world, and preach the gospel to every
creature.
16 He that believeth and is baptized shall be saved; but he that believeth not shall be
damned.
17 And these signs shall follow them that believe; In my name shall they cast out
devils; they shall speak with new tongues;
18 They shall take up serpents; and if they drink any deadly thing, it shall not hurt
them; they shall lay hands on the sick, and they shall recover. (Mark 16:15-18)

Jesus did many more works, but those written down are sufficient to testify to the correctness of his teaching

30 ¶ And many other signs truly did Jesus in the presence of his disciples, which are not
written in this book:
31 But these are written, that ye might believe that Jesus is the Christ, the Son of God;
and that believing ye might have life through his name. (John 20:30-31)

178 - THE MORNING MEAL

1 After these things Jesus shewed himself again to the disciples at the sea of Tiberias;
and on this wise shewed he *himself.*
2 There were together Simon Peter, and Thomas called Didymus, and Nathanael of
Cana in Galilee, and the *sons* of Zebedee, and two other of his disciples.
3 Simon Peter saith unto them, I go a-fishing. They say unto him, We also go with
thee. They went forth, and entered into a ship immediately; and that night they caught
nothing.
4 But when the morning was now come, Jesus stood on the shore: but the disciples
knew not that it was Jesus.
5 Then Jesus saith unto them, Children, have ye any meat? They answered him, No.

6 And he said unto them, Cast the net on the right side of the ship, and ye shall find.
They cast therefore, and now they were not able to draw it for the multitude of fishes.
7 Therefore that disciple whom Jesus loved saith unto Peter, It is the Lord. Now when
Simon Peter heard that it was the Lord, he girt *his* fisher's coat *unto him*, (for he was
naked,) and did cast himself into the sea.
8 And the other disciples came in a little ship; (for they were not far from land, but as it
were two hundred cubits,) dragging the net with fishes.
9 As soon then as they were come to land, they saw a fire of coals there, and fish laid
thereon, and bread.
10 Jesus saith unto them, Bring of the fish which ye have now caught.
11 Simon Peter went up, and drew the net to land full of great fishes, an hundred and
fifty and three: and for all there were so many, yet was not the net broken.
12 Jesus saith unto them, Come *and* dine. And none of the disciples durst ask him,
Who art thou? knowing that it was the Lord.
13 Jesus then cometh, and taketh bread, and giveth them, and fish likewise.
14 This is now the third time that Jesus shewed himself to his disciples, after that he
was risen from the dead.
15 ¶ So when they had dined, Jesus saith to Simon Peter, Simon, *son* of Jonas, lovest
thou me more than these? He saith unto him, Yea, Lord; thou knowest that I love thee.
He saith unto him, Feed my lambs.
16 He saith to him again the second time, Simon, *son* of Jonas, lovest thou me? He
saith unto him, Yea, Lord; thou knowest that I love thee. He saith unto him, Feed my
sheep.
17 He saith unto him the third time, Simon, *son* of Jonas, lovest thou me? Peter was
grieved because he said unto him the third time, Lovest thou me? And he said unto
him, Lord, thou knowest all things; thou knowest that I love thee. Jesus saith unto him,
Feed my sheep.
18 Verily, verily, I say unto thee, When thou wast young, thou girdedst thyself, and
walkedst whither thou wouldest: but when thou shalt be old, thou shalt stretch forth thy
hands, and another shall gird thee, and carry *thee* whither thou wouldest not.
19 This spake he, signifying by what death he should glorify God. And when he had
spoken this, he saith unto him, Follow me.
20 Then Peter, turning about, seeth the disciple whom Jesus loved following; which
also leaned on his breast at supper, and said, Lord, which is he that betrayeth thee?
21 Peter seeing him saith to Jesus, Lord, and what *shall* this man *do*?
22 Jesus saith unto him, If I will that he tarry till I come, what *is that* to thee? follow
thou me.
23 Then went this saying abroad among the brethren, that that disciple should not die:
yet Jesus said not unto him, He shall not die; but, If I will that he tarry till I come, what
is that to thee?
24 This is the disciple which testifieth of these things, and wrote these things: and we
know that his testimony is true. (John 21:1-24)

179 – FINAL INSTRUCTIONS AND THE RETURN TO GLORY

16 ¶ Then the eleven disciples went away into Galilee, into a mountain where Jesus had
appointed them.
17 And when they saw him, they worshipped him: but some doubted.

18 And Jesus came and spake unto them, saying, All power is given unto me in heaven
and in earth.
19 ¶ Go ye therefore, and teach all nations, baptizing them in the name of the Father,
and of the Son, and of the Holy Ghost:
20 Teaching them to observe all things whatsoever I have commanded you: and, lo, I
am with you alway, *even* unto the end of the world. Amen. (Matt 28:16-20)
50 ¶ And he led them out as far as to Bethany, and he lifted up his hands, and blessed
them.
51 And it came to pass, while he blessed them, he was parted from them, and carried up
into heaven. (Luke 24:50-51)
19 ¶ So then after the Lord had spoken unto them, he was received up into heaven, and
sat on the right hand of God. (Mark 16:19)
52 And they worshipped him, and returned to Jerusalem with great joy:
53 And were continually in the temple, praising and blessing God. Amen. (Luke 24:52-53)
20 And they went forth, and preached every where, the Lord working with *them*, and
confirming the word with signs following. Amen. (Mark 16:20)
25 And there are also many other things which Jesus did, the which, if they should be
written every one, I suppose that even the world itself could not contain the books that
should be written. Amen. (John 21:25)

Part II

THE COMBINED GOSPELS

of

(Matthew, Mark, Luke, and John)

compiled from

The King James Bible of 1611

and

arranged in chronological order

with notes

THE COMBINED GOSPELS
WITH
NOTES
(MATTHEW, MARK, LUKE AND JOHN)
COMPILED IN CHRONOLOGICAL ORDER FROM
THE AUTHORIZED KING JAMES VERSION OF THE BIBLE

CHAPTER 1
THE ETERNAL ORDER OF BEING

Where wast thou "when the morning stars sang together, and all the sons of God shouted for joy?" – Job. God and Christ are eternally one. "Principle and its idea is one, and this one is God, omnipotent, omniscient, and omnipresent Being, and His reflection is man and the universe." "All reality is in God and His creation, harmonious and eternal. That which He makes is good, and He makes all that is made. Therefore the only reality of sin, sickness, or death is the awful fact that unrealities seem real to human, erring belief, until God strips of their disguise." - MBE. Jesus proved these statements to be true, and through his teaching and example showed mankind the pathway to heaven, harmony.

1 In the beginning was the Word, and the Word was with God, and the Word was God.
2 The same was in the beginning with God.
3 All things were made by him; and without him was not any thing made that was
made.
4 In him was life; and the life was the light of men.
5 And the light shineth in darkness; and the darkness comprehended it not. (John 1:1-5)

CHAPTER 2
THE PURPOSE OF THE GOSPELS

1 Forasmuch as many have taken in hand to set forth in order a declaration of those
things which are most surely believed among us,
2 Even as they delivered them unto us, which from the beginning were eyewitnesses,
and ministers of the word;
3 It seemed good to me also, having had perfect understanding of all things from the
very first, to write unto thee in order, most excellent Theophilus,
4 That thou mightest know the certainty of those things, wherein thou hast been
instructed. (Luke 1:1-4)

CHAPTER 3
THE MISSION JOHN THE BAPTIST

6 ¶ There was a man sent from God, whose name *was* John.
7 The same came for a witness, to bear witness of the Light, that all *men* through him
might believe.
8 He was not that Light, but *was sent* to bear witness of that Light.
9 *That* was the true Light, which lighteth every man that cometh into the world.
10 He was in the world, and the world was made by him, and the world knew him not.
11 He came unto his own, and his own received him not.
12 But as many as received him, to them gave he power to become the sons of God,
even to them that believe on his name:
13 Which were born, not of blood, nor of the will of the flesh, nor of the will of man,
but of God. (John 1:6-13)

CHAPTER 4
ELISABETH CONCEIVES JOHN THE BAPTIST

Zacharias served during the course of Abia, the Old Testament Abijah. See I Chronicles 24:10.

5 ¶ There was in the days of Herod, the king of Judæa, a certain priest named
Zacharias, of the course of Abia: and his wife *was* of the daughters of Aaron, and her
name *was* Elisabeth.
6 And they were both righteous before God, walking in all the commandments and
ordinances of the Lord blameless.
7 And they had no child, because that Elisabeth was barren, and they both were *now*
well stricken in years. (Luke 1:5-7)

Gabriel appears to Zacharias

The angel Gabriel appeared to Zacharias during the 2nd administration of Abia, 12-18 Silvan (June 13-19, 5 B.C.)

8 And it came to pass, that while he executed the priest's office before God in the order
of his course,
9 According to the custom of the priest's office, his lot was to burn incense when he
went into the temple of the Lord.
10 And the whole multitude of the people were praying without at the time of incense.
11 And there appeared unto him an angel of the Lord standing on the right side of the
altar of incense.
12 And when Zacharias saw *him*, he was troubled, and fear fell upon him.
13 But the angel said unto him, Fear not, Zacharias: for thy prayer is heard; and thy
wife Elisabeth shall bear thee a son, and thou shalt call his name John.
14 And thou shalt have joy and gladness; and many shall rejoice at his birth.
15 For he shall be great in the sight of the Lord, and shall drink neither wine nor strong
drink; and he shall be filled with the Holy Ghost, even from his mother's womb.
16 And many of the children of Israel shall he turn to the Lord their God.
17 And he shall go before him in the spirit and power of Elias, to turn the hearts of the
fathers to the children, and the disobedient to the wisdom of the just; to make ready a
people prepared for the Lord.
18 And Zacharias said unto the angel, Whereby shall I know this? for I am an old man,
and my wife well stricken in years.
19 And the angel answering said unto him, I am Gabriel, that stand in the presence of
God; and am sent to speak unto thee, and to shew thee these glad tidings.
20 And, behold, thou shalt be dumb, and not able to speak, until the day that these
things shall be performed, because thou believest not my words, which shall be fulfilled
in their season.
21 And the people waited for Zacharias, and marvelled that he tarried so long in the
temple.
22 And when he came out, he could not speak unto them: and they perceived that he
had seen a vision in the temple: for he beckoned unto them, and remained speechless.
23 And it came to pass, that, as soon as the days of his ministration were accomplished,
he departed to his own house. (Luke 1:8-23)

Elisabeth conceived on or about the 23rd of Silvan (June 24, 5 B.C.)

24 And after those days his wife Elisabeth conceived, and hid herself five months,
saying,

25 Thus hath the Lord dealt with me in the days wherein he looked on *me*, to take away
my reproach among men. (Luke 1:24-25)

CHAPTER 5
MARY CONCEIVES CHRIST JESUS

26 And in the sixth month the angel Gabriel was sent from God unto a city of Galilee,
named Nazareth,
27 To a virgin espoused to a man whose name was Joseph, of the house of David; and
the virgin's name *was* Mary.
28 And the angel came in unto her, and said, Hail, *thou that art* highly favoured, the
Lord *is* with thee: blessed *art* thou among women.
29 And when she saw *him*, she was troubled at his saying, and cast in her mind what
manner of salutation this should be.
30 And the angel said unto her, Fear not, Mary: for thou hast found favour with God.
31 And, behold, thou shalt conceive in thy womb, and bring forth a son, and shalt call
his name JESUS.
32 He shall be great, and shall be called the Son of the Highest: and the Lord God shall
give unto him the throne of his father David:
33 And he shall reign over the house of Jacob for ever; and of his kingdom there shall
be no end.
34 Then said Mary unto the angel, How shall this be, seeing I know not a man?
35 And the angel answered and said unto her, The Holy Ghost shall come upon thee,
and the power of the Highest shall overshadow thee: therefore also that holy thing
which shall be born of thee shall be called the Son of God. (Luke 1:26-35)

Mary conceived in the sixth month of Elisabeth's pregnancy
(on the 1st of Tebeth, the Gentile December 25, 5 B.C.)

36 And, behold, thy cousin Elisabeth, she hath also conceived a son in her old age: and
this is the sixth month with her, who was called barren.
37 For with God nothing shall be impossible.
38 And Mary said, Behold the handmaid of the Lord; be it unto me according to thy
word. And the angel departed from her. (Luke 1:36-38)

Jesus was born of Mary. The corporeal man Jesus was human. Mary's conception of him was spiritual, for only purity could reflect Truth and Love, which were plainly incarnate in the good and pure Christ Jesus. - MBE

14 And the Word was made flesh, and dwelt among us, (and we beheld his glory, the
glory as of the only begotten of the Father,) full of grace and truth. (John 1:14)

CHAPTER 6
THE LEGAL & ROYAL GENEALOGY OF JESUS

"The Lord God shall give unto him the throne of his father (ancestor) David." - Luke

The *Royal* Line from Abraham through King David to Joseph, the husband of Mary who was *legally* the father of Jesus.

1 The book of the generation of Jesus Christ, the son of David, the son of Abraham.
2 Abraham begat Isaac; and Isaac begat Jacob; and Jacob begat Judas and his brethren;
3 And Judas begat Phares and Zara of Thamar; and Phares begat Esrom; and Esrom
begat Aram;
4 And Aram begat Aminadab; and Aminadab begat Naasson; and Naasson begat
Salmon;
5 And Salmon begat Booz of Rachab; and Booz begat Obed of Ruth; and Obed begat

Jesse;
6 And Jesse begat David the king; and David the king begat Solomon of her *that had*
been the wife of Urias;
7 And Solomon begat Roboam; and Roboam begat Abia; and Abia begat Asa;
8 And Asa begat Josaphat; and Josaphat begat Joram; and Joram begat Ozias;
9 And Ozias begat Joatham; and Joatham begat Achaz; and Achaz begat Ezekias;
10 And Ezekias begat Manasses; and Manasses begat Amon; and Amon begat Josias;
11 And Josias begat Jechonias and his brethren, about the time they were carried away
to Babylon:
12 And after they were brought to Babylon, Jechonias begat Salathiel; and Salathiel
begat Zorobabel;
13 And Zorobabel begat Abiud; and Abiud begat Eliakim; and Eliakim begat Azor;
14 And Azor begat Sadoc; and Sadoc begat Achim; and Achim begat Eliud;
15 And Eliud begat Eleazar; and Eleazar begat Matthan; and Matthan begat Jacob;
16 And Jacob begat Joseph the husband of Mary, of whom was born Jesus, who is
called Christ.
17 So all the generations from Abraham to David *are* fourteen generations; and from
David until the carrying away into Babylon *are* fourteen generations; and from the
carrying away into Babylon unto Christ *are* fourteen generations. (Matt. 1:1-17)

CHAPTER 7
MARY VISITS ELISABETH

39 And Mary arose in those days, and went into the hill country with haste, into a city
of Juda;
40 And entered into the house of Zacharias, and saluted Elisabeth.
41 And it came to pass, that, when Elisabeth heard the salutation of Mary, the babe
leaped in her womb; and Elisabeth was filled with the Holy Ghost: (Luke 1:39-41)

Elisabeth blesses Mary rejoicing in the fulfillment of the promises spoken through the angel Gabriel: Luke 1:30-35 p. 177.

42 And she spake out with a loud voice, and said, Blessed *art* thou among women, and
blessed *is* the fruit of thy womb.
43 And whence *is* this to me, that the mother of my Lord should come to me?
44 For, lo, as soon as the voice of thy salutation sounded in mine ears, the babe leaped
in my womb for joy.
45 And blessed *is* she that believed: for there shall be a performance of those things
which were told her from the Lord. (Luke 1:42-45)

Mary's Magnificat. Magnify, *μεγαλύνω megalynō*, to esteem highly, extol, celebrate. soul & spirit mean spiritual sense.

46 And Mary said, My soul doth magnify the Lord,
47 And my spirit hath rejoiced in God my Saviour. (Luke 1:46-47)

Low estate, *ταπείνωσις tapeinōsis*. Mary, by overcoming self-will was enabled to bring forth according to the divine will.

48 For he hath regarded the low estate of his handmaiden: for, behold, from henceforth
all generations shall call me blessed.
49 For he that is mighty hath done to me great things; and holy *is* his name.
50 And his mercy *is* on them that fear him from generation to generation. . (Luke 1:48-50)

Note how Mary's submission to God's will revealed how God, divine Love overturns and reverses mortal error.

51 He hath shewed strength with his arm; he hath scattered the proud in the imagination
of their hearts.
52 He hath put down the mighty from *their* seats, and exalted them of low degree.
53 He hath filled the hungry with good things; and the rich he hath sent empty away.

54 He hath holpen his servant Israel, in remembrance of *his* mercy;
55 As he spake to our fathers, to Abraham, and to his seed for ever.
56 And Mary abode with her about three months, and returned to her own house. (Luke
1:51-56)

CHAPTER 8

THE BIRTH AND PROPHECY OF JOHN THE BAPTIST

The birth of John the Baptist was on or about the 7th day of Nisan, the Gentile March 28 or 29, 4 B.C.

57 Now Elisabeth's full time came that she should be delivered; and she brought forth a
son.
58 And her neighbours and her cousins heard how the Lord had shewed great mercy
upon her; and they rejoiced with her. (Luke 1:57-58)

Zacharias confirms the word of Elisabeth that their son is to be named John.

59 And it came to pass, that on the eighth day they came to circumcise the child; and
they called him Zacharias, after the name of his father.
60 And his mother answered and said, Not *so*; but he shall be called John.
61 And they said unto her, There is none of thy kindred that is called by this name.
62 And they made signs to his father, how he would have him called.
63 And he asked for a writing table, and wrote, saying, His name is John. And they
marvelled all. (Luke 1:59-63)

Zacharias foretells that John will be the Forerunner announcing the fulfillment of prophecy, deliverance from our enemies through Christ, Truth.

64 And his mouth was opened immediately, and his tongue *loosed*, and he spake, and
praised God.
65 And fear came on all that dwelt round about them: and all these sayings were noised
abroad throughout all the hill country of Judæa.
66 And all they that heard *them* laid *them* up in their hearts, saying, What manner of
child shall this be! And the hand of the Lord was with him.
67 And his father Zacharias was filled with the Holy Ghost, and prophesied, saying,
68 Blessed *be* the Lord God of Israel; for he hath visited and redeemed his people,
69 And hath raised up an horn of salvation for us in the house of his servant David;
70 As he spake by the mouth of his holy prophets, which have been since the world
began: (Luke 1:64-70)

Enemies, *ἐχθρός echthros*. More than political enemies and invading armies, but all sin, disease and death!

71 That we should be saved from our enemies, and from the hand of all that hate us;
72 To perform the mercy *promised* to our fathers, and to remember his holy covenant;
73 The oath which he sware to our father Abraham,
74 That he would grant unto us, that we being delivered out of the hand of our enemies
might serve him without fear,
75 In holiness and righteousness before him, all the days of our life.
76 And thou, child, shalt be called the prophet of the Highest: for thou shalt go before
the face of the Lord to prepare his ways; (Luke 1:71-76)

"Knowledge of salvation" is rendered "Science and Health" in Wyclif's translation of the New Testament.

77 To give knowledge of salvation unto his people by the remission of their sins,
78 Through the tender mercy of our God; whereby the dayspring from on high hath
visited us,
79 To give light to them that sit in darkness and *in* the shadow of death, to guide our
feet into the way of peace.
80 And the child grew, and waxed strong in spirit, and was in the deserts till the day of

his shewing unto Israel. (Luke 1:77-80)

CHAPTER 9
THE IMMACULATE CONCEPTION REVEALED TO JOSEPH

18 ¶ Now the birth of Jesus Christ was on this wise: When as his mother Mary was
espoused to Joseph, before they came together, she was found with child of the Holy
Ghost.
19 Then Joseph her husband, being a just *man*, and not willing to make her a public
example, was minded to put her away privily.
20 But while he thought on these things, behold, the angel of the Lord appeared unto
him in a dream, saying, Joseph, thou son of David, fear not to take unto thee Mary thy
wife: for that which is conceived in her is of the Holy Ghost.
21 And she shall bring forth a son, and thou shalt call his name JESUS: for he shall
save his people from their sins.
22 Now all this was done, that it might be fulfilled which was spoken of the Lord by the
prophet, saying, (Matt.1:18-22)

Emmanuel, *Ἐμμανουήλ Emmanouēl*, "God (Ēl) with us." Isa. 7:14; 8:8. A term for Christ, the divine title of Jesus.

23 Behold, a virgin shall be with child, and shall bring forth a son, and they shall call
his name Emmanuel, which being interpreted is, God with us.
24 Then Joseph being raised from sleep did as the angel of the Lord had bidden him,
and took unto him his wife:
25 And knew her not till she had brought forth her firstborn son: and he called his name
JESUS. (Matt.1:23-25)

CHAPTER 10
BETHLEHEM AND THE BIRTH OF JESUS

The birth of Jesus would have occurred on the 15th of Tisri, the Gentile September 29, 4 B.C.

1 And it came to pass in those days, that there went out a decree from Cæsar Augustus,
that all the world should be taxed.
2 (*And* this taxing was first made when Cyrenius was governor of Syria.)
3 And all went to be taxed, every one into his own city.
4 And Joseph also went up from Galilee, out of the city of Nazareth, into Judæa, unto
the city of David, which is called Bethlehem; (because he was of the house and lineage
of David:)
5 To be taxed with Mary his espoused wife, being great with child.
6 And so it was, that, while they were there, the days were accomplished that she
should be delivered.
7 And she brought forth her firstborn son, and wrapped him in swaddling clothes, and
laid him in a manger; because there was no room for them in the inn.
8 And there were in the same country shepherds abiding in the field, keeping watch
over their flock by night.
9 And, lo, the angel of the Lord came upon them, and the glory of the Lord shone
round about them: and they were sore afraid.
10 And the angel said unto them, Fear not: for, behold, I bring you good tidings of great
joy, which shall be to all people.
11 For unto you is born this day in the city of David a Saviour, which is Christ the
Lord.
12 And this *shall be* a sign unto you; Ye shall find the babe wrapped in swaddling

clothes, lying in a manger.
13 And suddenly there was with the angel a multitude of the heavenly host praising
God, and saying,
14 Glory to God in the highest, and on earth peace, good will toward men.
15 And it came to pass, as the angels were gone away from them into heaven, the
shepherds said one to another, Let us now go even unto Bethlehem, and see this thing
which is come to pass, which the Lord hath made known unto us.
16 And they came with haste, and found Mary, and Joseph, and the babe lying in a
manger.
17 And when they had seen *it*, they made known abroad the saying which was told
them concerning this child.
18 And all they that heard *it* wondered at those things which were told them by the
shepherds.
19 But Mary kept all these things, and pondered *them* in her heart.
20 And the shepherds returned, glorifying and praising God for all the things that they
had heard and seen, as it was told unto them. (Luke 2:1-20)

CHAPTER 11
SIMEON AND ANNA TESTIFY CONCERNING JESUS

21 And when eight days were accomplished for the circumcising of the child, his name
was called JESUS, which was so named of the angel before he was conceived in the
womb. (Luke 2:21)

Jesus was presented in Jerusalem before being taken home to Nazareth. See Exodus 13:2, 8-15 for the significance of the presentation and the promise of deliverance. For the symbolic meaning of circumcision see Lev. 12:1-8.

22 And when the days of her purification according to the law of Moses were
accomplished, they brought him to Jerusalem, to present *him* to the Lord;
23 (As it is written in the law of the Lord, Every male that openeth the womb shall be
called holy to the Lord;)
24 And to offer a sacrifice according to that which is said in the law of the Lord, A pair
of turtledoves, or two young pigeons.
25 And, behold, there was a man in Jerusalem, whose name *was* Simeon; and the same
man *was* just and devout, waiting for the consolation of Israel: and the Holy Ghost was
upon him.
26 And it was revealed unto him by the Holy Ghost, that he should not see death,
before he had seen the Lord's Christ.
27 And he came by the Spirit into the temple: and when the parents brought in the child
Jesus, to do for him after the custom of the law,
28 Then took he him up in his arms, and blessed God, and said,
29 Lord, now lettest thou thy servant depart in peace, according to thy word:
30 For mine eyes have seen thy salvation,
31 Which thou hast prepared before the face of all people; (Luke 2:22-31)

Moses and the prophets brought enlightenment to Israel. Jesus would glorify Israel by bringing Christ to enlighten the Gentiles.

32 A light to lighten the Gentiles, and the glory of thy people Israel.
33 And Joseph and his mother marvelled at those things which were spoken of him.
(Luke 2:32-33)

Simeon foretells Mary's anguish due to the rejection Jesus would endure for exposing religious hypocrisy, Phariseeism.

34 And Simeon blessed them, and said unto Mary his mother, Behold, this *child* is set

for the fall and rising again of many in Israel; and for a sign which shall be spoken
against;
35 (Yea, a sword shall pierce through thy own soul also,) that the thoughts of many
hearts may be revealed.
36 And there was one Anna, a prophetess, the daughter of Phanuel, of the tribe of Aser:
she was of a great age, and had lived with an husband seven years from her virginity;
37 And she *was* a widow of about fourscore and four years, which departed not from
the temple, but served *God* with fastings and prayers night and day.
38 And she coming in that instant gave thanks likewise unto the Lord, and spake of him
to all them that looked for redemption in Jerusalem.
39 And when they had performed all things according to the law of the Lord, they
returned into Galilee, to their own city Nazareth. (Luke 2:34-39)

CHAPTER 12
THE EARLY YEARS

After the family departed for home, wise men arrive in Jerusalem to honor the new born "King of the Jews."

1 Now when Jesus was born in Bethlehem of Judæa in the days of Herod the king,
behold, there came wise men from the east to Jerusalem,
2 Saying, Where is he that is born King of the Jews? for we have seen his star in the
east, and are come to worship him.
3 When Herod the king had heard *these things*, he was troubled, and all Jerusalem with
him. (Matt. 2:1-3)

Political and religious intolerance to Truth conspired to know WHERE the birth took place.

4 And when he had gathered all the chief priests and scribes of the people together, he
demanded of them where Christ should be born.
5 And they said unto him, In Bethlehem of Judæa: for thus it is written by the prophet,
6 And thou Bethlehem, *in* the land of Juda, art not the least among the princes of Juda:
for out of thee shall come a Governor, that shall rule my people Israel.
7 Then Herod, when he had privily called the wise men, inquired of them diligently
what time the star appeared. (Matt. 2:4-7)

Herod directed the wise men to Bethlehem with instructions to return and tell him where the child was located.

8 And he sent them to Bethlehem, and said, Go and search diligently for the young
child; and when ye have found *him*, bring me word again, that I may come and worship
him also. (Matt. 2:8)

The star did not reappear until *after* the wise men departed from Jerusalem.

9 When they had heard the king, they departed; and, lo, the star, which they saw in the
east, went before them, till it came and stood over where the young child was.
10 When they saw the star, they rejoiced with exceeding great joy. (Matt 2:9-10)

The wise men found the young child alone with Mary ***in the house***. By this time Jesus could be nearly two years of age.

11 ¶ And when they were come into the house, they saw the young child with Mary his
mother, and fell down, and worshipped him: and when they had opened their treasures,
they presented unto him gifts; gold, and frankincense, and myrrh. (Matt. 2:11)

The wise men were compelled to ignore Herod's request to report back to him. An instance of divine protection.

12 And being warned of God in a dream that they should not return to Herod, they
departed into their own country another way. (Matt. 2:12)

Joseph was told in a dream to flee with his family into Egypt, and he obeyed. Another instance of divine protection,

13 And when they were departed, behold, the angel of the Lord appeareth to Joseph in a
dream, saying, Arise, and take the young child and his mother, and flee into Egypt, and

be thou there until I bring thee word: for Herod will seek the young child to destroy
him.
14 When he arose, he took the young child and his mother by night, and departed into
Egypt:
15 And was there until the death of Herod: that it might be fulfilled which was spoken
of the Lord by the prophet, saying, Out of Egypt have I called my son. (Matt. 2:13-15)

Herod displayed his real intention by ordering the slaughter of innocent children under the age of two years.

16 ¶ Then Herod, when he saw that he was mocked of the wise men, was exceeding
wroth, and sent forth, and slew all the children that were in Bethlehem, and in all the
coasts thereof, from two years old and under, according to the time which he had
diligently inquired of the wise men.
17 Then was fulfilled that which was spoken by Jeremy the prophet, saying,
18 In Rama was there a voice heard, lamentation, and weeping, and great mourning,
Rachel weeping *for* her children, and would not be comforted, because they are not.
19 ¶ But when Herod was dead, behold, an angel of the Lord appeareth in a dream to
Joseph in Egypt,
20 Saying, Arise, and take the young child and his mother, and go into the land of
Israel: for they are dead which sought the young child's life.
21 And he arose, and took the young child and his mother, and came into the land of
Israel. (Matt. 2:16-21)

Archelaus was the son of Herod the Great & Malthace, and brother to Herod Antipas, who beheaded John the Baptist.

22 But when he heard that Archelaus did reign in Judæa in the room of his father
Herod, he was afraid to go thither: notwithstanding, being warned of God in a dream,
he turned aside into the parts of Galilee: (Matt. 2:22)

The prophecy was SPOKEN not written. Nazarene signifies being separated or appointed for a divine purpose. See Num. 6:13-21; Judg. 13:1-24 and Amos 2:11 & 12. The family returned home to Nazareth after their flight into Egypt.

23 And he came and dwelt in a city called Nazareth: that it might be fulfilled which was
spoken by the prophets, He shall be called a Nazarene. (Matt. 2:23)
40 And the child grew, and waxed strong in spirit, filled with wisdom: and the grace of
God was upon him. (Luke 2:40)

CHAPTER 13
JESUS VISITS JERUSALEM AT THE AGE OF TWELVE

41 Now his parents went to Jerusalem every year at the feast of the passover.
42 And when he was twelve years old, they went up to Jerusalem after the custom of
the feast. (Luke 2:41-42)

Joseph and Mary thought Jesus was with friends and relatives in the caravan, when actually he never left Jerusalem.

43 And when they had fulfilled the days, as they returned, the child Jesus tarried behind
in Jerusalem; and Joseph and his mother knew not *of it*.
44 But they, supposing him to have been in the company, went a day's journey; and
they sought him among *their* kinsfolk and acquaintance.
45 And when they found him not, they turned back again to Jerusalem, seeking him.
46 And it came to pass, that after three days they found him in the temple, sitting in the
midst of the doctors, both hearing them, and asking them questions.
47 And all that heard him were astonished at his understanding and answers.
48 And when they saw him, they were amazed: and his mother said unto him, Son, why
hast thou thus dealt with us? behold, thy father and I have sought thee sorrowing. (Luke
2:43-48)

No disrespect. Jesus expected his parents to look for him in the temple grounds. Where else would he be?

49 And he said unto them, How is it that ye sought me? wist ye not that I must be about my Father's business? (Luke 2:49)

His reply, not understood by Joseph and Mary, was based on Psalm 40: "I have preached righteousness in the great congregation … I have not concealed thy lovingkindness and thy truth from the great congregation." See Psalm 40.

50 And they understood not the saying which he spake unto them.

51 And he went down with them, and came to Nazareth, and was subject unto them: but his mother kept all these sayings in her heart.

52 And Jesus increased in wisdom and stature, and in favour with God and man. (Luke 2:50-52)

CHAPTER 14
JOHN THE BAPTIST PREPARING THE WAY

According to the Gospel of Mark

Mark's Gospel begins with John the Baptist in the wilderness, baptizing in preparation to receive the Messiah.

1 The beginning of the gospel of Jesus Christ, the Son of God;

2 As it is written in the prophets, Behold, I send my messenger before thy face, which shall prepare thy way before thee.

3 The voice of one crying in the wilderness, Prepare ye the way of the Lord, make his paths straight.

4 John did baptize in the wilderness, and preach the baptism of repentance for the remission of sins.

5 And there went out unto him all the land of Judæa, and they of Jerusalem, and were all baptized of him in the river of Jordan, confessing their sins. (Mark 1:1-5)

The simple apparel and diet of John the Baptist. A girdle of skin means a girdle made of leather. See Matthew 3:4.

6 And John was clothed with camel's hair, and with a girdle of a skin about his loins; and he did eat locusts and wild honey; (Mark 1:6)

John declared that Jesus would bring a spiritual baptism; a moral and mental cleansing.

7 And preached, saying, There cometh one mightier than I after me, the latchet of whose shoes I am not worthy to stoop down and unloose.

8 I indeed have baptized you with water: but he shall baptize you with the Holy Ghost. (Mark 1:7-8)

According to the Gospel of Matthew

To Matthew, earlier events and the fulfillment of prophecy, serve to further define John's role as the Forerunner.

1 In those days came John the Baptist, preaching in the wilderness of Judæa, (Matt. 3:1)

John, in quoting from Isaiah, is imploring *all* of the people to join with him in preparing to receive the Messiah. Repent is *μετανοέω metanoeō* meaning not just to change your thinking, but to put on the Mind of Christ. See Phil. 2:5.

2 And saying, Repent ye: for the kingdom of heaven is at hand.

3 For this is he that was spoken of by the prophet Esaias, saying, The voice of one crying in the wilderness, Prepare ye the way of the Lord, make his paths straight. (Matt. 3:2-3)

John's unpretentious apparel and diet. See Jesus' comments Matthew 11:7-15 & Luke 7:24-28. Meat means food.

4 And the same John had his raiment of camel's hair, and a leathern girdle about his loins; and his meat was locusts and wild honey.

5 Then went out to him Jerusalem, and all Judæa, and all the region round about Jordan,

6 And were baptized of him in Jordan, confessing their sins. (Matt. 3:4-6)

John rebuked the Pharisees and Sadducees for hypocrisy, for their attitude of religious and national superiority.

7 ¶ But when he saw many of the Pharisees and Sadducees come to his baptism, he said unto them, O generation of vipers, who hath warned you to flee from the wrath to come?

8 Bring forth therefore fruits meet for repentance:
9 And think not to say within yourselves, We have Abraham to *our* father: for I say
unto you, that God is able of these stones to raise up children unto Abraham.
10 And now also the axe is laid unto the root of the trees: therefore every tree which
bringeth not forth good fruit is hewn down, and cast into the fire. (Matt. 3:7-10)

John warns the Pharisees and Sadducees that the baptism of Christ is more severe than his; it is spiritual purification by fire. "Jesus said, 'I have cast fire upon the world, and see, I am guarding it until it blazes.'" - *The Coptic Gospel of Thomas*

11 I indeed baptize you with water unto repentance: but he that cometh after me is
mightier than I, whose shoes I am not worthy to bear: he shall baptize you with the
Holy Ghost, and *with* fire:
12 Whose fan *is* in his hand, and he will throughly purge his floor, and gather his wheat
into the garner; but he will burn up the chaff with unquenchable fire. (Matt 3:11-12)

According to the Gospel of Luke

Luke's Gospel supplements by naming political and religious figures that date the beginning of Jesus' ministry at 26 A.D.

1 Now in the fifteenth year of the reign of Tiberius Cæsar, Pontius Pilate being
governor of Judæa, and Herod being tetrarch of Galilee, and his brother Philip tetrarch
of Ituræa and of the region of Trachonitis, and Lysanias the tetrarch of Abilene,
2 Annas and Caiaphas being the high priests, the word of God came unto John the son
of Zacharias in the wilderness.
3 And he came into all the country about Jordan, preaching the baptism of repentance
for the remission of sins; (Luke 3:1-3)

Both the coming of the Messiah, and the Forerunner announcing it, were foretold in scripture. See Isaiah 40:3-5.

4 As it is written in the book of the words of Esaias the prophet, saying, The voice of
one crying in the wilderness, Prepare ye the way of the Lord, make his paths straight.
5 Every valley shall be filled, and every mountain and hill shall be brought low; and the
crooked shall be made straight, and the rough ways *shall be* made smooth;
6 And all flesh shall see the salvation of God. (Luke 3:4-6)

John's rebuke was general, not just for the Pharisees and Sadducees.

7 Then said he to the multitude that came forth to be baptized of him, O generation of
vipers, who hath warned you to flee from the wrath to come? (Luke 3:7)

Jesus later rebuked his Jerusalem disciples who, as descendants of Abraham, thought they needn't repent. See Jn. 8:33

8 Bring forth therefore fruits worthy of repentance, and begin not to say within
yourselves, We have Abraham to *our* father: for I say unto you, That God is able of
these stones to raise up children unto Abraham.
9 And now also the axe is laid unto the root of the trees: every tree therefore which
bringeth not forth good fruit is hewn down, and cast into the fire. (Luke 3:8-9)

The truly repentant, those who sincerely desired to change for the better, asked John what they must do.

10 And the people asked him, saying, What shall we do then?
11 He answereth and saith unto them, He that hath two coats, let him impart to him that
hath none; and he that hath meat, let him do likewise.
12 Then came also publicans to be baptized, and said unto him, Master, what shall we
do?
13 And he said unto them, Exact no more than that which is appointed you.
14 And the soldiers likewise demanded of him, saying, And what shall we do? And he
said unto them, Do violence to no man, neither accuse *any* falsely; and be content with
your wages. (Luke 3:10-14)

John the Baptist openly declared that he was not the Messiah. Messiah is the Hebrew word for Christ.

15 And as the people were in expectation, and all men mused in their hearts of John,
whether he were the Christ, or not;

16 John answered, saying unto *them* all, I indeed baptize you with water; but one
mightier than I cometh, the latchet of whose shoes I am not worthy to unloose: he shall
baptize you with the Holy Ghost and with fire:
17 Whose fan *is* in his hand, and he will throughly purge his floor, and will gather the
wheat into his garner; but the chaff he will burn with fire unquenchable.
18 And many other things in his exhortation preached he unto the people. (Luke 3:15-18)

This is a parenthetic remark about the persecution and imprisonment John the Baptist would later endure.

19 But Herod the tetrarch, being reproved by him for Herodias his brother Philip's wife,
and for all the evils which Herod had done,
20 Added yet this above all, that he shut up John in prison. (Luke 3:19-20)

CHAPTER 15

THE BAPTISM OF JESUS THE CHRIST

"Let it be, for it is fitting that all things be fulfilled in this way." *The Gospel of the Ebionites*. Jesus' concessions (in certain cases) to material methods were for the advancement of spiritual good. - MBE

According to the Gospel of Matthew

13 ¶ Then cometh Jesus from Galilee to Jordan unto John, to be baptized of him. (Matt 3:13)

John realized that what Jesus was bringing into the world would meet mankind's greatest need, purification by Spirit.

14 But John forbad him, saying, I have need to be baptized of thee, and comest thou to
me? (Matt 3:14)

The reason for this baptism is given in Jn. 1:31-33. That [Jesus] should be made manifest (i.e. made known, or identified) in Israel as the Messiah.

15 And Jesus answering said unto him, Suffer *it to be so* now: for thus it becometh us
to fulfil all righteousness. Then he suffered him. (Matt 3:15)

The baptism of Jesus by the Holy Ghost exemplified "the new birth" that reveals man as the child of God.

16 And Jesus, when he was baptized, went up straightway out of the water: and, lo, the
heavens were opened unto him, and he saw the Spirit of God descending like a dove,
and lighting upon him: (Matt 3:16)

John heard through Soul-sense that Jesus was the Messiah who would reveal through Christ, man's sonship with God.

17 And lo a voice from heaven, saying, This is my beloved Son, in whom I am well
pleased. (Matt 3:17)

According to the Gospel of Mark

Only the gospel of Mark mentions that Nazareth was the hometown of Jesus at the time of his baptism.

9 And it came to pass in those days, that Jesus came from Nazareth of Galilee, and was
baptized of John in Jordan.
10 And straightway coming up out of the water, he saw the heavens opened, and the
Spirit like a dove descending upon him: (Mark 1:9-10)

Mark states that what John and others heard was audible.

11 And there came a voice from heaven, *saying*, Thou art my beloved Son, in whom I
am well pleased. (Mark 1:11)

According to the Gospel of John

John the Baptist declared his mission secondary to that of Jesus, who would reveal everyone's pre-existence in Christ.

15 ¶ John bare witness of him, and cried, saying, This was he of whom I spake, He that
cometh after me is preferred before me: for he was before me. (John 1:15)

Here John the Beloved disciple declares it was through grace that Jesus made the Christ, Truth available to everyone.

16 And of his fulness have all we received, and grace for grace. (John 1:16)

Moses brought a sense of grace through the law, and Jesus presented a fuller sense of grace through Christ. And what is grace but seeing all creation through the eyes of God by having the Mind that was in Christ Jesus? (Gen 1:31 & Phil. 2:5)

17 For the law was given by Moses, *but* grace and truth came by Jesus Christ. (John 1:17)

God, Spirit is unseen to the physical senses. Jesus made God known to humanity through his demonstration of Christ.

18 No man hath seen God at any time; the only begotten Son, which is in the bosom of
the Father, he hath declared *him*.

19 ¶ And this is the record of John, when the Jews sent priests and Levites from
Jerusalem to ask him, Who art thou?

20 And he confessed, and denied not; but confessed, I am not the Christ. (John 1:18-20)

John rejected rumors that he was Elijah reincarnated or the prophet foretold by Moses. See (Deut. 18:15)

21 And they asked him, What then? Art thou Elias? And he saith, I am not. Art thou
that prophet? And he answered, No. (John 1:21)

John plainly declares himself to be the Forerunner whose role was to prepare mankind to receive Christ.

22 Then said they unto him, Who art thou? that we may give an answer to them that
sent us. What sayest thou of thyself?

23 He said, I *am* the voice of one crying in the wilderness, Make straight the way of the
Lord, as said the prophet Esaias.

24 And they which were sent were of the Pharisees.

25 And they asked him, and said unto him, Why baptizest thou then, if thou be not that
Christ, nor Elias, neither that prophet? (John 1:22-25)

John answered that his baptism symbolized the moral purification required in preparation for submergence in Spirit.

26 John answered them, saying, I baptize with water: but there standeth one among you,
whom ye know not; (John 1:26)

Science so reverses the evidence before the corporeal human senses, as to make this Scriptural testimony true in our hearts, "The last shall be first and the first last," so that God and His idea may be to us what divinity really is and must of necessity be, --- all-inclusive. - MBE

27 He it is, who coming after me is preferred before me, whose shoe's latchet I am not
worthy to unloose.

28 These things were done in Bethabara beyond Jordan, where John was baptizing. (John
1:27-28)

According to the Gospel of Luke

21 Now when all the people were baptized, it came to pass, that Jesus also being
baptized, and praying, the heaven was opened, (Luke 3:21)

The real man being linked by Science to his Maker, mortals need only turn from sin to find Christ, the real man and his relation to God, and to recognize the divine sonship. - MBE

22 And the Holy Ghost descended in a bodily shape like a dove upon him, and a voice
came from heaven, which said, Thou art my beloved Son; in thee I am well pleased.
(Luke 3:22)

CHAPTER 16

THE NATURAL GENEALOGY OF JESUS – THE SON OF MAN

("Born of a woman, Jesus' advent in the flesh partook partly of Mary's earthly condition, although he was endowed with the Christ, the divine Spirit, without measure." - MBE)

Jesus began his ministry at about the age of thirty.

23 And Jesus himself began to be about thirty years of age, (Luke 3:23 *to* 1st,)

The natural line begins at Joseph the son (son-in-law) of Heli, father of Mary the mother of Jesus, and ends at Adam.

23 being (as was supposed) the son of Joseph, which was *the son* of Heli,

24 Which was *the son* of Matthat, which was *the son* of Levi, which was *the son* of
Melchi, which was *the son* of Janna, which was *the son* of Joseph,

25 Which was *the son* of Mattathias, which was *the son* of Amos, which was *the son* of
Naum, which was *the son* of Esli, which was *the son* of Nagge,

26 Which was *the son* of Maath, which was *the son* of Mattathias, which was *the son* of
Semei, which was *the son* of Joseph, which was *the son* of Juda,

27 Which was *the son* of Joanna, which was *the son* of Rhesa, which was *the son* of

Zorobabel, which was *the son* of Salathiel, which was *the son* of Neri,
28 Which was *the son* of Melchi, which was *the son* of Addi, which was *the son* of
Cosam, which was *the son* of Elmodam, which was *the son* of Er,
29 Which was *the son* of Jose, which was *the son* of Eliezer, which was *the son* of
Jorim, which was *the son* of Matthat, which was *the son* of Levi,
30 Which was *the son* of Simeon, which was *the son* of Juda, which was *the son* of
Joseph, which was *the son* of Jonan, which was *the son* of Eliakim,
31 Which was *the son* of Melea, which was *the son* of Menan, which was *the son* of
Mattatha, which was *the son* of Nathan, which was *the son* of David,
32 Which was *the son* of Jesse, which was *the son* of Obed, which was *the son* of Booz,
which was *the son* of Salmon, which was *the son* of Naasson,
33 Which was *the son* of Aminadab, which was *the son* of Aram, which was *the son* of
Esrom, which was *the son* of Phares, which was *the son* of Juda,
34 Which was *the son* of Jacob, which was *the son* of Isaac, which was *the son* of
Abraham, which was *the son* of Thara, which was *the son* of Nachor,
35 Which was *the son* of Saruch, which was *the son* of Ragau, which was *the son* of
Phalec, which was *the son* of Heber, which was *the son* of Sala,
36 Which was *the son* of Cainan, which was *the son* of Arphaxad, which was *the son* of
Sem, which was *the son* of Noe, which was *the son* of Lamech,
37 Which was *the son* of Mathusala, which was *the son* of Enoch, which was *the son* of
Jared, which was *the son* of Maleleel, which was *the son* of Cainan,
38 Which was *the son* of Enos, which was *the son* of Seth, which was *the son* of Adam,
which was *the son* of God. (Luke 3:23-38 *being*)

CHAPTER 17
JESUS AND HIS FIRST SIX DISCIPLES

The "LAMB OF GOD. The spiritual idea of Love; self-immolation; innocence and purity; sacrifice" - MBE.

29 ¶ The next day John seeth Jesus coming unto him, and saith, Behold the Lamb of
God, which taketh away the sin of the world.
30 This is he of whom I said, After me cometh a man which is preferred before me: for
he was before me.
31 And I knew him not: but that he should be made manifest to Israel, therefore am I
come baptizing with water.
32 And John bare record, saying, I saw the Spirit descending from heaven like a dove,
and it abode upon him.
33 And I knew him not: but he that sent me to baptize with water, the same said unto
me, Upon whom thou shalt see the Spirit descending, and remaining on him, the same
is he which baptizeth with the Holy Ghost.
34 And I saw, and bare record that this is the Son of God.
35 ¶ Again the next day after John stood, and two of his disciples;
36 And looking upon Jesus as he walked, he saith, Behold the Lamb of God! (John 1:29-36)

Two of John the Baptist's disciples, Andrew and John, leave John the Baptist to become disciples of Jesus.

37 And the two disciples heard him speak, and they followed Jesus.
38 Then Jesus turned, and saw them following, and saith unto them, What seek ye?
They said unto him, Rabbi, (which is to say, being interpreted, Master,) where dwellest
thou?

39 He saith unto them, Come and see. They came and saw where he dwelt, and abode
with him that day: for it was about the tenth hour.
40 One of the two which heard John *speak*, and followed him, was Andrew, Simon
Peter's brother. (John 1:37-40)

Andrew, in telling his brother Simon (Peter) about Jesus, refers to Jesus as the Messiah. Apparently he already saw it.

41 He first findeth his own brother Simon, and saith unto him, We have found the
Messias, which is, being interpreted, the Christ.
42 And he brought him to Jesus. (John 1:41-42 *to* 1st.)

Jesus, seeing Simon called him by name and then said: "thou shalt be called Cephas," *Petros* a stone. See Luke 4:3

42 And when Jesus beheld him, he said, Thou art Simon the son of Jona: thou shalt be
called Cephas, which is by interpretation, A stone. (John 1:42 *And*)

Philip, *Amator equorum* lover of horses, means a native of Philippi, a city of Macedonia (Greece). See Jn. 12:20-23

43 ¶ The day following Jesus would go forth into Galilee, and findeth Philip, and saith
unto him, Follow me. (John 1:43)

There were many Greeks living in Galilee at this time, and it appears that Philip took up residence in Bethsaida.

44 Now Philip was of Bethsaida, the city of Andrew and Peter. (John 1:44)

Philip introduced Nathanael, which means "gift of God." He became the sixth disciple of Jesus.

45 Philip findeth Nathanael, and saith unto him, We have found him, of whom Moses
in the law, and the prophets, did write, Jesus of Nazareth, the son of Joseph.
46 And Nathanael said unto him, Can there any good thing come out of Nazareth?
Philip saith unto him, Come and see.
47 Jesus saw Nathanael coming to him, and saith of him, Behold an Israelite indeed, in
whom is no guile!
48 Nathanael saith unto him, Whence knowest thou me? Jesus answered and said unto
him, Before that Philip called thee, when thou wast under the fig tree, I saw thee. (John 1:45-48)

Nathanael, seeing this spiritual insight addressed Jesus as Rabbi (Master), "the King of Israel," "the Son of God."

49 Nathanael answered and saith unto him, Rabbi, thou art the Son of God; thou art the
King of Israel.
50 Jesus answered and said unto him, Because I said unto thee, I saw thee under the fig
tree, believest thou? thou shalt see greater things than these.
51 And he saith unto him, Verily, verily, I say unto you, Hereafter ye shall see heaven
open, and the angels of God ascending and descending upon the Son of man. (John 1:49-51)

CHAPTER 18

WATER INTO WINE

(May Christ, Truth, be present at every bridal altar to turn the water into wine and to give to human life an inspiration by which man's spiritual and eternal existence may be discerned. - MBE)

1 And the third day there was a marriage in Cana of Galilee; and the mother of Jesus
was there:
2 And both Jesus was called, and his disciples, to the marriage. (John 2:1-2)

Mary knew the time for Jesus to show forth his ability to reflect "power from on high" had arrived, and he complied.

3 And when they wanted wine, the mother of Jesus saith unto him, They have no wine. (John 2:3)

Compared to overcoming death, Jesus apparently considered changing water into wine a small demonstration.

4 Jesus saith unto her, Woman, what have I to do with thee? mine hour is not yet come. (John 2:4)

These are the last words of Mary that are recorded in the Bible. We would do well to take her instruction to heart.

5 His mother saith unto the servants, Whatsoever he saith unto you, do *it*.
6 And there were set there six waterpots of stone, after the manner of the purifying of

the Jews, containing two or three firkins apiece.
7 Jesus saith unto them, Fill the waterpots with water. And they filled them up to the
brim.
8 And he saith unto them, Draw out now, and bear unto the governor of the feast. And
they bare *it*.
9 When the ruler of the feast had tasted the water that was made wine, and knew not
whence it was: (but the servants which drew the water knew;) the governor of the feast
called the bridegroom, (John 2:5-9)

Christ produces good wine (true inspiration). It is far superior to (poor wine) human doctrines, ways, and means.

10 And saith unto him, Every man at the beginning doth set forth good wine; and when
men have well drunk, then that which is worse; *but* thou hast kept the good wine until
now.
11 This beginning of miracles did Jesus in Cana of Galilee, and manifested forth his
glory; and his disciples believed on him.
12 ¶ After this he went down to Capernaum, he, and his mother, and his brethren, and
his disciples: and they continued there not many days. (John 2:10-12)

CHAPTER 19
THE FIRST TEMPLE CLEANSING

("The word *temple* also means *body*." "We need a clean body and a clean mind, --- a body rendered pure by Mind as well as washed by water." - MBE)

13 ¶ And the Jews' passover was at hand, and Jesus went up to Jerusalem,
14 And found in the temple those that sold oxen and sheep and doves, and the changers
of money sitting:
15 And when he had made a scourge of small cords, he drove them all out of the
temple, and the sheep, and the oxen; and poured out the changers' money, and
overthrew the tables;
16 And said unto them that sold doves, Take these things hence; make not my Father's
house an house of merchandise.
17 And his disciples remembered that it was written, The zeal of thine house hath eaten
me up. (John 2:13-17)

The carnal mind rejects Truth. Here Jesus' confrontation with ecclesiasticism begins. See Stephen's words, Acts 7:51.

18 ¶ Then answered the Jews and said unto him, What sign shewest thou unto us,
seeing that thou doest these things? (John 2:18)

Jesus foretells his resurrection. This remark was later perverted by the scribes and priests and used against him.

19 Jesus answered and said unto them, Destroy this temple, and in three days I will
raise it up. (John 2:19)

The carnal mind interprets everything materially. However "the wisdom of this world is foolishness with God." I Cor. 3:19

20 Then said the Jews, Forty and six years was this temple in building, and wilt thou
rear it up in three days?
21 But he spake of the temple of his body.
22 When therefore he was risen from the dead, his disciples remembered that he had
said this unto them; and they believed the scripture, and the word which Jesus had said.
(John 2:20-22)

The Passover is a high sabbath. Any miracles done on the "feast day" were considered major violations of the sabbath.

23 ¶ Now when he was in Jerusalem at the passover, in the feast *day*, many believed in
his name, when they saw the miracles which he did. (John 2:23)

Jesus realized that regardless of any personal relationship or professed loyalty, mortal man is not trustworthy.

24 But Jesus did not commit himself unto them, because he knew all *men*,

25 And needed not that any should testify of man: for he knew what was in man. (John 2:24-25)

CHAPTER 20
THE NEED FOR SPIRITUAL REBIRTH

Seeing ye have purified your souls in obeying the truth through the Spirit unto unfeigned love of the brethren, *see that ye* love one another with a pure heart fervently: Being born again, not of corruptible seed, but of incorruptible, by the word of God, which liveth and abideth for ever. - I Pet. 1:22-23. "The new birth is not the work of a moment. It begins with moments, and goes on with years; moments of surrender to God, of childlike trust and joyful adoption of good; moments of self-abnegation, self-consecration, heaven-born hope, and spiritual love." - MBE

A night meeting with Nicodemus, a Pharisee and leading member of the Sanhedrin, who later became a disciple.

1 There was a man of the Pharisees, named Nicodemus, a ruler of the Jews: (John 3:1)

"We know." Here Nicodemus states that the members of the Sanhedrin knew Jesus was sent and empowered by God.

2 The same came to Jesus by night, and said unto him, Rabbi, we know that thou art a teacher come from God: for no man can do these miracles that thou doest, except God be with him. (John 3:2)

Jesus answered the implied question: "How is the healing done?" with the answer, "through a spiritual rebirth." The word translated "again" is ἄνωθεν *anōthen,* and means from above, from a higher place, from the very first, from the beginning.

3 Jesus answered and said unto him, Verily, verily, I say unto thee, Except a man be born again, he cannot see the kingdom of God. (John 3:3)

Jesus is speaking spiritually whereas Nicodemus is hearing and reasoning from a strictly material basis of belief.

4 Nicodemus saith unto him, How can a man be born when he is old? can he enter the second time into his mother's womb, and be born? (John 3:4)

Born of water and of Spirit: washing away the characteristics of the "old man" and submergence in Spirit IS the new birth.

5 Jesus answered, Verily, verily, I say unto thee, Except a man be born of water and *of* the Spirit, he cannot enter into the kingdom of God. (John 3:5)

Spirit and flesh (matter) are terms representing opposites that can no more unite than light and darkness.

6 That which is born of the flesh is flesh; and that which is born of the Spirit is spirit. (John 3:6)

Ye means "all of you." Hence the entire Sanhedrin, and everyone else for that matter, requires a spiritual rebirth.

7 Marvel not that I said unto thee, Ye must be born again. (John 3:7)

Realizing one's true self to be spiritual, not material, and living this truth is the new birth, unseen to the physical senses.

8 The wind bloweth where it listeth, and thou hearest the sound thereof, but canst not tell whence it cometh, and whither it goeth: so is every one that is born of the Spirit.

9 Nicodemus answered and said unto him, How can these things be? (John 3:8-9)

Human philosophy and scholastic theology cannot explain how the transformation from matter to Spirit takes place.

10 Jesus answered and said unto him, Art thou a master of Israel, and knowest not these things? (John 3:10)

Jesus' teaching of the Father and His Christ is not theory. He proved it to be reality, practical Truth leading to eternal Life.

11 Verily, verily, I say unto thee, We speak that we do know, and testify that we have seen; (John 3:11 *to* ;)

The carnal mind rejects Truth calling all error, sin, disease and death realities, while denying the existence of God.

11 and ye receive not our witness. (John 3:11 2nd *and*)

Spiritual teaching appears unreasonable to the carnal mind and therefore incomprehensible and unrealistic.

12 If I have told you earthly things, and ye believe not, how shall ye believe, if I tell you *of* heavenly things? (John 3:12)

The only true identity of Jesus and every man is Christ, the divine image and likeness of God that has never left heaven!

13 And no man hath ascended up to heaven, but he that came down from heaven, *even* the Son of man which is in heaven. (John 3:13)

A mystical statement foretelling the crucifixion. It is also a metaphysical statement that Christ Jesus has shown us the way to rise above the material sense of existence and find our true being in God, Spirit Who is eternal Life.

14 ¶ And as Moses lifted up the serpent in the wilderness, even so must the Son of man be lifted up:

15 That whosoever believeth in him should not perish, but have eternal life. (John 3:14-15)

The only man God created is spiritual and eternal. Jesus came to reveal spiritual manhood the truth about everyone.
16 ¶ For God so loved the world, that he gave his only begotten Son, that whosoever
believeth in him should not perish, but have everlasting life.
17 For God sent not his Son into the world to condemn the world; but that the world
through him might be saved.
18 ¶ He that believeth on him is not condemned: but he that believeth not is condemned
already, because he hath not believed in the name of the only begotten Son of God. (John 3:16-18)

Condemnation is self-inflicted. God through Christ condemns, or destroys sin, disease and death, but never man.
19 And this is the condemnation, that light is come into the world, and men loved
darkness rather than light, because their deeds were evil.
20 For every one that doeth evil hateth the light, neither cometh to the light, lest his
deeds should be reproved.
21 But he that doeth truth cometh to the light, that his deeds may be made manifest, that
they are wrought in God. (John 3:19-21)

CHAPTER 21

(TEMPTATION - REJECTION - VICTORY - DOMINION

(Jesus was tempted on two separate occasions)

1 And Jesus being full of the Holy Ghost returned from Jordan, and was led by the
Spirit into the wilderness,
2 Being forty days tempted of the devil. And in those days he did eat nothing: and
when they were ended, he afterward hungered. (Luke 4:1-2)

The first assault of evil suggestions

The 1st temptation: command *this stone* (singular) that it be made bread, i.e. seek satisfaction in matter.
3 And the devil said unto him, If thou be the Son of God, command this stone that it be
made bread.
4 And Jesus answered him, saying, It is written, That man shall not live by bread alone,
but by every word of God.
5 And the devil, taking him up into an high mountain, shewed unto him all the
kingdoms of the world in a moment of time. (Luke 4:3-5)

The 2nd temptation: seek to acquire political position and authority by admitting that evil can result in good.
6 And the devil said unto him, All this power will I give thee, and the glory of them:
for that is delivered unto me; and to whomsoever I will I give it.
7 If thou therefore wilt worship me, all shall be thine.
8 And Jesus answered and said unto him, Get thee behind me, Satan: for it is written,
Thou shalt worship the Lord thy God, and him only shalt thou serve. (Luke 4:6-8)

The 3rd temptation: acquire ecclesiastical power and prestige by living contrary to what the Scriptures teach.
9 And he brought him to Jerusalem, and set him on a pinnacle of the temple, and said
unto him, If thou be the Son of God, cast thyself down from hence:
10 For it is written, He shall give his angels charge over thee, to keep thee:
11 And in *their* hands they shall bear thee up, lest at any time thou dash thy foot against
a stone. (Luke 4:9-11)

Tempt, *ἐκπειράζω ekpeirazō*, here meaning to do what one knows is contrary to the divine will; to be wilfully disobedient.
12 And Jesus answering said unto him, It is said, Thou shalt not tempt the Lord thy
God. (Luke 4:12)

The devil departs for a season, *καιρός kairos,* to a point when things are brought to crisis, to the final decision point.
13 And when the devil had ended all the temptation, he departed from him for a season.
(Luke 4:13)

A period of more preaching, teaching, and healing

14 ¶ And Jesus returned in the power of the Spirit into Galilee: and there went out a
fame of him through all the region round about.
15 And he taught in their synagogues, being glorified of all. (Luke 4:14-15)

Jesus announces his God-appointed mission to the people in his hometown of Nazareth

16 ¶ And he came to Nazareth, where he had been brought up: and, as his custom was,
he went into the synagogue on the sabbath day, and stood up for to read.
17 And there was delivered unto him the book of the prophet Esaias. And when he had
opened the book, he found the place where it was written,
18 The Spirit of the Lord *is* upon me, because he hath anointed me to preach the gospel
to the poor; he hath sent me to heal the brokenhearted, to preach deliverance to the
captives, and recovering of sight to the blind, to set at liberty them that are bruised,
19 To preach the acceptable year of the Lord.
20 And he closed the book, and he gave *it* again to the minister, and sat down. And the
eyes of all them that were in the synagogue were fastened on him.
21 And he began to say unto them, This day is this scripture fulfilled in your ears. (Luke 4:16-21)

Jesus is mocked by the people living in his hometown
(Rejection despite reports of successful healing and teaching from other regions. *See John 4:44*)

Wondered, *θαυμάζω thaumazō*, not admiration but feelings of doubt or uncertainty; a curious concern. They doubted!

22 And all bare him witness, and wondered at the gracious words which proceeded out
of his mouth. And they said, Is not this Joseph's son?
23 And he said unto them, Ye will surely say unto me this proverb, Physician, heal
thyself: whatsoever we have heard done in Capernaum, do also here in thy country.
24 And he said, Verily I say unto you, No prophet is accepted in his own country. (Luke 4:22-24)

Jesus confronts their skepticism, their unbelief. Unbelief, *ἀπιστία apistia*, disbelief, resistance to accepting truth.

25 But I tell you of a truth, many widows were in Israel in the days of Elias, when the
heaven was shut up three years and six months, when great famine was throughout all
the land;
26 But unto none of them was Elias sent, save unto Sarepta, *a city* of Sidon, unto a
woman *that was* a widow.
27 And many lepers were in Israel in the time of Eliseus the prophet; and none of them
was cleansed, saving Naaman the Syrian. (Luke 4:25-27)

The people of Nazareth attempt to murder Jesus

28 And all they in the synagogue, when they heard these things, were filled with wrath,
29 And rose up, and thrust him out of the city, and led him unto the brow of the hill
whereon their city was built, that they might cast him down headlong. (Luke 4:28-29)

Jesus knew he was being protected by his heavenly Father. Mortal mind can neither see nor destroy spiritual man!

30 But he passing through the midst of them went his way, (Luke 4:30)

Jesus is driven back into the wilderness to face the second assault of evil suggestions

A summary account according to the Gospel of Mark

12 And immediately the spirit driveth him into the wilderness.
13 And he was there in the wilderness forty days, tempted of Satan; and was with the
wild beasts; and the angels ministered unto him. (Mark 1:12-13)

A full and detailed account of the second assault recorded in the Gospel of Matthew

1 Then was Jesus led up of the Spirit into the wilderness to be tempted of the devil.

2 And when he had fasted forty days and forty nights, he was afterward an hungered. (Matt. 4:1-2)

The first time "the tempter" was called "the devil." Now the devil is called "the tempter", i.e. the one who tempted before.

3 And when the tempter came to him, he said, (Matt. 4:3 *to* 2nd ,)

This time the 1st temptation is "stones" (plural). Whereas in the 1st assault the 1st temptation was a "stone" (singular).

3 If thou be the Son of God, command that these stones be made bread.

4 But he answered and said, It is written, Man shall not live by bread alone, but by every word that proceedeth out of the mouth of God. (Matt. 4:3-4 *lf*)

Here the 2nd temptation is elevation to a position of ecclesiastical authority. In the 1st assault this was the 3rd temptation.

5 Then the devil taketh him up into the holy city, and setteth him on a pinnacle of the temple, (Matt. 4:5)

Here the 3rd temptation is to acquire ecclesiastical power in exchange for betraying his highest understanding of right.

6 And saith unto him, If thou be the Son of God, cast thyself down: for it is written, He shall give his angels charge concerning thee: and in *their* hands they shall bear thee up, lest at any time thou dash thy foot against a stone. (Matt. 4:6)

Note Jesus reply: "it is written ***again***" i.e. "to repeat, it is written." Not simply "it is written"!

7 Jesus said unto him, It is written again, Thou shalt not tempt the Lord thy God. (Matt. 4:7)

Note this 3rd temptation is a repetition of what the first time was the 2nd temptation. The word *again* means for the 2nd time.

8 Again, the devil taketh him up into an exceeding high mountain, and sheweth him all the kingdoms of the world, and the glory of them;

9 And saith unto him, All these things will I give thee, if thou wilt fall down and worship me. (Matt. 4:8-9)

Here Jesus asserted his dominion by rejecting all evil suggestions and remaining faithful to the First Commandment.

10 Then saith Jesus unto him, Get thee hence, Satan: for it is written, Thou shalt worship the Lord thy God, and him only shalt thou serve. (Matt. 4:10)

Adherence to Truth opened *the way*. The reward: evil suggestions knocking at the door of thought were silenced, and in their place messages of Truth and Love filled consciousness!

11 Then the devil leaveth him, and, behold, angels came and ministered unto him. (Matt. 4:11)

CHAPTER 22
QUESTIONS ABOUT BAPTISM

Prior to being imprisoned, John the Baptist and his disciples were baptizing at the same time as Jesus and his disciples.

22 ¶ After these things came Jesus and his disciples into the land of Judæa; and there he tarried with them, and baptized.

23 ¶ And John also was baptizing in Aenon near to Salim, because there was much water there: and they came, and were baptized.

24 For John was not yet cast into prison. (John 3:22-24)

The "question" raised by the Pharisees was intended to create division between Jesus and his disciples and John and his disciples.

25 ¶ Then there arose a question between *some* of John's disciples and the Jews about purifying. (John 3:25)

John the Baptist's disciples complain to him that more and more people are going to Jesus and his disciples.

26 And they came unto John, and said unto him, Rabbi, he that was with thee beyond Jordan, to whom thou barest witness, behold, the same baptizeth, and all *men* come to him. (John 3:26)

John the Baptist, free from envy or jealousy, rejoiced that the number following Jesus was increasing!

27 John answered and said, A man can receive nothing, except it be given him from heaven.

28 Ye yourselves bear me witness, that I said, I am not the Christ, but that I am sent
before him.
29 He that hath the bride is the bridegroom: but the friend of the bridegroom, which
standeth and heareth him, rejoiceth greatly because of the bridegroom's voice: this my
joy therefore is fulfilled.
30 He must increase, but I *must* decrease. (John 3:27-30)

Here John the Baptist makes a clear distinction between mortal man and the immortal man that Jesus came to bear witness to through Christ.

31 He that cometh from above is above all: he that is of the earth is earthly, and
speaketh of the earth: he that cometh from heaven is above all.
32 And what he hath seen and heard, that he testifieth; and no man receiveth his
testimony.
33 He that hath received his testimony hath set to his seal that God is true.
34 For he whom God hath sent speaketh the words of God: for God giveth not the Spirit
by measure *unto him.*
35 The Father loveth the Son, and hath given all things into his hand.
36 He that believeth on the Son hath everlasting life: and he that believeth not the Son
shall not see life; but the wrath of God abideth on him. (John 3:31-36)

From this experience early in his ministry, Jesus was alerted to the adversarial intentions of the Pharisees.

1 When therefore the Lord knew how the Pharisees had heard that Jesus made and
baptized more disciples than John, (John 4:1)

A statement that although Jesus did not himself baptize, he did not force his disciples to stop the practice.

2 (Though Jesus himself baptized not, but his disciples,) (John 4:2)

It is likely that one reason Jesus left Judæa for Galilee was to maintain harmony with John and his disciples. This was also an opportunity to teach his disciples by example to not concern themselves with "Who shall be the greatest."

3 He left Judæa, and departed again into Galilee. (John 4:3)

In his trip North through Samaria, Jesus gives a foundational lesson on the nature of God and the meaning of worship.

4 And he must needs go through Samaria. (John 4:4)

CHAPTER 23
THE TRUE GOD AND THE TRUE WORSHIP

5 Then cometh he to a city of Samaria, which is called Sychar, near to the parcel of
ground that Jacob gave to his son Joseph. (John 4:5)

Jesus arrived at "Jacob's well" at about twelve o'clock noon.

6 Now Jacob's well was there. Jesus therefore, being wearied with *his* journey, sat thus
on the well: *and* it was about the sixth hour.
7 There cometh a woman of Samaria to draw water: Jesus saith unto her, Give me to
drink.
8 (For his disciples were gone away unto the city to buy meat.)
9 Then saith the woman of Samaria unto him, How is it that thou, being a Jew, askest
drink of me, which am a woman of Samaria? (John 4:6-9 *to* ?)

A parenthetical statement explaining the woman's question since the Jews generally viewed Samaritans with contempt.

9 for the Jews have no dealings with the Samaritans.
10 Jesus answered and said unto her, If thou knewest the gift of God, and who it is that
saith to thee, Give me to drink; thou wouldest have asked of him, and he would have
given thee living water. (John 4:9-10 *for*)

Jesus was speaking spiritually. Like Nicodemus, the woman was reasoning from a material basis and did not understand.

11 The woman saith unto him, Sir, thou hast nothing to draw with, and the well is deep:
from whence then hast thou that living water?
12 Art thou greater than our father Jacob, which gave us the well, and drank thereof

himself, and his children, and his cattle? (John 4:11-12)
Jesus explained that he was not speaking of H_2O, but what it symbolizes, that which man thirsts for, eternal Life.
13 Jesus answered and said unto her, Whosoever drinketh of this water shall thirst again:
14 But whosoever drinketh of the water that I shall give him shall never thirst; but the water that I shall give him shall be in him a well of water springing up into everlasting life. (John 4:13-14)
The woman displayed a receptive thought. "Blessed *are* the poor in spirit: for theirs is the kingdom of heaven." - Jesus
15 The woman saith unto him, Sir, give me this water, that I thirst not, neither come hither to draw. (John 4:15)
Jesus next sought to determine the woman's integrity.
16 Jesus saith unto her, Go, call thy husband, and come hither. (John 4:16)
The woman, by her honest reply, displayed forthrightness, a foundation on which she could understand more.
17 The woman answered and said, I have no husband. Jesus said unto her, Thou hast well said, I have no husband:
18 For thou hast had five husbands; and he whom thou now hast is not thy husband: in that saidst thou truly. (John 4:17-18)
The woman's spiritual intuition, "Christ in you, the hope of glory" Col. 1:27, was awakened.
19 The woman saith unto him, Sir, I perceive that thou art a prophet.
20 Our fathers worshipped in this mountain; and ye say, that in Jerusalem is the place where men ought to worship. (John 4:19-20)
Jesus replied that a material sense of worship (both location and deity) must give place to a more spiritual idea of worship.
21 Jesus saith unto her, Woman, believe me, the hour cometh, when ye shall neither in this mountain, nor yet at Jerusalem, worship the Father. (John 4:21)
"Salvation is of the Jews" refers to what was revealed through the Prophets and recorded in the Hebrew Scriptures.
22 Ye worship ye know not what: we know what we worship: for salvation is of the Jews. (John 4:22)
The statement that follows applies to mankind universally and always.
23 But the hour cometh, and now is, when the true worshippers shall worship the Father in spirit and in truth: for the Father seeketh such to worship him. (John 4:23)
Jesus defines God as "Spirit." The word "is" was added by the Revisers, and the "a" was previously added to the text.
24 God *is* a Spirit: and they that worship him must worship *him* in spirit and in truth. (John 4:24)
This Samaritan woman obviously knew something of the Hebrew Scriptures and the prophecies concerning a Messiah.
25 The woman saith unto him, I know that Messias cometh, which is called Christ: when he is come, he will tell us all things. (John 4:25)
Jesus declared the presence of the Christ to be in the ever-present NOW. The word "he" was added by the revisers.
26 Jesus saith unto her, I that speak unto thee am *he*. (John 4:26)
The disciples apparently entertained judgmental and perhaps carnal thoughts about his conversing with a woman.
27 ¶ And upon this came his disciples, and marvelled that he talked with the woman: yet no man said, What seekest thou? or, Why talkest thou with her?
28 The woman then left her waterpot, and went her way into the city, and saith to the men, (John 4:27-28)
The Samaritan men proved more open minded to what "a woman" had to say than did the disciples after the resurrection.
29 Come, see a man, which told me all things that ever I did: is not this the Christ
30 Then they went out of the city, and came unto him. (John 4:29-30)
Interim: After the woman left, Jesus used the opportunity to teach the disciples.
31 In the mean while his disciples prayed him, saying, Master, eat.
32 But he said unto them, I have meat to eat that ye know not of. (John 4:31-32)
Jesus was speaking symbolically to teach *spiritually*. His disciples were interpreting what he said *literally*.
33 Therefore said the disciples one to another, Hath any man brought him *ought* to eat? (John 4:33)

Jesus then explained what the symbols meant. Generally meat meant food, but here it meant that which truly satisfies.

34 Jesus saith unto them, My meat is to do the will of him that sent me, and to finish his
work. (John 4:34)

Grain, ready for harvest has a glistening white appearance. The point being made is that harvest time is always NOW.

35 Say not ye, There are yet four months, and *then* cometh harvest? behold, I say unto
you, Lift up your eyes, and look on the fields; for they are white already to harvest.
36 And he that reapeth receiveth wages, and gathereth fruit unto life eternal: that both
he that soweth and he that reapeth may rejoice together.
37 And herein is that saying true, One soweth, and another reapeth.
38 I sent you to reap that whereon ye bestowed no labour: other men laboured, and ye
are entered into their labours. (John 4:35-38)

The unbiased thought will at least check things out before deciding.

39 ¶ And many of the Samaritans of that city believed on him for the saying of the
woman, which testified, He told me all that ever I did.
40 So when the Samaritans were come unto him, they besought him that he would tarry
with them: and he abode there two days. (John 4:39-40)

"Blessed *are* they which do hunger and thirst after righteousness: for they shall be filled," even Samaritans! - Jesus

41 And many more believed because of his own word; (John 4:41)

Apparently, among the Samaritans, some recognized who Jesus was before some of his own disciples.

42 And said unto the woman, Now we believe, not because of thy saying: for we have
heard *him* ourselves, and know that this is indeed the Christ, the Saviour of the world.
(John 4:42)

Two days later Jesus departed Samaria for Galilee..

43 ¶ Now after two days he departed thence, and went into Galilee.
44 For Jesus himself testified, that a prophet hath no honour in his own country. (John
4:43-44)

CHAPTER 24
JOHN THE BAPTIST IS CAST INTO PRISON

According to the Gospel of Matthew

12 ¶ Now when Jesus had heard that John was cast into prison, he departed into Galilee;
(Matt 4:12)

According to the Gospel of Mark

14 Now after that John was put in prison, Jesus came into Galilee, preaching the gospel
of the kingdom of God,
15 And saying, The time is fulfilled, and the kingdom of God is at hand: repent ye, and
believe the gospel. (Mark 1:14-15)

CHAPTER 25
JESUS DEPARTS NAZARETH TO DWELL IN CAPERNAUM

According to the Gospel of Matthew

John's Gospel indicates that Jesus went to Nazareth first and then immediately relocated to Capernaum.

13 And leaving Nazareth, he came and dwelt in Capernaum, which is upon the sea
coast, in the borders of Zabulon and Nephthalim: (Matt. 4:13)

Matthew saw this relocation from Nazareth to Capernaum as fulfilling prophecy. – Isaiah 9:1 & 2.

14 That it might be fulfilled which was spoken by Esaias the prophet, saying,
15 The land of Zabulon, and the land of Nephthalim, *by* the way of the sea, beyond
Jordan, Galilee of the Gentiles;
16 The people which sat in darkness saw great light; and to them which sat in the region
and shadow of death light is sprung up. (Matt. 4:14-16)

Repent *μετανοέω, metanoeō,* change your mind. Not from evil to good thoughts, but from the human to the divine Mind.

17 ¶ From that time Jesus began to preach, and to say, Repent: for the kingdom of
heaven is at hand. (Matt. 4:17)

According to the Gospel of John

An open reception in Galilee, where no one knew his family tree, and where he was away from the Jerusalem elitists.

45 Then when he was come into Galilee, the Galilæans received him, having seen all
the things that he did at Jerusalem at the feast: for they also went unto the feast. (John 4:45)

While in Cana Jesus healed a nobleman's son that was in Capernaum

46 So Jesus came again into Cana of Galilee, where he made the water wine. And there
was a certain nobleman, whose son was sick at Capernaum.
47 When he heard that Jesus was come out of Judæa into Galilee, he went unto him,
and besought him that he would come down, and heal his son: for he was at the point of
death. (John 4:46-47)

Jesus urged his listeners to rely on God, Spirit and not to place so much reliance on material sense testimony.

48 Then said Jesus unto him, Except ye see signs and wonders, ye will not believe.
49 The nobleman saith unto him, Sir, come down ere my child die. (John 4:48-49)

Personal presence is not required to heal spiritually. It is about 21 miles as the crow flies between Cana and Capernaum.

50 Jesus saith unto him, Go thy way; thy son liveth. And the man believed the word
that Jesus had spoken unto him, and he went his way.
51 And as he was now going down, his servants met him, and told *him*, saying, Thy son
liveth.
52 Then inquired he of them the hour when he began to amend. And they said unto
him, Yesterday at the seventh hour the fever left him. (John 4:50-52)

The father realized the power of spiritual truth on human experience. Spirit being ever-present, its effect is instantaneous.

53 So the father knew that *it was* at the same hour, in the which Jesus said unto him,
Thy son liveth: and himself believed, and his whole house.
54 This *is* again the second miracle *that* Jesus did, when he was come out of Judæa into
Galilee. (John 4:53-54)

CHAPTER 26
THE FIRST CALLING OF PETER & ANDREW, JAMES & JOHN

According to the Gospel of Mark

16 Now as he walked by the sea of Galilee, he saw Simon and Andrew his brother
casting a net into the sea: for they were fishers.
17 And Jesus said unto them, Come ye after me, and I will make you to become fishers
of men.
18 And straightway they forsook their nets, and followed him.
19 And when he had gone a little further thence, he saw James the *son* of Zebedee, and
John his brother, who also were in the ship mending their nets.
20 And straightway he called them: and they left their father Zebedee in the ship with
the hired servants, and went after him. (Mark 1:16-20)

According to the Gospel of Matthew

18 ¶ And Jesus, walking by the sea of Galilee, saw two brethren, Simon called Peter,
and Andrew his brother, casting a net into the sea: for they were fishers.
19 And he saith unto them, Follow me, and I will make you fishers of men.

20 And they straightway left *their* nets, and followed him.
21 And going on from thence, he saw other two brethren, James *the son* of Zebedee,
and John his brother, in a ship with Zebedee their father, mending their nets; and he
called them.
22 And they immediately left the ship and their father, and followed him. (Matt 4:18-22)

CHAPTER 27
AN EXTENSIVE MINISTRY IN AND BEYOND GALILEE

23 ¶ And Jesus went about all Galilee, teaching in their synagogues, and preaching the
gospel of the kingdom, and healing all manner of sickness and all manner of disease
among the people.
24 And his fame went throughout all Syria: and they brought unto him all sick people
that were taken with divers diseases and torments, and those which were possessed with
devils, and those which were lunatic, and those that had the palsy; and he healed them.
25 And there followed him great multitudes of people from Galilee, and *from*
Decapolis, and *from* Jerusalem, and *from* Judæa, and *from* beyond Jordan. (Matt 4:23-25)

CHAPTER 28
THE SERMON ON THE MOUNT

"He was set," i.e. anchored in Truth. Nowhere does Jesus suggest that his teaching is too idealistic to be practical.

1 And seeing the multitudes, he went up into a mountain: and when he was set, his
disciples came unto him:
2 And he opened his mouth, and taught them, saying, (Matt 5:1-2)

The Beatitudes. Only when understood spiritually can it be seen how the following requirements lead to happiness.

3 Blessed *are* the poor in spirit: for theirs is the kingdom of heaven.
4 Blessed *are* they that mourn: for they shall be comforted.
5 Blessed *are* the meek: for they shall inherit the earth.
6 Blessed *are* they which do hunger and thirst after righteousness: for they shall be
filled.
7 Blessed *are* the merciful: for they shall obtain mercy.
8 Blessed *are* the pure in heart: for they shall see God.
9 Blessed *are* the peacemakers: for they shall be called the children of God.
10 Blessed *are* they which are persecuted for righteousness' sake: for theirs is the
kingdom of heaven.
11 Blessed are ye, when *men* shall revile you, and persecute *you*, and shall say all
manner of evil against you falsely, for my sake.
12 Rejoice, and be exceeding glad: for great *is* your reward in heaven: for so persecuted
they the prophets which were before you. (Matt 5:3-12)

The call to demonstrate. Knowing what to do is not enough. It must be put into practice.

13 ¶ Ye are the salt of the earth: but if the salt have lost his savour, wherewith shall it
be salted? it is thenceforth good for nothing, but to be cast out, and to be trodden under
foot of men.
14 Ye are the light of the world. A city that is set on an hill cannot be hid.
15 Neither do men light a candle, and put it under a bushel, but on a candlestick; and it
giveth light unto all that are in the house.
16 Let your light so shine before men, that they may see your good works, and glorify
your Father which is in heaven. (Matt 5:13-16)

Total compliance with the Ten Commandments is required. Jesus stressed the need to *live* the Commandments.

17 ¶ Think not that I am come to destroy the law, or the prophets: I am not come to
destroy, but to fulfil.
18 For verily I say unto you, Till heaven and earth pass, one jot or one tittle shall in no
wise pass from the law, till all be fulfilled.
19 Whosoever therefore shall break one of these least commandments, and shall teach
men so, he shall be called the least in the kingdom of heaven: but whosoever shall do
and teach *them*, the same shall be called great in the kingdom of heaven.
20 For I say unto you, That except your righteousness shall exceed *the righteousness* of
the scribes and Pharisees, ye shall in no case enter into the kingdom of heaven. (Matt 5:17-20)

Reconciliation with our fellow man is a necessary step in realizing our oneness with the divine.

21 ¶ Ye have heard that it was said by them of old time, Thou shalt not kill; and
whosoever shall kill shall be in danger of the judgment: (Matt 5:21)

The words 'without cause' are not present in some copies, nor in the Jewish Gospel." - *Gospel of the Nazareans.* This note from the *Gospel of the Nazareans* is consistent with everything Jesus taught.

22 But I say unto you, That whosoever is angry with his brother without a cause shall
be in danger of the judgment: and whosoever shall say to his brother, Raca, shall be in
danger of the council: but whosoever shall say, Thou fool, shall be in danger of hell
fire.
23 Therefore if thou bring thy gift to the altar, and there rememberest that thy brother
hath aught against thee;
24 Leave there thy gift before the altar, and go thy way; first be reconciled to thy
brother, and then come and offer thy gift. (Matt 5:22-24)

To "agree with thine adversary" does not mean to yield to the promptings of evil, but rather to come to terms with evil by identifying evil AS evil, and so avoid becoming its victim. God, good is All power. "Get thee hence, Satan." - Jesus.

25 Agree with thine adversary quickly, whiles thou art in the way with him; lest at any
time the adversary deliver thee to the judge, and the judge deliver thee to the officer,
and thou be cast into prison.
26 Verily I say unto thee, Thou shalt by no means come out thence, till thou hast paid
the uttermost farthing. (Matt 5:25-26)

Purity of thought is the standard. Impure thoughts must be rejected.

27 ¶ Ye have heard that it was said by them of old time, Thou shalt not commit
adultery:
28 But I say unto you, That whosoever looketh on a woman to lust after her hath
committed adultery with her already in his heart.
29 And if thy right eye offend thee, pluck it out, and cast *it* from thee: for it is profitable
for thee that one of thy members should perish, and not *that* thy whole body should be
cast into hell.
30 And if thy right hand offend thee, cut it off, and cast *it* from thee: for it is profitable
for thee that one of thy members should perish, and not *that* thy whole body should be
cast into hell.
31 It hath been said, Whosoever shall put away his wife, let him give her a writing of
divorcement:
32 But I say unto you, That whosoever shall put away his wife, saving for the cause of
fornication, causeth her to commit adultery: and whosoever shall marry her that is
divorced committeth adultery. (Matt 5:27-32)

The requirement to be upright and forthright.

33 ¶ Again, ye have heard that it hath been said by them of old time, Thou shalt not

forswear thyself, but shalt perform unto the Lord thine oaths:
34 But I say unto you, Swear not at all; neither by heaven; for it is God's throne:
35 Nor by the earth; for it is his footstool: neither by Jerusalem; for it is the city of the
great King.
36 Neither shalt thou swear by thy head, because thou canst not make one hair white or
black. (Matt 5:33-36)

"Yea, yea; Nay, nay" does not mean "Yes, yes; No, no." It means something is either right or wrong; no compromising!

37 But let your communication be, Yea, yea; Nay, nay: for whatsoever is more than
these cometh of evil. (Matt 5:37)

Reconciliation with our fellow man is required.

38 ¶ Ye have heard that it hath been said, An eye for an eye, and a tooth for a tooth:
39 But I say unto you, That ye resist not evil: but whosoever shall smite thee on thy
right cheek, turn to him the other also.
40 And if any man will sue thee at the law, and take away thy coat, let him have *thy*
cloak also.
41 And whosoever shall compel thee to go a mile, go with him twain.
42 Give to him that asketh thee, and from him that would borrow of thee turn not thou
away. (Matt 5:38-42)

Divine Love is the answer. It means to live love as God loves.

43 ¶ Ye have heard that it hath been said, Thou shalt love thy neighbour, and hate thine
enemy.
44 But I say unto you, Love your enemies, bless them that curse you, do good to them
that hate you, and pray for them which despitefully use you, and persecute you;
45 That ye may be the children of your Father which is in heaven: for he maketh his
sun to rise on the evil and on the good, and sendeth rain on the just and on the unjust.
46 For if ye love them which love you, what reward have ye? do not even the publicans
the same?
47 And if ye salute your brethren only, what do ye more *than others*? do not even the
publicans so? (Matt. 5:43-47)

The demand to be "perfect" is not an abstract statement. It means that 100% compliance with this teaching is required.

48 Be ye therefore perfect, even as your Father which is in heaven is perfect. (Matt. 5:48)

Sincerity is demanded. Hypocrisy not only deceives others, it is a destructive form self-deception and must be put off.

1 Take heed that ye do not your alms before men, to be seen of them: otherwise ye have
no reward of your Father which is in heaven.
2 Therefore when thou doest *thine* alms, do not sound a trumpet before thee, as the
hypocrites do in the synagogues and in the streets, that they may have glory of men.
Verily I say unto you, They have their reward.
3 But when thou doest alms, let not thy left hand know what thy right hand doeth:
4 That thine alms may be in secret: and thy Father which seeth in secret himself shall
reward thee openly. (Matt 6:1-4)

Fair seeming instead of a forthright character must be repudiated.

5 ¶ And when thou prayest, thou shalt not be as the hypocrites *are:* for they love to
pray standing in the synagogues and in the corners of the streets, that they may be seen
of men. Verily I say unto you, They have their reward.
6 But thou, when thou prayest, enter into thy closet, and when thou hast shut thy door,
pray to thy Father which is in secret; and thy Father which seeth in secret shall reward
thee openly.
7 But when ye pray, use not vain repetitions, as the heathen *do:* for they think that they

shall be heard for their much speaking.
8 Be not ye therefore like unto them: for your Father knoweth what things ye have need
of, before ye ask him. (Matt 6:5-8)

The Lord's Prayer. The emphasis is on self-examination and corrective action, acknowledging God as the *only* power.

9 After this manner therefore pray ye: Our Father which art in heaven, Hallowed be thy
name.
10 Thy kingdom come. Thy will be done in earth, as *it is* in heaven.
11 Give us this day our daily bread.
12 And forgive us our debts, as we forgive our debtors.
13 And lead us not into temptation, but deliver us from evil: For thine is the kingdom,
and the power, and the glory, for ever. Amen.
14 For if ye forgive men their trespasses, your heavenly Father will also forgive you:
15 But if ye forgive not men their trespasses, neither will your Father forgive your
trespasses. (Matt 6:9-15)

Mere outward display is condemned. hypocrites, ὑποκριτής *hypokritēs*, from theatre an actor, stage player, pretender.

16 ¶ Moreover when ye fast, be not, as the hypocrites, of a sad countenance: for they
disfigure their faces, that they may appear unto men to fast. Verily I say unto you,
They have their reward.
17 But thou, when thou fastest, anoint thine head, and wash thy face;
18 That thou appear not unto men to fast, but unto thy Father which is in secret: and thy
Father, which seeth in secret, shall reward thee openly. (Matt 6:16-18)

Materialism leads to darkness. Spirituality is the path to enlightenment. Duplicity also leads to darkness, so reject it.

19 ¶ Lay not up for yourselves treasures upon earth, where moth and rust doth corrupt,
and where thieves break through and steal:
20 But lay up for yourselves treasures in heaven, where neither moth nor rust doth
corrupt, and where thieves do not break through nor steal:
21 For where your treasure is, there will your heart be also.
22 The light of the body is the eye: if therefore thine eye be single, thy whole body
shall be full of light.
23 But if thine eye be evil, thy whole body shall be full of darkness. If therefore the
light that is in thee be darkness, how great *is* that darkness! (Matt 6:19-23)

It is impossible to serve both Spirit and matter, Truth and error, or good and evil.

24 ¶ No man can serve two masters: for either he will hate the one, and love the other;
or else he will hold to the one, and despise the other. Ye cannot serve God and
mammon. (Matt 6:24)

Obedient trustfulness is required. Notice the "take no thought" cautions. Do we think Jesus said it but didn't mean it?

25 Therefore I say unto you, Take no thought for your life, what ye shall eat, or what ye
shall drink; nor yet for your body, what ye shall put on. Is not the life more than meat,
and the body than raiment?
26 Behold the fowls of the air: for they sow not, neither do they reap, nor gather into
barns; yet your heavenly Father feedeth them. Are ye not much better than they?
27 Which of you by taking thought can add one cubit unto his stature?
28 And why take ye thought for raiment? Consider the lilies of the field, how they
grow; they toil not, neither do they spin:
29 And yet I say unto you, That even Solomon in all his glory was not arrayed like one
of these.
30 Wherefore, if God so clothe the grass of the field, which to-day is, and to-morrow is
cast into the oven, *shall he* not much more *clothe* you, O ye of little faith? (Matt 6:25-30)

Attend to the "First love" and all needs will be met.

31 Therefore take no thought, saying, What shall we eat? or, What shall we drink? or, Wherewithal shall we be clothed? (Matt. 6:31)

He was addressing Israelites, but as earlier noted: "He came unto his own, and his own received him not." John 1:11

32 (For after all these things do the Gentiles seek:) for your heavenly Father knoweth that ye have need of all these things. (Matt. 6:32)

Our "first love" (Rev. 2:4), should be to seek the spiritual state of consciousness called heaven, and NOT to make comfort or ease in matter the priority. See Luke 12:15-21.

33 But seek ye first the kingdom of God, and his righteousness; and all these things shall be added unto you.

34 Take therefore no thought for the morrow: for the morrow shall take thought for the things of itself. Sufficient unto the day *is* the evil thereof. (Matt. 6:33-34)

Do not judge according to material sense testimony since it will most likely lead to a state of self-righteousness.

1 Judge not, that ye be not judged.

2 For with what judgment ye judge, ye shall be judged: and with what measure ye mete, it shall be measured to you again.

3 And why beholdest thou the mote that is in thy brother's eye, but considerest not the beam that is in thine own eye?

4 Or how wilt thou say to thy brother, Let me pull out the mote out of thine eye; and, behold, a beam *is* in thine own eye?

5 Thou hypocrite, first cast out the beam out of thine own eye; and then shalt thou see clearly to cast out the mote out of thy brother's eye. (Matt 7:1-5)

Exercise divine wisdom by not imposing your understanding on the unreceptive.

6 ¶ Give not that which is holy unto the dogs, neither cast ye your pearls before swine, lest they trample them under their feet, and turn again and rend you. (Matt 7:6)

Persistence and expectancy of good is required.

7 ¶ Ask, and it shall be given you; seek, and ye shall find; knock, and it shall be opened unto you:

8 For every one that asketh receiveth; and he that seeketh findeth; and to him that knocketh it shall be opened.

9 Or what man is there of you, whom if his son ask bread, will he give him a stone?

10 Or if he ask a fish, will he give him a serpent?

11 If ye then, being evil, know how to give good gifts unto your children, how much more shall your Father which is in heaven give good things to them that ask him? (Matt 7:7-11)

The Golden Rule.

12 Therefore all things whatsoever ye would that men should do to you, do ye even so to them: for this is the law and the prophets. (Matt 7:12)

The guidelines herein outlined are to be put into practice.

13 ¶ Enter ye in at the strait gate: for wide *is* the gate, and broad *is* the way, that leadeth to destruction, and many there be which go in thereat:

14 Because strait *is* the gate, and narrow *is* the way, which leadeth unto life, and few there be that find it. (Matt 7:13-14)

Deeds not words.

15 ¶ Beware of false prophets, which come to you in sheep's clothing, but inwardly they are ravening wolves.

16 Ye shall know them by their fruits. Do men gather grapes of thorns, or figs of thistles?

17 Even so every good tree bringeth forth good fruit; but a corrupt tree bringeth forth evil fruit.

18 A good tree cannot bring forth evil fruit, neither *can* a corrupt tree bring forth good fruit.
19 Every tree that bringeth not forth good fruit is hewn down, and cast into the fire.
20 Wherefore by their fruits ye shall know them. (Matt 7:15-20)

Pleading while wilfully persisting in evil is futile. Obedience to the Christ teaching is essential.

21 ¶ Not every one that saith unto me, Lord, Lord, shall enter into the kingdom of heaven; but he that doeth the will of my Father which is in heaven.
22 Many will say to me in that day, Lord, Lord, have we not prophesied in thy name? and in thy name have cast out devils? and in thy name done many wonderful works?
23 And then will I profess unto them, I never knew you: depart from me, ye that work iniquity. (Matt 7:21-23)

Again, knowing what is the right thing to do is not enough, this teaching must be put into practice.

24 ¶ Therefore whosoever heareth these sayings of mine, and doeth them, I will liken him unto a wise man, which built his house upon a rock:
25 And the rain descended, and the floods came, and the winds blew, and beat upon that house; and it fell not: for it was founded upon a rock.
26 And every one that heareth these sayings of mine, and doeth them not, shall be likened unto a foolish man, which built his house upon the sand:
27 And the rain descended, and the floods came, and the winds blew, and beat upon that house; and it fell: and great was the fall of it. (Matt 7:24-27)

Divine authority acknowledged. Jesus let the "I" go to the Father, therefore it was the Word of God that he spoke. The people were astonished because unlike the scribes and Pharisees, Jesus lived what he taught.

28 And it came to pass, when Jesus had ended these sayings, the people were astonished at his doctrine:
29 For he taught them as *one* having authority, and not as the scribes. (Matt 7:28-29)

CHAPTER 29
JESUS PROVES HIS TEACHING PRACTICAL

1 When he was come down from the mountain, great multitudes followed him. (Matt 8:1)

Wholeness and purity result from living Christ's teaching. Showing no fear, Jesus touched a leper, perhaps physically, but most definitely spiritually, and healed him.

2 And, behold, there came a leper and worshipped him, saying, Lord, if thou wilt, thou canst make me clean.
3 And Jesus put forth *his* hand, and touched him, saying, I will; be thou clean. And immediately his leprosy was cleansed. (Matt 8:2-3)

Literally, this instruction was to comply with Leviticus 14:4. More importantly, this healing of leprosy provided proof to the ecclesiastical authorities that what Jesus taught and practiced had divine authority.

4 And Jesus saith unto him, See thou tell no man; but go thy way, shew thyself to the priest, and offer the gift that Moses commanded, for a testimony unto them. (Matt 8:4)

CHAPTER 30
MORE HEALING IN CAPERNAUM
Healing the centurion's servant of palsy

5 ¶ And when Jesus was entered into Capernaum, there came unto him a centurion, beseeching him,
6 And saying, Lord, my servant lieth at home sick of the palsy, grievously tormented.
7 And Jesus saith unto him, I will come and heal him.
8 The centurion answered and said, Lord, I am not worthy that thou shouldest come under my roof: but speak the word only, and my servant shall be healed.
9 For I am a man under authority, having soldiers under me: and I say to this *man*, Go,

and he goeth; and to another, Come, and he cometh; and to my servant, Do this, and he
doeth *it*.
10 When Jesus heard *it*, he marvelled, and said to them that followed, Verily I say unto
you, I have not found so great faith, no, not in Israel.
11 And I say unto you, That many shall come from the east and west, and shall sit down
with Abraham, and Isaac, and Jacob, in the kingdom of heaven.
12 But the children of the kingdom shall be cast out into outer darkness: there shall be
weeping and gnashing of teeth.
13 And Jesus said unto the centurion, Go thy way; and as thou hast believed, *so* be it
done unto thee. And his servant was healed in the selfsame hour. (Matt 8:5-13)

Healing the man with an unclean spirit

According to the Gospel of Mark

21 And they went into Capernaum; and straightway on the sabbath day he entered into
the synagogue, and taught.
22 And they were astonished at his doctrine: for he taught them as one that had
authority, and not as the scribes.
23 And there was in their synagogue a man with an unclean spirit; and he cried out,
24 Saying, Let *us* alone; what have we to do with thee, thou Jesus of Nazareth? art thou
come to destroy us? I know thee who thou art, the Holy One of God.
25 And Jesus rebuked him, saying, Hold thy peace, and come out of him.
26 And when the unclean spirit had torn him, and cried with a loud voice, he came out
of him.
27 And they were all amazed, insomuch that they questioned among themselves,
saying, What thing is this? what new doctrine *is* this? for with authority commandeth he
even the unclean spirits, and they do obey him.
28 And immediately his fame spread abroad throughout all the region round about
Galilee. (Mark 1:21-28)

According to the Gospel of Luke

31 And came down to Capernaum, a city of Galilee, and taught them on the sabbath
days.
32 And they were astonished at his doctrine: for his word was with power.
33 ¶ And in the synagogue there was a man, which had a spirit of an unclean devil, and
cried out with a loud voice,
34 Saying, Let *us* alone; what have we to do with thee, *thou* Jesus of Nazareth? art thou
come to destroy us? I know thee who thou art; the Holy One of God.
35 And Jesus rebuked him, saying, Hold thy peace, and come out of him. And when
the devil had thrown him in the midst, he came out of him, and hurt him not.
36 And they were all amazed, and spake among themselves, saying, What a word *is*
this! for with authority and power he commandeth the unclean spirits, and they come
out.
37 And the fame of him went out into every place of the country round about. (Luke 4:31-37)

Simon Peter's mother-in-law is healed of a fever

According to the Gospel of Luke

38 ¶ And he arose out of the synagogue, and entered into Simon's house. And Simon's
wife's mother was taken with a great fever; and they besought him for her.

39 And he stood over her, and rebuked the fever; and it left her: and immediately she
arose and ministered unto them. (Luke 4:38-39)

According to the Gospel of Matthew

14 ¶ And when Jesus was come into Peter's house, he saw his wife's mother laid, and
sick of a fever.
15 And he touched her hand, and the fever left her: and she arose, and ministered unto
them. (Matt 8:14-15)

According to the Gospel of Mark

29 And forthwith, when they were come out of the synagogue, they entered into the
house of Simon and Andrew, with James and John.
30 But Simon's wife's mother lay sick of a fever, and anon they tell him of her.
31 And he came and took her by the hand, and lifted her up; and immediately the fever
left her, and she ministered unto them. (Mark 1:29-31)

Numerous healings in the evening

According to the Gospel of Mark

32 And at even, when the sun did set, they brought unto him all that were diseased, and
them that were possessed with devils.
33 And all the city was gathered together at the door.
34 And he healed many that were sick of divers diseases, and cast out many devils; and
suffered not the devils to speak, because they knew him. (Mark 1:32-34)

According to the Gospel of Matthew

16 ¶ When the even was come, they brought unto him many that were possessed with
devils: and he cast out the spirits with *his* word, and healed all that were sick:
17 That it might be fulfilled which was spoken by Esaias the prophet, saying, Himself
took our infirmities, and bare *our* sicknesses. (Matt 8:16-17)

According to the Gospel of Luke

40 ¶ Now when the sun was setting, all they that had any sick with divers diseases
brought them unto him; and he laid his hands on every one of them, and healed them.
41 And devils also came out of many, crying out, and saying, Thou art Christ the Son
of God. And he rebuking *them* suffered them not to speak: for they knew that he was
Christ. (Luke 4:40-41)

CHAPTER 31
PRAYER & PREACHING

According to the Gospel of Mark

35 And in the morning, rising up a great while before day, he went out, and departed
into a solitary place, and there prayed.
36 And Simon and they that were with him followed after him.
37 And when they had found him, they said unto him, All *men* seek for thee.
38 And he said unto them, Let us go into the next towns, that I may preach there also:
for therefore came I forth.
39 And he preached in their synagogues throughout all Galilee, and cast out devils. (Mark
1:35-39)

According to the Gospel of Luke

42 And when it was day, he departed and went into a desert place: and the people

sought him, and came unto him, and stayed him, that he should not depart from them.
43 And he said unto them, I must preach the kingdom of God to other cities also: for
therefore am I sent.
44 And he preached in the synagogues of Galilee. (Luke 4:42-44)

CHAPTER 32
THE FIRST GREAT CATCH OF FISHES

Peter, Andrew, James and John had returned to fishing. lake of Gennesaret is the Sea of Galilee. ship is a fishing boat.

1 And it came to pass, that, as the people pressed upon him to hear the word of God, he
stood by the lake of Gennesaret,
2 And saw two ships standing by the lake: but the fishermen were gone out of them,
and were washing *their* nets.
3 And he entered into one of the ships, which was Simon's, and prayed him that he
would thrust out a little from the land. And he sat down, and taught the people out of
the ship.
4 Now when he had left speaking, he said unto Simon, Launch out into the deep, and
let down your nets for a draught.
5 And Simon answering said unto him, Master, we have toiled all the night, and have
taken nothing: nevertheless at thy word I will let down the net.
6 And when they had this done, they enclosed a great multitude of fishes: and their net
brake.
7 And they beckoned unto *their* partners, which were in the other ship, that they should
come and help them. And they came, and filled both the ships, so that they began to
sink.
8 When Simon Peter saw *it*, he fell down at Jesus' knees, saying, Depart from me; for I
am a sinful man, O Lord.
9 For he was astonished, and all that were with him, at the draught of the fishes which
they had taken:
10 And so *was* also James, and John, the sons of Zebedee, which were partners with
Simon. (Luke 5:1-10 *to* 1st.)

The last and final call for Peter and Andrew, James and John.

10 And Jesus said unto Simon, Fear not; from henceforth thou shalt catch men. (Luke 5:10
2nd *And*)

These four left everything to follow Jesus. They faltered at the crucifixion, recommitted after the morning meal, and remained rock solid following the descent of the Holy Ghost on the Day of Pentecost.

11 And when they had brought their ships to land, they forsook all, and followed him.
(Luke 5:11)

CHAPTER 33
A LEPER'S BETRAYAL

According to the Gospel of Mark

40 And there came a leper to him, beseeching him, and kneeling down to him, and
saying unto him, If thou wilt, thou canst make me clean.
41 And Jesus, moved with compassion, put forth *his* hand, and touched him, and saith
unto him, I will; be thou clean.
42 And as soon as he had spoken, immediately the leprosy departed from him, and he
was cleansed.
43 And he straitly charged him, and forthwith sent him away;
44 And saith unto him, See thou say nothing to any man: but go thy way, shew thyself

to the priest, and offer for thy cleansing those things which Moses commanded, for a
testimony unto them. (Mark 1:40-44)

The lepers disobedience. Jesus was not being sneaky, he was protecting his mission from resistance.

45 But he went out, and began to publish *it* much, and to blaze abroad the matter,
insomuch that Jesus could no more openly enter into the city, but was without in desert
places: and they came to him from every quarter. (Mark 1:45)

According to the Gospel of Luke

12 ¶ And it came to pass, when he was in a certain city, behold a man full of leprosy:
who seeing Jesus fell on *his* face, and besought him, saying, Lord, if thou wilt, thou
canst make me clean.
13 And he put forth *his* hand, and touched him, saying, I will: be thou clean. And
immediately the leprosy departed from him.
14 And he charged him to tell no man: but go, and shew thyself to the priest, and offer
for thy cleansing, according as Moses commanded, for a testimony unto them.
15 But so much the more went there a fame abroad of him: and great multitudes came
together to hear, and to be healed by him of their infirmities.
16 ¶ And he withdrew himself into the wilderness, and prayed. (Luke 5:12-16)

CHAPTER 34
A TSUNAMI IS STILLED

Preparation for crossing. Only those who are committed can follow

18 ¶ Now when Jesus saw great multitudes about him, he gave commandment to depart
unto the other side.
19 And a certain scribe came, and said unto him, Master, I will follow thee
whithersoever thou goest. (Matt 8:18-19)

Mere emotional enthusiasm should be tempered by an assessment of the cost before committing.

20 And Jesus saith unto him, The foxes have holes, and the birds of the air *have* nests;
but the Son of man hath not where to lay *his* head.
21 And another of his disciples said unto him, Lord, suffer me first to go and bury my
father. (Matt 8:20-21)

"To the unwise helper our Master said, 'Follow me; and let the dead bury their dead.'" - MBE

22 But Jesus said unto him, Follow me; and let the dead bury their dead. (Matt 8:22)

The crossing

The ship was decked, not an open boat that could be filled with water; hence, it was being covered with the waves.

23 ¶ And when he was entered into a ship, his disciples followed him. (Matt 8:23)

Tempest, *σεισμός seismos*, a tsunami that can occur in an ocean or a large lake causing great turbulence and wind.

24 And, behold, there arose a great tempest in the sea, insomuch that the ship was
covered with the waves: but he was asleep.
25 And his disciples came to *him*, and awoke him, saying, Lord, save us: we perish.
26 And he saith unto them, Why are ye fearful, O ye of little faith? Then he arose, and
rebuked the winds and the sea; and there was a great calm.
27 But the men marvelled, saying, What manner of man is this, that even the winds and
the sea obey him! (Matt 8:24-27)

CHAPTER 35
THE HEALINGS OF TWO DEMONIACS IN GERGESA

Jesus was met by **two** demoniacs when coming ashore.

28 ¶ And when he was come to the other side into the country of the Gergesenes, there

met him two possessed with devils, coming out of the tombs, exceeding fierce, so that
no man might pass by that way. (Matt 8:28)
Insanity has no abiding place in Christ, therefore it is no part of true manhood.
29 And, behold, they cried out, saying, What have we to do with thee, Jesus, thou Son
of God? art thou come hither to torment us before the time? (Matt 8:29)
The swinish element in human nature must be destroyed, not the man.
30 And there was a good way off from them an herd of many swine feeding. (Matt 8:30)
Error, when seen as error, is doomed.
31 So the devils besought him, saying, If thou cast us out, suffer us to go away into the
herd of swine.
32 And he said unto them, Go. And when they were come out, they went into the herd
of swine: and, behold, the whole herd of swine ran violently down a steep place into the
sea, and perished in the waters. (Matt 8:31-32)
The belief that we are benefitted by error would cause us to cling to error.
33 And they that kept them fled, and went their ways into the city, and told every thing,
and what was befallen to the possessed of the devils.
34 And, behold, the whole city came out to meet Jesus: and when they saw him, they
besought *him* that he would depart out of their coasts. (Matt. 8:33-34)
There is no point arguing with a mind that is unreceptive to Truth.
1 And he entered into a ship, and passed over, and came into his own city. (Matt 9:1)

CHAPTER 36
A MAN IN CAPERNAUM IS HEALED OF THE PALSY

Demonstration is required to validate the words

According to the Gospel of Mark

1 And again he entered into Capernaum after *some* days; and it was noised that he was
in the house.
2 And straightway many were gathered together, insomuch that there was no room to
receive *them*, no, not so much as about the door: and he preached the word unto them.
3 And they come unto him, bringing one sick of the palsy, which was borne of four.
4 And when they could not come nigh unto him for the press, they uncovered the roof
where he was: and when they had broken *it* up, they let down the bed wherein the sick
of the palsy lay.
5 When Jesus saw their faith, he said unto the sick of the palsy, Son, thy sins be
forgiven thee.
6 But there were certain of the scribes sitting there, and reasoning in their hearts,
7 Why doth this *man* thus speak blasphemies? who can forgive sins but God only?
8 And immediately when Jesus perceived in his spirit that they so reasoned within
themselves, he said unto them, Why reason ye these things in your hearts?
9 Whether is it easier to say to the sick of the palsy, *Thy* sins be forgiven thee; or to
say, Arise, and take up thy bed, and walk?
10 But that ye may know that the Son of man hath power on earth to forgive sins, (he
saith to the sick of the palsy,)
11 I say unto thee, Arise, and take up thy bed, and go thy way into thine house.
12 And immediately he arose, took up the bed, and went forth before them all;
insomuch that they were all amazed, and glorified God, saying, We never saw it on this
fashion.
13 And he went forth again by the sea side; and all the multitude resorted unto him, and

he taught them. (Mark 2:1-13)

According to the Gospel of Matthew

2 And, behold, they brought to him a man sick of the palsy, lying on a bed: and Jesus
seeing their faith said unto the sick of the palsy; Son, be of good cheer; thy sins be
forgiven thee.
3 And, behold, certain of the scribes said within themselves, This *man* blasphemeth.
4 And Jesus knowing their thoughts said, Wherefore think ye evil in your hearts?
5 For whether is easier, to say, *Thy* sins be forgiven thee; or to say, Arise, and walk?
6 But that ye may know that the Son of man hath power on earth to forgive sins, (then
saith he to the sick of the palsy,) Arise, take up thy bed, and go unto thine house.
7 And he arose, and departed to his house.
8 But when the multitudes saw *it*, they marvelled, and glorified God, which had given
such power unto men. (Matt 9:2-8)

According to the Gospel of Luke

17 And it came to pass on a certain day, as he was teaching, that there were Pharisees
and doctors of the law sitting by, which were come out of every town of Galilee, and
Judæa, and Jerusalem: and the power of the Lord was *present* to heal them.
18 ¶ And, behold, men brought in a bed a man which was taken with a palsy: and they
sought *means* to bring him in, and to lay *him* before him.
19 And when they could not find by what *way* they might bring him in because of the
multitude, they went upon the housetop, and let him down through the tiling with *his*
couch into the midst before Jesus.
20 And when he saw their faith, he said unto him, Man, thy sins are forgiven thee.
21 And the scribes and the Pharisees began to reason, saying, Who is this which
speaketh blasphemies? Who can forgive sins, but God alone?
22 But when Jesus perceived their thoughts, he answering said unto them, What reason
ye in your hearts?
23 Whether is easier, to say, Thy sins be forgiven thee; or to say, Rise up and walk?
24 But that ye may know that the Son of man hath power upon earth to forgive sins, (he
said unto the sick of the palsy,) I say unto thee, Arise, and take up thy couch, and go
into thine house.
25 And immediately he rose up before them, and took up that whereon he lay, and
departed to his own house, glorifying God.
26 And they were all amazed, and they glorified God, and were filled with fear, saying,
We have seen strange things to-day. (Luke 5:17-26)

CHAPTER 37
THE CALLING OF MATTHEW (LEVI)

(Tax collectors were called publicans. Matthew was a custom house officer that became a disciple)

According to the Gospel of Mark

14 And as he passed by, he saw Levi the *son* of Alphæus sitting at the receipt of
custom, and said unto him, Follow me. And he arose and followed him. (Mark 2:14)

According to the Gospel of Matthew

9 ¶ And as Jesus passed forth from thence, he saw a man, named Matthew, sitting at the
receipt of custom: and he saith unto him, Follow me. And he arose, and followed him.
(Matt 9:9)

According to the Gospel of Luke

27 ¶ And after these things he went forth, and saw a publican, named Levi, sitting at the
receipt of custom: and he said unto him, Follow me.
28 And he left all, rose up, and followed him. (Luke 5:27-28)

CHAPTER 38
JESUS DECLARES THE PURPOSE OF HIS MISSION

The mission of Jesus was to destroy sin, not sinners

According to the Gospel of Luke

29 And Levi made him a great feast in his own house: and there was a great company
of publicans and of others that sat down with them.
30 But their scribes and Pharisees murmured against his disciples, saying, Why do ye
eat and drink with publicans and sinners?
31 And Jesus answering said unto them, They that are whole need not a physician; but
they that are sick.
32 I came not to call the righteous, but sinners to repentance. (Luke 5:29-32)

According to the Gospel of Matthew

10 ¶ And it came to pass, as Jesus sat at meat in the house, behold, many publicans and
sinners came and sat down with him and his disciples.
11 And when the Pharisees saw *it*, they said unto his disciples, Why eateth your Master
with publicans and sinners?
12 But when Jesus heard *that*, he said unto them, They that be whole need not a
physician, but they that are sick. (Matt 9:10-12)

Jesus quoting Hosea 6:6. "For I desire mercy and not sacrifice; and the knowledge of God more than burnt offerings."

13 But go ye and learn what *that* meaneth, I will have mercy, and not sacrifice: for I am
not come to call the righteous, but sinners to repentance. (Matt 9:13)

According to the Gospel of Mark

15 And it came to pass, that, as Jesus sat at meat in his house, many publicans and
sinners sat also together with Jesus and his disciples: for there were many, and they
followed him.
16 And when the scribes and Pharisees saw him eat with publicans and sinners, they
said unto his disciples, How is it that he eateth and drinketh with publicans and sinners?
17 When Jesus heard *it*, he saith unto them, They that are whole have no need of the
physician, but they that are sick: I came not to call the righteous, but sinners to
repentance. (Mark 2:15-17)

CHAPTER 39
NO MIXING ALLOWED

"The letter killeth, but the spirit giveth life" II Cor. 3:6

According to the Gospel of Mark

18 And the disciples of John and of the Pharisees used to fast: and they come and say
unto him, Why do the disciples of John and of the Pharisees fast, but thy disciples fast
not?
19 And Jesus said unto them, Can the children of the bridechamber fast, while the
bridegroom is with them? as long as they have the bridegroom with them, they cannot
fast.

20 But the days will come, when the bridegroom shall be taken away from them, and
then shall they fast in those days.
21 No man also seweth a piece of new cloth on an old garment: else the new piece that
filled it up taketh away from the old, and the rent is made worse.
22 And no man putteth new wine into old bottles: else the new wine doth burst the
bottles, and the wine is spilled, and the bottles will be marred: but new wine must be
put into new bottles. (Mark 2:18-22)

According to the Gospel of Luke

33 ¶ And they said unto him, Why do the disciples of John fast often, and make
prayers, and likewise *the disciples* of the Pharisees; but thine eat and drink?
34 And he said unto them, Can ye make the children of the bridechamber fast, while the
bridegroom is with them?
35 But the days will come, when the bridegroom shall be taken away from them, and
then shall they fast in those days.
36 ¶ And he spake also a parable unto them; No man putteth a piece of a new garment
upon an old; if otherwise, then both the new maketh a rent, and the piece that was *taken*
out of the new agreeth not with the old.
37 And no man putteth new wine into old bottles; else the new wine will burst the
bottles, and be spilled, and the bottles shall perish.
38 But new wine must be put into new bottles; and both are preserved.
39 No man also having drunk old *wine* straightway desireth new: for he saith, The old
is better. (Luke 5:33-39)

According to the Gospel of Matthew

14 ¶ Then came to him the disciples of John, saying, Why do we and the Pharisees fast
oft, but thy disciples fast not?
15 And Jesus said unto them, Can the children of the bridechamber mourn, as long as
the bridegroom is with them? but the days will come, when the bridegroom shall be
taken from them, and then shall they fast.
16 No man putteth a piece of new cloth unto an old garment, for that which is put in to
fill it up taketh from the garment, and the rent is made worse.
17 Neither do men put new wine into old bottles: else the bottles break, and the wine
runneth out, and the bottles perish: but they put new wine into new bottles, and both are
preserved. (Matt 9:14-17)

CHAPTER 40
DEATH OVERCOME AND HEMORRHAGING HEALED
(The first healing of death – A rulers daughter already deceased)

18 ¶ While he spake these things unto them, behold, there came a certain ruler, and
worshipped him, saying, My daughter is even now dead: but come and lay thy hand
upon her, and she shall live.
19 And Jesus arose, and followed him, and *so did* his disciples. (Matt 9:18-19)

On the way a woman is healed of hemorrhaging

20 ¶ And, behold, a woman, which was diseased with an issue of blood twelve years,
came behind *him*, and touched the hem of his garment:
21 For she said within herself, If I may but touch his garment, I shall be whole.

22 But Jesus turned him about, and when he saw her, he said, Daughter, be of good
comfort; thy faith hath made thee whole. And the woman was made whole from that
hour. (Matt 9:20-22)

The maiden is raised to life

23 And when Jesus came into the ruler's house, and saw the minstrels and the people
making a noise,
24 He said unto them, Give place: for the maid is not dead, but sleepeth. And they
laughed him to scorn.
25 But when the people were put forth, he went in, and took her by the hand, and the
maid arose.
26 And the fame hereof went abroad into all that land. (Matt 9:23-26)

CHAPTER 41
HEALING AND MOCKERY

Two men are healed of blindness

27 ¶ And when Jesus departed thence, two blind men followed him, crying, and saying,
Thou Son of David, have mercy on us.
28 And when he was come into the house, the blind men came to him: and Jesus saith
unto them, Believe ye that I am able to do this? They said unto him, Yea, Lord.
29 Then touched he their eyes, saying, According to your faith be it unto you.
30 And their eyes were opened; and Jesus straitly charged them, saying, See *that* no
man know *it*.
31 But they, when they were departed, spread abroad his fame in all that country. (Matt
9:27-31)

A mute is healed

32 ¶ As they went out, behold, they brought to him a dumb man possessed with a devil.
33 And when the devil was cast out, the dumb spake: (Matt 9:32-33 *to* :)

The people marvel whereas the Pharisees mock

The common people that either witnessed or received healing, expressed gratitude.

33 and the multitudes marvelled, saying, It was never so seen in Israel. (Matt 9:33 *and*)

The Pharisees, due to their envy and ignorance of the divine laws of healing, accused Jesus of practicing demonology.

34 But the Pharisees said, He casteth out devils through the prince of the devils. (Matt
9:34)

Despite the persecution the healing work goes on

35 And Jesus went about all the cities and villages, teaching in their synagogues, and
preaching the gospel of the kingdom, and healing every sickness and every disease
among the people. (Matt 9:35)

Jesus was moved with compassion! This is a way of saying that divine Love was the power that did the healing.

36 ¶ But when he saw the multitudes, he was moved with compassion on them, because
they fainted, and were scattered abroad, as sheep having no shepherd.
37 Then saith he unto his disciples, The harvest truly *is* plenteous, but the labourers *are*
few;
38 Pray ye therefore the Lord of the harvest, that he will send forth labourers into his
harvest. (Matt 9:36-38)

CHAPTER 42
THE DISCIPLES ARE TAUGHT TO HEAL

"Our Master's first article of faith propounded to his students was healing, and he proved his faith by his works." - MBE

1 And when he had called unto *him* his twelve disciples, he gave them power *against*
unclean spirits, to cast them out, and to heal all manner of sickness and all manner of
disease. (Matt 10:1)

The Apostles were first instructed in the art of spiritual healing, and then they were sent forth to preach and to heal.

2 Now the names of the twelve apostles are these; The first, Simon, who is called Peter,
and Andrew his brother; James *the son* of Zebedee, and John his brother;
3 Philip, and Bartholomew; Thomas, and Matthew the publican; James *the son* of
Alphæus, and Lebbæus, whose surname was Thaddæus;
4 Simon the Canaanite, and Judas Iscariot, who also betrayed him. (Matt 10:2-4)

These commands were given to the twelve at this time. Later, near the end of Jesus' ministry, they were changed.

5 These twelve Jesus sent forth, and commanded them, saying, (Matt 10:5 *to* 3rd,)

They were sent first to the house of Israel expecting to be received.

5 Go not into the way of the Gentiles, and into *any* city of the Samaritans enter ye not:
6 But go rather to the lost sheep of the house of Israel.
7 And as ye go, preach, saying, The kingdom of heaven is at hand. (Matt 10:5-7 *Go*)

Freely, *δωρεάν dōrean*, gratuitously, without restriction or expectation of being compensated.

8 Heal the sick, cleanse the lepers, raise the dead, cast out devils: freely ye have
received, freely give. (Matt 10:8)

The disciple must trust the laws of Spirit to meet every need.

9 Provide neither gold, nor silver, nor brass in your purses,
10 Nor scrip for *your* journey, neither two coats, neither shoes, nor yet staves: for the
workman is worthy of his meat. (Matt 10:9-10)

The disciple must be wise and to seek out, and abide with, only those who are receptive.

11 And into whatsoever city or town ye shall enter, inquire who in it is worthy; and
there abide till ye go thence.
12 And when ye come into an house, salute it.
13 And if the house be worthy, let your peace come upon it: (Matt 10:11-13 *to* :)

If rejected or abused, the disciple must simply move on, casting aside any sense of resentment.

13 but if it be not worthy, let your peace return to you.
14 And whosoever shall not receive you, nor hear your words, when ye depart out of
that house or city, shake off the dust of your feet.
15 Verily I say unto you, It shall be more tolerable for the land of Sodom and
Gomorrha in the day of judgment, than for that city. (Matt 10:13-15 *but*)

To be successful, the disciple must abide in the spirit of wisdom and love.

16 ¶ Behold, I send you forth as sheep in the midst of wolves: be ye therefore wise as
serpents, and harmless as doves. (Matt 10:16)

The disciple must have full trust in God, and place no reliance on human ways and means.

17 But beware of men: for they will deliver you up to the councils, and they will
scourge you in their synagogues; (Matt 10:17)

Persecution is inevitable for those who practice Christ-healing. for my sake = because of me, on my account.

18 And ye shall be brought before governors and kings for my sake, for a testimony
against them and the Gentiles. (Matt 10:18)

When required to answer know: "the Father which sent me gave me a commandment, what I should say." - John 12:49.

19 But when they deliver you up, take no thought how or what ye shall speak: for it
shall be given you in that same hour what ye shall speak.
20 For it is not ye that speak, but the Spirit of your Father which speaketh in you. (Matt
10:19-20)

The followers of Jesus will be persecuted, even by those closest to them, including their family.
21 And the brother shall deliver up the brother to death, and the father the child: and the
children shall rise up against *their* parents, and cause them to be put to death.
22 And ye shall be hated of all *men* for my name's sake: but he that endureth to the end
shall be saved.
23 But when they persecute you in this city, flee ye into another: for verily I say unto
you, Ye shall not have gone over the cities of Israel, till the Son of man be come. (Matt 10:21-23)

Don't murmur when persecuted because persecution confirms discipleship. *(See Matt 5:10-12)*
24 The disciple is not above *his* master, nor the servant above his lord.
25 It is enough for the disciple that he be as his master, and the servant as his lord. If
they have called the master of the house Beelzebub, how much more *shall they call*
them of his household? (Matt 10:24-25)

Fear no person, but watch that *you* sin not! Whatever you need will be revealed in God's way at the appointed time.
26 Fear them not therefore: for there is nothing covered, that shall not be revealed; and
hid, that shall not be known.
27 What I tell you in darkness, *that* speak ye in light: and what ye hear in the ear, *that*
preach ye upon the housetops.
28 And fear not them which kill the body, but are not able to kill the soul: but rather
fear him which is able to destroy both soul and body in hell.
29 Are not two sparrows sold for a farthing? and one of them shall not fall on the
ground without your Father.
30 But the very hairs of your head are all numbered.
31 Fear ye not therefore, ye are of more value than many sparrows. (Matt 10:26-31)

confess me means to abide *in* me, where "*in*" is *ἐν en,* and denotes being or remaining within, to actually "put on Christ" - Gal. 2:27, and not to merely profess a belief in Christ.
32 Whosoever therefore shall confess me before men, him will I confess also before my
Father which is in heaven.
33 But whosoever shall deny me before men, him will I also deny before my Father
which is in heaven. (Matt 10:32-33)

Again, don't be alarmed if those nearest and dearest to you turn against you because of your fidelity to Christ.
34 Think not that I am come to send peace on earth: I came not to send peace, but a
sword.
35 For I am come to set a man at variance against his father, and the daughter against
her mother, and the daughter in law against her mother in law.
36 And a man's foes *shall be* they of his own household.
37 He that loveth father or mother more than me is not worthy of me: and he that loveth
son or daughter more than me is not worthy of me. (Matt 10:34-37)

The love of Christ must supersede self-love. The high goal remains ever the same, we must leave all for Christ.
38 And he that taketh not his cross, and followeth after me, is not worthy of me.
39 He that findeth his life shall lose it: and he that loseth his life for my sake shall find
it. (Matt 10:38-39)

He that receives a messenger of Christ receives Christ.
40 ¶ He that receiveth you receiveth me, and he that receiveth me receiveth him that
sent me. (Matt 10:40)

"In the name of" is a Hebraism that means "because he is." "little ones" humbly and obediently trust all to the Father.
41 He that receiveth a prophet in the name of a prophet shall receive a prophet's reward;
and he that receiveth a righteous man in the name of a righteous man shall receive a
righteous man's reward.
42 And whosoever shall give to drink unto one of these little ones a cup of cold *water*

only in the name of a disciple, verily I say unto you, he shall in no wise lose his reward. (Matt 10:41-42)

CHAPTER 43
UNBELIEF, CALLOUSNESS, AND INGRATITUDE REBUKED

1 And it came to pass, when Jesus had made an end of commanding his twelve
disciples, he departed thence to teach and to preach in their cities. (Matt 11:1)

John the Baptist questions if Jesus is the Messiah

The word *two* is not *duo*, two but *dia*, meaning *by*, or through his disciples. This was the Baptists first questioning. The second is recorded in Luke 7:19 where the word translated *two is* a number. See *TCB* for a fuller explanation.

2 Now when John had heard in the prison the works of Christ, he sent two of his
disciples, (Matt 11:2)

John the Baptist now doubting questions Jesus through his disciples if he really is the Messiah.

3 And said unto him, Art thou he that should come, or do we look for another? (Matt 11:3)

Jesus' reply is that the healing works verify that he is, and that John should not lose sight of what was revealed to him.

4 Jesus answered and said unto them, Go and shew John again those things which ye
do hear and see:

5 The blind receive their sight, and the lame walk, the lepers are cleansed, and the deaf
hear, the dead are raised up, and the poor have the gospel preached to them.

6 And blessed is *he*, whosoever shall not be offended in me. (Matt 11:4-6)

The multitude is admonished for not believing John the Baptist

Jesus remarks on how John the Baptist held firmly to his moral convictions, even though persecuted.

7 ¶ And as they departed, Jesus began to say unto the multitudes concerning John,
What went ye out into the wilderness to see? A reed shaken with the wind? (Matt 11:7)

John was unpretentious, genuine. He did not rely on material status or comfort to gain approval or to appear important.

8 But what went ye out for to see? A man clothed in soft raiment? behold, they that
wear soft *clothing* are in kings' houses. (Matt 11:8)

John was much more than a prophet – he was the Forerunner declaring prophecy fulfilled in the coming of Christ Jesus.

9 But what went ye out for to see? A prophet? yea, I say unto you, and more than a
prophet.

10 For this is *he*, of whom it is written, Behold, I send my messenger before thy face,
which shall prepare thy way before thee. (Matt 11:9-10)

Jesus said, "Among those born of women, from Adam until John the Baptist, there is no one superior to John the Baptist that his eyes should not be lowered (before him). Yet I have said, whichever one of you comes to be a child will be acquainted with the kingdom and will become superior to John." - *The Coptic Gospel of Thomas*

11 Verily I say unto you, Among them that are born of women there hath not risen a
greater than John the Baptist: notwithstanding he that is least in the kingdom of heaven
is greater than he.

12 And from the days of John the Baptist until now the kingdom of heaven suffereth
violence, and the violent take it by force. (Matt 11:11-12)

The prophets spoke of a future coming of the Messiah whereas John declared it fulfilled in the coming of Christ Jesus.

13 For all the prophets and the law prophesied until John. (Matt 11:13)

If the ecclesiastics had seen Jesus as John the Baptist did, they would have reckoned John as Elijah in metaphor.

14 And if ye will receive *it*, this is Elias, which was for to come. (Matt 11:14)

Ears to hear = spiritual discernment. The disciples did not understand at this time, but finally did. See Matt. 17:13

15 He that hath ears to hear, let him hear. (Matt 11:15)

Jesus points out mortal man's inconsistency

16 ¶ But whereunto shall I liken this generation? It is like unto children sitting in the
markets, and calling unto their fellows,

17 And saying, We have piped unto you, and ye have not danced; we have mourned

unto you, and ye have not lamented. (Matt 11:16-17)

Devil = demon. Mortal mind mocks the fact that Wisdom is justified in the righteous outcome it produces.

18 For John came neither eating nor drinking, and they say, He hath a devil.
19 The Son of man came eating and drinking, and they say, Behold a man gluttonous,
and a winebibber, a friend of publicans and sinners. But wisdom is justified of her
children. (Matt 11:18-19)

Ingratitude for healing rebuked

20 ¶ Then began he to upbraid the cities wherein most of his mighty works were done,
because they repented not:
21 Woe unto thee, Chorazin! woe unto thee, Bethsaida! for if the mighty works, which
were done in you, had been done in Tyre and Sidon, they would have repented long ago
in sackcloth and ashes.
22 But I say unto you, It shall be more tolerable for Tyre and Sidon at the day of
judgment, than for you.
23 And thou, Capernaum, which art exalted unto heaven, shalt be brought down to hell:
for if the mighty works, which have been done in thee, had been done in Sodom, it
would have remained until this day. (Matt 11:20-23)

Ingratitude brings punishment upon itself.

24 But I say unto you, That it shall be more tolerable for the land of Sodom in the day
of judgment, than for thee. (Matt 11:24)

Jesus expressed gratitude that the omnipotence of God was accessible only to babes, i.e. to the pure in heart.

25 ¶ At that time Jesus answered and said, I thank thee, O Father, Lord of heaven and
earth, because thou hast hid these things from the wise and prudent, and hast revealed
them unto babes.
26 Even so, Father: for so it seemed good in thy sight.
27 All things are delivered unto me of my Father: and no man knoweth the Son, but the
Father; neither knoweth any man the Father, save the Son, and *he* to whomsoever the
Son will reveal *him*. (Matt 11:25-27)

Contrary to appearances, the way through Christ is the surest, quickest, and easiest way

28 ¶ Come unto me, all *ye* that labour and are heavy laden, and I will give you rest.
29 Take my yoke upon you, and learn of me; for I am meek and lowly in heart: and ye
shall find rest unto your souls.
30 For my yoke *is* easy, and my burden is light. (Matt 11:28-30)

CHAPTER 44
PARALYSIS HEALED AT THE POOL OF BETHESDA

Jesus is in Jerusalem at the time of a feast, likely Purim celebrated on the 15th of Adar (Late February or early March)

1 After this there was a feast of the Jews; and Jesus went up to Jerusalem.
2 Now there is at Jerusalem by the sheep *market* a pool, which is called in the Hebrew
tongue Bethesda, having five porches.
3 In these lay a great multitude of impotent folk, of blind, halt, withered, waiting for
the moving of the water.
4 For an angel went down at a certain season into the pool, and troubled the water:
whosoever then first after the troubling of the water stepped in was made whole of
whatsoever disease he had.
5 And a certain man was there, which had an infirmity thirty and eight years.
6 When Jesus saw him lie, and knew that he had been now a long time *in that case*, he

saith unto him, Wilt thou be made whole?
7 The impotent man answered him, Sir, I have no man, when the water is troubled, to put me into the pool: but while I am coming, another steppeth down before me.
8 Jesus saith unto him, Rise, take up thy bed, and walk.
9 And immediately the man was made whole, and took up his bed, and walked: and on the same day was the sabbath. (John 5:1-9)

The objection was that the man carried his mat on the sabbath day. Bed, κράβαττος *krabattos*, a camp bed, mattress.

10 ¶ The Jews therefore said unto him that was cured, It is the sabbath day: it is not lawful for thee to carry *thy* bed.
11 He answered them, He that made me whole, the same said unto me, Take up thy bed, and walk.
12 Then asked they him, What man is that which said unto thee, Take up thy bed, and walk?
13 And he that was healed wist not who it was: for Jesus had conveyed himself away, a multitude being in *that* place.
14 Afterward Jesus findeth him in the temple, and said unto him, Behold, thou art made whole: sin no more, lest a worse thing come unto thee. (John 5:10-14)

The man healed complained to the Jews that he was only doing what Jesus told him to do.

15 The man departed, and told the Jews that it was Jesus, which had made him whole. (John 10:15)

Jesus' "crime" was that he refused to let a false sense of God, man, or the sabbath day leave error (evil) in control.

16 And therefore did the Jews persecute Jesus, and sought to slay him, because he had done these things on the sabbath day. (John 5:16)

Error, in the guise of theology, was inflamed when Jesus said that God alone controls man and the universe.

17 ¶ But Jesus answered them, My Father worketh hitherto, and I work.
18 Therefore the Jews sought the more to kill him, because he not only had broken the sabbath, but said also that God was his Father, making himself equal with God. (John 5:17-18)

Healing is the Father, divine Principle, Love, reaching humanity through Christ, divine Love expressed.

19 Then answered Jesus and said unto them, Verily, verily, I say unto you, The Son can do nothing of himself, but what he seeth the Father do: for what things soever he doeth, these also doeth the Son likewise.
20 For the Father loveth the Son, and sheweth him all things that himself doeth: and he will shew him greater works than these, that ye may marvel.
21 For as the Father raiseth up the dead, and quickeneth *them*; even so the Son quickeneth whom he will. (John 5:19-21)

Separating error from Truth reveals Life, and man who is Life's reflection, to be deathless.

22 For the Father judgeth no man, but hath committed all judgment unto the Son:
23 That all *men* should honour the Son, even as they honour the Father. He that honoureth not the Son honoureth not the Father which hath sent him.
24 Verily, verily, I say unto you, He that heareth my word, and believeth on him that sent me, hath everlasting life, and shall not come into condemnation; but is passed from death unto life.
25 Verily, verily, I say unto you, The hour is coming, and now is, when the dead shall hear the voice of the Son of God: and they that hear shall live.
26 For as the Father hath life in himself; so hath he given to the Son to have life in himself; (John 5:22-26)

The word authority is ἐξουσία *exousia*, a delegated power. The source of the power is of course, God. See vs.30.

27 And hath given him authority to execute judgment also, because he is the Son of

man.
28 Marvel not at this: for the hour is coming, in the which all that are in the graves shall
hear his voice,
29 And shall come forth; they that have done good, unto the resurrection of life; and
they that have done evil, unto the resurrection of damnation.
30 I can of mine own self do nothing: as I hear, I judge: and my judgment is just;
because I seek not mine own will, but the will of the Father which hath sent me. (John 5:27-30)

Jesus couldn't say it any clearer than he did; namely, that corporeal sense testimony does not bear witness to Truth.

31 If I bear witness of myself, my witness is not true. (John 5:31)

John the Baptist's witness, rejected by the Pharisees, was true because inspired by Spirit. As John, the Beloved Disciple said, "it is the Spirit that beareth witness, because the Spirit is truth." (I John 5:6). Matter, Spirit's opposite is error.

32 ¶ There is another that beareth witness of me; and I know that the witness which he
witnesseth of me is true.
33 Ye sent unto John, and he bare witness unto the truth.
34 But I receive not testimony from man: but these things I say, that ye might be saved.
35 He was a burning and a shining light: and ye were willing for a season to rejoice in
his light. (John 5:32-35)

The healing works done through the power of God provide greater testimony than the words of men.

36 ¶ But I have greater witness than *that* of John: for the works which the Father hath
given me to finish, the same works that I do, bear witness of me, that the Father hath
sent me.
37 And the Father himself, which hath sent me, hath borne witness of me. Ye have
neither heard his voice at any time, nor seen his shape.
38 And ye have not his word abiding in you: for whom he hath sent, him ye believe not.
(John 5:36-38)

This should read: "Ye search the scriptures." Reading the scriptures from a material standpoint doesn't reveal eternal life.

39 ¶ Search the scriptures; for in them ye think ye have eternal life: and they are they
which testify of me. (John 5:39)

The carnal mind "is enmity" to eternal life. To understand that God is Life, is to know eternal Life. See Jn. 17:3.

40 And ye will not come to me, that ye might have life.
41 I receive not honour from men.
42 But I know you, that ye have not the love of God in you. (John 5:40-42)

Since mortal mind loves human approval and hates Truth, it rejects Jesus and the Christ-healing he taught his disciples.

43 I am come in my Father's name, and ye receive me not: if another shall come in his
own name, him ye will receive.
44 How can ye believe, which receive honour one of another, and seek not the honour
that *cometh* from God only? (John 5:43-44)

Mortal mind rejected and continues to reject the testimony of Moses who foretold *"a prophet like unto me."* (Deut. 18:18*)*.

45 Do not think that I will accuse you to the Father: there is *one* that accuseth you, *even*
Moses, in whom ye trust. (John 5:45)
46 For had ye believed Moses, ye would have believed me: for he wrote of me.
47 But if ye believe not his writings, how shall ye believe my words? (John 5:46-47)

CHAPTER 45
DISPUTES CONCERNING THE SABBATH
(Ears of "corn" plucked on the Sabbath)

According to the Gospel of Mark

23 And it came to pass, that he went through the corn fields on the sabbath day; and his
disciples began, as they went, to pluck the ears of corn.

24 And the Pharisees said unto him, Behold, why do they on the sabbath day that which
is not lawful?
25 And he said unto them, Have ye never read what David did, when he had need, and
was an hungered, he, and they that were with him?
26 How he went into the house of God in the days of Abiathar the high priest, and did
eat the shewbread, which is not lawful to eat but for the priests, and gave also to them
which were with him? (Mark 2:23-26)

Seeing creation as God sees it is the sabbath that sets man free instead of enslaving him to ritual and tradition.

27 And he said unto them, The sabbath was made for man, and not man for the sabbath:
28 Therefore the Son of man is Lord also of the sabbath. (Mark 2:27-28)

According to the Gospel of Luke

1 And it came to pass on the second sabbath after the first, that he went through the
corn fields; and his disciples plucked the ears of corn, and did eat, rubbing *them* in *their*
hands.
2 And certain of the Pharisees said unto them, Why do ye that which is not lawful to do
on the sabbath days?
3 And Jesus answering them said, Have ye not read so much as this, what David did,
when himself was an hungered, and they which were with him;
4 How he went into the house of God, and did take and eat the shewbread, and gave
also to them that were with him; which it is not lawful to eat but for the priests alone?
5 And he said unto them, That the Son of man is Lord also of the sabbath. (Luke 6:1-5)

According to the Gospel of Matthew

1 At that time Jesus went on the sabbath day through the corn; and his disciples were
an hungered, and began to pluck the ears of corn, and to eat.
2 But when the Pharisees saw *it*, they said unto him, Behold, thy disciples do that
which is not lawful to do upon the sabbath day.
3 But he said unto them, Have ye not read what David did, when he was an hungered,
and they that were with him;
4 How he entered into the house of God, and did eat the shewbread, which was not
lawful for him to eat, neither for them which were with him, but only for the priests?
5 Or have ye not read in the law, how that on the sabbath days the priests in the temple
profane the sabbath, and are blameless?
6 But I say unto you, That in this place is *one* greater than the temple. (Matt 12:1-6)

Here Jesus quotes Hosea 6:6: "For I desired mercy, and not sacrifice," which is to say, brotherly love rather than ritual.

7 But if ye had known what *this* meaneth, I will have mercy, and not sacrifice, ye
would not have condemned the guiltless.
8 For the Son of man is Lord even of the sabbath day. (Matt 12:7-8)

CHAPTER 46
IT IS LAWFUL TO HEAL ON THE SABBATH DAYS!
(Healing the man with a withered hand)

According to the Gospel of Matthew

9 And when he was departed thence, he went into their synagogue:
10 ¶ And, behold, there was a man which had *his* hand withered. And they asked him,
saying, Is it lawful to heal on the sabbath days? that they might accuse him.
11 And he said unto them, What man shall there be among you, that shall have one

sheep, and if it fall into a pit on the sabbath day, will he not lay hold on it, and lift *it*
out?
12 How much then is a man better than a sheep? Wherefore it is lawful to do well on
the sabbath days.
13 Then saith he to the man, Stretch forth thine hand. And he stretched *it* forth; and it
was restored whole, like as the other. (Matt 12:9-13)

The first mention of a plot to kill Jesus. The Gospel of Mark tells us that the plot included the Herodians. See Mark 3:6

14 ¶ Then the Pharisees went out, and held a council against him, how they might
destroy him.
15 But when Jesus knew *it*, he withdrew himself from thence: (Matt 12:14-15 *to* :)

According to the Gospel of Luke

6 And it came to pass also on another sabbath, that he entered into the synagogue and
taught: and there was a man whose right hand was withered.
7 And the scribes and Pharisees watched him, whether he would heal on the sabbath
day; that they might find an accusation against him.
8 But he knew their thoughts, and said to the man which had the withered hand, Rise
up, and stand forth in the midst. And he arose and stood forth.
9 Then said Jesus unto them, I will ask you one thing; Is it lawful on the sabbath days
to do good, or to do evil? to save life, or to destroy *it*?
10 And looking round about upon them all, he said unto the man, Stretch forth thy
hand. And he did so: and his hand was restored whole as the other. (Luke 6:6-10)

Madness, *ἄνοια anoia*, means an anger originating in a lack of understanding and love, a senseless rage.

11 And they were filled with madness; and communed one with another what they
might do to Jesus. (Luke 6:11)

According to the Gospel of Mark

1 And he entered again into the synagogue; and there was a man there which had a
withered hand.
2 And they watched him, whether he would heal him on the sabbath day; that they
might accuse him.
3 And he saith unto the man which had the withered hand, Stand forth.
4 And he saith unto them, Is it lawful to do good on the sabbath days, or to do evil? to
save life, or to kill? But they held their peace.
5 And when he had looked round about on them with anger, being grieved for the
hardness of their hearts, he saith unto the man, Stretch forth thine hand. And he
stretched *it* out: and his hand was restored whole as the other. (Mark 3:1-5)

An unholy alliance was formed to kill Jesus: government, the Herodians, together with religion, the Pharisees.

6 And the Pharisees went forth, and straightway took counsel with the Herodians
against him, how they might destroy him.
7 But Jesus withdrew himself with his disciples to the sea: (Mark 3:6-7 *to* :)

CHAPTER 47
MULTITUDES SEEK HEALING

(It was necessary for the multitudes to go out to Jesus because he was barred from entering the cities and towns)

According to the Gospel of Mark

7 and a great multitude from Galilee followed him, and from Judæa,
8 And from Jerusalem, and from Idumæa, and *from* beyond Jordan; and they about
Tyre and Sidon, a great multitude, when they had heard what great things he did, came

unto him.
9 And he spake to his disciples, that a small ship should wait on him because of the
multitude, lest they should throng him.
10 For he had healed many; insomuch that they pressed upon him for to touch him, as
many as had plagues.
11 And unclean spirits, when they saw him, fell down before him, and cried, saying,
Thou art the Son of God. (Mark 3:7-11 *and*)

Jesus charged them "not to make him known" since the more the *people* loved him the more the *Pharisees* hated him.

12 And he straitly charged them that they should not make him known. (Mark 3:12)

According to the Gospel of Matthew

15 and great multitudes followed him, and he healed them all;
16 And charged them that they should not make him known:
17 That it might be fulfilled which was spoken by Esaias the prophet, saying,
18 Behold my servant, whom I have chosen; my beloved, in whom my soul is well
pleased: I will put my spirit upon him, and he shall shew judgment to the Gentiles. (Matt 12:15-18)

The quote below is from Isa. 42:2. The Hebrew, צָעַק *tsa`aq,* means to outcry, clamor. The Greek *κραυγάζω kraugazō*, is to clamor – cry out. Jesus wanted to do his work without fanfare to avoid even greater resistance from the Pharisees.

19 He shall not strive, nor cry; neither shall any man hear his voice in the streets. (Matt 12:19)

Isaiah foresaw that the Gentiles would accept the Messiah's message first, and only later would the Jewish people.

20 A bruised reed shall he not break, and smoking flax shall he not quench, till he send
forth judgment unto victory.
21 And in his name shall the Gentiles trust. (Matt 12:20-21)

CHAPTER 48
MORE PREPARATION TO PREACH AND HEAL

According to the Gospel of Mark

13 And he goeth up into a mountain, and calleth *unto him* whom he would: and they
came unto him.
14 And he ordained twelve, that they should be with him, and that he might send them
forth to preach,
15 And to have power to heal sicknesses, and to cast out devils:
16 And Simon he surnamed Peter;
17 And James the *son* of Zebedee, and John the brother of James; and he surnamed
them Boanerges, which is, The sons of thunder:
18 And Andrew, and Philip, and Bartholomew, and Matthew, and Thomas, and James
the *son* of Alphæus, and Thaddæus, and Simon the Canaanite,
19 And Judas Iscariot, which also betrayed him: (Mark 3:13-19 *to* :)

According to the Gospel of Luke

12 And it came to pass in those days, that he went out into a mountain to pray, and
continued all night in prayer to God.
13 ¶ And when it was day, he called *unto him* his disciples: and of them he chose
twelve, whom also he named apostles;
14 Simon, (whom he also named Peter,) and Andrew his brother, James and John,
Philip and Bartholomew,
15 Matthew and Thomas, James the *son* of Alphæus, and Simon called Zelotes,
16 And Judas *the brother* of James, and Judas Iscariot, which also was the traitor. (Luke

6:12-16)
Jesus taught to preach and heal by example, and he expected his followers to heal as well as to teach and preach.
17 ¶ And he came down with them, and stood in the plain, and the company of his
disciples, and a great multitude of people out of all Judæa and Jerusalem, and from the
sea coast of Tyre and Sidon, which came to hear him, and to be healed of their diseases;
18 And they that were vexed with unclean spirits: and they were healed.
19 And the whole multitude sought to touch him: for there went virtue out of him, and
healed *them* all. (Luke 6:17-19)

CHAPTER 49
THE SERMON ON THE PLAIN

The following blessings were spoken directly to his disciples. poor *πτωχός ptōchos*. It is a blessing to know our need for the things of Spirit for that makes us receptive to Christ, Truth.

20 ¶ And he lifted up his eyes on his disciples, and said, Blessed *be ye* poor: for yours
is the kingdom of God. (Luke 6:20)

hunger *πεινάω peinaō*, weep κλαίω klaiō. Desiring the spiritual and yielding up the material, while it may appear to be a sacrifice now makes room for lasting peace and joy.

21 Blessed *are ye* that hunger now: for ye shall be filled. Blessed *are ye* that weep
now: for ye shall laugh. (Luke 6:21)

Being mocked, belittled and rebuffed by those clinging to materialism is proof that you are on the right path. Rejoice!

22 Blessed are ye, when men shall hate you, and when they shall separate you *from
their company*, and shall reproach *you*, and cast out your name as evil, for the Son of
man's sake.
23 Rejoice ye in that day, and leap for joy: for, behold, your reward *is* great in heaven:
for in the like manner did their fathers unto the prophets. (Luke 6:22-23)

Here Jesus addresses the entire assembly on the woes caused by relying on matter and rejecting Spirit.

24 But woe unto you that are rich! for ye have received your consolation.
25 Woe unto you that are full! for ye shall hunger. Woe unto you that laugh now! for
ye shall mourn and weep.
26 Woe unto you, when all men shall speak well of you! for so did their fathers to the
false prophets. (Luke 6:24-26)

Jesus gave instruction on overcoming matter because the love of matter is a stumbling block on the pathway to holiness.

27 ¶ But I say unto you which hear, Love your enemies, do good to them which hate
you,
28 Bless them that curse you, and pray for them which despitefully use you.
29 And unto him that smiteth thee on the *one* cheek offer also the other; and him that
taketh away thy cloak forbid not *to take thy* coat also.
30 Give to every man that asketh of thee; and of him that taketh away thy goods ask
them not again.
31 And as ye would that men should do to you, do ye also to them likewise.
32 For if ye love them which love you, what thank have ye? for sinners also love those
that love them.
33 And if ye do good to them which do good to you, what thank have ye? for sinners
also do even the same.
34 And if ye lend *to them* of whom ye hope to receive, what thank have ye? for sinners
also lend to sinners, to receive as much again.
35 But love ye your enemies, and do good, and lend, hoping for nothing again; and
your reward shall be great, and ye shall be the children of the Highest: for he is kind
unto the unthankful and *to* the evil.

36 Be ye therefore merciful, as your Father also is merciful.
37 Judge not, and ye shall not be judged: condemn not, and ye shall not be condemned:
forgive, and ye shall be forgiven:
38 Give, and it shall be given unto you; good measure, pressed down, and shaken
together, and running over, shall men give into your bosom. For with the same
measure that ye mete withal it shall be measured to you again. (Luke 6:27-38)

We must correct our own errors before we can effectively help anyone else overcome theirs.

39 And he spake a parable unto them, Can the blind lead the blind? shall they not both
fall into the ditch?
40 The disciple is not above his master: but every one that is perfect shall be as his
master.
41 And why beholdest thou the mote that is in thy brother's eye, but perceivest not the
beam that is in thine own eye?
42 Either how canst thou say to thy brother, Brother, let me pull out the mote that is in
thine eye, when thou thyself beholdest not the beam that is in thine own eye? Thou
hypocrite, cast out first the beam out of thine own eye, and then shalt thou see clearly to
pull out the mote that is in thy brother's eye.
43 For a good tree bringeth not forth corrupt fruit; neither doth a corrupt tree bring forth
good fruit.
44 For every tree is known by his own fruit. For of thorns men do not gather figs, nor
of a bramble bush gather they grapes.
45 A good man out of the good treasure of his heart bringeth forth that which is good;
and an evil man out of the evil treasure of his heart bringeth forth that which is evil: for
of the abundance of the heart his mouth speaketh. (Luke 6:39-45)

Jesus again decries mere professions of fidelity, and demands divinely impelled obedience.

46 ¶ And why call ye me, Lord, Lord, and do not the things which I say?
47 Whosoever cometh to me, and heareth my sayings, and doeth them, I will shew you
to whom he is like:
48 He is like a man which built an house, and digged deep, and laid the foundation on a
rock: and when the flood arose, the stream beat vehemently upon that house, and could
not shake it: for it was founded upon a rock.
49 But he that heareth, and doeth not, is like a man that without a foundation built an
house upon the earth; against which the stream did beat vehemently, and immediately it
fell; and the ruin of that house was great. (Luke 6:46-49)

CHAPTER 50
THE CENTURION'S SERVENT IS HEALED

(Jesus, back home in Capernaum, heals the servant of a Roman military officer)

1 Now when he had ended all his sayings in the audience of the people, he entered into
Capernaum.
2 And a certain centurion's servant, who was dear unto him, was sick, and ready to die.
3 And when he heard of Jesus, he sent unto him the elders of the Jews, beseeching him
that he would come and heal his servant.
4 And when they came to Jesus, they besought him instantly, saying, That he was
worthy for whom he should do this:
5 For he loveth our nation, and he hath built us a synagogue.
6 Then Jesus went with them. And when he was now not far from the house, the

centurion sent friends to him, saying unto him, Lord, trouble not thyself: for I am not
worthy that thou shouldest enter under my roof:
7 Wherefore neither thought I myself worthy to come unto thee: but say in a word, and
my servant shall be healed.
8 For I also am a man set under authority, having under me soldiers, and I say unto
one, Go, and he goeth; and to another, Come, and he cometh; and to my servant, Do
this, and he doeth *it*.
9 When Jesus heard these things, he marvelled at him, and turned him about, and said
unto the people that followed him, I say unto you, I have not found so great faith, no,
not in Israel.
10 And they that were sent, returning to the house, found the servant whole that had
been sick. (Luke 7:1-10)

CHAPTER 51
A WIDOW'S SON IS RAISED TO LIFE
(The 2nd instance of death overcome)

11 ¶ And it came to pass the day after, that he went into a city called Nain; and many of
his disciples went with him, and much people.
12 Now when he came nigh to the gate of the city, behold, there was a dead man
carried out, the only son of his mother, and she was a widow: and much people of the
city was with her.
13 And when the Lord saw her, he had compassion on her, and said unto her, Weep not.
14 And he came and touched the bier: and they that bare *him* stood still. And he said,
Young man, I say unto thee, Arise.
15 And he that was dead sat up, and began to speak. And he delivered him to his
mother.
16 And there came a fear on all: and they glorified God, saying, That a great prophet is
risen up among us; and, That God hath visited his people.
17 And this rumour of him went forth throughout all Judæa, and throughout all the
region round about. (Luke 7:11-17)

The word shewed is *ἀπαγγέλλω apaggellō* and means to bring word, to declare, to report.

18 And the disciples of John shewed him of all these things. (Luke 7:18)

CHAPTER 52
JESUS TESTIFIES CONCERNING JOHN THE BAPTIST

Jesus replies for the second time to John's questioning whether or not he is the Messiah. two is a number; a certain two.

19 ¶ And John calling *unto him* two of his disciples sent *them* to Jesus, saying, Art thou
he that should come? or look we for another?
20 When the men were come unto him, they said, John Baptist hath sent us unto thee,
saying, Art thou he that should come? or look we for another?
21 And in that same hour he cured many of *their* infirmities and plagues, and of evil
spirits; and unto many *that were* blind he gave sight.
22 Then Jesus answering said unto them, Go your way, and tell John what things ye
have seen and heard; how that the blind see, the lame walk, the lepers are cleansed, the
deaf hear, the dead are raised, to the poor the gospel is preached. (Luke 7:19-22)

Perhaps a warning to John the Baptist not to fall away, i.e. that he should not renege on what he originally proclaimed.

23 And blessed is *he*, whosoever shall not be offended in me. (Luke 7:23)

Jesus, for the 2nd time declares that John the Baptist is more than a prophet, since John did not speak of the future. John declared prophecy fulfilled in the coming of Jesus Christ! For the 1st questioning see Matt. 11:10 & 11 page 216.

24 ¶ And when the messengers of John were departed, he began to speak unto the
people concerning John, What went ye out into the wilderness for to see? A reed
shaken with the wind?
25 But what went ye out for to see? A man clothed in soft raiment? Behold, they which
are gorgeously apparelled, and live delicately, are in kings' courts.
26 But what went ye out for to see? A prophet? Yea, I say unto you, and much more
than a prophet.
27 This is *he*, of whom it is written, Behold, I send my messenger before thy face,
which shall prepare thy way before thee.
28 For I say unto you, Among those that are born of women there is not a greater
prophet than John the Baptist: (Luke 7:24-28 *to :*)

He who has *accepted* Jesus and the kingdom of God is greater than John the Baptist who *proclaimed* it, but now doubts.

28 but he that is least in the kingdom of God is greater than he. (Luke 7:28 *but*)

CHAPTER 53
PHARISEES REBUKED FOR REJECTING JOHN AND JESUS

The people, including the publicans who were baptized by John, rightly acknowledged that Jesus was sent from God.

29 And all the people that heard *him*, and the publicans, justified God, being baptized
with the baptism of John. (Luke 7:29)

The Pharisees and lawyers however, being filled with arrogance and pride, were both unwilling and unable to see it.

30 But the Pharisees and lawyers rejected the counsel of God against themselves, being
not baptized of him. (Luke 7:30)

What follows is Jesus' assessment of the Pharisees and lawyers for refusing to acknowledge who he was.

31 ¶ And the Lord said, Whereunto then shall I liken the men of this generation? and to
what are they like? (Luke 7:31)

The Pharisees proved themselves to be remarkably *incongruous* in what they professed to be, and actually were; while on the other hand they were remarkably *consistent* in rejecting Truth's messengers.

32 They are like unto children sitting in the marketplace, and calling one to another,
and saying, We have piped unto you, and ye have not danced; we have mourned to you,
and ye have not wept. (Luke 7:32)

John, who was neither gluttonous nor a heavy drinker, the Pharisees said was crazy.

33 For John the Baptist came neither eating bread nor drinking wine; and ye say, He
hath a devil. (Luke 7:33)

The Pharisees said Jesus was a glutton, drunkard, and friend of extortionists and the impure because he healed them.

34 The Son of man is come eating and drinking; and ye say, Behold a gluttonous man,
and a winebibber, a friend of publicans and sinners! (Luke 7:34)

Jesus and John will be justified for having done the works of Wisdom; John for proclaiming, and Jesus for fulfilling.

35 But wisdom is justified of all her children. (Luke 7:35)

CHAPTER 54
A LESSON IN LOVE
The 1st anointing of Jesus. The woman who anointed him is unnamed

36 ¶ And one of the Pharisees desired him that he would eat with him. And he went
into the Pharisee's house, and sat down to meat. (Luke 7:36)

The uninvited and unnamed "guest"

Did this anointing take place in Magdala, and was this "strange woman" Mary Magdalene? Note that Luke informs us that immediately afterwards "the twelve" and certain women, including Mary Magdalene who had several healings, accompany Jesus.

37 And, behold, a woman in the city, which was a sinner, when she knew that *Jesus* sat

at meat in the Pharisee's house, brought an alabaster box of ointment,
38 And stood at his feet behind *him* weeping, and began to wash his feet with tears, and
did wipe *them* with the hairs of her head, and kissed his feet, and anointed *them* with
the ointment. (Luke 7:37-38)

Criticism of the host

39 Now when the Pharisee which had bidden him saw *it*, he spake within himself,
saying, This man, if he were a prophet, would have known who and what manner of
woman *this is* that toucheth him: for she is a sinner. (Luke 7:39)

Jesus had read Simon the Pharisees' thought, and now the lesson begins

40 And Jesus answering said unto him, Simon, I have somewhat to say unto thee. And
he saith, Master, say on.
41 There was a certain creditor which had two debtors: the one owed five hundred
pence, and the other fifty.
42 And when they had nothing to pay, he frankly forgave them both. Tell me therefore,
which of them will love him most?
43 Simon answered and said, I suppose that *he*, to whom he forgave most. And he said
unto him, Thou hast rightly judged. (Luke 7:40-43)

Self-righteousness contrasted to genuine repentance

Do we like Simon see only flesh and blood, or do we see beyond the veil as Jesus taught, and behold God's perfect man?

44 And he turned to the woman, and said unto Simon, Seest thou this woman? I
entered into thine house, thou gavest me no water for my feet: but she hath washed my
feet with tears, and wiped *them* with the hairs of her head.
45 Thou gavest me no kiss: but this woman since the time I came in hath not ceased to
kiss my feet.
46 My head with oil thou didst not anoint: but this woman hath anointed my feet with
ointment.
47 Wherefore I say unto thee, Her sins, which are many, are forgiven; for she loved
much: but to whom little is forgiven, *the same* loveth little. (Luke 7:44-47)

The conclusion

48 And he said unto her, Thy sins are forgiven. (Luke 7:48)

The attempt of self-righteousness to justify itself

49 And they that sat at meat with him began to say within themselves, Who is this that
forgiveth sins also? (Luke 7:49)

Human opinions cannot overthrow the law of God. Jesus knew this woman was now striving to live his teaching

50 And he said to the woman, Thy faith hath saved thee; go in peace. (Luke 7:50)

CHAPTER 55
SOME QUALITIES NEEDED TO BE A SUCCESSFUL DISCIPLE

The Apostles and "certain women" accompany Jesus

1 And it came to pass afterward, that he went throughout every city and village,
preaching and shewing the glad tidings of the kingdom of God: and the twelve *were*
with him,
2 And certain women, which had been healed of evil spirits and infirmities, Mary
called Magdalene, out of whom went seven devils,

3 And Joanna the wife of Chuza Herod's steward, and Susanna, and many others,
which ministered unto him of their substance. (Luke 8:1-3)

Potential followers gathered and were taught in parables

4 ¶ And when much people were gathered together, and were come to him out of every
city, he spake by a parable: (Luke 8:4)

The Parable of the Sower
(This is the 1st recorded use of this parable)

5 A sower went out to sow his seed: and as he sowed, some fell by the way side; and it
was trodden down, and the fowls of the air devoured it.
6 And some fell upon a rock; and as soon as it was sprung up, it withered away,
because it lacked moisture.
7 And some fell among thorns; and the thorns sprang up with it, and choked it.
8 And other fell on good ground, and sprang up, and bare fruit an hundredfold. And
when he had said these things, he cried, He that hath ears to hear, let him hear. (Luke 8:5-8)

Not understanding, the disciples request an explanation

9 ¶ And his disciples asked him, saying, What might this parable be?
10 And he said, Unto you it is given to know the mysteries of the kingdom of God: but
to others in parables; that seeing they might not see, and hearing they might not
understand. (Luke 8:9-10)

Jesus interprets the parable to his disciples

The sower is Jesus and the seed is his teaching.

11 Now the parable is this: The seed is the word of God. (Luke 8:11)

Those by the way side believe without actually understanding.

12 Those by the way side are they that hear; then cometh the devil, and taketh away the
word out of their hearts, lest they should believe and be saved. (Luke 8:12)

Those on the rock lack fortitude and moral courage so that when tested fall away, i.e. they become unfaithful and desert.

13 They on the rock *are they*, which, when they hear, receive the word with joy; and
these have no root, which for a while believe, and in time of temptation fall away. (Luke 8:13)

Those that fall among thorns become immersed in self and matter making them spiritually unfruitful.

14 And that which fell among thorns are they, which, when they have heard, go forth,
and are choked with cares and riches and pleasures of *this* life, and bring no fruit to
perfection. (Luke 8:14)

They on good ground are sincere, faithful, and so become empowered to demonstrate Jesus' teaching.

15 But that on the good ground are they, which in an honest and good heart, having
heard the word, keep *it*, and bring forth fruit with patience. (Luke 8:15)

The disciples are told they must be unselfish and openly declare the truth through *living* it

16 ¶ No man, when he hath lighted a candle, covereth it with a vessel, or putteth *it*
under a bed; but setteth *it* on a candlestick, that they which enter in may see the light.
17 For nothing is secret, that shall not be made manifest; neither *any thing* hid, that
shall not be known and come abroad. (Luke 8:16-17)

A correct understanding increases through practice, whereas mere belief perishes

18 Take heed therefore how ye hear: for whosoever hath, to him shall be given; and
whosoever hath not, from him shall be taken even that which he seemeth to have. (Luke 8:18)

CHAPTER 56
DECLARED INSANE BY HIS FAMILY

(The word friends is *παρά para*, it means those near; kinsfolk i.e. his mother, brothers, and sisters)

19 and they went into an house.
20 And the multitude cometh together again, so that they could not so much as eat
bread. (Mark 3:19-20 *and*)

To be beside oneself means to be insane. Here we are being told that the family of Jesus accused him of insanity.

21 And when his friends heard *of it*, they went out to lay hold on him: for they said, He
is beside himself. (Mark 3:21)

CHAPTER 57
ACCUSED OF HEALING THROUGH BEELZEBUB

Next the scribes from Jerusalem accuse Jesus of utilizing the highest form of malpractice

22 ¶ And the scribes which came down from Jerusalem said, He hath Beelzebub, and
by the prince of the devils casteth he out devils.
23 And he called them *unto him*, and said unto them in parables, How can Satan cast
out Satan?
24 And if a kingdom be divided against itself, that kingdom cannot stand.
25 And if a house be divided against itself, that house cannot stand.
26 And if Satan rise up against himself, and be divided, he cannot stand, but hath an
end.
27 No man can enter into a strong man's house, and spoil his goods, except he will first
bind the strong man; and then he will spoil his house.
28 Verily I say unto you, All sins shall be forgiven unto the sons of men, and
blasphemies wherewith soever they shall blaspheme: (Mark 3:22-28)

The accusation that Jesus healed through evil is a denial of Christ, Truth. It is the sin against the Holy Ghost.

29 But he that shall blaspheme against the Holy Ghost hath never forgiveness, but is in
danger of eternal damnation: (Mark 3:29)

Jesus did not let the accusation that he healed through demonology go unchallenged. He was no mesmerist!

30 Because they said, He hath an unclean spirit. (Mark 3:30)

The *Pharisees* repeated the accusation of the scribes when they witnessed a healing. The people knew better

22 ¶ Then was brought unto him one possessed with a devil, blind, and dumb: and he
healed him, insomuch that the blind and dumb both spake and saw.
23 And all the people were amazed, and said, Is not this the son of David?
24 But when the Pharisees heard *it*, they said, This *fellow* doth not cast out devils, but
by Beelzebub the prince of the devils. (Matt 12:22-24)

Jesus exposed the hypocrisy of the Pharisees with the same arguments he used with the scribes

25 And Jesus knew their thoughts, and said unto them, Every kingdom divided against
itself is brought to desolation; and every city or house divided against itself shall not
stand:
26 And if Satan cast out Satan, he is divided against himself; how shall then his
kingdom stand? (Matt 12:25-26)

Jesus exposed the Pharisees and their disciples (children = disciples or pupils) as the actual practitioners of demonology.

27 And if I by Beelzebub cast out devils, by whom do your children cast *them* out?
therefore they shall be your judges. (Matt 12:27)

Jesus declared that his healing was done through Christ, the power of God operating in human experience.

28 But if I cast out devils by the Spirit of God, then the kingdom of God is come unto
you. (Matt 12:28)

The method used by Jesus does not cooperate with evil, it exposes and destroys evil.

29 Or else how can one enter into a strong man's house, and spoil his goods, except he
first bind the strong man? and then he will spoil his house.
30 He that is not with me is against me; and he that gathereth not with me scattereth
abroad. (Matt 12:29-30)

The sin against the Holy Ghost, being a denial of Truth, is not forgiven because it leaves error in control.

31 ¶ Wherefore I say unto you, All manner of sin and blasphemy shall be forgiven unto
men: but the blasphemy *against* the *Holy* Ghost shall not be forgiven unto men.
32 And whosoever speaketh a word against the Son of man, it shall be forgiven him:
but whosoever speaketh against the Holy Ghost, it shall not be forgiven him, neither in
this world, neither in the *world* to come. (Matt 12:31-32)

Jesus calls out the Pharisees for their hypocrisy

To make, *ποιέω, poieō*, here means to identify a tree (the teaching), as either good or evil by its fruit (the results),

33 Either make the tree good, and his fruit good; or else make the tree corrupt, and his
fruit corrupt: for the tree is known by *his* fruit.
34 O generation of vipers, how can ye, being evil, speak good things? for out of the
abundance of the heart the mouth speaketh.
35 A good man out of the good treasure of the heart bringeth forth good things: and an
evil man out of the evil treasure bringeth forth evil things.
36 But I say unto you, That every idle word that men shall speak, they shall give
account thereof in the day of judgment.
37 For by thy words thou shalt be justified, and by thy words thou shalt be condemned.
(Matt 12:33-37)

Jesus exposes the materialism of certain scribes and Pharisees

38 ¶ Then certain of the scribes and of the Pharisees answered, saying, Master, we
would see a sign from thee. (Matt 12:38)

The corrupting effect of relying on material sense testimony rather trusting spiritual intuition is pointed out.

39 But he answered and said unto them, An evil and adulterous generation seeketh after
a sign; and there shall no sign be given to it, but the sign of the prophet Jonas: (Matt 12:39)

Jesus would be in the tomb three days: Wednesday, Nisan 14 before sunset, until after sunset the beginning of Nisan 18.

40 For as Jonas was three days and three nights in the whale's belly; so shall the Son of
man be three days and three nights in the heart of the earth. (Matt 12:40)

Self-justification and pride forestall repentance and reformation. The result is self-condemnation.

41 The men of Nineveh shall rise in judgment with this generation, and shall condemn
it: because they repented at the preaching of Jonas; and, behold, a greater than Jonas *is*
here.
42 The queen of the south shall rise up in the judgment with this generation, and shall
condemn it: for she came from the uttermost parts of the earth to hear the wisdom of
Solomon; and, behold, a greater than Solomon *is* here. (Matt 12:41-42)

Jesus exposes the error of casting out "devils" through Beelzebub

43 When the unclean spirit is gone out of a man, he walketh through dry places,
seeking rest, and findeth none.
44 Then he saith, I will return into my house from whence I came out; and when he is
come, he findeth *it* empty, swept, and garnished.
45 Then goeth he, and taketh with himself seven other spirits more wicked than
himself, and they enter in and dwell there: and the last *state* of that man is worse than
the first. Even so shall it be also unto this wicked generation. (Matt 12:43-45)

CHAPTER 58
GOD'S FAMILY ARE THOSE WHO DO HIS WILL

(Immortals, or God's children in divine Science, are one harmonious family; but mortals, or the "children of men" in material sense, are discordant and ofttimes false brethren. - MBE)

According to the Gospel of Mark

Read this remembering Mark 3:21 where the family of Jesus sought to "lay hold on him" on the grounds of insanity.

31 ¶ There came then his brethren and his mother, and, standing without, sent unto him,
calling him.
32 And the multitude sat about him, and they said unto him, Behold, thy mother and thy
brethren without seek for thee. (Mark 3:31-32)

Imagine how alone Jesus must have felt at being misunderstood and falsely accused of insanity by his own family!

33 And he answered them, saying, Who is my mother, or my brethren?
34 And he looked round about on them which sat about him, and said, Behold my
mother and my brethren!
35 For whosoever shall do the will of God, the same is my brother, and my sister, and
mother. (Mark 3:33-35)

According to the Gospel of Luke

19 ¶ Then came to him *his* mother and his brethren, and could not come at him for the
press.
20 And it was told him *by certain* which said, Thy mother and thy brethren stand
without, desiring to see thee.
21 And he answered and said unto them, My mother and my brethren are these which
hear the word of God, and do it. (Luke 8:19-21)

According to the Gospel of Matthew

46 ¶ While he yet talked to the people, behold, *his* mother and his brethren stood
without, desiring to speak with him.
47 Then one said unto him, Behold, thy mother and thy brethren stand without, desiring
to speak with thee.
48 But he answered and said unto him that told him, Who is my mother? and who are
my brethren? (Matt 12:46-48)

God is our Father and our Mother, our Minister and the great Physician: He is man's only real relative on earth and in heaven. David sang, "Whom have I in heaven beside thee? and there is none upon earth that I desire beside thee. - MBE

49 And he stretched forth his hand toward his disciples, and said, Behold my mother
and my brethren!
50 For whosoever shall do the will of my Father which is in heaven, the same is my
brother, and sister, and mother. (Matt 12:49-50)

CHAPTER 59
CHRISTIANITY IN PARABLES

1 The same day went Jesus out of the house, and sat by the sea side.
2 And great multitudes were gathered together unto him, so that he went into a ship,
and sat; and the whole multitude stood on the shore.
3 And he spake many things unto them in parables, saying, (Matt 13:1-3 *to* 2nd ,)

The Parable of the Sower (2nd time)

3 Behold, a sower went forth to sow;
4 And when he sowed, some *seeds* fell by the way side, and the fowls came and
devoured them up:

5 Some fell upon stony places, where they had not much earth: and forthwith they sprung up, because they had no deepness of earth:
6 And when the sun was up, they were scorched; and because they had no root, they withered away.
7 And some fell among thorns; and the thorns sprung up, and choked them:
8 But other fell into good ground, and brought forth fruit, some an hundredfold, some sixtyfold, some thirtyfold.
9 Who hath ears to hear, let him hear. (Matt 13:3-9 *Behold*)

Jesus tells his disciples why he teaches in parables

In the soil of an "honest and good heart" the seed must be sown; else it beareth not much fruit, for the swinish element in human nature uproots it. Jesus' parable of "the sower" shows the care our Master took not to impart to dull ears and gross hearts the spiritual teachings which dulness and grossness could not accept. Reading the thoughts of the people, he said: "Give not that which is holy unto the dogs, neither cast ye your pearls before swine." - MBE

10 And the disciples came, and said unto him, Why speakest thou unto them in parables?
11 He answered and said unto them, Because it is given unto you to know the mysteries of the kingdom of heaven, but to them it is not given.
12 For whosoever hath, to him shall be given, and he shall have more abundance: but whosoever hath not, from him shall be taken away even that he hath.
13 Therefore speak I to them in parables: because they seeing see not; and hearing they hear not, neither do they understand. (Matt 13:10-13)

A statement by Jesus that Isaiah's prophecy, foretelling the resistance of the carnal mind, was being fulfilled.

14 And in them is fulfilled the prophecy of Esaias, which saith, By hearing ye shall hear, and shall not understand; and seeing ye shall see, and shall not perceive:
15 For this people's heart is waxed gross, and *their* ears are dull of hearing, and their eyes they have closed; lest at any time they should see with *their* eyes, and hear with *their* ears, and should understand with *their* heart, and should be converted, and I should heal them. (Matt 13:14-15)

The disciples were truly blessed to see what the prophets and many others had hoped to see and hear, and didn't.

16 But blessed *are* your eyes, for they see: and your ears, for they hear.
17 For verily I say unto you, That many prophets and righteous *men* have desired to see *those things* which ye see, and have not seen *them*; and to hear *those things* which ye hear, and have not heard *them*. (Matt 13:16-17)

Jesus interprets the Parable of the Sower for the 2nd time

In this parable Jesus is the sower, his teaching the seed, and those that hear are the soil where the seed is cast.

18 ¶ Hear ye therefore the parable of the sower. (Matt 13:18)

Those receiving seed by the wayside believe without really understanding.

19 When any one heareth the word of the kingdom, and understandeth *it* not, then cometh the wicked *one*, and catcheth away that which was sown in his heart. This is he which received seed by the way side. (Matt 13:19)

They who receive the seed in stony places lack courage and conviction and so fall away when persecuted.

20 But he that received the seed into stony places, the same is he that heareth the word, and anon with joy receiveth it;
21 Yet hath he not root in himself, but dureth for a while: for when tribulation or persecution ariseth because of the word, by and by he is offended.

They who receive the seed among the thorns are immersed in self and buried in matter, and fail to practice the teaching.

22 He also that received seed among the thorns is he that heareth the word; and the care of this world, and the deceitfulness of riches, choke the word, and he becometh unfruitful. (Matt 13:22)

Those receiving seed in good ground understand the teaching and are able to put the Christ-teaching into practice.
23 But he that received seed into the good ground is he that heareth the word, and
understandeth *it*; which also beareth fruit, and bringeth forth, some an hundredfold,
some sixty, some thirty. (Matt 13:23)

The Parable of the Wheat and the Tares

24 ¶ Another parable put he forth unto them, saying, The kingdom of heaven is likened
unto a man which sowed good seed in his field: (Matt 13:24)
A warning to his disciples to watch so that tares (false teaching) doesn't contaminate the wheat (his true teaching).
25 But while men slept, his enemy came and sowed tares among the wheat, and went
his way. (Matt 13:25)
Jesus here foretells that despite this warning his teaching will become adulterated.
26 But when the blade was sprung up, and brought forth fruit, then appeared the tares
also. (Matt 13:26)
Jesus also saw there would be a tendency to focus on the uprooting the tares (false teaching).
27 So the servants of the householder came and said unto him, Sir, didst not thou sow
good seed in thy field? from whence then hath it tares?
28 He said unto them, An enemy hath done this. The servants said unto him, Wilt thou
then that we go and gather them up? (Matt 13:27-28)
Jesus foretold that uprooting the tares would result in uprooting the good seed also. Christians would do well to heed the counsel of Gamaliel. See Acts 5:12-39, specifically verses 34, 38 & 39.
29 But he said, Nay; lest while ye gather up the tares, ye root up also the wheat with
them. (Matt 13:29)
Stay focused on understanding the true teaching and trust God to reveal the means to eliminate the false.
30 Let both grow together until the harvest: and in the time of harvest I will say to the
reapers, Gather ye together first the tares, and bind them in bundles to burn them: but
gather the wheat into my barn. (Matt 13:30)

The Parable of the Mustard Seed (1st Time)

31 ¶ Another parable put he forth unto them, saying, The kingdom of heaven is like to a
grain of mustard seed, which a man took, and sowed in his field: (Matt 13:31)
Students of Jesus' teaching, first called "followers of the way" and later renamed "Christians," would multiply greatly.
32 Which indeed is the least of all seeds: but when it is grown, it is the greatest among
herbs, and becometh a tree, so that the birds of the air come and lodge in the branches
thereof. (Matt 13:32)

The Parable of Leaven Hid by a Woman in Three Measures of Meal (1st Time)

This parable is the fourth, and therefore the climax, foretelling that his true teaching would be restored through a woman.
33 ¶ Another parable spake he unto them; The kingdom of heaven is like unto leaven,
which a woman took, and hid in three measures of meal, till the whole was leavened.
(Matt 13:33)

All teaching was done by parables

34 All these things spake Jesus unto the multitude in parables; and without a parable
spake he not unto them:
35 That it might be fulfilled which was spoken by the prophet, saying, I will open my
mouth in parables; I will utter things which have been kept secret from the foundation
of the world. (Matt 13:34-35)

The multitude is sent away

(Teaching from here to the end of this chapter was in private to his disciples)

36 Then Jesus sent the multitude away, and went into the house: (Matt 13:36 *to* :)

Jesus interprets the Parable of the Wheat and the Tares

36 and his disciples came unto him, saying, Declare unto us the parable of the tares of the field. (Matt 13:36 *and*)

Jesus is the Son of man that sows the seed (teaches the true way) .

37 He answered and said unto them, He that soweth the good seed is the Son of man; (Matt 13:37)

The world is human consciousness. The good seed is his pure teaching. The tares are deviations from his teaching.

38 The field is the world; the good seed are the children of the kingdom; but the tares are the children of the wicked *one*; (Matt 13:38)

The devil, "a liar," is the wicked one. Spiritualization of consciousness is the end of the world. Angels are God's thoughts.

39 The enemy that sowed them is the devil; the harvest is the end of the world; and the reapers are the angels. (Matt 13:39)

The exposure of all mortal and material belief to the light of Christ, Truth destroys error as light destroys darkness.

40 As therefore the tares are gathered and burned in the fire; so shall it be in the end of this world. (Matt 13:40)

This is fully explained in the "Revelation of Jesus Christ" recorded by John the Beloved Disciple just as Jesus foretold.

41 The Son of man shall send forth his angels, and they shall gather out of his kingdom all things that offend, and them which do iniquity;

42 And shall cast them into a furnace of fire: there shall be wailing and gnashing of teeth. (Matt 13:41-42)

Then shall man in God's image and likeness be understood to be the only true man, and God be glorified in His reflection.

43 Then shall the righteous shine forth as the sun in the kingdom of their Father. (Matt 13:43 to 1st.)

A statement that those with ears (spiritual discernment) will understand correctly what has been taught.

43 Who hath ears to hear, let him hear. (Matt 13: 43 *Who*)

Parable of the Hid Treasure

"The kingdom" may seem hidden because it is invisible to the physical senses, but it is nevertheless "at hand." But in order to see it we must be "willing to leave all for Christ, for Truth, and so be counted among sinners." – MBE

44 ¶ Again, the kingdom of heaven is like unto treasure hid in a field; the which when a man hath found, he hideth, and for joy thereof goeth and selleth all that he hath, and buyeth that field. (Matt 13:44)

Parable of the Pearl of Great Price

The kingdom of heaven is worth more than all earthly possessions, but to attain it we must willingly exchange "the objects of sense for the ideas of Soul." "We are not Christian Scientists until we leave all for Christ." - MBE

45 ¶ Again, the kingdom of heaven is like unto a merchant man, seeking goodly pearls:

46 Who, when he had found one pearl of great price, went and sold all that he had, and bought it. (Matt 13:45-46)

Parable of the Net Cast into the Sea

This, the seventh and final parable, foretells how the "wheat" (Truth) and the "tares" (false beliefs) are separated.

47 ¶ Again, the kingdom of heaven is like unto a net, that was cast into the sea, and gathered of every kind: (Matt 13:47)

Error must be identified in human consciousness so that it can be relinquished for Truth.

48 Which, when it was full, they drew to shore, and sat down, and gathered the good into vessels, but cast the bad away. (Matt 13:48)

Truth and error cannot coexist any more than can light and darkness. Light always dispels the darkness!

49 So shall it be at the end of the world: the angels shall come forth, and sever the wicked from among the just, (Matt 13:49)

Though human belief may resist, it will ultimately be forced to yield to Truth. Then it will be free from every form of evil.

50 And shall cast them into the furnace of fire: there shall be wailing and gnashing of teeth. (Matt 13:50)

The critical question

Jesus asked his disciples: Have you understood this teaching? They said they did, but we shall see they really didn't.

51 Jesus saith unto them, Have ye understood all these things? They say unto him,
Yea, Lord. (Matt 13:51)

If *you* have '*thine* age shall be clearer than the noonday; thou shalt shine forth, thou shalt be as the morning." Job 11:17

52 Then said he unto them, Therefore every scribe *which is* instructed unto the kingdom
of heaven is like unto a man *that is* an householder, which bringeth forth out of his
treasure *things* new and old. (Matt 13:52)

CHAPTER 60
THE NEXT DAY: REVIEW AND DEPARTURE

1 And he began again to teach by the sea side: and there was gathered unto him a great
multitude, so that he entered into a ship, and sat in the sea; and the whole multitude was
by the sea on the land.
2 And he taught them many things by parables, and said unto them in his doctrine, (Mark
4:1-2)

The Parable of the Sower (3rd time)

3 Hearken; Behold, there went out a sower to sow:
4 And it came to pass, as he sowed, some fell by the way side, and the fowls of the air
came and devoured it up.
5 And some fell on stony ground, where it had not much earth; and immediately it
sprang up, because it had no depth of earth:
6 But when the sun was up, it was scorched; and because it had no root, it withered
away.
7 And some fell among thorns, and the thorns grew up, and choked it, and it yielded no
fruit.
8 And other fell on good ground, and did yield fruit that sprang up and increased; and
brought forth, some thirty, and some sixty, and some an hundred.
9 And he said unto them, He that hath ears to hear, let him hear. (Mark 4:3-9)

Jesus repeats his reason for teaching in parables. Remember that we, like the disciples, are not always quick learners.

10 And when he was alone, they that were about him with the twelve asked of him the
parable.
11 And he said unto them, Unto you it is given to know the mystery of the kingdom of
God: but unto them that are without, all *these* things are done in parables:
12 That seeing they may see, and not perceive; and hearing they may hear, and not
understand; lest at any time they should be converted, and *their* sins should be forgiven
them.
13 And he said unto them, Know ye not this parable? and how then will ye know all
parables? (Mark 4:10-13)

Instruction on how to understand this parable and all parables

14 ¶ The sower soweth the word.
15 And these are they by the way side, where the word is sown; but when they have
heard, Satan cometh immediately, and taketh away the word that was sown in their
hearts.
16 And these are they likewise which are sown on stony ground; who, when they have
heard the word, immediately receive it with gladness;
17 And have no root in themselves, and so endure but for a time: afterward, when

affliction or persecution ariseth for the word's sake, immediately they are offended.
18 And these are they which are sown among thorns; such as hear the word,
19 And the cares of this world, and the deceitfulness of riches, and the lusts of other
things entering in, choke the word, and it becometh unfruitful.
20 And these are they which are sown on good ground; such as hear the word, and
receive *it*, and bring forth fruit, some thirtyfold, some sixty, and some an hundred. (Mark 4:14-20)

Demonstration, actually putting this teaching into practice, validates that it has been understood

21 ¶ And he said unto them, Is a candle brought to be put under a bushel, or under a
bed? and not to be set on a candlestick?
22 For there is nothing hid, which shall not be manifested; neither was any thing kept
secret, but that it should come abroad.
23 If any man have ears to hear, let him hear. (Mark 4:21-23)

Greater enlightenment can only come by putting into practice what is already understood

24 And he said unto them, Take heed what ye hear: with what measure ye mete, it shall
be measured to you: and unto you that hear shall more be given.
25 For he that hath, to him shall be given: and he that hath not, from him shall be taken
even that which he hath. (Mark 4:24-25)

A new parable - The Kingdom of God and Harvest Time

26 ¶ And he said, So is the kingdom of God, as if a man should cast seed into the
ground;
27 And should sleep, and rise night and day, and the seed should spring and grow up,
he knoweth not how.
28 For the earth bringeth forth fruit of herself; first the blade, then the ear, after that the
full corn in the ear. (Mark 4:26-28)

We must not procrastinate. When we finally understand something we must immediately put it into practice.

29 But when the fruit is brought forth, immediately he putteth in the sickle, because the
harvest is come. (Mark 4:29)

The Parable the Mustard Seed (2nd time)

30 ¶ And he said, Whereunto shall we liken the kingdom of God? or with what
comparison shall we compare it?
31 *It is* like a grain of mustard seed, which, when it is sown in the earth, is less than all
the seeds that be in the earth:
32 But when it is sown, it groweth up, and becometh greater than all herbs, and
shooteth out great branches; so that the fowls of the air may lodge under the shadow of
it. (Mark 4:30-32)

All teaching to the multitudes was done in parables

33 And with many such parables spake he the word unto them, as they were able to
hear *it*.
34 But without a parable spake he not unto them: (Mark 4:33-34 to :)

Only the disciples were given the interpretation of the parables

34 and when they were alone, he expounded all things to his disciples. (Mark 4:34 *and*)

Departure across the sea (lake) at day's end

According to the Gospel of Matthew

53 ¶ And it came to pass, *that* when Jesus had finished these parables, he departed

thence. (Matt 13:53)

According to the Gospel of Mark

35 And the same day, when the even was come, he saith unto them, Let us pass over
unto the other side. (Mark 4:35)

CHAPTER 61
A TEMPEST IS STILLED

According to the Gospel of Mark

36 And when they had sent away the multitude, they took him even as he was in the
ship. And there were also with him other little ships. (Mark 4:36)

Storm, *λαῖλαψ lailaps*, a tempestuous wind. This vessel was open, uncovered. This allowed waves to swamp the boat.

37 And there arose a great storm of wind, and the waves beat into the ship, so that it
was now full.
38 And he was in the hinder part of the ship, asleep on a pillow: and they awake him,
and say unto him, Master, carest thou not that we perish?
39 And he arose, and rebuked the wind, and said unto the sea, Peace, be still. And the
wind ceased, and there was a great calm.
40 And he said unto them, Why are ye so fearful? how is it that ye have no faith?
41 And they feared exceedingly, and said one to another, What manner of man is this,
that even the wind and the sea obey him? (Mark 4:37-41)

According to the Gospel of Luke

22 ¶ Now it came to pass on a certain day, that he went into a ship with his disciples:
and he said unto them, Let us go over unto the other side of the lake. And they
launched forth.
23 But as they sailed he fell asleep: and there came down a storm of wind on the lake;
and they were filled *with water*, and were in jeopardy.
24 And they came to him, and awoke him, saying, Master, master, we perish. Then he
arose, and rebuked the wind and the raging of the water: and they ceased, and there was
a calm.
25 And he said unto them, Where is your faith? And they being afraid wondered,
saying one to another, What manner of man is this! for he commandeth even the winds
and water, and they obey him. (Luke 8:22-25)

CHAPTER 62
HEALING THE DEMONIAC IN GADARA

According to the Gospel of Luke

26 ¶ And they arrived at the country of the Gadarenes, which is over against Galilee.
27 And when he went forth to land, there met him out of the city a certain man, which
had devils long time, and ware no clothes, neither abode in *any* house, but in the tombs.
28 When he saw Jesus, he cried out, and fell down before him, and with a loud voice
said, What have I to do with thee, Jesus, *thou* Son of God most high? I beseech thee,
torment me not.
29 (For he had commanded the unclean spirit to come out of the man. For oftentimes it
had caught him: and he was kept bound with chains and in fetters; and he brake the
bands, and was driven of the devil into the wilderness.)
30 And Jesus asked him, saying, What is thy name? And he said, Legion: because
many devils were entered into him. (Luke 8:26-30)

The people demanded assurance that the "devils" would not return, i.e. they wanted proof the healing was permanent.

31 And they besought him that he would not command them to go out into the deep.

32 And there was there an herd of many swine feeding on the mountain: and they besought him that he would suffer them to enter into them. And he suffered them. (Luke 8:31-32)

Proof is given that the "devils" were destroyed. For the significance see Matthew 12:43-45 (*to* 1st. , and Luke 11:21-26.

33 Then went the devils out of the man, and entered into the swine: and the herd ran violently down a steep place into the lake, and were choked. (Luke 8:33)

When the healing was reported to "city officials", who most likely knew of the demoniac, they were alarmed

34 When they that fed *them* saw what was done, they fled, and went and told *it* in the city and in the country.

35 Then they went out to see what was done; and came to Jesus, and found the man, out of whom the devils were departed, sitting at the feet of Jesus, clothed, and in his right mind: and they were afraid.

36 They also which saw *it* told them by what means he that was possessed of the devils was healed. (Luke 8:34-36)

Jesus complied with the request that he depart, consistent with his teaching, "neither cast ye your pearls before swine."

37 ¶ Then the whole multitude of the country of the Gadarenes round about besought him to depart from them; for they were taken with great fear: and he went up into the ship, and returned back again. (Luke 8:37)

Jesus knew that God had healed the man, so he told the man to show what "great things *God* had done." Instead, the man published what great things *Jesus* had done, causing even greater envy and resistance.

38 Now the man out of whom the devils were departed besought him that he might be with him: but Jesus sent him away, saying,

39 Return to thine own house, and shew how great things God hath done unto thee. And he went his way and published throughout the whole city how great things Jesus had done unto him. (Luke 8:38-39)

According to the Gospel of Mark

1 And they came over unto the other side of the sea, into the country of the Gadarenes.

2 And when he was come out of the ship, immediately there met him out of the tombs a man with an unclean spirit,

3 Who had *his* dwelling among the tombs; and no man could bind him, no, not with chains:

4 Because that he had been often bound with fetters and chains, and the chains had been plucked asunder by him, and the fetters broken in pieces: neither could any *man* tame him.

5 And always, night and day, he was in the mountains, and in the tombs, crying, and cutting himself with stones. (Mark 5:1-5)

To worship here means to give homage, to acknowledge and to show respect by prostration.

6 But when he saw Jesus afar off, he ran and worshipped him,

7 And cried with a loud voice, and said, What have I to do with thee, Jesus, *thou* Son of the most high God? I adjure thee by God, that thou torment me not.

8 For he said unto him, Come out of the man, *thou* unclean spirit.

9 And he asked him, What *is* thy name? And he answered, saying, My name *is* Legion: for we are many. (Mark 5:6-9)

A request for proof that the unclean spirit was destroyed and the healing permanent. See Matt. 12:43-45 & Luke 44:24-26

10 And he besought him much that he would not send them away out of the country.

11 Now there was there nigh unto the mountains a great herd of swine feeding.

12 And all the devils besought him, saying, Send us into the swine, that we may enter
into them. (Mark 5:10-12)

Proof that the 'unclean spirit' had been destroyed was provided when the swine perished in the lake.

13 And forthwith Jesus gave them leave. And the unclean spirits went out, and entered
into the swine: and the herd ran violently down a steep place into the sea, (they were
about two thousand;) and were choked in the sea. (Mark 5:13)

When the incident was reported, the city officials and people in the countryside, reacted with fear.

14 And they that fed the swine fled, and told *it* in the city, and in the country. And they
went out to see what it was that was done.
15 And they come to Jesus, and see him that was possessed with the devil, and had the
legion, sitting, and clothed, and in his right mind: and they were afraid.
16 And they that saw *it* told them how it befell to him that was possessed with the devil,
and *also* concerning the swine. (Mark 5:14-16)

Jesus was implored to leave the country. Pray, *παρακαλέω parakaleō*, here means to beg, entreat, beseech.

17 And they began to pray him to depart out of their coasts.
18 And when he was come into the ship, he that had been possessed with the devil
prayed him that he might be with him. (Mark 15:17-18)

Jesus used the word Lord meaning God. The man was told to share with his friends the power of God to heal.

19 Howbeit Jesus suffered him not, but saith unto him, Go home to thy friends, and tell
them how great things the Lord hath done for thee, and hath had compassion on thee.
20 And he departed, and began to publish in Decapolis how great things Jesus had done
for him: and all *men* did marvel. (Mark 5:19-20)

CHAPTER 63
BACK IN CAPERNAUM AND MORE HEALING

According to the Gospel of Luke

"The people," desiring spiritual freedom, enthusiastically awaited Jesus' return. The Pharisees and elders however, saw his message of liberation as a threat to their domination, control, and exploitation of the people.

40 And it came to pass, that, when Jesus was returned, the people *gladly* received him:
for they were all waiting for him. (Luke 8:40)

Jairus a ruler of the synagogue asks Jesus to heal his dying daughter
(A different healing than the one reported in Matt. 9:18-19, 23-26. There the daughter had already died.)
(This is the 3rd account of Jesus raising the dead)

41 ¶ And, behold, there came a man named Jairus, and he was a ruler of the synagogue:
and he fell down at Jesus' feet, and besought him that he would come into his house:
42 For he had one only daughter, about twelve years of age, and she lay a-dying. But
as he went the people thronged him. (Luke 8:41-42)

Jesus is delayed in order to heal a woman who has suffered for twelve years with an illness
(A different healing from Matt. 9:20-22 where there is no mention of physicians, or discussion of "who touched me?")

43 ¶ And a woman having an issue of blood twelve years, which had spent all her living
upon physicians, neither could be healed of any,
44 Came behind *him*, and touched the border of his garment: and immediately her issue
of blood stanched.
45 And Jesus said, Who touched me? When all denied, Peter and they that were with
him said, Master, the multitude throng thee and press *thee*, and sayest thou, Who
touched me?
46 And Jesus said, Somebody hath touched me: for I perceive that virtue is gone out of
me.

47 And when the woman saw that she was not hid, she came trembling, and falling
down before him, she declared unto him before all the people for what cause she had
touched him, and how she was healed immediately.
48 And he said unto her, Daughter, be of good comfort: thy faith hath made thee whole;
go in peace. (Luke 8:43-48)

The walk to the home of Jairus resumes even though informed that the daughter was now dead

49 ¶ While he yet spake, there cometh one from the ruler of the synagogue's *house*,
saying to him, Thy daughter is dead; trouble not the Master.
50 But when Jesus heard *it*, he answered him, saying, Fear not: believe only, and she
shall be made whole. (Luke 8:49-50)

Note the words of Jesus that contradict the physical evidence of death.

51 And when he came into the house, he suffered no man to go in, save Peter, and
James, and John, and the father and the mother of the maiden.
52 And all wept, and bewailed her: but he said, Weep not; she is not dead, but sleepeth.
(Luke 8:51-52)

The carnal mind mocks spiritual vision and would impugn the power of Christ.

53 And they laughed him to scorn, knowing that she was dead. (Luke 8:53)

Faithless thoughts were put out, and the maid was addressed as being present and alive.

54 And he put them all out, and took her by the hand, and called, saying, Maid, arise.
55 And her spirit came again, and she arose straightway: and he commanded to give her
meat. (Luke 8:54-55)

After the healing her parents were told to rejoice in private and to NOT discuss with others what they had seen.

56 And her parents were astonished: but he charged them that they should tell no man
what was done. (Luke 8:56)

According to the Gospel of Mark

The people gathered to receive Jesus. The Pharisees came only to ridicule him.

21 And when Jesus was passed over again by ship unto the other side, much people
gathered unto him: and he was nigh unto the sea. (Mark 5:21)

Jairus requests that Jesus heal his dying daughter

22 And, behold, there cometh one of the rulers of the synagogue, Jairus by name; and
when he saw him, he fell at his feet,
23 And besought him greatly, saying, My little daughter lieth at the point of death: *I
pray thee*, come and lay thy hands on her, that she may be healed; and she shall live.
24 And *Jesus* went with him; and much people followed him, and thronged him. (Mark
5:22-24)

Jesus is delayed in order to heal a woman of a twelve-year illness

25 And a certain woman, which had an issue of blood twelve years,
26 And had suffered many things of many physicians, and had spent all that she had,
and was nothing bettered, but rather grew worse,
27 When she had heard of Jesus, came in the press behind, and touched his garment.
28 For she said, If I may touch but his clothes, I shall be whole.
29 And straightway the fountain of her blood was dried up; and she felt in *her* body that
she was healed of that plague.
30 And Jesus, immediately knowing in himself that virtue had gone out of him, turned
him about in the press, and said, Who touched my clothes?
31 And his disciples said unto him, Thou seest the multitude thronging thee, and sayest
thou, Who touched me?

32 And he looked round about to see her that had done this thing.
33 But the woman fearing and trembling, knowing what was done in her, came and fell
down before him, and told him all the truth.
34 And he said unto her, Daughter, thy faith hath made thee whole; go in peace, and be
whole of thy plague. (Mark 5:25-34)

Jesus resumes walking to the home of Jairus

35 While he yet spake, there came from the ruler of the synagogue's *house certain*
which said, Thy daughter is dead: why troublest thou the Master any further?
36 As soon as Jesus heard the word that was spoken, he saith unto the ruler of the
synagogue, Be not afraid, only believe. (Mark 5:35-36)

The physical evidence of death not deemed final by Jesus.

37 And he suffered no man to follow him, save Peter, and James, and John the brother
of James.
38 And he cometh to the house of the ruler of the synagogue, and seeth the tumult, and
them that wept and wailed greatly.
39 And when he was come in, he saith unto them, Why make ye this ado, and weep?
the damsel is not dead, but sleepeth. (Mark 5:37-39)

The mourners refused to see anything but the physical evidence, and so they mocked what Jesus said to them.

40 And they laughed him to scorn. (Mark 5:40 *to* 1st.)

It was not persons, so much as materialistic and faithless beliefs, that Jesus put out.

40 But when he had put them all out, he taketh the father and the mother of the damsel,
and them that were with him, and entereth in where the damsel was lying.
41 And he took the damsel by the hand, and said unto her, Talitha cumi; which is, being
interpreted, Damsel, I say unto thee, arise. (Mark 5:40-41 *But*)

Astonished, *ἐξίστημι existēmi*. The parents were ecstatic, thrilled to see their daughter restored to life.

42 And straightway the damsel arose, and walked; for she was *of the age* of twelve
years. And they were astonished with a great astonishment.
43 And he charged them straitly that no man should know it; and commanded that
something should be given her to eat. (Mark 5:42-43)

CHAPTER 64
HEALING IN NAZARETH FORESTALLED BY UNBELIEF

According to the Gospel of Matthew

The people of Nazareth, hearing reports of Jesus and his ability to heal discount them as fantastic exaggerations.

54 And when he was come into his own country, he taught them in their synagogue,
insomuch that they were astonished, and said, Whence hath this *man* this wisdom, and
these mighty works? (Matt 13:54)

The invisible Christ was imperceptible to the so-called personal senses, whereas Jesus appeared as a bodily existence. – MBE.

55 Is not this the carpenter's son? is not his mother called Mary? and his brethren,
James, and Joses, and Simon, and Judas?
56 And his sisters, are they not all with us? Whence then hath this *man* all these
things? (Matt 13:55-56)

It was envy and mockery that prevented them from seeing the Christ. offended in him means to be put off by him.

57 And they were offended in him. But Jesus said unto them, A prophet is not without
honour, save in his own country, and in his own house. (Matt 13:57)

"Unbelief" is the result of taking no account of Spirit, and of reckoning life solely on the basis of physical sense testimony.

58 And he did not many mighty works there because of their unbelief. (Matt 13:58)

According to the Gospel of Mark

1 And he went out from thence, and came into his own country; and his disciples
follow him. (Mark 6:1)

The word astonished is, ἐκπλήσσω ekplēssō. It means to expel by a blow, reject, to strike out with panic, shock.

2 And when the sabbath day was come, he began to teach in the synagogue: and many
hearing *him* were astonished, saying, From whence hath this *man* these things? and
what wisdom *is* this which is given unto him, that even such mighty works are wrought
by his hands? (Mark 6:2)

The townsfolk, seeing Jesus as just another mortal, failed to see Christ, his divine nature. See John 7:24

3 Is not this the carpenter, the son of Mary, the brother of James, and Joses, and of
Juda, and Simon? and are not his sisters here with us? (Mark 6:3 *to* 2nd ?)

Personal opinion prevented accepting Christ. See John 7:24. Offended, σκανδαλίζω, *skandalizō*, to disapprove of.

3 And they were offended at him.
4 But Jesus said unto them, A prophet is not without honour, but in his own country,
and among his own kin, and in his own house. (Mark 6:3-4 *And*)

The effect of "unbelief." Unbelief, ἀπιστία *apistia,* is more resistant than disbelief; it is opposition to Truth.

5 And he could there do no mighty work, save that he laid his hands upon a few sick
folk, and healed *them*.
6 And he marvelled because of their unbelief. And he went round about the villages,
teaching. (Mark 6:5-6)

CHAPTER 65
THE APOSTLES ARE SENT AGAIN TO PREACH AND TO HEAL

According to the Gospel of Mark

7 ¶ And he called *unto him* the twelve, and began to send them forth by two and two;
and gave them power over unclean spirits;
8 And commanded them that they should take nothing for *their* journey, save a staff
only; no scrip, no bread, no money in *their* purse:
9 But *be* shod with sandals; and not put on two coats.
10 And he said unto them, In what place soever ye enter into an house, there abide till
ye depart from that place.
11 And whosoever shall not receive you, nor hear you, when ye depart thence, shake
off the dust under your feet for a testimony against them. Verily I say unto you, It shall
be more tolerable for Sodom and Gomorrha in the day of judgment, than for that city.
12 And they went out, and preached that men should repent.
13 And they cast out many devils, and anointed with oil many that were sick, and
healed *them*. (Mark 6:7-13)

According to the Gospel of Luke

1 Then he called his twelve disciples together, and gave them power and authority over
all devils, and to cure diseases.
2 And he sent them to preach the kingdom of God, and to heal the sick.
3 And he said unto them, Take nothing for *your* journey, neither staves, nor scrip,
neither bread, neither money; neither have two coats apiece.
4 And whatsoever house ye enter into, there abide, and thence depart.
5 And whosoever will not receive you, when ye go out of that city, shake off the very
dust from your feet for a testimony against them.
6 And they departed, and went through the towns, preaching the gospel, and healing
every where. (Luke 9:1-6)

CHAPTER 66
ACCOUNTS OF JOHN THE BAPTISTS BEHEADING

According to the Gospel of Luke (A summary statement)

7 ¶ Now Herod the tetrarch heard of all that was done by him: and he was perplexed, because that it was said of some, that John was risen from the dead;

8 And of some, that Elias had appeared; and of others, that one of the old prophets was risen again. (Luke 9:7-8)

Herod's demented reason for desiring to see was Jesus based on guilt and superstition.

9 And Herod said, John have I beheaded: but who is this, of whom I hear such things? And he desired to see him. (Luke 9:9)

According to the Gospel of Matthew (A more detailed account)

Spiritualism: speculation that Jesus was actually John the Baptist returned from the dead in a corporeal form.

1 At that time Herod the tetrarch heard of the fame of Jesus,

2 And said unto his servants, This is John the Baptist; he is risen from the dead; and therefore mighty works do shew forth themselves in him. (Matt 14:1-2)

Herod Antipas imprisoned John the Baptist to pacify Herodias, who before was the wife of his brother Philip.

3 ¶ For Herod had laid hold on John, and bound him, and put *him* in prison for Herodias' sake, his brother Philip's wife.

4 For John said unto him, It is not lawful for thee to have her. (Matt 14:3-4)

The main reason Herod Antipas hadn't already executed John the Baptist was fear of rebellion.

5 And when he would have put him to death, he feared the multitude, because they counted him as a prophet. (Matt 14:5)

The trap to have John the Baptist executed was set by Herodias.

6 But when Herod's birthday was kept, the daughter of Herodias danced before them, and pleased Herod. (Matt 14:6)

Herod fell into a trap set by Herodias through pride and indiscretion.

7 Whereupon he promised with an oath to give her whatsoever she would ask. (Matt 14:7)

According to Josephus, the grotesque request of Salome originated with her resentful mother, Herodias.

8 And she, being before instructed of her mother, said, Give me here John Baptist's head in a charger. (Matt 14:8)

A lesson in how pride, passion, and indiscretion can cause a person to do something they know is wrong.

9 And the king was sorry: nevertheless for the oath's sake, and them which sat with him at meat, he commanded *it* to be given *her*.

10 And he sent, and beheaded John in the prison.

11 And his head was brought in a charger, and given to the damsel: and she brought *it* to her mother. (Matt 14:9-11)

The response of John's disciples to his beheading. (Note the connection of John's disciples to Jesus)

12 And his disciples came, and took up the body, and buried it, and went and told Jesus. (Matt 14:12)

Even in this time of sorrow Jesus was able to show loving care for the people by healing the sick.

13 ¶ When Jesus heard *of it*, he departed thence by ship into a desert place apart: and when the people had heard *thereof*, they followed him on foot out of the cities.

14 And Jesus went forth, and saw a great multitude, and was moved with compassion toward them, and he healed their sick. (Matt 14:13-14)

According to the Gospel of Mark (The most complete account)

14 And king Herod heard *of him*; (for his name was spread abroad:) and he said, That John the Baptist was risen from the dead, and therefore mighty works do shew forth themselves in him.

15 Others said, That it is Elias. And others said, That it is a prophet, or as one of the

prophets.
16 But when Herod heard *thereof*, he said, It is John, whom I beheaded: he is risen
from the dead. (Mark 6:14-16)

Herod Antipas imprisoned John to appease his wife, Herodias.

17 For Herod himself had sent forth and laid hold upon John, and bound him in prison
for Herodias' sake, his brother Philip's wife: for he had married her.
18 For John had said unto Herod, It is not lawful for thee to have thy brother's wife.
19 Therefore Herodias had a quarrel against him, and would have killed him; but she
could not: (Mark 6:17-19)

Another reason for Herod's reluctance to execute John the Baptist, he *knew* that John was just and holy.

20 For Herod feared John, knowing that he was a just man and an holy, and observed
him; and when he heard him, he did many things, and heard him gladly. (Mark 6:20)

The trap: A sensual and hypnotic dance performed for a conceited degenerate.

21 And when a convenient day was come, that Herod on his birthday made a supper to
his lords, high captains, and chief *estates* of Galilee;
22 And when the daughter of the said Herodias came in, and danced, and pleased Herod
and them that sat with him, the king said unto the damsel, Ask of me whatsoever thou
wilt, and I will give *it* thee. (Mark 6:21-22)

The foolish promise from a heated brain.

23 And he sware unto her, Whatsoever thou shalt ask of me, I will give *it* thee, unto the
half of my kingdom. (Mark 6:23)

The monstrous request.

24 And she went forth, and said unto her mother, What shall I ask? And she said, The
head of John the Baptist.
25 And she came in straightway with haste unto the king, and asked, saying, I will that
thou give me by and by in a charger the head of John the Baptist. (Mark 6:24-25)

The consequences of being a pleaser of men rather than a doer of God's will, guilt and sorrow.

26 And the king was exceeding sorry; *yet* for his oath's sake, and for their sakes which
sat with him, he would not reject her. (Mark 6:26)

Herod, imitating Roman customs, had armed detectives who served as body guards and also performed executions.

27 And immediately the king sent an executioner, and commanded his head to be
brought: and he went and beheaded him in the prison.
28 And brought his head in a charger, and gave it to the damsel: and the damsel gave it
to her mother.
29 And when his disciples heard *of it*, they came and took up his corpse, and laid it in a
tomb. (Mark 6:27-29)

CHAPTER 67

THE LOAVES AND FISHES MULTIPLIED (1ST OCCASION)

(Four accounts of the same event that involved 5,000 men plus women and children)

According to the Gospel of Mark

From these accounts we see how little opportunity Jesus and the Apostles had for rest and relaxation.

30 And the apostles gathered themselves together unto Jesus, and told him all things,
both what they had done, and what they had taught.
31 And he said unto them, Come ye yourselves apart into a desert place, and rest a
while: for there were many coming and going, and they had no leisure so much as to
eat.
32 And they departed into a desert place by ship privately. (Mark 6:30-32)

Even though the elitists refused to endorse Jesus or his message, the common people welcomed it.

33 And the people saw them departing, and many knew him, and ran afoot thither out

of all cities, and outwent them, and came together unto him.
34 And Jesus, when he came out, saw much people, and was moved with compassion
toward them, because they were as sheep not having a shepherd: and he began to teach
them many things. (Mark 6:33-34)
Jesus never worked *from* the problem. He worked from the standpoint of God as All-in-all. The result was healing!
35 And when the day was now far spent, his disciples came unto him, and said, This is
a desert place, and now the time *is* far passed:
36 Send them away, that they may go into the country round about, and into the
villages, and buy themselves bread: for they have nothing to eat.
37 He answered and said unto them, Give ye them to eat. (Mark 6:35-37 *to* 1st.)
Jesus saw every trial as an opportunity to teach and to grow spiritually.
37 And they say unto him, Shall we go and buy two hundred pennyworth of bread, and
give them to eat?
38 He saith unto them, How many loaves have ye? go and see. And when they knew,
they say, Five, and two fishes. (Mark 6:37-38 *And*)
Jesus looked up to heaven with gratitude, never doubting, because he knew that supply invariably meets demand.
39 And he commanded them to make all sit down by companies upon the green grass.
40 And they sat down in ranks, by hundreds, and by fifties.
41 And when he had taken the five loaves and the two fishes, he looked up to heaven,
and blessed, and brake the loaves, and gave *them* to his disciples to set before them; and
the two fishes divided he among them all.
42 And they did all eat, and were filled. (Mark 6:39-42)
This lesson in gratitude as an important step in demonstrating that supply is unlimited.
43 And they took up twelve baskets full of the fragments, and of the fishes.
44 And they that did eat of the loaves were about five thousand men. (Mark 6:43-44)

According to the Gospel of Luke

The actual location is difficult to determine. All accounts describe a remote place where they could be alone.
10 ¶ And the apostles, when they were returned, told him all that they had done. And
he took them, and went aside privately into a desert place belonging to the city called
Bethsaida.
11 And the people, when they knew *it*, followed him: and he received them, and spake
unto them of the kingdom of God, and healed them that had need of healing. (Luke 9:10-11)
Questions of supply are also subject to the laws of God, and can therefore be healed.
12 And when the day began to wear away, then came the twelve, and said unto him,
Send the multitude away, that they may go into the towns and country round about, and
lodge, and get victuals: for we are here in a desert place.
13 But he said unto them, Give ye them to eat. And they said, We have no more but
five loaves and two fishes; except we should go and buy meat for all this people.
14 For they were about five thousand men. (Luke 9:12-14 *to* 1st.)
Jesus illustrates how order is an integral part of a harmonious universe.
14 And he said to his disciples, Make them sit down by fifties in a company.
15 And they did so, and made them all sit down.
16 Then he took the five loaves and the two fishes, and looking up to heaven, he
blessed them, and brake, and gave to the disciples to set before the multitude. (Luke 9:14-16 *And)*
In the scientific relation of God to man, we find that whatever blesses one blesses all, as Jesus showed with the loaves and fishes, --- Spirit, not matter, being the source of supply. - MBE
17 And they did eat, and were all filled: and there was taken up of fragments that
remained to them twelve baskets. (Luke 9:17)

According to the Gospel of Matthew

15 ¶ And when it was evening, his disciples came to him, saying, This is a desert place, and the time is now past; send the multitude away, that they may go into the villages, and buy themselves victuals.

16 But Jesus said unto them, They need not depart; give ye them to eat.

17 And they say unto him, We have here but five loaves, and two fishes.

18 He said, Bring them hither to me.

19 And he commanded the multitude to sit down on the grass, and took the five loaves, and the two fishes, and looking up to heaven, he blessed, and brake, and gave the loaves to *his* disciples, and the disciples to the multitude.

20 And they did all eat, and were filled: and they took up of the fragments that remained twelve baskets full.

21 And they that had eaten were about five thousand men, beside women and children. (Matt 14:15-21)

According to the Gospel of John

1 After these things Jesus went over the sea of Galilee, which is *the sea* of Tiberias.

2 And a great multitude followed him, because they saw his miracles which he did on them that were diseased. (John 6:1-2)

Jesus and his disciples were seeking a refuge from the crowds.

3 And Jesus went up into a mountain, and there he sat with his disciples.

4 And the passover, a feast of the Jews, was nigh.

5 ¶ When Jesus then lifted up *his* eyes, and saw a great company come unto him, he saith unto Philip, Whence shall we buy bread, that these may eat?

6 And this he said to prove him: for he himself knew what he would do.

7 Philip answered him, Two hundred pennyworth of bread is not sufficient for them, that every one of them may take a little.

8 One of his disciples, Andrew, Simon Peter's brother, saith unto him,

9 There is a lad here, which hath five barley loaves, and two small fishes: but what are they among so many? (John 6:3-9)

If seed is necessary to produce wheat, and wheat to produce flour, or if one animal can originate another, how then can we account for their primal origin? How were the loaves and fishes multiplied on the shores of Galilee, --- and that, too, without meal or monad from which loaf or fish could come? - MBE

10 And Jesus said, Make the men sit down. Now there was much grass in the place. So the men sat down, in number about five thousand.

11 And Jesus took the loaves; and when he had given thanks, he distributed to the disciples, and the disciples to them that were set down; and likewise of the fishes as much as they would.

12 When they were filled, he said unto his disciples, Gather up the fragments that remain, that nothing be lost.

13 Therefore they gathered *them* together, and filled twelve baskets with the fragments of the five barley loaves, which remained over and above unto them that had eaten. (John 6:10-13)

CHAPTER 68
JESUS ESCAPES BEING MADE A KING

Apparently the people likened the multiplying of the loaves and fishes to the manna that fell from the sky feeding the children of Israel in the wilderness. From this they reasoned that Jesus must be the "prophet . . . like unto me" foretold by Moses. See Deut.18:15. But that is not what likened Jesus to Moses. What likened Jesus to Moses was the meekness to have God, the one infinite Mind, be his I AM, or Ego. God is the Mind that was in both Jesus and Moses. - Phil 2:5.

14 Then those men, when they had seen the miracle that Jesus did, said, This is of a

truth that prophet that should come into the world. (John 6:14)

Jesus escaped to avoid being made a king. (Recall the temptations. See Luke 4:9-12 & Matt. 4:5-7, pages 15-17)

15 ¶ When Jesus therefore perceived that they would come and take him by force, to
make him a king, he departed again into a mountain himself alone. (John 6:15)

CHAPTER 69
LAWS OF NATURE AND PHYSICS NULLIFIED

According to the Gospel of John
(The only account when a boat, and everyone in it, is instantaneously transported its destination)

16 And when even was *now* come, his disciples went down unto the sea, (John 6:16)

Ship is, *πλοῖον ploion*. The remains of a fishing vessel dated the 1st century AD was discovered in the sea of Galilee in 1986. It measured 27 feet long 7½ feet wide with a fairly flat bottom. It could be rowed and had a mast for sailing. TCB

17 And entered into a ship, and went over the sea toward Capernaum. And it was now
dark, and Jesus was not come to them. (John 6:17)

This wind is not a gentle breeze, *πνεῦμα pneuma*, but a great wind, *ἄνεμος anemos*, a very strong tempestuous wind.

18 And the sea arose by reason of a great wind that blew. (John 6:18)

The disciples had rowed between 3⅛ to 3¾ miles, about half way across, when they saw Jesus walking toward them.

19 So when they had rowed about five and twenty or thirty furlongs, they see Jesus
walking on the sea, and drawing nigh unto the ship: and they were afraid.
20 But he saith unto them, It is I; be not afraid. (John 6:19-20)

Only John mentions the boat, and everyone in it, being instantly transported to the shore.

21 Then they willingly received him into the ship: and immediately the ship was at the
land whither they went. (John 6:21)

According to the Gospel of Mark
(This account supplements by giving the time when Jesus walked upon the sea)

Jesus sent the disciples to Bethsaida which lies on the shore of lake Galilee about 3½ miles Northeast of Capernaum.

45 And straightway he constrained his disciples to get into the ship, and to go to the
other side before unto Bethsaida, while he sent away the people.
46 And when he had sent them away, he departed into a mountain to pray.
47 And when even was come, the ship was in the midst of the sea, and he alone on the
land.
48 And he saw them toiling in rowing; for the wind was contrary unto them: (Mark 6:45-48
to :)

It was sometime between 3 and 6 a.m. when the disciples saw Jesus about to pass by them, “walking” on the sea.

48 and about the fourth watch of the night he cometh unto them, walking upon the sea,
and would have passed by them.
49 But when they saw him walking upon the sea, they supposed it had been a spirit, and
cried out:
50 For they all saw him, and were troubled. And immediately he talked with them, and
saith unto them, Be of good cheer: it is I; be not afraid. (Mark 6:48-50 *and*)

The storm is stilled and the disciples are extremely amazed. Note how strongly the human mind resists the truth

51 And he went up unto them into the ship; and the wind ceased: and they were sore
amazed in themselves beyond measure, and wondered.
52 For they considered not *the miracle* of the loaves: for their heart was hardened. (Mark
6:51-52)

The boat came ashore south of Capernaum, in the region of Gennesaret

53 And when they had passed over, they came into the land of Gennesaret, and drew to
the shore. (Mark 6:53)

According to the Gospel of Matthew
(The only account that mentions Peter's brief “walk” on the water until overcome by fear)

22 ¶ And straightway Jesus constrained his disciples to get into a ship, and to go before

him unto the other side, while he sent the multitudes away. (Matt 14:22)

The example set by Jesus: Pray to keep the light burning, don't wait until moments of darkness

23 And when he had sent the multitudes away, he went up into a mountain apart to
pray: and when the evening was come, he was there alone. (Matt 14:23)

The disciples were alone in the boat. Human experience can feel overwhelming and lonely until the Christ appears.

24 But the ship was now in the midst of the sea, tossed with waves: for the wind was
contrary. (Matt 14:24)

Matthew writes that Jesus walked to the ship in the fourth watch meaning sometime between 3 and 6 a.m.

25 And in the fourth watch of the night Jesus went unto them, walking on the sea.

26 And when the disciples saw him walking on the sea, they were troubled, saying, It is
a spirit; and they cried out for fear.

27 But straightway Jesus spake unto them, saying, Be of good cheer; it is I; be not
afraid. (Matt 14:25-27)

Peter walked on the sea until overcome by fear. Nevertheless, he had demonstrated a higher law available to everyone!

28 And Peter answered him and said, Lord, if it be thou, bid me come unto thee on the
water.

29 And he said, Come. And when Peter was come down out of the ship, he walked on
the water, to go to Jesus.

30 But when he saw the wind boisterous, he was afraid; and beginning to sink, he cried,
saying, Lord, save me. (Matt 14:28-30)

Peter was rescued and chastened for lack of faith. Why the fear? The same reason we fear; physical sense testimony! Jesus said to Peter "O thou of little faith." We must ask, little faith in what? Do we answer, too little faith in God, and let it go at that? Note, Jesus asked Peter why he *doubted*. From this it would seem that Jesus must have had discussions with his disciples about what we call the "laws of nature and of physics," and how to affect physical phenomenon with the transcendent laws of Spirit. It would also appear that PRAYER was the connection Jesus utilized to access these superior laws of Mind or Spirit. Shouldn't Christians, in this more enlightened age, be looking in this direction for answers? Maybe we should expand our view of Jesus and instead of seeing him as a miracle worker who could mysteriously overrule the so-called laws of nature, we should begin to see him as a divine Scientist, accessing the Laws of Spirit, God that are able to bring harmony to what at times appears to be a very tumultuous material universe. Jesus came to lift us out of sin, but maybe there is more to sin than we understand. How much more can we learn from him about the laws of God, Spirit?

31 And immediately Jesus stretched forth *his* hand, and caught him, and said unto him,
O thou of little faith, wherefore didst thou doubt? (Matt 14:31)

The storm is stilled. Jesus was not a show-off. He was illustrating divine laws for everyone to learn and practice. Are we interested? If not why not?

32 And when they were come into the ship, the wind ceased.

33 Then they that were in the ship came and worshipped him, saying, Of a truth thou art
the Son of God.

34 ¶ And when they were gone over, they came into the land of Gennesaret. (Matt 14:32-34)

CHAPTER 70
EVENTS IN GENNESARET

According to the Gospel of Matthew

The people of Gennesaret came to Jesus seeking to be healed.

35 And when the men of that place had knowledge of him, they sent out into all that
country round about, and brought unto him all that were diseased;

36 And besought him that they might only touch the hem of his garment: and as many
as touched were made perfectly whole. (Matt 14:35-36)

According to the Gospel of Mark

The people of Gennesaret knew about Jesus and were confident that he could heal their illnesses.

54 And when they were come out of the ship, straightway they knew him,

55 And ran through that whole region round about, and began to carry about in beds
those that were sick, where they heard he was. (Mark 6:54-55)

His reputation inspired faith among the common folk, while at the same time it engendered envy among the elites.
56 And whithersoever he entered, into villages, or cities, or country, they laid the sick
in the streets, and besought him that they might touch if it were but the border of his
garment: and as many as touched him were made whole. (Mark 6:56)

CHAPTER 71
SPIRITUAL TEACHING REJECTED BY MANY

Mortals seek Christ for material benefits but are blind to their real need, spiritual transformation.
22 ¶ The day following, when the people which stood on the other side of the sea saw
that there was none other boat there, save that one whereinto his disciples were entered,
and that Jesus went not with his disciples into the boat, but *that* his disciples were gone
away alone;
23 (Howbeit there came other boats from Tiberias nigh unto the place where they did
eat bread, after that the Lord had given thanks:)
24 When the people therefore saw that Jesus was not there, neither his disciples, they
also took shipping, and came to Capernaum, seeking for Jesus. (John 6:22-24)

The natural man is chastened for not seeking the things of Spirit (See I Cor. 22:14)

25 And when they had found him on the other side of the sea, they said unto him,
Rabbi, when camest thou hither?
26 Jesus answered them and said, Verily, verily, I say unto you, Ye seek me, not
because ye saw the miracles, but because ye did eat of the loaves, and were filled.
27 Labour not for the meat which perisheth, but for that meat which endureth unto
everlasting life, which the Son of man shall give unto you: for him hath God the Father
sealed. (John 6:25-27)
Jesus rebuked mortal man's desire to use spiritual means for material gain.
28 Then said they unto him, What shall we do, that we might work the works of God?
29 Jesus answered and said unto them, This is the work of God, that ye believe on him
whom he hath sent. (John 6:28-29)
The people desired physical evidence to confirm spiritual truth, because to them matter was substance.
30 They said therefore unto him, What sign shewest thou then, that we may see, and
believe thee? what dost thou work?
31 Our fathers did eat manna in the desert; as it is written, He gave them bread from
heaven to eat. (John 6:30-31)
Jesus said plainly that manna from the sky (material food), is not bread (divine Truth), from heaven.
32 Then Jesus said unto them, Verily, verily, I say unto you, Moses gave you not that
bread from heaven; (John 6:32 *to* ;)
Christ, Truth *is* the bread from heaven.
32 but my Father giveth you the true bread from heaven.
33 For the bread of God is he which cometh down from heaven, and giveth life unto the
world.
34 Then said they unto him, Lord, evermore give us this bread.
35 And Jesus said unto them, I am the bread of life: he that cometh to me shall never
hunger; and he that believeth on me shall never thirst. (John 6:32-35 *but*)
Even though the truth Jesus taught could bring them lasting satisfaction, they weren't interested.
36 But I said unto you, That ye also have seen me, and believe not. (John 6:36)

Separating those that only believe from those that truly understand

The spiritually minded, being drawn to Christ, will find and follow the pathway to eternal life.

37 All that the Father giveth me shall come to me; and him that cometh to me I will in no wise cast out.

38 For I came down from heaven, not to do mine own will, but the will of him that sent me.

39 And this is the Father's will which hath sent me, that of all which he hath given me I should lose nothing, but should raise it up again at the last day.

40 And this is the will of him that sent me, that every one which seeth the Son, and believeth on him, may have everlasting life: and I will raise him up at the last day. (John 6:37-40)

The carnally minded did not understand what Jesus was saying because they took the symbols he was using literally.

41 The Jews then murmured at him, because he said, I am the bread which came down from heaven. (John 6:41)

The Jews only saw Jesus as the son of Joseph and Mary. The spiritual, or Christ Jesus, was unseen by them.

42 And they said, Is not this Jesus, the son of Joseph, whose father and mother we know? how is it then that he saith, I came down from heaven? (John 6:42)

Only those willing to leave matter for Spirit will come to the Truth, "because the Spirit is truth." I Jn. 5:6.

43 Jesus therefore answered and said unto them, Murmur not among yourselves.

44 No man can come to me, except the Father which hath sent me draw him: and I will raise him up at the last day.

45 It is written in the prophets, And they shall be all taught of God. Every man therefore that hath heard, and hath learned of the Father, cometh unto me. (John 6:43-45)

The word seen is *ὁράω horaō*. It means to perceive, know, or become acquainted by experience.

46 Not that any man hath seen the Father, save he which is of God, he hath seen the Father. (John 6:46)

In saying "I am that bread of life," Jesus meant that he embodied what he taught, the Truth that is Life.

47 Verily, verily, I say unto you, He that believeth on me hath everlasting life.

48 I am that bread of life.

49 Your fathers did eat manna in the wilderness, and are dead.

50 This is the bread which cometh down from heaven, that a man may eat thereof, and not die. (John 6:47-50)

Christ, Truth is the bread that when eaten and assimilated (accepted and lived), becomes flesh (is embodied as us).

51 I am the living bread which came down from heaven: if any man eat of this bread, he shall live for ever: and the bread that I will give is my flesh, which I will give for the life of the world. (John 6:51)

The Pharisees never understood because they insisted on taking the symbols Jesus used literally. Why? Because they didn't care at all about Spirit, God, the infinite Being that Jesus called Father. Why didn't they care about the things of Spirit? Because they were convinced that matter was substance when it is absolutely obvious that no one ever takes anything material with them when the time comes to move on. Is there any greater blindness than that?

52 The Jews therefore strove among themselves, saying, How can this man give us *his* flesh to eat? (John 6:52)

Jesus spoke symbolically of his flesh and his blood. To eat his flesh and to drink his blood meant to partake of his Life.

53 Then Jesus said unto them, Verily, verily, I say unto you, Except ye eat the flesh of the Son of man, and drink his blood, ye have no life in you.

54 Whoso eateth my flesh, and drinketh my blood, hath eternal life; and I will raise him up at the last day.

55 For my flesh is meat indeed, and my blood is drink indeed.

56 He that eateth my flesh, and drinketh my blood, dwelleth in me, and I in him.

57 As the living Father hath sent me, and I live by the Father: so he that eateth me, even he shall live by me. (John 6:53-57)

The bread the children of Israel ate in the wilderness fell from the sky. The generation that Moses led out of Egypt perished before reaching the promise land. The bread from heaven spoken of by Jesus is the Christ, Truth, eternal Life.

58 This is that bread which came down from heaven: not as your fathers did eat manna,
and are dead: he that eateth of this bread shall live for ever.
59 These things said he in the synagogue, as he taught in Capernaum. (John 6:58-59)

Some disciples reject the Christ teaching

Jesus had many students throughout Galilee and also in Jerusalem that proved unable to accept his teaching.

60 Many therefore of his disciples, when they had heard *this*, said, This is an hard
saying; who can hear it? (John 6:60)

Jesus asks if what he is saying will cause some disciples to leave. Notice that his teaching is becoming more absolute.

61 When Jesus knew in himself that his disciples murmured at it, he said unto them,
Doth this offend you? (John 6:61)

If what these disciples have seen so far is not enough to convince them, will his ascension?

62 *What* and if ye shall see the Son of man ascend up where he was before? (John 6:62)

Jesus' core teaching was: "There is no life, truth, intelligence, nor substance in matter." "Life is Spirit." - MBE

63 It is the spirit that quickeneth; the flesh profiteth nothing: the words that I speak unto
you, *they* are spirit, and *they* are life. (John 6:63)

Spiritual receptivity is an absolute necessity to understand Jesus. It enables one to accept Christ, the true idea of Life.

64 But there are some of you that believe not. For Jesus knew from the beginning who
they were that believed not, and who should betray him. (John 6:64)

The carnal mind being enmity against God will not accept spiritual teaching; only the Mind that is God can. See Phil. 2:5. This fact shouldn't bother us because the Mind that is God is already here, it is already everyone's true Mind. Everything Jesus is teaching and showing us, is telling us this is true. Paul put it this way: "For who hath known the mind of the Lord, that he may instruct him? But we have the mind of Christ." - I Cor. 2:16. So, let's get better acquainted with this Mind.

65 And he said, Therefore said I unto you, that no man can come unto me, except it
were given unto him of my Father. (John 6:65)

Many disciples left Jesus due to ecclesiastical and scholastic pride. This illustrates the importance of the first Beatitude: "Blessed *are* the poor in spirit: for theirs is the kingdom of heaven." – Matt 5:3. See Matt.13:18-21 and John 12:42-43.

66 ¶ From that *time* many of his disciples went back, and walked no more with him.
(John 6:66)

The twelve are asked if they too will "go away"

67 Then said Jesus unto the twelve, Will ye also go away?
68 Then Simon Peter answered him, Lord, to whom shall we go? thou hast the words of
eternal life.
69 And we believe and are sure that thou art that Christ, the Son of the living God. (John
6:67-69)

For the 1st time the betrayal of Judas Iscariot is mentioned

Devil, *διάβολος diabolos*, traducer, calumniator. Jesus already knew what Judas was contemplating.

70 Jesus answered them, Have not I chosen you twelve, and one of you is a devil?
71 He spake of Judas Iscariot *the son* of Simon: for he it was that should betray him,
being one of the twelve. (John 6:70-71)

CHAPTER 72
GOD'S COMMANDMENTS MOCKED BY MEN'S TRADITIONS

According to the Gospel of Mark

1 Then came together unto him the Pharisees, and certain of the scribes, which came
from Jerusalem.
2 And when they saw some of his disciples eat bread with defiled, that is to say, with
unwashen, hands, they found fault.
3 For the Pharisees, and all the Jews, except they wash *their* hands oft, eat not, holding

the tradition of the elders. (Mark 7:1-3)

to hold κρατέω *krateō* here means to hold fast, i.e. not to discard or let go. We would say "to stubbornly cling on to."

4 And *when they come* from the market, except they wash, they eat not. And many
other things there be, which they have received to hold, *as* the washing of cups, and
pots, brasen vessels, and of tables. (Mark 7:4)

The Pharisees and scribes objected to Jesus because he did not conform to their "traditions." Do we do that?

5 Then the Pharisees and scribes asked him, Why walk not thy disciples according to
the tradition of the elders, but eat bread with unwashen hands? (Mark 7:5)

Jesus exposed the hypocrisy of demanding others to abide by practices and traditions that they themselves did not follow.

6 He answered and said unto them, Well hath Esaias prophesied of you hypocrites, as it
is written, (Mark 7:6 to 3rd ,)

The scripture quoted below is Isaiah 29:13 with the wording slightly modified to fit the situation. "me" refers to God.

6 This people honoureth me with *their* lips, but their heart is far from me.

7 Howbeit in vain do they worship me, teaching *for* doctrines the commandments of
men. (Mark 7:6-7 *This*)

The foolishness of disobeying God's commandments while holding fast to man-made traditions is exposed.

8 For laying aside the commandment of God, ye hold the tradition of men, *as* the
washing of pots and cups: and many other such like things ye do.

9 And he said unto them, Full well ye reject the commandment of God, that ye may
keep your own tradition. (Mark 7:8-9)

Below is an example of nullifying a commandment by a man-made tradition: *(Ex. 20:10; 21:17 and Lev. 20:9).*

10 For Moses said, Honour thy father and thy mother; and, Whoso curseth father or
mother, let him die the death: (Mark 7:10)

The tradition: If a son pledged money as a gift to God, meaning *the temple*, money that should have been used to care for his parents, that pledge was binding and the son was not permitted to do anything more for his parents. Thus the son's money pledged to the temple, meaning the ecclesiastics, was made a higher priority than the care of his parents.

11 But ye say, If a man shall say to his father or mother, *It is* Corban, that is to say, a
gift, by whatsoever thou mightest be profited by me; *he shall be free.*

12 And ye suffer him no more to do ought for his father or his mother; (Mark 7:11-12)

The result of the tradition is that the fourth commandment, to honor father and mother, is nullified.

13 Making the word of God of none effect through your tradition, which ye have
delivered: and many such like things do ye. (Mark 7:13)

What Jesus taught negated the teaching and tradition of the scribes and Pharisees. Another reason they hated him.

14 ¶ And when he had called all the people *unto him*, he said unto them, Hearken unto
me every one *of you*, and understand:

15 There is nothing from without a man, that entering into him can defile him: but the
things which come out of him, those are they that defile the man.

16 If any man have ears to hear, let him hear. (Mark 7:14-16)

The dullness of the disciples addressed, v. 18 "so" is *οὔτω(ς) hoytō(s)* likewise, as the scribes and Pharisees

17 And when he was entered into the house from the people, his disciples asked him
concerning the parable.

18 And he saith unto them, Are ye so without understanding also? Do ye not perceive,
that whatsoever thing from without entereth into the man, *it* cannot defile him;

19 Because it entereth not into his heart, but into the belly, and goeth out into the
draught, purging all meats?

20 And he said, That which cometh out of the man, that defileth the man.

21 For from within, out of the heart of men, proceed evil thoughts, adulteries,
fornications, murders,

22 Thefts, covetousness, wickedness, deceit, lasciviousness, an evil eye, blasphemy,
pride, foolishness:

23 All these evil things come from within, and defile the man. (Mark 7:17-23)

According to the Gospel of Matthew

1 Then came to Jesus scribes and Pharisees, which were of Jerusalem, saying, (Matt 15:1)

The Pharisees objected to Jesus' non-conformity because it showed their traditions pointless and weakened their authority.

2 Why do thy disciples transgress the tradition of the elders? for they wash not their
hands when they eat bread. (Matt 15:2)

Jesus' reply pointed out a much greater transgression than the refusal to conform to a tradition.

3 But he answered and said unto them, Why do ye also transgress the commandment of
God by your tradition? (Matt 15:3)

More important than traditions are God's Commandments. In this case the fourth: "Honor thy father and thy mother."

4 For God commanded, saying, Honour thy father and mother: and, He that curseth
father or mother, let him die the death. (Matt 15:4)

A pledge to the temple released a man from the care of his parents. (On Matthew 15:5. *The Jewish Gospel* says, "That which you would have had as a benefit from us is now an offering [to the Temple?]. *Gospel of the Nazareans* MS 1412)

5 But ye say, Whosoever shall say to *his* father or *his* mother, *It is* a gift, by whatsoever
thou mightest be profited by me;
6 And honour not his father or his mother, *he shall be free.* (Matt 15:5-6 to 1st.)

The hypocrisy: Violating the fourth commandment through a man-made tradition that transfers wealth to the ecclesiastics while leaving a man's parents destitute.

6 Thus have ye made the commandment of God of none effect by your tradition.
7 *Ye* hypocrites, well did Esaias prophesy of you, saying, (Matt 15:6-7 *Thus*)

The scripture quoted is Isa. 29:13 with the wording slightly modified. Jesus applied this prophecy to the scribes and Pharisees pointing out the hypocrisy of saying one thing to sound good but doing the opposite, which is evil.

8 This people draweth nigh unto me with their mouth, and honoureth me with *their*
lips; but their heart is far from me. (Matt 15:8)

Man-made pretenses do not gain the divine ear. Why? Because God is Truth, and Truth and error do not commune.

9 But in vain they do worship me, teaching *for* doctrines the commandments of men.
(Matt 15:9)

Jesus was telling the people that what the scribes and Pharisees taught was not only foolish, but at times cruel, even murderous.

10 ¶ And he called the multitude, and said unto them, Hear, and understand:
11 Not that which goeth into the mouth defileth a man; but that which cometh out of the
mouth, this defileth a man. (Matt 15:10-11)

Jesus was unconcerned that the Pharisees were offended, because he knew that Truth is the only way to uncover and destroy error. Here we see Jesus' absolute conviction in the ultimate victory of Truth, God and His Christ, over all error.

12 Then came his disciples, and said unto him, Knowest thou that the Pharisees were
offended, after they heard this saying?
13 But he answered and said, Every plant, which my heavenly Father hath not planted,
shall be rooted up.
14 Let them alone: they be blind leaders of the blind. And if the blind lead the blind,
both shall fall into the ditch. (Matt 15:12-14)

The Master was disappointed that his disciples still didn't understand. Are we yielding to Spirit any sooner?

Verse 16 "yet" is *ἀκμὴν akmēn* meaning even now; verse 17 "yet" is *οὔπω oupō* meaning do ye not yet?

15 Then answered Peter and said unto him, Declare unto us this parable.
16 And Jesus said, Are ye also yet without understanding? (Matt 15:15-16)

The need is to purify our motives (thoughts), and not to only wash our hands (a tradition). It is by purifying the motives that what is right and good gets done. As for the washing of hands, do we suppose that thieves and murderers would have ceased their criminal behavior if they had been more diligent in keeping their hands washed?

17 Do not ye yet understand, that whatsoever entereth in at the mouth goeth into the
belly, and is cast out into the draught?
18 But those things which proceed out of the mouth come forth from the heart; and they
defile the man.

19 For out of the heart proceed evil thoughts, murders, adulteries, fornications, thefts,
false witness, blasphemies:
20 These are *the things* which defile a man: but to eat with unwashen hands defileth not
a man. (Matt 15:17-20)

CHAPTER 73
A CANAANITE CHILD HEALED

According to the Gospel of Matthew

21 ¶ Then Jesus went thence, and departed into the coasts of Tyre and Sidon.
22 And, behold, a woman of Canaan came out of the same coasts, and cried unto him,
saying, Have mercy on me, O Lord, *thou* son of David; my daughter is grievously
vexed with a devil.
23 But he answered her not a word. And his disciples came and besought him, saying,
Send her away; for she crieth after us.
24 But he answered and said, I am not sent but unto the lost sheep of the house of
Israel.
25 Then came she and worshipped him, saying, Lord, help me. (Matt 15:21-25)

dogs = puppies. Puppies once mature dogs were not cared for in the East. Gentiles were in general regarded by the Jews as "dogs." Jesus' ministry was to the Jews, therefore the woman had no claim, even as a puppy. meet = right, fair. Jesus was not being rude or cruel, he was at this point obediently taking the Word of God to the children of Israel first. Why? Because they were better? No! Because they supposedly were more grounded in the understanding of but ONE God and His Commandments, and therefore they were expected to be better prepared and more willing to receive it.

26 But he answered and said, It is not meet to take the children's bread, and to cast *it* to
dogs.
27 And she said, Truth, Lord: yet the dogs eat of the crumbs which fall from their
masters' table. (Matt 15:26-27)

Faith, *πίστις pistis*, conviction of the truth, assurance. It is here being contrasted to the disciples lack of faith, conviction.

28 Then Jesus answered and said unto her, O woman, great *is* thy faith: be it unto thee
even as thou wilt. And her daughter was made whole from that very hour.
29 And Jesus departed from thence, and came nigh unto the sea of Galilee; and went up
into a mountain, and sat down there. (Matt 15:28-29)

According to the Gospel of Mark

24 ¶ And from thence he arose, and went into the borders of Tyre and Sidon, and
entered into an house, and would have no man know *it*: but he could not be hid.
25 For a *certain* woman, whose young daughter had an unclean spirit, heard of him,
and came and fell at his feet:
26 The woman was a Greek, a Syrophenician by nation; and she besought him that he
would cast forth the devil out of her daughter.
27 But Jesus said unto her, Let the children first be filled: for it is not meet to take the
children's bread, and to cast *it* unto the dogs.
28 And she answered and said unto him, Yes, Lord: yet the dogs under the table eat of
the children's crumbs.
29 And he said unto her, For this saying go thy way; the devil is gone out of thy
daughter.
30 And when she was come to her house, she found the devil gone out, and her
daughter laid upon the bed.
31 ¶ And again, departing from the coasts of Tyre and Sidon, he came unto the sea of
Galilee, through the midst of the coasts of Decapolis. (Mark 7:24-31)

CHAPTER 74
HEALING IN THE REGION OF DECAPOLIS

(Except for Scythopolis these "cities" were east of the Jordan River and Lake Galilee)

The healing of a deaf mute

32 And they bring unto him one that was deaf, and had an impediment in his speech;
and they beseech him to put his hand upon him.
33 And he took him aside from the multitude, and put his fingers into his ears, and he
spit, and touched his tongue;
34 And looking up to heaven, he sighed, and saith unto him, Ephphatha, that is, Be
opened.
35 And straightway his ears were opened, and the string of his tongue was loosed, and
he spake plain.
36 And he charged them that they should tell no man: but the more he charged them, so
much the more a great deal they published *it*;
37 And were beyond measure astonished, saying, He hath done all things well:
he maketh both the deaf to hear, and the dumb to speak. (Mark 7:32-37)

A summary of the many healings that were done

30 And great multitudes came unto him, having with them *those that were* lame, blind,
dumb, maimed, and many others, and cast them down at Jesus' feet; and he healed
them:
31 Insomuch that the multitude wondered, when they saw the dumb to speak, the
maimed to be whole, the lame to walk, and the blind to see: and they glorified the God
of Israel. (Matt 15:30-31)

CHAPTER 75
THE LOAVES AND FISHES ARE MULTIPLIED (2ND OCCASION)

(4,000 men plus women and children)

According to the Gospel of Matthew

32 ¶ Then Jesus called his disciples *unto him*, and said, I have compassion on the
multitude, because they continue with me now three days, and have nothing to eat: and
I will not send them away fasting, lest they faint in the way. (Matt 15:32)

Had the disciples already forgotten feeding the 5,000? Wilderness means a desert place. To fill means to satisfy.

33 And his disciples say unto him, Whence should we have so much bread in the
wilderness, as to fill so great a multitude? (Matt 15:33)

Jesus never saw limitation, so the question could have been asked to awaken the disciples to God's ever-present supply.

34 And Jesus saith unto them, How many loaves have ye? And they said, Seven, and a
few little fishes.
35 And he commanded the multitude to sit down on the ground. (Matt 15:34-35)

Seven symbolizes spiritual perfection. Gratitude opens thought to behold the presence of whatever is needed.

36 And he took the seven loaves and the fishes, and gave thanks, and brake *them*, and
gave to his disciples, and the disciples to the multitude.
37 And they did all eat, and were filled: (Matt 15:36-37 *to* :)

Here baskets *σπυρίς spyris*, is a hamper or *large* basket. In the first occasion of multiplying the loaves and fishes recorded in Matt. 14:15-21 the word translated baskets is *κόφινος kophinos*, meaning *small* baskets.

37 and they took up of the broken *meat* that was left seven baskets full.
38 And they that did eat were four thousand men, beside women and children.
39 And he sent away the multitude, and took ship, and came into the coasts of Magdala.
(Matt 15:37-39 *and*)

1 In those days the multitude being very great, and having nothing to eat, Jesus called
his disciples *unto him*, and saith unto them,
2 I have compassion on the multitude, because they have now been with me three days,
and have nothing to eat:
3 And if I send them away fasting to their own houses, they will faint by the way: for
divers of them came from far. (Mark 8:1-3)

What did the disciples think was the source when the five thousand men plus women and children were fed?

4 And his disciples answered him, From whence can a man satisfy these *men* with
bread here in the wilderness? (Mark 8:4)

When Jesus asked his disciples "how many loaves have ye" what should they have answered?

5 And he asked them, How many loaves have ye? And they said, Seven. (Mark 8:5)

Notice that Jesus expressed gratitude BEFORE any confirmation that the need was met, and how gratitude for the indestructible relationship between God and man was expressed BEFORE Jesus raised Lazarus. See Jn. 11:41-43.

6 And he commanded the people to sit down on the ground: and he took the seven
loaves, and gave thanks, and brake, and gave to his disciples to set before *them*; and
they did set *them* before the people.
7 And they had a few small fishes: and he blessed, and commanded to set them also
before *them*. (Mark 8:6-7)

"Broken meat" means fragments or pieces of food. Nothing was wasted. Gratitude and wastefulness do not coexist.

8 So they did eat, and were filled: and they took up of the broken *meat* that was left
seven baskets. (Mark 8:8)

Note the compassion. The multitude was not dismissed until the need was met.

9 And they that had eaten were about four thousand: and he sent them away. (Mark 8:9)

CHAPTER 76
BEWARE OF EVIL DOCTRINES

(Spiritual teaching must always be by symbols." - MBE

The first warning: Beware the teaching of the Pharisees and Herod

Dalmanutha is likely on the western shore of Lake Galilee since Matthew 15:39 mentions "the region of" Magdala."

10 ¶ And straightway he entered into a ship with his disciples, and came into the parts
of Dalmanutha.
11 And the Pharisees came forth, and began to question with him, seeking of him a sign
from heaven, tempting him.
12 And he sighed deeply in his spirit, and saith, Why doth this generation seek after a
sign? verily I say unto you, There shall no sign be given unto this generation.
13 And he left them, and entering into the ship again departed to the other side.
14 ¶ Now *the disciples* had forgotten to take bread, neither had they in the ship with
them more than one loaf. (Mark 8:10-14)

The disciples again interpret a symbol literally. See Mark 3:6 p. 221 for the significance of the Pharisees and Herod.

15 And he charged them, saying, Take heed, beware of the leaven of the Pharisees, and
of the leaven of Herod.
16 And they reasoned among themselves, saying, *It is* because we have no bread. (Mark
8:15-16)

Jesus *again* chastened the disciples for their spiritual dullness. your heart hardened = your receptivity closed.

17 And when Jesus knew *it*, he saith unto them, Why reason ye, because ye have no
bread? perceive ye not yet, neither understand? have ye your heart yet hardened?
18 Having eyes, see ye not? and having ears, hear ye not? and do ye not remember?
19 When I brake the five loaves among five thousand, how many baskets full of
fragments took ye up? They say unto him, Twelve.

20 And when the seven among four thousand, how many baskets full of fragments took
ye up? And they said, Seven.
21 And he said unto them, How is it that ye do not understand? (Mark 8:17-21)

The second warning is against the teaching of the Pharisees and Sadducees

Jesus knew the generation to be wicked and adulterous, seeking the material more than the spiritual. - MBE

1 The Pharisees also with the Sadducees came, and tempting desired him that he would
shew them a sign from heaven. (Matt 16:1)

Both Jew and Gentile may have acute corporeal senses, but mortals need spiritual sense. - MBE

2 He answered and said unto them, When it is evening, ye say, *It will be* fair weather:
for the sky is red.
3 And in the morning, *It will be* foul weather to-day: for the sky is red and lowering.
(Matt 16:2-3 to 1st.)

His thrusts at materialism were sharp but needed. He never spared hypocrisy the sternest condemnation. – MBE

3 O *ye* hypocrites, ye can discern the face of the sky; but can ye not *discern* the signs of
the times? (Matt 16:3 *O ye)*

The carnal mind, being the source and essence of materialism, is "enmity against God (Life)." Rom 8:7

4 A wicked and adulterous generation seeketh after a sign; (Matt 16:4 *to ;*)

Jesus knew that a sign would be given --- but it would be largely misunderstood or ignored. See Luke 16:31

4 and there shall no sign be given unto it, but the sign of the prophet Jonas. And he left
them, and departed.
5 And when his disciples were come to the other side, they had forgotten to take bread.
(Matt. 16:4-5 *and*)

Jesus persisted, this time warning against the teaching of the Pharisees and the Sadducees.

6 ¶ Then Jesus said unto them, Take heed and beware of the leaven of the Pharisees
and of the Sadducees. (Matt 16:6)

The disciples again reasoned erroneously because they still did not *understand* the symbolism Jesus was using.

7 And they reasoned among themselves, saying, *It is* because we have taken no bread.
(Matt 16:7)

Here the word translated *faith* is more about *understanding* than about *trusting* or *believing*.

8 *Which* when Jesus perceived, he said unto them, O ye of little faith, why reason ye
among yourselves, because ye have brought no bread?
9 Do ye not yet understand, neither remember the five loaves of the five thousand, and
how many baskets ye took up?
10 Neither the seven loaves of the four thousand, and how many baskets ye took up?
(Matt 16:8-10)

Desiring that they understand what he was saying *in the future*, he reminded them *again* that he had to speak in parables when teaching spiritual truth.

11 How is it that ye do not understand that I spake *it* not to you concerning bread, that
ye should beware of the leaven of the Pharisees and of the Sadducees? (Matt 16:8-11)

The disciples finally understood, at least intellectually.

12 Then understood they how that he bade *them* not beware of the leaven of bread, but
of the doctrine of the Pharisees and of the Sadducees. (Matt 16:12)

CHAPTER 77
A MAN IN BETHSAIDA HEALED OF BLINDNESS

(A correct view of man as spiritual not material heals blindness)

22 ¶ And he cometh to Bethsaida; and they bring a blind man unto him, and besought
him to touch him.
23 And he took the blind man by the hand, and led him out of the town; and when he
had spit on his eyes, and put his hands upon him, he asked him if he saw ought.
24 And he looked up, and said, I see men as trees, walking.

25 After that he put *his* hands again upon his eyes, and made him look up: and he was
restored, and saw every man clearly.
26 And he sent him away to his house, saying, Neither go into the town, nor tell *it* to
any in the town. (Mark 8:22-26)

CHAPTER 78

PETER'S REALIZATION THAT JESUS IS THE CHRIST

(This probably occurred on three separate occasions since the settings are different and three words translated *charged* are used! Jesus hoped to instill in his disciples that he was the Messiah so they would not betray him.)

According to the Gospel of Mark

Whom do *men* say that I am?

27 ¶ And Jesus went out, and his disciples, into the towns of Cæsarea Philippi: and by
the way he asked his disciples, saying unto them, Whom do men say that I am?
28 And they answered, John the Baptist: but some *say*, Elias; and others, One of the
prophets. (Mark 8:27-28)

Jesus, not caring about general opinion, but what his disciples understood, asked: Who do ALL of you say I am?

29 And he saith unto them, But whom say ye that I am? (Mark 8:29 to ?)

Andrew recognized Jesus from the very start as the Christ, the Son of the living God. Peter now sees it for himself.

29 And Peter answereth and saith unto him, Thou art the Christ. (Mark 8:29 *And*)

The word "charged" is *ἐπιτιμάω; epitimaō,* a strong word meaning to censure severely, charge sharply.

30 And he charged them that they should tell no man of him. (Mark 8:30)

According to the Gospel of Matthew

Cæsarea Philippi is a city located about 25 miles north of Lake Galilee, capital city of the tetrarchy of Philip.

13 ¶ When Jesus came into the coasts of Cæsarea Philippi, he asked his disciples,
saying, Whom do men say that I the Son of man am?
14 And they said, Some *say that thou art* John the Baptist: some, Elias; and others,
Jeremias, or one of the prophets. (Matt 16:13-14)

What Jesus really wanted to know is who his disciples thought he was.

15 He saith unto them, But whom say ye that I am? (Matt 16:15)

It is one thing to merely repeat what others are saying, and quite another to see it for yourself. Peter's time had arrived.

16 And Simon Peter answered and said, Thou art the Christ, the Son of the living God.
(Matt 16:16)

Jesus declared Peter's spiritual insight a blessing because one can only build on an absolute conviction of the truth.

17 And Jesus answered and said unto him, Blessed art thou, Simon Bar-jona: for flesh
and blood hath not revealed *it* unto thee, but my Father which is in heaven. (Matt 16:17)

The name Peter received a new meaning (no longer a stone, but a Rock). Jesus' church (the society that would eventually be called Christianity) was to be built on the understanding of Christ, the Truth that Jesus brought to humanity.

18 And I say also unto thee, That thou art Peter, and upon this rock I will build my
church; and the gates of hell shall not prevail against it. (Matt 16:18)

The significance of Peter's realization: greater access to divine power through a clearer understanding of spiritual reality.

19 And I will give unto thee the keys of the kingdom of heaven: and whatsoever thou
shalt bind on earth shall be bound in heaven: and whatsoever thou shalt loose on earth
shall be loosed in heaven. (Matt 16:19)

The word charged is *διαστέλλω diastellō,* even stronger language. It means to admonish, or order to keep silent.

20 Then charged he his disciples that they should tell no man that he was Jesus the
Christ. (Matt 16:20)

According to the Gospel of Luke

18 ¶ And it came to pass, as he was alone praying, his disciples were with him: and he
asked them, saying, Whom say the people that I am? (Luke 9:18)

The disciples again reply with an answer that reveals a belief in spiritualism among the people.

19 They answering said, John the Baptist; but some *say*, Elias; and others *say*, that one
of the old prophets is risen again. (Luke 9:19)

Jesus needed his disciples to examine their thinking, so he repeated, repeated, and repeated the question. Jesus knew that the disciples needed to understand who he was, so that when the testing time came they would NOT desert him.

20 He said unto them, But whom say ye that I am? Peter answering said, The Christ of God. (Luke 9:20)

Straitly, strictly, under penalty, *πολύς polys*. Charged, *ἐπιτιμάω epitimaō* AND commanded, *παραγγέλλω paraggellō* is even stronger than before. At this point the Kingdom and the King have been proclaimed. Now begins the period of his ministry where the King is rejected. Ultimately the Kingdom will also be rejected.

21 And he straitly charged them, and commanded *them* to tell no man that thing; (Luke 9:21)

CHAPTER 79

THE 1ST ANNOUNCEMENT OF SUFFERINGS

(Note how this followed immediately after the declarations of who he was. Luke 9:22; Mark 8:31; Matt. 16:21. Jesus is clearly attempting to prepare the Apostles for what is soon to happen, so that they won't lose faith and desert the cause.)

According to the Gospel of Luke

22 Saying, The Son of man must suffer many things, and be rejected of the elders and chief priests and scribes, and be slain, and be raised the third day. (Luke 9:22)

The demand of discipleship. ALL of Jesus teaching aims toward one objective: to teach us how to leave all for Christ.

23 ¶ And he said to *them* all, If any *man* will come after me, let him deny himself, and take up his cross daily, and follow me. (Luke 9:23)

The goal: to lay aside the mortal self (the old man) and to put on the immortal self (the new man).

24 For whosoever will save his life shall lose it: but whosoever will lose his life for my sake, the same shall save it. (Luke 9:24)

To "lose himself" or to "lose his own soul" is to lose sight of our true nature in Christ, God's own "image and likeness."

25 For what is a man advantaged, if he gain the whole world, and lose himself, or be cast away?

26 For whosoever shall be ashamed of me and of my words, of him shall the Son of man be ashamed, when he shall come in his own glory, and *in his* Father's, and of the holy angels. (Luke 9:25-26)

According to the Gospel of Matthew

21 ¶ From that time forth began Jesus to shew unto his disciples, how that he must go unto Jerusalem, and suffer many things of the elders and chief priests and scribes, and be killed, and be raised again the third day. (Matt 16:21)

Mortal mind's first priority is to preserve a corporeal sense of self-hood.

22 Then Peter took him, and began to rebuke him, saying, Be it far from thee, Lord: this shall not be unto thee. (Matt 16:22)

Jesus rebukes the tendency of the human being to cling to this mortal sense of selfhood.

23 But he turned, and said unto Peter, Get thee behind me, Satan: thou art an offence unto me: for thou savourest not the things that be of God, but those that be of men. (Matt 16:23)

To take up the cross means to give up the material sense of life to make place for the spiritual sense of life.

24 ¶ Then said Jesus unto his disciples, If any *man* will come after me, let him deny himself, and take up his cross, and follow me.

25 For whosoever will save his life shall lose it: and whosoever will lose his life for my sake shall find it.

26 For what is a man profited, if he shall gain the whole world, and lose his own soul? or what shall a man give in exchange for his soul?

27 For the Son of man shall come in the glory of his Father with his angels; and then he shall reward every man according to his works. (Matt 16:24-27)

According to the Gospel of Mark

31 And he began to teach them, that the Son of man must suffer many things, and be

rejected of the elders, and *of* the chief priests, and scribes, and be killed, and after three
days rise again.
32 And he spake that saying openly. (Mark 8:31-32 *to* 1st.)

Jesus rebuked Peter's emotional response. When on the cross, Jesus was illustrating "the pathway" to eternal Life. It is to lay aside the mortal sense of self. Over and over again, this is the message. We can be reborn spiritually only by first laying aside the material. Are we any more willing to this than was Peter and the other disciples?

32 And Peter took him, and began to rebuke him.
33 But when he had turned about and looked on his disciples, he rebuked Peter, saying,
Get thee behind me, Satan: for thou savourest not the things that be of God, but the
things that be of men. (Mark 8:32-33 *And*)

Next Jesus tells the people what they must do to inherit eternal life: Put off the mortal for the immortal.

34 ¶ And when he had called the people *unto him* with his disciples also, he said unto
them, Whosoever will come after me, let him deny himself, and take up his cross, and
follow me.
35 For whosoever will save his life shall lose it; but whosoever shall lose his life for my
sake and the gospel's, the same shall save it. (Mark 8:34-35)

soul *ψυχή psychē*. In v. 35 translated life. The danger of losing the awareness of our *identity* in the likeness of the divine.

36 For what shall it profit a man, if he shall gain the whole world, and lose his own
soul?
37 Or what shall a man give in exchange for his soul?
38 Whosoever therefore shall be ashamed of me and of my words in this adulterous and
sinful generation; of him also shall the Son of man be ashamed, when he cometh in the
glory of his Father with the holy angels. (Mark 8:36-38)

CHAPTER 80
A PROPHECY CONCERNING THE KINGDOM OF GOD

(John the Beloved Disciple did see the kingdom of God. *(See Rev. 21)*. There is no record of his death. Jesus spoke the words below in 28 A.D. The Revelation of Jesus Christ came to John sixty-eight years later, in 96 A.D. Hence the words of Jesus to Peter concerning John: "If I will that he tarry till I come, what *is that* to thee? follow thou me." John 21:22)

According to the Gospel of Mark

1 And he said unto them, Verily I say unto you, That there be some of them that stand
here, which shall not taste of death, till they have seen the kingdom of God come with
power. (Mark 9:1)

According to the Gospel of Matthew

28 Verily I say unto you, There be some standing here, which shall not taste of death,
till they see the Son of man coming in his kingdom. (Matt 16:28)

According to the Gospel of Luke

27 But I tell you of a truth, there be some standing here, which shall not taste of death,
till they see the kingdom of God. (Luke 9:27)

CHAPTER 81
TRANSFIGURATION – THE FIRST RESURRECTION

(Transfigured is *μεταμορφόω metamorphoō, to* change to another form, transform. For what & how see II Cor. 3)

According to the Gospel of Luke

28 ¶ And it came to pass about an eight days after these sayings, he took Peter and John
and James, and went up into a mountain to pray.
29 And as he prayed, the fashion of his countenance was altered, and his raiment *was*
white *and* glistering.
30 And, behold, there talked with him two men, which were Moses and Elias:

31 Who appeared in glory, and spake of his decease which he should accomplish at
Jerusalem.
32 But Peter and they that were with him were heavy with sleep: and when they were
awake, they saw his glory, and the two men that stood with him.
33 And it came to pass, as they departed from him, Peter said unto Jesus, Master, it is
good for us to be here: and let us make three tabernacles; one for thee, and one for
Moses, and one for Elias: not knowing what he said. (Luke 9:28-33)

"No man hath seen God at any time." See John 1:18 (to ;).

34 While he thus spake, there came a cloud, and overshadowed them: and they feared
as they entered into the cloud.
35 And there came a voice out of the cloud, saying, This is my beloved Son: hear him.
36 And when the voice was past, Jesus was found alone. And they kept *it* close, and
told no man in those days any of those things which they had seen. (Luke 9:34-36)

According to the Gospel of Matthew

1 And after six days Jesus taketh Peter, James, and John his brother, and bringeth them
up into an high mountain apart,
2 And was transfigured before them: and his face did shine as the sun, and his raiment
was white as the light.
3 And, behold, there appeared unto them Moses and Elias talking with him.
4 Then answered Peter, and said unto Jesus, Lord, it is good for us to be here: if thou
wilt, let us make here three tabernacles; one for thee, and one for Moses, and one for
Elias. (Matt 17:1-4)

"No man hath seen God at any time;" See John 1:18(to ;). If they haven't seen God, they haven't seen the real man, God's image and likeness. Jesus came to show us both, for they are One since cause and effect can never be separated.

5 While he yet spake, behold, a bright cloud overshadowed them: and behold a voice
out of the cloud, which said, This is my beloved Son, in whom I am well pleased; hear
ye him.
6 And when the disciples heard *it*, they fell on their face, and were sore afraid.
7 And Jesus came and touched them, and said, Arise, and be not afraid.
8 And when they had lifted up their eyes, they saw no man, save Jesus only. (Matt 17:5-8)

"Until the Son of man be risen ***again*** from the dead" implies that his transfiguration was a resurrection.

9 And as they came down from the mountain, Jesus charged them, saying, Tell the
vision to no man, until the Son of man be risen again from the dead. (Matt 17:9)

According to the Gospel of Mark

2 ¶ And after six days Jesus taketh *with him* Peter, and James, and John, and leadeth
them up into an high mountain apart by themselves: and he was transfigured before
them.
3 And his raiment became shining, exceeding white as snow; so as no fuller on earth
can white them.
4 And there appeared unto them Elias with Moses: and they were talking with Jesus.
5 And Peter answered and said to Jesus, Master, it is good for us to be here: and let us
make three tabernacles; one for thee, and one for Moses, and one for Elias.
6 For he wist not what to say; for they were sore afraid. (Mark 9:2-6)

"No man hath seen God at any time", See John. 1:18 (to ;), because God is not a corporeal being, God is Spirit and therefore man must be spiritual. Spiritual man cannot be seen by the material senses any more than can God, Spirit.

7 And there was a cloud that overshadowed them: and a voice came out of the cloud,
saying, This is my beloved Son: hear him.
8 And suddenly, when they had looked round about, they saw no man any more, save

Jesus only with themselves.
9 And as they came down from the mountain, he charged them that they should tell no
man what things they had seen, till the Son of man were risen from the dead.
10 And they kept that saying with themselves, questioning one with another what the
rising from the dead should mean. (Mark 9:7-10)

CHAPTER 82
THE 2ND ANNOUNCEMENT OF SUFFERINGS
(Mark 9:12 & Matthew 17:12)

According to the Gospel of Mark

11 ¶ And they asked him, saying, Why say the scribes that Elias must first come?
12 And he answered and told them, Elias verily cometh first, and restoreth all things;
and how it is written of the Son of man, that he must suffer many things, and be set at
nought.
13 But I say unto you, That Elias is indeed come, and they have done unto him
whatsoever they listed, as it is written of him. (Mark 9:11-13)

According to the Gospel of Matthew

10 And his disciples asked him, saying, Why then say the scribes that Elias must first
come?
11 And Jesus answered and said unto them, Elias truly shall first come, and restore all
things.
12 But I say unto you, That Elias is come already, and they knew him not, but have
done unto him whatsoever they listed. Likewise shall also the Son of man suffer of
them.
13 Then the disciples understood that he spake unto them of John the Baptist. (Matt 17:10-13)

CHAPTER 83
THREE CASES OF OVERCOMING UNBELIEF

The 1st Case: The case of a lunatic. Occurred when *Jesus and the disciples* were come to the multitude

Lunacy. Lunatic = lunatic, *σεληνιάζομαι selēniazomai,* epileptic (moon-struck) because believed caused by the moon.

14 ¶ And when they were come to the multitude, there came to him a *certain* man,
kneeling down to him, and saying,
15 Lord, have mercy on my son: for he is lunatic, and sore vexed: for ofttimes he falleth
into the fire, and oft into the water. (Matt 17:14-15)

The disciples inability to heal exposed.

16 And I brought him to thy disciples, and they could not cure him. (Matt 17:16)

The root cause of the inability to heal: The faithlessness of mortal conception, i.e. of mortal belief.

17 Then Jesus answered and said, O faithless and perverse generation, how long shall I
be with you? how long shall I suffer you? bring him hither to me. (Matt 17:17)

The "devil" of unbelief rebuked. Jesus did not *believe*, for as he said "I *knew* that Thou hearest me always." John 11:42

18 And Jesus rebuked the devil; and he departed out of him: and the child was cured
from that very hour. (Matt 17:18)

A soul-searching question.

19 Then came the disciples to Jesus apart, and said, Why could not we cast him out?
(Matt 17:19)

Jesus replies it is ***unbelief,*** a firmly held conviction that matter is substance and Spirit an illusion, that prevents the healing.

20 And Jesus said unto them, Because of your unbelief: for verily I say unto you, If ye
have faith as a grain of mustard seed, ye shall say unto this mountain, Remove hence to

yonder place; and it shall remove; and nothing shall be impossible unto you. (Matt 17:20)

Prayer: the acknowledgment God's power. Fasting: to refrain from accepting material sense testimony, the basis of fear, as absolute or final.

21 Howbeit this kind goeth not out but by prayer and fasting. (Matt 17:21)

The 2nd Case: The case of a dumb (speechless) child. Occurred when *Jesus was come to his disciples*

The scribes were joined together disputing with Jesus' disciples. Questioning, συζητέω syzēteō, disputing, arguing.

14 ¶ And when he came to *his* disciples, he saw a great multitude about them, and the
scribes questioning with them.

15 And straightway all the people, when they beheld him, were greatly amazed, and
running to *him* saluted him. (Mark 9:14-15)

Jesus confronted the scribes by asking them why they were ganging up on his disciples. This defense of his disciples, despite the fact they had not achieved a healing, shows that he rebuked them for the sole purpose of gaining their full attention to what he was teaching them so that they would become better healers.

16 And he asked the scribes, What question ye with them? (Mark 9:16)

A case of dumbness. Dumb, *ἄλαλος alalos,* speechless. Believed to be a defect of demoniacs.

17 And one of the multitude answered and said, Master, I have brought unto thee my
son, which hath a dumb spirit;

18 And wheresoever he taketh him, he teareth him: and he foameth, and gnasheth with
his teeth, and pineth away: (Mark 9:17-18 *to* :)

The disciples were unsuccessful in healing the man's son, and the scribes were mocking them.

18 and I spake to thy disciples that they should cast him out; and they could not. (Mark 9:18 *and*)

Jesus' reply: O faithless generation. Man born of the flesh, material *generation*, has no knowledge of, nor trust in, Spirit.

19 He answereth him, and saith, O faithless generation, how long shall I be with you?
how long shall I suffer you? bring him unto me. (Mark 9:19)

Jesus' fearless example.

20 And they brought him unto him: and when he saw him, straightway the spirit tare
him; and he fell on the ground, and wallowed foaming.

21 And he asked his father, How long is it ago since this came unto him? And he said,
Of a child.

22 And ofttimes it hath cast him into the fire, and into the waters, to destroy him: but if
thou canst do any thing, have compassion on us, and help us. (Mark 9:20-22)

The demand made on the father – accept the possibility of healing.

23 Jesus said unto him, If thou canst believe, all things *are* possible to him that
believeth. (Mark 9:23)

The impediment to healing was exposed, it was *unbelief*, i.e. a strongly held conviction that healing was not possible.

24 And straightway the father of the child cried out, and said with tears, Lord, I believe;
help thou mine unbelief. (Mark 9:24)

Jesus heals the difficulty and forestalls a relapse. Note the chemicalization when the error was uncovered by Jesus.

25 When Jesus saw that the people came running together, he rebuked the foul spirit,
saying unto him, *Thou* dumb and deaf spirit, I charge thee, come out of him, and enter
no more into him.

26 And *the spirit* cried, and rent him sore, and came out of him: and he was as one
dead; insomuch that many said, He is dead.

27 But Jesus took him by the hand, and lifted him up; and he arose. (Mark 9:25-27)

Another soul-searching question.

28 And when he was come into the house, his disciples asked him privately, Why could
not we cast him out? (Mark 9:28)

The need is to reject material sense testimony as conclusive, and hold firmly to God's all-power and all-presence.

29 And he said unto them, This kind can come forth by nothing, but by prayer and
fasting. (Mark 9:29)

The 3rd case, convulsions: The *next day,* after coming down from "the hill," meaning the mountain

37 ¶ And it came to pass, that on the next day, when they were come down from the
hill, much people met him. (Luke 9:37)

A father's call for help.

38 And, behold, a man of the company cried out, saying, Master, I beseech thee, look
upon my son: for he is mine only child. (Luke 9:38)

A case of convulsions believed caused by an "unclean spirit." In today's terminology a false belief. See vs. 42.

39 And, lo, a spirit taketh him, and he suddenly crieth out; and it teareth him that he
foameth again, and bruising him hardly departeth from him. (Luke 9:39)

Apparently the father had asked the disciples to cure his son, and again they had been unable to effect a cure.

40 And I besought thy disciples to cast him out; and they could not. (Luke 9:40)

Jesus' appraisal of the situation. The faithless and perverse generation is the belief that man, not God, is the creator.

41 And Jesus answering said, O faithless and perverse generation, how long shall I be
with you, and suffer you? Bring thy son hither. (Luke 9:41)

Jesus rejected the belief that man originates in matter, and affirmed the truth that man is spiritual and therefore whole.

42 And as he was yet a-coming, the devil threw him down, and tare *him*. And Jesus
rebuked the unclean spirit, and healed the child, and delivered him again to his father.
(Luke 9:42)

CHAPTER 84

THE 3RD ANNOUNCEMENT OF SUFFERINGS

(Luke 9:44; Matt. 17:22; Mark 9:31)

According to the Gospel of Luke

The manifestation of God's power is both instructional and redemptive. The time is drawing closer, and Jesus' words are getting more intense. He wants his disciples to understand so they won't desert him.

43 ¶ And they were all amazed at the mighty power of God. But while they wondered
every one at all things which Jesus did, he said unto his disciples, (Luke 9:43)

Listen to how forcefully Jesus urges his disciples to pay attention to what he is telling them so as not to forget it.

44 Let these sayings sink down into your ears: for the Son of man shall be delivered
into the hands of men.

45 But they understood not this saying, and it was hid from them, that they perceived it
not: and they feared to ask him of that saying. (Luke 9:44-45)

According to the Gospel of Mark

30 ¶ And they departed thence, and passed through Galilee; and he would not that any
man should know *it*.

31 For he taught his disciples, and said unto them, The Son of man is delivered into the
hands of men, (Mark 9:30-31 *to* 3rd,)

What appears to be defeat will culminate in the resurrection (victory over death AND the grave). They must not lose faith!

31 and they shall kill him; and after that he is killed, he shall rise the third day.

32 But they understood not that saying, and were afraid to ask him. (Mark 9:31-32 *and*)

According to the Gospel of Matthew

22 ¶ And while they abode in Galilee, Jesus said unto them, The Son of man shall be
betrayed into the hands of men: (Matt 17:22)

The Son of man (Jesus) will be killed (apparent defeat) but the final outcome will be resurrection (victory over death).

23 And they shall kill him, and the third day he shall be raised again. (Matt 17:23)

The disciples were exceedingly sorrowful because their sense of doom outweighed their expectation of victory.

23 And they were exceeding sorry. (Matt 17:23 *And*)

CHAPTER 85

MONEY FOR THE TAXES

24 ¶ And when they were come to Capernaum, they that received tribute *money* came
to Peter, and said, Doth not your master pay tribute?

25 He saith, Yes. And when he was come into the house, Jesus prevented him, saying,
What thinkest thou, Simon? of whom do the kings of the earth take custom or tribute?
of their own children, or of strangers?
26 Peter saith unto him, Of strangers. Jesus saith unto him, Then are the children free.
27 Notwithstanding, lest we should offend them, go thou to the sea, and cast an hook,
and take up the fish that first cometh up; and when thou hast opened his mouth, thou
shalt find a piece of money: that take, and give unto them for me and thee. (Matt 17:24-27)

CHAPTER 86
WHO SHALL BE THE GREATEST?

(The 1st recorded incident)

According to the Gospel of Mark

Jesus rebuked the Apostles for the division caused by the self-seeking desire for position and power.

33 ¶ And he came to Capernaum: and being in the house he asked them, What was it
that ye disputed among yourselves by the way? (Mark 9:33)

The disciples could not reply because convicted by a guilty conscience. This shows that they knew better.

34 But they held their peace: for by the way they had disputed among themselves, who
should be the greatest. (Mark 9:34)

Wrong motives bring disappointment.

35 And he sat down, and called the twelve, and saith unto them, If any man desire to be
first, *the same* shall be last of all, and servant of all. (Mark 9:35)

Jesus AGAIN uses a child to represent the state of mind desired.

36 And he took a child, and set him in the midst of them: and when he had taken him in
his arms, he said unto them, (Mark 9:36)

"Such children" are to be received in Christ's name. Meekness is required to receive Christ and to understand God.

37 Whosoever shall receive one of such children in my name, receiveth me: and
whosoever shall receive me, receiveth not me, but him that sent me. (Mark 9:37)

According to the Gospel of Matthew

Who is the greatest, *μείζων meizōn,* greater, larger, elder, stronger.

1 At the same time came the disciples unto Jesus, saying, Who is the greatest in the
kingdom of heaven? (Matt 18:1)

The required state of mind (innocence, purity, selflessness) is *symbolized* by a child.

2 And Jesus called a little child unto him, and set him in the midst of them, (Matt 18:2)

What it means to "receive a child in my name." Converted, *στρέφω strephō*, is to re-establish our God-given identity.

3 And said, Verily I say unto you, Except ye be converted, and become as little
children, ye shall not enter into the kingdom of heaven. (Matt 18:3)

Jesus again points to his first Beatitude: 'Blessed are the poor in spirit, for theirs is the kingdom of heaven?"

4 Whosoever therefore shall humble himself as this little child, the same is greatest in
the kingdom of heaven. (Matt 18:4)

The Christ-like nature of a child must replace pride and self-seeking or true dominion and peace will be unattainable.

5 And whoso shall receive one such little child in my name receiveth me. (Matt 18:5)

According to the Gospel of Luke

The disciples arguing among themselves. Reasoning, *διαλογισμός dialogismos*, disputing, arguing.

46 ¶ Then there arose a reasoning among them, which of them should be greatest. (Luke
9:46)

The error uncovered. The child symbolizes man's original nature in God's image and likeness, pure and spiritual.

47 And Jesus, perceiving the thought of their heart, took a child, and set him by him,
(Luke 9:47)

The ideal nature of a little child (Christlikeness rather than self-seeking). Sadly, the lesson was yet to be learned!

48 And said unto them, Whosoever shall receive this child in my name receiveth me:
and whosoever shall receive me receiveth him that sent me: for he that is least among

you all, the same shall be great. (Luke 9:48)

CHAPTER 87
EXCLUSIVENESS AND ENVY MUST BE UNSELFED

(Denomination means *division*. Christianity is One)

One infinite God, good, unifies men and nations; constitutes the brotherhood of man; ends wars; fulfills the Scripture, "Love thy neighbor as thyself;" annihilates pagan and Christian idolatry, --- whatever is wrong in social, civil, criminal, political, and religious codes; equalizes the sexes; annuls the curse on man, and leaves nothing that can sin, suffer, be punished or destroyed. - MBE

According to the Gospel of Luke

49 ¶ And John answered and said, Master, we saw one casting out devils in thy name;
and we forbad him, because he followeth not with us.
50 And Jesus said unto him, Forbid *him* not: for he that is not against us is for us. (Luke 9:49-50)

According to the Gospel of Mark

38 ¶ And John answered him, saying, Master, we saw one casting out devils in thy
name, and he followeth not us: and we forbad him, because he followeth not us.
39 But Jesus said, Forbid him not: for there is no man which shall do a miracle in my
name, that can lightly speak evil of me.
40 For he that is not against us is on our part. (Mark 9:38-40)

Christ advocates against cliques. Obedience to this instruction will heal the division between denominaions of Christians due to doctrinal differences! Question. Does everyone within a denomination see things exactly the same way? Were the twelve apostles in total agreement, did they have the same level of understanding? If each and every disciple of Jesus was required to have the same understanding that Jesus had, how many disciples would he have kept? NONE!

41 For whosoever shall give you a cup of water to drink in my name, because ye belong
to Christ, verily I say unto you, he shall not lose his reward. (Mark 9:41)

CHAPTER 88
AVOID OFFENSES

According to the Gospel of Luke

To offend, *σκανδαλίζω skandalizō*, to put a stumbling block or impediment, cause one to distrust or to fall away.

42 And whosoever shall offend one of *these* little ones that believe in me, it is better for
him that a millstone were hanged about his neck, and he were cast into the sea. (Mark 9:42)

Therefore watch and refrain from doing whatever would lead a sincere seeker for Truth (a little one) to fall away.

43 And if thy hand offend thee, cut if off: it is better for thee to enter into life maimed,
than having two hands to go into hell, into the fire that never shall be quenched:
44 Where their worm dieth not, and the fire is not quenched.
45 And if thy foot offend thee, cut it off: it is better for thee to enter halt into life, than
having two feet to be cast into hell, into the fire that never shall be quenched:
46 Where their worm dieth not, and the fire is not quenched.
47 And if thine eye offend thee, pluck it out: it is better for thee to enter into the
kingdom of God with one eye, than having two eyes to be cast into hell fire:
48 Where their worm dieth not, and the fire is not quenched.
49 For every one shall be salted with fire, and every sacrifice shall be salted with salt.
50 Salt *is* good: but if the salt have lost his saltness, wherewith will ye season it? Have
salt in yourselves, and have peace one with another. (Mark 9:43-50)

According to the Gospel of Matthew

The penalty is severe for causing a "little one," namely a sincere seeker for Christ, to stumble or fall aside.

6 But whoso shall offend one of these little ones which believe in me, it were better for
him that a millstone were hanged about his neck, and *that* he were drowned in the depth

of the sea.
7 ¶ Woe unto the world because of offences! for it must needs be that offences come;
but woe to that man by whom the offence cometh! (Matt 18:6-7)

Therefore unself, put off or cast aside and refrain from doing whatever would cause another to stumble or to fall away.

8 Wherefore if thy hand or thy foot offend thee, cut them off, and cast *them* from thee:
it is better for thee to enter into life halt or maimed, rather than having two hands or two
feet to be cast into everlasting fire.
9 And if thine eye offend thee, pluck it out, and cast *it* from thee: it is better for thee to
enter into life with one eye, rather than having two eyes to be cast into hell fire. (Matt
18:8-9)

Don't cause a sincere seeker to be led astray. Despise, *καταφρονέω kataphroneō*, to think little of, contemn, disdain. "Their angels . . . behold the face of my Father which is in heaven" i.e. their harmonious thoughts reflect God, Spirit.

10 Take heed that ye despise not one of these little ones; for I say unto you, That in
heaven their angels do always behold the face of my Father which is in heaven. (Matt
18:10)

The example Jesus set is to not acquire worldly power but to reflect divine Love. Note how his teaching at this point in his ministry is moving more and more toward emphasizing the need to love. Not a human self-centered sense of love, but to become divine Love!!

11 For the Son of man is come to save that which was lost.
12 How think ye? if a man have an hundred sheep, and one of them be gone astray,
doth he not leave the ninety and nine, and goeth into the mountains, and seeketh that
which is gone astray?
13 And if so be that he find it, verily I say unto you, he rejoiceth more of that *sheep*,
than of the ninety and nine which went not astray.
14 Even so it is not the will of your Father which is in heaven, that one of these little
ones should perish. (Matt 18:11-14)

CHAPTER 89
LOVE ENOUGH TO SEEK RECONCILIATION

15 ¶ Moreover if thy brother shall trespass against thee, go and tell him his fault
between thee and him alone: if he shall hear thee, thou hast gained thy brother.
16 But if he will not hear *thee*, *then* take with thee one or two more, that in the mouth
of two or three witnesses every word may be established.
17 And if he shall neglect to hear them, tell *it* unto the church: but if he neglect to hear
the church, let him be unto thee as an heathen man and a publican. (Matt 18:15-17)

Everything must be worked out either here and now, or else later on. So why not NOW and escape the suffering!

18 Verily I say unto you, Whatsoever ye shall bind on earth shall be bound in heaven:
and whatsoever ye shall loose on earth shall be loosed in heaven.
19 Again I say unto you, That if two of you shall agree on earth as touching any thing
that they shall ask, it shall be done for them of my Father which is in heaven.
20 For where two or three are gathered together in my name, there am I in the midst of
them. (Matt 18:18-20)

The requirement to forgive (to reverse the error and behold the truth) has no limit.

21 ¶ Then came Peter to him, and said, Lord, how oft shall my brother sin against me,
and I forgive him? till seven times?
22 Jesus saith unto him, I say not unto thee, Until seven times: but, Until seventy times
seven. (Matt 18:21-22)

A parable illustrating a proper sense of forgiveness. To forgive does not mean to overlook or to merely pardon, for that would leave sin unpunished and therefore subject to being repeated. For Christ's terms of forgiveness see John 8:11.

23 ¶ Therefore is the kingdom of heaven likened unto a certain king, which would take
account of his servants.

24 And when he had begun to reckon, one was brought unto him, which owed him ten
thousand talents. (Matt 18:23-24)

The **righteous** use of power and authority is to empower others to do what is right.

25 But forasmuch as he had not to pay, his lord commanded him to be sold, and his
wife, and children, and all that he had, and payment to be made.
26 The servant therefore fell down, and worshipped him, saying, Lord, have patience
with me, and I will pay thee all.
27 Then the lord of that servant was moved with compassion, and loosed him, and
forgave him the debt. (Matt 18:25-27)

The **unrighteous** use of power and authority includes seeing only the faults of other's and not correcting our own,

28 But the same servant went out, and found one of his fellowservants, which owed
him an hundred pence: and he laid hands on him, and took *him* by the throat, saying,
Pay me that thou owest.
29 And his fellowservant fell down at his feet, and besought him, saying, Have patience
with me, and I will pay thee all.
30 And he would not: but went and cast him into prison, till he should pay the debt. (Matt
18:28-30)

Here retribution is demanded. Retribution is not revenge. The punishment was administered to bring about reform.

31 So when his fellowservants saw what was done, they were very sorry, and came and
told unto their lord all that was done.
32 Then his lord, after that he had called him, said unto him, O thou wicked servant, I
forgave thee all that debt, because thou desiredst me:
33 Shouldest not thou also have had compassion on thy fellowservant, even as I had
pity on thee?
34 And his lord was wroth, and delivered him to the tormentors, till he should pay all
that was due unto him. (Matt 18:31-34)

"To remit the penalty due for sin, would be for Truth to pardon error. We cannot escape the penalty due for sin." – M.B.E.

35 So likewise shall my heavenly Father do also unto you, if ye from your hearts
forgive not every one his brother their trespasses. (Matt 18:35)

CHAPTER 90
TREACHEROUS ADVICE REJECTED

Galilee is North. Jewry (*Ἰουδαία Ioudaia*) refers to the hostile group centered South in Jerusalem, plotting to kill Jesus.

1 After these things Jesus walked in Galilee: for he would not walk in Jewry, because
the Jews sought to kill him. (John 7:1)

The Feast of Tabernacles is eight days (Tishri 15-21). On the Gentile calendar the end of September or early October.

2 Now the Jews' feast of tabernacles was at hand. (John 7:2)

Jesus' brethren, ἀδελφός a*delphos*, kinsfolk, mocked him to encourage an open display, knowing it might prove fatal.

3 His brethren therefore said unto him, Depart hence, and go into Judæa, that thy
disciples also may see the works that thou doest.
4 For *there is* no man *that* doeth any thing in secret, and he himself seeketh to be
known openly. If thou do these things, shew thyself to the world. (John 7:3-4)

A parenthetic remark telling why his bethren (brothers and sisters) proposed such perilous advice.

5 For neither did his brethren believe in him. (John 7:5)

Jesus responded that he would act under divine direction, not according to their malicious promptings.

6 Then Jesus said unto them, My time is not yet come: but your time is alway ready.
(John 7:6)

Jesus to his brethren: "you conform to the world, so it loves you, whereas I uncover its evil, and so it hates me."

7 The world cannot hate you; but me it hateth, because I testify of it, that the works
thereof are evil. (John 7:7)

Jesus acted according to divine direction, whereas his brethren were motivated by destructive human emotions.
8 Go ye up unto this feast: I go not up yet unto this feast; for my time is not yet full
come. (John 7:8)
Therefore, Jesus ignored the "advice" of his brethren, and for the time being he remained in Galilee.
9 When he had said these words unto them, he abode *still* in Galilee. (John 7:9)
A parenthetic remark that Jesus went to Jerusalem later, but with discretion and under divine direction.
10 ¶ But when his brethren were gone up, then went he also up unto the feast, not
openly, but as it were in secret. (John 7:10)
The words Jesus spoke earlier were now confirmed: "A man's foes *shall be* they of his own household." – Matt10:36
1 And it came to pass, *that* when Jesus had finished these sayings, he departed from
Galilee, (Matt 19:1 *to* 3rd,)

CHAPTER 91
FROM GALILEE THROUGH SAMARIA TOWARD JUDÆA

(During this journey Jesus declared his mission to mankind in unmistakable words – to save men's lives.)

51 ¶ And it came to pass, when the time was come that he should be received up, he
stedfastly set his face to go to Jerusalem,
52 And sent messengers before his face: and they went, and entered into a village of the
Samaritans, to make ready for him.
53 And they did not receive him, because his face was as though he would go to
Jerusalem.
54 And when his disciples James and John saw *this*, they said, Lord, wilt thou that we
command fire to come down from heaven, and consume them, even as Elias did?
55 But he turned, and rebuked them, and said, Ye know not what manner of spirit ye
are of.
56 For the Son of man is not come to destroy men's lives, but to save *them*. And they
went to another village. (Luke 9:51-56)

CHAPTER 92
EXCUSES - EXCUSES - EXCUSES

57 ¶ And it came to pass, that, as they went in the way, a certain *man* said unto him,
Lord, I will follow thee whithersoever thou goest.
58 And Jesus said unto him, Foxes have holes, and birds of the air *have* nests; but the
Son of man hath not where to lay *his* head.
59 And he said unto another, Follow me. But he said, Lord, suffer me first to go and
bury my father.
60 Jesus said unto him, Let the dead bury their dead: but go thou and preach the
kingdom of God.
61 And another also said, Lord, I will follow thee; but let me first go bid them farewell,
which are at home at my house.
62 And Jesus said unto him, No man, having put his hand to the plough, and looking
back, is fit for the kingdom of God. (Luke 9:57-62)

CHAPTER 93
SEVENTY MORE DISCIPLES APPOINTED

1 After these things the Lord appointed other seventy also, and sent them two and two
before his face into every city and place, whither he himself would come.
2 Therefore said he unto them, The harvest truly *is* great, but the labourers *are* few:

pray ye therefore the Lord of the harvest, that he would send forth labourers into his harvest.
3 Go your ways: behold, I send you forth as lambs among wolves. (Luke 10:1-3)
These were an additional seventy disciples sent out with instructions. No: purse βαλλάντιον *ballantion*, money bag; scrip πήρα *pēra*, a bag to hold money collected begging; shoes, ὑπόδημα *hypodēma*, sandals, 2nd pair; salute = greetings.
4 Carry neither purse, nor scrip, nor shoes: and salute no man by the way.
5 And into whatsoever house ye enter, first say, Peace *be* to this house.
6 And if the son of peace be there, your peace shall rest upon it: if not, it shall turn to you again.
7 And in the same house remain, eating and drinking such things as they give: for the labourer is worthy of his hire. Go not from house to house. (Luke 10:4-7)
Work with the receptive; those who permit you to share the truth. It is quality of thought, not how many that matters.
8 And into whatsoever city ye enter, and they receive you, eat such things as are set before you:
9 And heal the sick that are therein, and say unto them, The kingdom of God is come nigh unto you. (Luke 10:8-9)
Depart from the unreceptive who are not yet ready to receive.
10 But into whatsoever city ye enter, and they receive you not, go your ways out into the streets of the same, and say, (Luke 10:10)
With no judgment or resentment simply brush aside the unreceptive attitude that rejects Christ.
11 Even the very dust of your city, which cleaveth on us, we do wipe off against you: (Luke 10:10-11 *to* :)
Do not be discouraged, another's lack of receptivity cannot prevent you, or anyone else, from entering the kingdom.
11 notwithstanding be ye sure of this, that the kingdom of God is come nigh unto you. (Luke 10:11 *notwithstanding*)
The consequences of rejecting Truth are unavoidable, namely suffering.
12 But I say unto you, that it shall be more tolerable in that day for Sodom, than for that city.
13 Woe unto thee, Chorazin! woe unto thee, Bethsaida! for if the mighty works had been done in Tyre and Sidon, which have been done in you, they had a great while ago repented, sitting in sackcloth and ashes.
14 But it shall be more tolerable for Tyre and Sidon at the judgment, than for you.
15 And thou, Capernaum, which art exalted to heaven, shalt be thrust down to hell.
16 He that heareth you heareth me; and he that despiseth you despiseth me; and he that despiseth me despiseth him that sent me. (Luke 10:12-16)
The seventy returned rejoicing in their dominion over devils, evils (plural, meaning various false beliefs, or errors).
17 ¶ And the seventy returned again with joy, saying, Lord, even the devils are subject unto us through thy name. (Luke 10:17)
The success of these disciples showed that the false teaching of Phariseeism was being exposed and would in time be replaced by Truth.
18 And he said unto them, I beheld Satan as lightning fall from heaven. (Luke 10:18)
It was the Christ that Jesus taught, and that gave his followers, disciples or students, power over all claims of evil.
19 Behold, I give unto you power to tread on serpents and scorpions, and over all the power of the enemy: and nothing shall by any means hurt you. (Luke 10:19)
While dominion over evil is encouraging, realizing your present spiritual being in Christ is the real reason for rejoicing. To have your name written in heaven is to know that your true identity is spiritual, and therefore harmonious and eternal.
20 Notwithstanding in this rejoice not, that the spirits are subject unto you; but rather rejoice, because your names are written in heaven. (Luke 10:20)
Since the power of God is omnipotent, we should be grateful that only the spiritually minded can exercise divine power.
21 In that hour Jesus rejoiced in spirit, and said, I thank thee, O Father, Lord of heaven and earth, that thou hast hid these things from the wise and prudent, and hast revealed them unto babes: even so, Father; for so it seemed good in thy sight. (Luke 10:21)

The true nature of God and of man can only be discerned through spiritual sense.

22 All things are delivered to me of my Father: and no man knoweth who the Son is,
but the Father; and who the Father is, but the Son, and *he* to whom the Son will reveal
him. (Luke 10:22)

Truly these disciples were blessed to witness the things they saw and heard. And we are blessed they were recorded!

23 ¶ And he turned him unto *his* disciples, and said privately, Blessed *are* the eyes
which see the things that ye see:
24 For I tell you, that many prophets and kings have desired to see those things which
ye see, and have not seen *them*; and to hear those things which ye hear, and have not
heard *them*. (Luke 10:23-24)

CHAPTER 94
ETERNAL LIFE IS NOT FOR SALE

25 ¶ And, behold, a certain lawyer stood up, and tempted him, saying, Master, what
shall I do to inherit eternal life? (Luke 10:25)

Jesus referred the lawyer to Deuteronomy, chapter ten verse twelve, knowing he would likely have memorized it.

26 He said unto him, What is written in the law? how readest thou?
27 And he answering said, Thou shalt love the Lord thy God with all thy heart, and
with all thy soul, and with all thy strength, and with all thy mind; and thy neighbour as
thyself. (Luke 10:26-27)

In essence Jesus' reply was: "You have given the right answer, now you must put it into practice."

28 And he said unto him, Thou hast answered right: this do, and thou shalt live. (Luke
10:28)

Knowing that his cunning had been exposed the lawyer sought to justify himself.

29 But he, willing to justify himself, said unto Jesus, And who is my neighbour? (Luke
10:29)

Jesus replied with a parable involving a Samaritan, doubtless a rebuke to the lawyer's illusory *superiority* complex.

30 And Jesus answering said, A certain *man* went down from Jerusalem to Jericho, and
fell among thieves, which stripped him of his raiment, and wounded *him*, and departed,
leaving *him* half dead.
31 And by chance there came down a certain priest that way: and when he saw him, he
passed by on the other side.
32 And likewise a Levite, when he was at the place, came and looked *on him*, and
passed by on the other side.
33 But a certain Samaritan, as he journeyed, came where he was: and when he saw him,
he had compassion *on him*,
34 And went to *him*, and bound up his wounds, pouring in oil and wine, and set him on
his own beast, and brought him to an inn, and took care of him.
35 And on the morrow when he departed, he took out two pence, and gave *them* to the
host, and said unto him, Take care of him; and whatsoever thou spendest more, when I
come again, I will repay thee. (Luke 10:30-35)

There was only one answer the lawyer could give, and that answer would reinforce: "this ***do***, and thou shalt live."

36 Which now of these three, thinkest thou, was neighbour unto him that fell among the
thieves? (Luke 10:36)

Jesus approved the answer, and then having exposed the foolishness of self-justification, repeated the demand for proof.

37 And he said, He that shewed mercy on him. Then said Jesus unto him, Go, and do
thou likewise. (Luke 10:37)

CHAPTER 95
ARRIVAL IN THE REGION OF JUDÆA

According to the Gospel of Matthew

1 and came into the coasts of Judæa beyond Jordan;

2 And great multitudes followed him; and he healed them there. (Matt 19:1-2 2nd *and*)

According to the Gospel of Mark

1 And he arose from thence, and cometh into the coasts of Judæa by the farther side of
Jordan: and the people resort unto him again; and, as he was wont, he taught them
again. (Mark 10:1)

CHAPTER 96
THE ONE THING NEEDFUL

38 ¶ Now it came to pass, as they went, that he entered into a certain village: and a
certain woman named Martha received him into her house.
39 And she had a sister called Mary, which also sat at Jesus' feet, and heard his word.
40 But Martha was cumbered about much serving, and came to him, and said, Lord,
dost thou not care that my sister hath left me to serve alone? bid her therefore that she
help me.
41 And Jesus answered and said unto her, Martha, Martha, thou art careful and troubled
about many things:
42 But one thing is needful: and Mary hath chosen that good part, which shall not be
taken away from her. (Luke 10:38-42)

CHAPTER 97
JESUS AT THE FEAST OF TABERNACLES

(An eight-day celebration. Tishri 15-21 is equivalent to the Gentile end of September or early October)

Mortal opinion seldom gets it right because the Christ is unseen by the eyes and is incomprehensible to mortal mind.

11 Then the Jews sought him at the feast, and said, Where is he?
12 And there was much murmuring among the people concerning him: for some said,
He is a good man: others said, Nay; but he deceiveth the people. (John 7:11-12)

Many were aware of the execution being planned and knew it was wrong. It was cowardice that gave free reign to evil.

13 Howbeit no man spake openly of him for fear of the Jews. (John 7:13)

Midst of the feast = about the fourth day of the feast. Jesus didn't teach in the *temple*, but in the *temple grounds.* Only the priests were permitted to enter the temple.

14 ¶ Now about the midst of the feast Jesus went up into the temple, and taught. (John 7:14)

Jesus Declares Himself Openly to the People

The Jews (ecclesiastical & political elites) mocked Jesus for exposing their burdensome demands on the people.

15 And the Jews marvelled, saying, How knoweth this man letters, having never
learned? (John 7:15)

The Christ-teaching has a divine, not a human origin. There is no division or contradiction in that teaching!

16 Jesus answered them, and said, My doctrine is not mine, but his that sent me. (John 7:16)

Obedience to the will of God proves the Christ teaching to have a divine origin. The proof that Jesus provided was healing sin, disease, and death. When understood and practiced, his teaching will produce the same results today!

17 If any man will do his will, he shall know of the doctrine, whether it be of God, or
whether I speak of myself. (John 7:17)

The Jews interpreted the Scriptures to glorify themselves. Jesus' interpretation of scripture frees mankind to glorify God.

18 He that speaketh of himself seeketh his own glory: but he that seeketh his glory that
sent him, the same is true, and no unrighteousness is in him. (John 7:18)

Moses taught "Thou shalt not kill", and yet here they were, scheming to have him, an innocent man, executed.

19 Did not Moses give you the law, and *yet* none of you keepeth the law? Why go ye
about to kill me? (John 7:19)

The bystanders who were ignorant of what was being planned, thought Jesus crazy to think anyone wanted to kill him.

20 The people answered and said, Thou hast a devil: who goeth about to kill thee? (John 7:20)

The word marvel θαυμάζω, *thaumazō* means to wonder, to question. The people were told that Jesus profaned the sabbath day by healing on it. The *Gospel of Thomas* records Jesus as saying "If you do not observe the Sabbath as a Sabbath, you will not see the father." The meaning of the sabbath is given in Gen. 1:31- Gen. 2:3 where it is declared God saw everything finished, perfect, and to remain so forever. This is to see "the Sabbath as a Sabbath." This is what Jesus saw, and what made healing possible. Jesus honored the Sabbath as the ever-present and eternal reality of God, good.

21 Jesus answered and said unto them, I have done one work, and ye all marvel. (John 7:21)

"His disciples said to [Jesus], 'Is circumcision beneficial or not?' He said to them, "If it were beneficial, their father would beget them already circumcised from their mother. Rather, the true circumcision in spirit has become completely profitable." *The Coptic Gospel of Thomas.* Circumcision, a surgical operation, is a tradition that preceded Moses and the Commandments. It was performed by a priest on the eighth day of a young male child's life, be it a sabbath day or not.

22 Moses therefore gave unto you circumcision; (not because it is of Moses, but of the fathers;) and ye on the sabbath day circumcise a man. (John 7:22)

Question: Why was it considered okay to surgically remove a child's foreskin on the sabbath but not okay to heal that same child as an adult on the sabbath? Answer: Only man-made tradition and erroneous human belief.

23 If a man on the sabbath day receive circumcision, that the law of Moses should not be broken; are ye angry at me, because I have made a man every whit whole on the sabbath day?

24 Judge not according to the appearance, but judge righteous judgment. (John 7:23-24)

From this we know that the plot to kill Jesus had been leaked, and so some were already aware of it.

25 Then said some of them of Jerusalem, Is not this he, whom they seek to kill? (John 7:25)

Some saw the courage Jesus displayed in face of the plot to kill him as testifying to his being Christ.

26 But, lo, he speaketh boldly, and they say nothing unto him. Do the rulers know indeed that this is the very Christ? (John 7:26)

No matter in what form the Christ appears, mortal man will always criticize the manner of its appearing.

27 Howbeit we know this man whence he is: but when Christ cometh, no man knoweth whence he is. (John 7:27)

Because mortal man does not know the true nature of God, he cannot recognize the Christ, God's reflection or image and likeness.

28 Then cried Jesus in the temple as he taught, saying, Ye both know me, and ye know whence I am: and I am not come of myself, but he that sent me is true, whom ye know not.

29 But I know him: for I am from him, and he hath sent me. (John 7:28-29)

God governs ALL regardless of what mortal mind believes.

30 Then they sought to take him: but no man laid hands on him, because his hour was not yet come. (John 7:30)

It was healing that caused many who were sitting on the fence to realize that Jesus was indeed the Messiah.

31 And many of the people believed on him, and said, When Christ cometh, will he do more miracles than these which this *man* hath done? (John 7:31)

The Pharisees and chief priests then sent temple guards to arrest Jesus

Elites always seek to manipulate the masses, and often resort to misinformation and violence to accomplish their end.

32 ¶ The Pharisees heard that the people murmured such things concerning him; and the Pharisees and the chief priests sent officers to take him. (John 7:32)

Jesus, in foretelling his crucifixion, intimates that it will culminate in his disappearance in the ascension.

33 Then said Jesus unto them, Yet a little while am I with you, and *then* I go unto him that sent me.

34 Ye shall seek me, and shall not find *me*: and where I am, *thither* ye cannot come. (John 7:33-34)

Mortal man, reasoning on the basis of matter, never grasps the spiritual meaning.

35 Then said the Jews among themselves, Whither will he go, that we shall not find him? will he go unto the dispersed among the Gentiles, and teach the Gentiles?

36 What *manner of* saying is this that he said, Ye shall seek me, and shall not find *me*: and where I am, *thither* ye cannot come? (John 7:35-36)

Jesus addressed the people again on the eighth day of the Feast of Tabernacles
(See Lev. 23:34-36)

A prophecy foretelling the outpouring of the Spirit of God, or Holy Ghost, on the Day of Pentecost. See Acts 2:1-41.
37 In the last day, that great *day* of the feast, Jesus stood and cried, saying, If any man
thirst, let him come unto me, and drink.
38 He that believeth on me, as the scripture hath said, out of his belly shall flow rivers
of living water.
39 (But this spake he of the Spirit, which they that believe on him should receive: for
the Holy Ghost was not yet *given*; because that Jesus was not yet glorified.) (John 7:37-39)
Many saw in Jesus the fulfilling of Moses' prophecy. Deut. 15:15. Later by Peter – Acts 3:22 and Stephen Acts7:37
40 ¶ Many of the people therefore, when they heard this saying, said, Of a truth this is
the Prophet.
41 Others said, This is the Christ. But some said, Shall Christ come out of Galilee?
(John 7:40-41)
Reasoning based on ignorance is foolishness. Jesus *was* born in Bethlehem, fled to Egypt, and grew up in Nazareth.
42 Hath not the scripture said, That Christ cometh of the seed of David, and out of the
town of Bethlehem, where David was?
43 So there was a division among the people because of him.
44 And some of them would have taken him; but no man laid hands on him. (John 7:42-44)

The reaction of the chief priests and Pharisees to Jesus escaping arrested

45 ¶ Then came the officers to the chief priests and Pharisees; and they said unto them,
Why have ye not brought him?
46 The officers answered, Never man spake like this man.
47 Then answered them the Pharisees, Are ye also deceived?
48 Have any of the rulers or of the Pharisees believed on him?
49 But this people who knoweth not the law are cursed. (John 7:45-49)

Nicodemus defends Jesus. Obviously Nicodemus felt the presence of Christ at their late night meeting. Jn. 3:1-2

50 Nicodemus saith unto them, (he that came to Jesus by night, being one of them,)
51 Doth our law judge *any* man, before it hear him, and know what he doeth?
52 They answered and said unto him, Art thou also of Galilee? Search, and look: for
out of Galilee ariseth no prophet. (John 7:50-52)
While "every man" was free to go to his own house, Jesus was forced to "camp out" to escape arrest.
53 And every man went unto his own house.
1 Jesus went unto the mount of Olives. (John 7:53; 8:1)

CHAPTER 98
A CRUEL AND HEARTLESS PLAN TO ENTRAP JESUS
(Another attempt to entrap Jesus by victimizing a "woman taken in adultery.")

2 And early in the morning he came again into the temple, and all the people came unto
him; and he sat down, and taught them.
3 And the scribes and Pharisees brought unto him a woman taken in adultery; and when
they had set her in the midst,
4 They say unto him, Master, this woman was taken in adultery, in the very act.
5 Now Moses in the law commanded us, that such should be stoned: but what sayest
thou?
6 This they said, tempting him, that they might have to accuse him. But Jesus stooped
down, and with *his* finger wrote on the ground, *as though he heard them not.*
7 So when they continued asking him, he lifted up himself, and said unto them, He that

is without sin among you, let him first cast a stone at her.
8 And again he stooped down, and wrote on the ground.
9 And they which heard *it*, being convicted by *their own* conscience, went out one by
one, beginning at the eldest, *even* unto the last: and Jesus was left alone, and the woman
standing in the midst.
10 When Jesus had lifted up himself, and saw none but the woman, he said unto her,
Woman, where are those thine accusers? hath no man condemned thee?

Jesus required genuine repentance, "go and sin no more," as the condition for forgiveness. See Luke 17:3 & John 5:14.

11 She said, No man, Lord. And Jesus said unto her, Neither do I condemn thee: go,
and sin no more. (John 8:2-11)

CHAPTER 99
THE LIGHT OF THE WORLD

12 ¶ Then spake Jesus again unto them, saying, I am the light of the world: he that
followeth me shall not walk in darkness, but shall have the light of life.
13 The Pharisees therefore said unto him, Thou bearest record of thyself; thy record is
not true.
14 Jesus answered and said unto them, Though I bear record of myself, *yet* my record is
true; for I know whence I came, and whither I go; but ye cannot tell whence I come,
and whither I go.
15 Ye judge after the flesh; I judge no man.
16 And yet if I judge, my judgment is true: for I am not alone, but I and the Father that
sent me.
17 It is also written in your law, that the testimony of two men is true.
18 I am one that bear witness of myself, and the Father that sent me beareth witness of
me.
19 Then said they unto him, Where is thy Father? Jesus answered, Ye neither know
me, nor my Father: if ye had known me, ye should have known my Father also. (John 8:12-19)

Jesus knew, "My times *are* in Thy hand" and that God would "deliver [him] from the hand of [his] enemies." Ps. 31:15

20 These words spake Jesus in the treasury, as he taught in the temple: and no man laid
hands on him; for his hour was not yet come.
21 Then said Jesus again unto them, I go my way, and ye shall seek me, and shall die in
your sins: whither I go, ye cannot come. (John 8:20-21)

The darkness of material belief displayed by the Pharisees.

22 Then said the Jews, Will he kill himself? because he saith, Whither I go, ye cannot
come. (John 8:22)

"He that is of the earth is earthly, and speaketh of the earth: he that cometh from heaven is above all" – John the Baptist (John 3:31). To Jesus, his and everyone's true being was Christ. That is why he said we are to "call no *man* [our] father upon the earth: for One is [our] Father, which is in heaven." Matt. 23:9.

23 And he said unto them, Ye are from beneath; I am from above: ye are of this world;
I am not of this world. (John 8:23)

Having given up a personal sense of ego Jesus was declaring his "**I**" to be the "I AM THAT I AM." Exodus 3:14.

24 I said therefore unto you, that ye shall die in your sins: for if ye believe not that I am
he, ye shall die in your sins. (John 8:24)

Jesus said at the *beginning* of this discourse when referring to the Christ: "I am the light of the world." Therefore, it is the I AM, divine Mind, or Spirit that is the light of the world.

25 Then said they unto him, Who art thou? And Jesus saith unto them, Even *the same*
that I said unto you from the beginning. (John 8:25)

The Father of Jesus, being God, is not only true, but is Truth!

26 I have many things to say and to judge of you: but he that sent me is true; and I

speak to the world those things which I have heard of him.
27 They understood not that he spake to them of the Father. (John 8:26-27)
Jesus knew that his resurrection and ascension, following the crucifixion, would validate all that he taught. Note that the word "he" is in italics because it is a later addition by the revisers. Jesus was speaking as Christ, hence he said "ye (all of you) know that I am."
28 Then said Jesus unto them, When ye have lifted up the Son of man, then shall ye know that I am *he*, and *that* I do nothing of myself; but as my Father hath taught me, I speak these things. (John 8:28)
A declaration of the eternal unity of Principle and idea. Obedience, doing the will of God, is the essence of oneness.
29 And he that sent me is with me: the Father hath not left me alone; for I do always those things that please him.
30 As he spake these words, many believed on him. (John 8:29-30)

CHAPTER 100
JESUS CONFUTES THE HOSTILE DISCIPLES AT JERUSALEM

Demonstration is required to be a true disciple

31 Then said Jesus to those Jews which believed on him, If ye continue in my word, *then* are ye my disciples indeed;
32 And ye shall know the truth, and the truth shall make you free. (John 8:31-32)
John the Baptist earlier warned against believing in ancestral or genealogical superiority. See Matt. 3:9 & Luke 3:8.
33 ¶ They answered him, We be Abraham's seed, and were never in bondage to any man: how sayest thou, Ye shall be made free? (John 8:33)
Mortal man, regardless of human ancestry, is in bondage because sin enslaves and would make man mortal.
34 Jesus answered them, Verily, verily, I say unto you, Whosoever committeth sin is the servant of sin.
35 And the servant abideth not in the house for ever: *but* the Son abideth ever. (John 8:34-35)
Only Christ, the understanding of man's origin and relation to God made practical, can free from sin and mortality.
36 If the Son therefore shall make you free, ye shall be free indeed. (John 8:36)
Jesus knew that some of his disciples in Jerusalem were involved in the plot to kill him.
37 I know that ye are Abraham's seed; but ye seek to kill me, because my word hath no place in you. (John 8:37)
"That which is born of the flesh is flesh; and that which is born of the Spirit is spirit[ual]" hence "Ye must be born again."
38 I speak that which I have seen with my Father: and ye do that which ye have seen with your father. (John 8:38)
Question. Where does God fit into any of the arguments used by these unfaithful disciples? Answer. Nowhere!
39 They answered and said unto him, Abraham is our father. (John 8:39 *to* 1st.)
Thoughts and actions, not genetic lineage testify to one's real origin and character.
39 Jesus saith unto them, If ye were Abraham's children, ye would do the works of Abraham.
40 But now ye seek to kill me, a man that hath told you the truth, which I have heard of God: this did not Abraham. (John 8:39-40 *Jesus*)
Plotting to kill Jesus is impossible for a child of God. Calling God their father was a subterfuge.
41 Ye do the deeds of your father. Then said they to him, We be not born of fornication; we have one Father, *even* God. (John 8:41)
Their intentions originated in evil, not God, good. On the contrary, the actions of Jesus testified to a divine origin.
42 Jesus said unto them, If God were your Father, ye would love me: for I proceeded forth and came from God; neither came I of myself, but he sent me. (John 8:42)
When focused on doing evil it is not possible to hear the voice of Truth.
43 Why do ye not understand my speech? *even* because ye cannot hear my word. (John 8:43)

The devil, evil, is a self-constituted liar whose offspring is a lie. The lie and liar are one, and is all there is to the "devil."

44 Ye are of *your* father the devil, and the lusts of your father ye will do. He was a murderer from the beginning, and abode not in the truth, because there is no truth in him. When he speaketh a lie, he speaketh of his own: for he is a liar, and the father of it. (John 8:44)

A liar can neither accept the truth, believe the truth, nor testify to Truth.

45 And because I tell *you* the truth, ye believe me not. (John 8:45)

Their refusal to accept his witness exposed the origin of their malice, whereas they had no evidence to convict him of sin.

46 Which of you convinceth me of sin? And if I say the truth, why do ye not believe me? (John 8:46)

They could not accept his witness because their thoughts, being carnal, rejected Truth.

47 He that is of God heareth God's words: ye therefore hear *them* not, because ye are not of God. (John 8:47)

Having lost that argument, they next said that being from Nazareth he must be Samaritan and therefore demonic.

48 Then answered the Jews, and said unto him, Say we not well that thou art a Samaritan, and hast a devil? (John 8:48)

There is nothing demonic about doing the will of God, but it is evil to slander any one that honors God.

49 Jesus answered, I have not a devil; but I honour my Father, and ye do dishonour me.

50 And I seek not mine own glory: there is one that seeketh and judgeth. (John 8:49-50)

Jesus proved his next statement true when he raised Lazarus, and then again shortly after that, in his own resurrection.

51 Verily, verily, I say unto you, If a man keep my saying, he shall never see death. (John 8:51)

These materially minded, disloyal students next replied with arguments based solely on physical sense testimony.

52 Then said the Jews unto him, Now we know that thou hast a devil. Abraham is dead, and the prophets; and thou sayest, If a man keep my saying, he shall never taste of death.

53 Art thou greater than our father Abraham, which is dead? and the prophets are dead: whom makest thou thyself?

54 Jesus answered, If I honour myself, my honour is nothing: it is my Father that honoureth me; of whom ye say, that he is your God:

55 Yet ye have not known him; but I know him: and if I should say, I know him not, I shall be a liar like unto you: but I know him, and keep his saying. (John 8:52-55)

Jesus then declared his pre-existence in Christ "before the world began." See II Tim 1:9. "Before Abraham was, I am." Here we are told that divine Mind, the great I AM is eternal Life and Truth and Love.

56 Your father Abraham rejoiced to see my day: and he saw *it*, and was glad. (John 8:56)

Reasoning based on sense testimony is incapable of comprehending spiritual truth.

57 Then said the Jews unto him, Thou art not yet fifty years old, and hast thou seen Abraham? (John 8:57)

Jesus declares his Christ-being. It is Christ that honors God by making the "I AM THAT I AM" known. Ex. 3:14

58 Jesus said unto them, Verily, verily, I say unto you, Before Abraham was, I am. (John 8:58)

The hatred of Truth displayed by the "Jews" was over-ruled by the protection of divine Love that sustained Jesus.

59 Then took they up stones to cast at him: but Jesus hid himself, and went out of the temple, going through the midst of them, and so passed by. (John 8:59)

CHAPTER 101
HEALING A MAN BORN BLIND

1 And as *Jesus* passed by, he saw a man which was blind from *his* birth.

2 And his disciples asked him, saying, Master, who did sin, this man, or his parents, that he was born blind? (John 9:1-2)

The disciples saw a condemned mortal. Jesus saw the opportunity to reveal the truth that God created man perfect.

3 Jesus answered, Neither hath this man sinned, nor his parents: but that the works of

God should be made manifest in him.
4 I must work the works of him that sent me, while it is day: the night cometh, when no man can work.
5 As long as I am in the world, I am the light of the world. (John 9:3-5)

Jesus spat on the ground, not on the man, displaying contempt for the belief that man is a mortal, created materially.

6 When he had thus spoken, he spat on the ground, and made clay of the spittle, and he anointed the eyes of the blind man with the clay, (John 9:6)

Washing away the clay symbolized eradicating the belief that man was, is, or ever will be material. *(See Genesis 2:6-7).*

7 And said unto him, Go, wash in the pool of Siloam, (which is by interpretation, Sent.) (John 9:7 to 1st.)

The man's obedience demonstrated his receptivity, and opened the way for his sight to be restored.

7 He went his way therefore, and washed, and came seeing. (John 9:7 *He*)

The carnal mind thinks healing by Spirit is impossible, causing the testimony of anyone healed spiritually to be ridiculed.

8 ¶ The neighbours therefore, and they which before had seen him that he was blind, said, Is not this he that sat and begged?
9 Some said, This is he: others *said*, He is like him: *but* he said, I am *he*.
10 Therefore said they unto him, How were thine eyes opened? (John 9:8-10)

Telling what Jesus said and the man did, does not explain HOW the healing was accomplished.

11 He answered and said, A man that is called Jesus made clay, and anointed mine eyes, and said unto me, Go to the pool of Siloam, and wash: and I went and washed, and I received sight.
12 Then said they unto him, Where is he? He said, I know not.
13 ¶ They brought to the Pharisees him that aforetime was blind.
14 And it was the sabbath day when Jesus made the clay, and opened his eyes.
15 Then again the Pharisees also asked him how he had received his sight. He said unto them, He put clay upon mine eyes, and I washed, and do see. (John 9:11-15)

Tradition, social pressure, and beliefs tenaciously held to prevent the Christ, Truth from operating in human experience.

16 Therefore said some of the Pharisees, This man is not of God, because he keepeth not the sabbath day. Others said, How can a man that is a sinner do such miracles? And there was a division among them.
17 They say unto the blind man again, What sayest thou of him, that he hath opened thine eyes? He said, He is a prophet. (John 9:16-17)

The parents knew their son was telling the truth, but they were terrified at the prospect of being excommunicated.

18 But the Jews did not believe concerning him, that he had been blind, and received his sight, until they called the parents of him that had received his sight.
19 And they asked them, saying, Is this your son, who ye say was born blind? how then doth he now see?
20 His parents answered them and said, We know that this is our son, and that he was born blind:
21 But by what means he now seeth, we know not; or who hath opened his eyes, we know not: he is of age; ask him: he shall speak for himself. (John 9:18-21)

This parenthetical remark explains how the ecclesiastics dominated the people through fear.

22 These *words* spake his parents, because they feared the Jews: for the Jews had agreed already, that if any man did confess that he was Christ, he should be put out of the synagogue.
23 Therefore said his parents, He is of age; ask him.
24 Then again called they the man that was blind, and said unto him, Give God the praise: we know that this man is a sinner. (John 9:22-24)

There is nothing more powerful than the facts! This man's honesty and conviction threatened the questioner's authority.

25 He answered and said, Whether he be a sinner *or no*, I know not: one thing I know,

that, whereas I was blind, now I see.
26 Then said they to him again, What did he to thee? how opened he thine eyes? (John
9:25-26)
Simple honesty unmasks callous hypocrisy.
27 He answered them, I have told you already, and ye did not hear: wherefore would ye
hear *it* again? will ye also be his disciples? (John 9:27)
Self-righteous indignation. How could they KNOW that God spake only to Moses and not to Jesus? A belief! The fact is that in their state of self-righteousness, self-importance and self-will, THEY could NOT hear the voice of God.
28 Then they reviled him, and said, Thou art his disciple; but we are Moses' disciples.
29 We know that God spake unto Moses: *as for* this *fellow*, we know not from whence
he is. (John 9:28-29)
Marvellous, θαυμαστός *thaumastos*, beyond belief, inconceivable. The man healed thought it inconceivable that these men could not to see that God had sent Jesus. Three years earlier Nicodemus told Jesus that the Pharisees *knew* he was "a teacher come from God." Jn. 3:2. What had changed when even more proof had been provided? ENVY!
30 The man answered and said unto them, Why herein is a marvellous thing, that ye
know not from whence he is, and *yet* he hath opened mine eyes.
31 Now we know that God heareth not sinners: but if any man be a worshipper of God,
and doeth his will, him he heareth.
32 Since the world began was it not heard that any man opened the eyes of one that was
born blind.
33 If this man were not of God, he could do nothing. (John 9:30-33)
The man was ex-communicated for speaking the truth. Error can only operate by hiding the truth. The good news is that error cannot destroy Truth, but Truth does annihilate error. Since they could not argue against the Truth and win, they commenced to attack person!
34 They answered and said unto him, Thou wast altogether born in sins, and dost thou
teach us? And they cast him out.
35 Jesus heard that they had cast him out; and when he had found him, he said unto
him, Dost thou believe on the Son of God?
36 He answered and said, Who is he, Lord, that I might believe on him?
37 And Jesus said unto him, Thou hast both seen him, and it is he that talketh with thee.
(John 9:34-37)
Gratitude is expressed for blessings received. *worshipped, προσκυνέω proskyneō,* prostration in respect or gratitude.
38 And he said, Lord, I believe. And he worshipped him. (John 9:38)
Jesus came so we could "judge" between what is true and what is false, so that the Christ, Truth we were blind to would be seen, and the error we believed was true would no longer be seen as true. In short, when a lie is once seen to be a lie, it no longer has any power over us.
39 ¶ And Jesus said, For judgment I am come into this world, that they which see not
might see; and that they which see might be made blind. (John 9:39)
Self-righteousness is a self-imposed blindness that causes a person to cling to error.
40 And *some* of the Pharisees which were with him heard these words, and said unto
him, Are we blind also? (John 9:40)
The Pharisees were condemning themselves because they knew what was right and they willfully chose to do evil.
41 Jesus said unto them, If ye were blind, ye should have no sin: but now ye say, We
see; therefore your sin remaineth. (John 9:41)
A parable exposing the unfaithful stewardship of the Pharisees, in this case for ex-communicating a man for being honest.
1 Verily, verily, I say unto you, He that entereth not by the door into the sheepfold, but
climbeth up some other way, the same is a thief and a robber.
2 But he that entereth in by the door is the shepherd of the sheep.
3 To him the porter openeth; and the sheep hear his voice: and he calleth his own sheep
by name, and leadeth them out.
4 And when he putteth forth his own sheep, he goeth before them, and the sheep follow
him: for they know his voice.

5 And a stranger will they not follow, but will flee from him: for they know not the
voice of strangers.
6 This parable spake Jesus unto them: but they understood not what things they were
which he spake unto them.
7 Then said Jesus unto them again, Verily, verily, I say unto you, I am the door of the
sheep.
8 All that ever came before me are thieves and robbers: but the sheep did not hear
them.
9 I am the door: by me if any man enter in, he shall be saved, and shall go in and out,
and find pasture.
10 The thief cometh not, but for to steal, and to kill, and to destroy: I am come that they
might have life, and that they might have *it* more abundantly.
11 I am the good shepherd: the good shepherd giveth his life for the sheep.
12 But he that is an hireling, and not the shepherd, whose own the sheep are not, seeth
the wolf coming, and leaveth the sheep, and fleeth: and the wolf catcheth them, and
scattereth the sheep.
13 The hireling fleeth, because he is an hireling, and careth not for the sheep.
14 I am the good shepherd, and know my *sheep*, and am known of mine.
15 As the Father knoweth me, even so know I the Father: and I lay down my life for the
sheep. (John 10:1-15)

Universal salvation is through Christ. He came to his own first. Their rejection of Christ can't keep it from the receptive.

16 And other sheep I have, which are not of this fold: them also I must bring, and they
shall hear my voice; and there shall be one fold, *and* one shepherd. (John 10:16)

To follow Jesus is to give up the temporal for the eternal. This is the will of "Our Father which [is] in heaven." Mat. 6:9.

17 Therefore doth my Father love me, because I lay down my life, that I might take it
again. (John 10:17)

Jesus could have withdrawn himself from his enemies. He had power to lay down a human sense of life for his spiritual identity in the likeness of the divine; but he allowed men to attempt the destruction of the mortal body in order that he might furnish the proof of immortal life. - MBE. This is what Jesus meant by power "from on high." Lk. 24:49.

18 No man taketh it from me, but I lay it down of myself. I have power to lay it down,
and I have power to take it again. This commandment have I received of my Father.
(John 10:18)

How are false statements to be separated from true statements? Moses gave instruction on how to know if what a prophet spoke was actually "the word which the LORD hath spoken." See Deut. 18:21 & 22.

19 ¶ There was a division therefore again among the Jews for these sayings.
20 And many of them said, He hath a devil, and is mad; why hear ye him?
21 Others said, These are not the words of him that hath a devil. Can a devil open the
eyes of the blind? (John 10:19-21)

CHAPTER 102
MORE INSTRUCTION ON PRAYER

1 And it came to pass, that, as he was praying in a certain place, when he ceased, one
of his disciples said unto him, Lord, teach us to pray, as John also taught his disciples.
(Luke 11:1)

The objective: Lay aside human will so that the harmony of the divine will may prevail "on earth as it [does] in heaven.'

2 And he said unto them, When ye pray, say, Our Father which art in heaven, Hallowed
be thy name. Thy kingdom come. Thy will be done, as in heaven, so in earth.
3 Give us day by day our daily bread.
4 And forgive us our sins; for we also forgive every one that is indebted to us. And
lead us not into temptation; but deliver us from evil. (Luke 11:2-4)

A key ingredient for success in prayer: an unremitting expectancy of good.
5 And he said unto them, Which of you shall have a friend, and shall go unto him at
midnight, and say unto him, Friend, lend me three loaves;
6 For a friend of mine in his journey is come to me, and I have nothing to set before
him?
7 And he from within shall answer and say, Trouble me not: the door is now shut, and
my children are with me in bed; I cannot rise and give thee.
8 I say unto you, Though he will not rise and give him, because he is his friend, yet
because of his importunity he will rise and give him as many as he needeth.
9 And I say unto you, Ask, and it shall be given you; seek, and ye shall find; knock,
and it shall be opened unto you.
10 For every one that asketh receiveth; and he that seeketh findeth; and to him that
knocketh it shall be opened. (Luke 11:5-10)

Trust God to provide whatever us needed, and know that it will be good, even better than anything you could outline.
11 If a son shall ask bread of any of you that is a father, will he give him a stone? or if
he ask a fish, will he for a fish give him a serpent?
12 Or if he shall ask an egg, will he offer him a scorpion?
13 If ye then, being evil, know how to give good gifts unto your children: how much
more shall *your* heavenly Father give the Holy Spirit to them that ask him? (Luke 11:11-13)

CHAPTER 103
CHRIST-HEALING OPPOSED TO DEMONOLOGY

A demon (false belief) is cast out and the dumb speaks

14 ¶ And he was casting out a devil, and it was dumb. And it came to pass, when the
devil was gone out, the dumb spake; and the people wondered. (Luke 11:14)

Jesus is again accused of using demonology

Accusations of demonology. Beelzebub,. Βεελζεβούλ Beelzeboul. Heb. בַּעַל זְבוּב Ba`al Zĕbuwb*; Gr. Baal-zebub, "Lord of the flies," a Philistine deity at Ekron. Later changed to Beel-zebub, Lord of the dunghill, also "prince of idols or idolatry."*

Question. If what follows was said of Jesus, what will be said of his followers?
15 But some of them said, He casteth out devils through Beelzebub the chief of the
devils.
16 And others, tempting *him*, sought of him a sign from heaven. (Luke 11:15-16)

The self-destructive nature of erroneous methods exposed

17 But he, knowing their thoughts, said unto them, Every kingdom divided against
itself is brought to desolation; and a house *divided* against a house falleth.
18 If Satan also be divided against himself, how shall his kingdom stand? because ye
say that I cast out devils through Beelzebub. (Luke 11:17-18)

What students practice is sometimes a window through which can be seen what they have learned from their teacher.
19 And if I by Beelzebub cast out devils, by whom do your sons cast *them* out?
therefore shall they be your judges. (Luke 11:19)

Jesus healed with the "finger of God," the divine Spirit or Holy Ghost. The carnal mind uses matter and human will.
20 But if I with the finger of God cast out devils, no doubt the kingdom of God is come
upon you. (Luke 11:20)

Either the fear or the practice of erroneous methods leaves evil in control.
21 When a strong man armed keepeth his palace, his goods are in peace: (Luke 11:21)

The carnal mind, when bound by omnipotent Mind, is rendered powerless.
22 But when a stronger than he shall come upon him, and overcome him, he taketh
from him all his armour wherein he trusted, and divideth his spoils. (Luke 11:22)

Spirit and matter can no more mix than can Truth and error, good and evil, or light and darkness.

23 He that is not with me is against me: and he that gathereth not with me scattereth. (Luke 11:23)

To guard against relapse, error must be reduced to its common denominator – NOTHING real or actual. Just error!

24 When the unclean spirit is gone out of a man, he walketh through dry places, seeking rest; and finding none, he saith, I will return unto my house whence I came out.
25 And when he cometh, he findeth *it* swept and garnished.
26 Then goeth he, and taketh *to him* seven other spirits more wicked than himself; and they enter in, and dwell there: and the last *state* of that man is worse than the first. (Luke 11:24-26)

Blessings come from being faithful, fidelity to Truth, by putting Truth into practice

27 ¶ And it came to pass, as he spake these things, a certain woman of the company lifted up her voice, and said unto him, Blessed *is* the womb that bare thee, and the paps which thou hast sucked.
28 But he said, Yea rather, blessed *are* they that hear the word of God, and keep it. (Luke 11:27-28)

CHAPTER 104
QUESTIONS CONCERNING DIVORCE AND CELIBACY

1st Question: Does the law provide for a man to divorce his wife?

Man means husband, *ἀνήρ anēr*. put away, *ἀπολύω apolyō*, used of divorce means to bid depart, to send away.

2 ¶ And the Pharisees came to him, and asked him, Is it lawful for a man to put away *his* wife? tempting him. (Mark 10:2)

A fundamental question: Is Law based on Principle or is it merely a device at the disposal of the powerful to camouflage injustice? Notice, Jesus asked: "What did Moses command", and they answered what Moses *permitted*, or *allowed.*

3 And he answered and said unto them, What did Moses command you? (Mark 10:3)

Moses (not the Law!) suffered, ἐπιτρέπω *epitrepō*, gave license *permitting* a man to divorce his wife.

4 And they said, Moses suffered to write a bill of divorcement, and to put *her* away. (Mark 10:4)

Moses wrote a precept, *ἐντολ entolē,* a magistrates order or edict, that allowed for divorce under duress.

5 And Jesus answered and said unto them, For the hardness of your heart he wrote you this precept. (Mark 10:5)

Jesus declared law to be divine: "male and female created He them." Gen. 1:27. Human law should pattern the divine!

6 But from the beginning of the creation God made them male and female. (Mark 10:6)

The word man is *ἄνθρωπος anthrōpos*, a human being. The compulsion to marry is to find completeness in oneness.

7 For this cause shall a man leave his father and mother, and cleave to his wife;
8 And they twain shall be one flesh: so then they are no more twain, but one flesh. (Mark 10:7-8)

The mandates of mortal man should not override the Law of God. True completeness is in spiritual oneness.

9 What therefore God hath joined together, let not man put asunder. (Mark 10:9)

Additional private instruction with the disciples

10 And in the house his disciples asked him again of the same *matter*.
11 And he saith unto them, Whosoever shall put away his wife, and marry another, committeth adultery against her.
12 And if a woman shall put away her husband, and be married to another, she committeth adultery. (Mark 10:10-12)

2nd Question: Can a man divorce his wife for any reason he chooses?

Jesus declared plainly in verse 9 below that the answer is NO! Marriage or divorce is not a whimsical matter. every = any.

3 ¶ The Pharisees also came unto him, tempting him, and saying unto him, Is it lawful for a man to put away his wife for every cause? (Matt 19:3)

Jesus referred the Pharisees to Genesis 1:26-28 that reads: "male and female" not "males and females."

4 And he answered and said unto them, Have ye not read, that he which made *them* at
the beginning made them male and female,
5 And said, For this cause shall a man leave father and mother, and shall cleave to his
wife: and they twain shall be one flesh? (Matt 19:4-5)

Jesus is attempting to get the Pharisees to look above the human sense of marriage to see its spiritual significance.

6 Wherefore they are no more twain, but one flesh. What therefore God hath joined
together, let not man put asunder. (Matt 19:6)

The Pharisees then ask: Why then did Moses make provision for divorce?

7 They say unto him, Why did Moses then command to give a writing of divorcement,
and to put her away? (Matt 19:7)

Jesus answered that Moses provided for it due to political expediency. (After 40 years in the wilderness Deut. 24:1-4).

8 He saith unto them, Moses because of the hardness of your hearts suffered you to put
away your wives: but from the beginning it was not so. (Matt 19:8)

In response to "every cause" Jesus replied that there is only one reason that justifies a man to divorce his wife.

9 And I say unto you, Whosoever shall put away his wife, except *it be* for fornication,
and shall marry another, committeth adultery: and whoso marrieth her which is put
away doth commit adultery. (Matt 19:9)

What about of celibacy

10 ¶ His disciples say unto him, If the case of the man be so with *his* wife, it is not good
to marry. (Matt 19:10)

Jesus replied that a life of celibacy is only for those who are spiritually mature.

11 But he said unto them, All *men* cannot receive this saying, save *they* to whom it is
given. (Matt 19:11)

The three kinds of eunuchs

(It would appear that this discussion arose because being a eunuch implies a celibate life,)

(1) eunuchs, *εὐνοῦχος eunouchos*, emasculated from birth, from *ἐκ ek*, meaning from out of [the womb].

12 For there are some eunuchs, which were so born from *their* mother's womb: (Matt 19:12 to 1st :)

(2) euncuhs, *εὐνουχίζω eunouchizō,* should read "were made eunuchs ***by*** men, surgically.

12 and there are some eunuchs, which were made eunuchs of men, (Matt 19:12 1st *and* to 2nd:)

(3) euncuhs, *εὐνουχίζω eunouchizō*, self-imposed through abstinence.

12 and there be eunuchs, which have made themselves eunuchs for the kingdom of
heaven's sake. (Matt 19:12 2nd *and* to 1st.)

The third is an individual choice that must come from the heart, not surgically or otherwise. See I Cor. 7:1-11.

12 He that is able to receive *it*, let him receive *it*. (Matt 19:12 *He*)

CHAPTER 105
THE "EVIL GENERATION" CONFRONTED

Evil generation, *πονηρός ponēros, of a bad nature, morally blind.* The Pharisees plotting to kill him exemplified this evil.

29 ¶ And when the people were gathered thick together, he began to say, This is an evil
generation: they seek a sign; and there shall no sign be given it, but the sign of Jonas
the prophet. (Luke 11:29)

Jesus again foretells his resurrection

30 For as Jonas was a sign unto the Ninevites, so shall also the Son of man be to this
generation. (Luke 11:30)

The Queen of Sheba and the sinful men of Nineveh were more receptive to Truth than was that "evil generation."

31 The queen of the south shall rise up in the judgment with the men of this generation,
and condemn them: for she came from the utmost parts of the earth to hear the wisdom
of Solomon; and, behold, a greater than Solomon *is* here.

32 The men of Nineve shall rise up in the judgment with this generation, and shall condemn it: for they repented at the preaching of Jonas; and, behold, a greater than Jonas *is* here. (Luke 11:31-32)

The "evil generation" is called out for secretly plotting to kill him. Verse 35 warns them to cease their plotting

A right life has nothing to hide! Candlestick = lampstand symbolizing living the truth. Light, *φέγγος pheggos*, the truth.

33 No man, when he hath lighted a candle, putteth *it* in a secret place, neither under a bushel, but on a candlestick, that they which come in may see the light. (Luke 11:33)

1st light (source of), *λύχνος lychnos*. Body, the person, you. Eye, Mind. 2nd light (illumination of), *φωτεινός phōteinos*.

34 The light of the body is the eye: therefore when thine eye is single, thy whole body also is full of light; but when *thine eye* is evil, thy body also *is* full of darkness. (Luke 11:34)

Light, *φῶς phōs*, the same word for light used by John: "God is light." I Jn. 1:5. It is the light of Christ Jn. 1:4, 5, 7, 8 & 9.

35 Take heed therefore that the light which is in thee be not darkness. (Luke 11:35)

A statement on the power of a consciousness illumined by divine Mind to shed healing and comfort upon the receptive.

36 If thy whole body therefore *be* full of light, having no part dark, the whole shall be full of light, as when the bright shining of a candle doth give thee light. (Luke 11:36)

CHAPTER 106
AN UNPLEASANT DINNER IN THE HOME OF A PHARISEE

Preoccupation with outer appearances rebuked

Pharisee, *Φαρισαῖος Pharisaios*. Bitter enemies of Jesus and his cause are severely rebuked by him for their avarice, ambition, hollow reliance on outward works, and affectation of piety in order to gain notoriety. See *Strong's Concordance*

37 ¶ And as he spake, a certain Pharisee besought him to dine with him: and he went in, and sat down to meat.

38 And when the Pharisee saw *it*, he marvelled that he had not first washed before dinner. (Luke 11:37-38)

The Pharisee's *unspoken* criticism is confronted by Jesus. Ravening, *ἁρπαγή harpagē*, plundering, robbery, extortion.

39 And the Lord said unto him, Now do ye Pharisees make clean the outside of the cup and the platter; but your inward part is full of ravening and wickedness. (Luke 11:39)

"Jesus said, 'Why do you wash the outside of the cup? Do you not realize that he who made the inside is the same one who made the outside?'" *The Coptic Gospel of Thomas*

40 *Ye* fools, did not he that made that which is without make that which is within also?

41 But rather give alms of such things as ye have; and, behold, all things are clean unto you.

42 But woe unto you, Pharisees! for ye tithe mint and rue and all manner of herbs, and pass over judgment and the love of God: these ought ye to have done, and not to leave the other undone.

43 Woe unto you, Pharisees! for ye love the uppermost seats in the synagogues, and greetings in the markets.

44 Woe unto you, scribes and Pharisees, hypocrites! for ye are as graves which appear not, and the men that walk over *them* are not aware *of them*. (Luke 11:40-44)

A lawyer complains that not only the Pharisees, but the lawyers also, are offended by his remarks

45 ¶ Then answered one of the lawyers, and said unto him, Master, thus saying thou reproachest us also. (Luke 11:45)

The lawyers were also rebuked for burdening the people with legal demands they would not comply with themselves.

46 And he said, Woe unto you also, *ye* lawyers! for ye lade men with burdens grievous to be borne, and ye yourselves touch not the burdens with one of your fingers.

47 Woe unto you! for ye build the sepulchres of the prophets, and your fathers killed

them.
48 Truly ye bear witness that ye allow the deeds of your fathers: for they indeed killed them, and ye build their sepulchres.
49 Therefore also said the wisdom of God, I will send them prophets and apostles, and *some* of them they shall slay and persecute:
50 That the blood of all the prophets, which was shed from the foundation of the world, may be required of this generation; (Luke 11:46-50)

Knowing that Cain slew Abel out of envy, we know that the prophet Zechariah the son of Berechiah (Zech. 1:1) was slain out of ENVY also, the same dark emotion that impelled the Pharisees to frame and murder Jesus.

51 From the blood of Abel unto the blood of Zacharias, which perished between the altar and the temple: verily I say unto you, It shall be required of this generation. (Luke 11:51)

Jesus said, "The Pharisees and the scribes have taken the keys of knowledge (gnosis) and hidden them. They themselves have not entered, nor have they allowed to enter those who wish to. You, however, be as wise as serpents and as innocent as doves." *The Coptic Gospel of Thomas.* Hinder *κωλύω kōlyō*, prevent, forbid.

52 Woe unto you, lawyers! for ye have taken away the key of knowledge: ye entered not in yourselves, and them that were entering in ye hindered. (Luke 11:52)

Attempts at entrapment persist

53 And as he said these things unto them, the scribes and the Pharisees began to urge *him* vehemently, and to provoke him to speak of many things:
54 Laying wait for him, and seeking to catch something out of his mouth, that they might accuse him. (Luke 11:53-54)

CHAPTER 107
WARNINGS

Warnings for the disciples

The disciples are warned to not be deceived by the hypocritical teaching and practice of the Pharisees.

1 In the mean time, when there were gathered together an innumerable multitude of people, insomuch that they trode one upon another, he began to say unto his disciples first of all, Beware ye of the leaven of the Pharisees, which is hypocrisy.
1 For there is nothing covered, that shall not be revealed; neither hid, that shall not be
2 known.
3 Therefore whatsoever ye have spoken in darkness shall be heard in the light; and that which ye have spoken in the ear in closets shall be proclaimed upon the housetops. (Luke 12:1-3)

Jesus could say to not be intimidated by threats of bodily harm because he was fully conscious of man's spiritual being. The thing to fear is sin, i.e. to acknowledge a power beside God, Spirit, the only true power. Matter cannot destroy Spirit!

4 And I say unto you my friends, Be not afraid of them that kill the body, and after that have no more that they can do.
5 But I will forewarn you whom ye shall fear: Fear him, which after he hath killed hath power to cast into hell; yea, I say unto you, Fear him.
6 Are not five sparrows sold for two farthings, and not one of them is forgotten before God?
7 But even the very hairs of your head are all numbered. Fear not therefore: ye are of more value than many sparrows. (Luke 12:4-7)

Fear not to confess, *ὁμολογέω homologeō*, to declare openly your trust in Christ.

8 Also I say unto you, Whosoever shall confess me before men, him shall the Son of man also confess before the angels of God:
9 But he that denieth me before men shall be denied before the angels of God.
10 And whosoever shall speak a word against the Son of man, it shall be forgiven him:

but unto him that blasphemeth against the Holy Ghost it shall not be forgiven.
11 And when they bring you unto the synagogues, and *unto* magistrates, and powers,
take ye no thought how or what thing ye shall answer, or what ye shall say:
12 For the Holy Ghost shall teach you in the same hour what ye ought to say. (Luke 12:8-12)

Warnings for the people

[A man said] to him, "Tell my brothers to divide my father's possessions with me." He said to him, "O man, who has made me a divider?" He turned to his disciples and said to them, "I am not a divider, am I?" *The Coptic Gospel of Thomas.* Be not covetous, *πλεονεξία pleonexia*, greed, the desire to have more; extortion. Note the relation of covetousness to envy.

13 ¶ And one of the company said unto him, Master, speak to my brother, that he divide
the inheritance with me.
14 And he said unto him, Man, who made me a judge or a divider over you?
15 And he said unto them, Take heed, and beware of covetousness: for a man's life
consisteth not in the abundance of the things which he possesseth. (Luke 12:13-15)

Jesus said, "There was a rich man who had much money." He said, 'I shall put my money to use so that I may sow, reap, plant, and fill my storehouse with produce, with the result that I shall lack nothing.' Such were his intentions, but that same night he died. Let him who has ears hear." *The Coptic Gospel of Thomas*

16 And he spake a parable unto them, saying, The ground of a certain rich man brought
forth plentifully:
17 And he thought within himself, saying, What shall I do, because I have no room
where to bestow my fruits?
18 And he said, This will I do: I will pull down my barns, and build greater; and there
will I bestow all my fruits and my goods.
19 And I will say to my soul, Soul, thou hast much goods laid up for many years; take
thine ease, eat, drink, *and* be merry. (Luke 12:16-19)

There is no life, truth, intelligence, nor substance in matter. All is infinite Mind and its infinite manifestation, for God is All-in-all. Spirit is immortal Truth; matter is mortal error. Spirit is the real and eternal; matter is the unreal and temporal. - MBE. Soul, *ψυχή psuchē*, here best rendered "life" but also soul mind, heart according to the context.

20 But God said unto him, *Thou* fool, this night thy soul shall be required of thee: then
whose shall those things be, which thou hast provided?
21 So *is* he that layeth up treasure for himself, and is not rich toward God. (Luke 12:20-21)

More warnings spoken to the disciples

Avoid preoccupation with personal gratification and vanity. Note Jesus is here repeating his instruction in Matthew 6.

22 ¶ And he said unto his disciples, Therefore I say unto you, Take no thought for your
life, what ye shall eat; neither for the body, what ye shall put on.
23 The life is more than meat, and the body *is more* than raiment. (Luke 12:22-23)

Concerning apparel: Indulge in neither vanity nor fear of lack.

24 Consider the ravens: for they neither sow nor reap; which neither have storehouse
nor barn; and God feedeth them: how much more are ye better than the fowls?
25 And which of you with taking thought can add to his stature one cubit?
26 If ye then be not able to do that thing which is least, why take ye thought for the
rest?
27 Consider the lilies how they grow: they toil not, they spin not; and yet I say unto
you, that Solomon in all his glory was not arrayed like one of these.
28 If then God so clothe the grass, which is to-day in the field, and to-morrow is cast
into the oven; how much more *will he clothe* you, O ye of little faith? (Luke 12:24-28)

Avoid being anxious about food and drink.

29 And seek not ye what ye shall eat, or what ye shall drink, neither be ye of doubtful
mind.
30 For all these things do the nations of the world seek after: and your Father knoweth

that ye have need of these things. (Luke 12:29-30)
Keep priorities in order. "I do not maintain that anyone can exist in the flesh without food and raiment; but I do believe that the real man is immortal and that he lives in Spirit, not matter." - MBE
31 ¶ But rather seek ye the kingdom of God; and all these things shall be added unto
you.
32 Fear not, little flock; for it is your Father's good pleasure to give you the kingdom.
(Luke 12:31-32)
The pathway to redemption requires exchanging reliance on matter for total reliance on God, named Spirit by Jesus.
33 Sell that ye have, and give alms; provide yourselves bags which wax not old, a
treasure in the heavens that faileth not, where no thief approacheth, neither moth
corrupteth.
34 For where your treasure is, there will your heart be also. (Luke 12:33-34)
Keep a faithful watch. Lights, *λύχνος lychnos*, the candle that is placed on the lightstand, your Christ consciousness.
35 Let your loins be girded about, and *your* lights burning;
36 And ye yourselves like unto men that wait for their lord, when he will return from
the wedding; that when he cometh and knocketh, they may open unto him immediately.
37 Blessed *are* those servants, whom the lord when he cometh shall find watching:
verily I say unto you, that he shall gird himself, and make them to sit down to meat, and
will come forth and serve them.
38 And if he shall come in the second watch, or come in the third watch, and find *them*
so, blessed are those servants.
39 And this know, that if the goodman of the house had known what hour the thief
would come, he would have watched, and not have suffered his house to be broken
through.
40 Be ye therefore ready also: for the Son of man cometh at an hour when ye think not.
(Luke 12:35-40)

Warnings spoken in reply to a question asked by Peter

Peter asked Jesus what he meant by *ye* (vs. 40). Did he mean the group of disciples present, or did he mean everyone?
41 ¶ Then Peter said unto him, Lord, speakest thou this parable unto us, or even to all?
(Luke 12:41)
Jesus answers: Each and every "disciple" present is a servant required to patiently and faithfully execute his watch.
42 And the Lord said, Who then is that faithful and wise steward, whom his lord shall
make ruler over his household, to give *them their* portion of meat in due season?
43 Blessed is that servant, whom his lord when he cometh shall find so doing.
44 Of a truth I say unto you, that he will make him ruler over all that he hath. (Luke 12:42-
44)
Any disciple who fails to fully carry out his assigned watch will be regarded as unfaithful.
45 But and if that servant say in his heart, My lord delayeth his coming; and shall begin
to beat the menservants and maidens, and to eat and drink, and to be drunken; (Luke 12:45)
46 The lord of that servant will come in a day when he looketh not for *him*, and at an
hour when he is not aware, and will cut him in sunder, and will appoint him his portion
with the unbelievers. (Luke 12:45-46)
The disciple is held to a higher standard simply because he knows what is expected of him.
47 And that servant, which knew his lord's will, and prepared not *himself*, neither did
according to his will, shall be beaten with many *stripes*.
48 But he that knew not, and did commit things worthy of stripes, shall be beaten with
few *stripes*. (Luke 12:47-48 to 1st .)
The greater a disciples' understanding the more that is expected of him since we are required to live up to our highest understanding!
48 For unto whomsoever much is given, of him shall be much required: and to whom
men have committed much, of him they will ask the more. (Luke 12:48 *For*)

The fiery baptism has already started

"Jesus said, 'I have cast fire upon the world, and see, I am guarding it until it blazes.'" "Jesus said, 'He who is near me is near the fire, and he who is far from me is far from the kingdom.'" Both quotations are from *The Coptic Gospel of Thomas*. Fire. Fear; remorse; lust; hatred; destruction; affliction purifying and elevating man. - MBE

49 I am come to send fire on the earth; and what will I, if it be already kindled?

50 But I have a baptism to be baptized with; and how am I straitened till it be accomplished! (Luke 12:49-50)

Error would prevent, if possible, the unfolding of Christ, Truth.

51 Suppose ye that I am come to give peace on earth? I tell you, Nay; but rather division:

52 For from henceforth there shall be five in one house divided, three against two, and two against three.

53 The father shall be divided against the son, and the son against the father; the mother against the daughter, and the daughter against the mother; the mother in law against her daughter in law, and the daughter in law against her mother in law. (Luke 12:51-53)

More warnings for the people

Mortals pride themselves on material perceptiveness, but the real need is to exercise spiritual intuition.

54 ¶ And he said also to the people, When ye see a cloud rise out of the west, straightway ye say, There cometh a shower; and so it is.

55 And when *ye see* the south wind blow, ye say, There will be heat; and it cometh to pass. (Luke 12:54-55)

Mortals must look beyond fading, finite forms, if they would gain the true sense of things. - MBE

56 *Ye* hypocrites, ye can discern the face of the sky and of the earth; but how is it that ye do not discern this time? (Luke 12:56)

Here, the people are admonished to be alert and to correct their own errors.

57 Yea, and why even of yourselves judge ye not what is right? (Luke 12:57)

Come to terms with self-righteousness and self-justification, and then take immediate corrective action.

58 ¶ When thou goest with thine adversary to the magistrate, *as thou art* in the way, give diligence that thou mayest be delivered from him; lest he hale thee to the judge, and the judge deliver thee to the officer, and the officer cast thee into prison.

59 I tell thee, thou shalt not depart thence, till thou hast paid the very last mite. (Luke 12:58-59)

CHAPTER 108
TOTAL REPENTANCE REQUIRED

1 There were present at that season some that told him of the Galilæans, whose blood Pilate had mingled with their sacrifices.

2 And Jesus answering said unto them, Suppose ye that these Galilæans were sinners above all the Galilæans, because they suffered such things?

3 I tell you, Nay: but, except ye repent, ye shall all likewise perish.

4 Or those eighteen, upon whom the tower in Siloam fell, and slew them, think ye that they were sinners above all men that dwelt in Jerusalem?

5 I tell you, Nay: but, except ye repent, ye shall all likewise perish. (Luke 13:1-5)

Parable of the Fig Tree

(The Fig Tree: A symbol of Jesus' three-year mission to bring Christ to Israel. The vineyard: Ecclesiastical Judaism)

6 ¶ He spake also this parable; A certain *man* had a fig tree planted in his vineyard; and he came and sought fruit thereon, and found none.

7 Then said he unto the dresser of his vineyard, Behold, these three years I come seeking fruit on this fig tree, and find none: cut it down; why cumbereth it the ground?

8 And he answering said unto him, Lord, let it alone this year also, till I shall dig about
it, and dung *it*:
9 And if it bear fruit, *well*: and if not, *then* after that thou shalt cut it down.
10 And he was teaching in one of the synagogues on the sabbath. (Luke 13:6-10)

Resistance to Christ shown in opposition to spiritual healing

11 ¶ And, behold, there was a woman which had a spirit of infirmity eighteen years,
and was bowed together, and could in no wise lift up *herself*.
12 And when Jesus saw her, he called *her* to *him*, and said unto her, Woman, thou art
loosed from thine infirmity.
13 And he laid *his* hands on her: and immediately she was made straight, and glorified
God.
14 And the ruler of the synagogue answered with indignation, because that Jesus had
healed on the sabbath day, and said unto the people, There are six days in which men
ought to work: in them therefore come and be healed, and not on the sabbath day.
15 The Lord then answered him, and said, *Thou* hypocrite, doth not each one of you on
the sabbath loose his ox or *his* ass from the stall, and lead *him* away to watering? (Luke 13:11-15)

"Daughter of Abraham." A female descendant of Abraham that should be valued the same as any male descendant.

16 And ought not this woman, being a daughter of Abraham, whom Satan hath bound,
lo, these eighteen years, be loosed from this bond on the sabbath day?
17 And when he had said these things, all his adversaries were ashamed: and all the
people rejoiced for all the glorious things that were done by him. (Luke 13:16-17)

Two Parables Uniting The Male & The Female to the Kingdom of Heaven
The Male: The Parable of the Mustard Seed (For the 3rd time)

18 ¶ Then said he, Unto what is the kingdom of God like? and whereunto shall I
resemble it?
19 It is like a grain of mustard seed, which a man took, and cast into his garden; and it
grew, and waxed a great tree; and the fowls of the air lodged in the branches of it. (Luke 13:18-19)

The Female: The Parable of the Leaven Hid in Three Measures of Meal ("And again" i.e. for the 2nd time)

20 And again he said, Whereunto shall I liken the kingdom of God?
21 It is like leaven, which a woman took and hid in three measures of meal, till the
whole was leavened.
22 And he went through the cities and villages, teaching, and journeying toward
Jerusalem. (Luke 13:20-22)

CHAPTER 109
IN JERSUALEM AT THE FEAST OF DEDICATION
(The Hebrew Chislev 26. The Gentile early December.)

22 ¶ And it was at Jerusalem the feast of the dedication, and it was winter.
23 And Jesus walked in the temple in Solomon's porch. (John 10:22-23)

Efforts to entrap Jesus resume. "came round about" = surrounded. "make us to doubt" = hold us in suspense, to wonder.

24 Then came the Jews round about him, and said unto him, How long dost thou make
us to doubt? If thou be the Christ, tell us plainly.
25 Jesus answered them, I told you, and ye believed not: the works that I do in my
Father's name, they bear witness of me.
26 But ye believe not, because ye are not of my sheep, as I said unto you.

27 My sheep hear my voice, and I know them, and they follow me:
28 And I give unto them eternal life; and they shall never perish, neither shall any *man*
pluck them out of my hand.
29 My Father, which gave *them* me, is greater than all; and no *man* is able to pluck
them out of my Father's hand. (John 10:24-29)

One, *εἷς heis*. Remove "*my*" added by the revisers and it reads, "I and the Father," one essence expressed as Christ.

30 I and *my* Father are one. (John 10:30)

The statement of Jesus: "'I and my Father are one,' separated him from the scholastic theology of the rabbis.' - M.B.E.

31 Then the Jews took up stones again to stone him.
32 Jesus answered them, Many good works have I shewed you from my Father; for
which of those works do ye stone me?
33 The Jews answered him, saying, For a good work we stone thee not; but for
blasphemy; and because that thou, being a man, makest thyself God. (John 10:31-33)

See Psalm 82. For the meaning of "gods" see Gen. 3:5. Jesus showed that the charge of blasphemy was fallacious.

34 Jesus answered them, Is it not written in your law, I said, Ye are gods?
35 If he called them gods, unto whom the word of God came, and the scripture cannot
be broken; (John 10:34-35)

Note Jesus plainly declared he was not God, but "the Son of God", the Son or effect, showing forth God, the cause.

36 Say ye of him, whom the Father hath sanctified, and sent into the world, Thou
blasphemest; because I said, I am the Son of God? (John 10:36)

The works of Jesus demonstrated *sonship* with God. He repeatedly said his "I" was God, the divine Mind. See Phil. 2:5.

37 If I do not the works of my Father, believe me not. (John 10:37)

The "I" that is the Father, is the divine Principle, Love that empowered Jesus, the Son of Man, to do the healing works.

38 But if I do, though ye believe not me, believe the works: that ye may know, and
believe, that the Father *is* in me, and I in him. (John 10:38)

Self-righteousness, driven by envy to destroy Christ, remained the driving force to unjustly murder the man Jesus.

39 Therefore they sought again to take him: but he escaped out of their hand, (John 10:39)

CHAPTER 110
TEACHNG IN RETREAT BEYOND JORDAN

Jesus had to retreat from Jerusalem again, this time for about three months.

40 And went away again beyond Jordan into the place where John at first baptized; and
there he abode. (John 10:40)

The unbiased thought acknowledged that the healing works of Jesus validated his teaching.

41 And many resorted unto him, and said, John did no miracle: but all things that John
spake of this man were true.
42 And many believed on him there. (John 10:41-42)

The way to enter the kingdom is straight and narrow

23 Then said one unto him, Lord, are there few that be saved? And he said unto them,
24 ¶ Strive to enter in at the strait gate: for many, I say unto you, will seek to enter in,
and shall not be able.
25 When once the master of the house is risen up, and hath shut to the door, and ye
begin to stand without, and to knock at the door, saying, Lord, Lord, open unto us; and
he shall answer and say unto you, I know you not whence ye are:
26 Then shall ye begin to say, We have eaten and drunk in thy presence, and thou hast
taught in our streets.
27 But he shall say, I tell you, I know you not whence ye are; depart from me, all *ye*
workers of iniquity.
28 There shall be weeping and gnashing of teeth, when ye shall see Abraham, and

Isaac, and Jacob, and all the prophets, in the kingdom of God, and you *yourselves* thrust out.
29 And they shall come from the east, and *from* the west, and from the north, and *from* the south, and shall sit down in the kingdom of God.
30 And, behold, there are last which shall be first, and there are first which shall be last. (Luke 13:23-30)

CHAPTER 111
JESUS REPLIES TO HEROD'S THREATS

31 ¶ The same day there came certain of the Pharisees, saying unto him, Get thee out, and depart hence: for Herod will kill thee. (Luke 13:31)

A mystical statement foretelling the healing work Jesus would accomplish during his three days in the tomb.

32 And he said unto them, Go ye, and tell that fox, Behold, I cast out devils, and I do cures to-day and to-morrow, and the third *day* I shall be perfected. (Luke 13:32)

Out of = outside of. Jesus did his work openly and stated plainly that the only place he would be killed was in *Jerusalem*.

33 Nevertheless I must walk to-day, and to-morrow, and the *day* following: for it cannot be that a prophet perish out of Jerusalem. (Luke 13:33)

The history of ecclesiasticism is one of killing the prophets. "PROPHET. A spiritual seer." - MBE

34 O Jerusalem, Jerusalem, which killest the prophets, and stonest them that are sent unto thee; (Luke 13:34 *to* ;)

The appearing of the Messiah or Christ, in whatever form, has repeatedly been rejected by ecclesiasticism.

34 how often would I have gathered thy children together, as a hen *doth gather* her brood under *her* wings, and ye would not! (Luke 13:34 *how*)

Jesus referred to the temple in Jerusalem operating under the control of ecclesiastical despots as "*your house,*" since it no longer functioned as "God's House." Due to their corrupt management it would be totally destroyed, left desolate.

35 Behold, your house is left unto you desolate: (Luke 13:35 to ;)

The ecclesiastics would not see God and His Christ until they acknowledged that Jesus came in fulfillment of Ps. 118:26.

35 and verily I say unto you, Ye shall not see me, until *the time* come when ye shall say, Blessed *is* he that cometh in the name of the Lord. (Luke 13:35 *and*)

CHAPTER 112
DINING WITH A CHIEF PHARISEE

An event held for the purpose of entrapping Jesus?

Jesus was *invited* to dinner, he didn't just happen to be there.

1 And it came to pass, as he went into the house of one of the chief Pharisees to eat bread on the sabbath day, (Luke 14:1 to 2nd ,)

The "guests," no doubt participants in a plot to entrap Jesus, were fully aware of what was to take place.

1 that they watched him. (Luke 14:1 *that*)

The man with the dropsy didn't just happen to be there either, he was a dupe in this attempt to entrap Jesus.

2 And, behold, there was a certain man before him which had the dropsy. (Luke 14:2)

Fearlessly confronting the lawyers and Pharisees, Jesus argued God's law, the law of Love

3 And Jesus answering spake unto the lawyers and Pharisees, saying, Is it lawful to heal on the sabbath day? (Luke 14:3)

Their reply was thunderous in its display of SILENT, LOVELESS legality. They refused to answer an obvious truth.

4 And they held their peace. (Luke 14:4 to 1st .)

Jesus' response in healing the man was a glorious symphony of praise to God, Whose Law is divine Love.

4 And he took *him*, and healed him, and let him go; (Luke 14:4 *and*)

Heartless hypocrisy exposed

(Remedy: The 5th Beatitude - "Blessed are the merciful for they shall obtain mercy")

The Companion Bible states that the word *onos*, ass is actually *huios*, son and should read "son," not "ass." Jesus was making the point that it would not be God's will for a father to leave his son who had fallen into a pit on the sabbath left until after the sabbath was over. A loving God would most certainly not object to a man being healed on the sabbath.

5 And answered them, saying, Which of you shall have an ass or an ox fallen into a pit,

and will not straightway pull him out on the sabbath day?
6 And they could not answer him again to these things. (Luke 14:5-6)

A parable rebuking pride and self-glorification – "Who shall be the greatest"
(More teaching on the 1st Beatitude - "Blessed *are* the poor in spirit: for theirs is the kingdom of heaven.")

7 ¶ And he put forth a parable to those which were bidden, when he marked how they
chose out the chief rooms; saying unto them,
8 When thou art bidden of any *man* to a wedding, sit not down in the highest room; lest
a more honourable man than thou be bidden of him;
9 And he that bade thee and him come and say to thee, Give this man place; and thou
begin with shame to take the lowest room.
10 But when thou art bidden, go and sit down in the lowest room; that when he that
bade thee cometh, he may say unto thee, Friend, go up higher: then shalt thou have
worship in the presence of them that sit at meat with thee.
11 For whosoever exalteth himself shall be abased; and he that humbleth himself shall
be exalted. (Luke 14:7-11)

Jesus then rebuked the host for self-seeking

12 ¶ Then said he also to him that bade him, When thou makest a dinner or a supper,
call not thy friends, nor thy brethren, neither thy kinsmen, nor *thy* rich neighbours; lest
they also bid thee again, and a recompence be made thee.
13 But when thou makest a feast, call the poor, the maimed, the lame, the blind:
14 And thou shalt be blessed; for they cannot recompense thee: for thou shalt be
recompensed at the resurrection of the just. (Luke 14:12-14)

Remarks directed at the Pharisees and lawyers for rejecting invitations to the Kingdom

A remark made by a lawyer that he and the other Pharisees were specially chosen to inherit "the kingdom of God."
15 ¶ And when one of them that sat at meat with him heard these things, he said unto
him, Blessed *is* he that shall eat bread in the kingdom of God. (Luke 14:15)

A Parable: The Great Supper
(What good is it to be "chosen to eat bread in the kingdom of God" if you decline the invitation?)

The "great supper" is the kingdom of God. The first bidding to attend the supper was extended by John the Baptist.
16 Then said he unto him, A certain man made a great supper, and bade many: (Luke
14:16)
The second bidding was by Jesus to those previously invited by John the Baptist.
17 And sent his servant at supper time to say to them that were bidden, Come; for all
things are now ready. (Luke 14:17)
Among those in attendance were many that made, and continued to make, excuses for not accepting the invitation.
18 And they all with one *consent* began to make excuse. The first said unto him, I have
bought a piece of ground, and I must needs go and see it: I pray thee have me excused.
19 And another said, I have bought five yoke of oxen, and I go to prove them: I pray
thee have me excused.
20 And another said, I have married a wife, and therefore I cannot come. (Luke 14:18-20)
Later, the Apostles and Paul would extend invitations, but only those who were desperate would accept them.
21 So that servant came, and shewed his lord these things. Then the master of the
house being angry said to his servant, Go out quickly into the streets and lanes of the
city, and bring in hither the poor, and the maimed, and the halt, and the blind. (Luke 14:21)
Since the kingdom of God is infinite, and there is room for ***all*** to attend, another invitation would be extended.
22 And the servant said, Lord, it is done as thou hast commanded, and yet there is
room. (Luke 14:22)

This invitation came centuries later, but was again rejected, as were the previous invitations.

23 And the lord said unto the servant, Go out into the highways and hedges, and
compel *them* to come in, that my house may be filled. (Luke 14:23)

Conclusion. The Christ must be accepted before "the great supper" can be attended.

24 For I say unto you, That none of those men which were bidden shall taste of my
supper. (Luke 14:24)

CHAPTER 113
THE COST OF DISCIPLESHIP

25 ¶ And there went great multitudes with him: and he turned, and said unto them, (Luke 14:25)

Jesus tells the multitude that ties to the flesh must be replaced by bonds of spiritual love.

26 If any *man* come to me, and hate not his father, and mother, and wife, and children,
and brethren, and sisters, yea, and his own life also, he cannot be my disciple. (Luke 14:26)

To reflect divine Love, all forms of self-love must be overcome.

27 And whosoever doth not bear his cross, and come after me, cannot be my disciple.
(Luke 14:27)

Before entering the pathway, the cost should be determined. The cost is to leave *ALL* for Christ. (See verse 33 below.)

28 For which of you, intending to build a tower, sitteth not down first, and counteth the
cost, whether he have *sufficient* to finish *it*? (Luke 14:28)

Haply, *μήποτε mēpote*, peradventure, perhaps, possibly, if by chance.

29 Lest haply, after he hath laid the foundation, and is not able to finish *it*, all that
behold *it* begin to mock him,
30 Saying, This man began to build, and was not able to finish. (Luke 14:29-30)

A person should not enter the pathway until fully prepared and totally committed.

31 Or what king, going to make war against another king, sitteth not down first, and
consulteth whether he be able with ten thousand to meet him that cometh against him
with twenty thousand?
32 Or else, while the other is yet a great way off, he sendeth an ambassage, and desireth
conditions of peace. (Luke 14:31-32)

It is all or nothing, there is no compromising. See Rev. 3:14-22.

33 So likewise, whosoever he be of you that forsaketh not all that he hath, he cannot be
my disciple. (Luke 14:33)

The salt (disciple) must not be contaminated with materialism. "It is the spirit that quickeneth the flesh profiteth nothing."

34 ¶ Salt *is* good: but if the salt have lost his savour, wherewith shall it be seasoned?
35 It is neither fit for the land, nor yet for the dunghill; *but* men cast it out. He that hath
ears to hear, let him hear. (Luke 14:34-35)

CHAPTER 114
SALVATION COMES THROUGH GRACE NOT PRIVILEGE

The "the poor in spirit" are those who have been rendered heavenly hungry.

1 Then drew near unto him all the publicans and sinners for to hear him. (Luke 15:1)

The self-righteous (the prideful and arrogant), blind to their spiritual poverty, criticize those who are awakening.

2 And the Pharisees and scribes murmured, saying, This man receiveth sinners, and
eateth with them.
3 ¶ And he spake this parable unto them, saying, (Luke 15:2-3)

Parable of the Lost Sheep

4 What man of you, having an hundred sheep, if he lose one of them, doth not leave the
ninety and nine in the wilderness, and go after that which is lost, until he find it?
5 And when he hath found *it*, he layeth *it* on his shoulders, rejoicing.
6 And when he cometh home, he calleth together *his* friends and neighbours, saying

unto them, Rejoice with me; for I have found my sheep which was lost. (Luke 15:4-6)

Whereas "the publicans and sinners" realized they were in the wilderness, the "Pharisees" didn't know they're lost.

7 I say unto you, that likewise joy shall be in heaven over one sinner that repenteth,
more than over ninety and nine just persons, which need no repentance. (Luke 15:7)

Parable of the Lost Coin

(The First Commandment is my favorite text. It demonstrates Christian Science. - MBE)

8 ¶ Either what woman having ten pieces of silver, if she lose one piece, doth not light
a candle, and sweep the house, and seek diligently till she find *it*?
9 And when she hath found *it*, she calleth *her* friends and *her* neighbours together,
saying, Rejoice with me; for I have found the piece which I had lost. (Luke 15:8-9)

The divine Principle of the First Commandment bases the Science of being, by which man demonstrates health, holiness, and life eternal. - MBE

10 Likewise, I say unto you, there is joy in the presence of the angels of God over one
sinner that repenteth. (Luke 15:10)

Parable of the Prodigal Son

(In this parable the younger son symbolizes the publicans and sinners and the elder son the Pharisees. Question: Who is most likely to enter the kingdom first: the repentant younger son or the self-righteous elder son? See Luke 18:9-14)

11 ¶ And he said, A certain man had two sons: (Luke 15:11)

The sensualism of the younger son leads to pain and suffering

The younger son represents the publicans and sinners.

12 And the younger of them said to *his* father, Father, give me the portion of goods that
falleth *to me*. And he divided unto them *his* living. (Luke 15:12)

The wilderness experience of the younger son begins with the belief that he can have a great time with his new "friends.'

13 And not many days after the younger son gathered all together, and took his journey
into a far country, and there wasted his substance with riotous living. (Luke 15:13)

The wake-up call comes through suffering and his "friends" vanish because there is nothing more they can take from him.

14 And when he had spent all, there arose a mighty famine in that land; and he began to
be in want. (Luke 15:14)

The effort to escape suffering causes him to look to human ways and means for relief, rather than to God.

15 And he went and joined himself to a citizen of that country; and he sent him into his
fields to feed swine. (Luke 15:15)

Desperation leads to disappointment; disappointment to anguish; anguish to questioning; and questioning to awakening.

16 And he would fain have filled his belly with the husks that the swine did eat: and no
man gave unto him. (Luke 15:16)

The awakening came "when he came to himself." That's what we must do. It's a spiritual rebirth, called being born again.

17 And when he came to himself, he said, How many hired servants of my father's have
bread enough and to spare, and I perish with hunger! (Luke 15:17)

Turning thought toward Truth and away from error, he realized: I am a child of God! I must stop being a sinning mortal!

18 I will arise and go to my father, and will say unto him, Father, I have sinned against
heaven, and before thee,
19 And am no more worthy to be called thy son: make me as one of thy hired servants.
(Luke 15:18-19)

Realization was then followed by taking right action.

20 And he arose, and came to his father. (Luke 15:20 to 1st .)

Man, whether believing himself to be a publican, or a Pharisee, is never outside the focal distance of God, infinite Love.

20 But when he was yet a great way off, his father saw him, and had compassion, and
ran, and fell on his neck, and kissed him. (Luke 15:20 *But*)

The acknowledgment of having erred, and the commitment to turn from it, is to "put off the old man with his deeds."

21 And the son said unto him, Father, I have sinned against heaven, and in thy sight,
and am no more worthy to be called thy son. (Luke 15:21)

God sees His sons and daughters in His image and likeness. See Gen 1:26 & 27, 31 *to* (1st.). This is the grace of God!

22 But the father said to his servants, Bring forth the best robe, and put *it* on him; and
put a ring on his hand, and shoes on *his* feet:

23 And bring hither the fatted calf, and kill *it*; and let us eat, and be merry: (Luke 15:22-23)

Death is a term at times used for the erroneous belief of being separated from the Father, Who is the only real Life.

24 For this my son was dead, and is alive again; he was lost, and is found. And they
began to be merry. (Luke 15:24)

The envy and self-righteousness of the elder son make him miserable

Pharisaism with its ecclesiastical despotism and self-righteousness, is represented by the "elder son."

25 Now his elder son was in the field: and as he came and drew nigh to the house, he
heard music and dancing.

26 And he called one of the servants, and asked what these things meant. (Luke 15:25-26)

The elder son is told that his brother has "come to himself," recognized his mistakes, repented, and is now home.

27 And he said unto him, Thy brother is come; and thy father hath killed the fatted calf,
because he hath received him safe and sound. (Luke 15:27)

The elder son's anger for his brother's safe return represents the Pharisees' hatred of Jesus and their resentment toward the people who accepted his teaching. It's called ENVY.

28 And he was angry, and would not go in: therefore came his father out, and entreated
him. (Luke 15:28)

The elder son, being *envious* of the father's love for his brother, displays resentment, complaining, and annoyance. "Self-will, self-justification, and self-love . . . wars against spirituality and is the law of sin and death"- MBE

29 And he answering said to *his* father, Lo, these many years do I serve thee, neither
transgressed I at any time thy commandment: and yet thou never gavest me a kid, that I
might make merry with my friends:

30 But as soon as this thy son was come, which hath devoured thy living with harlots,
thou hast killed for him the fatted calf. (Luke 15:29-30)

We are to behold our fellow man as Jesus taught, in the Christ-light, and to see everyone through the eyes of Love.

31 And he said unto him, Son, thou art ever with me, and all that I have is thine.

32 It was meet that we should make merry, and be glad: for this thy brother was dead,
and is alive again; and was lost, and is found. (Luke 15:31-32)

CHAPTER 115
INTEGRITY AND THE FIRST COMMANDMENT

In this parable the Pharisees are being rebuked for their dishonest stewardship

Parable of the Unjust Steward

(The Pharisees are symbolized by the self-seeking steward whose methods are generally applauded by the world)

A household steward Is accused of mismanagement, apparently a lesser infraction than he is about to commit!

1 And he said also unto his disciples, There was a certain rich man, which had a
steward; and the same was accused unto him that he had wasted his goods. (Luke 16:1)

The steward's employer demands an accounting before releasing him.

2 And he called him, and said unto him, How is it that I hear this of thee? give an
account of thy stewardship; for thou mayest be no longer steward. (Luke 16:2)

Believing he is smarter than his employer he devises a scheme. His "I cannot dig" is I WILL not dig. Ashamed = too proud.

3 Then the steward said within himself, What shall I do? for my lord taketh away from
me the stewardship: I cannot dig; to beg I am ashamed. (Luke 16:3)

The plan is to get debtors of his employer to offer him employment "in their houses" by embezzling *for* them while he still has access to his employers accounts.

4 I am resolved what to do, that, when I am put out of the stewardship, they may
receive me into their houses.

5 So he called every one of his lord's debtors *unto him*, and said unto the first, How
much owest thou unto my lord? (Luke 16:4-5)

He "takes" 50% of the amount owed his employer and "gives" it to his employer's debtor for a possible future benefit.

6 And he said, An hundred measures of oil. And he said unto him, Take thy bill, and sit down quickly, and write fifty. (Luke 16:6)

The unjust steward then "takes" 20% on behalf of another debtor.

7 Then said he to another, And how much owest thou? And he said, An hundred measures of wheat. And he said unto him, Take thy bill, and write fourscore. (Luke 16:7)

Wisely, *φρονίμως phronimōs*, prudently, shrewd in the management of practical affairs, cunning. In this context conceited, mindful of one's self interest even at the expense of another. The unjust steward is commended for his deceitfulness. It's sad but true, that mortals often consider being shrewd or cunning wiser than being just or honest.

8 And the lord commended the unjust steward, because he had done wisely: for the children of this world are in their generation wiser than the children of light. (Luke 16:8)

Jesus asks his disciples a question intended to be overheard by the Pharisees

"And I say unto you" should read "And say I unto you" with a "?" at the end, for it is a question to which the answer is No!

9 And I say unto you, Make to yourselves friends of the mammon of unrighteousness; that, when ye fail, they may receive you into everlasting habitations. (Luke 16:9)

Fidelity is a virtue, and dishonesty an evil, whether in large or small matters.

10 He that is faithful in that which is least is faithful also in much: and he that is unjust in the least is unjust also in much. (Luke 16:10)

If we do not demonstrate faithfulness in earthly affairs, we will not be entrusted with heavenly affairs.

11 If therefore ye have not been faithful in the unrighteous mammon, who will commit to your trust the true *riches*? (Luke 16:11)

The same principle that applies to that which is yours must be applied to that which is another's.

12 And if ye have not been faithful in that which is another man's, who shall give you that which is your own? (Luke 16:12)

The First Commandment is supreme
(This is a rebuke to the Pharisees, who like the unjust steward have been stealing from the people under the guise of serving God)

The First Commandment is primary. Jesus declared emphatically that "God is Spirit", the antipode of matter (mammon).

13 ¶ No servant can serve two masters: for either he will hate the one, and love the other; or else he will hold to the one, and despise the other. Ye cannot serve God and mammon. (Luke 16:13)

CHAPTER 116
COVETOUSNESS REBUKED

The Pharisees are reproved for making void the law and the prophets

In the following four verses Jesus plainly states that hypocrisy is doomed whereas the Law is infallible.

14 And the Pharisees also, who were covetous, heard all these things: and they derided him.

15 And he said unto them, Ye are they which justify yourselves before men; but God knoweth your hearts: for that which is highly esteemed among men is abomination in the sight of God.

16 The law and the prophets *were* until John: since that time the kingdom of God is preached, and every man presseth into it. (Luke 16:14-16)

Heaven AND earth will not pass, leaving *only* heaven, until God's law is obeyed on earth "as it is in heaven."

17 And it is easier for heaven and earth to pass, than one tittle of the law to fail. (Luke 16:17)

The Pharisees are then rebuked for making void the law regarding divorce
(Violating thou shalt not covert leads to breaking thou shalt not commit adultery)

18 Whosoever putteth away his wife, and marrieth another, committeth adultery: and whosoever marrieth her that is put away from *her* husband committeth adultery. (Luke 16:18)

A Parable that overturns the Pharisees' erroneous teaching regarding death

A warning to the Pharisees symbolized by a rich man, and a prophecy concerning Lazarus soon to be resurrected.

19 ¶ There was a certain rich man, which was clothed in purple and fine linen, and
fared sumptuously every day:
20 And there was a certain beggar named Lazarus, which was laid at his gate, full of
sores,
21 And desiring to be fed with the crumbs which fell from the rich man's table:
moreover the dogs came and licked his sores.
22 And it came to pass, that the beggar died, and was carried by the angels into
Abraham's bosom: the rich man also died, and was buried;
23 And in hell he lift up his eyes, being in torments, and seeth Abraham afar off, and
Lazarus in his bosom.
24 And he cried and said, Father Abraham, have mercy on me, and send Lazarus, that
he may dip the tip of his finger in water, and cool my tongue; for I am tormented in this
flame.
25 But Abraham said, Son, remember that thou in thy lifetime receivedst thy good
things, and likewise Lazarus evil things: but now he is comforted, and thou art
tormented. (Luke 16:19-25)

It is impossible for different states of consciousness, the material and the spiritual, to communicate with one another.

26 And beside all this, between us and you there is a great gulf fixed: so that they which
would pass from hence to you cannot; neither can they pass to us, that *would come* from
thence.
27 Then he said, I pray thee therefore, father, that thou wouldest send him to my
father's house:
28 For I have five brethren; that he may testify unto them, lest they also come into this
place of torment.
29 Abraham saith unto him, They have Moses and the prophets; let them hear them.
30 And he said, Nay, father Abraham: but if one went unto them from the dead, they
will repent. (Luke 16:26-30)

Jesus knew that even after raising Lazarus and overcoming death and the grave, he would still be rejected.

31 And he said unto him, If they hear not Moses and the prophets, neither will they be
persuaded, though one rose from the dead. (Luke 16:31)

CHAPTER 117
DOING "THAT WHICH IS OUR DUTY TO DO"

The disciples addressed

Do not ***offend**, σκάνδαλον skandalon,* means do not place a snare, trap, trap stick, impediment, stumbling block, or enticement to error or sin in the way, *thereby* causing those who are struggling to enter in, to instead fall away.

1 Then said he unto the disciples, It is impossible but that offences will come: but woe
unto him, through whom they come! (Luke 17:1)

A "little one" is one who has adopted the spirit of the Beatitudes and earnestly strives to do the Father's will.

2 It were better for him that a millstone were hanged about his neck, and he cast into
the sea, than that he should offend one of these little ones. (Luke 17:2)

"First cast out the beam out of thine own eye." (Matt. 7:5). Jesus taught that neither the person nor society is benefitted when evil is justified and not forsaken. Forgiveness demands repentance of ourselves and of others. See Jn. 8:11.

3 ¶ Take heed to yourselves: If thy brother trespass against thee, rebuke him; and if he
repent, forgive him.
4 And if he trespass against thee seven times in a day, and seven times in a day turn
again to thee, saying, I repent: thou shalt forgive him. (Luke 17:3-4)

The Apostles appeal to Jesus to help them better understand and demonstrate what he is telling them.

5 And the apostles said unto the Lord, Increase our faith. (Luke 17:5)

The sycamine or mulberry tree was used medicinally. "When we come to have more faith in the truth of being than we have in error, more faith in Spirit than in matter, more faith in living than in dying, more faith in God than in man, then no material suppositions can prevent us from healing the sick and destroying error." - MBE

6 And the Lord said, If ye had faith as a grain of mustard seed, ye might say unto this sycamine tree, Be thou plucked up by the root, and be thou planted in the sea; and it should obey you. (Luke 17:6)

A servant (disciple) must perform his duties with no expectation of gratitude, appreciation, or praise.

7 But which of you, having a servant plowing or feeding cattle, will say unto him by and by, when he is come from the field, Go and sit down to meat?

8 And will not rather say unto him, Make ready wherewith I may sup, and gird thyself, and serve me, till I have eaten and drunken; and afterward thou shalt eat and drink?

9 Doth he thank that servant because he did the things that were commanded him? I trow not. (Luke 17:7-9)

Jesus expected, as a minimum, that we would comply with everything he *commanded* us to do, for it is merely "that which is our duty to do." But he hoped we would strive to do everything he taught, and even more, of *our own free will.*

10 So likewise ye, when ye shall have done all those things which are commanded you, say, We are unprofitable servants: we have done that which was our duty to do. (Luke 17:10)

CHAPTER 118

"BUT WHERE ARE THE NINE?"

(Jesus demonstrated 'that which is our duty to do" when he healed the nine ungrateful, as well as the one grateful, leper)

11 ¶ And it came to pass, as he went to Jerusalem, that he passed through the midst of Samaria and Galilee. (Luke 17:11)

Ten lepers called on Jesus for healing. Ten symbolizes the perfection of the divine order. There are Ten Commandments.

12 And as he entered into a certain village, there met him ten men that were lepers, which stood afar off:

13 And they lifted up *their* voices, and said, Jesus, Master, have mercy on us. (Luke 17:12-13)

Jesus required the lepers to show their trust and obedience BEFORE there was any evidence of healing.

14 And when he saw *them*, he said unto them, Go shew yourselves unto the priests. (Luke 17:14 to 1st .)

Obedience and trust opened the way for *all ten* to be healed. Ten is significant as to why they could *all* be healed. In the divine order of being man, God's image and likeness, is always and forever spiritual and perfect. Healing doesn't change anything, it simply reveals the present perfection of being. The question is: are we truly grateful for what God *has* done?

14 And it came to pass, that, as they went, they were cleansed. (Luke 17:14 *And*)

Only one, a Samaritan, looked upon with disdain by the Jews, turned back to express gratitude.

15 And one of them, when he saw that he was healed, turned back, and with a loud voice glorified God,

16 And fell down on *his* face at his feet, giving him thanks: and he was a Samaritan. (Luke 17:15-16)

Note, only the *grateful* Samaritan received the blessing of having his healing ratified by the Master. The word stranger is *ἀλλογενής allogenēs*, used only here. It means of another race, a foreigner. The implications are profound.

17 And Jesus answering said, Were there not ten cleansed? but where *are* the nine?

18 There are not found that returned to give glory to God, save this stranger.

19 And he said unto him, Arise, go thy way: thy faith hath made thee whole. (Luke 17:17-19)

CHAPTER 119

WHEN THE KINGDOM OF GOD WILL COME

His disciples said to him, "When will the kingdom come?" <Jesus said,> "It will not come by waiting for it. It will not be a matter of saying 'here it is' or 'there it is.' Rather, the kingdom of the father is spread out upon the earth, and men do not see it." *The Coptic Gospel of Thomas*

20 ¶ And when he was demanded of the Pharisees, when the kingdom of God should

come, he answered them and said, (Luke 17:20 *to* 3rd,)
The material senses do not reveal the kingdom of God.
20 The kingdom of God cometh not with observation: (Luke 17:20 *The*)
It makes no sense to expect that which is spiritual to conform to matter. Spirit is omnipresent; matter is separation.
21 Neither shall they say, Lo here! or, lo there! (Luke 17:21 *to* !)
Only Christ, the hope of glory, reveals "the kingdom of God" (present perfection), already NOW within you. See Col. 1:27
21 for, behold, the kingdom of God is within you. (Luke 17:21 *for*)

CHAPTER 120
END OF THE WORLD ORDER

(All must give place to the spiritual fact by the translation of man and the universe back into Spirit" - MBE)

Jesus said, "Many times have you desired to hear these words which I am saying to you, and you have no one else to hear them from. There will be days when you will look for me and will not find me." – *The Coptic Gospel of Thomas*

22 And he said unto the disciples, The days will come, when ye shall desire to see one
of the days of the Son of man, and ye shall not see *it*. (Luke 17:22)
Don't listen to the Pharisees. They know not the way to the kingdom of God, therefore don't follow after them
23 And they shall say to you, See here; or, see there: go not after *them*, nor follow *them*.
(Luke 17:23)
Spiritual man, made in the image and likeness of God, your real ever-present being, reflects the Christ light.
24 For as the lightning, that lighteneth out of the one *part* under heaven, shineth unto
the other *part* under heaven; so shall also the Son of man be in his day. (Luke 17:24)

4th Announcement of sufferings

25 But first must he suffer many things, and be rejected of this generation. (Luke 17:25)
History will continue to repeat itself until all error is totally destroyed.
26 And as it was in the days of Noe, so shall it be also in the days of the Son of man.
27 They did eat, they drank, they married wives, they were given in marriage, until the
day that Noe entered into the ark, and the flood came, and destroyed them all.
28 Likewise also as it was in the days of Lot; they did eat, they drank, they bought, they
sold, they planted, they builded;
29 But the same day that Lot went out of Sodom it rained fire and brimstone from
heaven, and destroyed *them* all. (Luke 17:26-29)
The only way to see "the Son of man" is to leave all for Christ. Therefore don't cling to material persons, places, or things.
30 Even thus shall it be in the day when the Son of man is revealed.
31 In that day, he which shall be upon the housetop, and his stuff in the house, let him
not come down to take it away: and he that is in the field, let him likewise not return
back.
32 Remember Lot's wife. (Luke 17:30-32)
If we have been listening we recognize this as the constant message: the material or corporeal is mortal and temporal, the spiritual is the real and eternal. To lose our life means to lay off the mortal for the immortal. Jesus called it taking up the cross; Paul referred to it when he said "I die daily." In other words, each day Paul strove to put off more of the mortal nature. Here, to seek to save our life means to cling tenaciously to the sinning nature, and to resist leaving all for Christ!
33 Whosoever shall seek to save his life shall lose it; and whosoever shall lose his life
shall preserve it. (Luke 17:33)
The spiritual is real and eternal; the material must be left behind. "If we observe our mental processes, we shall find that we are perpetually arguing with ourselves; yet each mortal is not two personalities, but one. In like manner good and evil talk to one another; yet they are not two but one, for evil is naught, and good only is reality." "Nothing is real and eternal --- nothing is Spirit, --- but God and His idea." - MBE
34 I tell you, in that night there shall be two *men* in one bed; the one shall be taken, and
the other shall be left.
35 Two *women* shall be grinding together; the one shall be taken, and the other left.
36 Two *men* shall be in the field; the one shall be taken, and the other left.
37 And they answered and said unto him, Where, Lord? (Luke 17:34-37 *to* ?)

body = carcass, a lifeless mortal body. eagles = vultures. The material is left for the vultures whereas that which is born of the Spirit is spiritual and eternal. Therefore, to that which is spiritual there is neither death, nor vultures.

37 And he said unto them, Wheresoever the body *is*, thither will the eagles be gathered together. (Luke 17:37 *And*)

CHAPTER 121
EVEN MORE INSTRUCTION ON PRAYER

Avenge ≠ Revenge. Avenge, ἐκδικέω *ekdikeō,* to vindicate [the widow's] right, to do [the widow] justice, to protect [her].

1 And he spake a parable unto them *to this end*, that men ought always to pray, and not to faint;
2 Saying, There was in a city a judge, which feared not God, neither regarded man:
3 And there was a widow in that city; and she came unto him, saying, Avenge me of mine adversary.
4 And he would not for a while: but afterward he said within himself, Though I fear not God, nor regard man;
5 Yet because this widow troubleth me, I will avenge her, lest by her continual coming she weary me.
6 And the Lord said, Hear what the unjust judge saith.
7 And shall not God avenge his own elect, which cry day and night unto him, though he bear long with them?
8 I tell you that he will avenge them speedily. Nevertheless when the Son of man cometh, shall he find faith on the earth? (Luke 18:1-8)

Conceit nullifies prayer

9 And he spake this parable unto certain which trusted in themselves that they were righteous, and despised others:
10 Two men went up into the temple to pray; the one a Pharisee, and the other a publican.
11 The Pharisee stood and prayed thus with himself, God, I thank thee, that I am not as other men *are*, extortioners, unjust, adulterers, or even as this publican.
12 I fast twice in the week, I give tithes of all that I possess.
13 And the publican, standing afar off, would not lift up so much as *his* eyes unto heaven, but smote upon his breast, saying, God be merciful to me a sinner. (Luke 18:9-13)

Justified, *δικαιόω dikaioō*, in this context to judge, declare, pronounce, righteous and therefore acceptable.

14 I tell you, this man went down to his house justified *rather* than the other: for every one that exalteth himself shall be abased; and he that humbleth himself shall be exalted. (Luke 18:14)

CHAPTER 122
THE RESURRECTION OF LAZARUS

(The 4th incident where Jesus proves that life is eternal.)

Lazarus is declared by mortal mind to be sick, *ἀσθενέω, astheneō*, meaning feeble, without strength, powerless, failing.

1 Now a certain *man* was sick, *named* Lazarus, of Bethany, the town of Mary and her sister Martha. (John 11:1)

A parenthetical statement specifying which Mary, by identifying her with the 2nd anointing that will soon to take place.

2 (It was *that* Mary which anointed the Lord with ointment, and wiped his feet with her hair, whose brother Lazarus was sick.) (John 11:2)

Mary was a disciple (See Luke 10:38-42). She and her sister Martha maintained correspondence with Jesus.

3 Therefore his sisters sent unto him, saying, Lord, behold, he whom thou lovest is sick. (John 11:3)

Jesus never accepted the belief in a power other than God, Life, and so he immediately nullified the claim of death.

4 When Jesus heard *that*, he said, This sickness is not unto death, but for the glory of God, that the Son of God might be glorified thereby. (John 11:4)

A necessary explanation since to the unenlightened human mind his words might appear to be callous, uncaring.

5 Now Jesus loved Martha, and her sister, and Lazarus. (John 11:5)

Jesus acted according to God's time (eternal Life), not by the reckoning of mortals, (birth to death; beginning and ending).

6 When he had heard therefore that he was sick, he abode two days still in the same place where he was.

7 Then after that saith he to *his* disciples, Let us go into Judæa again. (John 11:6-7)

The Jews will lie to Pilate. The Hebrew law did provide for the death penalty for certain violations. Jesus was innocent!

8 *His* disciples say unto him, Master, the Jews of late sought to stone thee; and goest thou thither again? (John 11:8)

To avoid stumbling men must walk in the light, *phōs*, of Christ. Jesus had been praying for Lazarus these two days.

9 Jesus answered, Are there not twelve hours in the day? If any man walk in the day, he stumbleth not, because he seeth the light of this world.

10 But if a man walk in the night, he stumbleth, because there is no light in him. (John 11:9-10)

Sleepeth, *κοιμάω koimaō*, has fallen asleep. awake him, *ἐξυπνίζω exypnizō*, wake him up. Jesus was attempting to lift the thought of his disciples higher than the belief that what mortals call death is final.

11 These things said he: and after that he saith unto them, Our friend Lazarus sleepeth; but I go, that I may awake him out of sleep. (John 11:11)

Reasoning from a purely material basis the disciples interpreted what Jesus said according to sense testimony.

12 Then said his disciples, Lord, if he sleep, he shall do well.

13 Howbeit Jesus spake of his death: but they thought that he had spoken of taking of rest in sleep. (John 11:12-13)

The disciples did not yet understand God as omnipresent and eternal Life, so Jesus had to reply according to their belief.

14 Then said Jesus unto them plainly, Lazarus is dead. (John 11:14)

Being some distance from Jerusalem, Jesus knew Lazarus would have been "dead" for at least three days.

15 And I am glad for your sakes that I was not there, to the intent ye may believe; nevertheless let us go unto him. (John 11:15)

Thomas was certain that this trip to Jerusalem meant certain death for all of them, not only for Jesus.

16 Then said Thomas, which is called Didymus, unto his fellow-disciples, Let us also go, that we may die with him. (John 11:16)

Jesus was confronting the belief that after three days "the spirit" permanently departs the body.

17 Then when Jesus came, he found that he had *lain* in the grave four days already.

18 Now Bethany was nigh unto Jerusalem, about fifteen furlongs off:

19 And many of the Jews came to Martha and Mary, to comfort them concerning their brother. (John 11:17-19)

The word "still" is a later addition. Remove the word *still* and it reads: "but Mary sat in the house," i.e. she didn't go.

20 Then Martha, as soon as she heard that Jesus was coming, went and met him: but Mary sat *still* in the house.

21 Then said Martha unto Jesus, Lord, if thou hadst been here, my brother had not died.

22 But I know, that even now, whatsoever thou wilt ask of God, God will give *it* thee.

23 Jesus saith unto her, Thy brother shall rise again.

24 Martha saith unto him, I know that he shall rise again in the resurrection at the last day. (John 11:20-24)

The only "I am" Jesus identified with is God. This understanding IS the resurrection above all mortal sense testimony.

25 Jesus said unto her, I am the resurrection, and the life: he that believeth in me, though he were dead, yet shall he live: (John 11:25)

The "Me" that Jesus spoke of was Christ, his true and divine nature, the Son of God which is God in expression.

26 And whosoever liveth and believeth in me shall never die. Believest thou this?

27 She saith unto him, Yea, Lord: I believe that thou art the Christ, the Son of God,
which should come into the world. (John 11:26-27)

The following suggests that Martha stole away from the "mourners" so she could call Mary privately.

28 And when she had so said, she went her way, and called Mary her sister secretly,
saying, The Master is come, and calleth for thee.
29 As soon as she heard *that*, she arose quickly, and came unto him.
30 Now Jesus was not yet come into the town, but was in that place where Martha met
him.
31 The Jews then which were with her in the house, and comforted her, when they saw
Mary, that she rose up hastily and went out, followed her, saying, She goeth unto the
grave to weep there. (John 11:28-31)

Note below how Jesus responded when Mary arrived accompanied by a group of so-called "comforters."

32 Then when Mary was come where Jesus was, and saw him, she fell down at his feet,
saying unto him, Lord, if thou hadst been here, my brother had not died. (John 11:32)

Jesus groaned, *ἐμβριμάομαι embrimaomai*, derived from a word meaning to snort with anger, probably indignant at the feigned sorrow of the Jews, some that were plotting to kill him, and would later plot to kill Lazarus also.

33 When Jesus therefore saw her weeping, and the Jews also weeping which came with
her, he groaned in the spirit, and was troubled,
34 And said, Where have ye laid him? They said unto him, Lord, come and see. (John
11:33-34)

Jesus wept, not for Lazarus, but because Mary doubted.

35 Jesus wept.
36 Then said the Jews, Behold how he loved him! (John 11:35-36)

Had Jesus healed Lazarus sooner they would have said it was through Beelzebub. It is also likely that in this group were some who later on would propose murdering Lazarus simply because his resurrection validated what Jesus taught.

37 And some of them said, Could not this man, which opened the eyes of the blind,
have caused that even this man should not have died? (John 11:37)

Jesus again "groaned in himself," that is to say, he was again indignant at the malice of some so-called comforters.

38 Jesus therefore again groaning in himself cometh to the grave. It was a cave, and a
stone lay upon it. (John 11:38)

Eternal Life confronts the error that man has a life apart from God!

39 Jesus said, Take ye away the stone. Martha, the sister of him that was dead, saith
unto him, Lord, by this time he stinketh: for he hath been *dead* four days. (John 11:39)

Jesus rebuked the belief voiced by Martha that there was no hope. Despite all they had witnessed, she still doubted.

40 Jesus saith unto her, Said I not unto thee, that, if thou wouldest believe, thou
shouldest see the glory of God? (John 11:40)

Jesus had doubtless been praying the past few days to realize Lazarus could never actually die. "Jesus restored Lazarus by the understanding that Lazarus had never died, not by an admission that his body had died and then lived again. Had Jesus believed that Lazarus had lived or died in his body, the Master would have stood on the same plane of belief as those who buried the body, and he could not have resuscitated it." - MBE

41 Then they took away the stone *from the place* where the dead was laid. (John 11:41 *to*
1st.)

Jesus demonstrated his absolute conviction that righteous prayer is answered and that Lazarus was even then alive.

41 And Jesus lifted up *his* eyes, and said, Father, I thank thee that thou hast heard me.
42 And I knew that thou hearest me always: but because of the people which stand by I
said *it*, that they may believe that thou hast sent me.
43 And when he thus had spoken, he cried with a loud voice, Lazarus, come forth. (John
11:41-43 *And*)

The human mind must be loosed from the belief that man lives or dies in a material body.

44 And he that was dead came forth, bound hand and foot with graveclothes: and his
face was bound about with a napkin. Jesus saith unto them, Loose him, and let him go.
(John 11:44)

CHAPTER 123
OPPOSING REACTIONS TO RAISING LAZARUS

Many came to understand that Jesus had raised Lazarus from the dead through Christ.

45 Then many of the Jews which came to Mary, and had seen the things which Jesus
did, believed on him. (John 11:45)

Some, plotting to execute Jesus, reported to the Pharisees that Jesus had raised Lazarus to life.

46 But some of them went their ways to the Pharisees, and told them what things Jesus
had done. (John 11:46)

Envy. The chief priests and Pharisees assembled to discuss how to stop Jesus' ministry, for to them it was *too* successful.

47 ¶ Then gathered the chief priests and the Pharisees a council, and said, What do we?
for this man doeth many miracles. (John 11:47)

Jesus to them was a threat to *their* authority and *their* nation, for they said "OUR place and nation;" not God's nation.

48 If we let him thus alone, all *men* will believe on him: and the Romans shall come
and take away both our place and nation. (John 11:48)

The murderous nature of ecclesiastical despotism strives to eliminate any threat to personal control over others.
Maintaining ***their*** place, positions of authority, was their reason for executing Jesus. Saving the nation was a ruse!

49 And one of them, *named* Caiaphas, being the high priest that same year, said unto
them, Ye know nothing at all,
50 Nor consider that it is expedient for us, that one man should die for the people, and
that the whole nation perish not. (John 11:49-50)

The Jews regarded any *ex cathedra* utterance of the High Priest as inspired. should die = was about to die" TCB p. 1548.
Prophesied, *προφητεύω prophēteuō*. Caiaphas used the office of High Priest to advance his murderous proposition.
Hiding his real reason, preservation of rank and authority, he used fear and greed to influence the members of his faction.

51 And this spake he not of himself: but being high priest that year, he prophesied that
Jesus should die for that nation; (John 11:51)

Caiaphas also imagined that executing Jesus would result in the dispersed Jews uniting in rebellion against Rome.

52 And not for that nation only, but that also he should gather together in one the
children of God that were scattered abroad. (John 11:52)

So from that time forward every day was spent by members of the Sanhedrin devising a plan to execute Jesus.

53 Then from that day forth they took counsel together for to put him to death. (John 11:53)

Another retreat, this one was about 16 miles north-east of Jerusalem to Ephraim, now named *Ophrah*. TCB

54 Jesus therefore walked no more openly among the Jews; but went thence unto a
country near to the wilderness, into a city called Ephraim, and there continued with his
disciples. (John 11:54)

CHAPTER 124
TWO REQUIREMENTS TO ENTER THE KINGDOM

The 1st requirement: Childlikeness (purity, innocency)

According to the Gospel of Luke

15 And they brought unto him also infants, that he would touch them: but when *his*
disciples saw *it*, they rebuked them.
16 But Jesus called them *unto him*, and said, Suffer little children to come unto me, and
forbid them not: for of such is the kingdom of God.
17 Verily I say unto you, Whosoever shall not receive the kingdom of God as a little
child shall in no wise enter therein. (Luke 18:15-17)

According to the Gospel of Mark

13 ¶ And they brought young children to him, that he should touch them: and *his*
disciples rebuked those that brought *them*.
14 But when Jesus saw *it*, he was much displeased, and said unto them, Suffer the little
children to come unto me, and forbid them not: for of such is the kingdom of God.

15 Verily I say unto you, Whosoever shall not receive the kingdom of God as a little
child, he shall not enter therein.
16 And he took them up in his arms, put *his* hands upon them, and blessed them. (Mark
10:13-16)

According to the Gospel of Matthew

13 ¶ Then were there brought unto him little children, that he should put *his* hands on
them, and pray: and the disciples rebuked them.
14 But Jesus said, Suffer little children, and forbid them not, to come unto me: for of
such is the kingdom of heaven.
15 And he laid *his* hands on them, and departed thence. (Matt 19:13-15)

The 2nd requirement: Keep the Commandments (Obedience)

According to the Gospel of Matthew

Jesus was not swayed by flattery! He knew God, Spirit to be good, the source of any and all good that he expressed.

16 ¶ And, behold, one came and said unto him, Good Master, what good thing shall I
do, that I may have eternal life?
17 And he said unto him, Why callest thou me good? *there is* none good but one, *that
is*, God: (Matt 19:16-17 to :)

There are no shortcuts to eternal life. Obedience to ***all*** of the Commandments is required.

17 but if thou wilt enter into life, keep the commandments.
18 He saith unto him, Which? (Matt 19:17-18 but *to* ?)

It's not negotiable. Jesus listed the Commandments relating to treatment of our fellow man first. See Matt 22:35-40.

18 Jesus said, Thou shalt do no murder, Thou shalt not commit adultery, Thou shalt not
steal, Thou shalt not bear false witness,
19 Honour thy father and *thy* mother: and, Thou shalt love thy neighbour as thyself.
20 The young man saith unto him, All these things have I kept from my youth up: what
lack I yet? (Matt 19:18-20 *Jesus*)

If thou wilt be perfect = if you will obey *every* Commandment. The First Commandment includes all of the others.

21 Jesus said unto him, If thou wilt be perfect, go *and* sell that thou hast, and give to the
poor, and thou shalt have treasure in heaven: and come *and* follow me. (Matt 19:21)

The love of mammon, having other gods before the Me that is Spirit, results in violating the First Commandment.

22 But when the young man heard that saying, he went away sorrowful: for he had
great possessions. (Matt 19:22)

Rich, *πλούσιος plousios*, abundance. See note above Mk 10:24. Hardly, *δυσκόλως dyskolōs*, with great difficulty.

23 ¶ Then said Jesus unto his disciples, Verily I say unto you, That a rich man shall
hardly enter into the kingdom of heaven. (Matt 19:23)

Again, *πάλιν palin*. Jesus is using a metaphor to repeat, for emphasis a crucial point. See Matt. 6:19-24; 7:13-14, 21.

24 And again I say unto you, It is easier for a camel to go through the eye of a needle,
than for a rich man to enter into the kingdom of God. (Matt 19:24)

The disciples' amazement (shock) was due to their hearing that a rich man could NOT buy his way into the kingdom.

25 When his disciples heard *it*, they were exceedingly amazed, saying, Who then can be
saved? (Matt 19:25)

Metaphysics is above physics, and matter does not enter into metaphysical premises or conclusions. - MBE

26 But Jesus beheld *them*, and said unto them, With men this is impossible; but with
God all things are possible. (Matt 19:26)

According to the Gospel of Luke

18 And a certain ruler asked him, saying, Good Master, what shall I do to inherit eternal
life?
19 And Jesus said unto him, Why callest thou me good? none *is* good, save one, *that is*,

God.
20 Thou knowest the commandments, Do not commit adultery, Do not kill, Do not
steal, Do not bear false witness, Honour thy father and thy mother.
21 And he said, All these have I kept from my youth up. (Luke 18:18-21)

Keep the First Commandment and have but one God, Spirit for it includes all of the others. This is what it means to leave all for Christ.

22 Now when Jesus heard these things, he said unto him, Yet lackest thou one thing:
sell all that thou hast, and distribute unto the poor, and thou shalt have treasure in
heaven: and come, follow me.
23 And when he heard this, he was very sorrowful: for he was very rich.
24 And when Jesus saw that he was very sorrowful, he said, How hardly shall they that
have riches enter into the kingdom of God!
25 For it is easier for a camel to go through a needle's eye, than for a rich man to enter
into the kingdom of God.
26 And they that heard *it* said, Who then can be saved? (Luke 18:22-26)

When man is governed by God, the ever-present Mind who understands all things, man knows that with God all things are possible. The only way to this living Truth, which heals the sick, is found in the Science of Mind as taught and demonstrated by Christ Jesus. - MBE

27 And he said, The things which are impossible with men are possible with God. (Luke
18:27)

According to the Gospel of Mark

17 ¶ And when he was gone forth into the way, there came one running, and kneeled to
him, and asked him, Good Master, what shall I do that I may inherit eternal life?
18 And Jesus said unto him, Why callest thou me good? *there is* none good but one,
that is, God.
19 Thou knowest the commandments, Do not commit adultery, Do not kill, Do not
steal, Do not bear false witness, Defraud not, Honour thy father and mother.
20 And he answered and said unto him, Master, all these have I observed from my
youth. (Mark 10:17-20)

In order to keep the First Commandment all of the others must be kept. Keeping them all constitutes leaving all for Christ.

21 Then Jesus beholding him loved him, and said unto him, One thing thou lackest: go
thy way, sell whatsoever thou hast, and give to the poor, and thou shalt have treasure in
heaven: and come, take up the cross, and follow me.
22 And he was sad at that saying, and went away grieved: for he had great possessions.
23 ¶ And Jesus looked round about, and saith unto his disciples, How hardly shall they
that have riches enter into the kingdom of God!
24 And the disciples were astonished at his words. (Mark 10:21-24 *to* 1st.)

The difficulty is NOT in having abundance, but TRUSTING in matter rather than in Spirit, God. See John 10:10

24 But Jesus answereth again, and saith unto them, Children, how hard is it for them
that trust in riches to enter into the kingdom of God! (Mark 10:24 *But*)

Literal explanations for this metaphor, *e.g.* a "needle gate," a small gate within or next to the main gate may be interesting, but the point is that there is no material means to accomplish a spiritual end. See Mk. 10:27 below.

25 It is easier for a camel to go through the eye of a needle, than for a rich man to enter
into the kingdom of God.
26 And they were astonished out of measure, saying among themselves, Who then can
be saved? (Mark 10:24-26 *But*)

Scripture informs us that "with God all things are possible," --- all good is possible to Spirit; but our prevalent theories practically deny this, and make healing possible only through matter. These theories must be untrue, for the Scripture is true. Christianity is not false, but religions which contradict its Principle are false. - MBE

27 And Jesus looking upon them saith, With men *it is* impossible, but not with God: for
with God all things are possible. (Mark 10:27)

CHAPTER 125
WHAT'S IN IT FOR ME?

Jesus replies to the Apostles in answer to Peter's concern about being rewarded

According to the Gospel of Luke

28 Then Peter said, Lo, we have left all, and followed thee,
29 And he said unto them, Verily I say unto you, There is no man that hath left house,
or parents, or brethren, or wife, or children, for the kingdom of God's sake,
30 Who shall not receive manifold more in this present time, and in the world to come
life everlasting. (Luke 18:28-30)

According to the Gospel of Mark

28 ¶ Then Peter began to say unto him, Lo, we have left all, and have followed thee.
29 And Jesus answered and said, Verily I say unto you, There is no man that hath left
house, or brethren, or sisters, or father, or mother, or wife, or children, or lands, for my
sake, and the gospel's,
30 But he shall receive an hundredfold now in this time, houses, and brethren, and
sisters, and mothers, and children, and lands, with persecutions; and in the world to
come eternal life.
31 But many *that are* first shall be last; and the last first. (Mark 10:28-31)

According to the Gospel of Matthew

27 ¶ Then answered Peter and said unto him, Behold, we have forsaken all, and
followed thee; what shall we have therefore?
28 And Jesus said unto them, Verily I say unto you, That ye which have followed me,
in the regeneration when the Son of man shall sit in the throne of his glory, ye also shall
sit upon twelve thrones, judging the twelve tribes of Israel.
29 And every one that hath forsaken houses, or brethren, or sisters, or father, or mother,
or wife, or children, or lands, for my name's sake, shall receive an hundredfold, and
shall inherit everlasting life.
30 But many *that are* first shall be last; and the last *shall be* first. (Matt 19:27-30)

The answer to Peter's Question: "What shall we have therefore?" is expanded in The Parable of the Householder

The laborers hired early in the morning refers to the first disciples, the twelve Apostles.

1 For the kingdom of heaven is like unto a man *that is* an householder, which went out
early in the morning to hire labourers into his vineyard. (Matt 20:1)

Wages were agreed upon before labor began. "A penny a day" symbolizes inheriting the kingdom.

2 And when he had agreed with the labourers for a penny a day, he sent them into his
vineyard. (Matt 20:2)

The "third hour of the day" (Acts 2:15), foretells the day of Pentecost when others would be "hired."

3 And he went out about the third hour, and saw others standing idle in the
marketplace,
4 And said unto them; Go ye also into the vineyard, and whatsoever is right I will give
you. And they went their way. (Matt 20:3-4)

The 6th hour foretells Peter's vision (Acts 10:9) and Cornelius' the 9th hour (Acts 10:3, 30) when more would be "hired."

5 Again he went out about the sixth and ninth hour, and did likewise. (Matt 20:5)

The eleventh hour foretells the end is near. Who is to say we are right now not in the eleventh hour?"

6 And about the eleventh hour he went out, and found others standing idle, and saith
unto them, Why stand ye here all the day idle?
7 They say unto him, Because no man hath hired us. He saith unto them, Go ye also

into the vineyard; and whatsoever is right, *that* shall ye receive.
8 So when even was come, the lord of the vineyard saith unto his steward, Call the
labourers, and give them *their* hire, beginning from the last unto the first.
9 And when they came that *were hired* about the eleventh hour, they received every
man a penny.
10 But when the first came, they supposed that they should have received more; and
they likewise received every man a penny.
11 And when they had received *it*, they murmured against the goodman of the house,
12 Saying, These last have wrought *but* one hour, and thou hast made them equal unto
us, which have borne the burden and heat of the day. (Matt 20:6-12)

Why murmur? A penny IS the kingdom, "Son, thou art ever with me, and all that I have is thine." (Luke: 15:31).

13 But he answered one of them, and said, Friend, I do thee no wrong: didst not thou
agree with me for a penny? (Matt 20:13)

God, divine Love, bestows all good on ***all***. What more can we ask for? Mortals, thinking materially see only limitation.

14 Take *that* thine *is*, and go thy way: I will give unto this last, even as unto thee. (Matt 20:14)

The belief in limitation does not make God's law, the law of infinite good evil, unlawful, or unjust!

15 Is it not lawful for me to do what I will with mine own? Is thine eye evil, because I
am good? (Matt 20:15)

Spiritual consciousness, whether deemed of less importance than other concerns or simply ignored, will ultimately become first (primary), because it is only through spiritual sense that one can "enter" the kingdom. See I Cor. 15:50

16 So the last shall be first, and the first last: for many be called, but few chosen. (Matt 20:16)

THE SEVENTH DAY BEFORE PASSOVER

(The 8th day of Nisan the Gentile Wednesday sunset to Thursday sunset)

CHAPTER 126

THE 5TH ANNOUNCEMENT OF SUFFERINGS

(Mark 10:33; Matthew 20:18-19 & Luke 18:31-33)

According to the Gospel of Mark

"They were amazed", *θαμβέω thambeō*, terrified, frightened.

32 ¶ And they were in the way going up to Jerusalem; and Jesus went before them: and
they were amazed; and as they followed, they were afraid. And he took again the
twelve, and began to tell them what things should happen unto him,
33 *Saying*, Behold, we go up to Jerusalem; and the Son of man shall be delivered unto
the chief priests, and unto the scribes; and they shall condemn him to death, and shall
deliver him to the Gentiles:
34 And they shall mock him, and shall scourge him, and shall spit upon him, and shall
kill him: and the third day he shall rise again. (Mark 10:32-34)

According to the Gospel of Matthew

17 ¶ And Jesus going up to Jerusalem took the twelve disciples apart in the way, and
said unto them,
18 Behold, we go up to Jerusalem; and the Son of man shall be betrayed unto the chief
priests and unto the scribes, and they shall condemn him to death,
19 And shall deliver him to the Gentiles to mock, and to scourge, and to crucify *him*:
and the third day he shall rise again. (Matt 20:17-19)

According to the Gospel of Luke

31 ¶ Then he took *unto him* the twelve, and said unto them, Behold, we go up to

Jerusalem, and all things that are written by the prophets concerning the Son of man
shall be accomplished.
32 For he shall be delivered unto the Gentiles, and shall be mocked, and spitefully
entreated, and spitted on:
33 And they shall scourge *him*, and put him to death: and the third day he shall rise
again.
34 And they understood none of these things: and this saying was hid from them,
neither knew they the things which were spoken. (Luke 18:31-34)

CHAPTER 127
PETITIONING FOR POSITIONS OF AUTHORITY

First, James and John petition for themselves

35 ¶ And James and John, the sons of Zebedee, come unto him, saying, Master, we
would that thou shouldest do for us whatsoever we shall desire.
36 And he said unto them, What would ye that I should do for you?
37 They said unto him, Grant unto us that we may sit, one on thy right hand, and the
other on thy left hand, in thy glory.
38 But Jesus said unto them, Ye know not what ye ask: can ye drink of the cup that I
drink of? and be baptized with the baptism that I am baptized with?
39 And they said unto him, We can. And Jesus said unto them, Ye shall indeed drink
of the cup that I drink of; and with the baptism that I am baptized withal shall ye be
baptized:
40 But to sit on my right hand and on my left hand is not mine to give; but *it shall be
given to them* for whom it is prepared.
41 And when the ten heard *it*, they began to be much displeased with James and John.
(Mark 10:35-41)

Next, Salome the mother of James and John petitions for her two sons

20 ¶ Then came to him the mother of Zebedee's children with her sons, worshipping
him, and desiring a certain thing of him.
21 And he said unto her, What wilt thou? She saith unto him, Grant that these my two
sons may sit, the one on thy right hand, and the other on the left, in thy kingdom. (Matt 20:20-21)

It doesn't matter who petitions, the requirements remain the same! It is a matter of Principle, not person. Acts 10:34-35

22 But Jesus answered and said, Ye know not what ye ask. Are ye able to drink of the
cup that I shall drink of, and to be baptized with the baptism that I am baptized with?
They say unto him, We are able.
23 And he saith unto them, Ye shall drink indeed of my cup, and be baptized with the
baptism that I am baptized with: but to sit on my right hand, and on my left, is not mine
to give, but *it shall be given to them* for whom it is prepared of my Father.
24 And when the ten heard *it*, they were moved with indignation against the two
brethren. (Matt 20:23-24)

CHAPTER 128
JESUS ADVISES AGAINST A HIERARCHY

According to the Gospel of Matthew

25 But Jesus called them *unto him*, and said, Ye know that the princes of the Gentiles
exercise dominion over them, and they that are great exercise authority upon them.

26 But it shall not be so among you: but whosoever will be great among you, let him be
your minister;
27 And whosoever will be chief among you, let him be your servant:
28 Even as the Son of man came not to be ministered unto, but to minister, and to give
his life a ransom for many. (Matt 20:25-28)

According to the Gospel of Mark

42 But Jesus called them *to him*, and saith unto them, Ye know that they which are
accounted to rule over the Gentiles exercise lordship over them; and their great ones
exercise authority upon them.
43 But so shall it not be among you: but whosoever will be great among you, shall be
your minister:
44 And whosoever of you will be the chiefest, shall be servant of all.
45 For even the Son of man came not to be ministered unto, but to minister, and to give
his life a ransom for many. (Mark 10:42-45)

CHAPTER 129
APPROACHING JERICHO "A CERTAIN" BLIND MAN IS HEALED

35 ¶ And it came to pass, that as he was come nigh unto Jericho, a certain blind man sat
by the way side begging:
36 And hearing the multitude pass by, he asked what it meant.
37 And they told him, that Jesus of Nazareth passeth by.
38 And he cried, saying, Jesus, *thou* son of David, have mercy on me.
39 And they which went before rebuked him, that he should hold his peace: but he cried
so much the more, *Thou* son of David, have mercy on me.
40 And Jesus stood, and commanded him to be brought unto him: and when he was
come near, he asked him,
41 Saying, What wilt thou that I shall do unto thee? And he said, Lord, that I may
receive my sight.
42 And Jesus said unto him, Receive thy sight: thy faith hath saved thee.
43 And immediately he received his sight, and followed him, glorifying God: and all
the people, when they saw *it*, gave praise unto God. (Luke 18:35-43)

Arrival in Jericho

46 ¶ And they came to Jericho: (Mark 10:46 to :)

CHAPTER 130
JESUS AND ZACCHÆUS

(Jesus is the guest of Zacchæus Thursday night, the evening and night of Nisan 9)

1 And *Jesus* entered and passed through Jericho.
2 And, behold, *there was* a man named Zacchæus, which was the chief among the
publicans, and he was rich.
3 And he sought to see Jesus who he was; and could not for the press, because he was
little of stature.
4 And he ran before, and climbed up into a sycomore tree to see him: for he was to pass
that *way*.
5 And when Jesus came to the place, he looked up, and saw him, and said unto him,
Zacchæus, make haste, and come down; for to-day I must abide at thy house.

6 And he made haste, and came down, and received him joyfully. (Luke 19:1-6)

Note the reaction of the Pharisees to a man who actually did what Jesus earlier told the rich young man to do. See Matt. 19:21, Luke 18:22 & Mark 10:21 pgs. 304 & 305. Would the ecclesiastics have murmured if Zacchæus had pledged "the half of his goods" to the ***temple*** rather than to the poor? Re-read Matthew 15:1-6 p. 253 for the answer.

7 And when they saw *it*, they all murmured, saying, That he was gone to be guest with
a man that is a sinner.
8 And Zacchæus stood, and said unto the Lord; Behold, Lord, the half of my goods I
give to the poor; and if I have taken any thing from any man by false accusation, I
restore *him* fourfold.
9 And Jesus said unto him, This day is salvation come to this house, forsomuch as he
also is a son of Abraham.
10 For the Son of man is come to seek and to save that which was lost. (Luke 19:7-10)

THE SIXTH DAY BEFORE PASSOVER

(The 9th day of Nisan, the Gentile Thursday sunset to Friday sunset)

CHAPTER 131

BLINDNESS HEALED LEAVING AND DEPARTING JERICHO

Bartimæus" is healed of blindness "as [Jesus] *went out of* Jericho with his disciples"

46 and as he went out of Jericho with his disciples and a great number of people, blind
Bartimæus, the son of Timæus, sat by the highway side begging.
47 And when he heard that it was Jesus of Nazareth, he began to cry out, and say,
Jesus, *thou* son of David, have mercy on me.
48 And many charged him that he should hold his peace: but he cried the more a great
deal, *Thou* son of David, have mercy on me.
49 And Jesus stood still, and commanded him to be called. And they call the blind
man, saying unto him, Be of good comfort, rise; he calleth thee.
50 And he, casting away his garment, rose, and came to Jesus.
51 And Jesus answered and said unto him, What wilt thou that I should do unto thee?
The blind man said unto him, Lord, that I might receive my sight.
52 And Jesus said unto him, Go thy way; thy faith hath made thee whole. And
immediately he received his sight, and followed Jesus in the way. (Mark 10:46-52 *and*)

Two more blind men are healed of blindness further along "as they *departed from* Jericho"

29 And as they departed from Jericho, a great multitude followed him.
30 ¶ And, behold, two blind men sitting by the way side, when they heard that Jesus
passed by, cried out, saying, Have mercy on us, O Lord, *thou* son of David.
31 And the multitude rebuked them, because they should hold their peace: but they
cried the more, saying, Have mercy on us, O Lord, *thou* son of David.
32 And Jesus stood still, and called them, and said, What will ye that I shall do unto
you?
33 They say unto him, Lord, that our eyes may be opened.
34 So Jesus had compassion *on them*, and touched their eyes: and immediately their
eyes received sight, and they followed him. (Matt 20:29-34)

CHAPTER 132
THE BRUTALITY OF WORLDLY RULERSHIP

(The Messiahship anticipated by the Jews was "of the earth, earthy." Jesus was a disappointment to them because they anticipated a revolutionary military leader who would free them from Roman rulership. So, they used their power to blackmail Pilate if he refused to execute Jesus, because Jesus was a threat to their control over the people.)

11 And as they heard these things, he added and spake a parable, because he was nigh
to Jerusalem, and because they thought that the kingdom of God should immediately
appear. (Luke 19:11)

The Parable of the Pounds

(A parable based on what happened after Herod the Great and his son Archélaus received the sovereignty from Rome)

12 He said therefore, A certain nobleman went into a far country to receive for himself
a kingdom, and to return.
13 And he called his ten servants, and delivered them ten pounds, and said unto them,
Occupy till I come.
14 But his citizens hated him, and sent a message after him, saying, We will not have
this *man* to reign over us.
15 And it came to pass, that when he was returned, having received the kingdom, then
he commanded these servants to be called unto him, to whom he had given the money,
that he might know how much every man had gained by trading.
16 Then came the first, saying, Lord, thy pound hath gained ten pounds.
17 And he said unto him, Well, thou good servant: because thou hast been faithful in a
very little, have thou authority over ten cities.
18 And the second came, saying, Lord, thy pound hath gained five pounds.
19 And he said likewise to him, Be thou also over five cities.
20 And another came, saying, Lord, behold, *here is* thy pound, which I have kept laid
up in a napkin:
21 For I feared thee, because thou art an austere man: thou takest up that thou layedst
not down, and reapest that thou didst not sow.
22 And he saith unto him, Out of thine own mouth will I judge thee, *thou* wicked
servant. Thou knewest that I was an austere man, taking up that I laid not down, and
reaping that I did not sow:
23 Wherefore then gavest not thou my money into the bank, that at my coming I might
have required mine own with usury?
24 And he said unto them that stood by, Take from him the pound, and give *it* to him
that hath ten pounds.
25 (And they said unto him, Lord, he hath ten pounds.) (Luke 19:12-25)

A remark by Jesus describing how worldly government works: The rich and powerful strive to take everything.

26 For I say unto you, That unto every one which hath shall be given; and from him
that hath not, even that he hath shall be taken away from him. (Luke 19:26)

Absolute power in the hands of mortal man is deadly.

27 But those mine enemies, which would not that I should reign over them, bring
hither, and slay *them* before me. (Luke 19:27)

Jesus continues the ascent toward Jerusalem

28 ¶ And when he had thus spoken he went before, ascending up to Jerusalem. (Luke 19:28)

A plan to arrest Jesus was already in effect

55 ¶ And the Jews' passover was nigh at hand: and many went out of the country up to

Jerusalem before the passover, to purify themselves.
56 Then sought they for Jesus, and spake among themselves, as they stood in the
temple, What think ye, that he will not come to the feast?
57 Now both the chief priests and the Pharisees had given a commandment, that, if any
man knew where he were, he should shew *it*, that they might take him. (John 11:55-57)

CHAPTER 133
JESUS ON HIS FIRST ENTRY INTO JERUSALEM IS UNKNOWN
Preparation for the 1st entry into Jerusalem from Bethphage

1 And when they drew nigh unto Jerusalem, and were come to Bethphage, unto the
2 mount of Olives, then sent Jesus two disciples,
2 Saying unto them, Go into the village over against you, and straightway ye shall find
an ass tied, and a colt with her: loose *them*, and bring *them* unto me.
3 And if any *man* say ought unto you, ye shall say, The Lord hath need of them; and
straightway he will send them.
4 All this was done, that it might be fulfilled which was spoken by the prophet, saying,
(Matt 21:1-4)

On his first entry Jesus rode on an ass leading a colt, thereby fulfilling the prophecy of Isaiah 62:11.

5 Tell ye the daughter of Sion, Behold, thy King cometh unto thee, meek, and sitting
upon an ass, and a colt the foal of an ass.
6 And the disciples went, and did as Jesus commanded them, (Matt 21:5-6)
7 And brought the ass, and the colt, and put on them their clothes, and they set *him*
thereon. (Matt 21:5-7)

The general population did not recognize Jesus. Only "the multitude", meaning a group of Jesus' disciples, knew him.

8 And a very great multitude spread their garments in the way; others cut down
branches from the trees, and strawed *them* in the way.
9 And the multitudes that went before, and that followed, cried, saying, Hosanna to the
son of David: Blessed *is* he that cometh in the name of the Lord; Hosanna in the
highest. (Matt 21:8-9)

The people of Jerusalem said: "Who is this?" simply because Jesus was largely unrecognized by the general population.

10 And when he was come into Jerusalem, all the city was moved, saying, Who is this?
(Matt 21:10)

It was the disciples in Jerusalem that knew Jesus. At that time Jesus had many, a multitude of disciples in Jerusalem.

11 And the multitude said, This is Jesus the prophet of Nazareth of Galilee. (Matt 21:11)

CHAPTER 134
THE SECOND TEMPLE CLEANSING
(Ecclesiastical despotism resents both cleansing the temple grounds and healing the human body)

This is the 2nd time Jesus overthrew the tables. The 1st occasion was at the beginning of his ministry. See John 2:15.

12 ¶ And Jesus went into the temple of God, and cast out all them that sold and bought
in the temple, and overthrew the tables of the moneychangers, and the seats of them
that sold doves,
13 And said unto them, It is written, My house shall be called the house of prayer; but
ye have made it a den of thieves. (Matt 21:12-13)

The ecclesiastics were "sore displeased" because they were envious of the people's approval of Jesus.

14 And the blind and the lame came to him in the temple; and he healed them.
15 And when the chief priests and scribes saw the wonderful things that he did, and the
children crying in the temple, and saying, Hosanna to the son of David; they were sore
displeased,
16 And said unto him, Hearest thou what these say? And Jesus saith unto them, Yea;

have ye never read, Out of the mouth of babes and sucklings thou hast perfected praise? (Matt 21:14-16)

After leaving the temple Jesus spent the night in Bethany

17 ¶ And he left them, and went out of the city into Bethany; and he lodged there. (Matt 21:17)

Late Friday afternoon the 9th day of Nisan, just before the start of the regular weekly sabbath, and six days before the Passover Feast, one of three High Sabbaths. The other two are Pentecost and Tabernacles.

1 Then Jesus six days before the passover came to Bethany, where Lazarus was which had been dead, whom he raised from the dead. (John 12:1)

THE FIFTH DAY BEFORE PASSOVER

(The 10h day of Nisan the Gentile Friday sunset to Saturday sunset)

(¶ Speak ye unto all the congregation of Israel, saying, In the tenth *day* of this month they shall take to them every man a lamb, according to the house of *their* fathers, a lamb for an house: And if the household be too little for the lamb, let him and his neighbour next unto his house take *it* according to the number of the souls; every man according to his eating shall make your count for the lamb. Your lamb shall be without blemish, a male of the first year: ye shall take *it* out from the sheep, or from the goats: And ye shall keep it up until the fourteenth day of the same month: and the whole assembly of the congregation of Israel shall kill it in the evening. Exodus 12:1-6)

CHAPTER 135
THE SECOND ANOINTING

Jesus attended a supper prepared and served by Martha Saturday afternoon, the 10th of Nisan, a regular weekly sabbath.

2 There they made him a supper; and Martha served: but Lazarus was one of them that sat at the table with him. (John 12:2)

Mary, the sister of Martha and Lazarus, administered the 2nd anointing. The 1st anointing is recorded in Luke 7:36-50.

3 Then took Mary a pound of ointment of spikenard, very costly, and anointed the feet of Jesus, and wiped his feet with her hair: and the house was filled with the odour of the ointment. (John 12:3)

Judas Iscariot is named as the only disciple to protest the cost of the ointment at this anointing.

4 Then saith one of his disciples, Judas Iscariot, Simon's *son*, which should betray him, (John 12:4)

Where is the love for the Master? In the remark in verse 6 below, John reveals the real reason for Judas' protest.

5 Why was not this ointment sold for three hundred pence, and given to the poor?

6 This he said, not that he cared for the poor; but because he was a thief, and had the bag, and bare what was put therein. (John 12:5-6)

Jesus knew that there wouldn't be sufficient time after the crucifixion to properly prepare his body for burial.

7 Then said Jesus, Let her alone: against the day of my burying hath she kept this. (John 12:7)

The lust for money caused Judas' to betray Jesus, and the remorse he felt for his betrayal resulted in his suicide.

8 For the poor always ye have with you; but me ye have not always. (John 12:8)

The carnal mind, loving a spectacle, came more to see Lazarus, than Jesus who had raised him from the dead. Lazarus had become a celebrity and a target, someone whose existence was seen as a threat the Pharisees' control over the people.

9 Much people of the Jews therefore knew that he was there: and they came not for Jesus' sake only, but that they might see Lazarus also, whom he had raised from the dead. (John 12:9)

The carnal mind relishes the opportunity to destroy anything or anyone that witnesses for Truth.

10 ¶ But the chief priests consulted that they might put Lazarus also to death; (John 12:10)

"Went away," meaning they left the faction led by Caiaphas, and instead became followers of Jesus and his teaching.

11 Because that by reason of him many of the Jews went away, and believed on Jesus. (John 12:11)

THE FOURTH DAY BEFORE PASSOVER

(The 11h day of Nisan, the Gentile Saturday sunset to Sunday sunset)

CHAPTER 136

THE SECOND OR TRIUMPHAL ENTRY INTO JERUSALEM

According to the Gospel of John

The "next day" was Sunday. By this time the people knew that it was Jesus who had raised Lazarus!

12 ¶ On the next day much people that were come to the feast, when they heard that
Jesus was coming to Jerusalem,
13 Took branches of palm trees, and went forth to meet him, (John 12:12-13 *to* 2nd,)

This time the entry was from Bethany, and the people were informed beforehand it was Jesus who would be entering.

13 and cried, Hosanna: Blessed *is* the King of Israel that cometh in the name of the
Lord. (John 12:13 *and*)

This time there is only the animal that Jesus rode upon, a "young ass." There is no mention of a colt following behind.

14 And Jesus, when he had found a young ass, sat thereon; as it is written,
15 Fear not, daughter of Sion; behold, thy King cometh, sitting on an ass's colt.
16 These things understood not his disciples at the first: but when Jesus was glorified,
then remembered they that these things were written of him, and *that* they had done
these things unto him. (John 12:14-16)

There were more people this time because the entry was pre-announced, and Jesus was now known to the people.

17 The people therefore that was with him when he called Lazarus out of his grave, and
raised him from the dead, bare record.
18 For this cause the people also met him, for that they heard that he had done this
miracle. (John 12:17-18)

The carnal mind reacts: The greater the recognition and approval of Jesus, the greater the ENVY felt by the Pharisees.

19 The Pharisees therefore said among themselves, Perceive ye how ye prevail
nothing? behold, the world is gone after him. (John 12:19)

According to the Gospel of Luke

29 And it came to pass, when he was come nigh to Bethphage and Bethany, at the
mount called *the mount* of Olives, he sent two of his disciples,
30 Saying, Go ye into the village over against *you*; in the which at your entering ye
shall find a colt tied, whereon yet never man sat: loose him, and bring *him hither*.
31 And if any man ask you, Why do ye loose *him*? thus shall ye say unto him, Because
the Lord hath need of him.
32 And they that were sent went their way, and found even as he had said unto them.
33 And as they were loosing the colt, the owners thereof said unto them, Why loose ye
the colt?
34 And they said, The Lord hath need of him.
35 And they brought him to Jesus: and they cast their garments upon the colt, and they
set Jesus thereon.
36 And as he went, they spread their clothes in the way.
37 And when he was come nigh, even now at the descent of the mount of Olives, the
whole multitude of the disciples began to rejoice and praise God with a loud voice for
all the mighty works that they had seen;
38 Saying, Blessed *be* the King that cometh in the name of the Lord: peace in heaven,
and glory in the highest. (Luke 19:29-38)

The Pharisees criticized Jesus because many disciples shouted praises as he rode toward Jerusalem.

39 And some of the Pharisees from among the multitude said unto him, Master, rebuke
thy disciples.

40 And he answered and said unto them, I tell you that, if these should hold their peace,
the stones would immediately cry out. (Luke 19:39-40)

The name Jerusalem means "the possession of peace; the abode of harmony." Jesus wept for its forthcoming destruction.

41 ¶ And when he was come near, he beheld the city, and wept over it,
42 Saying, If thou hadst known, even thou, at least in this thy day, the things *which belong* unto thy peace! but now they are hid from thine eyes.
43 For the days shall come upon thee, that thine enemies shall cast a trench about thee, and compass thee round, and keep thee in on every side,
44 And shall lay thee even with the ground, and thy children within thee; and they shall not leave in thee one stone upon another; because thou knewest not the time of thy visitation. (Luke 19:41-44)

According to the Gospel of Mark

1 And when they came nigh to Jerusalem, unto Bethphage and Bethany, at the mount of Olives, he sendeth forth two of his disciples,
2 And saith unto them, Go your way into the village over against you: and as soon as ye be entered into it, ye shall find a colt tied, whereon never man sat; loose him, and bring *him*.
3 And if any man say unto you, Why do ye this? say ye that the Lord hath need of him; and straightway he will send him hither.
4 And they went their way, and found the colt tied by the door without in a place where two ways met; and they loose him.
5 And certain of them that stood there said unto them, What do ye, loosing the colt?
6 And they said unto them even as Jesus had commanded: and they let them go.
7 And they brought the colt to Jesus, and cast their garments on him; and he sat upon him. (Mark 11:1-7)

Many who cheered believed that Jesus, as the Messiah, would usher in a military revolt against Rome resulting in political and economic freedom. Most had no conception of the moral and spiritual freedom he was working to inaugurate.

8 And many spread their garments in the way: and others cut down branches off the trees, and strawed *them* in the way.
9 And they that went before, and they that followed, cried, saying, Hosanna; Blessed *is* he that cometh in the name of the Lord:
10 Blessed *be* the kingdom of our father David, that cometh in the name of the Lord: Hosanna in the highest.
11 And Jesus entered into Jerusalem, and into the temple: and when he had looked round about upon all things, and now the eventide was come, (Mark 11:8-11 *to* 3rd,)

In the evening Jesus and the twelve returned to Bethany.

11 he went out unto Bethany with the twelve. (Mark 11:11 *he*)

THE THIRD DAY BEFORE PASSOVER

(The 12th day of Nisan the Gentile Sunday sunset to Monday sunset)

CHAPTER 137
THE BARREN FIG TREE

According to the Gospel of Mark

It is Monday morning, the 12th of Nisan. The fig tree represents the corrupt and despotic religion of Israel at the time.

12 ¶ And on the morrow, when they were come from Bethany, he was hungry:
13 And seeing a fig tree afar off having leaves, he came, if haply he might find anything thereon: and when he came to it, he found nothing but leaves; for the time of figs was not *yet*.

14 And Jesus answered and said unto it, No man eat fruit of thee hereafter for ever.
And his disciples heard *it.* (Mark 11:12-14)

According to the Gospel of Matthew

18 Now in the morning as he returned into the city, he hungered. (Matt 21:18)

Under the corrupt Pharisees, the ecclesiatsics held out an empty promise (leaves only) but no figs (salvation for the people). This is what Jesus despised when he said: "let no fruit grow on thee henceforth forever."

19 And when he saw a fig tree in the way, he came to it, and found nothing thereon, but
leaves only, and said unto it, Let no fruit grow on thee henceforward for ever. (Matt 21:19 *to* 1st.)

CHAPTER 138
THE THIRD TEMPLE CLEANSING

(Jesus overthrows the *gods* of ecclesiastical despotism, *money* and *power*)

According to the Gospel of Mark

Jesus casts out the merchants and overthrows the tables of the money changers for the third and last time.

15 ¶ And they come to Jerusalem: and Jesus went into the temple, and began to cast out
them that sold and bought in the temple, and overthrew the tables of the
moneychangers, and the seats of them that sold doves; (Mark 11:15)

This is the only occasion when Jesus prevented vessel (merchandise), from being carried through the temple area.

16 And would not suffer that any man should carry *any* vessel through the temple.
17 And he taught, saying unto them, Is it not written, My house shall be called of all
nations the house of prayer? but ye have made it a den of thieves. (Mark 11:16-17)

According to the Gospel of Luke

45 And he went into the temple, and began to cast out them that sold therein, and them
that bought;
46 Saying unto them, It is written, My house is the house of prayer: but ye have made it
a den of thieves. (Luke 19:45-46)

CHAPTER 139
PREACHING IN THE TEMPLE GROUNDS

The people came to hear the truth. The Pharisees came to spy and gather information to formulate an accusation.

47 And he taught daily in the temple. (Luke 19:47 to 1st.)

"Certain Greeks", Ἕλλην *Hellēnes,* a Greek-speaking person, especially a non-Jew, a Gentile.

20 ¶ And there were certain Greeks among them that came up to worship at the feast:
(John 12:20)

Philip was called directly by Jesus (Jn. 1:43). Had Jesus foreseen Philip as a link to bring his teaching to the Gentiles?

21 The same came therefore to Philip, which was of Bethsaida of Galilee, and desired
him, saying, Sir, we would see Jesus.
22 Philip cometh and telleth Andrew: and again Andrew and Philip tell Jesus. (John 12:21-22)

In Cana Jesus said to Mary: "Mine hour is not yet come." Now he says: "The hour is come." He had been rejected by his own nation. He realized he had done what he could to bring his message to mankind, and now the Gentiles, represented by the Greeks, would be an avenue to preserve and extend his message for all mankind as would Paul and the Comforter. It was time to glorify the true, or spiritual Jesus, whom we call Christ Jesus, to validate all that he had taught..

23 ¶ And Jesus answered them, saying, The hour is come, that the Son of man should
be glorified. (John 12:23)

His crucifixion, resurrection, and ascension would attract multitudes to his teaching as the pathway to eternal life.

24 Verily, verily, I say unto you, Except a corn of wheat fall into the ground and die, it
abideth alone: but if it die, it bringeth forth much fruit. (John 12:24)

There is no life in matter, therefore what is called mortal life must be exchanged for life in and of Spirit.

25 He that loveth his life shall lose it; and he that hateth his life in this world shall keep
it unto life eternal.
26 If any man serve me, let him follow me; and where I am, there shall also my servant

be: if any man serve me, him will *my* Father honour.
27 Now is my soul troubled; and what shall I say? Father, save me from this hour: but
for this cause came I unto this hour.
28 Father, glorify thy name. Then came there a voice from heaven, *saying*, I have both
glorified *it*, and will glorify *it* again.
29 The people therefore, that stood by, and heard *it*, said that it thundered: others said,
An angel spake to him.
30 Jesus answered and said, This voice came not because of me, but for your sakes.
(John 12:25-30)

Whatever form evil, called the devil, Satan, prince of this world, or death would take, the resurrection and ascension would prove it powerless. "The pride of priesthood is the prince of this world."- MBE

31 Now is the judgment of this world: now shall the prince of this world be cast out.
(John 12:31)

Jesus foretells that the crucifixion will result in the resurrection, climax in the ascension, and draw all men to Christ by letting his "I" go unto the Father, that is to say, by submitting entirely to the will of God. This is The Pathway to Glory!

32 And I, if I be lifted up from the earth, will draw all *men* unto me.
33 This he said, signifying what death he should die. (John 12:32-33)

The terms "Son of God" and "Son of man" that before were not understood are now explained to the people,

34 The people answered him, We have heard out of the law that Christ abideth for ever:
and how sayest thou, The Son of man must be lifted up? who is this Son of man? (John 12:34).

Light, *φῶς phōs*, The Son of God (Christ) made manifest as the Son of man (spiritual man) through Jesus. *Phōs* is the Greek word translated light all six times in the following three verses: Jn. 12:35 2x, Jn. 12:36 3x & Jn. 12:46 1x.

35 Then Jesus said unto them, Yet a little while is the light with you. Walk while ye
have the light, lest darkness come upon you: for he that walketh in darkness knoweth
not whither he goeth.
36 While ye have light, believe in the light, that ye may be the children of light. These
things spake Jesus, and departed, and did hide himself from them. (John 12:35-36)

Stubborn resistance to Truth. "Mortal mind sees what it believes as certainly as it believes what it sees." - MBE

37 ¶ But though he had done so many miracles before them, yet they believed not on
him:
38 That the saying of Esaias the prophet might be fulfilled, which he spake, Lord, who
hath believed our report? and to whom hath the arm of the Lord been revealed?
39 Therefore they could not believe, because that Esaias said again,
40 He hath blinded their eyes, and hardened their heart; that they should not see with
their eyes, nor understand with *their* heart, and be converted, and I should heal them.
41 These things said Esaias, when he saw his glory, and spake of him. (John 12:37-41)

Jesus had followers, some even members of the Sanhedrin, who for fear of being excommunicated remained silent.

42 ¶ Nevertheless among the chief rulers also many believed on him; but because of the
Pharisees they did not confess *him*, lest they should be put out of the synagogue:
43 For they loved the praise of men more than the praise of God.
44 ¶ Jesus cried and said, He that believeth on me, believeth not on me, but on him that
sent me.
45 And he that seeth me seeth him that sent me.
46 I am come a light into the world, that whosoever believeth on me should not abide in
darkness. (John 12:42-46)

He came not to ***judge***, *κρίνω krinō*, condemn, damn, but to ***save***, *σῴζω sōzō*, to heal, make whole. Jesus brought a full salvation, not only from sin, but from sickness, disease, death and all other forms of evil or error, called hell.

47 And if any man hear my words, and believe not, I judge him not: for I came not to
judge the world, but to save the world.
48 He that rejecteth me, and receiveth not my words, hath one that judgeth him: the

word that I have spoken, the same shall judge him in the last day.
49 For I have not spoken of myself; but the Father which sent me, he gave me a
commandment, what I should say, and what I should speak.
50 And I know that his commandment is life everlasting: whatsoever I speak therefore,
even as the Father said unto me, so I speak. (John 12:47-50)

The opposition of the chief priests and scribes was due to envy

According to the Gospel of Mark

18 And the scribes and chief priests heard *it*, and sought how they might destroy him:
for they feared him, because all the people was astonished at his doctrine. (Mark 11:18)

According to the Gospel of Luke

47 But the chief priests and the scribes and the chief of the people sought to destroy
him,
48 And could not find what they might do: for all the people were very attentive to hear
him. (Luke 19:47-48 *But*)

Jesus departed Jerusalem for the night

19 And when even was come, he went out of the city. (Mark 11:19)

THE SECOND DAY BEFORE PASSOVER

(The 13h day of Nisan the Gentile Monday sunset to Tuesday sunset)

CHAPTER 140
LESSONS FROM THE WITHERED FIG TREE

According to the Gospel of Matthew

On the way to the temple the disciples notice the fig tree that Jesus cursed the previous day already "withered away," foretelling the end of the Pharisees whose ecclesiastical control was destined to perish due to its corruption.

19 And presently the fig tree withered away.
20 And when the disciples saw *it*, they marvelled, saying, How soon is the fig tree
withered away!
21 Jesus answered and said unto them, Verily I say unto you, If ye have faith, and
doubt not, ye shall not only do this *which is done* to the fig tree, but also if ye shall say
unto this mountain, Be thou removed, and be thou cast into the sea; it shall be done.
22 And all things, whatsoever ye shall ask in prayer, believing, ye shall receive. (Matt
21:19-22 *And*)

According to the Gospel of Mark

20 ¶ And in the morning, as they passed by, they saw the fig tree dried up from the
roots.
21 And Peter calling to remembrance saith unto him, Master, behold, the fig tree which
thou cursedst is withered away. (Mark 11:20-21)

Trust God to not only eliminate false teaching but to also wipe out every manifestation of error opposed to Christ, Truth.

22 And Jesus answering saith unto them, Have faith in God.
23 For verily I say unto you, That whosoever shall say unto this mountain, Be thou
removed, and be thou cast into the sea; and shall not doubt in his heart, but shall believe
that those things which he saith shall come to pass; he shall have whatsoever he saith.
24 Therefore I say unto you, What things soever ye desire, when ye pray, believe that
ye receive *them*, and ye shall have *them*. (Mark 11:22-24)

Effective prayer must Include forgiveness

25 And when ye stand praying, forgive, if ye have ought against any: that your Father

also which is in heaven may forgive you your trespasses.
26 But if ye do not forgive, neither will your Father which is in heaven forgive your
trespasses. (Mark 11:25-26)

CHAPTER 141
DISPUTING WITH THE PRIESTS, SCRIBES, AND ELDERS

The question of authority

According to the Gospel of Mark

27 ¶ And they come again to Jerusalem: and as he was walking in the temple, there
come to him the chief priests, and the scribes, and the elders,
28 And say unto him, By what authority doest thou these things? and who gave thee
this authority to do these things?
29 And Jesus answered and said unto them, I will also ask of you one question, and
answer me, and I will tell you by what authority I do these things.
30 The baptism of John, was *it* from heaven, or of men? answer me.
31 And they reasoned with themselves, saying, If we shall say, From heaven; he will
say, Why then did ye not believe him?
32 But if we shall say, Of men; they feared the people: for all *men* counted John, that he
was a prophet indeed.
33 And they answered and said unto Jesus, We cannot tell. And Jesus answering saith
unto them, Neither do I tell you by what authority I do these things. (Mark 11:27-33)

According to the Gospel of Matthew

23 ¶ And when he was come into the temple, the chief priests and the elders of the
people came unto him as he was teaching, and said, By what authority doest thou these
things? and who gave thee this authority?
24 And Jesus answered and said unto them, I also will ask you one thing, which if ye
tell me, I in like wise will tell you by what authority I do these things.
25 The baptism of John, whence was it? from heaven, or of men? And they reasoned
with themselves, saying, If we shall say, From heaven; he will say unto us, Why did ye
not then believe him?
26 But if we shall say, Of men; we fear the people; for all hold John as a prophet.
27 And they answered Jesus, and said, We cannot tell. And he said unto them, Neither
tell I you by what authority I do these things. (Matt 21:23-27)

According to the Gospel of Luke

1 And it came to pass, *that* on one of those days, as he taught the people in the temple,
and preached the gospel, the chief priests and the scribes came upon *him* with the
elders,
2 And spake unto him, saying, Tell us, by what authority doest thou these things? or
who is he that gave thee this authority?
3 And he answered and said unto them, I will also ask you one thing; and answer me:
4 The baptism of John, was it from heaven, or of men?
5 And they reasoned with themselves, saying, If we shall say, From heaven; he will
say, Why then believed ye him not?
6 But and if we say, Of men; all the people will stone us: for they be persuaded that
John was a prophet.
7 And they answered, that they could not tell whence *it was*.

8 And Jesus said unto them, Neither tell I you by what authority I do these things. (Luke 20:1-8)

A Parable. Two Sons and the Vineyard.

(A parable exposing ecclesiastical self-will. What will it be: self-will, the human mind, or God's will, the divine Mind?)

Sons = children. In this parable the first son symbolizes the "publicans and harlots' who repent, change their mind.

28 ¶ But what think ye? A *certain* man had two sons; and he came to the first, and said, Son, go work to-day in my vineyard.

29 He answered and said, I will not: but afterward he repented, and went. (Matt 21:28-29)

The second son is the priests, scribes, and elders who in their conceit feign to do God's will while doing their own.

30 And he came to the second, and said likewise. And he answered and said, I *go*, sir: and went not.

31 Whether of them twain did the will of *his* father? They say unto him, The first. Jesus saith unto them, Verily I say unto you, That the publicans and the harlots go into the kingdom of God before you.

32 For John came unto you in the way of righteousness, and ye believed him not; but the publicans and the harlots believed him: and ye, when ye had seen *it*, repented not afterward, that ye might believe him. (Matt 21:30-32)

A Parable: The Unfaithful Husbandmen. The stone is the Ten Commandments obeyed in the Christ-teaching

(A parable exposing the infidelity, self-serving, and rejection of Christ by the ecclesiastical elitists.)

According to the Gospel of Mark

1 And he began to speak unto them by parables. A *certain* man planted a vineyard, and set an hedge about *it*, and digged *a place for* the winefat, and built a tower, and let it out to husbandmen, and went into a far country.

2 And at the season he sent to the husbandmen a servant, that he might receive from the husbandmen of the fruit of the vineyard.

3 And they caught *him*, and beat him, and sent *him* away empty.

4 And again he sent unto them another servant; and at him they cast stones, and wounded *him* in the head, and sent *him* away shamefully handled.

5 And again he sent another; and him they killed, and many others; beating some, and killing some.

6 Having yet therefore one son, his wellbeloved, he sent him also last unto them, saying, They will reverence my son.

7 But those husbandmen said among themselves, This is the heir; come, let us kill him, and the inheritance shall be ours.

8 And they took him, and killed *him*, and cast *him* out of the vineyard.

9 What shall therefore the lord of the vineyard do? he will come and destroy the husbandmen, and will give the vineyard unto others.

10 And have ye not read this scripture; The stone which the builders rejected is become the head of the corner:

11 This was the Lord's doing, and it is marvellous in our eyes? (Mark 12:1-11)

According to the Gospel of Luke

9 Then began he to speak to the people this parable; A certain man planted a vineyard, and let it forth to husbandmen, and went into a far country for a long time.

10 And at the season he sent a servant to the husbandmen, that they should give him of the fruit of the vineyard: but the husbandmen beat him, and sent *him* away empty.

11 And again he sent another servant: and they beat him also, and entreated *him* shamefully, and sent *him* away empty.

12 And again he sent a third: and they wounded him also, and cast *him* out.
13 Then said the lord of the vineyard, What shall I do? I will send my beloved son: it
may be they will reverence *him* when they see him.
14 But when the husbandmen saw him, they reasoned among themselves, saying, This
is the heir: come, let us kill him, that the inheritance may be ours.
15 So they cast him out of the vineyard, and killed *him*. What therefore shall the lord
of the vineyard do unto them?
16 He shall come and destroy these husbandmen, and shall give the vineyard to others.
And when they heard *it*, they said, God forbid.
17 And he beheld them, and said, What is this then that is written, The stone which the
builders rejected, the same is become the head of the corner?
18 Whosoever shall fall upon that stone shall be broken; but on whomsoever it shall
fall, it will grind him to powder. (Luke 20:9-18)

According to the Gospel of Matthew

33 ¶ Hear another parable: There was a certain householder, which planted a vineyard,
and hedged it round about, and digged a winepress in it, and built a tower, and let it out
to husbandmen, and went into a far country:
34 And when the time of the fruit drew near, he sent his servants to the husbandmen,
that they might receive the fruits of it.
35 And the husbandmen took his servants, and beat one, and killed another, and stoned
another.
36 Again, he sent other servants more than the first: and they did unto them likewise.
37 But last of all he sent unto them his son, saying, They will reverence my son.
38 But when the husbandmen saw the son, they said among themselves, This is the
heir; come, let us kill him, and let us seize on his inheritance.
39 And they caught him, and cast *him* out of the vineyard, and slew *him*.
40 When the lord therefore of the vineyard cometh, what will he do unto those
husbandmen?
41 They say unto him, He will miserably destroy those wicked men, and will let out *his*
vineyard unto other husbandmen, which shall render him the fruits in their seasons.
42 Jesus saith unto them, Did ye never read in the scriptures, The stone which the
builders rejected, the same is become the head of the corner: this is the Lord's doing,
and it is marvellous in our eyes?
43 Therefore say I unto you, The kingdom of God shall be taken from you, and given to
a nation bringing forth the fruits thereof.
44 And whosoever shall fall on this stone shall be broken: but on whomsoever it shall
fall, it will grind him to powder.
45 And when the chief priests and Pharisees had heard his parables, they perceived that
he spake of them. (Matt 21:33-45)

Why Jesus was not arrested in public

According to the Gospel of Matthew

46 But when they sought to lay hands on him, they feared the multitude, because they
took him for a prophet. (Matt 21:46)

According to the Gospel of Mark

12 And they sought to lay hold on him, but feared the people: for they knew that he had
spoken the parable against them: and they left him, and went their way. (Mark 12:12)

19 ¶ And the chief priests and the scribes the same hour sought to lay hands on him;
and they feared the people: for they perceived that he had spoken this parable against
them. (Luke 20:19)

CHAPTER 142

IMPOSTORS ARE TO BE CAST OUT

(The Parable of the Marriage of the King's Son)

Part 1: The Children of Israel, the Bidden Guests

The ecclesiastics and politicians (priests, scribes and elders of the people) are the unworthy intruders to be cast out.

1 And Jesus answered and spake unto them again by parables, and said, (Matt 22:1)

The wedding feast or marriage prepared by the king (God) is the realization of our union, spiritual oneness with God.

2 The kingdom of heaven is like unto a certain king, which made a marriage for his
son, (Matt 22:2)

John the Baptist, followed by Jesus and the Apostles and disciples, extended invitations to the "marriage."

3 And sent forth his servants to call them that were bidden to the wedding: and they
would not come. (Matt 22:3)

Later, the "Jews" that would hear the Apostles on the Day of Pentecost would be invited to the marriage.

4 Again, he sent forth other servants, saying, Tell them which are bidden, Behold, I
have prepared my dinner: my oxen and *my* fatlings *are* killed, and all things *are* ready:
come unto the marriage. (Matt 22:4)

Instead of accepting the invitation they would continue to pursue their worldly quest for power and wealth.

5 But they made light of *it*, and went their ways, one to his farm, another to his
merchandise: (Matt 22:5)

Next would be the: (1) Spiteful treatment (Acts 4:1-3; 5:40-41; 11:19), and (2) slaying (Acts 7:54-60; 12-2) of his followers.

6 And the remnant took his servants, and entreated *them* spitefully, and slew *them*. (Matt
22:6)

The destruction of Jerusalem foretold. Why? Because the kingdom is *wholly spiritual*, the *holy city* within us. Rev. 21:2.

7 But when the king heard *thereof*, he was wroth: and he sent forth his armies, and
destroyed those murderers, and burned up their city. (Matt 22:7)

Part 2: The Gentiles, the Replacement Guests

The wedding invitation is perpetual, but to attend one must be "clothed and in his right mind." Spiritually minded. Mk. 5:15.

8 Then saith he to his servants, The wedding is ready, but they which were bidden were
not worthy. (Matt 22:8)

The invitation (opportunity) to attend is extended to everyone.

9 Go ye therefore into the highways, and as many as ye shall find, bid to the marriage.
(Matt 22:9)

Both those who are prepared to leave all for Christ, and those who are not, will desire entrance to the wedding feast.

10 So those servants went out into the highways, and gathered together all as many as
they found, both bad and good: and the wedding was furnished with guests. (Matt 22:10)

But the carnal man, not truly "hungering and thirsting after righteousness" will not be clothed in a "wedding garment."

11 ¶ And when the king came in to see the guests, he saw there a man which had not on
a wedding garment: (Matt 22:11)

Question: Why would anyone expect to be admitted to a marriage ceremony if not properly attired?

12 And he saith unto him, Friend, how camest thou in hither not having a wedding
garment? (Matt 22:12 *to* ?)

The carnally minded man will be speechless, for he will have no answer for his subterfuge.

12 And he was speechless. (Matt 22:12 *And*)

There is no fooling God, the one Mind. We know this is true, because the "still small voice" speaks to everyone. I Ki.16:12.

13 Then said the king to the servants, Bind him hand and foot, and take him away, and
cast *him* into outer darkness; there shall be weeping and gnashing of teeth. (Matt 22:13)

All are called, but only those committed to be Christlike are "chosen." "God is no respecter of persons" – Acts 10:34

14 For many are called, but few *are* chosen. (Matt 22:14)

CHAPTER 143
FAILED ATTEMPTS TO ENTRAP JESUS

The 1st trap set by the Pharisees concerns paying Roman taxes.

3 [they came] to him and began rigorously testing him, saying, "Teacher Jesus, we know that you have come from God. For the things you do give a testimony that is beyond all the prophets. And so, tell us: is it right to pay the kings the things that relate to their rule? Shall we pay them or not?"

But when Jesus understood their thought, he became incensed and said to them, "Why do you call me teacher with your mouth, when you do not listen to what I say? Well did Isaiah prophecy about you, 'This people honors me with their lips, but their heart is far from me. In vain do they worship me *teaching for doctrines the commandments of men*.'" – From the *Papyrus Egerton 2: The Unknown Gospel* p. 28. The text in italics is Matt. 15:9.

The faction that wanted Jesus dead faced two problems: (1) He had broken no Mosaic law worthy of stoning; (2) If they executed him anyway, they feared a rebellion. So they plotted to have the Romans execute him. But since Jesus was neither an insurrectionist nor a criminal there was no violation of Roman law to present to Pilate. So they sought to use false witnesses and frame him. The following accounts show their failure to manufacture a legitimate charge of tax evasion. Nevertheless they did charge him with insurrection for: (1) "forbidding to give tribute to Cæsar" (Luke 23:2), and (2) for seeking to be a king (John 19:12), and used these charges to blackmail Pilate to crucify Jesus.

According to the Gospel of Luke

20 And they watched *him*, and sent forth spies, which should feign themselves just
men, that they might take hold of his words, that so they might deliver him unto the
power and authority of the governor.
21 And they asked him, saying, Master, we know that thou sayest and teachest rightly,
neither acceptest thou the person *of any*, but teachest the way of God truly:
22 Is it lawful for us to give tribute unto Cæsar, or no?
23 But he perceived their craftiness, and said unto them, Why tempt ye me?
24 Shew me a penny. Whose image and superscription hath it? They answered and
said, Cæsar's.
25 And he said unto them, Render therefore unto Cæsar the things which be Cæsar's,
and unto God the things which be God's.
26 And they could not take hold of his words before the people: and they marvelled at
his answer, and held their peace. (Luke 20:20-26)

According to the Gospel of Mark

13 ¶ And they send unto him certain of the Pharisees and of the Herodians, to catch him
in *his* words. (Mark 12:13)
14 And when they were come, they say unto him, Master, we know that thou art true,
and carest for no man: for thou regardest not the person of men, but teachest the way of
God in truth: Is it lawful to give tribute to Cæsar, or not?
15 Shall we give, or shall we not give? But he, knowing their hypocrisy, said unto
them, Why tempt ye me? bring me a penny, that I may see *it*.
16 And they brought *it*. And he saith unto them, Whose *is* this image and
superscription? And they said unto him, Cæsar's.
17 And Jesus answering said unto them, Render to Cæsar the things that are Cæsar's,
and to God the things that are God's. And they marvelled at him. (Mark 12:13-17)

According to the Gospel of Matthew

15 ¶ Then went the Pharisees, and took counsel how they might entangle him in *his*
talk.
16 And they sent out unto him their disciples with the Herodians, saying, Master, we
know that thou art true, and teachest the way of God in truth, neither carest thou for any
man: for thou regardest not the person of men.
17 Tell us therefore, What thinkest thou? Is it lawful to give tribute unto Cæsar, or not?

18 But Jesus perceived their wickedness, and said, Why tempt ye me, *ye* hypocrites?
19 Shew me the tribute money. And they brought unto him a penny.
20 And he saith unto them, Whose *is* this image and superscription?
21 They say unto him, Cæsar's. Then saith he unto them, Render therefore unto Cæsar
the things which are Cæsar's; and unto God the things that are God's.
22 When they had heard *these words*, they marvelled, and left him, and went their way.
(Matt 22:15-22)

The 2nd trap was set by the Sadducees on a theological question to manufacture charges of blasphemy

According to the Gospel of Matthew

23 ¶ The same day came to him the Sadducees, which say that there is no resurrection,
and asked him,
24 Saying, Master, Moses said, If a man die, having no children, his brother shall marry
his wife, and raise up seed unto his brother.
25 Now there were with us seven brethren: and the first, when he had married a wife,
deceased, and, having no issue, left his wife unto his brother:
26 Likewise the second also, and the third, unto the seventh.
27 And last of all the woman died also.
28 Therefore in the resurrection whose wife shall she be of the seven? for they all had
her.
29 Jesus answered and said unto them, Ye do err, not knowing the scriptures, nor the
power of God.
30 For in the resurrection they neither marry, nor are given in marriage, but are as the
angels of God in heaven.
31 But as touching the resurrection of the dead, have ye not read that which was spoken
unto you by God, saying,
32 I am the God of Abraham, and the God of Isaac, and the God of Jacob? God is not
the God of the dead, but of the living.
33 And when the multitude heard *this*, they were astonished at his doctrine. (Matt 22:23-33)

According to the Gospel of Luke

27 ¶ Then came to *him* certain of the Sadducees, which deny that there is any
resurrection; and they asked him,
28 Saying, Master, Moses wrote unto us, If any man's brother die, having a wife, and he
die without children, that his brother should take his wife, and raise up seed unto his
brother.
29 There were therefore seven brethren: and the first took a wife, and died without
children.
30 And the second took her to wife, and he died childless.
31 And the third took her; and in like manner the seven also: and they left no children,
and died.
32 Last of all the woman died also.
33 Therefore in the resurrection whose wife of them is she? for seven had her to wife.
34 And Jesus answering said unto them, The children of this world marry, and are
given in marriage:
35 But they which shall be accounted worthy to obtain that world, and the resurrection
from the dead, neither marry, nor are given in marriage:
36 Neither can they die any more: for they are equal unto the angels; and are the

children of God, being the children of the resurrection.
37 Now that the dead are raised, even Moses shewed at the bush, when he calleth the
Lord the God of Abraham, and the God of Isaac, and the God of Jacob.
38 For he is not a God of the dead, but of the living: for all live unto him. (Luke 20:27-38)

According to the Gospel of Mark

18 ¶ Then come unto him the Sadducees, which say there is no resurrection; and they
asked him, saying,
19 Master, Moses wrote unto us, If a man's brother die, and leave *his* wife *behind him*,
and leave no children, that his brother should take his wife, and raise up seed unto his
brother.
20 Now there were seven brethren: and the first took a wife, and dying left no seed.
21 And the second took her, and died, neither left he any seed: and the third likewise.
22 And the seven had her, and left no seed: last of all the woman died also.
23 In the resurrection therefore, when they shall rise, whose wife shall she be of them?
for the seven had her to wife.
24 And Jesus answering said unto them, Do ye not therefore err, because ye know not
the scriptures, neither the power of God?
25 For when they shall rise from the dead, they neither marry, nor are given in
marriage; but are as the angels which are in heaven.
26 And as touching the dead, that they rise: have ye not read in the book of Moses, how
in the bush God spake unto him, saying, I *am* the God of Abraham, and the God of
Isaac, and the God of Jacob?
27 He is not the God of the dead, but the God of the living: ye therefore do greatly err.
(Mark 12:18-27)

The Pharisees then redouble their effort to entrap Jesus

34 ¶ But when the Pharisees had heard that he had put the Sadducees to silence, they
were gathered together. (Matt 22:34)

The 3rd trap was set by a lawyer and a scribe to accuse Jesus of false teaching

According to the Gospel of Matthew

Lawyer = a teacher of the Hebrew law. Tempting, *πειράζω peirazō*, cunningly, in a manner to entice him to err.

35 Then one of them, *which was* a lawyer, asked *him a question*, tempting him, and
saying,
36 Master, which *is* the great commandment in the law?
37 Jesus said unto him, Thou shalt love the Lord thy God with all thy heart, and with all
thy soul, and with all thy mind.
38 This is the first and great commandment.
39 And the second *is* like unto it, Thou shalt love thy neighbour as thyself.
40 On these two commandments hang all the law and the prophets. (Matt 22:35-40)

According to the Gospel of Mark

28 ¶ And one of the scribes came, and having heard them reasoning together, and
perceiving that he had answered them well, asked him, Which is the first
commandment of all?
29 And Jesus answered him, The first of all the commandments *is*, Hear, O Israel; The
Lord our God is one Lord:
30 And thou shalt love the Lord thy God with all thy heart, and with all thy soul, and

with all thy mind, and with all thy strength: this *is* the first commandment.
31 And the second *is* like, *namely* this, Thou shalt love thy neighbour as thyself. There
is none other commandment greater than these.
32 And the scribe said unto him, Well, Master, thou hast said the truth: for there is one
God; and there is none other but he:
33 And to love him with all the heart and with all the understanding, and with all the
soul, and with all the strength, and to love *his* neighbour as himself, is more than all
whole burnt offerings and sacrifices.
34 And when Jesus saw that he answered discreetly, he said unto him, Thou art not far
from the kingdom of God. (Mark 12:28-34 to 1st.)

Attempts to entrap Jesus cease

34 And no man after that durst ask him *any question.* (Mark 12:34 *And*)

According to the Gospel of Luke

39 ¶ Then certain of the scribes answering said, Master, thou hast well said.
40 And after that they durst not ask him any *question at all.* (Luke 20:39-40)

CHAPTER 144
THE DIVINITY OF THE CHRIST

The divinity of the Christ was made manifest in the humanity of Jesus. The Christ was the Spirit which Jesus implied in his own statements: "I am the way, the truth, and the life;" "I and my Father are one." This Christ, or divinity of the man Jesus, was his divine nature, the godliness which animated him. [Jesus is] the highest human corporeal concept of the divine idea, rebuking and destroying error and bringing to light man's immortality. [Christ is] the divine manifestation of God, which come to the flesh to destroy incarnate error. Jesus is the human man, and Christ is the divine idea; hence the duality of Jesus the Christ. - MBE

According to the Gospel of Matthew

41 ¶ While the Pharisees were gathered together, Jesus asked them, (Matt 22:41)

Jesus question to the Pharisees: Whose son is Christ? In other words: Is Christ of human or divine parentage?

42 Saying, What think ye of Christ? whose son is he? (Matt 22:42 *to* 2nd ?)

The Pharisees identified Christ as a corporeal person descended from David, a human king, a mortal.

42 They say unto him, *The Son* of David. (Matt 22:42 *They*)

In spirit = spiritually. Jesus declared the Pharisees reasoning invalid based on David's own words: Psalm 110:1.

43 He saith unto them, How then doth David in spirit call him Lord, saying, (Matt 22:43)

The LORD (Jehovah or God) said unto my (David's) Lord (Christ), "sit thou on my right hand . . . "

44 The LORD said unto my Lord, Sit thou on my right hand, till I make thine enemies
thy footstool? (Matt 22:44)

Conclusion. If David called Christ "my Lord", Christ cannot be David's son. Christ is the Son of God, not the son of a man.

45 If David then call him Lord, how is he his son? (Matt 22:45)

According to the Gospel of Mark

35 ¶ And Jesus answered and said, while he taught in the temple, How say the scribes
that Christ is the son of David?
36 For David himself said by the Holy Ghost, The LORD said to my Lord, Sit thou on
my right hand, till I make thine enemies thy footstool.
37 David therefore himself calleth him Lord; and whence is he *then* his son? And the
common people heard him gladly. (Mark 12:35-37)

According to the Gospel of Luke

41 And he said unto them, How say they that Christ is David's son?
42 And David himself saith in the book of Psalms, The LORD said unto my Lord, Sit
thou on my right hand,

43 Till I make thine enemies thy footstool.
44 David therefore calleth him Lord, how is he then his son? (Luke 20:41-44)

CHAPTER 145
BEWARE OF THE SCRIBES

According to the Gospel of Luke

45 ¶ Then in the audience of all the people he said unto his disciples,
46 Beware of the scribes, which desire to walk in long robes, and love greetings in the
markets, and the highest seats in the synagogues, and the chief rooms at feasts;
47 Which devour widows' houses, and for a shew make long prayers: the same shall
receive greater damnation. (Luke 20:45-47)

According to the Gospel of Mark

38 ¶ And he said unto them in his doctrine, Beware of the scribes, which love to go in
long clothing, and *love* salutations in the marketplaces,
39 And the chief seats in the synagogues, and the uppermost rooms at feasts:
40 Which devour widows' houses, and for a pretence make long prayers: these shall
receive greater damnation. (Mark 12:38-40)

CHAPTER 146
A CERTAIN POOR WIDOW A PROPHECY

According to the Gospel of Mark

41 ¶ And Jesus sat over against the treasury, and beheld how the people cast money into
the treasury: and many that were rich cast in much.
42 And there came a certain poor widow, and she threw in two mites, which make a
farthing.
43 And he called *unto him* his disciples, and saith unto them, Verily I say unto you,
That this poor widow hath cast more in, than all they which have cast into the treasury:
44 For all *they* did cast in of their abundance; but she of her want did cast in all that she
had, *even* all her living. (Mark 12:41-44)

According to the Gospel of Luke

1 And he looked up, and saw the rich men casting their gifts into the treasury.
2 And he saw also a certain poor widow casting in thither two mites.
3 And he said, Of a truth I say unto you, that this poor widow hath cast in more than
they all:
4 For all these have of their abundance cast in unto the offerings of God: but she of her
penury hath cast in all the living that she had. (Luke 21:1-4)

No more questions from that day forth

46 And no man was able to answer him a word, neither durst any *man* from that day
forth ask him any more *questions*. (Matt 22:46)

CHAPTER 147
PHARISEEISM (SELF-RIGHTEOUSNESS) CONDEMNED

Jesus addresses the multitude and the disciples

1 Then spake Jesus to the multitude, and to his disciples,
2 Saying, The scribes and the Pharisees sit in Moses' seat: (Matt 23:1-2)

Obey the Law of Moses, the Ten Commandments, but don't be a hypocrite like the Pharisees that only pretend.

3 All therefore whatsoever they bid you observe, *that* observe and do; but do not ye after their works: for they say, and do not. (Matt 23:3)

They make demands on others that they don't comply with themselves.

4 For they bind heavy burdens and grievous to be borne, and lay *them* on men's shoulders; but they *themselves* will not move them with one of their fingers. (Matt 23:4)

Their outward display of righteousness is to gain *human* approval. It has nothing to do with keeping the Commandments.

5 But all their works they do for to be seen of men: they make broad their phylacteries, and enlarge the borders of their garments, (Matt 23:5)

Their thoughts and actions are driven by "Who shall be the greatest."

6 And love the uppermost rooms at feasts, and the chief seats in the synagogues, (Matt 23:6)

Believing themselves to be superior to others, they love to be called "My Master, My Master."

7 And greetings in the markets, and to be called of men, Rabbi, Rabbi. (Matt 23:7)

Christ alone is the Master of everyone.

8 But be not ye called Rabbi: for one is your Master, *even* Christ; and all ye are brethren. (Matt 23:8)

Father is strictly a divine appellative. Adam, Abraham, Moses and David are NOT fathers, they are mortal *ancestors*.

9 And call no *man* your father upon the earth: for one is your Father, which is in heaven. (Matt 23:9)

Seek not personal control of others. Be governed by Christ yourself, and permit others to do likewise.

10 Neither be ye called masters: for one is your Master, *even* Christ. (Matt 23:10)

With Christ as your Master there is no concern about "Who shall be the greatest."

11 But he that is greatest among you shall be your servant. (Matt 23:11)

Pride and self-seeking lead to a down fall. Overcoming mortal selfhood leads to sonship in Christ.

12 And whosoever shall exalt himself shall be abased; and he that shall humble himself shall be exalted. (Matt 23:12)

Jesus Addresses the Pharisees Directly

"Jesus was unselfish." "He was inspired by God, by Truth and Love, in all that he said and did. The motives of his persecutors were pride, envy, cruelty, and vengeance, inflicted on the physical Jesus, but aimed at the divine Principle, Love, which rebuked their sensuality." "He rebuked sinners pointedly and unflinchingly, because he was their friend; hence the cup he drank." - MBE

13 ¶ But woe unto you, scribes and Pharisees, hypocrites! for ye shut up the kingdom of heaven against men: for ye neither go in *yourselves*, neither suffer ye them that are entering to go in.

14 Woe unto you, scribes and Pharisees, hypocrites! for ye devour widows' houses, and for a pretence make long prayer: therefore ye shall receive the greater damnation.

15 Woe unto you, scribes and Pharisees, hypocrites! for ye compass sea and land to make one proselyte, and when he is made, ye make him twofold more the child of hell than yourselves. (Matt 23:13-15)

The Pharisees care nothing about the presence of God the temple signifies, they only care for the money collected there.

16 Woe unto you, *ye* blind guides, which say, Whosoever shall swear by the temple, it is nothing; but whosoever shall swear by the gold of the temple, he is a debtor!

17 *Ye* fools and blind: for whether is greater, the gold, or the temple that sanctifieth the gold?

18 And, Whosoever shall swear by the altar, it is nothing; but whosoever sweareth by the gift that is upon it, he is guilty.

19 *Ye* fools and blind: for whether *is* greater, the gift, or the altar that sanctifieth the gift?

20 Whoso therefore shall swear by the altar, sweareth by it, and by all things thereon.

21 And whoso shall swear by the temple, sweareth by it, and by him that dwelleth
therein.
22 And he that shall swear by heaven, sweareth by the throne of God, and by him that
sitteth thereon. (Matt 23:16-22)

The Pharisees made small donations of various kinds, but failed to administer justice, faithful stewardship, and mercy.

23 Woe unto you, scribes and Pharisees, hypocrites! for ye pay tithe of mint and anise
and cummin, and have omitted the weightier *matters* of the law, judgment, mercy, and
faith: these ought ye to have done, and not to leave the other undone.
24 *Ye* blind guides, which strain at a gnat, and swallow a camel. (Matt 23:23-24)

The scribes and Pharisees attend to hygienic cleansing but neglected to purify their thoughts and actions.

25 Woe unto you, scribes and Pharisees, hypocrites! for ye make clean the outside of
the cup and of the platter, but within they are full of extortion and excess.
26 *Thou* blind Pharisee, cleanse first that *which is* within the cup and platter, that the
outside of them may be clean also.
27 Woe unto you, scribes and Pharisees, hypocrites! for ye are like unto whited
sepulchres, which indeed appear beautiful outward, but are within full of dead *men's*
bones, and of all uncleanness.
28 Even so ye also outwardly appear righteous unto men, but within ye are full of
hypocrisy and iniquity. (Matt 23:25-28)

The scribes and Pharisees hid their murderous nature under an outward display of feigned holiness.

29 Woe unto you, scribes and Pharisees, hypocrites! because ye build the tombs of the
prophets, and garnish the sepulchres of the righteous,
30 And say, If we had been in the days of our fathers, we would not have been
partakers with them in the blood of the prophets.
31 Wherefore ye be witnesses unto yourselves, that ye are the children of them which
killed the prophets.
32 Fill ye up then the measure of your fathers.
33 *Ye* serpents, *ye* generation of vipers, how can ye escape the damnation of hell?
34 ¶ Wherefore, behold, I send unto you prophets, and wise men, and scribes: and *some*
of them ye shall kill and crucify; and *some* of them shall ye scourge in your
synagogues, and persecute *them* from city to city:
35 That upon you may come all the righteous blood shed upon the earth, from the blood
of righteous Abel unto the blood of Zacharias son of Barachias, whom ye slew between
the temple and the altar.
36 Verily I say unto you, All these things shall come upon this generation.
37 O Jerusalem, Jerusalem, *thou* that killest the prophets, and stonest them which are
sent unto thee, how often would I have gathered thy children together, even as a hen
gathereth her chickens under *her* wings, and ye would not!
38 Behold, your house is left unto you desolate.
39 For I say unto you, Ye shall not see me henceforth, till ye shall say, Blessed *is* he
that cometh in the name of the Lord. (Matt 23:29-39)

CHAPTER 148
THE FIRST PORTION OF JESUS' PROPHECY
Delivered in the temple area

5 ¶ And as some spake of the temple, how it was adorned with goodly stones and gifts,
he said,
6 *As for* these things which ye behold, the days will come, in the which there shall not

be left one stone upon another, that shall not be thrown down.
7 And they asked him, saying, Master, but when shall these things be? and what sign
will there be when these things shall come to pass?
8 And he said, Take heed that ye be not deceived: for many shall come in my name,
saying, I am *Christ*; and the time draweth near: go ye not therefore after them.
9 But when ye shall hear of wars and commotions, be not terrified: for these things
must first come to pass; but the end *is* not by and by.
10 Then said he unto them, Nation shall rise against nation, and kingdom against
kingdom:
11 And great earthquakes shall be in divers places, and famines, and pestilences; and
fearful sights and great signs shall there be from heaven.
12 But before all these, they shall lay their hands on you, and persecute *you*, delivering
you up to the synagogues, and into prisons, being brought before kings and rulers for
my name's sake.
13 And it shall turn to you for a testimony.
14 Settle *it* therefore in your hearts, not to meditate before what ye shall answer:
15 For I will give you a mouth and wisdom, which all your adversaries shall not be able
to gainsay nor resist.
16 And ye shall be betrayed both by parents, and brethren, and kinsfolks, and friends;
and *some* of you shall they cause to be put to death.
17 And ye shall be hated of all *men* for my name's sake.
18 But there shall not an hair of your head perish.
19 In your patience possess ye your souls.
20 And when ye shall see Jerusalem compassed with armies, then know that the
desolation thereof is nigh.
21 Then let them which are in Judæa flee to the mountains; and let them which are in
the midst of it depart out; and let not them that are in the countries enter thereinto.
22 For these be the days of vengeance, that all things which are written may be
fulfilled.
23 But woe unto them that are with child, and to them that give suck, in those days! for
there shall be great distress in the land, and wrath upon this people.
24 And they shall fall by the edge of the sword, and shall be led away captive into all
nations: and Jerusalem shall be trodden down of the Gentiles, until the times of the
Gentiles be fulfilled.
25 ¶ And there shall be signs in the sun, and in the moon, and in the stars; and upon the
earth distress of nations, with perplexity; the sea and the waves roaring;
26 Men's hearts failing them for fear, and for looking after those things which are
coming on the earth: for the powers of heaven shall be shaken.
27 And then shall they see the Son of man coming in a cloud with power and great
glory.
28 And when these things begin to come to pass, then look up, and lift up your heads;
for your redemption draweth nigh.
29 And he spake to them a parable; Behold the fig tree, and all the trees;
30 When they now shoot forth, ye see and know of your own selves that summer is
now nigh at hand.
31 So likewise ye, when ye see these things come to pass, know ye that the kingdom of

God is nigh at hand.
32 Verily I say unto you, This generation shall not pass away, till all be fulfilled.
33 Heaven and earth shall pass away: but my words shall not pass away.
34 ¶ And take heed to yourselves, lest at any time your hearts be overcharged with
surfeiting, and drunkenness, and cares of this life, and *so* that day come upon you
unawares.
35 For as a snare shall it come on all them that dwell on the face of the whole earth.
36 Watch ye therefore, and pray always, that ye may be accounted worthy to escape all
these things that shall come to pass, and to stand before the Son of man.
37 And in the day time he was teaching in the temple; and at night he went out, and
abode in the mount that is called *the mount* of Olives.
38 And all the people came early in the morning to him in the temple, for to hear him.
(Luke 21:5-38)

CHAPTER 149
DEPARTURE FROM THE TEMPLE AREA

According to the Gospel of Matthew

1 And Jesus went out, and departed from the temple: (Matt 24:1 *to* :)

The disciples' admiration of the temple's architectural magnificence.

1 and his disciples came to *him* for to shew him the buildings of the temple.
(Matt 24:1 *and*)

Jesus foretells the temple's destruction.

2 And Jesus said unto them, See ye not all these things? verily I say unto you, There
shall not be left here one stone upon another, that shall not be thrown down. (Matt 24:2)

According to the Gospel of Mark

1 And as he went out of the temple, (Mark 13:1 *to* 1st,)

Nothing we can say or believe regarding matter is immortal, for matter is temporal and is therefore a mortal phenomenon, a human concept, sometimes beautiful, always erroneous. - MBE

1 one of his disciples saith unto him, Master, see what manner of stones and what
buildings *are here!* (Mark 13:1 *one*)

Jesus foretells the destruction of the temple. For the answer as to why it was to be destroyed see Matt. 21:13 & 27:25.

2 And Jesus answering said unto him, Seest thou these great buildings? there shall not
be left one stone upon another, that shall not be thrown down. (Mark 13:2)

CHAPTER 150
THE SECOND PORTION OF JESUS' PROPHECY

(Delivered at the Mount of Olives across from the temple)

The following address was to Peter, Andrew, James, and John in private

3 And as he sat upon the mount of Olives over against the temple, Peter and James and
John and Andrew asked him privately,
4 Tell us, when shall these things be? and what *shall be* the sign when all these things
shall be fulfilled?
5 And Jesus answering them began to say, Take heed lest any *man* deceive you:
6 For many shall come in my name, saying, I am *Christ*; and shall deceive many.
7 And when ye shall hear of wars and rumours of wars, be ye not troubled: for *such*
things must needs be; but the end *shall* not *be* yet.
8 For nation shall rise against nation, and kingdom against kingdom: and there shall be
earthquakes in divers places, and there shall be famines and troubles: these *are* the
beginnings of sorrows.

9 ¶ But take heed to yourselves: for they shall deliver you up to councils; and in the
synagogues ye shall be beaten: and ye shall be brought before rulers and kings for my
sake, for a testimony against them.
10 And the gospel must first be published among all nations.
11 But when they shall lead *you*, and deliver you up, take no thought beforehand what
ye shall speak, neither do ye premeditate: but whatsoever shall be given you in that
hour, that speak ye: for it is not ye that speak, but the Holy Ghost.
12 Now the brother shall betray the brother to death, and the father the son; and
children shall rise up against *their* parents, and shall cause them to be put to death.
13 And ye shall be hated of all *men* for my name's sake: but he that shall endure unto
the end, the same shall be saved.
14 ¶ But when ye shall see the abomination of desolation, spoken of by Daniel the
prophet, standing where it ought not, (let him that readeth understand,) then let them
that be in Judæa flee to the mountains:
15 And let him that is on the housetop not go down into the house, neither enter *therein*,
to take any thing out of his house:
16 And let him that is in the field not turn back again for to take up his garment.
17 But woe to them that are with child, and to them that give suck in those days!
18 And pray ye that your flight be not in the winter.
19 For *in* those days shall be affliction, such as was not from the beginning of the
creation which God created unto this time, neither shall be.
20 And except that the Lord had shortened those days, no flesh should be saved: but for
the elect's sake, whom he hath chosen, he hath shortened the days.
21 And then if any man shall say to you, Lo, here *is* Christ; or, lo, *he is* there; believe
him not:
22 For false Christs and false prophets shall rise, and shall shew signs and wonders, to
seduce, if *it were* possible, even the elect.
23 But take ye heed: behold, I have foretold you all things.
24 ¶ But in those days, after that tribulation, the sun shall be darkened, and the moon
shall not give her light,
25 And the stars of heaven shall fall, and the powers that are in heaven shall be shaken.
26 And then shall they see the Son of man coming in the clouds with great power and
glory.
27 And then shall he send his angels, and shall gather together his elect from the four
winds, from the uttermost part of the earth to the uttermost part of heaven.
28 Now learn a parable of the fig tree; When her branch is yet tender, and putteth forth
leaves, ye know that summer is near:
29 So ye in like manner, when ye shall see these things come to pass, know that it is
nigh, *even* at the doors.
30 Verily I say unto you, that this generation shall not pass, till all these things be done.
31 Heaven and earth shall pass away: but my words shall not pass away.
32 ¶ But of that day and *that* hour knoweth no man, no, not the angels which are in
heaven, neither the Son, but the Father.
33 Take ye heed, watch and pray: for ye know not when the time is.
34 *For the Son of man is* as a man taking a far journey, who left his house, and gave
authority to his servants, and to every man his work, and commanded the porter to

watch. (Mark 13:3-34)

A warning to Peter, Andrew, James and John who would soon be asked to watch with him in the garden of Gethsemane.

35 Watch ye therefore: for ye know not when the master of the house cometh, at even,
or at midnight, or at the cockcrowing, or in the morning:
36 Lest coming suddenly he find you sleeping.
37 And what I say unto you I say unto all, Watch. (Mark 13:35-37)

This portion of the address was spoken in private to all the disciples

3 ¶ And as he sat upon the mount of Olives, the disciples came unto him privately,
saying, Tell us, when shall these things be? and what *shall be* the sign of thy coming,
and of the end of the world?
4 And Jesus answered and said unto them, Take heed that no man deceive you.
5 For many shall come in my name, saying, I am Christ; and shall deceive many.
6 And ye shall hear of wars and rumours of wars: see that ye be not troubled: for all
these things must come to pass, but the end is not yet.
7 For nation shall rise against nation, and kingdom against kingdom: and there shall be
famines, and pestilences, and earthquakes, in divers places.
8 All these *are* the beginning of sorrows.
9 Then shall they deliver you up to be afflicted, and shall kill you: and ye shall be hated
of all nations for my name's sake.
10 And then shall many be offended, and shall betray one another, and shall hate one
another.
11 And many false prophets shall rise, and shall deceive many.
12 And because iniquity shall abound, the love of many shall wax cold.
13 But he that shall endure unto the end, the same shall be saved.
14 And this gospel of the kingdom shall be preached in all the world for a witness unto
all nations; and then shall the end come.
15 When ye therefore shall see the abomination of desolation, spoken of by Daniel the
prophet, stand in the holy place, (whoso readeth, let him understand:)
16 Then let them which be in Judæa flee into the mountains:
17 Let him which is on the housetop not come down to take any thing out of his house:
18 Neither let him which is in the field return back to take his clothes.
19 And woe unto them that are with child, and to them that give suck in those days!
20 But pray ye that your flight be not in the winter, neither on the sabbath day:
21 For then shall be great tribulation, such as was not since the beginning of the world
to this time, no, nor ever shall be.
22 And except those days should be shortened, there should no flesh be saved: but for
the elect's sake those days shall be shortened.
23 Then if any man shall say unto you, Lo, here *is* Christ, or there; believe *it* not.
24 For there shall arise false Christs, and false prophets, and shall shew great signs and
wonders; insomuch that, if *it were* possible, they shall deceive the very elect.
25 Behold, I have told you before.
26 Wherefore if they shall say unto you, Behold, he is in the desert; go not forth:
behold, *he is* in the secret chambers; believe *it* not.
27 For as the lightning cometh out of the east, and shineth even unto the west; so shall
also the coming of the Son of man be.
28 For wheresoever the carcase is, there will the eagles be gathered together.

29 Immediately after the tribulation of those days shall the sun be darkened, and the
moon shall not give her light, and the stars shall fall from heaven, and the powers of the
heavens shall be shaken:
30 And then shall appear the sign of the Son of man in heaven: and then shall all the
tribes of the earth mourn, and they shall see the Son of man coming in the clouds of
heaven with power and great glory.
31 And he shall send his angels with a great sound of a trumpet, and they shall gather
together his elect from the four winds, from one end of heaven to the other.
32 Now learn a parable of the fig tree; When his branch is yet tender, and putteth forth
leaves, ye know that summer *is* nigh:
33 So likewise ye, when ye shall see all these things, know that it is near, *even* at the
doors.
34 Verily I say unto you, This generation shall not pass, till all these things be fulfilled.
35 Heaven and earth shall pass away, but my words shall not pass away.
36 ¶ But of that day and hour knoweth no *man*, no, not the angels of heaven, but my
Father only.
37 But as the days of Noe *were*, so shall also the coming of the Son of man be.
38 For as in the days that were before the flood they were eating and drinking, marrying
and giving in marriage, until the day that Noe entered into the ark,
39 And knew not until the flood came, and took them all away; so shall also the coming
of the Son of man be.
40 Then shall two be in the field; the one shall be taken, and the other left.
41 Two *women shall be* grinding at the mill; the one shall be taken, and the other left.
42 ¶ Watch therefore: for ye know not what hour your Lord doth come.
43 But know this, that if the goodman of the house had known in what watch the thief
would come, he would have watched, and would not have suffered his house to be
broken up.
44 Therefore be ye also ready: for in such an hour as ye think not the Son of man
cometh.
45 Who then is a faithful and wise servant, whom his lord hath made ruler over his
household, to give them meat in due season?
46 Blessed *is* that servant, whom his lord when he cometh shall find so doing.
47 Verily I say unto you, That he shall make him ruler over all his goods.
48 But and if that evil servant shall say in his heart, My lord delayeth his coming;
49 And shall begin to smite *his* fellowservants, and to eat and drink with the drunken;
50 The lord of that servant shall come in a day when he looketh not for *him*, and in an
hour that he is not aware of,
51 And shall cut him asunder, and appoint *him* his portion with the hypocrites: there
shall be weeping and gnashing of teeth. (Matt 24:3-51)

Three parables addressed to his disciples alone

The Parable of the Ten Virgins
(The need to maintain inspiration in order to keep the spiritual light burning)

1 Then shall the kingdom of heaven be likened unto ten virgins, which took their
lamps, and went forth to meet the bridegroom.
2 And five of them were wise, and five *were* foolish.
3 They that *were* foolish took their lamps, and took no oil with them:

4 But the wise took oil in their vessels with their lamps.
5 While the bridegroom tarried, they all slumbered and slept.
6 And at midnight there was a cry made, Behold, the bridegroom cometh; go ye out to
meet him.
7 Then all those virgins arose, and trimmed their lamps.
8 And the foolish said unto the wise, Give us of your oil; for our lamps are gone out.
9 But the wise answered, saying, *Not so*; lest there be not enough for us and you: but go
ye rather to them that sell, and buy for yourselves.
10 And while they went to buy, the bridegroom came; and they that were ready went in
with him to the marriage: and the door was shut.
11 Afterward came also the other virgins, saying, Lord, Lord, open to us.
12 But he answered and said, Verily I say unto you, I know you not.
13 Watch therefore, for ye know neither the day nor the hour wherein the Son of man
cometh. (Matt 25:1-13)

The Parable of The Talents

(Each disciple is required to put into practice what they understand, be it much or little)

Jesus would soon depart and these disciples would become responsible to keep the light of his teaching burning brightly.

14 ¶ For *the kingdom of heaven is* as a man travelling into a far country, *who* called his
own servants, and delivered unto them his goods. (Matt 25:14)

A recognition that the disciples would have varying degrees of understanding.

15 And unto one he gave five talents, to another two, and to another one; to every man
according to his several ability; and straightway took his journey. (Matt 25:15)

The disciples are being told that whatever has been understood by them must put into practice.

16 Then he that had received the five talents went and traded with the same, and made
them other five talents.
17 And likewise he that *had received* two, he also gained other two. (Matt 25:16-17)

A warning that even the smallest understanding must be utilized. If not put into practice it will become useless.

18 But he that had received one went and digged in the earth, and hid his lord's money.
(Matt 25:18)

However long and alone, the disciple must persist. The reckoning takes place in individual consciousness.

19 After a long time the lord of those servants cometh, and reckoneth with them. (Matt
25:19)

Demonstrating what is understood results in ever greater understanding.

20 And so he that had received five talents came and brought other five talents, saying,
Lord, thou deliveredst unto me five talents: behold, I have gained beside them five
talents more.
21 His lord said unto him, Well done, *thou* good and faithful servant: thou hast been
faithful over a few things, I will make thee ruler over many things: enter thou into the
joy of thy lord.
22 He also that had received two talents came and said, Lord, thou deliveredst unto me
two talents: behold, I have gained two other talents beside them.
23 His lord said unto him, Well done, good and faithful servant; thou hast been faithful
over a few things, I will make thee ruler over many things: enter thou into the joy of thy
lord. (Matt 25:20-23)

Principle is imperative. You cannot mock it by human will. Science is a divine demand, not a human. Always right, its divine Principle never repents, but maintains the claim of Truth by quenching error. - MBE

24 Then he which had received the one talent came and said, Lord, I knew thee that
thou art an hard man, reaping where thou hast not sown, and gathering where thou hast
not strawed: (Matt 25:24)

Spiritual understanding originates in divine Mind. It is on loan from God and must be utilized, not buried in material belief.

25 And I was afraid, and went and hid thy talent in the earth: lo, *there* thou hast *that is* thine. (Matt 25:25)

If men understood their real spiritual source to be all blessedness, they would struggle for recourse to the spiritual and be at peace; but the deeper the error into which mortal mind is plunged, the more intense the opposition to spirituality, till error yields to Truth. - MBE

26 His lord answered and said unto him, *Thou* wicked and slothful servant, thou knewest that I reap where I sowed not, and gather where I have not strawed: (Matt 25:26)

Paul and John had a clear apprehension that, as mortal man achieves no worldly honors except by sacrifice, so he must gain heavenly riches by forsaking all worldliness. Then he will have nothing in common with the worldling's affections, motives, and aims. Judge not the future advancement of Christian Science by the steps already taken, lest you yourself be condemned for failing to take the first step. - MBE

27 Thou oughtest therefore to have put my money to the exchangers, and *then* at my coming I should have received mine own with usury.

28 Take therefore the talent from him, and give *it* unto him which hath ten talents.

29 For unto every one that hath shall be given, and he shall have abundance: but from him that hath not shall be taken away even that which he hath.

30 And cast ye the unprofitable servant into outer darkness: there shall be weeping and gnashing of teeth. (Matt 25:27-30)

Separating the sheep from the goats

(The supreme teaching – Unconditional love)

Spiritual man, what each one of us really is, reflecting God's thoughts has dominion over the whole earth.

31 ¶ When the Son of man shall come in his glory, and all the holy angels with him, then shall he sit upon the throne of his glory: (Matt 25:31)

All nations, *ἔθνος, ethnos*, qualities of thought, are separated as a shepherd divides the sheep from the goats.

32 And before him shall be gathered all nations: and he shall separate them one from another, as a shepherd divideth *his* sheep from the goats: (Matt 25:32)

Sheep, spiritual thoughts on the right and goats, material thoughts on the left.

33 And he shall set the sheep on his right hand, but the goats on the left. (Matt 25:33)

Spiritual thoughts are manifested in acts of self-less love.

34 Then shall the King say unto them on his right hand, Come, ye blessed of my Father, inherit the kingdom prepared for you from the foundation of the world:

35 For I was an hungered, and ye gave me meat: I was thirsty, and ye gave me drink: I was a stranger, and ye took me in:

36 Naked, and ye clothed me: I was sick, and ye visited me: I was in prison, and ye came unto me. (Matt 25:34-36)

True love is a spontaneous outpouring with no expectancy of a reward.

37 Then shall the righteous answer him, saying, Lord, when saw we thee an hungered, and fed *thee*? or thirsty, and gave *thee* drink?

38 When saw we thee a stranger, and took *thee* in? or naked, and clothed *thee*?

39 Or when saw we thee sick, or in prison, and came unto thee? (Matt 25:37-39)

He that loveth his brother whom he hath seen necessarily loves God whom he hath not seen.

40 And the King shall answer and say unto them, Verily I say unto you, Inasmuch as ye have done *it* unto one of the least of these my brethren, ye have done *it* unto me. (Matt 25:40)

Goat thoughts are material thoughts of self: self-love, self-justification, self-pity, self-glorification, just plain selfishness.

41 Then shall he say also unto them on the left hand, Depart from me, ye cursed, into everlasting fire, prepared for the devil and his angels:

42 For I was an hungered, and ye gave me no meat: I was thirsty, and ye gave me no drink:

43 I was a stranger, and ye took me not in: naked, and ye clothed me not: sick, and in

prison, and ye visited me not. (Matt 25:41-43)
Selfishness cannot see beyond self.

44 Then shall they also answer him, saying, Lord, when saw we thee an hungered, or
athirst, or a stranger, or naked, or sick, or in prison, and did not minister unto thee? (Matt 25:44)

"He that loveth not his brother whom he hath seen, how can he love God whom he hath not seen not seen?" (I John 4:20)

45 Then shall he answer them, saying, Verily I say unto you, Inasmuch as ye did *it* not
to one of the least of these, ye did *it* not to me. (Matt 25:45)

Thoughts originating in divine Mind are eternal; thoughts originating in mortal mind punish themselves until expunged.

46 And these shall go away into everlasting punishment: but the righteous into life
eternal. (Matt 25:46)

CHAPTER 151
THE 6TH ANNOUNCEMENT OF SUFFERINGS
(Matthew 26:1-2)

1 And it came to pass, when Jesus had finished all these sayings, he said unto his
disciples,
2 Ye know that after two days is *the feast of* the passover, and the Son of man is
betrayed to be crucified. (Matt 26:1-2)

CHAPTER 152
PLOTTING TO KILL JESUS WITHOUT CREATING AN UPROAR

According to the Gospel of Luke

1 Now the feast of unleavened bread drew nigh, which is called the Passover.
2 And the chief priests and scribes sought how they might kill him; for they feared the
people. (Luke 22:1-2)

According to the Gospel of Mark

1 After two days was *the feast of* the passover, and of unleavened bread: and the chief
priests and the scribes sought how they might take him by craft, and put *him* to death.
2 But they said, Not on the feast *day*, lest there be an uproar of the people. (Mark 14:1-2)

According to the Gospel of Matthew

Caiaphas held a secret council to finalize a plan to execute Jesus in a manner that would not create a rebellion.

3 Then assembled together the chief priests, and the scribes, and the elders of the
people, unto the palace of the high priest, who was called Caiaphas,
4 And consulted that they might take Jesus by subtilty, and kill *him*.
5 But they said, Not on the feast *day*, lest there be an uproar among the people. (Matt 26:3-5)

CHAPTER 153
THE THIRD ANOINTING

This anointing should not be confused with the anointing three days earlier by Mary, the sister of Martha and Lazarus. There are similarities to the first anointing much earlier in his ministry. The woman is unnamed, the ointment is in an alabaster box, and it takes place in the home of a man named Simon. This time however, it is Simon the leper, not Simon the Pharisee; the head and not the feet are anointed; and it is the disciples that protest the expense of the ointment.

According to the Gospel of Matthew

Although Simon was a common name, it is noteworthy that Judas Iscariot was called "the son of Simon." Jn. 6:71 & 13:26.

6 ¶ Now when Jesus was in Bethany, in the house of Simon the leper, (Matt 26:6)

This woman is not identified, but being allowed to enter, she was likely someone known by those in attendance.

7 There came unto him a woman having an alabaster box of very precious ointment,
and poured it on his head, as he sat *at meat*. (Matt 26:7)

This time it is the disciples, and not only Judas or the host, that protest the expense of the ointment. Verse 10 suggests that there was also perhaps resentment or jealousy directed at the woman who anointed him.

8 But when his disciples saw *it*, they had indignation, saying, To what purpose *is* this

waste?
9 For this ointment might have been sold for much, and given to the poor.
10 When Jesus understood *it*, he said unto them, Why trouble ye the woman? for she hath wrought a good work upon me. (Matt 26:8-10)

Jesus repeats the same reply to the disciples that he gave to Judas three days before. Where is the compassion?

11 For ye have the poor always with you; but me ye have not always. (Matt 26:11)

This anointing took place less than two days before his body was placed in a tomb.

12 For in that she hath poured this ointment on my body, she did *it* for my burial. (Matt 26:12)

The woman is unnamed, but her act is immortal. Could this have been Jesus' most faithful female disciple?

13 Verily I say unto you, Wheresoever this gospel shall be preached in the whole world, *there* shall also this, that this woman hath done, be told for a memorial of her. (Matt 26:13)

According to the Gospel of Mark

3 ¶ And being in Bethany in the house of Simon the leper, as he sat at meat, there came a woman having an alabaster box of ointment of spikenard very precious; and she brake the box, and poured *it* on his head.
4 And there were some that had indignation within themselves, and said, Why was this waste of the ointment made?
5 For it might have been sold for more than three hundred pence, and have been given to the poor. And they murmured against her.
6 And Jesus said, Let her alone; why trouble ye her? she hath wrought a good work on me.
7 For ye have the poor with you always, and whensoever ye will ye may do them good: but me ye have not always.
8 She hath done what she could: she is come aforehand to anoint my body to the burying.
9 Verily I say unto you, Wheresoever this gospel shall be preached throughout the whole world, *this* also that she hath done shall be spoken of for a memorial of her. (Mark 14:4-9)

THE DAY BEFORE PASSOVER

(The 14th day of Nisan the Gentile Tuesday sunset to Wednesday sunset)

(And in the fourteenth day of the first month [Nisan] *is* the passover of the LORD." Numbers 28:16)
(And in the fifteenth day of this month [Nisan] *is* the feast: [when the Passover Lamb is eaten]." Numbers 28:17)
(The first day [of the feast on the 15th of Nisan] *shall be* [*is*] an holy convocation [High Sabbath]: Numbers 28:18 *The*)

CHAPTER 154

JUDAS ARRANGES THE BETRAYAL OF JESUS

After sunset on Tuesday, the evening of the 14th of Nisan. With other disciples protesting Jesus' third anointing, did Judas now feel justified? "The greed for gold strengthened his ingratitude, and for a time quieted his remorse." - MBE

According to the Gospel of Mark

Judas conspired against Jesus. The world's ingratitude and hatred towards that just man effected his betrayal. - MBE

10 ¶ And Judas Iscariot, one of the twelve, went unto the chief priests, to betray him unto them.
11 And when they heard *it*, they were glad, and promised to give him money. And he sought how he might conveniently betray him. (Mark 14:10-11)

According to the Gospel of Matthew

14 ¶ Then one of the twelve, called Judas Iscariot, went unto the chief priests, (Matt 26:14)

The traitor's price was thirty pieces of silver and the smiles of the Pharisees. - MBE. Also see Ex. 21:32.

15 And said *unto them*, What will ye give me, and I will deliver him unto you? And

they covenanted with him for thirty pieces of silver. (Matt 26:15)
He chose his time, when the people were in doubt concerning Jesus' teachings. - MBE
16 And from that time he sought opportunity to betray him. (Matt 26:16)

According to the Gospel of Luke

3 ¶ Then entered Satan into Judas surnamed Iscariot, being of the number of the
twelve. (Luke 22:3)
Note: not only the chief priests, but officers of the Temple Guard were involved in the scheme to have Jesus executed.
4 And he went his way, and communed with the chief priests and captains, how he
might betray him unto them.
5 And they were glad, and covenanted to give him money.
6 And he promised, and sought opportunity to betray him unto them in the absence of
the multitude. (Luke 22:4-6)

CHAPTER 155
PREPARATION FOR THE "LAST SUPPER"

The 14th of Nisan is the day of unleavened bread when lambs are killed in the afternoon. The Hebrew day begins after sunset. (see Gen.1:5, 8, 13 etc.). "The Last Supper" took place the night of the 14th of Nisan, about 24 hours before the passover feast when lamb is eaten. Therefore, lamb was not part of the "passover" meal Jesus shared with his disciples. The passover lambs were being slain while Jesus, the Lamb of God as John the Baptist called him, was on the cross.

Jesus must have made arrangements in advance for the last supper. He sent two disciples, Peter and John to made the final preparations. They would then inform those who were to attend the location.

According to the Gospel of Matthew

17 ¶ Now the first *day* of the *feast of* unleavened bread the disciples came to Jesus,
saying unto him, Where wilt thou that we prepare for thee to eat the passover?
18 And he said, Go into the city to such a man, and say unto him, The Master saith, My
time is at hand; I will keep the passover at thy house with my disciples.
19 And the disciples did as Jesus had appointed them; and they made ready the
passover. (Matt 26:17-19)

According to the Gospel of Mark

12 ¶ And the first day of unleavened bread, when they killed the passover, his disciples
said unto him, Where wilt thou that we go and prepare that thou mayest eat the
passover?
13 And he sendeth forth two of his disciples, and saith unto them, Go ye into the city,
and there shall meet you a man bearing a pitcher of water: follow him.
14 And wheresoever he shall go in, say ye to the goodman of the house, The Master
saith, Where is the guestchamber, where I shall eat the passover with my disciples?
15 And he will shew you a large upper room furnished *and* prepared: there make ready
for us.
16 And his disciples went forth, and came into the city, and found as he had said unto
them: and they made ready the passover. (Mark 14:12-16)

According to the Gospel of Luke

7 ¶ Then came the day of unleavened bread, when the passover must be killed.
8 And he sent Peter and John, saying, Go and prepare us the passover, that we may eat.
9 And they said unto him, Where wilt thou that we prepare?
10 And he said unto them, Behold, when ye are entered into the city, there shall a man
meet you, bearing a pitcher of water; follow him into the house where he entereth in.
11 And ye shall say unto the goodman of the house, The Master saith unto thee, Where
is the guestchamber, where I shall eat the passover with my disciples?
12 And he shall shew you a large upper room furnished: there make ready.

13 And they went, and found as he had said unto them: and they made ready the passover. (Luke 22:7-13)

THE LAST SUPPER

CHAPTER 156

SUPPER - FOOT WASHING - THE NEW TESTAMENT

The Passover, which Jesus ate with his disciples in the month Nisan on the night before his crucifixion, was a mournful occasion, a sad supper taken at the close of day, in the twilight of a glorious career with shadows fast falling around; and this supper closed forever Jesus' ritualism or concessions to matter. - MBE

The timing and reason for Jesus' "last supper" with his disciples

This supper that Jesus shared with his disciples took place 24 hours "before the feast of the passover" where lamb would be eaten. Jesus would already be in the sepulchre while the regular "passover" was being celebrated.

1 Now before the feast of the passover, when Jesus knew that his hour was come that he should depart out of this world unto the Father, having loved his own which were in the world, he loved them unto the end. (John 13:1)

The arrival of Jesus and the Apostles

According to the Gospel of Mark

Other disciples were already present when Jesus arrived with the twelve.

17 And in the evening he cometh with the twelve. (Mark 14:17)

According to the Gospel of Matthew

Jesus and the twelve sat (reclined) together.

20 Now when the even was come, he sat down with the twelve. (Matt 26:20)

According to the Gospel of Luke

14 And when the hour was come, he sat down, and the twelve apostles with him. (Luke 22:14)

During the meal Jesus announces that he will be betrayed

According to the Gospel of Luke

15 And he said unto them, With desire I have desired to eat this passover with you before I suffer:
16 For I say unto you, I will not any more eat thereof, until it be fulfilled in the kingdom of God.
17 And he took the cup, and gave thanks, and said, Take this, and divide *it* among yourselves:
18 For I say unto you, I will not drink of the fruit of the vine, until the kingdom of God shall come.
19 ¶ And he took bread, and gave thanks, and brake *it*, and gave unto them, saying, This is my body which is given for you: this do in remembrance of me. (Luke 22:15-19)

According to the Gospel of Matthew

21 And as they did eat, he said, Verily I say unto you, that one of you shall betray me.
22 And they were exceeding sorrowful, and began every one of them to say unto him, Lord, is it I?
23 And he answered and said, He that dippeth *his* hand with me in the dish, the same shall betray me.
24 The Son of man goeth as it is written of him: but woe unto that man by whom the Son of man is betrayed! it had been good for that man if he had not been born.
25 Then Judas, which betrayed him, answered and said, Master, is it I? He said unto

him, Thou hast said. (Matt 26:21-25)

According to the Gospel of Mark

18 And as they sat and did eat, Jesus said, Verily I say unto you, One of you which
eateth with me shall betray me.
19 And they began to be sorrowful, and to say unto him one by one, *Is* it I? and another
said, Is it I?
20 And he answered and said unto them, *It is* one of the twelve, that dippeth with me in
the dish.
21 The Son of man indeed goeth, as it is written of him: but woe to that man by whom
the Son of man is betrayed! good were it for that man if he had never been born. (Mark 14:18-21)

Washing the disciple's feet

This establishes that Jesus washed the Apostles feet after everyone had eaten the regular meal.

2 And supper being ended, the devil having now put into the heart of Judas Iscariot,
Simon's *son*, to betray him;
3 Jesus knowing that the Father had given all things into his hands, and that he was
come from God, and went to God;
4 He riseth from supper, and laid aside his garments; and took a towel, and girded
himself.
5 After that he poureth water into a basin, and began to wash the disciples' feet, and to
wipe *them* with the towel wherewith he was girded.
6 Then cometh he to Simon Peter: and Peter saith unto him, Lord, dost thou wash my
feet?
7 Jesus answered and said unto him, What I do thou knowest not now; but thou shalt
know hereafter.
8 Peter saith unto him, Thou shalt never wash my feet. Jesus answered him, If I wash
thee not, thou hast no part with me.
9 Simon Peter saith unto him, Lord, not my feet only, but also *my* hands and *my* head.
10 Jesus saith to him, He that is washed needeth not save to wash *his* feet, but is clean
every whit: and ye are clean, but not all.
11 For he knew who should betray him; therefore said he, Ye are not all clean.
12 So after he had washed their feet, and had taken his garments, and was set down
again, he said unto them, Know ye what I have done to you?
13 Ye call me Master and Lord: and ye say well; for *so* I am. (John 13:2-13)

Jesus had taught the true understanding of God; now the Apostles must watch that his understanding remain pure.

14 If I then, *your* Lord and Master, have washed your feet; ye also ought to wash one
another's feet. (John 13:14)

"Jesus established what he said by demonstration, thus making his acts of higher importance than his words." - MBE

15 For I have given you an example, that ye should do as I have done to you. (John 13:15)

Instead of arguing about "Who shall be the greatest," concentrate on putting into practice what you have been taught.

16 Verily, verily, I say unto you, The servant is not greater than his lord; neither he that
is sent greater than he that sent him. (John 13:16)

It is not enough to know the right thing to do, it must be done.

17 If ye know these things, happy are ye if ye do them. (John 13:17)

Jesus *again* announces that he will be betrayed, and that the betrayer would be an Apostle

According to the Gospel of John

Concerning the betrayal to take place almost immediately, Jesus quotes from the 41st Psalm, verse 9.

18 I speak not of you all: I know whom I have chosen: but that the scripture may be

fulfilled, He that eateth bread with me hath lifted up his heel against me.
19 Now I tell you before it come, that, when it is come to pass, ye may believe that I am *he*.
20 Verily, verily, I say unto you, He that receiveth whomsoever I send receiveth me; and he that receiveth me receiveth him that sent me.
21 When Jesus had thus said, he was troubled in spirit, and testified, and said, Verily, verily, I say unto you, that one of you shall betray me. (John 13:18-21)

Doubting, ἀπορέω, *aporeō*, means perplexed or wondering.

22 Then the disciples looked one on another, doubting of whom he spake. (John 13:22)

According to the Gospel of Luke

20 Likewise also the cup after supper, saying, This cup *is* the new testament in my blood, which is shed for you.
21 ¶ But, behold, the hand of him that betrayeth me *is* with me on the table.
22 And truly the Son of man goeth, as it was determined: but woe unto that man by whom he is betrayed!
23 And they began to inquire among themselves, which of them it was that should do this thing. (Luke 22:20 -23)

Judas Iscariot leaves the others to carry out the betrayal

23 Now there was leaning on Jesus' bosom one of his disciples, whom Jesus loved.
24 Simon Peter therefore beckoned to him, that he should ask who it should be of whom he spake.
25 He then lying on Jesus' breast saith unto him, Lord, who is it?
26 Jesus answered, He it is, to whom I shall give a sop, when I have dipped *it*. And when he had dipped the sop, he gave *it* to Judas Iscariot, *the son* of Simon. (John 13:23-26)

The sop did not *cause* Satan to enter Judas, who instead of repenting, hardened his heart. Self-will led to his tragedy.

27 And after the sop Satan entered into him. (John 13:27 to 1st.)

Jesus did not tell Judas to betray him, Judas had already committed himself and was merely awaiting the opportunity.

27 Then said Jesus unto him, That thou doest, do quickly.
28 Now no man at the table knew for what intent he spake this unto him.
29 For some *of them* thought, because Judas had the bag, that Jesus had said unto him, Buy *those things* that we have need of against the feast; or, that he should give something to the poor.
30 He then having received the sop went immediately out: and it was night. (John 13:27-30 *Then*)

After eating and washing the disciples feet, the New Testament, *διαθήκη diathēkēis*, is announced
("The disciples had eaten, yet Jesus prayed and gave them bread." - MBE)

According to the Gospel of Mark

Bread, a hard biscuit that required breaking to be eaten; a metaphor for Truth that must be *explained* to be understood.

22 ¶ And as they did eat, Jesus took bread, and blessed, and brake *it*, and gave to them, and said, Take, eat: this is my body. (Mark 14:22)

Cup, a metaphor for his experience. For blood of the New testament read Jer. 31:31-34. It is forsaking all that is mortal.

23 And he took the cup, and when he had given thanks, he gave *it* to them: and they all drank of it.
24 And he said unto them, This is my blood of the new testament, which is shed for many.
25 Verily I say unto you, I will drink no more of the fruit of the vine, until that day that I drink it new in the kingdom of God. (Mark 14:23-25)

"This is" = this represents. Body is substance, a metaphor for the Christ, Truth that constituted the very being of Jesus.

26 ¶ And as they were eating, Jesus took bread, and blessed *it*, and brake *it*, and gave *it*
to the disciples, and said, Take, eat; this is my body.
27 And he took the cup, and gave thanks, and gave *it* to them, saying, Drink ye all of it;
28 For this is my blood of the new testament, which is shed for many for the remission
of sins.
29 But I say unto you, I will not drink henceforth of this fruit of the vine, until that day
when I drink it new with you in my Father's kingdom. (Matt 26:26-29)

The "new" commandment (ἐντολή, entolē)

31 ¶ Therefore, when he was gone out, Jesus said, Now is the Son of man glorified, and
God is glorified in him.
32 If God be glorified in him, God shall also glorify him in himself, and shall
straightway glorify him.
33 Little children, yet a little while I am with you. Ye shall seek me: and as I said unto
the Jews, Whither I go, ye cannot come; so now I say to you. (John 13:31-33)

It is "new" because it is "*as I have loved, ἀγαπάω agapaō you,*" totally self-less, even unto the laying down of his life.

34 A new commandment I give unto you, That ye love one another; as I have loved
you, that ye also love one another. (John 13:34)

Here Jesus uses *ἀγάπη agape*, love me, to which Peter replies with *φιλέω phileō*, a friend. See John 21:15-17.

35 By this shall all *men* know that ye are my disciples, if ye have love one to another.
(John 13:35)

Peter's 1st profession of loyalty

36 ¶ Simon Peter said unto him, Lord, whither goest thou? Jesus answered him,
Whither I go, thou canst not follow me now; but thou shalt follow me afterwards.
37 Peter said unto him, Lord, why cannot I follow thee now? I will lay down my life
for thy sake. (John 13:36-37)

Jesus' 1st warning to Peter that he will deny him

38 Jesus answered him, Wilt thou lay down thy life for my sake? Verily, verily, I say
unto thee, The cock shall not crow, till thou hast denied me thrice. (John 13:38)

Jesus had just washed their feet and here they were again arguing over "who shall be the greatest."
(See Mark 9:34 for the first occasion. This is within minutes of the Master speaking the words of John 13:14-17.)

24 ¶ And there was also a strife among them, which of them should be accounted the
greatest.
25 And he said unto them, The kings of the Gentiles exercise lordship over them; and
they that exercise authority upon them are called benefactors.
26 But ye *shall* not *be* so: but he that is greatest among you, let him be as the younger;
and he that is chief, as he that doth serve.
27 For whether *is* greater, he that sitteth at meat, or he that serveth? *is* not he that sitteth
at meat? but I am among you as he that serveth.
28 Ye are they which have continued with me in my temptations.
29 And I appoint unto you a kingdom, as my Father hath appointed unto me;
30 That ye may eat and drink at my table in my kingdom, and sit on thrones judging the
twelve tribes of Israel. (Luke 22:24-30)

Peter is warned that he was at that very moment being tested

31 ¶ And the Lord said, Simon, Simon, behold, Satan hath desired *to have* you, that he

may sift *you* as wheat:
32 But I have prayed for thee, that thy faith fail not: and when thou art converted,
strengthen thy brethren. (Luke 22:31-32)

Peter's 2nd profession of loyalty

33 And he said unto him, Lord, I am ready to go with thee, both into prison, and to
death. (Luke 22:33)

Jesus' 2nd warning to Peter

34 And he said, I tell thee, Peter, the cock shall not crow this day, before that thou shalt
thrice deny that thou knowest me. (Luke 22:34)

The following discourses constitute an integral part of the "Last Supper."

CHAPTER 157
REVISED INSTRUCTIONS FOR CHANGED CONDITIONS

For earlier instructions given when the kingdom of God was being proclaimed see Luke 9:1-6; 10:1-11 & Matt. 10:1-14.

35 And he said unto them, When I sent you without purse, and scrip, and shoes, lacked
ye any thing? And they said, Nothing. (Luke 22:35)

New instructions were required because the kingdom of God had been rejected by the Jews.

36 Then said he unto them, But now, he that hath a purse, let him take *it*, and likewise
his scrip: and he that hath no sword, let him sell his garment, and buy one. (Luke 22:36)

Jesus tells what will soon take place. It was foretold nearly 600 years earlier. See Isa. 53:12.

37 For I say unto you, that this that is written must yet be accomplished in me, (Luke 22:37 to 1st.)

The quotation Jesus used: ". . . he was numbered with the transgressors" is from Isa. 53:12. The total number will be five: Jesus, *two malefactors* who will accompany him to the site, and later *two thieves* will be brought out and crucified.

37 And he was reckoned among the transgressors: (Luke 22:37 *And to* :)

This scripture would be accomplished in less than 24 hours. "have an end" = the things prophesied will be fulfilled.

37 for the things concerning me have an end. (Luke 22:37 2nd *for*)

One can feel Jesus' frustration. These men had been with him for over three years, and they still could not discern when he was speaking to them symbolically. When he said to sell their garment and buy a sword he did not mean to purchase a material weapon to cut off the ear of the high priest's servant. He meant to put on "the sword of the Spirit." Eph. 6:17,

38 And they said, Lord, behold, here *are* two swords. And he said unto them, It is
enough. (Luke 22:38)

CHAPTER 158
DISCOURSE ON THE COMFORTER

1 Let not your heart be troubled: ye believe in God, believe also in me.
2 In my Father's house are many mansions: if *it were* not *so*, I would have told you. I
go to prepare a place for you.
3 And if I go and prepare a place for you, I will come again, and receive you unto
myself; that where I am, *there* ye may be also.
4 And whither I go ye know, and the way ye know.
5 Thomas saith unto him, Lord, we know not whither thou goest; and how can we
know the way?
6 Jesus saith unto him, I am the way, the truth, and the life: no man cometh unto the
Father, but by me.
7 If ye had known me, ye should have known my Father also: and from henceforth ye
know him, and have seen him. (John 14:1-7)

Philip expresses his desire to see the Father, Spirit in the form of a corporeal being, an impossibility.

8 Philip saith unto him, Lord, shew us the Father, and it sufficeth us. (John 14:8)

"No man hath seen God at any time." The Christ, at one with Him "hath declared him." See John 1:18.

9 Jesus saith unto him, Have I been so long time with you, and yet hast thou not known

me, Philip? he that hath seen me hath seen the Father; and how sayest thou *then*, Shew us the Father? (John 14:9)

The healing works show forth the presence of the Father, for it is God Who "doeth the works."

10 Believest thou not that I am in the Father, and the Father in me? the words that I speak unto you I speak not of myself: but the Father that dwelleth in me, he doeth the works. (John 14:10)

Jesus in substance is saying: The only "I" is the Father Whose will I do. The works you have seen prove this to be true.

11 Believe me that I *am* in the Father, and the Father in me: or else believe me for the very works' sake. (John 14:11)

The understanding that God, divine Mind is the only "I" is the key to doing the works.

12 Verily, verily, I say unto you, He that believeth on me, the works that I do shall he do also; and greater *works* than these shall he do; because I go unto my Father. (John 14:12)

Christ is God manifested. The "I" that is God does the works that appear to humanity through Christ.

13 And whatsoever ye shall ask in my name, that will I do, that the Father may be glorified in the Son.
14 If ye shall ask any thing in my name, I will do *it*. (John 14:13-14)

The test of true love

15 If ye love me, keep my commandments. (John 14:15)

The "other" Comforter the Father will send is incorporeal and therefore ever-present

16 And I will pray the Father, and he shall give you another Comforter, that he may abide with you for ever; (John 14:16)

The Comforter: "Which is Christ in you, the hope of glory", is invisible, incorporeal. Col 1:27.

17 *Even* the Spirit of truth; whom the world cannot receive, because it seeth him not, neither knoweth him: but ye know him; for he dwelleth with you, and shall be in you. (John 14:17)

Here Jesus plainly tells the disciples that his "Second Coming " will be in the form of the Comforter.

18 I will not leave you comfortless: I will come to you.
19 Yet a little while, and the world seeth me no more; but ye see me: because I live, ye shall live also. (John 14:18-19)

The divine Mind, the One "I" will be known as All-in-all, and will be understood to be the only true and eternal Mind.

20 At that day ye shall know that I *am* in my Father, and ye in me, and I in you. (John 14:20)

The reward for fidelity

21 He that hath my commandments, and keepeth them, he it is that loveth me: and he that loveth me shall be loved of my Father, and I will love him, and will manifest myself to him. (John 14:21)

Christ is to be manifested as the Comforter.

22 Judas saith unto him, not Iscariot, Lord, how is it that thou wilt manifest thyself unto us, and not unto the world? (John 14:22)

If one truly loves Jesus, he will keep his words, which is to say, he will put the teaching of Jesus into practice.

23 Jesus answered and said unto him, If a man love me, he will keep my words: and my Father will love him, and we will come unto him, and make our abode with him. (John 14:23)

The consequences of infidelity

This love is *ἀγαπάω, agapaō*, divine, expressed through obedience to Mind, the origin of Jesus' teaching.

24 He that loveth me not keepeth not my sayings: and the word which ye hear is not mine, but the Father's which sent me.
25 These things have I spoken unto you, being *yet* present with you. (John 14:24-25)

The Comforter, Holy Ghost, will be sent to execute the office of Christ.

26 But the Comforter, *which is* the Holy Ghost, whom the Father will send in my name,
he shall teach you all things, and bring all things to your remembrance, whatsoever I
have said unto you. (John 14:26)

The peace of Christ is not merely a temporary cessation of hostilities, it is a proactive and permanent sense of Love.

27 Peace I leave with you, my peace I give unto you: not as the world giveth, give I
unto you. Let not your heart be troubled, neither let it be afraid. (John 14:27)

If you loved *ἀγαπάω agapaō* me, you would rejoice, and not wish to hold me back, but rather will you look forward to the day you will be with me in a much higher sense of being.

28 Ye have heard how I said unto you, I go away, and come *again* unto you. If ye
loved me, ye would rejoice, because I said, I go unto the Father: for my Father is
greater than I.

29 And now I have told you before it come to pass, that, when it is come to pass, ye
might believe. (John 14:28-29)

Jesus twice rejected the pride of priesthood at the very beginning of his career. See Luke 4:9-12 & Matt. 4:5-7. The pride of priesthood is the prince of this world. It has nothing in Christ. – MBE. Why is it the prince of this world? Because it is all about "who shall be the greatest." As we see here, Jesus KNEW that God is the only Great, and therefore THE Greatest.

30 Hereafter I will not talk much with you: for the prince of this world cometh, and
hath nothing in me.

31 But that the world may know that I love the Father; and as the Father gave me
commandment, even so I do. (John 14:30-31 to 1st.)

The call to rise to an even higher understanding of Christ

"Arise let us go hence" has nothing to do with getting up and going any place. Jesus was letting his disciples know that what he was about to say would elevate them to a higher state of consciousness in Spirit, so that later on when tempted, they would not falter. It was a wake-up call to rise above the material sense of things.

31 Arise, let us go hence. (John 14:31 *Arise*)

CHAPTER 159
DISCOURSE ON DEMONSTRATION

Demonstration demanded

1 I am the true vine, and my Father is the husbandman.

2 Every branch in me that beareth not fruit he taketh away: and every *branch* that
beareth fruit, he purgeth it, that it may bring forth more fruit. (John 15:1-2)

Clean, *καθαρός katharos*, in a similitude, like a vine well pruned, and so "clean" to bear fruit. Purged of false beliefs.

3 Now ye are clean through the word which I have spoken unto you. (John 15:3)

Fidelity to the teachings of Christ is required for demonstration.

4 Abide in me, and I in you. As the branch cannot bear fruit of itself, except it abide in
the vine; no more can ye, except ye abide in me.

5 I am the vine, ye *are* the branches: He that abideth in me, and I in him, the same
bringeth forth much fruit: for without me ye can do nothing.

6 If a man abide not in me, he is cast forth as a branch, and is withered; and men gather
them, and cast *them* into the fire, and they are burned. (John 15:4-6)

The conditional promise of demonstration.

7 If ye abide in me, and my words abide in you, ye shall ask what ye will, and it shall
be done unto you. (John 15:7)

Demonstration (bearing fruit) is the test of faithful discipleship.

8 Herein is my Father glorified, that ye bear much fruit; so shall ye be my disciples.

9 As the Father hath loved me, so have I loved you: continue ye in my love.

10 If ye keep my commandments, ye shall abide in my love; even as I have kept my
Father's commandments, and abide in his love.

11 These things have I spoken unto you, that my joy might remain in you, and *that* your

joy might be full. (John 15:8-11)

The New Commandment in Christ requires the fruits of Love, *ἀγαπάω; agapaō,* self-less love, AS Jesus loved. And how was that? He laid down his life by allowing men to crucify him. This he did for two reasons. First, the crucifixion was followed by his resurrection where he proved Life to be eternal. Next the ascension where he showed that eternal life is spiritual, not material. Second, the crucifixion exemplified what Jesus meant when he said to take up the cross. We are called to follow him, not by being crucified, but by putting off the old [material] man with his deeds, and putting on the new [spiritual] man, which after God is created in righteousness and true holiness. See Eph. 4:22-24.

12 This is my commandment, That ye love one another, as I have loved you. (John 15:12)

The Test and Proof of True Friendship (See John 21:17)

The word here translated love is *φίλος philos*, friend, an associate. Hence, there is no greater friendship than for a man to "lay down his life" for his friend. This verse explains why Peter was grieved when Jesus asked him if he was his *friend*, since he and the other disciples had deserted him after plecging their undying loyalty. (See Jn. 21:17)

13 Greater love hath no man than this, that a man lay down his life for his friends. (John 15:13)

Jesus saw *obedience* to his teaching as the test of genuine friendship. Here friendship is *φίλος philos.*

14 Ye are my friends, if ye do whatsoever I command you. (John 15:14)

Jesus' friendship, *φίλος philos* was genuine, and he would soon demonstrate, not just profess, his friendship.

15 Henceforth I call you not servants; for the servant knoweth not what his lord doeth: but I have called you friends; for all things that I have heard of my Father I have made known unto you. (John 15:15)

With discipleship comes persecution (See Matthew 5:11 & 12)

16 Ye have not chosen me, but I have chosen you, and ordained you, that ye should go and bring forth fruit, and *that* your fruit should remain: that whatsoever ye shall ask of the Father in my name, he may give it you. (John 15:16)

Only through obedience to these instructions do we fully "love one another."

17 These things I command you, that ye love one another. (John 15:17)

If the supreme "Demonstrator" of these teachings was hated, his disciples should be not alarmed if they too are hated.

18 If the world hate you, ye know that it hated me before *it hated* you. (John 15:18)

Goodness is persecuted because it threatens to destroy evil, and it does it in the same way that light destroys darkness. It just keeps pouring forth good until like any solvent, it dissolves the appearance of evil.

19 If ye were of the world, the world would love his own: but because ye are not of the world, but I have chosen you out of the world, therefore the world hateth you.

20 Remember the word that I said unto you, The servant is not greater than his lord. If they have persecuted me, they will also persecute you; if they have kept my saying, they will keep yours also. (John 15:19-20)

Ignorance of God makes it impossible to recognize His Christ.

21 But all these things will they do unto you for my name's sake, because they know not him that sent me. (John 15:21)

Willful rejection of Truth has no excuse.

22 If I had not come and spoken unto them, they had not had sin: but now they have no cloak for their sin. (John 15:22)

To hate Christ is to hate the Father, for they are one Being, just as cause and effect are one, though different in office.

23 He that hateth me hateth my Father also.

24 If I had not done among them the works which none other man did, they had not had sin: but now have they both seen and hated both me and my Father.

25 But *this cometh to pass*, that the word might be fulfilled that is written in their law, They hated me without a cause. (John 15:23-25)

Through the Comforter we shall bear witnesses to Christ, because in reality we have never been separated from Christ.

26 But when the Comforter is come, whom I will send unto you from the Father, *even* the Spirit of truth, which proceedeth from the Father, he shall testify of me:

27 And ye also shall bear witness, because ye have been with me from the beginning. (John 15:26-27)

CHAPTER 160

THE LAST HOUR REMINDER: TAKE CARE NOT TO DESERT

(Offended, *σκανδαλίζω skandalizō,* made to stumble, fall away, distrust, desert).

Having been forewarned that persecution is inevitable, a disciple should not be offended, i.e. run away, desert.

1 These things have I spoken unto you, that ye should not be offended.

2 They shall put you out of the synagogues: yea, the time cometh, that whosoever killeth you will think that he doeth God service.

3 And these things will they do unto you, because they have not known the Father, nor me.

4 But these things have I told you, that when the time shall come, ye may remember that I told you of them. And these things I said not unto you at the beginning, because I was with you. (John 16:1-4)

Whither, *ποῦ pou,* where, to what place. Interrogatively or relatively in a sense not physical; to a higher consciousness.

5 But now I go my way to him that sent me; and none of you asketh me, Whither goest thou?

6 But because I have said these things unto you, sorrow hath filled your heart. (John 16:5-6)

Jesus must depart because Christ, being the incorporeal Truth, cannot be received while clinging to corporeal personality.

7 Nevertheless I tell you the truth; It is expedient for you that I go away: for if I go not away, the Comforter will not come unto you; but if I depart, I will send him unto you. (John 16:7)

The Comforter will expose and denounce three aspects of the world (i.e. of the carnal mind):

8 And when he is come, he will reprove the world of sin, and of righteousness, and of judgment: (John 16:8)

First, the world is convicted of sin for rejecting Christ, not mere moral offences or infractions of ceremonies and traditions.

9 Of sin, because they believe not on me; (John 16:9)

Second, of the false righteousness of the hypocritical Pharisee convicted by their refusal to adopt the practice of: "Thy will not mine be done," as Jesus taught that we all must do..

10 Of righteousness, because I go to my Father, and ye see me no more; (John 16:10)

Third, the world belief in a personal devil is convicted by Jesus' teaching that the devil, evil is a lie and a liar. (John 8:44)

11 Of judgment, because the prince of this world is judged. (John 16:11)

The disciples were not able to hear more. Bear, *βαστάζω bastazō*, to take up in order to carry, to put upon one's self. Why? Because they were apparently still concerned with "Who shall be the greatest."

12 I have yet many things to say unto you, but ye cannot bear them now. (John 16:12)

In the absence of the personal Jesus, the impersonal Christ that Jesus called the Comforter, will reveal the whole of Truth.

13 Howbeit when he, the Spirit of truth, is come, he will guide you into all truth: for he shall not speak of himself; but whatsoever he shall hear, *that* shall he speak: and he will shew you things to come. (John 16:13)

The Comforter will explain everything that will make the teaching Jesus brought demonstrable, provable.

14 He shall glorify me: for he shall receive of mine, and shall shew *it* unto you. (John 16:14)

God is All-in-all, so everything real and good originates in God, and Christ is the full reflection or manifestation of God.

15 All things that the Father hath are mine: therefore said I, that he shall take of mine, and shall shew *it* unto you. (John 16:15)

Jesus told them that very soon he would be crucified and buried out of sight, and then rise from the dead and ascend.

16 A little while, and ye shall not see me: and again, a little while, and ye shall see me, because I go to the Father.

17 Then said *some* of his disciples among themselves, What is this that he saith unto us, A little while, and ye shall not see me: and again, a little while, and ye shall see me: and, Because I go to the Father?

18 They said therefore, What is this that he saith, A little while? we cannot tell what he saith.

19 Now Jesus knew that they were desirous to ask him, and said unto them, Do ye
inquire among yourselves of that I said, A little while, and ye shall not see me: and
again, a little while, and ye shall see me?
20 Verily, verily, I say unto you, That ye shall weep and lament, but the world shall
rejoice: and ye shall be sorrowful, but your sorrow shall be turned into joy. (John 16:16-20)

A brief parable on how the Comforter will come into the world
(A man child delivered of a woman. See Revelation chapter 12)

21 A woman when she is in travail hath sorrow, because her hour is come: but as soon
as she is delivered of the child, she remembereth no more the anguish, for joy that a
man is born into the world.
22 And ye now therefore have sorrow: but I will see you again, and your heart shall
rejoice, and your joy no man taketh from you.
23 And in that day ye shall ask me nothing. Verily, verily, I say unto you, Whatsoever
ye shall ask the Father in my name, he will give *it* you.
24 Hitherto have ye asked nothing in my name: ask, and ye shall receive, that your joy
may be full.
25 These things have I spoken unto you in proverbs: but the time cometh, when I shall
no more speak unto you in proverbs, but I shall shew you plainly of the Father. (John 16:21-25)

Love of Christ enables direct communion with the Father

Jesus here tells the disciples that through the Comforter, each individual will be in direct communion with God.

26 At that day ye shall ask in my name: and I say not unto you, that I will pray the
Father for you:
27 For the Father himself loveth you, because ye have loved me, and have believed that
I came out from God.
28 I came forth from the Father, and am come into the world: again, I leave the world,
and go to the Father. (John 16:26-28)

The disciples say they understood when they actually didn't

29 His disciples said unto him, Lo, now speakest thou plainly, and speakest no proverb.
30 Now are we sure that thou knowest all things, and needest not that any man should
ask thee: by this we believe that thou camest forth from God.
31 Jesus answered them, Do ye now believe? (John 16:29-31)

Jesus warns them for the 1st time that they will *all* desert him

"The Christian Scientist is alone with his own being and with the reality of things." - MBE

32 Behold, the hour cometh, yea, is now come, that ye shall be scattered, every man to
his own, and shall leave me alone: and yet I am not alone, because the Father is with
me. (John 16:32)

"Every mortal at some period, here or hereafter, must grapple with and overcome the mortal belief in a power opposed to God." - MBE

33 These things I have spoken unto you, that in me ye might have peace. In the world
ye shall have tribulation: but be of good cheer; I have overcome the world. (John 16:33)

CHAPTER 161
THE FAREWELL DISCOURSE

(What follows was spoken to comfort and encourage the disciples so they would not succumb to doubt and fear.)

1 These words spake Jesus, and lifted up his eyes to heaven, and said, Father, the hour
is come; glorify thy Son, that thy Son also may glorify thee:

2 As thou hast given him power over all flesh, that he should give eternal life to as
many as thou hast given him.
3 And this is life eternal, that they might know thee the only true God, and Jesus Christ,
whom thou hast sent.
4 I have glorified thee on the earth: I have finished the work which thou gavest me to
do. (John 17:1-4)

Jesus here declares his pre-existence, present existence, and eternal existence in Christ, his true, divine nature.

5 And now, O Father, glorify thou me with thine own self with the glory which I had
with thee before the world was. (John 17:5)

Jesus' manifestation of divine Love made God known to the disciples, and they are now with him in obedience to God.

6 I have manifested thy name unto the men which thou gavest me out of the world:
thine they were, and thou gavest them me; and they have kept thy word. (John 17:6)

Everything Jesus showed and taught the disciples originated in God, Who is the only cause and creator.

7 Now they have known that all things whatsoever thou hast given me are of thee. (John 17:7)

Everything Jesus taught his disciples came from God, and the disciples know this to be true.

8 For I have given unto them the words which thou gavest me; and they have received
them, and have known surely that I came out from thee, and they have believed that
thou didst send me. (John 17:8)

Pray, *ἐρωτάω erōtaō*, the asking of an inferior to a superior. Here praying for the disciples and not for "the world."

9 I pray for them: I pray not for the world, but for them which thou hast given me; for
they are thine. (John 17:9)

God is one. The allness of Deity is His oneness. - MBE. Man reflecting God, glorifies God.

10 And all mine are thine, and thine are mine; and I am glorified in them.
11 And now I am no more in the world, but these are in the world, and I come to thee.
Holy Father, keep through thine own name those whom thou hast given me, that they
may be one, as we *are*.
12 While I was with them in the world, I kept them in thy name: those that thou gavest
me I have kept, and none of them is lost, but the son of perdition; that the scripture
might be fulfilled.
13 And now come I to thee; and these things I speak in the world, that they might have
my joy fulfilled in themselves.
14 I have given them thy word; and the world hath hated them, because they are not of
the world, even as I am not of the world. (John 17:10-14)

The purpose of prayer is not to find a way to escape the challenges of the world, but to overcome the evils of the world.

15 I pray not that thou shouldest take them out of the world, but that thou shouldest
keep them from the evil. (John 17:15)

Yes! You too are in reality not of the world flesh and blood, but are of God spiritual and eternal.

16 They are not of the world, even as I am not of the world.
17 Sanctify them through thy truth: thy word is truth.
18 As thou hast sent me into the world, even so have I also sent them into the world.
19 And for their sakes I sanctify myself, that they also might be sanctified through the
truth. (John 17:16-19)

The following prayer of Jesus is intended to include everyone, and is effectual right NOW
(Here Jesus expands his prayer to include all who choose to follow his teaching and example)

20 Neither pray I for these alone, but for them also which shall believe on me through
their word;
21 That they all may be one; as thou, Father, *art* in me, and I in thee, that they also may
be one in us: that the world may believe that thou hast sent me.

22 And the glory which thou gavest me I have given them; that they may be one, even
as we are one: (John 17:20-22)

The way to perfection is through spiritual oneness with divine Love. Perfection will never be found in matter, it is spiritual.

23 I in them, and thou in me, that they may be made perfect in one; and that the world
may know that thou hast sent me, and hast loved them, as thou hast loved me.
24 Father, I will that they also, whom thou hast given me, be with me where I am; that
they may behold my glory, which thou hast given me: for thou lovedst me before the
foundation of the world.
25 O righteous Father, the world hath not known thee: but I have known thee, and these
have known that thou hast sent me.
26 And I have declared unto them thy name, and will declare *it*: that the love wherewith
thou hast loved me may be in them, and I in them. (John 17:23-26)

CHAPTER 162
DEPARTURE TO THE MOUNT OF OLIVES

According to the Gospel of Mark

26 ¶ And when they had sung an hymn, they went out into the mount of Olives. (Mark 14:26)

According to the Gospel of Matthew

30 And when they had sung an hymn, they went out into the mount of Olives. (Matt 26:30)

The disciples are warned for the 2nd time that they will all desert Jesus

31 Then saith Jesus unto them, All ye shall be offended because of me this night: for it
is written, I will smite the shepherd, and the sheep of the flock shall be scattered
abroad.
32 But after I am risen again, I will go before you into Galilee. (Matt 26:31-32)

Peter's 3rd declaration of loyalty that he will never deny or desert him

33 Peter answered and said unto him, Though all *men* shall be offended because of
thee, *yet* will I never be offended. (Matt 26:33)

Jesus' 3rd warning to Peter that he would deny him, emphasizing with the words "this night"

Before each of two cock crows there would be three denials, i.e. 3 denials 1st cock crow, 3 more denials 2nd cock crow.

34 Jesus said unto him, Verily I say unto thee, That this night, before the cock crow,
thou shalt deny me thrice. (Matt 26:34)

Peter's 4th and the disciples 1st declaration of loyalty, here adding: "even unto death"

35 Peter said unto him, Though I should die with thee, yet will I not deny thee.
Likewise also said all the disciples. (Matt 26:35)

According to the Gospel of John

1 When Jesus had spoken these words, he went forth with his disciples over the brook
Cedron, where was a garden, into the which he entered, and his disciples. (John 18:1)

CHAPTER 163
IN THE GARDEN

This first time Jesus prayed by himself. He withdrew "from them about a stone's cast"

39 ¶ And he came out, and went, as he was wont, to the mount of Olives; and his
disciples also followed him.

40 And when he was at the place, he said unto them, Pray that ye enter not into
temptation.
41 And he was withdrawn from them about a stone's cast, and kneeled down, and
prayed,
42 Saying, Father, if thou be willing, remove this cup from me: nevertheless not my
will, but thine, be done.
43 And there appeared an angel unto him from heaven, strengthening him.
44 And being in an agony he prayed more earnestly: and his sweat was as it were great
drops of blood falling down to the ground.
45 And when he rose up from prayer, and was come to his disciples, he found them
sleeping for sorrow,
46 And said unto them, Why sleep ye? rise and pray, lest ye enter into temptation. (Luke
22:39-46)

Jesus' 3rd warning to all the disciples that they would desert him

27 And Jesus saith unto them, All ye shall be offended because of me this night: for it is
written, I will smite the shepherd, and the sheep shall be scattered.
28 But after that I am risen, I will go before you into Galilee. (Mark 14:27-28)

Peter's 5th declaration of loyalty, this time adding, "even if all the others should desert"

What Peter say's here is the equivalent of: "I love you more than these." (See John 21:15)

29 But Peter said unto him, Although all shall be offended, yet *will* not I. (Mark 14:29)

Jesus' 4th warning to Peter that he will betray him, adding "this day, even in this night"
(Note: Peter is warned he will deny Jesus three times before each of two cock crows, for a total of six denials)

Jesus foretold that the cock would crow two times, and before each crowing Peter will have denied him three times.

30 And Jesus saith unto him, Verily I say unto thee, That this day, *even* in this night,
before the cock crow twice, thou shalt deny me thrice. (Mark 14:30)

Peter's 6th and final declaration of loyalty, including the words, "if I should die with thee"
(Note: six times Peter proclaims his fidelity, six times he will deny Jesus, and twice the cock will crow)

31 But he spake the more vehemently, If I should die with thee, I will not deny thee in
any wise. Likewise also said they all. (Mark 14:31)

This time Jesus takes Peter, James and John when he prays, while the others sit apart
(These three disciples fall asleep three times, and then Judas Iscariot arrives with the priests, Pharisees and guards.)

According to the Gospel of Mark

32 And they came to a place which was named Gethsemane: and he saith to his
disciples, Sit ye here, while I shall pray.
33 And he taketh with him Peter and James and John, and began to be sore amazed, and
to be very heavy;
34 And saith unto them, My soul is exceeding sorrowful unto death: tarry ye here, and
watch.
35 And he went forward a little, and fell on the ground, and prayed that, if it were
possible, the hour might pass from him.
36 And he said, Abba, Father, all things *are* possible unto thee; take away this cup from
me: nevertheless not what I will, but what thou wilt.
37 And he cometh, and findeth them sleeping, and saith unto Peter, Simon, sleepest
thou? couldest not thou watch one hour?
38 Watch ye and pray, lest ye enter into temptation. The spirit truly *is* ready, but the
flesh *is* weak.

39 And again he went away, and prayed, and spake the same words.
40 And when he returned, he found them asleep again, (for their eyes were heavy,)
neither wist they what to answer him.
41 And he cometh the third time, and saith unto them, Sleep on now, and take *your* rest:
it is enough, the hour is come; behold, the Son of man is betrayed into the hands of
sinners.
42 Rise up, let us go; lo, he that betrayeth me is at hand. (Mark 14:32-42)

According to the Gospel of Matthew

36 ¶ Then cometh Jesus with them unto a place called Gethsemane, and saith unto the
disciples, Sit ye here, while I go and pray yonder.
37 And he took with him Peter and the two sons of Zebedee, and began to be sorrowful
and very heavy.
38 Then saith he unto them, My soul is exceeding sorrowful, even unto death: tarry ye
here, and watch with me.
39 And he went a little farther, and fell on his face, and prayed, saying, O my Father, if
it be possible, let this cup pass from me: nevertheless not as I will, but as thou *wilt*.
40 And he cometh unto the disciples, and findeth them asleep, and saith unto Peter,
What, could ye not watch with me one hour?
41 Watch and pray, that ye enter not into temptation: the spirit indeed *is* willing, but the
flesh *is* weak.
42 He went away again the second time, and prayed, saying, O my Father, if this cup
may not pass away from me, except I drink it, thy will be done.
43 And he came and found them asleep again: for their eyes were heavy.
44 And he left them, and went away again, and prayed the third time, saying the same
words.
45 Then cometh he to his disciples, and saith unto them, Sleep on now, and take *your*
rest: behold, the hour is at hand, and the Son of man is betrayed into the hands of
sinners.
46 Rise, let us be going: behold, he is at hand that doth betray me. (Matt 26:36-46)

CHAPTER 164
THE BETRAYAL AND ARREST

Judas knew when and where Jesus would be when the people wouldn't be present

2 And Judas also, which betrayed him, knew the place: for Jesus ofttimes resorted
thither with his disciples.
3 Judas then, having received a band *of men* and officers from the chief priests and
Pharisees, cometh thither with lanterns and torches and weapons. (John 18:2-3)

The sign to confirm the identity of Jesus

According to the Gospel of Matthew

47 ¶ And while he yet spake, lo, Judas, one of the twelve, came, and with him a great
multitude with swords and staves, from the chief priests and elders of the people.
48 Now he that betrayed him gave them a sign, saying, Whomsoever I shall kiss, that
same is he: hold him fast. (Matt 26:47-48)

According to the Gospel of Mark

43 ¶ And immediately, while he yet spake, cometh Judas, one of the twelve, and with

him a great multitude with swords and staves, from the chief priests and the scribes and the elders.
44 And he that betrayed him had given them a token, saying, Whomsoever I shall kiss, that same is he; take him, and lead *him* away safely. (Mark 14:43-44)

Jesus addresses the entourage

4 Jesus therefore, knowing all things that should come upon him, went forth, and said unto them, Whom seek ye?
5 They answered him, Jesus of Nazareth. Jesus saith unto them, I am *he*. And Judas also, which betrayed him, stood with them.
6 As soon then as he had said unto them, I am *he*, they went backward, and fell to the ground.
7 Then asked he them again, Whom seek ye? And they said, Jesus of Nazareth.
8 Jesus answered, I have told you that I am *he*: if therefore ye seek me, let these go their way: (John 18:4-8)

A parenthetical remark of John that Jesus said this to fulfill John 17:12 (p. 350) where "kept" is *τηρέω tēreō* "guarded."

9 That the saying might be fulfilled, which he spake, Of them which thou gavest me have I lost none. (John 18:9)
47 ¶ And while he yet spake, behold a multitude, and he that was called Judas, one of the twelve, went before them, and drew near unto Jesus to kiss him. (Luke 22:47)

The kiss of betrayal (kiss, *καταφιλέω kataphileō*, an ostentatious embrace)

According to the Gospel of Mark

45 And as soon as he was come, he goeth straightway to him, and saith, Master, master; and kissed him. (Mark 14:45)

According to the Gospel of Matthew

49 And forthwith he came to Jesus, and said, Hail, master; and kissed him. (Matt 26:49)

The word Jesus used that is translated here friend is *ἑταῖρος hetairos*, comrade, not, *φίλος philos*, friend. Jesus is not asking Judas a question, he is telling him to proceed with what he came to do, to crry out his purpose. TCB p. 1373

50 And Jesus said unto him, Friend, wherefore art thou come? (Matt 26:50 *to* ?)

According to the Gospel of Luke

48 But Jesus said unto him, Judas, betrayest thou the Son of man with a kiss? (Luke 22:48)

The first effort to apprehend Jesus

According to the Gospel of Matthew

50 Then came they, and laid hands on Jesus, and took him. (Matt 26:50 *Then*)

According to the Gospel of Mark

46 ¶ And they laid their hands on him, and took him. (Mark 14:46)

Peter cuts off the right ear of the high priest's servant

According to the Gospel of Luke

49 When they which were about him saw what would follow, they said unto him, Lord, shall we smite with the sword?
50 ¶ And one of them smote the servant of the high priest, and cut off his right ear. (Luke 22:49-50)

According to the Gospel of Mark

47 And one of them that stood by drew a sword, and smote a servant of the high priest, and cut off his ear. (Mark 14:47)

According to the Gospel of Matthew

51 And, behold, one of them which were with Jesus stretched out *his* hand, and drew
his sword, and struck a servant of the high priest's, and smote off his ear. (Matt 26:51)

According to the Gospel of John

This act would later result in Peter being identified as a follower of Jesus, and to the third of his six denials.

10 Then Simon Peter having a sword drew it, and smote the high priest's servant, and
cut off his right ear. The servant's name was Malchus.
11 Then said Jesus unto Peter, Put up thy sword into the sheath: the cup which my
Father hath given me, shall I not drink it? (John 18:10-11)

Jesus restores the ear of Malchus

Suffer ye thus far i.e. "All of you, permit me to do this," to make clear that his reaching out was not a personal attack.

51 And Jesus answered and said, Suffer ye thus far. And he touched his ear, and healed
him. (Luke 22:51)

Jesus then rebuked the disciples for the use of physical force

52 Then said Jesus unto him, Put up again thy sword into his place: for all they that take
the sword shall perish with the sword.
53 Thinkest thou that I cannot now pray to my Father, and he shall presently give me
more than twelve legions of angels?
54 But how then shall the scriptures be fulfilled, that thus it must be? (Matt 26:52-54)

Jesus then addressed leaders of the mob

According to the Gospel of Luke

52 Then Jesus said unto the chief priests, and captains of the temple, and the elders,
which were come to him, Be ye come out, as against a thief, with swords and staves?
53 When I was daily with you in the temple, ye stretched forth no hands against me: but
this is your hour, and the power of darkness. (Luke 22:52-53)

According to the Gospel of Matthew

55 In that same hour said Jesus to the multitudes, Are ye come out as against a thief
with swords and staves for to take me? I sat daily with you teaching in the temple, and
ye laid no hold on me.
56 But all this was done, that the scriptures of the prophets might be fulfilled. (Matt 26:55-
56 to 1st .)

According to the Gospel of Mark

48 And Jesus answered and said unto them, Are ye come out, as against a thief, with
swords and *with* staves to take me?
49 I was daily with you in the temple teaching, and ye took me not: but the scriptures
must be fulfilled. (Mark 14:48-49)

All of the disciples are "offended," meaning they all desert Jesus

According to the Gospel of Matthew

56 Then all the disciples forsook him, and fled. (Matt 26:56 *Then*)

According to the Gospel of Mark

50 And they all forsook him, and fled. (Mark 14:50)

A certain young man, very likely Lazarus, escapes arrest
(This may answer the question: who heard and recorded the words Jesus prayed while in the garden?)

51 And there followed him a certain young man, having a linen cloth cast about *his*

naked *body*; and the young men laid hold on him:
52 And he left the linen cloth, and fled from them naked. (Mark 14:51-52)

The arrest

12 Then the band and the captain and officers of the Jews took Jesus, and bound him, (John 18:12)

CHAPTER 165
ECCLESIASTICAL TRIALS & PETER'S DENIALS

(The Jews question and abuse Jesus until "the morning was come" i.e. until after midnight. Matt. 27:1)

Took, *συλλαμβάνω syllambanō*, seized as to take a prisoner. Apparently Annas lived in the home of Caiaphas.
54 ¶ Then took they him, and led *him*, and brought him into the high priest's house.
And Peter followed afar off. (Luke 22:54)

Jesus was taken first to Annas for preliminary questioning

Annas was deposed the year Jesus began his ministry. Three others were then appointed and deposed before Caiaphas.
13 And led him away to Annas first; for he was father in law to Caiaphas, which was
the high priest that same year.
14 Now Caiaphas was he, which gave counsel to the Jews, that it was expedient that
one man should die for the people. (John 18:13-14)

Peter is granted admittance through "another disciple"
(Possibilities are Joseph of Arimathæa and Nicodemus, both were members of the Sanhedrin and disciples of Jesus.)

15 ¶ And Simon Peter followed Jesus, and *so did* another disciple: that disciple was
known unto the high priest, and went in with Jesus into the palace of the high priest.
16 But Peter stood at the door without. Then went out that other disciple, which was
known unto the high priest, and spake unto her that kept the door, and brought in Peter.
(John 18:15-16)

Peter's 1st denial is to a female doorkeeper

17 Then saith the damsel that kept the door unto Peter, Art not thou also *one* of this
man's disciples? He saith, I am not.
18 And the servants and officers stood there, who had made a fire of coals; for it was
cold: and they warmed themselves: and Peter stood with them, and warmed himself.
(John 18:17-18)

Preliminary questioning by Annas
(The purpose of this questioning was to formulate charges against Jesus. This was a fishing expedition, not a trial!)

19 ¶ The high priest then asked Jesus of his disciples, and of his doctrine.
20 Jesus answered him, I spake openly to the world; I ever taught in the synagogue, and
in the temple, whither the Jews always resort; and in secret have I said nothing.
21 Why askest thou me? ask them which heard me, what I have said unto them: behold,
they know what I said. (John 18:19-21)

The first physical assault on Jesus is by a temple guard

Annas, no longer the high priest, having previously held that position, was still addressed as the high priest.
22 And when he had thus spoken, one of the officers which stood by struck Jesus with
the palm of his hand, saying, Answerest thou the high priest so?
23 Jesus answered him, If I have spoken evil, bear witness of the evil: but if well, why
smitest thou me? (John 18:22-23)

When the preliminary questioning was finished Jesus was taken to Caiaphas

24 Now Annas had sent him bound unto Caiaphas the high priest. (John 18:24)

The chief priests, scribes and elders were waiting with Caiaphas for Jesus to be brought in

According to the Gospel of Mark

53 ¶ And they led Jesus away to the high priest: and with him were assembled all the
chief priests and the elders and the scribes. (Mark 14:53)

According to the Gospel of Matthew

57 ¶ And they that had laid hold on Jesus led *him* away to Caiaphas the high priest,
where the scribes and the elders were assembled. (Matt 26:57)

Peter followed at a distance, and then *sat* with others by a fire

According to the Gospel of Luke

55 And when they had kindled a fire in the midst of the hall, and were set down
together, Peter sat down among them. (Luke 22:55)

According to the Gospel of Mark

54 And Peter followed him afar off, even into the palace of the high priest: and he sat
with the servants, and warmed himself at the fire. (Mark 14:54)

According to the Gospel of Matthew

58 But Peter followed him afar off unto the high priest's palace, and went in, and sat
with the servants, to see the end. (Matt 26:58)

The strategy was to use false witnesses to establish that Jesus was guilty of blasphemy

(This was before the high priest, chief priests, elders and members of the Sanhedrin. If they were so faithful to Moses and the Commandments, what happened to the 9th, "Thou shalt not bear false witness against thy neighbour" Ex. 20:16?)

59 Now the chief priests, and elders, and all the council, sought false witness against
Jesus, to put him to death;
60 But found none: yea, though many false witnesses came, *yet* found they none. (Matt
26:59-60 to 1st.)

No legitimate charges could be established due to a lack of consistent testimony

55 And the chief priests and all the council sought for witness against Jesus to put him
to death; and found none.
56 For many bare false witness against him, but their witness agreed not together. (Mark
14:55-56)

The accusation that Jesus intended to destroy the temple could not be established

57 And there arose certain, and bare false witness against him, saying,
58 We heard him say, I will destroy this temple that is made with hands, and within
three days I will build another made without hands. (Mark 14:57-58)
60 At the last came two false witnesses,
61 And said, This *fellow* said, I am able to destroy the temple of God, and to build it in
three days. (Matt 26:60-61 *At*)

This accusation failed due to inconsistent testimony

59 But neither so did their witness agree together. (Mark 14:59)

Then the high priest demanded a reply from Jesus

According to the Gospel of Mark

60 And the high priest stood up in the midst, and asked Jesus, saying, Answerest thou
nothing? what *is it which* these witness against thee?
61 But he held his peace, and answered nothing. (Mark 14:60-61 *to* 1st.)

According to the Gospel of Matthew

62 And the high priest arose, and said unto him, Answerest thou nothing? what *is it which* these witness against thee?
63 But Jesus held his peace. (Matt 26:62-63 *to* 1st.)

The next strategy was to trick Jesus into saying something chargeable as blasphemy

63 And the high priest answered and said unto him, I adjure thee by the living God, that thou tell us whether thou be the Christ, the Son of God.
64 Jesus saith unto him, Thou hast said: nevertheless I say unto you, Hereafter shall ye see the Son of man sitting on the right hand of power, and coming in the clouds of heaven. (Matt 26:63-64 *And*)
61 Again the high priest asked him, and said unto him, Art thou the Christ, the Son of the Blessed?
62 And Jesus said, I am: and ye shall see the Son of man sitting on the right hand of power, and coming in the clouds of heaven. (Mark 14:61-62 *Again*)

The high priest orchestrates a demand for the death penalty for blasphemy

According to the Gospel of Mark

63 Then the high priest rent his clothes, and saith, What need we any further witnesses?
64 Ye have heard the blasphemy: what think ye? And they all condemned him to be guilty of death.
65 And some began to spit on him, and to cover his face, and to buffet him, and to say unto him, Prophesy: and the servants did strike him with the palms of their hands. (Mark 14:63-65)

According to the Gospel of Matthew

65 Then the high priest rent his clothes, saying, He hath spoken blasphemy; what further need have we of witnesses? behold, now ye have heard his blasphemy.
66 What think ye? They answered and said, He is guilty of death.
67 Then did they spit in his face, and buffeted him; and others smote *him* with the palms of their hands,
68 Saying, Prophesy unto us, thou Christ, Who is he that smote thee? (Matt 26:65-68)

Peter's 2rd denial is to a maid and a man while *sitting* by a fire

According to the Gospel of Luke

56 But a certain maid beheld him as he sat by the fire, and earnestly looked upon him, and said, This man was also with him.
57 And he denied him, saying, Woman, I know him not. (Luke 22:56-57)

According to the Gospel of Matthew

69 ¶ Now Peter sat without in the palace: and a damsel came unto him, saying, Thou also wast with Jesus of Galilee.
70 But he denied before *them* all, saying, I know not what thou sayest. (Matt 26:69-70)

According to the Gospel of Mark

66 ¶ And as Peter was beneath in the palace, there cometh one of the maids of the high priest:
67 And when she saw Peter warming himself, she looked upon him, and said, And thou also wast with Jesus of Nazareth.
68 But he denied, saying, I know not, neither understand I what thou sayest. (Mark 14:66-68 *to* 1st.)

Peter's 3rd denial is a little later, in the gateway or porch, while *standing* and warming himself with *others*

According to the Gospel of Luke

58 And after a little while another saw him, and said, Thou art also of them. And Peter
said, Man, I am not. (Luke 22:58)

According to the Gospel of Matthew

71 And when he was gone out into the porch, another *maid* saw him, and said unto
them that were there, This *fellow* was also with Jesus of Nazareth.
72 And again he denied with an oath, I do not know the man. (Matt 26:71-72)

According to the Gospel of John

25 And Simon Peter stood and warmed himself. They said therefore unto him, Art not
thou also *one* of his disciples? He denied *it*, and said, I am not.
26 One of the servants of the high priest, being *his* kinsman whose ear Peter cut off,
saith, Did not I see thee in the garden with him? (John 18:25-26)

When Peter denies for the 3rd time, a cock crows for the 1st time

According to the Gospel of John

27 Peter then denied again: and immediately the cock crew. (John 18:27)

According to the Gospel of Mark

68 And he went out into the porch; and the cock crew. (Mark 14:68 *And*)

Peter's 4th denial is a short time later while "beneath in the palace" to bystanders when questioned by a maid

According to the Gospel of Mark

69 And a maid saw him again, and began to say to them that stood by, This is *one* of
them.
70 And he denied it again. (Mark 14:69-70 *to* 1st.)

Peter's 5th denial is a little after when "they that stood by" noted his Galilæan accent

According to the Gospel of Mark

70 And a little after, they that stood by said again to Peter, Surely thou art *one* of them:
for thou art a Galilæan, and thy speech agreeth *thereto*.
71 But he began to curse and to swear, *saying*, I know not this man of whom ye speak.
(Mark 14:70-71 *And*)

According to the Gospel of Matthew

73 And after a while came unto *him* they that stood by, and said to Peter, Surely thou
also art *one* of them; for thy speech bewrayeth thee.
74 Then began he to curse and to swear, *saying*, I know not the man. (Matt 26:73-74 *to* 1st.)

Peter's 6th denial is an hour later in the midst of the hall to a group that again notes his Galilæan accent

According to the Gospel of Luke

59 And about the space of one hour after another confidently affirmed, saying, Of a
truth this *fellow* also was with him: for he is a Galilæan.
60 And Peter said, Man, I know not what thou sayest. (Luke 22:59-60 *to* 1st.)

A 2nd cock crow following the 2nd group of three denials

(This 2nd, "a cock crowing" around mid-night, being just before morning makes perfect sense. - Matt. 27:1 below)

According to the Gospel of Mark

The Gospel of Mark is very definite: "And the second time the cock crew!"

72 And the second time the cock crew. And Peter called to mind the word that Jesus
said unto him, Before the cock crow twice, thou shalt deny me thrice. (Mark 14:72 *to* 2nd.)

According to the Gospel of Luke

60 And immediately, while he yet spake, the cock crew.
61 And the Lord turned, and looked upon Peter. And Peter remembered the word of
the Lord, how he had said unto him, Before the cock crow, thou shalt deny me thrice.
(Luke 22:60-61 Beginning with the 2nd *And*)

According to the Gospel of Matthew

74 And immediately the cock crew.
75 And Peter remembered the word of Jesus, which said unto him, Before the cock
crow, thou shalt deny me thrice. (Matt 26:74-75 *to* 1st.)

Peter weeps bitterly

According to the Gospel of Matthew

75 And he went out, and wept bitterly. (Matt 26:75 *And*)

According to the Gospel of Luke

62 And Peter went out, and wept bitterly. (Luke 22:62)

According to the Gospel of Mark

72 And when he thought thereon, he wept. (Mark 14:72 3rd *And*)

More mocking and abuse

63 ¶ And the men that held Jesus mocked him, and smote *him*.
64 And when they had blindfolded him, they struck him on the face, and asked him,
saying, Prophesy, who is it that smote thee?
65 And many other things blasphemously spake they against him. (Luke 22:63-65)

A political charge that Jesus claimed to be "the King of the Jews" is fabricated

66 ¶ And as soon as it was day, the elders of the people and the chief priests and the
scribes came together, and led him into their council, saying,
67 Art thou the Christ? tell us. And he said unto them, If I tell you, ye will not believe:
68 And if I also ask *you*, ye will not answer me, nor let *me* go. (Luke 22:66-68)

It is now clear to Jesus that there would be no justice in human law, and that in God alone could he trust.

69 Hereafter shall the Son of man sit on the right hand of the power of God.
70 Then said they all, Art thou then the Son of God? And he said unto them, Ye say
that I am.
71 And they said, What need we any further witness? for we ourselves have heard of
his own mouth. (Luke 22:69-71)

The plan of Caiaphas to have the Romans execute Jesus is now put into play
(Jesus is taken to the Praetorium sometime shortly after mid-night: early in the Gentile Wednesday morning)

According to the Gospel of Matthew

1 When the morning was come, all the chief priests and elders of the people took
counsel against Jesus to put him to death:
2 And when they had bound him, they led *him* away, and delivered him to Pontius
Pilate the governor. (Matt 27:1-2)

According to the Gospel of Mark

1 And straightway in the morning the chief priests held a consultation with the elders
and scribes and the whole council, and bound Jesus, and carried *him* away, and
delivered *him* to Pilate. (Mark 15:1)

According to the Gospel of Luke

1 And the whole multitude of them arose, and led him unto Pilate. (Luke 23:1)

CHAPTER 166
JUDAS ISCARIOT'S ACTIONS CONCURRENT WITH THE TRIALS

Feeling remorse for betraying an innocent man that is soon to be executed Judas attempts to return the money.

3 ¶ Then Judas, which had betrayed him, when he saw that he was condemned,
repented himself, and brought again the thirty pieces of silver to the chief priests and
elders, (Matt 27:3)

Judas Iscariot is the 1st to witness that Jesus was innocent

The callous response of the chief priests was to ignore the innocence of Jesus and the statement of Judas.

4 Saying, I have sinned in that I have betrayed the innocent blood. And they said, What
is that to us? see thou *to that.*

5 And he cast down the pieces of silver in the temple, and departed, and went and
hanged himself. (Matt 27:4-5)

The chief priests motive, personal gain rather than justice, made their display of reverence for "the law" a mockery.

6 And the chief priests took the silver pieces, and said, It is not lawful for to put them
into the treasury, because it is the price of blood.

7 And they took counsel, and bought with them the potter's field, to bury strangers in.

8 Wherefore that field was called, The field of blood, unto this day. (Matt 27:6-8)

This prophecy was not written, it was spoken only.

9 Then was fulfilled that which was spoken by Jeremy the prophet, saying, And they
took the thirty pieces of silver, the price of him that was valued, whom they of the
children of Israel did value;

10 And gave them for the potter's field, as the Lord appointed me. (Matt 27:9-10)

CHAPTER 167
THE TRIAL BEFORE PILATE BEGINS

Jesus is taken Into the Praetorium while the Jews remain outside

28 ¶ Then led they Jesus from Caiaphas unto the hall of judgment: (John 18:28 to :)

In order that they might partake of the Passover "the Jews" did not enter the Praetorium. Did they actually believe that being ritually clean would absolve them from the crime of cold-blooded murder? Which was the lesser crime: Pharaoh's refusal to release the children of Israel from bondage or this envy motivated murder of a man *known* to be innocent?

28 and it was early; and they themselves went not into the judgment hall, lest they
should be defiled; but that they might eat the passover.

29 Pilate then went out unto them, and said, What accusation bring ye against this man?
(John 18:28-29 *and*)

Claiming to be the Son of God would not bring the death penalty under Roman Law. Hence their misleading reply.

30 They answered and said unto him, If he were not a malefactor, we would not have
delivered him up unto thee. (John 18:30)

Three false charges are presented to Pilate

2 And they began to accuse him, saying, (Luke 23:2 *to* 2nd,)

1st false charge: "perverting the nation," *διαστρέφω diastrephō*, inciting insurrection) – a lie.

2 We found this *fellow* perverting the nation, (Luke 23:2 *We to* 3rd,)

2nd false charge: tax evasion – a lie. *(See Matthew 17:24-27)*

2 and forbidding to give tribute to Cæsar, (Luke 23:2 *and to* 4th,)

3rd false charge: Claiming kingship, supposedly a challenge to the authority of Rome and Cæsar – another lie.

2 saying that he himself is Christ a King. (Luke 23:2 *saying*)

Jesus implies "Yes" to the question: Art thou the King of the Jews? meaning a spiritual, not an earthly dominion

According to the Gospel of Matthew

11 And Jesus stood before the governor: and the governor asked him, saying, Art thou
the King of the Jews? And Jesus said unto him, Thou sayest. (Matt 27:11)

According to the Gospel of Mark

2 And Pilate asked him, Art thou the King of the Jews? And he answering said unto him, Thou sayest *it.* (Mark 15:2)

According to the Gospel of Luke

3 And Pilate asked him, saying, Art thou the King of the Jews? And he answered him and said, Thou sayest *it.* (Luke 23:3)

Pilate is the 2nd to witness to Jesus' innocence, Judas having been the first

4 Then said Pilate to the chief priests and *to* the people, I find no fault in this man. (Luke 23:4)

Pilate's 1st plea to release Jesus is that he should be tried under ecclesiastical law, not Roman law

31 Then said Pilate unto them, Take ye him, and judge him according to your law. (John 18:31 to 1st.)

The Jews lied. There were violations that called for death by stoning! Jesus was framed and Pilate trapped

31 The Jews therefore said unto him, It is not lawful for us to put any man to death:
32 That the saying of Jesus might be fulfilled, which he spake, signifying what death he should die. (John 18:31-32 *The*). (See John 12:33 p. 317)

More accusations – the chief priests and elders

12 And when he was accused of the chief priests and elders, he answered nothing.
13 Then said Pilate unto him, Hearest thou not how many things they witness against thee?
14 And he answered him to never a word; insomuch that the governor marvelled greatly. (Matt 27:12-14)

More accusations – The chief priests only

3 And the chief priests accused him of many things: but he answered nothing. (Mark 15:3)

Pilate asks Jesus *AGAIN* why he does not reply

4 And Pilate asked him again, saying, Answerest thou nothing? behold how many things they witness against thee.
5 But Jesus yet answered nothing; so that Pilate marvelled. (Mark 15:4-5)

Pilate questions Jesus *AGAIN* as to the original charge

33 Then Pilate entered into the judgment hall again, and called Jesus, and said unto him, Art thou the King of the Jews? (John 18:33)

Jesus asks Pilate why he believes he is being tried: for a real crime or hearsay

34 Jesus answered him, Sayest thou this thing of thyself, or did others tell it thee of me?
35 Pilate answered, Am I a Jew? Thine own nation and the chief priests have delivered thee unto me: what hast thou done? (John 18:34-35)

Jesus responds that he claims no earthly kingship, and is no enemy to Rome, Cæsar, or to him

36 Jesus answered, My kingdom is not of this world: if my kingdom were of this world, then would my servants fight, that I should not be delivered to the Jews: but now is my kingdom not from hence. (John 18:36)

The answer is "Yes" for his life was a demonstration of God-given *dominion* over all sin, disease and even death. A king has dominion! Listen to John's words: "And hast made us unto our God kings and priests: and we shall reign on the earth." Rev. 5:10. We learn to claim and live our God-given dominion as we put off the old man with his deeds.

37 Pilate therefore said unto him, Art thou a king then? Jesus answered, Thou sayest that I am a king. (John 18:37 *to* 1st.)

Jesus makes sure that Pilate understands that his mission is not political, but spiritual

37 To this end was I born, and for this cause came I into the world, that I should bear
witness unto the truth. Every one that is of the truth heareth my voice. (John 18:37 *To*)

Pilates evasive reply was a ruse

38 Pilate saith unto him, What is truth? (John 18:38 *to* ?)

Pilates 2nd is the 3rd witnessing to Jesus' innocence

38 And when he had said this, he went out again unto the Jews, and saith unto them, I
find in him no fault *at all.* (John 18:38 *And*)

Violent reaction and more false accusations

5 And they were the more fierce, saying, He stirreth up the people, teaching throughout
all Jewry, beginning from Galilee to this place. (Luke 23:5)

CHAPTER 168
THE MOCK TRIAL BEFORE HEROD

Pilate's first attempt to release Jesus

Looking for a way out, Pilate sent Jesus to Herod, claiming that Herod had jurisdiction in the matter.

6 When Pilate heard of Galilee, he asked whether the man were a Galilæan.
7 And as soon as he knew that he belonged unto Herod's jurisdiction, he sent him to
Herod, who himself also was at Jerusalem at that time. (Luke 23:6-7)

Herod thinks Jesus is a magician, and his only interest is to be entertained

8 ¶ And when Herod saw Jesus, he was exceeding glad: for he was desirous to see him
of a long *season*, because he had heard many things of him; and he hoped to have seen
some miracle done by him. (Luke 23:8)

Jesus is unresponsive to Herod's questions because his mission was to awaken, not to entertain mankind. See Eph. 5:14.

9 Then he questioned with him in many words; but he answered him nothing. (Luke 23:9)

The chief priests and scribes that accompanied Jesus to Herod accuse him.

10 And the chief priests and scribes stood and vehemently accused him. (Luke 23:10)

Herod had his guards mock Jesus, and then he returned him to Pilate, possibly for refusing to do a "miracle," but more likely for political reasons as noted in Luke 23:12 below.

11 And Herod with his men of war set him at nought, and mocked *him*, and arrayed him
in a gorgeous robe, and sent him again to Pilate. (Luke 23:11)

Evil interests unite to destroy Truth

12 ¶ And the same day Pilate and Herod were made friends together: for before they
were at enmity between themselves. (Luke 23:12)

CHAPTER 169
THE TRIAL BEFORE PILATE RESUMES

Pilates 3rd is the 4th witnessing to Jesus' innocence

13 ¶ And Pilate, when he had called together the chief priests and the rulers and the
people,
14 Said unto them, Ye have brought this man unto me, as one that perverteth the
people: and, behold, I, having examined *him* before you, have found no fault in this
man touching those things whereof ye accuse him: (Luke 23:13-14)

Pilate declates that Herod's refusal to take action was the 5th witnessing to Jesus' innocence

15 No, nor yet Herod: for I sent you to him; and, lo, nothing worthy of death is done
unto him. (Luke 23:15)

The Passover tradition of the Roman Governor

According to the Gospel of Mark

6 Now at *that* feast he released unto them one prisoner, whomsoever they desired. (Mark 15:6)

According to the Gospel of Matthew

15 Now at *that* feast the governor was wont to release unto the people a prisoner, whom
they would. (Matt 27:15)

According to the Gospel of John

39 But ye have a custom, that I should release unto you one at the passover: (Jn. 18:39 *to* :)

According to the Gospel of Luke

Pilate makes another attempt to release Jesus.

16 I will therefore chastise him, and release *him*.
17 (For of necessity he must release one unto them at the feast.) (Luke 23:16-17)

The choice offered the mob: release Jesus who is innocent or Barabbas known for insurrection and murder
(Pilate probably offered this choice believing that the people would rather release Jesus than a murderer.)

According to the Gospel of Matthew

16 And they had then a notable prisoner, called Barabbas. (Matt 27:16)

Knowing the trial is unjust Pilate makes a 2nd attempt to release Jesus.

17 Therefore when they were gathered together, Pilate said unto them, Whom will ye
that I release unto you? Barabbas, or Jesus which is called Christ? (Matt 27:17)

Pilate didn't believe, he KNEW that Jesus was innocent and why he was being framed by the ecclesiastics: ENVY!

18 For he knew that for envy they had delivered him. (Matt 27:18)

Pilate's wife provides the 6th witnessing to Jesus' innocence

19 ¶ When he was set down on the judgment seat, his wife sent unto him, saying, Have
thou nothing to do with that just man: for I have suffered many things this day in a
dream because of him. (Matt 27:19)

The demand to release Barabbas is instigated by the chief priests and scribes.

20 But the chief priests and elders persuaded the multitude that they should ask
Barabbas, and destroy Jesus. (Matt 27:20)

Another attempt by Pilate to release Jesus.

21 The governor answered and said unto them, Whether of the twain will ye that I
release unto you? (Matt 27:21 *to* ?)

The mob, at the prompting of the chief priests and elders, demand that Pilate release of Barabbas.

21 They said, Barabbas. (Matt 27:21 *They*)

According to the Gospel of Mark

7 And there was *one* named Barabbas, *which lay* bound with them that had made
insurrection with him, who had committed murder in the insurrection.
8 And the multitude crying aloud began to desire *him to do* as he had ever done unto
them. (Mark 15:7-8)

Another attempt by Pilate to use this tradition as a means to release Jesus.

9 But Pilate answered them, saying, Will ye that I release unto you the King of the
Jews? (Mark 15:9)

A parenthetical statement that Pilate KNEW beyond any doubt that Jesus was innocent of all charges. It was ENVY!

10 For he knew that the chief priests had delivered him for envy. (Mark 15:10)

The mob, manipulated by the chief priests, demand the release of Barabbas.

11 But the chief priests moved the people, that he should rather release Barabbas unto them. (Mark 15:11)

According to the Gospel of Luke

18 And they cried out all at once, saying, Away with this *man*, and release unto us Barabbas:

19 (Who for a certain sedition made in the city, and for murder, was cast into prison.) (Luke 23:18-19)

According to the Gospel of John

Another attempt by Pilate to release Jesus.

39 will ye therefore that I release unto you the King of the Jews?

40 Then cried they all again, saying, Not this man, but Barabbas. Now Barabbas was a robber. (John 18:39-40 *will*)

The unyielding demand to crucify Jesus

According to the Gospel of Luke

Another attempt by Pilate to release Jesus.

20 Pilate therefore, willing to release Jesus, spake again to them.

21 But they cried, saying, Crucify *him*, crucify him. (Luke 23:20-21)

Pilate's 4th is the 7th witnessing to Jesus' innocence

22 And he said unto them the third time, Why, what evil hath he done? I have found no cause of death in him: (Luke 23:22 *to* :)

Another attempt by Pilate to release Jesus.

22 I will therefore chastise him, and let *him* go. (Luke 23:22 2nd *I*)

Another demand for crucifixion – instantaneous and insistent.

23 And they were instant with loud voices, requiring that he might be crucified. (Luke 23:23 to 1st.)

According to the Gospel of Mark

Another attempt by Pilate to release Jesus. Note verse 13 plainly states: "They cried out AGAIN."

12 And Pilate answered and said again unto them, What will ye then that I shall do *unto him* whom ye call the King of the Jews?

3 And they cried out again, Crucify him. (Mark 15:12-13)

Pilate's 4th is the 7th witnessing to Jesus' innocence.

14 Then Pilate said unto them, Why, what evil hath he done? (Mark 15:14 *to* ?)

Another demand for crucifixion – instantaneous and insistent.

14 And they cried out the more exceedingly, Crucify him. (Mark 15:14 *And*)

According to the Gospel of Matthew

Another attempt by Pilate to release Jesus.

22 Pilate saith unto them, What shall I do then with Jesus which is called Christ? (Matt 27:22 *to* ?)

Another demand for crucifixion – this time ***all*** said to crucify him.

22 *They* all say unto him, Let him be crucified. (Matt 27:22 *They*)

Pilate's 4th is the 7th witnessing to Jesus' innocence.

23 And the governor said, Why, what evil hath he done? (Matt 27:23 *to* ?)

Another demand for crucifixion – instantaneous and insistent.

23 But they cried out the more, saying, Let him be crucified. (Matt 27:23 *But*)

CHAPTER 170
SENTENCING

According to the Gospel of Luke

The mob, being manipulated by the ecclesiastics have Barabbas released. Jesus is delivered to be executed.

23 And the voices of them and of the chief priests prevailed.

24 And Pilate gave sentence that it should be as they required. (Luke 23:23-24 *And*)
Barabbas is released despite committing the crimes of sedition and murder.
25 And he released unto them him that for sedition and murder was cast into prison,
whom they had desired; but he delivered Jesus to their will. (Luke 23:25)

According to the Gospel of John

1 Then Pilate therefore took Jesus, and scourged *him.* (John 19:1)

According to the Gospel of Mark

Barabbas was released, Jesus to be put to death, because Pilate determined it to be politically expedient.
15 ¶ And *so* Pilate, willing to content the people, released Barabbas unto them, and
delivered Jesus, when he had scourged *him*, to be crucified. (Mark 15:15)

According to the Gospel of Matthew

Pilates' 5th is the 8th witnessing to Jesus' innocence. It occurs when Pilate washes his hands

Pilates' handwashing, being merely a ploy to absolve himself of guilt, was a disgusting display of self-deception.
24 ¶ When Pilate saw that he could prevail nothing, but *that* rather a tumult was made,
he took water, and washed *his* hands before the multitude, saying, I am innocent of the
blood of this just person: see ye *to it.* (Matt 27:24)
The people claimed responsibility for the murder of an innocent man, a called down a curse on the nation for this crime.
25 Then answered all the people, and said, His blood *be* on us, and on our children.
26 ¶ Then released he Barabbas unto them: and when he had scourged Jesus, he
delivered *him* to be crucified. (Matt 27:25-26)

CHAPTER 171
MALTREATMENT AFTER SENTENCING

Jesus is again taken into the Praetorium, this time to be tortured before crucifixion

According to the Gospel of Matthew

27 Then the soldiers of the governor took Jesus into the common hall, and gathered
unto him the whole band *of soldiers.* (Matt 27:27)
Purple robe (mock kingship). *The Companion Bible* states that scarlet should be translated purple. See Mark and John.
28 And they stripped him, and put on him a scarlet robe. (Matt 27:28)
Mock crown, a mock sceptre, mock homage, and mock praise.
29 ¶ And when they had platted a crown of thorns, they put *it* upon his head, and a reed
in his right hand: and they bowed the knee before him, and mocked him, saying, Hail,
King of the Jews! (Matt 27:29)
Spitting (contempt) and outright torture.
30 And they spit upon him, and took the reed, and smote him on the head. (Matt 27:30)

According to the Gospel of Mark

The purple, *πορφύρα porphyra,* robe, crown of thorns, and mock salutation.
16 And the soldiers led him away into the hall, called Praetorium; and they call together
the whole band.
17 And they clothed him with purple, and platted a crown of thorns, and put it about his
head,
18 And began to salute him, Hail, King of the Jews!
19 And they smote him on the head with a reed, and did spit upon him, and bowing
their knees worshipped him. (Mark 15:16-19)

According to the Gospel of John

The purple, *πορφύρα porphyra,* robe, crown of thorns, and mock salutation.
2 And the soldiers platted a crown of thorns, and put *it* on his head, and they put on

him a purple robe, (John 19:2)

Humiliation and physical abuse. "smote him." They didn't just slap him, they struck or punched him with their fists.

3 And said, Hail, King of the Jews! and they smote him with their hands. (John 19:3)

After torturing and mocking Jesus, Pilate makes a final but unsuccessful plea to have him released
(Perhaps Pilate thought this proof of torture would satisfy the Jews lust for revenge and that they would let Jesus go)

Pilates' 6th is the 9th witnessing to Jesus' innocence

4 Pilate therefore went forth again, and saith unto them, Behold, I bring him forth to
you, that ye may know that I find no fault in him.
5 Then came Jesus forth, wearing the crown of thorns, and the purple robe. And *Pilate*
saith unto them, Behold the man! (John 19:4-5)

This shows clearly there was no desire for justice. Apparently Pilate would have released Jesus as well as Barabbas.

6 When the chief priests therefore and officers saw him, they cried out, saying, Crucify
him, crucify *him*. (John 19:6 *to* 1st.)

Pilates 7th is the 10th witnessing to Jesus' innocence

6 Pilate saith unto them, Take ye him, and crucify *him*: for I find no fault in him. (John 19:6 Pilate)

The Jews contradict themselves. If there was such a law it, would have included the penalty they sought.

7 The Jews answered him, We have a law, and by our law he ought to die, because he
made himself the Son of God. (John 19:7)

Pilate fears --- what if it is true?

8 ¶ When Pilate therefore heard that saying, he was the more afraid;
9 And went again into the judgment hall, and saith unto Jesus, Whence art thou? (John 19:8-9 *to* ?)

To answer would prove pointless. *(See Luke 22:68)*

9 But Jesus gave him no answer. (John 19:9 *But*)

Pilate's pride reacts and he admits he could release Jesus.

10 Then saith Pilate unto him, Speakest thou not unto me? knowest thou not that I have
power to crucify thee, and have power to release thee? (John 19:10)

Jesus *chose* to submit. Pilate was a puppet and Judas a fool. Caiaphas and the Sanhedrin had the greater guilt. Jesus submitted to prove his dominion over death. (See the quotation before John 10:18 on page 280).

11 Jesus answered, Thou couldest have no power *at all* against me, except it were given
thee from above: therefore he that delivered me unto thee hath the greater sin.
12 And from thenceforth Pilate sought to release him: (John 19:11-12 *to* :)

Due to the threat of losing a position of power and prestige the carnal mind gave in to political blackmail.

12 but the Jews cried out, saying, If thou let this man go, thou art not Cæsar's friend:
whosoever maketh himself a king speaketh against Cæsar. (John 19:12 *but*)

What follows is Pilates final petition to the Jews to consent to the release of Jesus.

13 ¶ When Pilate therefore heard that saying, he brought Jesus forth, and sat down in
the judgment seat in a place that is called the Pavement, but in the Hebrew, Gabbatha.
(John 19:13)

Jesus is presented "at about the 6th hour" of the trial. (Around 6:00 a.m. on Wednesday Morning)

14 And it was the preparation of the passover, and about the sixth hour: and he saith
unto the Jews, Behold your King! (John 19:14)

The persistent effort of the Jews to destroy an innocent man was really the carnal mind attempting to destroy Christ. When will humanity learn that evil can never destroy good, for good is God in expression.

15 But they cried out, Away with *him*, away with *him*, crucify him. Pilate saith unto
them, Shall I crucify your King? (John 19:15 *to* ?)

When the chief priests replied that a pagan ruler was their King, they were admitting that mammon, *money* and *power*, was their god!

15 The chief priests answered, We have no king but Cæsar. (John 19:15 *The*)

Not long after sunrise Jesus was led away to be crucified

According to the Gospel of Matthew

31 And after that they had mocked him, they took the robe off from him, and put his own raiment on him, and led him away to crucify *him.* (Matt 27:31)

According to the Gospel of Mark

20 And when they had mocked him, they took off the purple from him, and put his own clothes on him, and led him out to crucify him. (Mark 15:20)

According to the Gospel of John

16 Then delivered he him therefore unto them to be crucified. And they took Jesus, and led *him away.* (John 19:16)

CHAPTER 172
THE WALK TO GOLGOTHA

skull, Heb. *Golgotha* = a head and shoulder elevation, Lat. *Calvaria*, Eng. *Calvary*. Cross, *σταυρός staurós*, a stake.

17 And he bearing his cross went forth into a place called *the place* of a skull, which is
called in the Hebrew Golgotha:
18 Where they crucified him, and two other with him, on either side one, and Jesus in
the midst. (John 19:17-18)

The Jews protested the wording on the 1st sign that named the crime for which Jesus was being executed

19 ¶ And Pilate wrote a title, and put *it* on the cross. And the writing was, JESUS OF NAZARETH THE KING OF THE JEWS. (John 19:19)

The order of the languages naming the charges was: Hebrew, Greek and Latin.

20 This title then read many of the Jews: for the place where Jesus was crucified was nigh to the city: and it was written in Hebrew, *and* Greek, *and* Latin. (John 19:20)

The Jews wanted Pilate to change the sign to read: "He said I am King of the Jews."

21 Then said the chief priests of the Jews to Pilate, Write not, The King of the Jews; but that he said, I am King of the Jews. (John 19:21)

Nevertheless, Pilate's sign was attached to the stake as written. It was later replaced by a second sign.

22 Pilate answered, What I have written I have written. (John 19:22)

Simon, a Cyrenian, is "compelled to bear the cross" beam

According to the Gospel of Matthew

32 And as they came out, they found a man of Cyrene, Simon by name: him they compelled to bear his cross. (Matt 27:32)

According to the Gospel of Mark

21 And they compel one Simon a Cyrenian, who passed by, coming out of the country, the father of Alexander and Rufus, to bear his cross. (Mark 15:21)

According to the Gospel of Luke

26 And as they led him away, they laid hold upon one Simon, a Cyrenian, coming out of the country, and on him they laid the cross, that he might bear *it* after Jesus. (Luke 23:26)

Jesus addresses the women on the sorrows of child bearing

27 ¶ And there followed him a great company of people, and of women, which also
bewailed and lamented him.
28 But Jesus turning unto them said, Daughters of Jerusalem, weep not for me, but
weep for yourselves, and for your children.

29 For, behold, the days are coming, in the which they shall say, Blessed *are* the barren,
and the wombs that never bare, and the paps which never gave suck.
30 Then shall they begin to say to the mountains, Fall on us; and to the hills, Cover us.
The pronoun *they* refers to the Romans. Symbolically, the *green tree* refers to Jesus, and the *dry* to the Hebrew nation.
31 For if they do these things in a green tree, what shall be done in the dry? (Luke 23:27-31)

Jesus is accompanied by two malefactors, *κακοῦργος kakourgos*, evildoers. Their crimes are not stated

32 And there were also two other, malefactors, led with him to be put to death. (Luke 23:32)

On the way to Golgotha Jesus is offered a pain killer that he refuses to drink

22 And they bring him unto the place Golgotha, which is, being interpreted, The place
of a skull.
"And they gave" = and they were offering. (As they were bringing him to Golgotha they were offering him ...)
23 And they gave him to drink wine mingled with myrrh: but he received *it* not. (Mark 15:22-23)

CHAPTER 173
THE CRUCIFIXION

At the site, before being crucified, Jesus refuses, for the second time, to drink a pain killer

33 And when they were come unto a place called Golgotha, that is to say, a place of a
skull,
34 ¶ They gave him vinegar to drink mingled with gall: and when he had tasted *thereof*,
he would not drink. (Matt 27:33-34)

The two *malefactors* led out with Jesus were crucified with him at the same time, one on each side

33 And when they were come to the place, which is called Calvary, there they crucified
him, and the malefactors, one on the right hand, and the other on the left. (Luke 23:33)

Jesus prays for his executioners. (John 19:23 states there were four, "four parts, to every soldier a part.")

34 ¶ Then said Jesus, Father, forgive them; for they know not what they do. (Luke 23:34 *to* 1st .)

Jesus is crucified.

35 And they crucified him, (Matt 27:35 *to* 1st,)

The Roman soldiers parted, *διαμερίζω diamerizō*, divided up Jesus' garments and cast lots for his coat

According to the Gospel of Luke

34 And they parted his raiment, and cast lots. (Luke 23:34 *And*)

According to the Gospel of John

23 ¶ Then the soldiers, when they had crucified Jesus, took his garments, and made four
parts, to every soldier a part; (John 19:23 *to* ;)
23 and also *his* coat: now the coat was without seam, woven from the top throughout.
24 They said therefore among themselves, Let us not rend it, but cast lots for it, whose
it shall be: (John 19:23-24 2nd *and to* 1st:)
In fulfillment of the scriptures. (See Ps. 22:18)
24 that the scripture might be fulfilled, which saith, They parted my raiment among
them, and for my vesture they did cast lots. (John 19:24 *that to* 1st.)
The actions of the Roman soldiers are summarized up to this point.
24 These things therefore the soldiers did. (John 19:24 *These*)

According to the Gospel of Mark

24 And when they had crucified him, they parted his garments, casting lots upon them,

what every man should take. (Mark 15:24)
A parenthetic note as to the time when Jesus was crucified: 9:00 a.m. on Wednesday the 14th of Nisan.
25 And it was the third hour, and they crucified him.
This is the indictment, it is not the writing on the sign placed over Jesus' head.
26 And the superscription of his accusation was written over, THE KING OF THE
JEWS. (Mark 15:25-26)

According to the Gospel of Matthew

35 and parted his garments, casting lots: (Matt 27:35 *and* to :)
In fulfillment of the scriptures. Psalms 22:18.
35 that it might be fulfilled which was spoken by the prophet, They parted my garments
among them, and upon my vesture did they cast lots. (Matt 27:35 *that*)
After the soldiers were done crucifying Jesus and the two malefactors, they sat down to keep watch.
36 And sitting down they watched him there; (Matt 27:36)

A 2nd sign with new wording arrives at the site and is used in place of the sign originally dictated by Pilate

Below is the wording on the sign that was placed on the stake. The order of the languages is not mentioned.
37 And set up over his head his accusation written, THIS IS JESUS THE KING OF
THE JEWS. (Matt 27:37)

Sometime later two *thieves, ληστής lēstēs*, robbers were brought out to be crucified

After the thieves were crucified the total became five in the order: (thief – malefactor – Jesus – malefactor – thief)
Five signifies grace. For by grace are ye saved through faith; and that not of yourselves: *it is* the gift of God. – Eph. 2:8

According to the Gospel of Matthew

"With him" means at the same place, but *not* at the same time *and* place, as were the two malefactors.
38 Then were there two thieves crucified with him, one on the right hand, and another
on the left. (Matt 27:38)

According to the Gospel of Mark

27 And with him they crucify two thieves; the one on his right hand, and the other on
his left.
28 And the scripture was fulfilled, which saith, And he was numbered with the
transgressors. (Mark 15:27-28)

The people and the rulers stood by mocking. A pain killer is offered and is again refused

35 And the people stood beholding. And the rulers also with them derided *him*, saying,
He saved others; let him save himself, if he be Christ, the chosen of God. (Luke 23:35)
Jesus is offered drink for the 3rd time, vinegar (sour wine), apparently to mock him.
36 And the soldiers also mocked him, coming to him, and offering him vinegar,
37 And saying, If thou be the king of the Jews, save thyself. (Luke 23:36-37)

A final sign, written in the order Greek, Latin, and Hebrew arrives and is put in place

The first sign was in the order Hebrew, Greek and Latin. This sign was in the order Greek, Latin and Hebrew
38 And a superscription also was written over him in letters of Greek, and Latin, and
Hebrew, THIS IS THE KING OF THE JEWS. (Luke 23:38)

The by-passers verbally abuse Jesus

According to the Gospel of Matthew

39 ¶ And they that passed by reviled him, wagging their heads,
40 And saying, Thou that destroyest the temple, and buildest *it* in three days, save
thyself. If thou be the Son of God, come down from the cross. (Matt 27:39-40)

According to the Gospel of Mark

29 And they that passed by railed on him, wagging their heads, and saying, Ah, thou

that destroyest the temple, and buildest *it* in three days,
30 Save thyself, and come down from the cross. (Mark 15:29-30)

The chief priests, scribes and elders are also there to mock Jesus

According to the Gospel of Matthew

41 Likewise also the chief priests mocking *him*, with the scribes and elders, said,
42 He saved others; himself he cannot save. If he be the King of Israel, let him now
come down from the cross, and we will believe him.
43 He trusted in God; let him deliver him now, if he will have him: for he said, I am the
Son of God. (Matt 27:41-43)

According to the Gospel of Mark

31 Likewise also the chief priests mocking said among themselves with the scribes, He
saved others; himself he cannot save.
32 Let Christ the King of Israel descend now from the cross, that we may see and
believe. (Mark 15:31-32 *to* 1st.)

Later the two thieves also rail on Jesus

According to the Gospel of Matthew

Crucified *with* him: for the malefactors, at the same place and time. For the two thieves it was later at the same place.

44 The thieves also, which were crucified with him, cast the same in his teeth. (Matt 27:44)

According to the Gospel of Mark

32 And they that were crucified with him reviled him. (Mark 15:32 *And*)

Jesus entrusts the care of his mother to John, the Beloved Disciple

25 ¶ Now there stood by the cross of Jesus his mother, and his mother's sister, Mary the
wife of Cleophas, and Mary Magdalene.
26 When Jesus therefore saw his mother, and the disciple standing by, whom he loved,
he saith unto his mother, Woman, behold thy son!
27 Then saith he to the disciple, Behold thy mother! And from that hour that disciple
took her unto his own *home*. (John 19:25-27)

Then one of the two malefactors railed on Jesus

39 ¶ And one of the malefactors which were hanged railed on him, saying, If thou be
Christ, save thyself and us.
40 But the other answering rebuked him, saying, Dost not thou fear God, seeing thou
art in the same condemnation? (Luke 23:39-40)

One of the malefactors testified to Jesus' innocence - the 11th witnessing to his innocence

41 And we indeed justly; for we receive the due reward of our deeds: but this man hath
done nothing amiss.
42 And he said unto Jesus, Lord, remember me when thou comest into thy kingdom.
43 And Jesus said unto him, Verily I say unto thee, To-day shalt thou be with me in
paradise. (Luke 23:41-43)

Next: Three hours of darkness from noon to 3:00 p.m.
(The ninth hour, 2:00 p.m. to 3:00 p.m., the same time the passover lambs were being slain)

According to the Gospel of Matthew

45 Now from the sixth hour there was darkness over all the land unto the ninth hour.
(Matt 27:45)

According to the Gospel of Mark

33 And when the sixth hour was come, there was darkness over the whole land until the
ninth hour. (Mark 15:33)

According to the Gospel of Luke

44 And it was about the sixth hour, and there was a darkness over all the earth until the
ninth hour.
45 And the sun was darkened, and the veil of the temple was rent in the midst. (Luke 23:44-45)

The cry of the Lord Jesus Christ. Pain killer offered and refused for the fourth time
(Was Jesus declaring defeat or victory? For the answer see Psalm 22 especially verses 22 – 31)

According to the Gospel of Matthew

46 And about the ninth hour Jesus cried with a loud voice, saying, Eli, Eli, lama
sabachthani? that is to say, My God, my God, why hast thou forsaken me?
47 Some of them that stood there, when they heard *that*, said, This *man* calleth for
Elias.
48 And straightway one of them ran, and took a spunge, and filled *it* with vinegar, and
put *it* on a reed, and gave him to drink.
49 The rest said, Let be, let us see whether Elias will come to save him. (Matt 27:46-49)

According to the Gospel of Mark

Jesus call is to Elohim, the God that "saw every thing that He had made, and, behold it was very good." Genesis 1:31

34 And at the ninth hour Jesus cried with a loud voice, saying, Eloi, Eloi, lama
sabachthani? which is, being interpreted, My God, my God, why hast thou forsaken
me?
35 And some of them that stood by, when they heard *it*, said, Behold, he calleth Elias.
36 And one ran and filled a spunge full of vinegar, and put *it* on a reed, and gave him to
drink, saying, Let alone; let us see whether Elias will come to take him down. (Mark 15:34-36)

Jesus requests something to drink

28 ¶ After this, Jesus knowing that all things were now accomplished, that the scripture
might be fulfilled, saith, I thirst.
29 Now there was set a vessel full of vinegar: and they filled a spunge with vinegar,
and put *it* upon hyssop, and put *it* to his mouth. (John 19:28-29)

"It is finished"
(Jesus "yielded or gave up" the ghost. He literally chose when to breath his last. Metaphysically, he yielded up forever the belief that man did, does, or ever will live ***in*** a material body).

According to the Gospel of John

30 When Jesus therefore had received the vinegar, he said, It is finished: and he bowed
his head, and gave up the ghost. (John 19:30)

According to the Gospel of Matthew

50 ¶ Jesus, when he had cried again with a loud voice, yielded up the ghost. (Matt 27:50)

According to the Gospel of Mark

37 And Jesus cried with a loud voice, and gave up the ghost. (Mark 15:37)

According to the Gospel of Luke

46 ¶ And when Jesus had cried with a loud voice, he said, Father, into thy hands I
commend my spirit: and having said thus, he gave up the ghost. (Luke 23:46)

CHAPTER 174
EVENTS IMMEDIATELY FOLLOWING

The Veil of the Temple is Rent

(The martyrdom of Jesus was the culminating sin of Pharisaism. It rent the veil of the temple. It revealed the false foundations and superstructure of superficial religion, tore from bigotry and superstition their coverings, and opened the sepulchre with divine Science, -- immortality and Love. - MBE)

According to the Gospel of Matthew

51 And, behold, the veil of the temple was rent in twain from the top to the bottom; and the earth did quake, and the rocks rent;
52 And the graves were opened; and many bodies of the saints which slept arose,
53 And came out of the graves after his resurrection, and went into the holy city, and appeared unto many. (Matt 27:51-53)

The unusual phenomenon that accompanied the passing of Jesus caused many to realize that he was **Christ** Jesus, the Son of God.

54 Now when the centurion, and they that were with him, watching Jesus, saw the earthquake, and those things that were done, they feared greatly, saying, Truly this was the Son of God. (Matt 27:54)

According to the Gospel of Mark

38 And the veil of the temple was rent in twain from the top to the bottom.
39 ¶ And when the centurion, which stood over against him, saw that he so cried out, and gave up the ghost, he said, Truly this man was the Son of God. (Mark 15:38-39)

The centurion's testimony was the 12th and final witnessing to Jesus' innocence

47 Now when the centurion saw what was done, he glorified God, saying, Certainly this was a righteous man. (Luke 23:47)

The lookers on must have realized the terrible evil they had witnessed, and so they departed in anguish. Just think how far humanity would have advanced if Jesus had not been crucified, but had remained with mankind to oversee the spread of his teaching and practice throughout the then known world! But first, it appears, that mankind needed to learn the power of Life, God, over death and of good over evil. So, let's begin to learn it and to exercise it. This would surely please Jesus.

48 And all the people that came together to that sight, beholding the things which were done, smote their breasts, and returned. (Luke 23:48)

Confirmation that *four* others were crucified with Jesus (Two malefactors AND two thieves)

The four crucified with Jesus must have been Jews for their bodies were taken down before the high sabbath.

31 The Jews therefore, because it was the preparation, that the bodies should not remain upon the cross on the sabbath day, (for that sabbath day was an high day,) besought Pilate that their legs might be broken, and *that* they might be taken away. (John 19:31)

Approaching from one side the legs of two were broken; 1st a thief, 2nd a malefactor, "the other crucified *with* him."

32 Then came the soldiers, and brake the legs of the first, and of the other which was crucified with him. (John 19:32)

Jesus is the 3rd. The other two are not mentioned, but continuing on it was a malefactor and then the other thief.

33 But when they came to Jesus, and saw that he was dead already, they brake not his legs: (John 19:33)

Proof that the corporeal Jesus was, to physical sense testimony, dead.

34 But one of the soldiers with a spear pierced his side, and forthwith came there out blood and water.
35 And he that saw *it* bare record, and his record is true: and he knoweth that he saith true, that ye might believe. (John 19:34-35)

Two prophecies fulfilled: The 1st, Exodus 12:46 & Numbers 9:12 and the 2nd, Zechariah 12:10.

36 For these things were done, that the scripture should be fulfilled, A bone of him shall not be broken.

37 And again another scripture saith, They shall look on him whom they pierced. (John 19:36-37)

The women who followed Jesus watched from a distance

According to the Gospel of Luke

49 And all his acquaintance, and the women that followed him from Galilee, stood afar off, beholding these things. (Luke 23:49)

According to the Gospel of Matthew

55 And many women were there beholding afar off, which followed Jesus from Galilee, ministering unto him:
56 Among which was Mary Magdalene, and Mary the mother of James and Joses, and the mother of Zebedee's children. (Matt 27:55-56)

According to the Gospel of Mark

40 There were also women looking on afar off: among whom was Mary Magdalene, and Mary the mother of James the less and of Joses, and Salome;
41 (Who also, when he was in Galilee, followed him, and ministered unto him;) and many other women which came up with him unto Jerusalem. (Mark 15:40-41)

Joseph of Arimathæa

According to the Gospel of Mark

A statement that the next day would be the high sabbath, celebrating the passover, when lamb is eaten.

42 ¶ And now when the even was come, because it was the preparation, that is, the day before the sabbath,
43 Joseph of Arimathæa, an honourable counsellor, which also waited for the kingdom of God, came, and went in boldly unto Pilate, and craved the body of Jesus. (Mark 15:42-43)

Pilate, doubting that Jesus could have died so quickly required "official" verification.

44 And Pilate marvelled if he were already dead: and calling *unto him* the centurion, he asked him whether he had been any while dead.
45 And when he knew *it* of the centurion, he gave the body to Joseph. (Mark 15:44-45)

Joseph took down the body. He and Nicodemus then hurriedly prepared it for burial.

46 And he bought fine linen, and took him down, and laid him in a sepulchre which was hewn out of a rock, (Mark 15:46 *to* 2nd,)

A stone was rolled over the entry *(Late afternoon on the 14th day of Nisan, the Gentile late Wednesday afternoon).*

46 and rolled a stone unto the door of the sepulchre. (Mark 15:46 3rd *and*)

The women were there watching, and so they knew where the body of Jesus was placed.

47 And Mary Magdalene and Mary *the mother* of Joses beheld where he was laid. (Mark 15:47)

According to the Gospel of Luke

50 ¶ And, behold, *there was* a man named Joseph, a counsellor; *and he was* a good man, and a just:
51 (The same had not consented to the counsel and deed of them;) *he was* of Arimathæa, a city of the Jews: who also himself waited for the kingdom of God.
52 This *man* went unto Pilate, and begged the body of Jesus.
53 And he took it down, and wrapped it in linen, and laid it in a sepulchre that was hewn in stone, wherein never man before was laid. (Luke 23:50-53)

Late Wednesday afternoon on the 14th of Nisan. The high sabbath, that would begin at sunset, was fast approaching.

54 And that day was the preparation, and the sabbath drew on. (Luke 23:54)

Having watched, the women knew where to come when both sabbaths were over to finish preparing the body for burial.

55 And the women also, which came with him from Galilee, followed after, and beheld the sepulchre, and how his body was laid. (Luke 23:55)

There were two sabbaths. The next day, Thursday Nisan 15th a high Sabbath, and Saturday the 17th the weekly sabbath.

56 And they returned, and prepared spices and ointments; and rested the sabbath day
according to the commandment. (Luke 23:56)

According to the Gospel of Matthew

57 When the even was come, there came a rich man of Arimathæa, named Joseph, who
also himself was Jesus' disciple: (Matt 27:57)

Joseph of Arimathæa asks Pilate for the body of Jesus.

58 He went to Pilate, and begged the body of Jesus. (Matt 27:58 *to* 1st.)

Pilate orders the body of Jesus to be turned over to Joseph of Arimathæa.

58 Then Pilate commanded the body to be delivered. (Matt 27:58 *Then*)

The body is wrapped in a linen shroud

59 And when Joseph had taken the body, he wrapped it in a clean linen cloth, (Matt 27:59)

The sepulchre Joseph of Arimathæa had hewn in a rock for his own burial was used to bury Jesus.

60 And laid it in his own new tomb, which he had hewn out in the rock: (Matt 27:60 *to* :)

Late on the 14th day of Nisan, the Gentile Wednesday afternoon, a stone was placed over the entry.

60 and he rolled a great stone to the door of the sepulchre, and departed. (Matt 27:60 *and*)

This explains how the women knew where to come three days later to finish preparing the body for burial.

61 And there was Mary Magdalene, and the other Mary, sitting over against the
sepulchre. (Matt 23:61)

According to the Gospel of John

38 ¶ And after this Joseph of Arimathæa, being a disciple of Jesus, but secretly for fear
of the Jews, besought Pilate that he might take away the body of Jesus: and Pilate gave
him leave. He came therefore, and took the body of Jesus. (John 19:38)

John adds that Nicodemus brought spices for burial.

39 And there came also Nicodemus, which at the first came to Jesus by night, and
brought a mixture of myrrh and aloes, about an hundred pound *weight*. (John 19:39)

Joseph and Nicodemus prepared the body for burial by wrapping it in linen with the spices. See John 20:6-7.

40 Then took they the body of Jesus, and wound it in linen clothes with the spices, as
the manner of the Jews is to bury. (John 19:40)

The body was placed in Joseph's newly hewn sepulchre.

41 Now in the place where he was crucified there was a garden; and in the garden a
new sepulchre, wherein was never man yet laid.
42 There laid they Jesus therefore because of the Jews' preparation *day*; for the
sepulchre was nigh at hand. (John 19:41-42)

THE THREE DAYS IN THE TOMB

Passover, a high sabbath, Thursday Nisan 15th, Friday Nisan 16th and the weekly sabbath, Saturday Nisan 17th 29 A.D.

THE FIRST DAY JESUS IS IN THE TOMB

(Passover, Thursday Nisan 15th which was a high sabbath)

CHAPTER 175

CONDUCTING BUSINESS IN VIOLATION OF A HIGH SABBATH

(The chief priests and Pharisees visit Pilate on Passover, the 15th of Nisan, to conduct business!)

62 ¶ Now the next day, that followed the day of the preparation, the chief priests and
Pharisees came together unto Pilate,
63 Saying, Sir, we remember that that deceiver said, while he was yet alive, After three
days I will rise again. (Matt 27:62-63)

The chief priests and Pharisees petition Pilate to have Roman soldiers seal and guard the tomb.

64 Command therefore that the sepulchre be made sure until the third day, lest his
disciples come by night, and steal him away, and say unto the people, He is risen from

the dead: so the last error shall be worse than the first. (Matt 27:64)

So Pilate gave the centurion Petronius and soldiers to guard the tomb. The elders and scribes came with them to the crypt. Everyone who was there, along with the centurion and the soldiers, rolled a great stone and placed it there before the entrance of the crypt. They smeared it with seven seals, pitched a tent there, and stood guard. – *The Gospel of Peter*

65 Pilate said unto them, Ye have a watch: go your way, make *it* as sure as ye can.
66 So they went, and made the sepulchre sure, sealing the stone, and setting a watch.
(Matt 27:65-66)

THE THIRD DAY AFTER PASSOVER

(The 18th day of Nisan, The Gentile Sunday)

CHAPTER 176

RESURRECTION DAY

(Sunday before dawn, three full days after his entombment late Wednesday afternoon just before sunset.)

Before sunrise the women go to the sepulchre to anoint the body of Jesus

(The 18th of Nisan before sunrise)

According to the Gospel of Matthew

1 In the end of the sabbath, as it began to dawn toward the first *day* of the week, came
Mary Magdalene and the other Mary to see the sepulchre. (Matt 28:1)

According to the Gospel of Luke

1 Now upon the first *day* of the week, very early in the morning, they came unto the
sepulchre, bringing the spices which they had prepared, and certain *others* with them.
(Luke 24:1)

According to the Gospel of Mark

1 And when the sabbath was past, Mary Magdalene, and Mary the *mother* of James,
and Salome, had bought sweet spices, that they might come and anoint him.
2 And very early in the morning the first *day* of the week, they came unto the sepulchre
at the rising of the sun. (Mark 16:1-2)

On their way to the tomb women discuss how the stone is to be rolled aside

Do we actually think that the stone needed to be rolled aside for Jesus to be outside the sepulchre? (See Matt.14:22-33; 17:1-2. Mk 9:1-3. Lk 28-30. Jn 6:15-21)

3 And they said among themselves, Who shall roll us away the stone from the door of
the sepulchre? (Mark 16:3)

Unknown to the women the stone had already been rolled aside

2 And, behold, there was a great earthquake: for the angel of the Lord descended from
heaven, and came and rolled back the stone from the door, and sat upon it.
3 His countenance was like lightning, and his raiment white as snow: (Matt 28:2-3)

The watchmen pass out from shock

4 And for fear of him the keepers did shake, and became as dead *men*. (Matt 28:4)

Upon arriving the women see the stone already rolled aside

According to the Gospel of Mark

4 And when they looked, they saw that the stone was rolled away: for it was very great.
(Mark 16:4)

According to the Gospel of Luke

2 And they found the stone rolled away from the sepulchre. (Luke 24:2)

Although the other women were with her, John mentions only Mary Magdalene

1 The first *day* of the week cometh Mary Magdalene early, when it was yet dark, unto

the sepulchre, and seeth the stone taken away from the sepulchre. (John 20:1)

Seeing the stone rolled aside, Mary left the other women, and ran to tell Peter and John

2 Then she runneth, and cometh to Simon Peter, and to the other disciple, whom Jesus
loved, and saith unto them, They have taken away the Lord out of the sepulchre, and we
know not where they have laid him. (John 20:2)

Peter and John ran to the sepulchre followed by Mary Magdalene

3 Peter therefore went forth, and that other disciple, and came to the sepulchre.
4 So they ran both together: (John 20:3-4 *to* :)

John arrived first, looked in, but did not enter.

4 and the other disciple did outrun Peter, and came first to the sepulchre.
5 And he stooping down, *and looking in*, saw the linen clothes lying; yet went he not
in. (John 20:4-5 *and*)

Upon arriving Peter immediately enters the sepulchre, sees the linen clothes neatly arranged, but does not see a body.

6 Then cometh Simon Peter following him, and went into the sepulchre, and seeth the
linen clothes lie,
7 And the napkin, that was about his head, not lying with the linen clothes, but
wrapped together in a place by itself. (John 20:6-7)

John, upon entering sees the same physical evidence, but unlike Peter, he "believes."

8 Then went in also that other disciple, which came first to the sepulchre, and he saw,
and believed. (John 20:8)

Even though both "knew not the scripture," Peter wondered, whereas John, seeing the same evidence, believed. Note it states "he must rise again" from the dead, perhaps implying that his transfiguration was indeed his first resurrection.

9 For as yet they knew not the scripture, that he must rise again from the dead. (John 20:9)

Following this *the disciples* (apparently meaning Peter and John) return home

10 Then the disciples went away again unto their own home. (John 20:10)

Peter and John didn't see the angel that rolled aside the stone, but the women did

5 And the angel answered and said unto the women, Fear not ye: for I know that ye
seek Jesus, which was crucified.
6 He is not here: for he is risen, as he said. (Matt 28:5-6 *to* 1st .)

The women, including Mary Magdalene who has returned, are invited to enter the sepulchre

6 Come, see the place where the Lord lay. (Matt 28:6 *Come*)

The women, not believing what they hear, and not seeing a body, are confused

3 And they entered in, and found not the body of the Lord Jesus. (Luke 24:3)

Two "men" in shining garments stand by the women

4 And it came to pass, as they were much perplexed thereabout, behold, two men stood
by them in shining garments: (Luke 24:4)

Mary Magdalene, standing outside weeping, looked into the sepulchre

11 ¶ But Mary stood without at the sepulchre weeping: and as she wept, she stooped
down, *and looked* into the sepulchre, (John 20:11)

Mary Magdalene saw two angels, one at either end of where the body of Jesus had been placed.

12 And seeth two angels in white sitting, the one at the head, and the other at the feet,
where the body of Jesus had lain. (John 20:12)

The two angels speak to Mary Magdalene, and she replies.

13 And they say unto her, Woman, why weepest thou? She saith unto them, Because

they have taken away my Lord, and I know not where they have laid him. (John 20:13)
Mary Magdalene then turns and looks away.

14 And when she had thus said, she turned herself back, (John 20:14 *to* 2nd,)
Jesus then appears to Mary Magdalene, but she does not recognize him.

14 and saw Jesus standing, and knew not that it was Jesus.

15 Jesus saith unto her, Woman, why weepest thou? whom seekest thou? She,
supposing him to be the gardener, saith unto him, Sir, if thou have borne him hence, tell
me where thou hast laid him, and I will take him away. (John 20:14-15 *and*)
Jesus addresses Mary Magdalene.

16 Jesus saith unto her, Mary. (John 20:16 *to* 1st.)
Hearing him speak her name, she recognizes his voice and turns, then reaching toward him addresses him as Master.

16 She turned herself, and saith unto him, Rabboni; which is to say, Master. (John 20:16 *She*)
Jesus exclaims "touch me not", ἅπτομαι *haptomai*, don't cling to me, i.e. let me go. *(See John 11:44 p. 302)*

17 Jesus saith unto her, Touch me not; for I am not yet ascended to my Father: (John 20:17 *to* :)

Concurrent with Mary encountering Jesus, the women inside were being addressed by one of the "young men"

5 And entering into the sepulchre, they saw a young man sitting on the right side,
clothed in a long white garment; and they were affrighted.
6 And he saith unto them, Be not affrighted: Ye seek Jesus of Nazareth, which was
crucified: he is risen; he is not here: behold the place where they laid him.
7 But go your way, tell his disciples and Peter that he goeth before you into Galilee:
there shall ye see him, as he said unto you. (Mark 16:5-7)

Being perplexed the women react in fear when the "young men" speak to them

5 And as they were afraid, and bowed down *their* faces to the earth, they said unto
them, Why seek ye the living among the dead? (Luke 24:5)
They are again told that Jesus is risen.

6 He is not here, but is risen: (Luke 24:6 *to* :)
It is then they remember what Jesus told them earlier in Galilee. These women, as well as the men were his disciples!

6 remember how he spake unto you when he was yet in Galilee,
7 Saying, The Son of man must be delivered into the hands of sinful men, and be
crucified, and the third day rise again. (Luke 24:6-7 *remember*)
The women remember that Jesus had indeed told them this would happen. They were able to see Jesus sooner after the resurrection than the men because they were more spiritually minded.

8 And they remembered his words, (Luke 24:8)

Mary Magdalene receives instruction from Jesus

17 but go to my brethren, and say unto them, I ascend unto my Father, and your Father;
and *to* my God, and your God. (John 20:17 *but*)

The other women, still in the tomb, receive instruction from the angel that had rolled aside the stone

7 And go quickly, and tell his disciples that he is risen from the dead; and, behold, he
goeth before you into Galilee; there shall ye see him: lo, I have told you. (Matt 28:7)

Mary Magdalene and the other women depart together, and as they are leaving, they encounter Jesus

8 And they departed quickly from the sepulchre with fear and great joy; and did run to
bring his disciples word.
9 ¶ And as they went to tell his disciples, behold, Jesus met them, saying, All hail. And
they came and held him by the feet, and worshipped him.
10 Then said Jesus unto them, Be not afraid: go tell my brethren that they go into

Galilee, and there shall they see me. (Matt 28:8-10)

After seeing Jesus they hurry to tell the disciples the good news

8 And they went out quickly, and fled from the sepulchre; for they trembled and were
amazed: neither said they any thing to any *man*; for they were afraid. (Mark 16:8)

Mary Magdalene tells the disciples that she has seen Jesus

18 Mary Magdalene came and told the disciples that she had seen the Lord, and *that* he
had spoken these things unto her. (John 20:18)

Mary Magdalene is not believed by the disciples

9 ¶ Now when *Jesus* was risen early the first *day* of the week, he appeared first to Mary
Magdalene, out of whom he had cast seven devils.
10 *And* she went and told them that had been with him, as they mourned and wept.
11 And they, when they had heard that he was alive, and had been seen of her, believed
not. (Mark 16:9-11)

The other women and Mary Magdalene tell *the rest of* the disciples, and they are not believed

9 And returned from the sepulchre, and told all these things unto the eleven, and to all
the rest.
10 It was Mary Magdalene, and Joanna, and Mary *the mother* of James, and other
women that were with them, which told these things unto the apostles.
11 And their words seemed to them as idle tales, and they believed them not. (Luke 24:9-11)

Peter, confused and unable to accept the resurrection, returns to the sepulchre by himself to look *again*

12 Then arose Peter, and ran unto the sepulchre; (Luke 24:12 *to* ;)

Peter, unlike John, sees only the physical evidence, and so he departs still confused and unbelieving

12 and stooping down, he beheld the linen clothes laid by themselves, and departed,
wondering in himself at that which was come to pass. (Luke 24:12 *and*)

In the meantime some of the watchmen report the empty tomb to the chief priests

11 ¶ Now when they were going, behold, some of the watch came into the city, and
shewed unto the chief priests all the things that were done. (Matt 28:11)

The chief priests and elders bribe the soldiers to testify falsely, to bear false witness contrary to the 9th Commandment.

12 And when they were assembled with the elders, and had taken counsel, they gave
large money unto the soldiers,
13 Saying, Say ye, His disciples came by night, and stole him *away* while we *slept.*
14 And if this come to the governor's ears, we will persuade him, and secure you.
15 So they took the money, and did as they were taught: and this saying is commonly
reported among the Jews until this day. (Matt 28:12-15)

The walk to Emmaus summarized

12 ¶ After that he appeared in another form unto two of them, as they walked, and went
into the country. (Mark 16:12)

A full account of the walk to Emmaus. (Three score furlongs is approximately 7½ miles)

13 ¶ And, behold, two of them went that same day to a village called Emmaus, which
was from Jerusalem *about* threescore furlongs.

14 And they talked together of all these things which had happened.
15 And it came to pass, that, while they communed *together* and reasoned, Jesus
himself drew near, and went with them. (Luke 24:13-15)
Being in a state of sorrow and confusion these two men do not recognize Jesus.
16 But their eyes were holden that they should not know him.
17 And he said unto them, What manner of communications *are* these that ye have one
to another, as ye walk, and are sad? (Luke 24:16-17)
Preoccupied with mourning his death they were unable to accept the report given by the women that he was alive.
18 And the one of them, whose name was Cleopas, answering said unto him, Art thou
only a stranger in Jerusalem, and hast not known the things which are come to pass
there in these days?
19 And he said unto them, What things? And they said unto him, Concerning Jesus of
Nazareth, which was a prophet mighty in deed and word before God and all the people:
20 And how the chief priests and our rulers delivered him to be condemned to death,
and have crucified him.
21 But we trusted that it had been he which should have redeemed Israel: and beside all
this, to-day is the third day since these things were done. (Luke 24:18-21)
Jesus is told that the women told them he was alive, and they refused to believe it.
22 Yea, and certain women also of our company made us astonished, which were early
at the sepulchre;
23 And when they found not his body, they came, saying, that they had also seen a
vision of angels, which said that he was alive. (Luke 24:22-23)
Because the testimony of the women had not been confirmed by a man it was automatically deemed unreliable.
24 And certain of them which were with us went to the sepulchre, and found *it* even so
as the women had said: but him they saw not. (Luke 24:24)
Jesus then rebukes them for placing greater reliance on physical sense testimony than on the Word of God.
25 Then he said unto them, O fools, and slow of heart to believe all that the prophets
have spoken:
26 Ought not Christ to have suffered these things, and to enter into his glory?
27 And beginning at Moses and all the prophets, he expounded unto them in all the
scriptures the things concerning himself. (Luke 24:25-27)
Jesus then tested these two to determine if they were now ready to receive even more of the Christ, Truth.
28 And they drew nigh unto the village, whither they went: and he made as though he
would have gone further.
29 But they constrained him, saying, Abide with us: for it is toward evening, and the
day is far spent. And he went in to tarry with them. (Luke 24:28-29)
When the bread of Truth was broken (explained), then their eyes (understanding) was opened.
30 And it came to pass, as he sat at meat with them, he took bread, and blessed *it*, and
brake, and gave to them.
31 And their eyes were opened, and they knew him; (Luke 24:30-31 to ;)
Once they understood, there was no longer any need for Jesus to remain physically present with them.
31 and he vanished out of their sight. (Luke 24:31 *and*)
Truth is known when our "heart burns within us", meaning when our spiritual consciousness is awakened.
32 And they said one to another, Did not our heart burn within us, while he talked with
us by the way, and while he opened to us the scriptures? (Luke 24:32)
When we see (understand) Truth and Love, there is an overwhelming desire to share it.
33 And they rose up the same hour, and returned to Jerusalem, and found the eleven
gathered together, and them that were with them, (Luke 24:33)
The eleven Apostles were discussing the appearing of Jesus to Simon Peter when they arrived back in Jerusalem.
34 Saying, The Lord is risen indeed, and hath appeared to Simon.

These two tell the Apostles how they were able to recognize Jesus when he explained the scriptures to them.

35 And they told what things *were done* in the way, and how he was known of them in
breaking of bread. (Luke 24:34-35)

Cleopas and his companion report their encounter of Jesus to other disciples, but they are *not* believed

13 And they went and told *it* unto the residue: (Mark 16:13 *to* :)

But the carnal mind rejects Truth, and regards their testimony, like that of the women to be mere fancy.

13 neither believed they them. (Mark 16:13 *neither*)

Jesus appears to all of the Apostles, except for Thomas, later that same day

According to the Gospel of Mark

14 ¶ Afterward he appeared unto the eleven as they sat at meat, and upbraided them
with their unbelief and hardness of heart, because they believed not them which had
seen him after he was risen. (Mark 16:14)

According to the Gospel of John

19 ¶ Then the same day at evening, being the first *day* of the week, when the doors
were shut where the disciples were assembled for fear of the Jews, came Jesus and
stood in the midst, (John 20:19 *to* 3rd,)

The first words Jesus speaks are to bless his disciples.

19 and saith unto them, Peace *be* unto you. (John 20:19 *and)*

Jesus' hands, feet, and side are examined.

20 And when he had so said, he shewed unto them *his* hands and his side. (John 20:20 *to 1st*.)

Once the fear was dispelled the disciples were able to rejoice.

20 Then were the disciples glad, when they saw the Lord. (John 20:20 *Then*)

The disciples are now prepared to go forth in a higher understanding because of what they have experienced.

21 Then said Jesus to them again, Peace *be* unto you: as *my* Father hath sent me, even
so send I you. (John 20:21)

To receive "the power from on High," is another way of saying to receive "the Holy Ghost."

22 And when he had said this, he breathed on *them*, and saith unto them, Receive ye the
Holy Ghost: (John 20:22)

The power of witnessing to the Comforter, which is the Holy Ghost, is what frees from all error.

23 Whose soever sins ye remit, they are remitted unto them; *and* whose soever *sins* ye
retain, they are retained. (John 20:23)

Thomas is not present on this occasion and remains doubtful.

24 ¶ But Thomas, one of the twelve, called Didymus, was not with them when Jesus
came.
25 The other disciples therefore said unto him, We have seen the Lord. But he said
unto them, Except I shall see in his hands the print of the nails, and put my finger into
the print of the nails, and thrust my hand into his side, I will not believe. (John 20:24-25)

According to the Gospel of Luke

36 ¶ And as they thus spake, Jesus himself stood in the midst of them, and saith unto
them, Peace *be* unto you.
37 But they were terrified and affrighted, and supposed that they had seen a spirit.
38 And he said unto them, Why are ye troubled? and why do thoughts arise in your
hearts?
39 Behold my hands and my feet, that it is I myself: handle me, and see; for a spirit
hath not flesh and bones, as ye see me have.
40 And when he had thus spoken, he shewed them *his* hands and *his* feet.

41 And while they yet believed not for joy, and wondered, he said unto them, Have ye
here any meat?
42 And they gave him a piece of a broiled fish, and of an honeycomb.
43 And he took *it*, and did eat before them.
44 And he said unto them, These *are* the words which I spake unto you, while I was yet
with you, that all things must be fulfilled, which were written in the law of Moses, and
in the prophets, and *in* the psalms, concerning me. (Luke 24:36-44)

First they had to be convinced that it was Jesus. Then they were ready to receive a fuller understanding of him.

45 Then opened he their understanding, that they might understand the scriptures, (Luke
24:45)

The crucifixion and resurrection made it possible for the disciples to receive a higher understanding of the scriptures.

46 And said unto them, Thus it is written, and thus it behoved Christ to suffer, and to
rise from the dead the third day:
47 And that repentance and remission of sins should be preached in his name among all
nations, beginning at Jerusalem.
48 And ye are witnesses of these things. (Luke 24:46-48)

Wait in Jerusalem for "the promise of the Father," "power from on high", two names for the Comforter or Holy Ghost.

49 ¶ And, behold, I send the promise of my Father upon you: but tarry ye in the city of
Jerusalem, until ye be endued with power from on high. (Luke 24:49)

THE DAYS PRECEDING THE ASCENSION

CHAPTER 177
PREPARATION FOR DEPARTURE

The 2nd appearing was eight days later with Thomas present. The number *eight* signifies *Resurrection* and *Regeneration,* the beginning of a new era or order. NIS, p. 200.

26 ¶ And after eight days again his disciples were within, and Thomas with them: *then*
came Jesus, the doors being shut, and stood in the midst, and said, Peace *be* unto you.
27 Then saith he to Thomas, Reach hither thy finger, and behold my hands; and reach
hither thy hand, and thrust *it* into my side: and be not faithless, but believing.
28 And Thomas answered and said unto him, My Lord and my God.
29 Jesus saith unto him, Thomas, because thou hast seen me, thou hast believed:
blessed *are* they that have not seen, and *yet* have believed. (John 20:26-29)

This second commission included speaking in new tongues (explaining the scriptures spiritually) and healing.

15 And he said unto them, Go ye into all the world, and preach the gospel to every
creature.
16 He that believeth and is baptized shall be saved; but he that believeth not shall be
damned. (Mark 16:15-16)

Jesus states for all time what is required if one truly "believes." By believe Jesus meant to understand and put into practice.

17 And these signs shall follow them that believe; In my name shall they cast out
devils; they shall speak with new tongues;
18 They shall take up serpents; and if they drink any deadly thing, it shall not hurt
them; they shall lay hands on the sick, and they shall recover. (Mark 16:17-18)

Jesus did many more works, but those written down are sufficient to testify to the correctness of his teaching.

30 ¶ And many other signs truly did Jesus in the presence of his disciples, which are not
written in this book:
31 But these are written, that ye might believe that Jesus is the Christ, the Son of God;
and that believing ye might have life through his name. (John 20:30-31)

CHAPTER 178
THE MORNING MEAL

What a contrast between our Lord's last supper and his last spiritual breakfast with his disciples in the bright morning hours at the joyful meeting on the shore of the Galilean Sea! His gloom had passed into glory, and his disciples' grief into repentance, — hearts chastened and pride rebuked. Convinced of the fruitlessness of their toil in the dark and wakened by their Master's voice, they changed their methods, turned away from material things, and cast their net on the right side. Discerning Christ, Truth, anew on the shore of time, they were enabled to rise somewhat from mortal sensuousness, or the burial of mind in matter, into newness of life as Spirit.

This spiritual meeting with our Lord in the dawn of a new light is the morning meal which Christian Scientists commemorate. They bow before Christ, Truth, to receive more of his reappearing and silently to commune with the divine Principle, Love. They celebrate their Lord's victory over death, his probation in the flesh after death, its exemplification of human probation, and his spiritual and final ascension above matter, or the flesh, when he rose out of material sight. – MBE.

1 After these things Jesus shewed himself again to the disciples at the sea of Tiberias; and on this wise shewed he *himself.*

2 There were together Simon Peter, and Thomas called Didymus, and Nathanael of Cana in Galilee, and the *sons* of Zebedee, and two other of his disciples. (John 21:1-2)

The commissions assigned to the disciples were being neglected, and their return to the old way was proving fruitless.

3 Simon Peter saith unto them, I go a-fishing. They say unto him, We also go with thee. They went forth, and entered into a ship immediately; and that night they caught nothing. (John 21:3)

Morning, is the coming of light, the beginning of a new day, and symbolizes greater spiritual unfoldment.

4 But when the morning was now come, Jesus stood on the shore: but the disciples knew not that it was Jesus. (John 21:4)

Jesus does not address them as friends but as children, *παιδίον paidon*, meaning "little boys or girls." After their desertion and return to the old way of living, he still sees in them, through the eyes of Love, their promise as children of God!

5 Then Jesus saith unto them, Children, have ye any meat? They answered him, No.
6 And he said unto them, Cast the net on the right side of the ship, and ye shall find.
They cast therefore, and now they were not able to draw it for the multitude of fishes.
7 Therefore that disciple whom Jesus loved saith unto Peter, It is the Lord. Now when
Simon Peter heard that it was the Lord, he girt *his* fisher's coat *unto him*, (for he was
naked,) and did cast himself into the sea.
8 And the other disciples came in a little ship; (for they were not far from land, but as it
were two hundred cubits,) dragging the net with fishes.
9 As soon then as they were come to land, they saw a fire of coals there, and fish laid
thereon, and bread.
10 Jesus saith unto them, Bring of the fish which ye have now caught.
11 Simon Peter went up, and drew the net to land full of great fishes, an hundred and
fifty and three: and for all there were so many, yet was not the net broken.
12 Jesus saith unto them, Come *and* dine. And none of the disciples durst ask him,
Who art thou? knowing that it was the Lord.
13 Jesus then cometh, and taketh bread, and giveth them, and fish likewise. (John 21:5-13)

This is the 3rd time Jesus appeared to his disciples. Three signifies something *solid, real, substantial, complete.* NIS

14 This is now the third time that Jesus shewed himself to his disciples, after that he was risen from the dead. (John 21:14)

The 1st question to Peter is "Do you love, *ἀγαπάω agapaō*, me more than these?" Peter answers, *φιλέω; phileō*, I'm your friend. "More than these" i.e. "more than the other disciples," because Peter had said he did. (See Mark 14:29 p. 352).

15 ¶ So when they had dined, Jesus saith to Simon Peter, Simon, *son* of Jonas, lovest thou me more than these? He saith unto him, Yea, Lord; thou knowest that I love thee. He saith unto him, Feed my lambs. (John 21:15)

The 2nd question to Peter is "lovest, *ἀγαπάω agapaō*, thou me?" No comparison, simply "do you love me?" Peter again answers, *φιλέω; phileō*, "Yes lord, you know that I am your friend." He did not answer "I love you."

16 He saith to him again the second time, Simon, *son* of Jonas, lovest thou me? He

saith unto him, Yea, Lord; thou knowest that I love thee. He saith unto him, Feed my sheep. (John 21:16)

The 3rd question to Peter is translated, "lovest, φιλέω *phileō*, thou me?" It means, "Simon, are you my *friend*?" Peter's answer is translated "you know I love, φιλέω *phileō,* thee"– I am your friend*).* Peter was grieved because he knew that he had failed Jesus as a friend. To understand why Peter was grieved. (See note above John 15:13 on page 347.)

17 He saith unto him the third time, Simon, *son* of Jonas, lovest thou me? Peter was
grieved because he said unto him the third time, Lovest thou me? And he said unto
him, Lord, thou knowest all things; thou knowest that I love thee. Jesus saith unto him,
Feed my sheep. (John 21:17)

Peter is told that he will be crucified. "The disciples' desertion of their Master in his last earthly struggle was punished; each one came to a violent death except for St. John, of whose death we have no record." - MBE

18 Verily, verily, I say unto thee, When thou wast young, thou girdedst thyself, and
walkedst whither thou wouldest: but when thou shalt be old, thou shalt stretch forth thy
hands, and another shall gird thee, and carry *thee* whither thou wouldest not.
19 This spake he, signifying by what death he should glorify God. And when he had
spoken this, he saith unto him, Follow me. (John 21:18-19)

The lesson has yet to be learned. It seems that at this point Peter was still concerned about "Who will be the greatest?"

20 Then Peter, turning about, seeth the disciple whom Jesus loved following; which
also leaned on his breast at supper, and said, Lord, which is he that betrayeth thee?
21 Peter seeing him saith to Jesus, Lord, and what *shall* this man *do*? (John 21:20-21)

Jesus in effect answered: "Mind your own business. John has his role to perform, and so have you." John faithfully carried out his role by giving us a better understanding of Jesus Christ in Revelation, written many years later while on Patmos.

22 Jesus saith unto him, If I will that he tarry till I come, what *is that* to thee? follow
thou me. (John 21:22)

The Master's teaching was again misinterpreted. But John knew what Jesus meant, and it is John who has given us the highest definition of God in these words: "And we have known and believed the love that God hath to us. God is love; and he that dwelleth in love dwelleth in God and God in him. I John 4:16. "A misplaced word changes the sense and misstates the Science of the Scriptures, as, for instance, to name Love as merely an attribute of God; but we can by special and proper capitalization speak of the love of Love, meaning by that what the beloved disciple meant in one of his epistles, when he said, "God is love." - MBE

23 Then went this saying abroad among the brethren, that that disciple should not die:
yet Jesus said not unto him, He shall not die; but, If I will that he tarry till I come, what
is that to thee? (John 21:23)

John gave oral and written testimony. But why should we trust John's testimony? Why did Jesus trust John to receive and record the Book of Revelation? Fidelity! "Jesus endured the shame, that he might pour his dear-bought bounty into barren lives. What was his earthly reward? He was forsaken by all save John, the beloved disciple, and a few women who bowed in silent woe beneath his cross. The earthly price of spirituality in a material age and the great moral distance between Christianity and sensualism preclude Christian Science from finding favor with the worldly-minded." - MBE

24 This is the disciple which testifieth of these things, and wrote these things: and we
know that his testimony is true. (John 21:24)

CHAPTER 179
FINAL INSTRUCTIONS AND THE RETURN TO GLORY

The apostles returned to the mountain where they were ordained, to witness the ascension.

16 ¶ Then the eleven disciples went away into Galilee, into a mountain where Jesus had
appointed them.
17 And when they saw him, they worshipped him: but some doubted.
18 And Jesus came and spake unto them, saying, All power is given unto me in heaven
and in earth. (Matt 28:16-18)

The following instructions comprise the 3rd commission, to bring the Christ, Truth to the Gentile nations.

19 ¶ Go ye therefore, and teach all nations, baptizing them in the name of the Father,
and of the Son, and of the Holy Ghost:
20 Teaching them to observe all things whatsoever I have commanded you: and, lo, I

am with you alway, *even* unto the end of the world. Amen. (Matt 28:19-20)

The last act of Jesus is to bless the disciples.

50 ¶ And he led them out as far as to Bethany, and he lifted up his hands, and blessed
them. (Luke 24:51)

The ascension --- the culmination of trustful obedience in the short span of a little more than thirty-three years..

51 And it came to pass, while he blessed them, he was parted from them, and carried up
into heaven. (Luke 24:51)

19 ¶ So then after the Lord had spoken unto them, he was received up into heaven, and
sat on the right hand of God. (Mark 16:19)

The disciples were filled with gratitude and joyfully returned to Jerusalem to carry out his instructions.

52 And they worshipped him, and returned to Jerusalem with great joy: (Luke 24:52)

They returned to the temple grounds to take up the work assigned them.

53 And were continually in the temple, praising and blessing God. Amen. (Luke 24:53)

Jesus' purpose is fulfilled only as we follow his example. That is what constitutes true worship. See John 8:31 & 32

20 And they went forth, and preached every where, the Lord working with *them*, and
confirming the word with signs following. Amen. (Mark 16:20)

A testimony to the magnitude of Jesus' words and works

25 And there are also many other things which Jesus did, the which, if they should be
written every one, I suppose that even the world itself could not contain the books that
should be written. Amen. (John 21:25)

NOW IT BEGINS

Jesus mapped out the path for others. He unveiled the Christ, the spiritual idea of divine Love.

The purpose and motive to live aright can be gained now. This point won, you have started as you should. You have begun at the numeration-table of Christian Science, and nothing but wrong intention can hinder your advancement. Working and praying with true motives, your Father will open the way. "Who did hinder you, that ye should not obey the truth?" - MBE

Part III

APPENDIXES

APPENDIX 1
PRONOUNS IN THE KING JAMES BIBLE

The Introduction mentions that the King James Bible of 1611 uses pronouns that today's reader may find so strange that he or she may decide to read a more modern "translation." However, with an open mind and a little bit of explanation it will be seen how valuable these unfamiliar pronouns are at putting into English the meaning recorded in the original languages. Since there are only a few of these strange sounding pronouns that you can easily learn, reading the Bible can quickly become a more enjoyable, meaningful and inspiring experience.

The Bible, like any textbook, is written in a precise language to accurately convey its message, and the pronouns it uses are a key factor in accomplishing that objective. The most important pronoun to understand is ***ye***, one of the most misunderstood yet frequently used pronouns in the Bible.

You and *Ye*

You is a pronoun of the second person *singular* or *plural* in any grammatical relation except that of the possessive. It refers to the *one* or *ones* being addressed. Ambiguity and even misunderstanding originates in the fact that the more modern "translations" only use the pronoun ***you***. The misunderstanding coming from the fact that ***you*** can be either singular or plural.

Ye on the other hand has been "used from the earliest times to the late 13th century only as a plural pronoun of the second person in the nominative case including direct address." It still survives archaically. Remembering that ***ye*** never means *you* as an individual but *you* as everyone forestalls the confusion.

Let's compare the King James Bible of 1611 to four other translations. Five illustrations will be enough to illustrate the value of the pronoun ***ye***.

1st Illustration: Matthew 3:1-3

In this illustration we will compare Matthew 3:1-3 in The King James Version (KJV) to five other translations.

The King James Version (KJV)

1 In those days came John the Baptist, preaching in the wilderness of Judaea,
2 And saying, Repent ye: for the kingdom of heaven is at hand.
3 For this is he that was spoken of by the prophet Esaias, saying, The voice of one crying in the wilderness, Prepare ye the way of the Lord, make his paths straight.

(1) The New Revised Standard Version (NRSV)

1 In those days John the Baptist appeared in the wilderness of Judea, proclaiming,
2 "Repent, for the kingdom of heaven has come near."
3 This is the voice of whom the prophet Isaiah spoke when he said,
"The voice of one crying out in

the wilderness:
'Prepare the way of the Lord,
make his paths straight.'"

(2) *George M. Lamsa Translation (Lamsa)*

1 In those days came John the Baptist; and he was preaching in the wilderness
of Judea,
2 Saying, Repent, for the kingdom of heaven is near,
3 For it was he of whom it was said by the prophet Isaiah, The voice which
cries in the wilderness, Prepare the way of the Lord, and strengthen his
highways.

(3) *The New Testament in Modern English by J.B. Phillips (Philips)*

1 In due course John the Baptist arrived, preaching in the Judaean desert:
2 "You must change your hearts and minds --- for the kingdom of Heaven has
arrived!"
3 This is the man whom the prophet Isaiah spoke about in the words:
The voice of one crying in the wilderness,
Make ready the way of the Lord,
Make his paths straight.

(4) *Revised English Bible (REB)*

1 In the course of time John the Baptist appeared in the Judaean wilderness,
proclaiming this message:
2 'Repent for the kingdom of Heaven is upon you!'
3 It was of him that the prophet Isaiah spoke when he said,
A voice cries in the wilderness,
'Prepare the way for the Lord;
clear a straight path for him.'

(5) *Living Bible (LB)*

1 While they were still living in Nazareth, John the Baptist began preaching out
in the Judean wilderness. His constant theme was,
2 "Turn from your sins . . . turn to God . . . for the Kingdom of Heaven is coming
soon."
3 Isaiah the prophet had told about John's ministry centuries before! He had
written,
" I hear a shout from the wilderness, 'Prepare a road for the Lord ---
straighten out the path where he will walk.'"

The King James Bible, by using ***ye*** in the second verse has John the Baptist calling upon everyone to change their thinking and behavior. The *NRSV*, *Lamsa*, and *REB* use no pronoun, and *Phillips* uses the ambiguous ***you***. *The Living Bible* by using the possessive form of you in the phrase "turn from your sins" results in a meaning different from all of the others. Only the KJV renders in English what was recorded in the original.

The third verse the KJV, Matt. 3:3, accurately quotes from Isaiah 40:3: "The voice of him that crieth in the wilderness, Prepare ***ye*** the way of the Lord". The *NRSV*, *Lamsa*, *Phillips*, *REB* and *LB* use no pronoun. Why? Apparently these "translators" thought this verse meant that John the Baptist alone was to "prepare the way of the Lord." The KJV however, by using the pronoun ***ye***, has John calling on the people to join with him in preparing the way of the Lord by their individual repentance. In other words, the receptivity and responsiveness of those who heard John speaking Isaiah's words were a necessary component in preparing way for the coming of the Messiah. Why? Because the coming of the Christ is *universal* and *timeless*, and can only appear to those who are prepared.

In the following four illustrations we will not compare the Authorized King James Version of 1611 to all of the other translations but will point out how the use of the pronoun ***ye*** in the KJV brings out the intended meaning.

2nd Illustration: Mark 13:32-37

In the following verses Peter, James, John, and Andrew comprise a group of four being addressed by Jesus in private. *See Mark 13:3-5*. The pronoun ***ye*** is used to show that Jesus was addressing all of them as a group. The pronoun ***you*** is used to show when he was making a point to each one individually.

Authorized KJV

32 ¶ But of that day and *that* hour knoweth no man, no, not the angels which are in heaven, neither the Son, but the Father.
33 Take ye heed, watch and pray: for ye know not when the time is.
34 *For the Son of man is* as a man taking a far journey, who left his house, and gave authority to his servants, and to every man his work, and commanded the porter to watch.
35 Watch ye therefore: for ye know not when the master of the house cometh, at even, or at midnight, or at the cockcrowing, or in the morning:
36 Lest coming suddenly he find you sleeping.
37 And what I say unto you I say unto all, Watch.

Peter, James, John, and Andrew are the ***ye*** Jesus is addressing as an all-inclusive group of four in verses 33 and 35. All four, with no exception, are called upon to watch and pray. Jesus is speaking to Peter, James, John, and Andrew individually in verse 36 by using the pronoun ***you***. By using the pronoun ***you*** in verse 37 Jesus is saying that his instruction to them individually to watch and pray applies to ALL, everyone. In other words, what applied to those four individually applies to everyone throughout all time.

3rd Illustration: Luke 22:51

The verse we are about to examine is preceded by: "And one of them smote the servant of the high priest, and cut off his right ear." Luke 22:50. The Gospel of John tells us the man's name was Malchus.

51 And Jesus answered and said, Suffer ye thus far. And he touched his ear, and healed him.

Translations vary widely. However, an understanding of the words ***ye*** and ***suffer*** make the meaning clear. The word translated "suffer" is the Greek ἐάω; *eaō* a verb meaning *to allow, permit, or let; to allow one to do as he wishes*. Peter had struck a blow contrary to Jesus' instructions. Jesus desired to restore the severed ear. He did not want what he was about to do to be misinterpreted as an attack. So he first addressed the entire assembly requesting them to stand down. The word ***ye*** means all of you, everyone. We would simply say: "I need all of you to let me do this." Then he healed Malchus. Jesus was not addressing Malchus alone. The word ***ye*** shows that everyone present, including Malchus was being instructed to "stand down."

4th Illustration: John 8:31-32.

31 Then said Jesus to those Jews which believed on him, If ye continue in my word, then are ye my disciples indeed;
32 And ye shall know the truth, and the truth shall make you free. *Authorized KJV.*

This is remarkable in its precision. Here the word ***ye*** makes it clear that Jesus was speaking to a group of his disciples in Jerusalem. He is making the point that merely believing in him personally is not enough. The word ***If*** establishes that true discipleship is conditional on what a disciple does, not merely on what he or she believes or professes to believe, or on membership in a group that is identified as his followers. Knowing what to do and actually doing it must be inseparable. In short, unless his teaching is lived it is for all practical purposes unknown.

In these two verses ***ye*** is used three times and ***you*** once. The requirement to "continue in [his] word," i.e. to do as he teaches, applies to all who claim to believe on him. The actual living of the Christ teaching is the Truth that "shall make you free." It is an individual choice with an individual outcome!

Look up these verses in the *NRSV* and you will see it uses only the pronoun ***you***. "If ***you*** continue in my word, ***you*** are truly my disciples." The Greek word translated ***truly*** in the *NRSV* is ἀληθῶς; *alēthōs* which can *mean truly, in reality, most certainly, indeed, surely*. While the word truly is arguably as correct as the word indeed, the translators of the KJV knew from the context that an important shade of meaning was being presented when they chose to use the word indeed. The word *deed* means "something that is done or effected by a responsible agent: act, action." – Webster. And since the whole point of these two verses is that deeds not words are what matter, it was an excellent word selection by the translators of the Authorized KJV. Not only did the translators of the *NRSV* change the word from *indeed* to *truly*, they also made a syntax alteration, which changed the emphasis and therefore the meaning. To be "truly my disciples" has not the force of conviction and commitment as to be "my disciples indeed," a phrase that emphasizes the action.

5th Illustration: John 3:7

The verse that follows is part of the first recorded meeting of Nicodemus with Jesus.

7 Marvel not that I said unto thee, Ye must be born again. Authorized KJV

Here we touch briefly on the word ***thee***. The word ***Thee*** is the objective case of ***Thou*** which is used as a nominative pronoun of the second person singular in biblical, ecclesiastical, solemn, or poetic language. It continues in use today by Friends (Quakers) as the universal form of address to one person in accordance with the belief in the quality of all persons before God. – Webster. We see the word ***Thou*** expressing reverence when capitalized and used in addressing the Supreme Being. When uncapitalized it conveys respect when used in addressing men and women.

Nicodemus was a member of the Sanhedrin. Whether he was sent by other members of the Sanhedrin or came of his own accord we are not told. As far as we know there were only two persons present: Jesus and Nicodemus. One thing is certain; the other members of the Sanhedrin knew that Jesus was "a teacher come from God." Nicodemus came desiring to learn how Jesus did "these miracles," i.e. his healing works. In his answer to Nicodemus Jesus pointed out the need for a rebirth, a topic that on the surface appeared completely unrelated to the question Nicodemus asked.

In this verse Jesus addressed Nicodemus saying: "Marvel not that I say unto thee." The pronoun ***thee*** is singular, so Jesus is addressing him individually and respectfully. The next phrase is "Ye must be born again." The pronoun ***Ye*** is plural. This means that Jesus is telling Nicodemus that not only he, individually must be "born again," but that every member of the Sanhedrin must also be born again *if* they truly wanted to do the miracles he did.

The *NRSV* translates this verse: "Do not be astounded that I said to you, 'You[p] must be born from above." The [p] directs the reader to a footnote that reads: "The Greek word for *you* here is plural." While it is helpful that the NRSV provides this information in a footnote, isn't much more direct to use the word **ye**? There are two distinct advantages in using ***ye*** rather than ***you***. With ***ye*** the reader instantly knows it is plural. Also, if this citation is read aloud from a translation that uses ***you*** in place of ***ye*** how would listeners don't know whether the pronoun ***you*** is singular or plural? They wouldn't! Normally one does not read footnotes when reading aloud since that would disrupt the flow of ideas. Even when reading silently, especially for comfort or inspiration, the tendency is to skip over footnotes.

The *Living Bible* translates: "so don't be surprised at my statement that you must be born again." Notice how the deeper meaning virtually vanishes!

The *New English Bible* is a little better but still does not bring out the intended meaning: "You ought not to be astonished, then, when I tell you that you must be born over again."

Phillips Modern English brings out the intended meaning better than the *New English Bible* by substituting "all of you" for "ye": "you must not be surprised that I told you that all of you must be born again."

We could go on. But isn't it obvious that the Authorized KJV is unsurpassed in its elegant simplicity, reverential tone, and faithful accuracy! Why not simply make the effort to get informed about a few words so the meaning will be clear?

Here is a simple guideline that may help in reading the Authorized KJV. ***You*** can be singular or plural. ***Ye*** is always plural, more than one person. The words ***thee***, ***thou***, ***thy***, ***thine***, ***hast***, ***doeth*** are always singular, one person. In this form the ***t*** always indicates the singular. In more modern English that is not the case when the letter "t" is present as in they, them, those and so on. Applying this to the Authorized KJV we know instantly how to read the text. For example:

> 29 And this *shall be* a sign unto thee [Singular to king Hezekiah], Ye [Plural, all of the inhabitants of Jerusalem] shall eat this year such things as grow of themselves, II Kings 19:29.
>
> 7 Marvel not that I [Singular - Jesus referring to the Christ he expressed] said unto thee [Singular - respectfully addressing Nicodemus], Ye [Plural - Nicodemus and all the Rulers of the Jews] must be born again. John 3:7

The reader may also find it useful to do his/her own research on additional words, some of which were only touched on in this discussion. Strong's Exhaustive Concordance has an appendix that lists verses where the following words, not included in the regular concordance appear: a – an – and – are – as – be – but – by – for – from – he – her – him – his – I – in – is – it – me – my – not – O – of – our – out – **shall** – **shalt** – she – that – the – **thee** – their – them – they – **thou** – **thy** – to – unto – up – upon – was – we – were – with – **ye** – **you**.

Hopefully this appendix has served to illustrate why the compiler elected to use the Authorized KJV to prepare a combined account of the four Gospels. It is also hoped that with this awareness the reader will more fully appreciate the great care the translators of the Authorized KJV took to present a faithful rendering in English of the original texts.

These remarks were not made to criticize other translations, or to suggest that you should not read them. Read whatever satisfies your need. The discussion of these pronouns is for those who desire gain the clearest understanding of what actually took place, or was said. Finally, be a thinker when your read, and pay attention to the context in which something is written, and you will be rewarded with more inspiration grounded in an accurate understanding.

Appendix 2 that begins on the next page is a table listing all occurrences of the word ***ye*** in the four Gospels. In Matthew the word ***ye*** appears 260 times in 191 verses; in Mark 115 times in 78 verses; in Luke 189 times in 137 verses and in John 233 times in 159 verses for a total of 797 times in the four Gospels.

What you have learned here applies to both the Old and the New Testaments.

APPENDIX 2

OCCURRENCES OF THE PRONOUN "YE" IN THE GOSPELS

No.	Book	Verse	No.	Book	Verse	No.	Book	Verse	No.	Book	Verse
	Matthew		60	Matt	10:27^{3}	120	Matt	21:28	180	Matt	26:41
1	Matt	2:8	61	Matt	10:31^{2}	121	Matt	21:32^{4}	181	Matt	26:55^{2}
2	Matt	3:2	62	Matt	11:4	122	Matt	21:42	182	Matt	26:64
3	Matt	3:3	63	Matt	11:7	123	Matt	22:9^{2}	183	Matt	26:65
4	Matt	5:11	64	Matt	11:8	124	Matt	22:18^{2}	184	Matt	26:66
5	Matt	5:13	65	Matt	11:9	125	Matt	22:29	185	Matt	27:17
6	Matt	5:14	66	Matt	11:14	126	Matt	22:31	186	Matt	27:21
7	Matt	5:20	67	Matt	11:17^{2}	127	Matt	22:42	187	Matt	27:24
8	Matt	5:21	68	Matt	11:28	128	Matt	23:3	188	Matt	27:65^{2}
9	Matt	5:27	69	Matt	11:29	129	Matt	23:8^{2}	189	Matt	28:5^{2}
10	Matt	5:33	70	Matt	12:3	130	Matt	23:10	190	Matt	28:13
11	Matt	5:38	71	Matt	12:5	131	Matt	23:13^{3}	191	Matt	28:19
12	Matt	5:39	72	Matt	12:7^{2}	132	Matt	23:14^{3}		**Mark**	
13	Matt	5:43	73	Matt	12:34	133	Matt	23:15^{2}	1	Mark	1:3
14	Matt	5:45	74	Matt	13:14^{2}	134	Matt	23:16	2	Mark	1:15
15	Matt	5:46^{2}	75	Matt	13:17^{2}	135	Matt	23:17	3	Mark	1:17
16	Matt	5:47^{2}	76	Matt	13:18	136	Matt	23:19	4	Mark	2:8
17	Matt	5:48	77	Matt	13:29^{2}	137	Matt	23:23^{2}	5	Mark	2:10
18	Matt	6:1^{2}	78	Matt	13:30	138	Matt	23:24	6	Mark	2:25
19	Matt	6:7	79	Matt	13:51	139	Matt	23:25	7	Mark	4:13^{2}
20	Matt	6:8^{3}	80	Matt	14:16	140	Matt	23:27	8	Mark	4:24^{2}
21	Matt	6:9	81	Matt	15:3	141	Matt	23:28^{2}	9	Mark	4:40^{2}
22	Matt	6:14	82	Matt	15:5	142	Matt	23:29	10	Mark	5:39
23	Matt	6:15	83	Matt	15:6	143	Matt	23:31^{2}	11	Mark	6:10^{2}
24	Matt	6:16	84	Matt	15:7	144	Matt	23:32	12	Mark	6:11
25	Matt	6:24	85	Matt	15:16	145	Matt	23:33^{3}	13	Mark	6:31
26	Matt	6:25^{3}	86	Matt	15:17	146	Matt	23:34^{2}	14	Mark	6:37
27	Matt	6:26	87	Matt	15:34	147	Matt	23:35	15	Mark	6:38
28	Matt	6:28	88	Matt	16:2	148	Matt	23:37	16	Mark	7:8^{2}
29	Matt	6:30	89	Matt	16:3^{2}	149	Matt	23:39^{2}	17	Mark	7:9^{2}
30	Matt	6:32	90	Matt	16:8^{2}	150	Matt	24:2	18	Mark	7:11
31	Matt	6:33	91	Matt	16:9^{2}	151	Matt	24:6^{2}	19	Mark	7:12
32	Matt	7:1	92	Matt	16:10	152	Matt	24:9	20	Mark	7:13^{2}
33	Matt	7:2^{3}	93	Matt	16:11^{2}	153	Matt	24:15	21	Mark	7:18^{2}
34	Matt	7:6	94	Matt	16:15	154	Matt	24:20	22	Mark	8:5
35	Matt	7:7	95	Matt	17:5	155	Matt	24:32	23	Mark	8:17^{4}
36	Matt	7:11	96	Matt	17:20^{2}	156	Matt	24:33^{2}	24	Mark	8:18^{3}
37	Matt	7:12^{2}	97	Matt	18:3^{2}	157	Matt	24:42	25	Mark	8:19
38	Matt	7:13	98	Matt	18:10	158	Matt	24:44^{2}	26	Mark	8:20
39	Matt	7:16	99	Matt	18:12	159	Matt	25:6	27	Mark	8:21
40	Matt	7:20	100	Matt	18:18^{2}	160	Matt	25:9	28	Mark	8:29
41	Matt	7:23	101	Matt	18:35	161	Matt	25:13	29	Mark	9:16
42	Matt	8:26^{2}	102	Matt	19:4	162	Matt	25:30	30	Mark	9:33
43	Matt	9:4	103	Matt	19:28^{2}	163	Matt	25:34	31	Mark	9:41
44	Matt	9:6	104	Matt	20:4	164	Matt	25:35^{3}	32	Mark	9:50
45	Matt	9:13	105	Matt	20:6	165	Matt	25:36^{3}	33	Mark	10:36
46	Matt	9:28	106	Matt	20:7^{2}	166	Matt	25:40^{2}	34	Mark	10:38^{3}
47	Matt	9:38	107	Matt	20:22^{3}	167	Matt	25:41	35	Mark	10:39^{2}
48	Matt	10:5	108	Matt	20:23	168	Matt	25:42^{2}	36	Mark	10:42
49	Matt	10:7	109	Matt	20:25	169	Matt	25:43^{2}	37	Mark	11:2^{2}
50	Matt	10:8	110	Matt	20:32	170	Matt	25:45^{2}	38	Mark	11:3^{2}
51	Matt	10:11^{2}	111	Matt	21:2	171	Matt	26:2	39	Mark	11:5
52	Matt	10:12	112	Matt	21:3	172	Matt	26:10	40	Mark	11:17
53	Matt	10:14	113	Matt	21:5	173	Matt	26:11^{2}	41	Mark	11:24^{4}
54	Matt	10:16	114	Matt	21:13	174	Matt	26:15	42	Mark	11:25^{2}
55	Matt	10:18	115	Matt	21:16	175	Matt	26:27	43	Mark	11:26
56	Matt	10:19^{2}	116	Matt	21:21^{3}	176	Matt	26:31	44	Mark	11:31
57	Matt	10:20	117	Matt	21:22^{2}	177	Matt	26:36	45	Mark	12:10
58	Matt	10:22	118	Matt	21:24	178	Matt	26:38	46	Mark	12:15
59	Matt	10:23^{2}	119	Matt	21:25	179	Matt	26:40	47	Mark	12:24^{2}

No.	Book	Verse	No.	Book	Verse	No.	Book	Verse	No.	Book	Verse
48	Mark	12:26	34	Luke	9:4	177	Luke	17:10^{2}	24	John	5:43^{2}
49	Mark	12:27	35	Luke	9:5	178	Luke	17:22^{2}	25	John	5:44
50	Mark	13:7^{2}	36	Luke	9:13	179	Luke	19:30^{2}	26	John	5:45
51	Mark	13:9^{2}	37	Luke	9:20	180	Luke	19:31^{2}	27	John	5:46^{2}
52	Mark	13:11^{4}	38	Luke	9:55^{2}	181	Luke	19:33	28	John	5:47^{2}
53	Mark	13:13	39	Luke	10:2	182	Luke	19:46	29	John	6:26^{3}
54	Mark	13:14	40	Luke	10:5	183	Luke	20:5	30	John	6:29
55	Mark	13:18	41	Luke	10:8	184	Luke	20:23	31	John	6:36
56	Mark	13:23	42	Luke	10:10	185	Luke	21:6	32	John	6:53^{2}
57	Mark	13:28	43	Luke	10:11	186	Luke	21:8^{2}	33	John	6:62
58	Mark	13:29^{2}	44	Luke	10:23	187	Luke	21:9	34	John	6:67
59	Mark	13:33^{2}	45	Luke	10:24^{2}	188	Luke	21:14	35	John	7:8
60	Mark	13:35^{2}	46	Luke	11:2	189	Luke	21:16	36	John	7:19
61	Mark	14:6	47	Luke	11:5	190	Luke	21:17	37	John	7:21
62	Mark	14:7^{4}	48	Luke	11:9	191	Luke	21:20	38	John	7:22
63	Mark	14:13	49	Luke	11:13	192	Luke	21:30	39	John	7:23
64	Mark	14:14	50	Luke	11:18	193	Luke	21:31^{3}	40	John	7:28^{3}
65	Mark	14:27	51	Luke	11:39	194	Luke	21:36^{2}	41	John	7:34^{2}
66	Mark	13:32	52	Luke	11:40	195	Luke	22:10	42	John	7:36^{2}
67	Mark	13:34	53	Luke	11:41	196	Luke	22:11	43	John	7:45
68	Mark	14:38^{2}	54	Luke	11:42^{2}	197	Luke	22:26	44	John	7:47
69	Mark	14:48	55	Luke	11:43	198	Luke	22:28	45	John	8:14
70	Mark	14:49	56	Luke	11:44	199	Luke	22:30	46	John	8:15
71	Mark	14:62	57	Luke	44:46^{3}	200	Luke	22:35	47	John	8:19^{3}
72	Mark	14:64^{2}	58	Luke	11:47	201	Luke	22:40	48	John	8:21^{2}
73	Mark	14:71	59	Luke	11:48^{3}	202	Luke	22:46^{2}	49	John	8:22
74	Mark	15:9	60	Luke	11:52^{3}	203	Luke	22:51	50	John	8:23^{2}
75	Mark	15:12^{2}	61	Luke	12:1	204	Luke	22:52	51	John	8:24^{3}
76	Mark	16:6	62	Luke	12:3^{2}	205	Luke	22:53	52	John	8:28^{2}
77	Mark	16:7	63	Luke	12:5	206	Luke	22:67	53	John	8:31^{2}
78	Mark	16:15	64	Luke	12:7	207	Luke	22:68	54	John	8:32
	Luke		65	Luke	12:11^{3}	208	Luke	22:70	55	John	8:33
1	Luke	2:12	66	Luke	12:12	209	Luke	23:14^{2}	56	John	8:36
2	Luke	2:49	67	Luke	12:22^{2}	210	Luke	23:15	57	John	8:37^{2}
3	Luke	3:4	68	Luke	12:24	211	Luke	24:5	58	John	8:38^{2}
4	Luke	4:23	69	Luke	12:26^{2}	212	Luke	24:17^{2}	59	John	8:39^{2}
5	Luke	5:22	70	Luke	12:28	213	Luke	24:38	60	John	8:40
6	Luke	5:24	71	Luke	12:29^{4}	214	Luke	24:39	61	John	8:41
7	Luke	5:30	72	Luke	12:30	215	Luke	24:41	62	John	8:42
8	Luke	5:34	73	Luke	12:31	216	Luke	24:48	63	John	8:43^{2}
9	Luke	6:2	74	Luke	12:33	217	Luke	24:49^{2}	64	John	8:44^{2}
10	Luke	6:3	75	Luke	12:36		**John**		65	John	8:45
11	Luke	6:20	76	Luke	12:40^{2}	1	John	1:26	66	John	8:46
12	Luke	6:21^{4}	77	Luke	12:51	2	John	1:38	67	John	8:47^{2}
13	Luke	6:22	78	Luke	12:54^{2}	3	John	1:51	68	John	8:49
14	Luke	6:23	79	Luke	12:55^{2}	4	John	3:7	69	John	8:54
15	Luke	6:24	80	Luke	12:56^{3}	5	John	3:11	70	John	8:55
16	Luke	6:25^{2}	81	Luke	12:57	6	John	3:12^{2}	71	John	9:19
17	Luke	6:31^{2}	82	Luke	13:2	7	John	3:28	72	John	9:27^{3}
18	Luke	6:32^{2}	83	Luke	13:3^{2}	8	John	4:20	73	John	9:30
19	Luke	6:33^{2}	84	Luke	13:4	9	John	4:21	74	John	9:41^{3}
20	Luke	6:34^{3}	85	Luke	13:5^{2}	10	John	4:22^{2}	75	John	10:20
21	Luke	6:35^{2}	86	Luke	13:25^{2}	11	John	4:32	76	John	10:25
22	Luke	6:36	87	Luke	13:26	12	John	4:35	77	John	10:26^{2}
23	Luke	6:37^{3}	88	Luke	13:27^{2}	13	John	4:38^{2}	78	John	10:32
24	Luke	6:38	89	Luke	13:28	14	John	4:48^{2}	79	John	10:34
25	Luke	6:46	90	Luke	13:32	15	John	5:20	80	John	10:36
26	Luke	7:22	91	Luke	13:34	16	John	5:33	81	John	10:38^{2}
27	Luke	7:24	92	Luke	13:35	17	John	5:34	82	John	11:15
28	Luke	7:25	93	Luke	16:9	18	John	5:35	83	John	11:34
29	Luke	7:26	94	Luke	16:11	19	John	5:37	84	John	11:39
30	Luke	7:32^{2}	95	Luke	16:12	20	John	5:38^{2}	85	John	11:49
31	Luke	7:33	96	Luke	16:13	21	John	5:39^{2}	86	John	11:56
32	Luke	7:34	97	Luke	16:15	22	John	5:40^{2}	87	John	12:8^{2}
33	Luke	8:18	98	Luke	17:6^{2}	23	John	5:42	88	John	12:19^{2}

No.	Book	Verse	No.	Book	Verse	No.	Book	Verse	No.	Book	Verse
89	John	12:35	107	John	14:14	125	John	15:17	143	John	16:32
90	John	12:36^2	108	John	14:15	126	John	15:18	144	John	16:33^2
91	John	13:10	109	John	14:17	127	John	15:19^2	145	John	18:4
92	John	13:11	110	John	14:19^2	128	John	15:27^2	146	John	18:7
93	John	13:12	111	John	14:20^2	129	John	16:1	147	John	15:8
94	John	13:13^2	112	John	14:24	130	John	16:4	148	John	18:29
95	John	13:14	113	John	14:28^3	131	John	16:10	149	John	18:31
96	John	13:15	114	John	14:29	132	John	16:12	150	John	18:39^2
97	John	13:17^3	115	John	15:3	133	John	16:16^2	151	John	19:4
98	John	13:19	116	John	15:4^2	134	John	16:17^2	152	John	19:6
99	John	13:33^2	117	John	15:5^2	135	John	16:19^3	153	John	19:35
100	John	13:34^2	118	John	15:7^2	136	John	16:20^2	154	John	20:22
101	John	13:35^2	119	John	15:8^2	137	John	16:22	155	John	20:23^2
102	John	14:1	120	John	15:9	138	John	16:23^2	156	John	20:31^2
103	John	14:3	121	John	15:10^2	139	John	16:24^2	157	John	21:5
104	John	14:4^2	122	John	15:12	140	John	16:26	158	John	21:6
105	John	14:7^3	123	John	15:14^2	141	John	16:27	159	John	21:10
106	John	14:13	124	John	15:16^3	142	John	16:31			

APPENDIX 3
THE SIGNIFICANCE OF ITALICIZED WORDS IN THE KING JAMES BIBLE

Begin reading the Authorized Version of the King James Bible and you will get no farther than Genesis 1:2 before encountering a word in italics.

I recall as a young man hearing a gentleman read the Bible aloud. I noticed he emphasized a lot of words that to me didn't seem very important, especially pronouns. I asked him why he emphasized certain and he replied: "because they are printed in italics so they need to be emphasized." I later learned that he was partly correct. Words are printed in italics to draw attention to them, but not for the reason he thought. His misunderstanding resulted in a manner of reading aloud that was actually distracting.

So why are certain words in the Bible printed in italics, and how should we read them? It is well to recall that our English Bible is translated from other languages: primarily Hebrew in the Old Testament and Greek in the New. The original documents can be likened to a child learning to write placing all of the letters in one unbroken stream. The parent, to understand what a child had written, would separate the letters into words, and then the words into sentences. Likewise, the translators of the original documents broke a stream of continuous Greek or Hebrew letters into words. The words were then arranged into sentences.

As an aside, the punctuation and capitalization, the breakdown into sentences, paragraphs, and chapters, and verse numbering are all additions by the translators to facilitate reading and study.

The next step was to translate the Greek and Hebrew text into equivalent English words. This is no easy task because there are some Hebrew or Greek words for which there is no single word in English to accurately convey its meaning. To further complicate things the Hebrew or Greek word may have more than one meaning, and the English word that was selected may have several meanings as well. Furthermore, the translators often worked with incomplete, severely faded or damaged originals, sometimes with portions of the text missing. Also, syntax varies between languages. For these reasons the translators sometimes thought it necessary to add words not in the original to assist the English reader. To alert the reader when this was done the compilers established the practice of printing any words they added in *italics*.

The following is quoted from Appendix 48 in *The Companion Bible*:

> The practice of indicating, by different types, words and phrases which were not in the Original Text, was, it is believed, first introduced by Sebastian Münster, of Basle, in a Latin version of the Old Testament published in 1534.
>
> The English New Testament (published at Geneva, 1557) and the Geneva Bible (1560) "put in that word which, lacking, made the sentence obscure, but set it in such letters as may easily be discerned from the common text." The example was followed and extended in the Bishops' Bible (1568, 1572), and the *roman* and *italic*[1] types of these Bibles (as distinguished from the *black letter* and *roman* type of previous Bibles) were introduced into the A.V. (1611).
>
> The following seem to have been the principles guiding the translators of the

A.V.: ---

1. To supply the omissions under the Figure *Ellipsis*, or what they considered the *Ellipsis*.
2. To supply the words necessary to give the sense, when the Figure Zeugma is employed.
3. Once, at least, to indicate a word or words of doubtful MS authority, 1 John 2.23 (first introduced in Cranmer's Bible---doubtless from the Vulgate). Perhaps also Judg. 16.2 and 20.9.
4. Where the English idiom differs from that of the Originals, and requires essential words to be added, which are not necessary in the Hebrew or Greek.

The use of large capital letters for certain words and phrases originated with the A.V. None of the previous or "former translations" have them.

The revisers abandoned this practice, but have not been consistent in the plan they substituted for it. In most of the cases they have used small capital letters; but in three cases (Jer. 23.6. Zech. 3.8; 6.12) they have used ordinary roman type.

The use of the large capital by the translators of the A.V. is destitute of any authority, and merely indicates the importance which they attached to such words and phrases thus indicated.

The Revised Edition of the King James Version and most "modern" translations no longer indicate words not included in the original texts. The following is from Appendix 7 in *The Companion Bible*.

The Revisers ill-advisedly decided that "all such words, now printed in italics, as are plainly implied in the Hebrew, and necessary in English, be printed in common type."

One of the consequences of this decision is that the verb "to be" is not distinguished from the verb "to become", so that the lessons conveyed by the A.V. "was" and "*was*" in Gen. 1.2; 3 and 4; 9 and 10; 11 and 12, are lost.

To summarize: italics in the A.V. indicate words that have been added that were not in the original texts. Knowing that a word is a later addition enables the reader to carefully consider its effect on the meaning. It may be helpful to illustrate by an example how an italicized word can affect the meaning.

17 For the law was given by Moses, *but* grace and truth came by Jesus Christ.
John 1:17

Note that the word "but" is italicized, meaning that it was added to the text "to bring out what the reviser thought to be the intended meaning." Before going forward let us examine the same scripture by changing the conjunction from "but" to "and."

17 For the law was given by Moses, *and* grace and truth came by Jesus Christ.
John 1:17

It is obvious that changing the conjunction "*but*" to "*and*" gives this verse a very different meaning. The addition of the conjunction "*but*" by the revisers separates the teaching of Moses and Jesus, whereas using the conjunction "*and*" unifies it.

Someone once told me that when Jesus came, the Ten Commandments, that came through Moses, were superseded by the Beatitudes, that came through Jesus Christ. This person cited Luke 16:16 as the authority for this opinion.

> 16 The law and the prophets *were* until John: since that time the kingdom of God is preached, and every man presseth into it. Luke 16:16.

This opinion, that with the coming of Jesus the Ten Commandments are now secondary, is not supported by Luke 16:16. The words "until John" means until John the Baptist came declaring prophecy fulfilled in these words: "The time is fulfilled, and the kingdom of God is at hand: repent ye, and believe the gospel." (Mark 1:15). Referring to these words of John, Jesus later said to the Pharisees and scribes: since that time the kingdom of God is preached, and every man presseth into it. (Luke 16:16). But nowhere does Jesus suggest that total obedience to the Ten Commandments is no longer required. Here is what he did say:

> 17 And it is easier for heaven and earth to pass, than one tittle of the law to fail. Luke 16:17.

Furthermore, Jesus is recorded to have said in Matthew:

> 17 ¶ Think not that I am come to destroy the law, or the prophets: I am not come to destroy, but to fulfil.
> 18 For verily I say unto you, Till heaven and earth pass, one jot or one tittle shall in no wise pass from the law, till all be fulfilled.
> 19 Whosoever therefore shall break one of these least commandments, and shall teach men so, he shall be called the least in the kingdom of heaven: but whosoever shall do and teach *them*, the same shall be called great in the kingdom of heaven.
> 20 For I say unto you, That except your righteousness shall exceed *the righteousness* of the scribes and Pharisees, ye shall in no case enter into the kingdom of heaven. Matt 5:17-19

Jesus came so that both the letter and the spirit of the Ten Commandments would be put into practice. What could possibly be more hypocritical than professing to have faith in Jesus and his teachings and then live a life contrary to the Ten Commandments? It is impossible to read the Gospels and not be aware of the importance Jesus placed on Moses and the Prophets.

> 1 And after six days Jesus taketh Peter, James, and John his brother, and bringeth them up into an high mountain apart,
> 2 And was transfigured before them: and his face did shine as the sun, and his raiment was white as the light.
> 3 And, behold, there appeared unto them Moses and Elias talking with him.
> 4 Then answered Peter, and said unto Jesus, Lord, it is good for us to be here: if thou wilt, let us make here three tabernacles; one for thee, and one for Moses, and one for Elias.
> 5 While he yet spake, behold, a bright cloud overshadowed them: and behold a voice out of the cloud, which said, This is my beloved Son, in whom I am well

pleased; hear ye him.
6 And when the disciples heard it, they fell on their face, and were sore afraid.
7 And Jesus came and touched them, and said, Arise, and be not afraid.
8 And when they had lifted up their eyes, they saw no man, save Jesus only.
Matt 17:1-8

The transfiguration illustrated how integral to the message of Christ Jesus was the teaching of the Law (Moses) and the Prophets (Elijah). Jesus ministry began with the message "repent ye, and believe the gospel." (Mark 1:14). Such a message would be meaningless if the Law was not in effect. So how can anyone reach the conclusion that with the coming of Jesus the Ten Commandments are now of less importance, a misunderstanding that may have originated, or is at least seen as implied in John 1:17 where the word "*but*" was added?

Two points must be made here. The first is that all words added by the revisers are not necessarily misleading and don't in many cases smooth out the text for the English reader. Second, the purpose of this discussion is not to argue over scriptural interpretation, but rather to point out the importance of paying attention to words that are printed in italics and to determine for yourself their effect on the meaning.

We have been discussing the effect of replacing the word "*but*" with "*and*" on the meaning of John 1:17. But the question is not what word should be added, but rather if the addition of any word helps or hinders in bringing out the intended meaning? Let us examine this verse once again as written in the original text.

17 For the law was given by Moses. Grace and truth came by Jesus Christ. John 1:17

What is not perfectly clear about this? How has anything but confusion and ambiguity been introduced by the addition of the word "*but*"? We should be grateful that the King James Bible identifies any words added by the revisers and enables us to decide for ourselves how much weight we choose to give to them.

19 When any one heareth the word of the kingdom, and understandeth it not, then cometh the wicked one, and catcheth away that which was sown in his heart. Matt 13:19 to *1st*.

Whatever we hear and understand correctly is ours forever. That should be motive enough to seek the correct understanding of the Scriptures!

As an aid to your being able to determine the significance you wish to ascribe to words added by the revisers a table of all italicized words added to each Gospel has been prepared. It may surprise you to know how many words have been added. In Matthew 469 words in 303 verses were added; in Mark 297 words in 197 verses; in Luke 587 words in 319 verses and in John 286 words in 204 verses. This makes a total of 1,639 words in 1023 verses were added in the four Gospels alone. With the myriad of new "translations" the ability of a student to identify these changes and determine their significance is gone. We can be thankful that the Authorized Version of the King James Bible continues to make this information available. Regardless of the English translation you prefer, you may find these tables useful.

APPENDIX 4

4.1 - TABLE OF ITALICIZED WORDS IN MATTHEW

(Page numbers apply to the Combined Gospels with Notes)

Book	Verse	Page	Partial text with italicized words	Count Here	Count Total
Matt	1:6	178	David the king begat Solomon of her *that had been the wife* of Urias	5	5
Matt	1:17	178	. . *are* fourteen generations; . . *are* fourteen generations; . . *are* fourteen	3	8
Matt	1:19	180	Then Joseph her husband, being a just *man*	1	9
Matt	2:3	182	When Herod the king had heard *these things*	2	11
Matt	2:6	182	And thou Bethlehem, *in* the land of Juda	1	12
Matt	2:8	182	Go and search diligently for the young child; and when ye have found *him*	1	13
Matt	2:18	183	Rachel weeping *for* her children, and would not be comforted, because they	1	14
Matt	3:9	185	We have Abraham to *our* father	1	15
Matt	3:11	185	he shall baptize you with the Holy Ghost, and *with* fire	1	16
Matt	3:12	185	Whose fan *is* in his hand	1	17
Matt	3:15	186	Suffer *it to be so* now: for thus it becometh us to fulfil all righteousness.	4	21
Matt	4:6	194	and in *their* hands they shall bear thee up,	1	22
Matt	4:15	197	Nephthalim, *by* the way of the sea, beyond Jordan, Galilee of the Gentiles	1	23
Matt	4:20	199	And they straightway left *their* nets, and followed him.	1	24
Matt	4:21	199	James *the son* of Zebedee	2	26
Matt	4:25	199	and *from* Decapolis, and *from* Jerusalem, and *from* Judaea, and *from* beyond	4	30
Matt	5:3	199	Blessed *are* the poor in spirit	1	31
Matt	5:4	199	Blessed *are* they that mourn	1	32
Matt	5:5	199	Blessed *are* the meek	1	33
Matt	5:6	199	Blessed *are* they which do hunger and thirst after righteousness	1	34
Matt	5:7	199	Blessed *are* the merciful	1	35
Matt	5:8	199	Blessed *are* the pure in heart	1	36
Matt	5:9	199	Blessed *are* the peacemakers	1	37
Matt	5:10	199	Blessed *are* they which are persecuted for righteousness' sake	1	38
Matt	5:11	199	Blessed are ye, when *men* shall revile you, and persecute *you*	2	40
Matt	5:12	199	Rejoice, and be exceeding glad: for great *is* your reward in heaven	1	41
Matt	5:19	200	but whosoever shall do and teach *them*	1	42
Matt	5:20	200	That except your righteousness shall exceed *the righteousness* of the scribes and	2	44
Matt	5:29	200	. . . pluck it out, and cast *it* from thee . .. and not *that* thy whole body	2	46
Matt	5:30	200	. . cut it off, and cast *it* from thee . . . and not *that* thy whole body	2	48
Matt	5:40	201	. . . let him have *thy* cloak also	1	49
Matt	5:47	201	And if ye salute your brethren only, what do ye more *than others*?	2	51
Matt	6:2	201	Therefore when thou doest *thine* alms	1	52
Matt	6:5	201	And when thou prayest, thou shalt not be as the hypocrites *are*	1	53
Matt	6:7	201	But when ye pray, use not vain repetitions, as the heathen *do*	1	54
Matt	6:10	202	Thy kingdom come. Thy will be done in earth, as *it is* in heaven	2	56
Matt	6:23	202	If therefore the light that is in thee be darkness, how great *is* that darkness!	1	57
Matt	6:30	202	. . . *shall he* not much more *clothe* you, O ye of little faith?	3	60
Matt	6:34	203	Sufficient unto the day *is* the evil thereof.	1	61
Matt	7:4	203	. . . and, behold, a beam *is* in thine own eye?	1	62
Matt	7:13	203	. . . for wide *is* the gate, and broad *is* the way	2	64
Matt	7:14	203	. . . Because strait *is* the gate, and narrow *is* the way	2	66
Matt	7:18	204	A good tree cannot bring forth evil fruit, neither *can* a corrupt tree bring forth	1	67
Matt	7:29	204	For he taught them as *one* having authority, and not as the scribes.	1	68
Matt	8:3	204	And Jesus put forth *his* hand, and touched him	1	69
Matt	8:9	204	. . . and I say to this *man*, Go, and he goeth . . . Do this, and he doeth *it*.	2	71
Matt	8:10	205	When Jesus heard *it*, he marvelled	1	72
Matt	8:13	205	Go thy way; and as thou hast believed, *so* be it done unto thee	1	73
Matt	8:16	206	and he cast out the spirits with *his* word, and healed all that were sick	1	74
Matt	8:17	206	Himself took our infirmities, and bare *our* sicknesses	1	75
Matt	8:20	208	. . . the birds of the air *have* nests; but the Son of man hath not where to lay *his*	2	77
Matt	8:25	208	And his disciples came to *him*, and awoke him	1	78
Matt	8:34	209	. . . they besought *him* that he would depart out of their coasts.	1	79
Matt	9:3	210	This *man* blasphemeth.	1	80
Matt	9:5	210	*Thy* sins be forgiven thee; or to say, Arise, and walk?	1	81
Matt	9:8	210	But when the multitudes saw *it*	1	82
Matt	9:11	211	And when the Pharisees saw *it*	1	83
Matt	9:12	211	But when Jesus heard *that*, he said unto them	1	84
Matt	9:13	211	But go ye and learn what *that* meaneth	1	85

Matt	9:19	212	And Jesus arose, and followed him, and *so did* his disciples.	2	87
Matt	9:20	212	. . . which was diseased with an issue of blood twelve years, came behind *him*	1	88
Matt	9:27	213	*Thou* Son of David, have mercy on us.	1	89
Matt	9:30	213	Jesus straitly charged them, saying, See *that* no man know *it*.	2	91
Matt	9:37	213	The harvest truly *is* plenteous, but the labourers *are* few	2	93
Matt	10:1	214	called unto *him* his twelve disciples, he gave them power *against* unclean spirits	2	95
Matt	10:2	214	James *the son* of Zebedee, and John his brother	2	97
Matt	10:3	214	James *the son* of Alphæus, and Lebbæus, whose surname was Thaddæus	2	99
Matt	10:5	214	Go not into the way of the Gentiles, and into *any* city of the Samaritans enter ye	1	100
Matt	10:10	214	Nor scrip for *your* journey, neither two coats	1	101
Matt	10:21	215	and the children shall rise up against *their* parents, and cause them to be put to	1	102
Matt	10:22	215	And ye shall be hated of all *men* for my name's sake	1	103
Matt	10:24	215	The disciple is not above *his* master, nor the servant above his lord	1	104
Matt	10:25	215	how much more *shall they call* them of his household?	3	107
Matt	10:27	215	in darkness, *that* speak ye in light: . . . in the ear, *that* preach ye upon the house	2	109
Matt	10:36	215	And a man's foes *shall be* they of his own household	2	111
Matt	10:42	215	one of these little ones a cup of cold *water* only in the name of	1	112
Matt	11:6	216	And blessed is *he*, whosoever shall not be offended in me	1	113
Matt	11:8	216	behold, they that wear soft *clothing* are in kings' houses	1	114
Matt	11:10	216	For this is *he*, of whom it is written	1	115
Matt	11:14	216	And if ye will receive *it*, this is Elias, which was for to come	1	116
Matt	11:27	217	save the Son, and *he* to whomsoever the Son will reveal *him*	2	118
Matt	11:28	217	Come unto me, all *ye* that labour and are heavy laden, and I will give you rest	1	119
Matt	11:30	217	For my yoke *is* easy, and my burden is light	1	120
Matt	12:2	220	But when the Pharisees saw *it*, they said unto him	1	121
Matt	12:6	220	But I say unto you, That in this place is *one* greater than the temple	1	122
Matt	12:7	220	But if ye had known what *this* meaneth, I will have mercy, and not sacrifice	1	123
Matt	12:10	220	And, behold, there was a man which had *his* hand withered	1	124
Matt	12:11	221	. . . if it fall into a pit on the sabbath day, will he not lay hold on it, and lift *it* out?	1	125
Matt	12:13	221	And he stretched *it* forth; and it was restored whole, like as the other	1	126
Matt	12:15	221	But when Jesus knew *it*, he withdrew himself from thence	1	127
Matt	12:24	229	But when the Pharisees heard *it*, they said, This *fellow* doth not cast out devils	2	129
Matt	12:27	229	. . . by whom do your children cast *them* out?	1	130
Matt	12:31	230	. . . the blasphemy *against* the *Holy* Ghost shall not be forgiven unto men	2	132
Matt	12:32	230	. . . it shall not be forgiven him, neither in this world, neither in the *world* to	1	133
Matt	12:33	230	. . . the tree corrupt, and his fruit corrupt: for the tree is known by *his* fruit	1	134
Matt	12:41	230	. . . behold, a greater than Jonas *is* here	1	135
Matt	12:42	230	. . . behold, a greater than Solomon *is* here	1	136
Matt	12:44	230	. . . and when he is come, he findeth *it* empty, swept, and garnished	1	137
Matt	12:45	230	. . . and the last *state* of that man is worse than the first	1	138
Matt	12:46	231	. . . behold, *his* mother and his brethren stood without, desiring to speak with him	1	139
Matt	13:4	231	. . . some *seeds* fell by the way side, and the fowls came and devoured them up	1	140
Matt	13:15	232	. . . and *their* ears . . . with *their* eyes . . . with *their* ears . . . with *their* heart	4	144
Matt	13:16	232	But blessed *are* your eyes, for they see: and your ears, for they hear	1	145
Matt	13:17	232	. . . *men* . . . *those things* . . . not seen *them* . . . *those things* . . . not heard *them*	7	152
Matt	13:19	232	. . . understandeth *it* not, then cometh the wicked *one*, and catcheth away	2	154
Matt	13:23	233	. . . and understandeth *it*; which also beareth fruit	1	155
Matt	13:38	234	. . . but the tares are the children of the wicked *one*	1	156
Matt	13:52	235	scribe *which is* instructed . . . man *that is* an householder . . . treasure *things*	5	161
Matt	13:53	236	. . . *that* when Jesus had finished these parables, he departed thence	1	162
Matt	13:54	241	Whence hath this *man* this wisdom, and *these* mighty works?	2	164
Matt	13:56	241	Whence then hath this *man* all these things?	1	165
Matt	14:3	243	. . . and put *him* in prison for Herodias' sake, his brother Philip's wife	1	166
Matt	14:9	243	and them which sat with him at meat, he commanded *it* to be given *her*	2	168
Matt	14:11	243	. . . and she brought *it* to her mother	1	169
Matt	14:13	243	When Jesus heard *of it*, he departed . . . when the people had heard *thereof*	3	172
Matt	14:19	246	and gave the loaves to *his* disciples, and the disciples to the multitude	1	173
Matt	14:31	248	And immediately Jesus stretched forth *his* hand, and caught him	1	174
Matt	15:5	253	Whosoever shall say to *his* father or *his* mother, *It is* a gift, by whatsoever	4	178
Matt	15:6	253	And honour not his father or his mother, *he shall be free*. Thus have	4	182
Matt	15:7	253	*Ye* hypocrites, well did Esaias prophesy of you, saying	1	183
Matt	15:8	253	. . . and honoureth me with *their* lips; but their heart is far from me	1	184
Matt	15:9	253	. . . teaching *for* doctrines the commandments of men	1	185
Matt	15:20	253	These are *the things* which defile a man	2	187
Matt	15:22	254	Have mercy on me, O Lord, *thou* son of David	1	188

Matt	15:26	254	It is not meet to take the children's bread, and to cast *it* to dogs	1	189
Matt	15:28	254	O woman, great *is* thy faith: be it unto thee even as thou wilt	1	190
Matt	15:30	255	having with them *those that were* lame, blind, dumb, maimed, and many others	3	193
Matt	15:32	255	Then Jesus called his disciples *unto him*, and said	2	195
Matt	15:36	255	. . . and gave thanks, and brake *them*, and gave to his disciples	1	196
Matt	15:37	255	. . . and they took up of the broken *meat* that was left seven baskets full	1	197
Matt	16:2	257	When it is evening, ye say, *It will be* fair weather: for the sky is red	3	200
Matt	16:3	257	And in the morning, *It will be* foul weather to-day: for the sky is red	5	205
Matt	16:7	257	. . . reasoned among themselves, saying, *It is* because we have taken no bread	2	207
Matt	16:8	257	*Which* when Jesus perceived, he said unto them, O ye of little faith	1	208
Matt	16:11	257	How is it that ye do not understand that I spake *it* not to you concerning bread	1	209
Matt	16:12	257	Then understood they how that he bade *them* not beware of the leaven of bread	1	210
Matt	16:14	258	Some *say that thou art* John the Baptist	4	214
Matt	16:17	258	. . . for flesh and blood hath not revealed *it* unto thee	1	215
Matt	16:24	259	If any *man* will come after me, let him deny himself	1	216
Matt	17:6	261	And when the disciples heard *it*, they fell on their face, and were sore afraid	1	217
Matt	17:14	262	. . . there came to him a *certain* man, kneeling down to him, and saying	1	218
Matt	17:24	264	. . . they that received tribute *money* came to Peter	1	219
Matt	18:6	266	. . . and *that* he were drowned in the depth of the sea	1	220
Matt	18:8	267	. . . cut them off, and cast *them* from thee	1	221
Matt	18:9	267	. . . pluck it out, and cast *it* from thee	1	222
Matt	18:13	267	. . . verily I say unto you, he rejoiceth more of that *sheep*	1	223
Matt	18:16	267	But if he will not hear *thee*, *then* take with thee one or two more	2	225
Matt	18:17	267	. . . tell *it* unto the church: but if he neglect to hear the church	1	226
Matt	18:28	268	. . . and he laid hands on him, and took *him* by the throat, saying, Pay me	1	227
Matt	19:1	269	And it came to pass, *that* when Jesus had finished these sayings	1	228
Matt	19:4	283	. . . he which made *them* at the beginning made them male and female	1	229
Matt	19:9	283	Whosoever shall put away his wife, except *it be* for fornication	2	231
Matt	19:10	283	If the case of the man be so with *his* wife, it is not good to marry	1	232
Matt	19:11	283	All *men* cannot receive this saying, save *they* to whom it is given	2	234
Matt	19:12	283	. . . born from *their* mother's womb . . . able to receive *it*, let him receive *it*	3	237
Matt	19:13	304	that he should put *his* hands on them, and pray	1	238
Matt	19:15	304	And he laid *his* hands on them, and departed thence	1	239
Matt	19:17	304	Why callest thou me good? *there is* none good but one, *that is*, God	4	243
Matt	19:19	304	Honour thy father and *thy* mother	1	244
Matt	19:21	304	. . . go *and* sell that thou hast . . . and come *and* follow me	2	246
Matt	19:25	304	When his disciples heard *it*, they were exceedingly amazed	1	247
Matt	19:26	304	But Jesus beheld *them*, and said unto them, With men this is impossible	1	248
Matt	19:30	306	But many *that are* first shall be last; and the last *shall be* first	4	252
Matt	20:1	306	For the kingdom of heaven is like unto a man *that is* an householder	2	254
Matt	20:7	307	and whatsoever is right, *that* shall ye receive	1	255
Matt	20:8	307	Call the labourers, and give them *their* hire, beginning from the last unto the	1	256
Matt	20:9	307	And when they came that *were hired* about the eleventh hour	2	258
Matt	20:11	307	And when they had received *it*, they murmured against the goodman of the	1	259
Matt	20:12	307	These last have wrought *but* one hour, and thou hast made them equal unto us	1	260
Matt	20:14	307	Take *that* thine *is*, and go thy way	2	262
Matt	20:19	307	. . . and to scourge, and to crucify *him*: and the third day he shall rise again	1	263
Matt	20:20	308	. . . worshipping *him*, and desiring a certain thing of him	1	264
Matt	20:23	308	. . . but *it shall be given to them* for whom it is prepared of my Father	6	270
Matt	20:24	308	And when the ten heard *it*, they were moved with indignation	1	271
Matt	20:25	308	But Jesus called them *unto him*, and said, Ye know that the princes of the	2	273
Matt	20:30	310	Have mercy on us, O Lord, *thou* son of David	1	274
Matt	20:31	310	Have mercy on us, O Lord, *thou* son of David	1	275
Matt	20:34	310	So Jesus had compassion *on them*, and touched their eyes	2	277
Matt	21:2	312	. . . find an ass tied, and a colt with her: loose *them*, and bring *them* unto me	2	279
Matt	21:3	312	And if any *man* say ought unto you, ye shall say	1	280
Matt	21:7	312	. . . and put on them their clothes, and they set *him* thereon	1	281
Matt	21:8	312	. . . others cut down branches from the trees, and strawed *them* in the way	1	282
Matt	21:9	312	Blessed *is* he that cometh in the name of the Lord; Hosanna in the highest	1	283
Matt	21:20	318	And when the disciples saw *it*, they marvelled, saying	1	284
Matt	21:21	318	. . . ye shall not only do this *which is done* to the fig tree	3	287
Matt	21:28	320	A *certain* man had two sons; and he came to the first, and said, Son	1	288
Matt	21:30	320	And he answered and said, I *go*, sir: and went not	1	289
Matt	21:31	320	Whether of them twain did the will of *his* father?	1	290
Matt	21:32	320	. . . and ye, when ye had seen *it*, repented not afterward, that ye might believe	1	291
Matt	21:39	321	And they caught him, and cast *him* out of the vineyard, and slew *him*	2	293

Matt	21:41	321	He will miserably destroy those wicked men, and will let out *his* vineyard unto	1	294
Matt	22:4	322	. . . my oxen and *my* fatlings *are* killed, and all things *are* ready: come unto the	3	297
Matt	22:5	322	But they made light of *it*, and went their ways	1	298
Matt	22:6	322	And the remnant took his servants, and entreated *them* spitefully, and slew *them*	2	300
Matt	22:7	322	But when the king heard *thereof*, he was wroth	1	301
Matt	22:13	322	. . . and cast *him* into outer darkness; there shall be weeping and gnashing of teeth	1	302
Matt	22:14	322	For many are called, but few *are* chosen	1	303
Matt	22:15	323	. . . took counsel how they might entangle him in *his* talk	1	304
Matt	22:16	323	. . . neither carest thou for any *man*: for thou regardest not the person of men	1	305
Matt	22:20	324	And he saith unto them, Whose *is* this image and superscription?	1	306
Matt	22:22	324	When they had heard *these words*, they marvelled, and left him, and went their	2	308
Matt	22:33	324	And when the multitude heard *this*, they were astonished at his doctrine	1	309
Matt	22:35	325	Then one of them, *which was* a lawyer, asked *him a question*, tempting him	5	314
Matt	22:36	325	Master, which *is* the great commandment in the law?	1	315
Matt	22:39	325	And the second *is* like unto it, Thou shalt love thy neighbour as thyself	1	316
Matt	22:42	326	They say unto him, *The Son* of David	2	318
Matt	22:46	327	. . . neither durst any *man* from that day forth ask him any more *questions*	2	320
Matt	23:3	328	All therefore whatsoever they bid you observe, *that* observe and do	1	321
Matt	23:4	328	. . . and lay *them* on men's shoulders; but they *themselves* will not move them	2	323
Matt	23:8	328	But be not ye called Rabbi: for one is your Master, *even* Christ	1	324
Matt	23:9	328	And call no *man* your father upon the earth: for one is your Father, which is in	1	325
Matt	23:10	328	Neither be ye called masters: for one is your Master, *even* Christ	1	326
Matt	23:13	328	. . . for ye neither go in *yourselves*, neither suffer ye them that are entering to go	1	327
Matt	23:16	328	Woe unto you, *ye* blind guides	1	328
Matt	23:17	328	*Ye* fools and blind: for whether is greater, the gold, or the temple	1	329
Matt	23:19	328	*Ye* fools and blind: for whether *is* greater, the gift, or the altar	2	331
Matt	23:23	329	and have omitted the weightier *matters* of the law, judgment, mercy, and faith	1	332
Matt	23:24	329	*Ye* blind guides, which strain at a gnat, and swallow a camel	1	333
Matt	23:26	329	*Thou* blind Pharisee, cleanse first that *which is* within the cup and platter	3	336
Matt	23:27	329	but are within full of dead *men's* bones, and of all uncleanness	1	337
Matt	23:33	329	*Ye* serpents, *ye* generation of vipers, how can ye escape the damnation of hell?	2	339
Matt	23:34	329	. . . and *some* of them . . . and *some* . . . persecute *them* from city to city	3	342
Matt	23:37	329	. . . Jerusalem, *thou* that killest . . . her chickens under *her* wings	2	344
Matt	23:39	329	Blessed *is* he that cometh in the name of the Lord	1	345
Matt	24:1	331	. . . and his disciples came to *him* for to shew him the buildings of the temple	1	346
Matt	24:3	333	. . . and what *shall be* the sign of thy coming, and of the end of the world?	2	348
Matt	24:6	333	. . . for all *these things* must come to pass, but the end is not yet	2	350
Matt	24:8	333	All these *are* the beginning of sorrows	1	351
Matt	24:23	333	Lo, here *is* Christ, or there; believe *it* not	2	353
Matt	24:24	333	. . . insomuch that, if *it were* possible, they shall deceive the very elect	2	355
Matt	24:26	333	. . . behold, *he is* in the secret chambers; believe *it* not	3	358
Matt	24:32	334	. . . and putteth forth leaves, ye know that summer *is* nigh	1	359
Matt	24:33	334	. . . when ye shall see all these things, know that it is near, *even* at the doors	1	360
Matt	24:36	334	. . . knoweth no *man*, no, not the angels of heaven, but my Father only	1	361
Matt	24:37	334	But as the days of Noe *were*, so shall also the coming of the Son of man be	1	362
Matt	24:41	334	Two *women shall be* grinding at the mill; the one shall be taken, and the other left	3	365
Matt	24:46	334	Blessed *is* that servant, whom his lord when he cometh shall find so doing	1	366
Matt	24:49	334	And shall begin to smite *his* fellowservants, and to eat and drink with the drunken	1	367
Matt	24:50	334	. . . in a day when he looketh not for *him*, and in an hour that he is not aware of	1	368
Matt	24:51	334	. . . and appoint *him* his portion with the hypocrites	1	369
Matt	25:2	334	And five of them were wise, and five *were* foolish	1	370
Matt	25:3	334	They that *were* foolish took their lamps, and took no oil with them	1	371
Matt	25:9	335	But the wise answered, saying, *Not so*; lest there be not enough	2	373
Matt	25:14	335	For *the kingdom of heaven is* as a man travelling into a far country, *who* called	6	379
Matt	25:16	335	. . . and made *them* other five talents	1	380
Matt	25:17	335	And likewise he that *had received* two, he also gained other two	2	382
Matt	25:21	335	His lord said unto him, Well done, *thou* good and faithful servant	1	383
Matt	25:25	336	. . . and went and hid thy talent in the earth: lo, *there* thou hast *that is* thine	3	386
Matt	25:26	336	His lord answered and said unto him, *Thou* wicked and slothful servant	1	387
Matt	25:27	336	. . . and *then* at my coming I should have received mine own with usury	1	388
Matt	25:28	336	Take therefore the talent from him, and give *it* unto him which hath ten talents	1	389
Matt	25:32	336	. . . as a shepherd divideth *his* sheep from the goats	1	390
Matt	25:37	336	. . . and fed *thee*? or thirsty, and gave *thee* drink?	2	392
Matt	25:38	336	When saw we thee a stranger, and took *thee* in? or naked, and clothed *thee*?	2	394
Matt	25:40	336	. . . have done *it* unto one of the least of these my brethren, ye have done *it* unto m	2	396
Matt	25:45	337	. . . Inasmuch as ye did *it* not to one of the least of these, ye did *it* not to me	2	398

Matt	26:2	337	Ye know that after two days is *the feast of* the passover	3	401
Matt	26:4	337	And consulted that they might take Jesus by subtilty, and kill *him*	1	402
Matt	26:5	337	Not on the feast *day*, lest there be an uproar among the people	1	403
Matt	26:7	337	. . . and poured it on his head, as he sat *at meat*	2	405
Matt	26:8	337	. . . his disciples saw *it* . . . saying, To what purpose *is* this waste?	2	407
Matt	26:10	338	When Jesus understood *it*, he said unto them, Why trouble ye the woman?	1	408
Matt	26:12	338	For in that she hath poured this ointment on my body, she did *it* for my burial	1	409
Matt	26:13	338	Wheresoever this gospel shall be preached ... *there* shall also this	1	410
Matt	26:15	338	And said *unto them*, What will ye give me, and I will deliver him unto you?	2	412
Matt	26:17	339	Now the first *day* of the *feast of* unleavened bread	3	415
Matt	26:23	340	He that dippeth *his* hand with me in the dish, the same shall betray me	1	416
Matt	26:26	343	Jesus took bread, and blessed *it*, and brake *it*, and gave *it* to the disciples	3	419
Matt	26:27	343	. . . and gave thanks, and gave *it* to them, saying, Drink ye all of it	1	420
Matt	26:33	351	Though all *men* shall be offended because of thee, *yet* will I never be offended	2	422
Matt	26:39	353	nevertheless not as I will, but as thou *wilt*	1	423
Matt	26:41	353	the spirit indeed *is* willing, but the flesh *is* weak	2	425
Matt	26:45	353	Sleep on now, and take *your* rest: behold, the hour is at hand	1	426
Matt	26:51	355	And, behold, one of them which were with Jesus stretched out *his* hand	1	427
Matt	26:57	357	. . . they that had laid hold on Jesus led *him* away to Caiaphas the high priest	1	428
Matt	26:60	357	. . . though many false witnesses came, *yet* found they none	1	429
Matt	26:61	357	This *fellow* said, I am able to destroy the temple of God	1	430
Matt	26:62	358	Answerest thou nothing? what *is it which* these witness against thee?	3	433
Matt	26:67	358	and others smote *him* with the palms of their hands	1	434
Matt	26:70	358	But he denied before *them* all, saying, I know not what thou sayest	1	435
Matt	26:71	359	another *maid* saw him, and said . . . This *fellow* was also with Jesus of Nazareth	2	437
Matt	26:73	359	. . . came unto *him* they that stood by . . . Surely thou also art *one* of them	2	439
Matt	26:74	359	he to curse and to swear, *saying*, I know not the man	1	440
Matt	27:2	360	. . . they led *him* away, and delivered him to Pontius Pilate the governor	1	441
Matt	27:4	361	And they said, What *is that* to us? see thou *to that.*	4	445
Matt	27:15	364	Now at *that* feast the governor was wont to release unto the people a prisoner	1	446
Matt	27:22	365	*They* all say unto him, Let him be crucified	1	447
Matt	27:24	366	. . . but *that* rather . . . washed *his* hands . . . see ye *to it*	4	451
Matt	27:25	366	Then answered all the people, and said, His blood *be* on us, and on our children	1	452
Matt	27:26	366	. . . and when he had scourged Jesus, he delivered *him* to be crucified	1	453
Matt	27:27	366	. . . and gathered unto him the whole band *of soldiers*	2	455
Matt	27:29	366	And when they had platted a crown of thorns, they put *it* upon his head	1	456
Matt	27:31	368	. . . and put his own raiment on him, and led him away to crucify *him*	1	457
Matt	27:34	369	. . . and when he had tasted *thereof*, he would not drink	1	458
Matt	27:40	370	Thou that destroyest the temple, and buildest *it* in three days, save thyself	1	459
Matt	27:41	371	Likewise also the chief priests mocking *him*, with the scribes and elders, said	1	460
Matt	27:47	372	Some of them that stood there, when they heard *that*, said, This *man* calleth for	2	462
Matt	27:48	372	. . . and filled *it* with vinegar, and put *it* on a reed, and gave him to drink	2	464
Matt	27:65	376	Pilate said unto them, Ye have a watch: go your way, make *it* as sure as ye can	1	465
Matt	28:1	376	. . . as it began to dawn toward the first *day* of the week	1	466
Matt	28:4	376	And for fear of him the keepers did shake, and became as dead *men*	1	467
Matt	28:13	379	Say ye, His disciples came by night, and stole him *away* while we *slept*	1	468
Matt	28:20	385	. . . lo, I am with you alway, *even* unto the end of the world. Amen	1	469

4.2 - TABLE OF ITALICIZED WORDS IN MARK

(Page numbers apply to the Combined Gospels with Notes)

Book	Verse	Page	Partial text with italicized words	Count Here	Count Total
Mark	1:11	186	And there came a voice from heaven, *saying*, Thou art my beloved Son	1	1
Mark	1:19	198	And . . . gone a little further thence, he saw James the *son* of Zebedee	1	2
Mark	1:24	205	Saying, Let *us* alone; what have we to do with thee, thou Jesus of Nazareth?	1	3
Mark	1:27	205	What thing is this? what new doctrine *is* this?	1	4
Mark	1:37	206	And when they had found him, they said unto him, All *men* seek for thee	1	5
Mark	1:41	207	And Jesus, moved with compassion, put forth *his* hand, and touched him	1	6
Mark	1:45	208	But he went out, and began to publish *it* much, and to blaze abroad the	1	7
Mark	2:1	209	And again he entered into Capernaum after *some* days	1	8
Mark	2:2	209	. . . insomuch that there was no room to receive *them*	1	9
Mark	2:4	209	. . . they uncovered the roof where he was: and when they had broken *it* up	1	10
Mark	2:7	209	Why doth this *man* thus speak blasphemies?	1	11
Mark	2:9	209	Whether is it easier to say to the sick of the palsy, *Thy* sins be forgiven	1	12

Mark	2:14	210	And as he passed by, he saw Levi the *son* of Alphæus sitting at the	1	13
Mark	2:17	211	When Jesus heard *it*, he saith unto them	1	14
Mark	3:5	221	And he stretched *it* out: and his hand was restored whole as the other	1	15
Mark	3:8	221	And from Jerusalem, and from Idumæa, and *from* beyond Jordan	1	16
Mark	3:13	222	And he goeth up into a mountain, and calleth *unto him* whom he would	2	18
Mark	3:17	222	And James the *son* of Zebedee, and John the brother of James	1	19
Mark	3:18	222	. . . and James the *son* of Alphæus, and Thaddæus, and Simon the Can	1	20
Mark	3:21	229	And when his friends heard *of it*, they went out to lay hold on him	2	22
Mark	3:23	229	And he called them *unto him*, and said unto them in parables	2	24
Mark	4:11	235	. . . but unto them that are without, all *these* things are done in parables	1	25
Mark	4:12	235	. . . lest at any time they should be converted, and *their* sins should be	1	26
Mark	4:20	236	. . . such as hear the word, and receive *it*, and bring forth fruit	1	27
Mark	4:31	236	*It is* like a grain of mustard seed, which, when it is sown in the earth	2	29
Mark	4:33	236	. . . many such . . . spake he the word unto them, as they were able to hear *it*.	1	30
Mark	5:3	238	Who had *his* dwelling among the tombs	1	31
Mark	5:4	238	. . . neither could any *man* tame him	1	32
Mark	5:7	238	What have I to do with thee, Jesus, *thou* Son of the most high God?	1	33
Mark	5:8	238	For he said unto him, Come out of the man, *thou* unclean spirit.	1	34
Mark	5:9	238	What *is* thy name? And he answered, saying, My name *is* Legion	2	36
Mark	5:14	239	And they that fed the swine fled, and told *it* in the city	1	37
Mark	5:16	239	And they that saw *it* told them . . . with the devil, and *also* concerning	2	39
Mark	5:20	239	. . . and all *men* did marvel	1	40
Mark	5:23	240	. . . *I pray thee*, come and lay thy hands on her, that she may be healed	3	43
Mark	5:24	240	And *Jesus* went with him	1	44
Mark	5:29	240	. . . and she felt in *her* body that she was healed of that plague	1	45
Mark	5:35	241	. . . there came from the ruler of the synagogue's *house certain* which said	2	47
Mark	5:42	241	. . . for she was *of the age* of twelve years	3	50
Mark	6:2	242	. . . hearing *him* were . . . this *man* these things? . . . what wisdom *is* this	3	53
Mark	6:5	242	. . . save that he laid his hands upon a few sick folk, and healed *them*	1	54
Mark	6:7	242	And he called *unto him* the twelve	2	56
Mark	6:8	242	. . . take nothing for *their* journey . . . no money in *their* purse	2	58
Mark	6:9	242	But *be* shod with sandals; and not put on two coats	1	59
Mark	6:13	242	. . . and anointed with oil many that were sick, and healed *them*	1	60
Mark	6:14	243	And king Herod heard *of him*; (for his name was spread abroad:)	2	62
Mark	6:16	244	But when Herod heard *thereof*, he said, It is John, whom I beheaded	1	63
Mark	6:21	244	high captains, and chief *estates* of Galilee	1	64
Mark	6:22	244	Ask of me whatsoever thou wilt, and I will give *it* thee	1	65
Mark	6:23	244	And he sware unto her, Whatsoever thou shalt ask of me, I will give *it* thee	1	66
Mark	6:26	244	And the king was exceeding sorry; *yet* for his oath's sake	1	67
Mark	6:29	244	And when his disciples heard *of it*, they came and took up his corpse	2	69
Mark	6:35	245	This is a desert place, and now the time *is* far passed	1	70
Mark	6:41	245	. . . and gave *them* to his disciples to set before them	1	71
Mark	6:52	247	For they considered not *the miracle* of the loaves: for their heart was	2	73
Mark	7:3	251	. . . except they wash *their* hands oft, eat not, holding the tradition of the	1	74
Mark	7:4	252	And *when they come* from the market . . . *as* the washing of cups	4	78
Mark	7:6	252	This people honoureth me with *their* lips, but their heart is far from me	1	79
Mark	7:7	252	. . . teaching *for* doctrines the commandments of men	1	80
Mark	7:8	252	. . . the tradition of men, *as* the washing of pots and cups	1	81
Mark	7:11	252	. . . *It is* Corban . . . mightest be profited by me; *he shall be free*	6	87
Mark	7:14	252	. . . the people *unto him* . . Hearken unto me every one *of you*	4	91
Mark	7:18	252	. . . from without entereth into the man, *it* cannot defile him	1	92
Mark	7:24	254	. . . and would have no man know *it*: but he could not be hid	1	93
Mark	7:25	254	For a *certain* woman, whose young daughter had an unclean spirit	1	94
Mark	7:27	254	. . . take the children's bread, and to cast *it* unto the dogs	1	95
Mark	7:36	255	. . . so much the more a great deal they published *it*;	1	96
Mark	8:1	256	Jesus called his disciples *unto him*, and saith unto them	2	98
Mark	8:4	256	From whence can a man satisfy these *men* with bread here in the wilderness?	1	99
Mark	8:6	256	. . . gave to his disciples to set before *them*; and they did set *them* before the	2	101
Mark	8:7	256	. . . and commanded to set them also before *them*	1	102
Mark	8:8	256	. . . they took up of the broken *meat* that was left seven baskets	1	103
Mark	8:14	256	Now *the disciples* had forgotten to take bread	2	105
Mark	8:15	256	Take heed, beware of the leaven of the Pharisees, and *of* the leaven of Herod	1	106
Mark	8:16	256	. . . saying, *It is* because we have no bread	2	108
Mark	8:17	256	. . . Jesus knew *it*, he saith unto them, Why reason ye, . . . ye have no bread?	1	109
Mark	8:25	258	After that he put *his* hands again upon his eyes, and made him look up	1	110
Mark	8:26	258	Neither go into the town, nor tell *it* to any in the town	1	111

Mark	8:28	258	And they answered, John the Baptist: but some *say*, Elias	1	112
Mark	8:31	260	. . . and *of* the chief priests, and scribes, and be killed, and after three days	1	113
Mark	8:34	260	And when he had called the people *unto him* with his disciples also	2	115
Mark	9:2	261	And after six days Jesus taketh *with him* Peter, and James, and John	2	117
Mark	9:14	263	And when he came to *his* disciples, he saw a great multitude	1	118
Mark	9:15	263	. . . were greatly amazed, and running to *him* saluted him	1	119
Mark	9:23	263	If thou canst believe, all things *are* possible to him that believeth	1	120
Mark	9:25	263	. . . saying unto him, *Thou* dumb and deaf spirit, I charge thee, come out of	1	121
Mark	9:26	263	And *the spirit* cried, and rent him sore, and came out of him: and he was as	2	123
Mark	9:30	264	. . . and he would not that any man should know *it*	1	124
Mark	9:34	265	. . . they had disputed among themselves, who *should be* the greatest	2	126
Mark	9:35	265	If any man desire to be first, *the same* shall be last of all, and servant of all	2	128
Mark	9:42	266	And whosoever shall offend one of *these* little ones that believe in me	1	129
Mark	9:50	266	Salt *is* good: but if the salt have lost his saltness, wherewith will ye season it?	1	130
Mark	10:2	282	. . . and asked him, Is it lawful for a man to put away *his* wife?	1	131
Mark	10:4	282	Moses suffered to write a bill of divorcement, and to put *her* away	1	132
Mark	10:10	282	. . . his disciples asked him again of the same *matter*	1	133
Mark	10:13	303	. . . and *his* disciples rebuked those that brought *them*	2	135
Mark	10:14	303	But when Jesus saw *it*, he was much displeased	1	136
Mark	10:16	304	And he took them up in his arms, put *his* hands upon them, and blessed	1	137
Mark	10:18	305	Why callest thou me good? *there is* none good but one, *that is*, God	4	141
Mark	10:27	305	With men *it is* impossible, but not with God: for with God . . . are possible	2	143
Mark	10:31	306	But many *that are* first shall be last; and the last first	2	145
Mark	10:33	307	*Saying*, Behold, we go up to Jerusalem; and the Son of man shall be delivered	1	146
Mark	10:40	308	. . . but *it shall be given to them* for whom it is prepared	6	152
Mark	10:41	308	And when the ten heard *it*, they began to be much . . . with James and John	1	153
Mark	10:42	309	But Jesus called them *to him*, and saith unto them	2	155
Mark	10:47	310	Jesus, *thou* son of David, have mercy on me	1	156
Mark	10:48	310	. . . but he cried the more a great deal, *Thou* son of David, have mercy on me	1	157
Mark	11:2	315	ye shall find a colt tied, whereon never man sat; loose him, and bring *him*	1	158
Mark	11:8	315	. . . and others cut down branches off the trees, and strawed *them* in the way	1	159
Mark	11:9	315	. . . cried, saying, Hosanna; Blessed *is* he that cometh in the name of the Lord	1	160
Mark	11:10	315	Blessed *be* the kingdom of our father David, that . . . in the name of the Lord	1	161
Mark	11:13	315	. . . he found nothing but leaves; for the time of figs was not *yet*	1	162
Mark	11:14	316	No man eat fruit of thee hereafter for ever. And his disciples heard *it*.	1	163
Mark	11:16	316	And would not suffer that any man should carry *any* vessel through the	1	164
Mark	11:18	318	And the scribes and chief priests heard *it*, and . . . how they might destroy him	1	165
Mark	11:24	318	. . . when ye pray, believe that ye receive *them*, and ye shall have *them*	2	167
Mark	11:30	319	The baptism of John, was *it* from heaven, or of men?	1	168
Mark	11:32	319	. . . for all *men* counted John, that he was a prophet indeed	1	169
Mark	12:1	320	A *certain* man planted a . . . , set an hedge about *it*, and digged *a place for*	5	174
Mark	12:3	320	And they caught *him*, and beat him, and sent *him* away empty	2	176
Mark	12:4	320	. . . and wounded *him* in the head, and sent *him* away shamefully handled	2	178
Mark	12:8	320	And they took him, and killed *him*, and cast *him* out of the vineyard	2	180
Mark	12:13	323	. . . certain of the Pharisees and of the Herodians, to catch him in *his* words	1	181
Mark	12:15	323	Why tempt ye me? bring me a penny, that I may see *it*	1	182
Mark	12:16	323	And they brought *it*. And he saith unto them, Whose *is* this image and	2	184
Mark	12:19	325	If a man's brother die, and leave *his* wife *behind him*, and leave no children	3	187
Mark	12:26	325	God spake unto him, saying, I *am* the God of Abraham, and the God of Isaac	1	188
Mark	12:29	325	The first of all the . . . *is*, Hear, O Israel; The Lord our God is one Lord:	1	189
Mark	12:30	326	. . . and with all thy strength: this *is* the first commandment	1	190
Mark	12:31	326	And the second *is* like, *namely* this, Thou shalt love thy neighbour as thyself	2	192
Mark	12:33	326	. . . and to love *his* neighbour as himself	1	193
Mark	12:34	326	And no man after that durst ask him *any question*.	2	195
Mark	12:37	326	. . . and whence is he *then* his son?	1	196
Mark	12:38	327	. . . which love to go in long clothing, and *love* salutations in the marketplaces	1	197
Mark	12:43	327	And he called *unto him* his disciples, and saith unto them	2	199
Mark	12:44	327	For all *they* did cast in of their abundance; but she . . . *even* all her living	2	201
Mark	13:1	331	Master, see what manner of stones and what buildings *are here!*	2	203
Mark	13:4	331	. . . and what *shall be* the sign when all these things shall be fulfilled?	2	205
Mark	13:5	331	Take heed lest any *man* deceive you	1	206
Mark	13:6	331	For many shall come in my name, saying, I am *Christ*; and shall deceive	1	207
Mark	13:7	331	. . . for *such things* must needs be; but the end *shall* not *be* yet	4	211
Mark	13:8	331	. . . these *are* the beginnings of sorrows	1	212
Mark	13:11	332	But when they shall lead *you*, and deliver you up	1	213
Mark	13:12	332	. . . and children shall rise up against *their* parents	1	214

Mark	13:13	332	And ye shall be hated of all *men* for my name's sake	1	215
Mark	13:15	332	. . . neither enter *therein*, to take any thing out of his house	1	216
Mark	13:19	332	For *in* those days shall be affliction	1	217
Mark	13:21	332	Lo, here *is* Christ; or, lo, *he is* there; believe *him* not	4	221
Mark	13:22	332	. . . to seduce, if *it were* possible, even the elect	2	223
Mark	13:29	332	know that it is nigh, *even* at the doors	1	224
Mark	13:32	332	But of that day and *that* hour knoweth no man	1	225
Mark	13:34	332	*For the Son of man is* as a man taking a far journey, who left his house	6	231
Mark	14:1	337	After two days was *the feast of* the passover, and . . . put *him* to death	4	235
Mark	14:2	337	Not on the feast *day*, lest there be an uproar of the people	1	236
Mark	14:3	338	and she brake the box, and poured *it* on his head	1	237
Mark	14:9	338	. . . the whole world, *this* also that she hath done shall be spoken of for a	1	238
Mark	14:11	338	And when they heard *it*, they were glad	1	239
Mark	14:15	339	And he will shew you a large upper room furnished *and* prepared	1	240
Mark	14:19	341	. . . one by one, *Is* it I? and another *said*, *Is* it I?	3	243
Mark	14:20	341	And he answered and said unto them, *It is* one of the twelve	2	245
Mark	14:22	342	Jesus took bread, and blessed, and brake *it*, and gave to them	1	246
Mark	14:23	342	. . . he gave *it* to them: and they all drank of it.	1	247
Mark	14:29	352	Although all shall be offended, yet *will* not I	1	248
Mark	14:30	352	. . this day, *even* in this night, before the cock crow twice, thou shalt deny	1	249
Mark	14:36	352	Abba, Father, all things *are* possible unto thee	1	250
Mark	14:38	352	The spirit truly *is* ready, but the flesh *is* weak	2	252
Mark	14:41	353	Sleep on now, and take *your* rest: it is enough, the hour is come	1	253
Mark	14:44	354	. . . take him, and lead *him* away safely	1	254
Mark	14:48	355	Are ye come out, as against a thief, with swords and *with* staves to take me?	1	255
Mark	14:51	355/6	. . . having a linen cloth cast about *his* naked *body*	2	257
Mark	14:60	357	Answerest thou nothing? what *is it which* these witness against thee?	3	260
Mark	14:69	359	This is *one* of them	1	261
Mark	14:70	359	. . . art *one* of them: for thou art a Galilæan, and thy speech agreeth *thereto*	2	263
Mark	14:71	359	. . . to curse and to swear, *saying*, I know not this man of whom ye speak	1	264
Mark	15:1	360	. . . and bound Jesus, and carried *him* away, and delivered *him* to Pilate	2	266
Mark	15:2	362	And he answering said unto him, Thou sayest *it*	1	267
Mark	15:6	364	. . . at *that* feast he released unto them one prisoner, whomsoever they	1	268
Mark	15:7	364	And there was *one* named Barabbas, *which lay* bound with them	3	271
Mark	15:8	364	And the multitude crying aloud began to desire *him to do* as he had ever done	3	274
Mark	15:12	365	What will ye then that I shall do *unto him* whom ye call the King of the Jews?	2	276
Mark	15:15	366	. . . *so* Pilate . . . delivered Jesus, when he had scourged *him*, to be crucified	2	278
Mark	15:17	366	. . . with purple, and platted a crown of thorns, and put it about his *head*	1	279
Mark	15:19	366	. . . and did spit upon him, and bowing *their* knees worshipped him	1	280
Mark	15:23	369	And they gave him to drink wine mingled with myrrh: but he received *it* not	1	281
Mark	15:29	371	Ah, thou that destroyest the temple, and buildest *it* in three days	1	282
Mark	15:35	372	. . . when they heard *it*, said, Behold, he calleth Elias	1	283
Mark	15:36	372	And one ran and filled a spunge full of vinegar, and put *it* on a reed	1	284
Mark	15:44	374	. . . and calling *unto him* the centurion, he asked him whether . . . any while	2	286
Mark	15:45	374	And when he knew *it* of the centurion, he gave the body to Joseph	1	287
Mark	15:47	374	And Mary Magdalene and Mary *the mother* of Joses beheld where he was	2	289
Mark	16:1	376	Mary Magdalene, and Mary the *mother* of James, and Salome	1	290
Mark	16:2	376	And very early in the morning the first *day* of the week	1	291
Mark	16:8	379	neither said they any thing to any *man*; for they were afraid	1	292
Mark	16:9	379	*Jesus* was risen early the first *day* of the week, he . . . to Mary Magdalene	2	294
Mark	16:10	379	*And* she went and told . . . that had been with him, as they mourned and wept	1	295
Mark	16:13	381	And they went and told *it* unto the residue: neither believed they them	1	296
Mark	16:20	385	the Lord working with *them*, and confirming the word with signs following	1	297

4.3 - TABLE OF ITALICIZED WORDS IN LUKE

(Page numbers apply to the Combined Gospels with Notes)

				Count	
Book	**Verse**	**Page**	**Partial text with italicized words**	**Here**	**Total**
Luke	1:5	176	. . . his wife *was* of the daughters of Aaron, and her name *was* Elisabeth	2	2
Luke	1:7	176	Elisabeth was barren, and they both were *now* well stricken in years	1	3
Luke	1:12	176	And when Zacharias saw *him*, he was troubled, and fear fell upon him	1	4
Luke	1:25	177	Thus hath the Lord dealt with me in the days wherein he looked on *me*	1	5
Luke	1:27	177	. . . and the virgin's name *was* Mary	1	6
Luke	1:28	177	Hail, *thou that art* highly favoured, the Lord *is* with thee: blessed *art* thou	5	11
Luke	1:29	177	And when she saw *him*, she was troubled at his saying	1	12

Luke	1:42	178	Blessed *art* thou among women, and blessed *is* the fruit of thy womb	2	14
Luke	1:43	178	And whence *is* this to me, that the mother of my Lord should come to me?	1	15
Luke	1:45	178	And blessed *is* she that believed	1	16
Luke	1:49	178	For he that is mighty hath done to me great things; and holy *is* his name	1	17
Luke	1:50	178	And his mercy *is* on them that fear him from generation to generation	1	18
Luke	1:52	178	He hath put down the mighty from *their* seats	1	19
Luke	1:54	179	He hath holpen his servant Israel, in remembrance of *his* mercy	1	20
Luke	1:60	179	And his mother answered and said, Not *so*; but he shall be called John	1	21
Luke	1:64	179	and his tongue *loosed*, and he spake, and praised God	1	22
Luke	1:66	179	And all they that heard *them* laid *them* up in their hearts, saying	2	24
Luke	1:68	179	Blessed *be* the Lord God of Israel; for he hath visited and redeemed his	1	25
Luke	1:72	179	To perform the mercy *promised* to our fathers, and to remember his holy	1	26
Luke	1:79	179	To give light to them that sit in darkness and *in* the shadow of death	1	27
Luke	2:2	180	*And* this taxing was first made when Cyrenius was governor of Syria	1	28
Luke	2:12	180	And this *shall be* a sign unto you; Ye shall find the babe wrapped	2	30
Luke	2:17	181	And when they had seen *it*, they made known abroad the saying	1	31
Luke	2:18	181	And all they that heard *it* wondered at those things which were told them	1	32
Luke	2:19	181	But Mary kept all these things, and pondered *them* in her heart	1	33
Luke	2:22	181	they brought him to Jerusalem, to present *him* to the Lord	1	34
Luke	2:25	181	. . . whose name *was* Simeon; and the same man *was* just and devout	2	36
Luke	2:34	181	Behold, this *child* is set for the fall and rising again of many in Israel	1	37
Luke	2:37	182	And she *was* a widow of about . . . . . and four years, which . . . served *God*	2	39
Luke	2:43	183	Jesus tarried behind in Jerusalem; and Joseph and his mother knew not *of it*	2	41
Luke	2:44	183	. . . and they sought him among *their* kinsfolk and acquaintance	1	42
Luke	3:5	185	. . . the crooked shall be made straight, and the rough ways *shall be* made	2	44
Luke	3:8	185	We have Abraham to *our* father	1	45
Luke	3:14	185	And the soldiers likewise demanded of him, saying, And what shall we do?	1	46
Luke	3:16	185	John answered, saying unto *them* all, I indeed baptize you with water	1	47
Luke	3:17	185	Whose fan *is* in his hand	1	48
Luke	3:23	187	. . . the son of Joseph, which was *the son* of Heli	2	50
Luke	3:24	187	. . . *the son* of Matthat , Levi, Melchi, Janna ,Joseph,	10	60
Luke	3:25	187	. . . *the son* of Mattathias, Amos, Naum, Esli, Nagge,	10	70
Luke	3:26	187	. . . *the son* of Maath, Mattathias, Semei, Joseph, Juda,	10	80
Luke	3:27	187	. . . *the son* of Joanna, Rhesa, Zorobabel, Salathiel, Neri,	10	90
Luke	3:28	188	. . . *the son* of Melchi, Addi, Cosam, Elmodam, Er,	10	100
Luke	3:29	188	. . . *the son* of Jose, Eliezer, Jorim, Matthat, Levi,	10	110
Luke	3:30	188	. . . *the son* of Simeon, Juda, Joseph, Jonan, Eliakim,	10	120
Luke	3:31	188	. . . *the son* of Melea, Menan, Mattatha, Nathan, David,	10	130
Luke	3:32	188	. . . *the son* of Jesse, Obed, Booz, Salmon, Naasson,	10	140
Luke	3:33	188	. . . *the son* of Aminadab, Aram, Esrom, Phares, Juda,	10	150
Luke	3:34	188	. . . Jacob, Isaac, Abraham, Thara, Nachor,	10	160
Luke	3:35	188	. . . *the son* of Saruch, Ragau, Phalec, Heber, Sala,	10	170
Luke	3:36	188	. . . *the son* of Cainan, Arphaxad, Sem, Noe, Lamech,	10	180
Luke	3:38	188	. . . *the son* of Enos, Seth, Adam, which was *the son* of God.	8	188
Luke	4:11	192	And in *their* hands they shall bear thee up, lest at any time thou dash thy foot	1	189
Luke	4:18	193	The Spirit of the Lord *is* upon me, because he hath anointed me to preach	1	190
Luke	4:20	193	And he closed the book, and he gave *it* again to the minister, and sat down	1	191
Luke	4:26	193	Sarepta, *a city* of Sidon, unto a woman *that was* a widow	4	195
Luke	4:34	205	Saying, Let *us* alone; what have we to do with thee, *thou* Jesus of Nazareth?	2	197
Luke	4:36	205	What a word *is* this!	1	198
Luke	4:41	206	And he rebuking *them* suffered them not to speak: for they knew that he was	1	199
Luke	5:2	207	. . . the fishermen were gone out of them, and were washing *their* nets	1	200
Luke	5:7	207	And they beckoned unto *their* partners, which were in the other ship	1	201
Luke	5:8	207	When Simon Peter saw *it*, he fell down at Jesus' knees, saying, Depart from me	1	202
Luke	5:10	207	And so *was* also James, and John, the sons of Zebedee	1	203
Luke	5:12	208	. . . behold a man full of leprosy: who seeing Jesus fell on *his* face, and	1	204
Luke	5:13	208	And he put forth *his* hand, and touched him, saying, I will: be thou clean	1	205
Luke	5:17	210	. . . and the power of the Lord was *present* to heal them	1	206
Luke	5:18	210	. . . and they sought *means* to bring him in, and to lay *him* before him	2	208
Luke	5:19	210	. . . could not find by what *way* they . . . let him down . . . with *his* couch	2	210
Luke	5:33	212	. . . and likewise *the disciples* of the Pharisees; but thine eat and drink?	2	212
Luke	5:36	212	. . . and the piece that was *taken* out of the new agreeth not with the old	1	213
Luke	5:39	212	No man also having drunk old *wine* straightway desireth new: . . . The old is	1	214
Luke	6:1	220	and his disciples plucked the ears of corn, and did eat, rubbing *them* in *their*	2	216
Luke	6:9	221	. . . to save life, or to destroy *it*?	1	217
Luke	6:13	222	And when it was day, he called *unto him* his disciples	2	219

Luke	6:15	222	James the *son* of Alphæus, and Simon called Zelotes	1	220
Luke	6:16	222	And Judas *the brother* of James	2	222
Luke	6:19	223	for there went virtue out of him, and healed *them* all	1	223
Luke	6:20	223	Blessed *be* ye poor: for yours is the kingdom of God	2	225
Luke	6:21	223	Blessed *are ye* that hunger now: . . . Blessed *are ye* that weep now	4	229
Luke	6:22	223	. . . separate you *from their company*, and shall reproach *you*	4	233
Luke	6:23	223	. . . for, behold, your reward *is* great in heaven	1	234
Luke	6:29	223	. . . on the *one* cheek offer also the other . . . and forbid not *to take thy* coat	4	238
Luke	6:30	223	. . . and of him that taketh away thy goods ask *them* not again	1	239
Luke	6:34	223	And if ye lend *to them* of whom ye hope to receive, what thank have ye?	2	241
Luke	6:35	223	. . . be the children of the Highest: for he is kind unto the unthankful and *to* the	1	242
Luke	7:8	225	Come, and he cometh; and to my servant, Do this, and he doeth *it*	1	243
Luke	7:14	225	and they that bare *him* stood still	1	244
Luke	7:19	225	And John calling *unto him* two of his disciples sent *them* to Jesus	3	247
Luke	7:21	225	. . . many of *their* infirmities and plagues . . . many *that were* blind he gave	3	250
Luke	7:23	225	And blessed is *he*, whosoever shall not be offended in me	1	251
Luke	7:27	226	This is *he*, of whom it is written, Behold, I send my messenger before thy face	1	252
Luke	7:29	226	And all the people that heard *him*, and the publicans	1	253
Luke	7:37	226	. . . when she knew that *Jesus* sat at meat in the Pharisee's house	1	254
Luke	7:38	226	. . . behind *him* weeping . . . did wipe *them* with the hairs. . . anointed *them*	3	257
Luke	7:39	226	. . . bidden him saw *it* . . . of woman *this is* that toucheth him	3	260
Luke	7:43	226	I suppose that *he*, to whom he forgave most	1	261
Luke	7:44	226	. . . and wiped *them* with the hairs of her head	1	262
Luke	7:47	226	. . . to whom little is forgiven, *the same* loveth little	2	264
Luke	8:1	227	. . . and the twelve *were* with him	1	265
Luke	8:13	228	They on the rock *are they*, which, when they hear, receive the word with joy	2	267
Luke	8:14	228	. . . cares and riches and pleasures of *this* life, and bring no fruit to perfection	1	268
Luke	8:15	228	. . . keep *it*, and bring forth fruit with patience	1	269
Luke	8:16	228	. . . or putteth *it* under a bed; but setteth *it* on a candlestick	2	271
Luke	8:17	228	. . . neither *any thing* hid, that shall not be known and come abroad	2	273
Luke	8:19	231	Then came to him *his* mother and his brethren	1	274
Luke	8:20	231	And it was told him *by certain* which said	2	276
Luke	8:23	237	and they were filled *with water*, and were in jeopardy	2	278
Luke	8:27	237	. . . neither abode in *any* house, but in the tombs	1	279
Luke	8:28	237	What have I to do with thee, Jesus, *thou* Son of God most high?	1	280
Luke	8:34	238	When they that fed *them* saw what was done . . . went and told *it* in the city	2	282
Luke	8:36	238	They also which saw *it* told them by what means he . . . was healed	1	283
Luke	8:40	239	. . . the people *gladly* received him: for they were all waiting for him	1	284
Luke	8:44	239	Came behind *him*, and touched the border of his garment	1	285
Luke	8:45	239	Master, the multitude throng thee and press *thee*, and . . . , Who touched me?	1	286
Luke	8:49	240	. . . there cometh one from the ruler of the synagogue's *house*, saying to him	1	287
Luke	8:50	240	But when Jesus heard *it*, he answered him, saying, Fear not	1	288
Luke	9:3	242	Take nothing for *your* journey, neither staves, nor scrip, neither bread	1	289
Luke	9:11	245	And the people, when they knew *it*, followed him	1	290
Luke	9:19	258	. . . but some *say*, Elias; and others *say*, that one of the old prophets is	2	292
Luke	9:21	259	And he straitly charged them, and commanded *them* to tell no man that thing	1	293
Luke	9:23	259	And he said to *them* all, If any *man* will come after me, let him deny himself	2	295
Luke	9:26	259	. . . when he shall come in his own glory, and *in his* Father's, and of the holy	2	297
Luke	9:29	260	the fashion of his countenance was altered, and his raiment *was* white *and*	2	299
Luke	9:36	261	And they kept *it* close, and told no man in those days	1	300
Luke	9:42	264	And as he was yet a-coming, the devil threw him down, and tare *him*	1	301
Luke	9:50	266	And Jesus said unto him, Forbid *him* not: for he that is not against us is for	1	302
Luke	9:54	269	And when his disciples James and John saw *this*, they said, Lord	1	303
Luke	9:56	269	For the Son of man is not come to destroy men's lives, but to save *them*	1	304
Luke	9:57	269	. . . as they went in the way, a certain *man* said unto him, Lord	1	305
Luke	9:58	269	. . . birds of the air *have* nests; but the Son of man hath not where to lay *his*	2	307
Luke	10:2	269	The harvest truly *is* great, but the labourers *are* few	1	308
Luke	10:5	270	And into whatsoever house ye enter, first say, Peace *be* to this house	1	309
Luke	10:22	271	. . . who the Father is, but the Son, and *he* to whom the Son will reveal *him*	2	311
Luke	10:23	271	. . . unto *his* disciples . . . Blessed *are* the eyes which see the things	2	313
Luke	10:24	271	. . . have not seen *them* . . . and have not heard *them*.	2	315
Luke	10:30	271	A certain *man* . . . and wounded *him* . . . leaving *him* half dead.	3	318
Luke	10:32	271	. . . came and looked *on him*, and passed by on the other side	2	320
Luke	10:33	271	But a certain Samaritan . . had compassion *on him*	1	321
Luke	10:34	271	And went to *him*, and bound up his wounds	1	322
Luke	10:35	271	. . . he took out two pence, and gave *them* to the host	1	323

Luke	11:11	281	. . . or *if he ask* a fish, will he for a fish give him a serpent?	2	325
Luke	11:13	281	. . . shall *your* heavenly Father give the Holy Spirit to them that ask him?	1	326
Luke	11:16	281	And others, tempting *him*, sought of him a sign from heaven	1	327
Luke	11:17	281	. . . and a house *divided* against a house falleth	1	328
Luke	11:19	281	. . . by whom do your sons cast *them* out?	1	329
Luke	11:25	282	And when he cometh, he findeth *it* swept and garnished	1	330
Luke	11:26	282	. . . and taketh *to him* seven other spirits . . . and the last *state* of that man	3	333
Luke	11:27	282	Blessed *is* the womb that bare thee, and the paps which thou hast sucked	1	334
Luke	11:28	282	But he said, Yea rather, blessed *are* they that hear the word of God, and	1	335
Luke	11:31	283	. . . and, behold, a greater than Solomon *is* here	1	336
Luke	11:32	284	and, behold, a greater than Solomon *is* here	1	337
Luke	11:33	284	No man, when he hath lighted a candle, putteth *it* in a secret place	1	338
Luke	11:34	284	but when *thine eye* is evil, thy body also *is* full of darkness	3	341
Luke	11:36	284	If thy whole body therefore *be* full of light, having no part dark	1	342
Luke	11:38	284	And when the Pharisee saw *it*, he marvelled that he had not first washed	1	343
Luke	11:40	284	*Ye* fools, did not he that made that which is without make . . . . within also?	1	344
Luke	11:44	284	. . . and the men that walk over *them* are not aware *of them*	3	347
Luke	11:46	284	And he said, Woe unto you also, *ye* lawyers!	1	348
Luke	11:49	285	I will send them prophets and apostles, and *some* of them they shall slay	1	349
Luke	11:53	285	. . . the scribes and the Pharisees began to urge *him* vehemently	1	350
Luke	12:11	286	And when they bring you unto the synagogues, and *unto* magistrates	1	351
Luke	12:19	286	. . . take thine ease, eat, drink, *and* be merry	1	352
Luke	12:20	286	*Thou* fool, this night thy soul shall be required of thee	1	353
Luke	12:21	286	So *is* he that layeth up treasure for himself, and is not rich toward God	1	354
Luke	12:23	286	The life is more than meat, and the body *is more* than raiment	2	356
Luke	12:28	286	how much more *will he clothe* you, O ye of little faith?	3	359
Luke	12:35	287	Let your loins be girded about, and *your* lights burning	1	360
Luke	12:37	287	Blessed *are* those servants, whom the lord when he cometh shall find watch	1	361
Luke	12:38	287	. . .if he shall come in the second watch, or . . . third watch, and find *them* so	1	362
Luke	12:42	287	. . . whom *his* lord shall make ruler . . . to give *them their* portion of meat	3	365
Luke	12:43	287	Blessed *is* that servant, whom his lord when he cometh shall find so doing	1	366
Luke	12:46	287	. . . he looketh not for *him*, and at an hour when he is not aware	1	367
Luke	12:47	287	. . . and prepared not *himself* . . . shall be beaten with many *stripes*	2	369
Luke	12:48	287	But he that knew not . . . shall be beaten with few *stripes*	1	370
Luke	12:55	288	And when *ye see* the south wind blow, ye say, There will be heat	2	372
Luke	12:56	288	*Ye* hypocrites, ye can discern the face of the sky and of the earth	1	373
Luke	12:58	288	When thou goest with thine adversary to the magistrate, *as thou art* in the way	3	376
Luke	13:6	288	A certain *man* had a fig tree planted in his vineyard	1	377
Luke	13:8	289	Lord, let it alone this year also, till I shall dig about it, and dung *it*	1	378
Luke	13:9	289	And if it bear fruit, *well*: and if not, *then* after that thou shalt cut it down	2	380
Luke	13:11	289	. . . and was bowed together, and could in no wise lift up *herself*	1	381
Luke	13:12	289	And when Jesus saw her, he called *her to him*, and said unto her	3	384
Luke	13:13	289	And he laid *his* hands on her: and immediately she was made straight	1	385
Luke	13:15	289	. . . said, Thou hypocrite . . . loose his ox or his ass . . . lead him away to . . .	3	388
Luke	13:27	290	. . . depart from me, all *ye* workers of iniquity	1	389
Luke	13:28	291	. . . in the kingdom of God, and you *yourselves* thrust out	1	390
Luke	13:29	291	. . . and *from* the west, and from the north, and *from* the south	2	392
Luke	13:32	291	I do cures to-day and to-morrow, and the third *day* I shall be perfected	1	393
Luke	13:33	291	Nevertheless I must walk to-day, and to-morrow, and the *day* following	1	394
Luke	13:34	291	. . . as a hen *doth gather* her brood under *her* wings, and ye would not!	3	397
Luke	13:35	291	. . . until *the time* come when ye shall say, Blessed *is* he that cometh in . . .	3	400
Luke	14:4	291	And they held their peace. And he took *him*, and healed him, and let him go	1	401
Luke	14:8	292	When thou art bidden of any *man* to a wedding, sit not down . . . room;	1	402
Luke	14:12	292	. . . neither thy kinsmen, nor *thy* rich neighbours; lest they also bid thee	1	403
Luke	14:15	292	Blessed *is* he that shall eat bread in the kingdom of God	1	404
Luke	14:18	292	And they all with one *consent* began to make excuse	1	405
Luke	14:23	293	. . . and compel *them* to come in, that my house may be filled	1	406
Luke	14:26	293	If any *man* come to me, and hate not his father, and mother, and . . .	1	407
Luke	14:28	293	. . . and counteth the cost, whether he have *sufficient* to finish *it*?	2	409
Luke	14:29	293	. . . and is not able to finish *it*, all that behold *it* begin to mock him	2	411
Luke	14:34	293	Salt *is* good: but if the salt have lost his savour, . . . shall it be seasoned?	1	412
Luke	14:35	293	It is neither fit for the land, nor yet for the dunghill; *but* men cast it out	1	413
Luke	15:5	293	And when he hath found *it*, he layeth *it* on his shoulders, rejoicing	2	415
Luke	15:6	293	And when he cometh home, he calleth together *his* friends and neighbours	1	416
Luke	15:8	294	. . . and sweep the house, and seek diligently till she find *it*?	1	417
Luke	15:9	294	And when she hath found *it*, she calleth *her* friends and *her* neighbours	3	420

Luke	15:12	294	. . . said to *his* father . . . that falleth *to me*. And he divided unto them *his*	4	424
Luke	15:22	295	. . . and put *it* on him; and put a ring on his hand, and shoes on *his* feet	2	426
Luke	15:23	295	And bring hither the fatted calf, and kill *it*; and let us eat, and be merry	1	427
Luke	15:29	295	And he answering said to *his* father, Lo, these many years do I serve thee	1	428
Luke	16:5	295	So he called every one of his lord's debtors *unto him*, and said unto the first	2	430
Luke	16:11	296	. . . who will commit to your trust the true *riches*?	1	431
Luke	16:16	296	The law and the prophets *were* until John: since . . . the kingdom of God is	1	432
Luke	16:18	296	. . . whosoever marrieth her that is put away from *her* husband committeth	1	433
Luke	16:26	297	. . . neither can they pass to us, that would *come from* thence	2	435
Luke	17:1	297	. . . offences will come: but woe *unto him*, through whom they come!	2	437
Luke	17:13	298	And they lifted up *their* voices, and said, Jesus, Master, have mercy on us	1	438
Luke	17:14	298	And when he saw *them*, he said unto them, Go shew yourselves unto the	1	439
Luke	17:16	298	And fell down on *his* face at his feet, giving him thanks	1	440
Luke	17:17	298	And Jesus . . . said, Were there not ten cleansed? but where *are* the nine?	1	441
Luke	17:22	299	. . . ye shall desire . . . of the days of the Son of man, and ye shall not see *it*	1	442
Luke	17:23	299	. . . go not after *them*, nor follow *them*	2	444
Luke	17:24	299	. . . of the one *part* under heaven, shineth unto the other *part* under	2	446
Luke	17:29	299	. . . it rained fire and brimstone from heaven, and destroyed *them* all	1	447
Luke	17:34	299	. . . in that night there shall be two *men* in one bed	1	448
Luke	17:35	299	Two *women* shall be grinding together; the one shall be taken	1	449
Luke	17:36	299	Two *men* shall be in the field; the one shall be taken, and the other left	1	450
Luke	17:37	300	Wheresoever the body *is*, thither will the eagles be gathered together	1	451
Luke	18:1	300	And he spake a parable unto them *to this end*, that men ought always to pray	3	454
Luke	18:11	300	I thank thee, that I am not as other men *are*, extortioners	1	455
Luke	18:13	300	would not lift up so much as *his* eyes unto heaven	1	456
Luke	18:14	300	I tell you, this man went down to his house justified *rather* than the other	1	457
Luke	18:15	303	. . . but when *his* disciples saw *it*, they rebuked them	2	459
Luke	18:16	304	But Jesus called them *unto him*, and said, Suffer little children to come	2	461
Luke	18:19	304	Why callest thou me good? none *is* good, save one, *that is*, God	3	464
Luke	18:26	305	And they that heard *it* said, Who then can be saved?	1	465
Luke	18:31	307	Then he took *unto him* the twelve, and said unto them	2	467
Luke	18:33	308	And they shall scourge *him*, and put him to death: and the third day he	1	468
Luke	18:38	309	And he cried, saying, Jesus, *thou* son of David, have mercy on me	1	469
Luke	18:39	309	. . . he cried so much the more, *Thou* son of David, have mercy on me	1	470
Luke	18:43	309	and all the people, when they saw *it*, gave praise unto God	1	471
Luke	19:1	309	And *Jesus* entered and passed through Jericho	1	472
Luke	19:2	309	And, behold, *there was* a man named Zacchaeus, which was the chief	2	474
Luke	19:4	309	. . . climbed up into a sycomore tree to see him: for he was to pass that *way*	1	475
Luke	19:7	310	And when they saw *it*, they all murmured	1	476
Luke	19:8	310	I restore *him* fourfold	1	477
Luke	19:14	311	We will not have this *man* to reign over us	1	478
Luke	19:20	311	Lord, behold, *here is* thy pound, which I have kept laid up in a napkin	2	480
Luke	19:22	311	Out of thine own mouth will I judge thee, *thou* wicked servant	1	481
Luke	19:24	311	Take from him the pound, and give *it* to him that hath ten pounds	1	482
Luke	19:27	311	But those mine enemies . . . bring hither, and slay *them* before me	1	483
Luke	19:29	314	. . . at the mount called *the mount* of Olives, he sent two of his disciples	2	485
Luke	19:30	314	Go ye into the village over against *you* . . . tied . . . and bring *him hither*	3	488
Luke	19:31	314	And if any man ask you, Why do ye loose *him*? thus shall ye say unto him	1	489
Luke	19:38	314	Blessed *be* the King that cometh in the name of the Lord	1	490
Luke	19:42	315	. . . the things *which belong* unto thy peace! but now they are hid from	2	492
Luke	20:1	319	And it came to pass, *that* on one of. . . the scribes came upon *him* with the	2	494
Luke	20:7	319	And they answered, that they could not tell whence *it was*	2	496
Luke	20:10	320	. . . but the husbandmen beat him, and sent *him* away empty	1	497
Luke	20:11	320	. . . and entreated *him* shamefully, and sent *him* away empty	2	499
Luke	20:12	320	And again he sent a third: and they wounded him also, and cast *him* out	1	500
Luke	20:13	320	I will send my beloved son: it may be they will reverence *him* when they	1	501
Luke	20:15	320	So they cast him out of the vineyard, and killed *him*	1	502
Luke	20:16	320	And when they heard *it*, they said, God forbid	1	503
Luke	20:20	323	And they watched *him*, and sent forth spies, which should feign themselves	1	504
Luke	20:21	323	. . . neither acceptest thou the person *of any*, but teachest the way of God truly	2	506
Luke	20:27	324	Then came to *him* certain of the Sadducees, which deny that there is any r	1	507
Luke	20:40	326	And after that they durst not ask him any *question at all*	3	510
Luke	21:6	329	*As for* these things which ye behold, the days will come	2	512
Luke	21:7	330	. . . and what sign *will there be* when these things shall come to pass?	3	515
Luke	21:8	330	for many shall come in my name, saying, I am *Christ*; and the time draweth	1	516
Luke	21:9	330	. . . but the end *is* not by and by	1	517

Luke	21:12	330	. . . and persecute *you*, delivering *you* up to the synagogues	2	519
Luke	21:14	330	Settle *it* therefore in your hearts, not to meditate before what ye shall answer	1	520
Luke	21:16	330	. . . and *some* of you shall they cause to be put to death	1	521
Luke	21:17	330	And ye shall be hated of all *men* for my name's sake	1	522
Luke	21:34	330	. . . and *so* that day come upon you unawares	1	523
Luke	21:37	330	. . . and abode in the mount that is called *the mount* of Olives	2	525
Luke	22:17	330	And he took the cup, and gave thanks, and said, Take this, and divide *it*	1	526
Luke	22:19	330	And he took bread, and gave thanks, and brake *it*	1	527
Luke	22:20	330	This cup *is* the new testament in my blood, which is shed for you	1	528
Luke	22:21	330	But, behold, the hand of him that betrayeth me *is* with me on the table	1	529
Luke	22:26	330	But ye *shall* not *be* so	2	531
Luke	22:27	330	For whether *is* greater . . . *is* not he that sitteth at meat?	2	533
Luke	22:31	330	Simon, behold, Satan hath desired *to have* you, that he may sift *you* as	3	536
Luke	22:36	331	But now, he that hath a purse, let him take *it*, and likewise *his* scrip	2	538
Luke	22:38	331	And they said, Lord, behold, here *are* two swords	1	539
Luke	22:54	356	Then took they him, and led *him*, and brought him into the high priest's	1	540
Luke	22:59	359	Of a truth this *fellow* also was with him: for he is a Galilæan	1	541
Luke	22:63	360	And the men that held Jesus mocked him, and smote *him*	1	542
Luke	22:68	360	And if I also ask *you*, ye will not answer me, nor let *me* go	2	544
Luke	23:2	361	We found this *fellow* perverting the nation, and . . . give tribute to Caesar	1	545
Luke	23:3	362	And he answered him and said, Thou sayest *it*	1	546
Luke	23:4	362	Then said Pilate to the chief priests and *to* the people, I find no fault in	1	547
Luke	23:8	363	. . . for he was desirous to see him of a long *season*	1	548
Luke	23:11	363	Herod with his men of war set him at nought, and mocked *him*	1	549
Luke	23:14	363	I, having examined *him* before you, have found no fault in this man	1	550
Luke	23:16	364	I will therefore chastise him, and release *him*	1	551
Luke	23:18	365	Away with this *man*, and release unto us Barabbas	1	552
Luke	23:21	365	But they cried, saying, Crucify *him*, crucify him	1	553
Luke	23:22	365	I will therefore chastise him, and let *him* go	1	554
Luke	23:26	368	. . . and on him they laid the cross, that he might bear *it* after Jesus	1	555
Luke	23:29	369	Blessed *are* the barren, and the wombs that never bare	1	556
Luke	23:35	370	And the rulers also with them derided *him*, saying, He saved others	1	557
Luke	23:50	374	. . . behold, *there was* a man named Joseph, a counsellor; *and he was* a	5	562
Luke	23:51	374	. . . *he was* of Arimathæa, a city of the Jews . . . waited for the	2	564
Luke	23:52	374	This *man* went unto Pilate, and begged the body of Jesus	1	565
Luke	24:1	376	. . . the first *day* of the week . . . and certain *others* with them	2	567
Luke	24:5	378	And as they were afraid, and bowed down *their* faces to the earth	1	568
Luke	24:10	379	. . . Mary *the mother* of James, and other *women that were* with them	5	573
Luke	24:13	379	. . . which was from Jerusalem *about* threescore furlongs	1	574
Luke	24:15	380	while they communed *together* and reasoned	1	575
Luke	24:17	380	What manner of communications *are* these that ye have one to another	1	576
Luke	24:24	380	. . . and found *it* even so as the women had said: but him they saw not	1	577
Luke	24:30	380	. . . he took bread, and blessed *it*, and brake, and gave to them	1	578
Luke	24:35	381	And they told what things *were done* in the way	2	580
Luke	24:36	381	Peace *be* unto you	1	581
Luke	24:40	381	And when he had thus spoken, he shewed them *his* hands and *his* feet	2	583
Luke	24:43	382	And he took *it*, and did eat before them	1	584
Luke	24:44	382	These *are* the words . . . *in* the prophets, and *in* the psalms, concerning me	3	587

4.4 - TABLE OF ITALICIZED WORDS IN JOHN

(Page numbers apply to the Combined Gospels with Notes)

Book	Verse	Page	Partial text with italicized words	Count Here	Count Total
John	1:6	175	There was a man sent from God, whose name *was* John	1	1
John	1:7	175	. . . that all *men* through him might believe	1	2
John	1:8	175	He was not that Light, but *was sent* to bear witness of that Light	2	4
John	1:9	175	*That* was the true Light, which lighteth every man that cometh into the	1	5
John	1:12	175	. . . *even* to them that believe on his name	1	6
John	1:17	186	For the law was given by Moses, *but* grace and truth came by Jesus Christ	1	7
John	1:18	187	. . . the only . . . Son, . . . in the bosom of the Father, he hath declared *him*	1	8
John	1:23	187	I *am* the voice of one crying in the wilderness	1	9
John	1:40	189	One of the two which heard John *speak*, and followed him, was Andrew	1	10
John	2:5	189	Whatsoever he saith unto you, do *it*	1	11
John	2:8	190	And they bare *it*	1	12
John	2:10	190	. . . then that which is worse; *but* thou hast kept the good wine until now	1	13

John	2:23	190	Now when he was in Jerusalem at the passover, in the feast *day*	1	14
John	2:24	190	But Jesus did not commit himself unto them, because he knew all *men*	1	15
John	3:5	191	Except a man be born of water and *of* the Spirit	1	16
John	3:12	191	. . . how shall ye believe, if I tell you *of* heavenly things?	1	17
John	3:13	191	. . . but he that came down from heaven, *even* the Son of man which is	1	18
John	3:25	194	Then there arose a question between *some* of John's disciples	1	19
John	3:26	194	. . . behold, the same baptizeth, and all *men* come to him	1	20
John	3:30	195	He must increase, but I *must* decrease	1	21
John	3:34	195	. . . for God giveth not the Spirit by measure *unto him*	2	23
John	4:6	195	. . . being wearied with *his* journey . . . *and* it was about the sixth hour	2	25
John	4:24	196	God *is* a Spirit: and they that worship him must worship *him* in spirit	2	27
John	4:26	196	Jesus saith unto her, I that speak unto thee am *he*	1	28
John	4:33	196	Hath any man brought him *ought* to eat?	1	29
John	4:35	197	Say not ye, There are yet four months, and *then* cometh harvest?	1	30
John	4:42	197	. . . for we have heard *him* ourselves	1	31
John	4:51	198	. . . his servants met him, and told *him*, saying, Thy son liveth	1	32
John	4:53	198	So the father knew that *it was* at the same hour	2	34
John	4:54	198	This *is* again the second miracle *that* Jesus did	2	36
John	5:2	217	Now there is at Jerusalem by the sheep *market* a pool	1	37
John	5:6	217	. . . and knew that he had been now a long time *in that case*	3	40
John	5:10	218	It is the sabbath day: it is not lawful for thee to carry *thy* bed	1	41
John	5:13	218	Jesus had conveyed himself away, a multitude being in *that* place	1	42
John	5:21	218	. . . the Father raiseth up the dead, and quickeneth *them*	1	43
John	5:23	218	That all *men* should honour the Son	1	44
John	5:36	219	But I have greater witness than *that* of John	1	45
John	5:44	219	. . . and seek not the honour that *cometh* from God only?	1	46
John	5:45	219	. . . there is *one* that accuseth you, *even* Moses, in whom ye trust	2	48
John	6:1	246	. . . things Jesus went over the sea of Galilee, which is *the sea* of Tiberias	2	50
John	6:5	246	Jesus then lifted up *his* eyes, and saw a great company come unto him	1	51
John	6:13	246	Therefore they gathered *them* together	1	52
John	6:16	247	16 And when even was *now* come, his disciples went down unto the sea	1	53
John	6:22	249	. . . but *that* his disciples were gone away alone	1	54
John	6:52	250	. . . How can this man give us *his* flesh to eat?	1	55
John	6:60	251	. . . they had heard *this*, said, This is an hard saying; who can hear it?	1	56
John	6:62	251	*What* and if ye shall see the Son of man ascend up where he was before?	1	57
John	6:63	251	. . . the words that I speak unto you, *they* are spirit, and *they* are life	2	59
John	6:66	251	. . . *time* many of his disciples went back, and walked no more with him	1	60
John	6:71	251	He spake of Judas Iscariot *the son* of Simon	2	62
John	7:4	268	For *there is* no man *that* doeth any thing in secret	3	65
John	7:9	269	When he had said these words unto them, he abode *still* in Galilee	1	66
John	7:17	272	. . . whether it be of God, or *whether* I speak of myself	1	67
John	7:19	272	Did not Moses give you the law, and *yet* none of you keepeth the law?	1	68
John	7:31	273	When Christ cometh, will he do more miracles . . . this *man* hath done?	1	69
John	7:33	273	Yet a little while am I with you, and *then* I go unto him that sent me	1	70
John	7:34	273	Ye shall seek me, and shall not find *me*: and where I am, *thither* ye cannot	2	72
John	7:36	273	What *manner of* saying . . . Ye shall . . . not find *me*: and . . . *thither* ye	4	76
John	7:37	274	In the last day, that great *day* of the feast	1	77
John	7:39	274	for the Holy Ghost was not yet *given*; because that Jesus was not yet	1	78
John	7:51	274	Doth our law judge *any* man, before it hear him, and know what he doeth?	1	79
John	8:6	274	. . . and with *his* finger wrote on the ground, *as though he heard them not*	7	86
John	8:9	275	. . . heard *it*, being convicted by *their own* conscience . . . *even* unto the	4	90
John	8:14	275	Though I bear record of myself, *yet* my record is true	1	91
John	8:24	275	. . . for if ye believe not that I am *he*, ye shall die in your sins	1	92
John	8:25	275	Even *the same* that I said unto you from the beginning	2	94
John	8:28	276	. . . then shall ye know that I am *he*, and *that* I do nothing of myself	2	96
John	8:31	276	If ye continue in my word, *then* are ye my disciples indeed	1	97
John	8:35	276	And the servant abideth not in the house for ever: *but* the Son abideth ever	1	98
John	8:41	276	We be not born of fornication; we have one Father, *even* God	1	99
John	8:43	276	. . . ye not understand my speech? *even* because ye cannot hear my word	1	100
John	8:44	277	Ye are of *your* father the devil, and the lusts of your father ye will do	1	101
John	8:45	277	And because I tell *you* the truth, ye believe me not	1	102
John	8:47	277	. . . ye therefore hear *them* not, because ye are not of God	1	103
John	8:56	277	Your father Abraham rejoiced to see my day: and he saw *it*, and was glad	1	104
John	9:1	277	And as *Jesus* passed by, he saw a man which was blind from *his* birth	2	106
John	9:9	278	Some said, This is he: others *said*, He is like him: *but* he said, I am *he*	3	109
John	9:22	278	These *words* spake his parents, because they feared the Jews	1	110

John	9:25	278	Whether he be a sinner *or no*, I know not: one thing I know . . . now I see	2	112
John	9:27	279	. . . you already, and ye did not hear: wherefore would ye hear *it* again?	1	113
John	9:29	279	We know that God spake unto Moses: *as for* this *fellow*, we know not	3	116
John	9:30	279	. . . ye know not from whence he is, and *yet* he hath opened mine eyes	1	117
John	9:40	279	And *some* of the Pharisees which were with him heard these words	1	118
John	10:10	280	I am come that they might have life, and that they might have *it* more	1	119
John	10:14	280	I am the good shepherd, and know my *sheep*, and am known of mine	1	120
John	10:16	280	. . . and they shall hear my voice; and there shall be one fold, *and* one	1	121
John	10:28	290	. . . and they shall never perish, neither shall any *man* pluck them out of	1	122
John	10:29	290	. . . gave *them* me, is greater than all; and no *man* is able to pluck *them* out	3	125
John	10:30	290	I and *my* Father are one	1	126
John	10:38	290	. . . that ye may know, and believe, that the Father *is* in me, and I in him	1	127
John	11:1	300	Now a certain *man* was sick, *named* Lazarus, of Bethany	2	129
John	11:2	300	It was *that* Mary which anointed the Lord with ointment	1	130
John	11:4	301	When Jesus heard *that*, he said, This sickness is not unto death	1	131
John	11:7	301	Then after that saith he to *his* disciples, Let us go into Judaea again	1	132
John	11:8	301	*His* disciples say unto him, Master, the Jews of late sought to stone thee	1	133
John	11:17	301	. . . Jesus came, he found that he had *lain* in the grave four days already	1	134
John	11:20	301	. . . but Mary sat *still* in the house	1	135
John	11:22	301	. . . that even now, whatsoever thou wilt ask of God, God will give *it* thee	1	136
John	11:29	302	As soon as she heard *that*, she arose quickly, and came unto him	1	137
John	11:39	302	Lord, by this time he stinketh: for he hath been *dead* four days	1	138
John	11:41	302	. . . the stone *from the place* . . . And Jesus lifted up *his* eyes	4	142
John	11:42	302	. . . but because of the people which stand by I said *it*	1	143
John	11:48	303	If we let him thus alone, all *men* will believe on him	1	144
John	11:49	303	And one of them, *named* Caiaphas, being the high priest that same year	1	145
John	11:57	312	. . man knew where he were, he should shew *it*, that they might take him	1	146
John	12:4	313	. . . one of his disciples, Judas Iscariot, Simon's *son*, which should betray	1	147
John	12:13	314	Blessed *is* the King of Israel that cometh in the name of the Lord	1	148
John	12:16	314	. . . and *that* they had done these things unto him	1	149
John	12:26	317	. . . if any man serve me, him will *my* Father honour	1	150
John	12:28	317	. . . from heaven, *saying*, I have both glorified *it*, and will glorify *it* again	3	153
John	12:29	317	. . . and heard *it*, said that it thundered: others said, An angel spake to him	1	154
John	12:32	317	And I, if I be lifted up from the earth, will draw all *men* unto me	1	155
John	12:40	317	. . . that they should not see with *their* eyes, nor understand with *their* heart	2	157
John	12:42	317	. . . but because of the Pharisees they did not confess *him*	1	158
John	13:2	341	. . . put into the heart of Judas Iscariot, Simon's *son*, to betray him	1	159
John	13:5	341	. . . and to wipe *them* with the towel wherewith he was girded	1	160
John	13:9	341	. . . saith unto him, Lord, not my feet only, but also *my* hands and *my* head	2	162
John	13:10	341	He that is washed needeth not save to wash *his* feet	1	163
John	13:13	341	Ye call me Master and Lord: and ye say well; for *so* I am	1	164
John	13:14	341	If I then, *your* Lord and Master, have washed your feet	1	165
John	13:19	342	when it is come to pass, ye may believe that I am *he*	1	166
John	13:26	342	. . . when I have dipped *it* . . . he gave *it* to Judas Iscariot, *the son* of Simon	4	170
John	13:29	342	For some *of them* thought . . . Buy *those things* that we have need	4	174
John	13:35	343	. . . all *men* know that ye are my disciples, if ye have love one to another	1	175
John	14:2	344	. . . if *it were* not *so*, I would have told you. I go to prepare a place for you	3	178
John	14:3	344	. . . that where I am, *there* ye may be also	1	179
John	14:9	345	. . . how sayest thou *then*, Shew us the Father?	1	180
John	14:11	345	Believe me that I *am* in the Father, and the Father in me	1	181
John	14:12	345	and greater *works* than these shall he do; because I go unto my Father.	1	182
John	14:14	345	If ye shall ask any thing in my name, I will do *it*	1	183
John	14:17	345	*Even* the Spirit of truth; whom the world cannot receive	1	184
John	14:20	345	. . . ye shall know that I *am* in my Father, and ye in me, and I in you	1	185
John	14:25	345	These things have I spoken unto you, being *yet* present with you	1	186
John	14:26	346	But the Comforter, *which is* the Holy Ghost, whom the Father will send	2	188
John	14:28	346	Ye have heard how I said unto you, I go away, and come *again* unto you	1	189
John	15:2	346	. . . *branch* that beareth fruit, he purgeth it, that it may bring forth more	1	190
John	15:5	346	I am the vine, ye *are* the branches: He that abideth in me	1	191
John	15:6	346	. . . and men gather them, and cast *them* into the fire, and they are burned	1	192
John	15:11	346	. . . that my joy might remain in you, and *that* your joy might be full	1	193
John	15:16	347	. . . and *that* your fruit should remain	1	194
John	15:18	347	If the world hate you, ye know that it hated me before *it hated* you	2	196
John	15:25	347	But *this cometh to pass*, that the word might be fulfilled	4	200
John	15:26	347	. . . whom I will send unto you from the Father, *even* the Spirit of truth	1	201
John	16:13	348	but whatsoever he shall hear, *that* shall he speak: and he will shew you	1	202

John	16:14	348	He shall glorify me: for he shall receive of mine, and shall shew *it* unto	1	203
John	16:15	348	. . . therefore said I, that he shall take of mine, and shall shew *it* unto you	1	204
John	16:17	348	Then said *some* of his disciples among themselves, What is this	1	205
John	16:23	349	Whatsoever ye shall ask the Father in my name, he will give *it* you	1	206
John	17:8	350	. . . have received *them*, and have known surely that I came out from thee	1	207
John	17:11	350	. . . that they may be one, as we *are*	1	208
John	17:21	350	That they all may be one; as thou, Father, *art* in me, and I in thee	1	209
John	17:26	351	And I have declared unto them thy name, and will declare *it*	1	210
John	18:3	353	Judas then, having received a band *of men* and officers from the chief	2	212
John	18:5	354	Jesus saith unto them, I am *he*	1	213
John	18:6	354	As soon then as he had said unto them, I am *he*, they went backward	1	214
John	18:8	354	Jesus answered, I have told you that I am *he*	1	215
John	18:15	356	And Simon Peter followed Jesus, and *so did* another disciple	2	217
John	18:17	356	Art not thou also *one* of this man's disciples? He saith, I am not	1	218
John	18:25	359	Art not thou also *one* of his disciples? He denied *it*, and said, I am not	2	220
John	18:26	359	. . . servants of the high priest, being *his* kinsman whose ear Peter cut off	1	221
John	18:38	363	I find in him no fault *at all*	2	223
John	19:1	366	Then Pilate therefore took Jesus, and scourged *him*	1	224
John	19:2	366	and put *it* on his head, and they put on him a purple robe	1	225
John	19:5	367	And *Pilate* saith unto them, Behold the man!	1	226
John	19:6	367	Crucify *him*, crucify *him*. . . Take ye him, and crucify *him*: for I find no	3	229
John	19:11	367	. . . have no power *at all* against me, except it were given thee from above	2	231
John	19:15	367	Away with *him*, away with *him*, crucify him	2	233
John	19:16	368	And they took Jesus, and led *him away*	1	234
John	19:17	368	And he bearing his cross went forth into a place called *the place* of a skull	2	236
John	19:19	368	And Pilate wrote a title, and put *it* on the cross	1	237
John	19:20	368	. . . and it was written in Hebrew, *and* Greek, *and* Latin	2	239
John	19:23	369	. . . and made four parts, to every soldier a part; and also *his* coat	1	240
John	19:25	371	. . . his mother's sister, Mary the *wife* of Cleophas, and Mary Magdalene	1	241
John	19:27	371	And from that hour that disciple took her unto his own *home*	1	242
John	19:29	372	. . . and put *it* upon hyssop, and put *it* to his mouth	2	244
John	19:31	373	. . . Pilate that their legs might be broken, and *that* they might be taken	1	245
John	19:35	373	And he that saw *it* bare record, and his record is true	1	246
John	19:38	375	. . . and Pilate gave *him* leave	1	247
John	19:39	375	. . . brought a mixture of myrrh and aloes, about an hundred pound *weight*	1	248
John	19:42	375	There laid they Jesus therefore because of the Jews' preparation *day*	1	249
John	20:1	376	The first *day* of the week cometh Mary Magdalene early	1	250
John	20:5	377	And he stooping down, *and looking in*, saw the linen clothes lying	3	253
John	20:11	377	. . . she stooped down, *and looked* into the sepulchre	2	255
John	20:17	378	I ascend unto my Father, and your Father; and *to* my God, and your God	1	256
John	20:18	379	and *that* he had spoken these things unto her	1	257
John	20:19	381	. . . being the first *day* of the week . . . Peace *be* unto you	2	259
John	20:20	381	And when he had so said, he shewed unto them *his* hands and his side	1	260
John	20:21	381	Peace *be* unto you: as *my* Father hath sent me, even so send I you	2	262
John	20:22	381	And when he had said this, he breathed on *them*, and saith unto them	1	263
John	20:23	381	. . . remitted unto them; *and* whose soever *sins* ye retain, they are	2	265
John	20:26	382	. . . *then* came Jesus . . . stood in the midst, and said, Peace *be* unto you	2	267
John	20:27	382	. . . and thrust *it* into my side: and be not faithless, but believing	1	268
John	20:29	382	. . . blessed *are* they that have not seen, and *yet* have believed	2	270
John	21:1	383	. . . and on this wise shewed he *himself*	1	271
John	21:2	383	and the *sons* of Zebedee, and two other of his disciples	1	272
John	21:7	383	he girt *his* fisher's coat *unto him*, (for he was naked,) and did cast himself	3	275
John	21:12	383	Jesus saith unto them, Come *and* dine	1	276
John	21:15	383	Simon, *son* of Jonas, lovest thou me more than these?	1	277
John	21:16	383	. . . again the second time, Simon, *son* of Jonas, lovest thou me?	1	278
John	21:17	384	. . . the third time, Simon, *son* of Jonas, lovest thou me?	1	279
John	21:18	384	. . . and another shall gird thee, and carry *thee* whither thou wouldest not	1	280
John	21:21	384	Peter seeing him saith to Jesus, Lord, and what *shall* this man *do*?	2	282
John	21:22	384	If I will that he tarry till I come, what *is that* to thee? follow thou me	2	284
John	21:23	384	. . . but, If I will that he tarry till I come, what *is that* to thee?	2	286

APPENDIX 5
CHECK POINT EVENTS
(5.1 - For use with the Combined Gospels without Notes)

Event	Concurrent Verses	Page(s) *
The baptism of Jesus the Christ	Mt 3:13-17; Mk 1:9-11; Jn 1:15-28; Lk 3:21-22	10-11
John the Baptist is cast into prison	Mt 4:12; Mk 1:14	19
The first calling Peter & Andrew, James & John	Mk 1:16-20; Mt 18:22	20
Simon Peter's mother-in-law is healed of a fever	Mt 8:14-15; Mk 4:29-31; Lk 4:38-39	25-27
Numerous healings in the evening	Mt 8:16-17; Mk 1:32-34; Lk 4:40-41	25-27
A man in Capernaum is healed of the palsy	Mk 2:1-12; Mt 9:2-8; Lk 5:17-26	29-30
The calling of Matthew (Levi)	Mk 2:14; Mt 9:9; Lk 5:27-28	30
The mission of Jesus	Lk 5:29-32; Mt 9:10-13; Mk 2:15-17	30-32
No mixing allowed	Mk 2:18-22; Lk 5:33-39; Mt 9:14-17	32
Disputes concerning the sabbath	Mk 2:23-28; Lk 6:1-5; Mt 12:1-8	38-39
It is lawful to heal on the sabbath days!	Mt 12:9-13; Lk 6:1-10; Mk 3:1-5	39-40
A tempest is stilled	Mk 4:36- 41; Lk 8:22-25	52-53
Healing the demoniac in Gadara	Lk 8:26-39; Mk 5:1-20	53-54
The loaves and the fishes multiplied (1st occasion)	Mk 6:30-44; Lk 9:10-17; Mt 14:15-21; Jn 6:1-13	59-60
Laws of nature and physics nullified	Jn 6:16-21; Mk 6:45-53; Mt 14:22-33	61-62
The loaves & fishes are multiplied (2nd occasion)	Mt 15:32-39; Mk 8:1-9	67-68
The 1st announcement of sufferings	Lk 9:22; Mt 16:21; Mk 8:31-32	70-71
Transfiguration – The first resurrection	Lk 9:28-36; Mt 17:1-9; Mk 9:2-13	71-72
The 2nd announcement of sufferings	Mk 9:12; Mt 17:12	72-73
The 3rd announcement of sufferings	Lk 9:43-45; Mk 9:30-32; Mt 17:22-23	74
Who shall be the greatest?	Mk 9:33-37; Mt 18:1-5; Lk. 9:46-48	75
Two requirements to enter the kingdom	Mk 10:13-16; Mt 19:13-15; Lk 18:15-17	103-105
What' in it for me?	Lk 18:28-30; Mk 10:28-31; Mt 19:27-30	105-106
The 5th announcement of sufferings	Mk 10:32-34; Mt 20:17-19; Lk 18:31-34	106-107
Disputing with the priests, scribes and elders	Mk 11:27-33; Lk 20:1-8; Mt 21:23-27	116-118
Why Jesus was not openly arrested	Mk 12:12; Lk 20:19; Mt 21:46	116-118
The divinity of the Christ	Mt 22:41-45; Mk 12:35-37; Lk 20:41-44	122
The 6th announcement of sufferings	Mt 26:1-2	131
Plotting to kill Jesus without creating an uproar	Lk 22:1-2; Mk 14:1-2; Mt 26:3-5	131-132
Judas arranges the betrayal of Jesus	Mk 14:10-11; Lk 22:3-6; Mt 26:14-16	132-133
Peter's 2nd denial	Lk 22:56-58; Mt 26:69-70; Mk 14:66-68 to 1st.	149-150
The 2nd Cock crew	Mk 14:72; Lk 22:60-61; Mt 26:74	151
Peter weeps	Mt 26:75; Lk 22:62; Mk 14:72	151
The Roman soldiers part Jesus' garments . . .	Lk 19 34 *And*; Jn 19:23-24; Mk 15:24; Mt 27:35-36	159
Three hours of darkness from noon to 3:00 p.m.	Mt 27:45; Mk 15:33; Lk 23:44-45	161
"It is finished"	Jn 19 30; Mt 24:50; Mk 15:37; Lk 23:46	162
Joseph of Arimathæa requests the body of Jesus	Mk 15:43; Lk 23:52; Mt 27:58; Jn 19:38;	163-164
The body of Jesus is placed in Joseph's sepulchre	Mk 15:46; Lk 23:53; Mt 27:60; Jn 19:41-42	163-164
Women witnesses to the burial	Mk 15:47; Lk 23:55; Mt:27:61	163-164

* Page numbers only apply to: The Combined Gospels *without* Notes.

APPENDIX 5
CHECK POINT EVENTS
(5.1 - For use with the Combined Gospels with Notes)

Event	Concurrent Verses	Page(s) **
The baptism of Jesus the Christ	Mt 3:13-17; Mk 1:9-11; Jn 1:15-28; Lk 3:21-22	186-187
John the Baptist is cast into prison	Mt 4:12; Mk 1:14	197
The first calling Peter & Andrew, James & John	Mk 1:16-20; Mt 18:22	198-199
Simon Peter's mother-in-law is healed of a fever	Lk 4:38-39; Mt 8:14-15; Mk 4:29-31	205-206
Numerous healings in the evening	Mt 8:16-17; Mk 1:32-34; Lk 4:40-41	206
A man in Capernaum is healed of the palsy	Mk 2:1-12; Mt 9:2-8; Lk 5:17-26	209-210
The calling of Matthew (Levi)	Mk 2:14; Mt 9:9; Lk 5:27-28	210-211
The mission of Jesus	Lk 5:29-32; Mt 9:10-13; Mk 2:15-17	211
No mixing allowed	Mk 2:18-22; Lk 5:33-39; Mt 9:14-17	211-212
Disputes concerning the sabbath	Mk 2:23-28; Lk 6:1-5; Mt 12:1-8	219-220
It is lawful to heal on the sabbath days!	Mt 12:9-13; Lk 6:1-10; Mk 3:1-5	220-221
A tempest is stilled	Mk 4:36- 41; Lk 8:22-25	237
Healing the demoniac in Gadara	Lk 8:26-39; Mk 5:1-20	237-239
The loaves and the fishes multiplied (1st occasion)	Mk 6:30-44; Lk 9:10-17; Mt 14:15-21; Jn 6:1-13	244-246
Laws of nature and physics nullified	Jn 6:16-21; Mk 6:45-53; Mt 14:22-33	247-248
The loaves & fishes are multiplied (2nd occasion)	Mt 15:32-39; Mk 8:1-9	255-256
The 1st announcement of sufferings	Lk 9:22; Mt 16:21; Mk 8:31-32	259-260
Transfiguration – The first resurrection	Lk 9:28-36; Mt 17:1-9; Mk 9:2-13	260-262
The 2nd announcement of sufferings	Mk 9:12; Mt 17:12	262
The 3rd announcement of sufferings	Lk 9:43-45; Mk 9:30-32; Mt 17:22-23	264
Who shall be the greatest?	Mk 9:33-37; Mt 18:1-5; Lk. 9:46-48	265-266
Two requirements to enter the kingdom	Mk 10:13-16; Mt 19:13-15; Lk 18:15-17	303-305
What' in it for me?	Lk 18:28-30; Mk 10:28-31; Mt 19:27-30	306
The 5th announcement of sufferings	Mk 10:32-34; Mt 20:17-19; Lk 18:31-34	307-308
Disputing with the priests, scribes and elders	Mk 11:27-33; Lk 20:1-8; Mt 21:23-27	319
Why Jesus was not openly arrested	Mt 21:46; Mk 12:12; Lk 20:19	321-322
The divinity of the Christ	Mt 22:41-45; Mk 12:35-37; Lk 20:41-44	326-327
The 6th announcement of sufferings	Mt 26:1-2	337
Plotting to kill Jesus without creating an uproar	Lk 22:1-2; Mk 14:1-2; Mt 26:3-5	337
Judas arranges the betrayal of Jesus	Mk 14:10-11; Mt 26:14-16; Lk 22:3-6	338-339
Peter's 2nd denial	Lk 22:56-58; Mt 26:69-70; Mk 14:66-68 to 1st.	358
The 2nd Cock crew	Mk 14:72; Lk 22:60-61; Mt 26:74	359-360
Peter weeps	Mt 26:75; Lk 22:62; Mk 14:72	360
The Roman soldiers part Jesus' garments . . .	Lk 19 34 *And*; Jn 19:23-24; Mk 15:24; Mt 27:35-36	369-370
Three hours of darkness from noon to 3:00 p.m.	Mt 27:45; Mk 15:33; Lk 23:44-45	371-372
"It is finished"	Jn 19 30; Mt 24:50; Mk 15:37; Lk 23:46	372
Joseph of Arimathæa requests the body of Jesus	Mk 15:43; Lk 23:52; Mt 27:58; Jn 19:38;	374-375
The body of Jesus is placed in Joseph's sepulchre	Mk 15:46; Lk 23:53; Mt 27:60; Jn 19:41-42	374-375
Women witnesses to the burial	Mk 15:47; Lk 23:55; Mt:27:61	374-375

** Page numbers only apply to: The Combined Gospels *with* Notes.

APPENDIX 6
LIST OF QUOTATIONS
(FOR USE WITH THE COMBINED GOSPELS with NOTES)

Inside Cover – front

That was the true Light, which lighteth every man that cometh into the world. – Jn 1:9

Thine ears shall hear a word behind thee, saying, This *is* the way, walk ye in it, when ye turn to the right hand, and when ye turn to the left." – Isa. 30:21.

Page iii

My words fly up, my thoughts remain below:
Words without thoughts never to heaven go. – Act III, Scene III Shakespeare's Hamlet

How think ye? – Matt 18:12

When ye pray, use not vain repetitions, as the heathen *do*: for they think that they shall be heard for their much speaking. Be not ye therefore like unto them: for your Father knoweth what things ye have need of, before ye ask him. – Matthew 6:7-8 *when*

But what think ye? – Matt 21:28

If we are not secretly yearning and openly striving for the accomplishment of all we ask, our prayers are "vain repetitions" such as the heathen use. If our petitions are sincere, we labor for what we ask; and our Father, who seeth in secret, will reward us openly. – S&H 13:6-12.

28 Jesus said, "I took my place in the midst of the world, and I appeared to them in flesh. I found all of them intoxicated; I found none of them thirsty. And my soul became afflicted for the sons of men, because they are blind in their hearts and do not have sight; for empty they came into the world, and empty too they seek to leave the world. But for the moment they are intoxicated. When they shake off their wine, then they will repent." - CGT p. 22.

Awake thou that sleepest, and arise from the dead, and Christ shall give thee light. - Eph 5:14 *Awake*

These things have I spoken unto you, that in me ye might have peace. In the world ye shall have tribulation: but be of good cheer; I have overcome the world. – John 16:33

Behold, the LORD hath proclaimed unto the end of the world, Say ye to the daughter of Zion, Behold, thy salvation cometh; behold, his reward *is* with him, and his work is before him. – Isa 62:11

To understand God strengthens hope, enthrones faith in Truth, and verifies Jesus' word: "Lo, I am with you alway, even unto the end of the world." - S&H 446:19-23

Page 169

When the morning stars sang together, and all the sons of God shouted for joy? - Job 38:7

Principle and its idea is one, and this one is God, omnipotent, omniscient, and omnipresent Being, and His reflection is man and the universe. - S&H 465:23

All reality is in God and His creation, harmonious and eternal. That which He makes is good, and He makes all that is made. Therefore the only reality of sin, sickness, or death is the awful fact that unrealities seem real to human, erring belief, until God strips of their disguise. - S&H 465:23

Page 177

Jesus was born of Mary. - S&H 332:29

The corporeal man Jesus was human. - S&H 332:17-18

Mary's conception of him was spiritual, for only purity could reflect Truth and Love, which were plainly incarnate in the good and pure Christ Jesus. – S&H 332:26-29.

The Lord God shall give unto him the throne of his father David. - Luke 1:32

Page 185

10 Jesus said, "I have cast fire upon the world, and see, I am guarding it until it blazes." - CGT p. 21

Page 186

4 "Let it be, for it is fitting that all things be fulfilled in this way." - The GOE p.13.

Jesus' concessions (in certain cases) to material methods were for the advancement of spiritual good. - S&H 56:4-6.

Page 187

Science so reverses the evidence before the corporeal human senses, as to make this Scriptural testimony true in our hearts, "The last shall be first and the first last," so that God and His idea may be to us what divinity really is and must of necessity be, --- all-inclusive. – S&H 116:5-10.

The real man being linked by Science to his Maker, mortals need only turn from sin to find Christ, the real man and his relation to God, and to recognize the divine sonship. – S&H 316:3-7.

Born of a woman, Jesus' advent in the flesh partook partly of Mary's earthly condition, although he was endowed with the Christ, the divine Spirit, without measure." – S&H 30:5-8.

Page 188

LAMB OF GOD. The spiritual idea of Love; self-immolation; innocence and purity; sacrifice – S&H 590:9-10.

Page 189

May Christ, Truth, be present at every bridal altar to turn the water into wine and to give to human life an inspiration by which man's spiritual and eternal existence may be discerned. - S&H 65:3-6

Page 190

The word *temple* also means *body*. - S&H 576:14-15.

We need a clean body and a clean mind, --- a body rendered pure by Mind as well as washed by water. - S&H 383:3-4.

Page 191

Seeing ye have purified your souls in obeying the truth through the Spirit unto unfeigned love of the brethren, *see that ye* love one another with a pure heart fervently: Being born again, not of corruptible seed, but of incorruptible, by the word of God, which liveth and abideth for ever. - I Pet. 1:22-23.

The new birth is not the work of a moment. It begins with moments, and goes on with years; moments of surrender to God, of childlike trust and joyful adoption of good; moments of self-abnegation, self-consecration, heaven-born hope, and spiritual love. – Mis. 15:13-17.

Page 196

Blessed *are* the poor in spirit: for theirs is the kingdom of heaven. – Matt 5:3.

Page 197

Blessed *are* they which do hunger and thirst after righteousness: for they shall be filled. - Matt 5:6

Page 200

The KJV states: That whosoever is angry with his brother without a cause shall be in danger of the judgment: (Matt. 5:22). This is implies that anger directed toward a person is justified, an implication contrary to the teaching of Jesus. - The Gospel of the Nazareans p. 11 records the following: "On Matthew 5:22. The words "without a cause" are not present in some copies, nor in the Jewish Gospel. (MS 1424).

Get thee hence, Satan. - Matt 4:10.

Page 208

To the unwise helper our Master said, "Follow me; and let the dead bury their dead." – Ret 86:24-2.

Page 211

For I desire mercy and not sacrifice; and the knowledge of God more than burnt offerings. – Hosea 6:6

The letter killeth, but the spirit giveth life. - II Cor. 3:6

Page 214

Our Master's first article of faith propounded to his disciples was healing, and he proved his faith by his works. – S&H 145:32-2.

Page 216

46 Jesus said, "Among those born of women, from Adam until John the Baptist, there is no one superior to John the Baptist that his eyes should not be lowered (before him). Yet I have said, whichever one of you comes to be a child will be acquainted with the kingdom and will become superior to John." - CGT p. 23-24.

Page 231

Immortals, or God's children in divine Science, are one harmonious family; but mortals, or the "children of men" in material sense, are discordant and ofttimes false brethren. - S&H 444:27-30.

God is our Father and our Mother, our Minister and the great Physician: He is man's only real relative on earth and in heaven. David sang, "Whom have I in heaven beside thee? and there is none upon earth that I desire beside thee. Mis. 151:13-17.

Page 232

In the soil of an "honest and good heart" the seed must be sown; else it beareth not much fruit, for the swinish element in human nature uproots it. S&H 272:6-8.

Jesus' parable of "the sower" shows the care our Master took not to impart to dull ears and gross hearts the spiritual teachings which dulness and grossness could not accept. Reading the thoughts of the people, he said: "Give not that which is holy unto the dogs, neither cast ye your pearls before swine." – S&H 272:13-18.

Page 234

Ye are of *your* father the devil, and the lusts of your father ye will do. He was a murderer from the beginning, and abode not in the truth, because there is no truth in him. When he speaketh a lie, he speaketh of his own: for he is a liar, and the father of it. - John 8:44.

Are you willing to leave all for Christ, for Truth, and so be counted among sinners? – S&H 9:25-26.

We must exchange "the objects of sense for the ideas of Soul." - S&H 269:14-16.

We are not Christian Scientists until we leave all for Christ. – S&H 192:5-6.

Page 238

Give not that which is holy unto the dogs, neither cast your pearls before swine, lest they trample them under their feet, and turn again and rend you. - Matt 7:6.

Page 241

The invisible Christ was imperceptible to the so-called personal senses, whereas Jesus appeared as a bodily existence – S&H 334:10-12.

Page 245

In the scientific relation of God to man, we find that whatever blesses one blesses all, as Jesus showed with the loaves and fishes, --- Spirit, not matter, being the source of supply. – S&H 206:15-18.

Page 246

If seed is necessary to produce wheat, and wheat to produce flour, or if one animal can originate another, how can we account for their primal origin? How were the loaves and fishes multiplied on the shores of Galilee, --- and that, too, without meal or monad from which loaf or fish could come? – S&H 89:32-5.

Page 256

Spiritual teaching must always be by symbols. S&H 575:14.

Page 257

Jesus knew the generation to be wicked and adulterous, seeking the material more than the spiritual. - S&H 85:24-26.

Both Jew and Gentile may have acute corporeal senses, but mortals need spiritual sense. – S&H 85:23-24.

His thrusts at materialism were sharp but needed. He never spared hypocrisy the sternest condemnation. - S&H 85:26-28.

Page 260

If I will that he tarry that I come, what is that to thee. Follow thou me. - John 21:22

Page 261

No man hath seen God at any time; - John 1:18 (*to* ;)

Page 266

One infinite God, good, unifies men and nations; constitutes the brotherhood of man; ends wars; fulfills the Scripture, "Love thy neighbor as thyself;" annihilates pagan and Christian idolatry, --- whatever is wrong in social, civil, criminal, political, and religious codes; equalizes the sexes; annuls the curse on man, and leaves nothing that can sin, suffer, be punished or destroyed. - S&H 340:23-29.

Page 268

To remit the penalty due for sin, would be for Truth to pardon error. - S&H 36:6-7.

We cannot escape the penalty due for sin. - S&H 6:1.

Page 269

And a man's foes shall be they of his own household. – Matt10:36

Page 273

27 If you do not observe the Sabbath as a Sabbath, you will not see the father. – COGT p. 22.

53 His disciples said to him, "Is circumcision beneficial or not?" He said to them, "If it were beneficial, their father would beget them already circumcised from their mother. Rather, the true circumcision in spirit has become completely profitable." - COGT p. 24.

Page 275

He that is of the earth is earthly, and speaketh of the earth: he that cometh from heaven is above all"- John. 3:31.

I AM THAT I AM. - Ex 3:14

I am the light of the world. - John 8:12 & 9:5.

Page 280

Jesus could have withdrawn himself from his enemies. He had power to lay down a human sense of life for his spiritual identity in the likeness of the divine; but he allowed men to attempt the destruction of the mortal body in order that he might furnish the proof of immortal life. – S&H 51:6-11.

Page 284

89 Jesus said, "Why do you wash the outside of the cup? Do you not realize that he who made the inside is the same one who made the outside?" COGT p.27.

Page 285

39 Jesus said, "The Pharisees and the scribes have taken the keys of knowledge (gnosis) and hidden them. They themselves have not entered, nor have they allowed to enter those who wish to. You however be wise as serpents and as innocent as doves." - COGT p.23.

Page 286

72 [A man said] to him, "Tell my brothers to divide my father's possessions with me." He said to him, "O man, who has made me a divider?" He turned to his disciples and said to them, "I am not a divider, am I?" - COGT p. 26.

63 Jesus said, "There was a rich man who had much money. He said, 'I shall put my money to use so that I may sow, reap, plant, and fill my storehouse with produce, with the result that I shall lack nothing.' Such were his intentions, but that same night he died. Let him who has ears hear." - COGT p. 25.

There is no life, truth, intelligence, nor substance in matter. All is infinite Mind and its infinite manifestation, for God is All-in-all. Spirit is immortal Truth; matter is mortal error. Spirit is the real and eternal; matter is the unreal and temporal. S&H 468:9-13.

Page 287

I do not maintain that anyone can exist in the flesh without food and raiment; but I do believe that the real man is immortal and that he lives in Spirit, not matter." – S&H 461:1-4

Page 288

10 Jesus said, "I have cast fire upon the world, and see, I am guarding it until it blazes." **82** Jesus said, "He who is near me is near the fire, and he who is far from me is far from the kingdom." - COGT pgs. 21 & 26.

Mortals must look beyond fading, finite forms it they would gain the true sense of things. S&H 264:7-8

Page 288

That statement of Jesus: "I and my Father are one," separated him from the scholastic theology of the rabbis. S&H 315:3-4.

Page 291

PROPHET. A spiritual seer; disappearance of material sense before the conscious facts of spiritual Truth." S&H 593:4-5.

Page 294

The First Commandment is my favorite text. It demonstrates Christian Science. - S&H

340:16-17.

The divine Principle of the First Commandment bases the Science of being, by which man demonstrates health, holiness, and life eternal. - S&H 340:20-22.

Page 295

Self-love is more opaque than a solid body. In patient obedience to a patient God, let us labor to dissolve with the universal solvent of Love the adamant of error, --- self-will, self-justification, and self-love, --- which wars against spirituality and is the law of sin and death. - S&H 242:15-20.

Page 297

Thou hypocrite, first cast out the beam out of thine own eye; and then shalt thou see clearly to cast out the mote out of thy brother's eye. - Matt. 7:5

Page 298

When we come to have more faith in the truth of being than we have in error, more faith in Spirit than in matter, more faith in living than in dying, more faith in God than in man, than no material suppositions can prevent us from healing the sick and destroying error. - S&H 368:14-19.

113 His disciples said to him, '"When will the kingdom come?" <Jesus said,> "It will not come by waiting for it. It will not be a matter of saying 'here it is' or 'there it is.' Rather, the kingdom of the father is spread out upon the earth, and men do not see it." - COGT p. 28.

Page 299

All must give place to the spiritual fact by the translation of man and the universe back into Spirit. S&H 209:21-22 *all.*

38 Jesus said, "Many times have you desired to hear these words which I am saying to you, and you have no one else to hear them from. There will be days when you will look for me and will not find me." – COGT p. 23.

If we observe our mental processes, we shall find that we are perpetually arguing with ourselves; yet each mortal is not two personalities, but one. In like manner good and evil talk to one another; yet they are not two but one, for evil is naught, and good only is reality." – Un 21:3-9.

Nothing is real and eternal --- nothing is Spirit, --- but God and His idea. S&H 71:1-2.

Page 302

Jesus restored Lazarus by the understanding that Lazarus had never died, not by an admission that his body had died and then lived again. Had Jesus believed that Lazarus had lived or died in his body, the Master would have stood on the same plane of belief as those who buried the body, and he could not have resuscitated it. - S&H 75:13-20

Page 304

Metaphysics is above physics, and matter does not enter into metaphysical premises or conclusions. – S&H 269:11-13.

Page 305

When man is governed by God, the ever-present Mind who understands all things, man knows that with God all things are possible. The only way to this living Truth, which heals the sick, is found in the Science of Mind as taught and demonstrated by Christ Jesus. – S&H 180:25-30.

Scripture informs us that "with God all things are possible," --- all good is possible to Spirit; but our prevalent theories practically deny this, and make healing possible only through matter. These theories must be untrue, for the Scripture is true. Christianity is not false, but religions which contradict its Principle are false. – S&H 232:9-15.

Page 313

Speak ye unto all the congregation of Israel, saying, In the tenth day of this month they shall take to them every man a lamb, according to the house of their fathers, a lamb for an house: And if the household be too little for the lamb, let him and his neighbour next unto his house take it according to the number of the souls; every man according to his eating shall make your count for the lamb. Your lamb shall be without blemish, a male of the first year: ye shall take it out from the sheep, or from the goats: And ye shall keep it up until the fourteenth day of the same month: and the whole assembly of the congregation of Israel shall kill it in the evening. - Ex 12:1-6.)

Page 317

The pride of priesthood is the prince of this world. S&H 270:22.

Mortal mind see what it believes as certainly as it believes what it see. S&H 86:29-30.

Page 323

3 . . . [they came] to him and began rigorously testing him, saying, "Teacher Jesus, we know that you have come from God. For the things you do give a testimony that is beyond all the prophets. And so, tell us: is it right to pay the kings the things that relate to their rule? Shall we pay them or not?"

But when Jesus understood their thought he became incensed and said to them, "Why do you call me teacher with your mouth, when you do not listen to what I say? Well did Isaiah prophecy about you, 'This people honors me with their lips, but their heart is far from me. In vain do they worship me *teaching for doctrines the commandments of men*."
- From the Papyrus Egerton 2: UNK p. 28. The text in italics: Matt. 15:9

Page 326

The divinity of the Christ was made manifest in the humanity of Jesus. S&H 25:31-32.

The Christ was the Spirit which Jesus implied in his own statements: "I am the way, the truth, and the life;" "I and my Father are one." This Christ, or divinity of the man Jesus, was his divine nature, the godliness which animated him. S&H 26:10-14.

[Jesus is] the highest human corporeal concept of the divine idea, rebuking and destroying error and bringing to light man's immortality. S&H 589:16-18.

[Christ is] the divine manifestation of God, which come to the flesh to destroy incarnate error. S&H 583:10-11.

Jesus is the human man, and Christ is the divine idea; hence the duality of Jesus the Christ. S&H 473:15-17.

Page 328

Jesus was unselfish. His spirituality separated him from sensuousness, and caused the selfish materialist to hate him; but it was this spirituality which enabled Jesus to heal the sick, cast out evil, and raise the dead. S&H 51:28-32.

He was inspired by God, by Truth and Love, in all that he said and did. The motives of his persecutors were pride, envy, cruelty, and vengeance, inflicted on the physical Jesus, but aimed at the divine Principle, Love, which rebuked their sensuality." S&H 51:23-27.

He rebuked sinners pointedly and unflinchingly, because he was their friend; hence the cup he drank. S&H 53:6-7.

Page 331

Nothing we can say or believe regarding matter is immortal, for matter is temporal and is therefore a mortal phenomenon, a human concept, sometimes beautiful, always erroneous. - S&H 277:29-32.

Page 335

Principle is imperative. You cannot mock it by human will. Science is a divine demand, not a human. Always right, its divine Principle never repents, but maintains the claim of Truth by quenching error. - S&H 329:21-25 *Principle.*

Page 336

If men understood their real spiritual source to be all blessedness, they would struggle for recourse to the spiritual and be at peace; but the deeper the error into which mortal mind is plunged, the more intense the opposition to spirituality, till error yields to Truth. - S&H 329:26-31 *If.*

Paul and John had a clear apprehension that, as mortal man achieves no worldly honors except by sacrifice, so he must gain heavenly riches by forsaking all worldliness. Then he will have nothing in common with the worldling's affections, motives, and aims. Judge not the future advancement of Christian Science by the steps already taken, lest you yourself be condemned for failing to take the first step. S&H 459:3-11.

Page 336

He that loveth not his brother whom he hath seen, how can he love God whom he hath not seen not seen? - (I John 4:20)

Page 338

And in the fourteenth day of the first month [Nisan] *is* the passover of the LORD. – Num. 28:16.

And in the fifteenth day of this month [Nisan] *is* the feast: [when the Passover Lamb is eaten] - Num. 28:17 (*to* :).

In the first day [of the feast on the 15th of Nisan] *shall be* [*is*] an holy convocation

[High Sabbath]: Num. 28:18 (*to ;*).

The greed for gold strengthened his ingratitude, and for a time quieted his remorse. - S&H 20-22.

Judas conspired against Jesus. The world's ingratitude and hatred towards that just man effected his betrayal. S&H 47:10-11.

The traitor's price was thirty pieces of silver and the smiles of the Pharisees. S&H 47:13-13.

Page 339

He chose his time, when the people were in doubt concerning Jesus' teachings. S&H 45:13-15.

Page 340

The Passover, which Jesus ate with his disciples in the month Nisan on the night before his crucifixion, was a mournful occasion, a sad supper taken at the close of day, in the twilight of a glorious career with shadows fast falling around; and this supper closed forever Jesus' ritualism or concessions to matter. S&H 32:28-2.

Page 341

Jesus established what he said by demonstration, thus making his acts of higher importance than his words. – S&H 473:26-28.

Page 342

The disciples had eaten, yet Jesus prayed and gave them bread. – S&H 32:21-23.

Page 344

"he was numbered with the transgressors." - Isa 53:12. The Hebrew word מָנָה (*manah*) translated "numbered" in Isaiah also has the meaning "reckoned" or "to reckon" as it was translated from the Greek word λογίζομαι (*logizomai*) in Luke 22:37.

And take the helmet of salvation, and the sword of the Spirit, which is the word of God: - Eph. 6:17.

No man hath seen God at any time; the only begotten Son, which is in the bosom of the Father, he hath declared *him*. - John 1:18.

Page 345

Believest thou not that I am in the Father, and the Father in me? the words that I speak unto you I speak not of myself: but of the Father that dwelleth in me, he doeth the works. - John 14:10.

Page 345

"Which is Christ in you, the hope of glory." - Col. 1:27

Page 346

The pride of priesthood is the prince of this world. It has nothing in Christ. – S&H 270:22-23.

Page 349

The Christian Scientist is alone with his own being and with the reality of things. – '01 20:8-9.

Every mortal at some period, here or hereafter, must grapple with and overcome the mortal belief in a power opposed to God. – S&H 569:3-5.

For I have not spoken of myself; but the Father which sent me, he gave me a commandment, what I should say, and what I should speak. - John 12:49.

(In English "what I should say, and what I should speak" mean the same thing. But was Jesus merely repeating himself with different phraseology? The word *say* in this text is εἶπον, *eipon* meaning to speak, to tell and deals with the subject itself [the what]. The word translated "speak" is λαλέω, *laleō* and refers to the words in which the message is delivered [the how]. From this we see it was not a mere repetition. Jesus was saying he was told by the Father not only what to say, but exactly how to say it.)

Page 350

God is one. The allness of Deity is His oneness. – S&H 267:5-6.

Page 357

Thou shalt not bear false witness against thy neighbour" Ex 20:16.

Page 370

For by grace are ye saved through faith; and that not of yourselves: *it is* the gift of God. – Eph. 2:8.

(The number five is significant. The fifth letter of the Hebrew alphabet ה (Hei or Hey) is used for the number five. When Abram was ninety-nine he came to the realization that the LORD (*Jehovah*) was in fact "the Almighty God" (*El Shaddai*) and heard the promise that he would become the father (founder) of many nations and the recipient of many blessings and his name was changed from Abram to Abraham by adding the letter ה - "h." With the addition of the same letter his wife's name was changed from Sarai to Sarah. These name changes signified that the blessings he and Sarah would receive were gifts of grace. The entire letter Paul wrote to the Ephesians is a tremendous source of insight and inspiration on the power of grace not only as it pertains to Jesus and the four who were crucified with him, but for all mankind.)

Page 376

31 So Pilate gave the centurion Petronius and soldiers to guard the tomb. The elders and scribes came with them to the crypt. **32** Everyone who was there, along with the centurion and the soldiers, rolled a great stone and placed it there before the entrance of the crypt. **33** They smeared it with seven seals, pitched a tent there, and stood guard. – GOP p. 33.

Page 383

What a contrast between our Lord's last supper and his last spiritual breakfast with his disciples in the bright morning hours at the joyful meeting on the shore of the Galilean Sea! His gloom had passed into glory, and his disciples' grief into repentance, — hearts chastened and pride rebuked. Convinced of the fruitlessness of their toil in the dark and wakened by their Master's voice, they changed their methods, turned away from material things, and cast their net on the right side. Discerning Christ, Truth, anew on the shore of time, they were enabled to rise somewhat from mortal sensuousness, or the burial of mind in matter, into newness of life as Spirit.

This spiritual meeting with our Lord in the dawn of a new light is the morning meal which Christian Scientists commemorate. They bow before Christ, Truth, to receive more of his reappearing and silently to commune with the divine Principle, Love. They celebrate their Lord's victory over death, his probation in the flesh after death, its exemplification of human probation, and his spiritual and final ascension above matter, or the flesh, when he rose out of material sight. S&H 34:29 – 35:18

Page 384

A misplaced word changes the sense and misstates the Science of the Scriptures, as, for instance, to name Love as merely an attribute of God; but we can by special and proper capitalization speak of the love of Love, meaning by that what the beloved disciple meant in one of his epistles, when he said, "God is love." S&H 319:27-1.

Jesus endured the shame, that he might pour his dear-bought bounty into barren lives. What was his earthly reward? He was forsaken by all save John, the beloved disciple, and a few women who bowed in silent woe beneath his cross. The earthly price of spirituality in a material age and the great moral distance between Christianity and sensualism preclude Christian Science from finding favor with the worldly-minded. S&H 36:10-18.

Page 368

Jesus mapped out the path for others. He unveiled the Christ, the spiritual idea of divine Love. S&H 38:24-26.

The purpose and motive to live aright can be gained now. This point won, you have started as you should. You have begun at the numeration-table of Christian Science, and nothing but wrong intention can hinder your advancement. Working and praying with true motives, your Father will open the way. "Who did hinder you, that ye should not obey the truth?" S&H 326:16-22.

APPENDIX 7
VERSE LOCATOR

(Page numbers apply to the Combined Gospels with Notes)

7.1 - VERSE LOCATOR FOR THE GOSPEL ACCORDING TO MATTHEW				
	Chapter:	Page	Chapter	
Book	Verse(s)	No.	No.	Title
MATT	1:1-17	177-178	6	THE LEGAL & ROYAL GENEALOGY OF JESUS
MATT	1:18-25	180	9	THE IMMACULATE CONCEPTION REVEALED TO JOSEPH
MATT	2:1-23	182-183	12	THE EARLY YEARS
MATT	3:1-12	184-185	14	JOHN THE BAPTIST PREPARING THE WAY
MATT	3:13-17	186	15	THE BAPTISM OF JESUS THE CHRIST
MATT	4:1-11	194	21	TEMPTATION – REJECTION – VICTORY - DOMINION
MATT	4:12	197	24	JOHN THE BAPTIST IS CAST INTO PRISON
MATT	4:13-17	197-198	25	JESUS LEAVES NAZARETH TO DWELL IN CAPERNAUM
MATT	4:18-22	198-199	26	THE FIRST CALLING OF PETER & ANDREW, JAMES & JOHN
MATT	4:23-25	199	27	AN EXTENSIVE MINISTRY IN AND BEYOND GALILEE
MATT	5:1-48	199-201	28	THE SERMON ON THE MOUNT
MATT	6:1-34	201-203	28	THE SERMON ON THE MOUNT
MATT	7:1-29	203-204	28	THE SERMON ON THE MOUNT
MATT	8:1-4	204	29	JESUS PROVES HIS TEACHING PRACTICAL
MATT	8:5-13	204-205	30	MORE HEALING IN CAPERNAUM
MATT	8:14-15	206	30	MORE HEALING IN CAPERNAUM
MATT	8:16-17	206	30	MORE HEALING IN CAPERNAUM
MATT	8:18-27	208	34	A TSUNAMI IS STILLED
MATT	8:28-34	208-209	35	THE HEALINGS OF TWO DEMONIACS IN GERGESA
MATT	9:1	209	35	THE HEALINGS OF TWO DEMONIACS IN GERGESA
MATT	9:2-8	210	36	A MAN IN CAPERNAUM IS HEALED OF THE PALSY
MATT	9:9	210	37	THE CALLING OF MATTHEW (LEVI)
MATT	9:10-13	211	38	JESUS DECLARES THE PURPOSE OF HIS MISSION
MATT	9:14-17	212	39	NO MIXING ALLOWED
MATT	9:18-26	212-213	40	DEATH OVERCOME AND HEMORRHAGING HEALED
MATT	9:27-38	213	41	HEALING AND MOCKERY
MATT	10:1-42	214-215	42	THE DISCIPLES ARE TAUGHT TO HEAL
MATT	11:1-30	216-217	43	UNBELIEF, CALLOUSNESS, AND INGRATITUDE REBUKED
MATT	12:1-8	220	45	DISPUTES CONCERNING THE SABBATH
MATT	12:9-15 *to* :	220-221	46	IT IS LAWFUL TO HEAL ON THE SABBATH DAYS!
MATT	12:15-21 *and*	222	47	MULTITUDES SEEK HEALING
MATT	12:22-45	229-230	57	ACCUSED OF HEALING THROUGH BEELZEBUB
MATT	12:46-50	231	58	GOD'S FAMILY ARE THOSE WHO DO HIS WILL
MATT	13:1-52	231-235	59	CHRISTIANITY IN PARABLES
MATT	13:53	236	60	THE NEXT DAY: REVIEW AND DEPARTURE
MATT	13:54-58	241	64	HEALING IN NAZARETH FORESTALLED BY UNBELIEF
MATT	14:1-14	243	66	ACCOUNTS OF JOHN THE BAPTISTS BEHEADING
MATT	14:15-21	246	67	THE LOAVES AND FISHES MULTIPLIED (1ST OCCASION)
MATT	14:22-34	247-248	69	LAWS OF NATURE AND PHYSICS NULLIFIED
MATT	14:35-36	248	70	EVENTS IN GENNESARET
MATT	15:1-20	253-254	72	GOD'S COMMANDMENTS MOCKED BY MEN'S TRADITIONS
MATT	15:21-29	254	73	A CANAANITE CHILD HEALED
MATT	15:30-31	255	74	HEALING IN THE REGION OF DECAPOLIS
MATT	15:32-39	255	75	THE LOAVES AND FISHES ARE MULTIPLIED (2ND OCCASION)
MATT	16:1-12	257	76	BEWARE OF EVIL DOCTRINES
MATT	16:13-20	258	78	PETER'S REALIZATION THAT JESUS IS THE CHRIST
MATT	16:21-27	259	79	THE 1ST ANNOUNCEMENT OF SUFFERINGS
MATT	16:28	260	80	A PROPHECY CONCERNING THE KINGDOM OF GOD
MATT	17:1-9	261	81	TRANSFIGURATION – THE FIRST RESURRECTION
MATT	17:10-13	262	82	THE 2ND ANNOUNCEMENT OF SUFFERINGS
MATT	17:14-21	262-263	83	THREE CASES OF OVERCOMING UNBELIEF
MATT	17:22-23	264	84	THE 3RD ANNOUNCEMENT OF SUFFERINGS
MATT	17:24-27	264-265	85	MONEY FOR THE TAXES
MATT	18:1-5	265	86	WHO SHALL BE THE GREATEST?
MATT	18:6-14	266-267	88	AVOID OFFENSES
MATT	18:15-35	267-268	89	LOVE ENOUGH TO SEEK RECONCILIATION
MATT	19:1 *to* 3rd,	269	90	TREACHEROUS ADVICE REJECTED
MATT	19:1-2 2nd *and*	271-272	95	ARRIVAL IN THE REGION OF JUDÆA

MATT	28:16-20	384-385	179	FINAL INSTRUCTIONS, THE RETURN TO GLORY AND THE FIRST FRUITS

7.2 - VERSE LOCATOR FOR THE GOSPEL ACCORDING TO MARK

7.3 - VERSE LOCATOR FOR THE GOSPEL ACCORDING TO LUKE

LUKE	4:1-30	192-193	21	TEMPTATION – REJECTION – VICTORY - DOMINION
LUKE	4:31-37, 38-39	205-206	30	MORE HEALING IN CAPERNAUM
LUKE	4:40-41	206	30	MORE HEALING IN CAPERNAUM
LUKE	4:42-44	206-207	31	PRAYER & PREACHING
LUKE	5:1-11	207	32	THE FIRST GREAT CATCH OF FISHES
LUKE	5:12-16	208	33	BETRAYED BY A LEPER
LUKE	5:17-26	210	36	A MAN IN CAPERNAUM IS HEALED OF THE PALSY
LUKE	5:27-28	211	37	THE CALLING OF MATTHEW (LEVI)
LUKE	5:29-32	211	38	JESUS DECLARES THE PURPOSE OF HIS MISSION
LUKE	5:33-39	212	39	NO MIXING ALLOWED
LUKE	6:1-5	220	45	DISPUTES CONCERNING THE SABBATH
LUKE	6:6-11	221	46	IT IS LAWFUL TO HEAL ON THE SABBATH DAYS!
LUKE	6:12-19	222-223	48	MORE PREPARATION TO PREAH AND HEAL
LUKE	6:20-49	223-224	49	THE SERMON ON THE PLAIN
LUKE	7:1-10	224-225	50	THE CENTURION'S SERVANT HEALED
LUKE	7:11-18	225	51	A WIDOW'S SON IS RAISED TO LIFE
LUKE	7:19-28	225-226	52	JESUS TESTIFIES CONCERNING JOHN THE BAPTIST
LUKE	7:29-35	225	53	PHARISEES REBUKED FOR REJECTING JOHN AND JESUS
LUKE	7:36-50	226-227	54	A LESSON IN LOVE
LUKE	8:1-18	227-228	55	SOME QUALITIES NEEDED TO BE A SUCCESSFUL DISCIPLE
LUKE	8:19-21	231	58	GOD'S FAMILY ARE THOSE WHO DO HIS WILL
LUKE	8:22-25	237	61	A TEMPEST IS STILLED
LUKE	8:26-39	237-238	62	HEALING THE DEMONIAC IN GADARA
LUKE	8:40-56	239-240	63	BACK IN CAPERNAUM AND MORE HEALING
LUKE	9:1-6	242	65	THE APOSTLES ARE SENT AGAIN TO PREACH AND TO HEAL
LUKE	9:7-9	243	66	ACCOUNTS OF JOHN THE BAPTISTS BEHEADING
LUKE	9:10-17	245	67	THE LOAVES AND FISHES MULTIPLIED (1ST OCCASION)
LUKE	9:18-21	258-259	78	PETER REALIZATION THAT JESUS IS THE CHRIST
LUKE	9:22-26	259	79	THE 1ST ANNOUNCEMENT OF SUFFERINGS
LUKE	9:27	260	80	A PROPHECY CONCERNING THE KINGDOM OF GOD
LUKE	9:28-36	260-261	81	TRANSFIGURATION – THE FIRST RESURRECTION
LUKE	9:37-42	264	83	THREE CASES OF OVERCOMING UNBELIEF
LUKE	9:43-45	264	84	THE 3RD ANNOUNCEMENT OF SUFFERINGS
LUKE	9:46-48	265-266	85	WHO SHALL BE THE GREATEST?
LUKE	9:49-50	266	86	EXCLUSIVENESS AND ENVY MUST BE UNSELFED
LUKE	9:42-50	266	88	AVOID OFFENSES
LUKE	9:51-56	269	91	FROM GALILEE THROUGH SAMARIA TOWARD JUDÆA
LUKE	9:57-62	269	92	EXCUSES – EXCUSES - EXCUSES
LUKE	10:1-24	269-271	93	SEVENTY MORE DISCIPLES APPOINTED
LUKE	10:25-37	271	94	ETERNAL LIFE IS NOT FOR SALE
LUKE	10:38-42	272	96	THE ONE THING NEEDFUL
LUKE	11:1-13	280-281	102	MORE INSTRUCTION ON PRAYER
LUKE	11:14-28	281282	103	CHRIST- HEALING OPPOSED TO DEMONOLOGY
LUKE	11:29-36	283-284	105	THE "EVIL GENERATION" CONFRONTED
LUKE	11:37-54	284-285	106	AN UNPLEASANT DINNER IN THE HOME OF A PHARISEE
LUKE	12:1-59	285-288	107	WARNINGS
LUKE	13:1-22	288-289	108	TOTAL REPENTANCE REQUIRED
LUKE	13:23-30	290-291	110	TEACHING IN RETREAT BEYOND JORDAN
LUKE	13:31-35	291	111	JESUS REPLIES TO WARNINGS THAT HEROD SEEKS TO KILL HIM
LUKE	14:1-24	291-293	112	DINING WITH A CHIEF PHARISEE
LUKE	14:25-35	293	113	THE COST OF DISCIPLESHIP
LUKE	15:1-32	293-295	114	SALVATION COMES THROUGH GRACE NOT PRIVILEGE
LUKE	16:1-13	295-296	115	INTEGRITY AND THE FIRST COMMANDMENT
LUKE	16:14-31	296-297	116	COVETOUSNESS REBUKED
LUKE	17:1-10	297-298	117	DOING "THAT WHICH IS OUR DUTY TO DO"
LUKE	17:11-19	298	118	"BUT WHERE ARE THE NINE?"
LUKE	17:20-21	298-299	119	WHEN THE KINGDOM OF GOD WILL COME
LUKE	17:22-37	299-300	120	END OF THE WORLD ORDER
LUKE	18:1-14	300	121	EVEN MORE INSTRUCTION ON PRAYER
LUKE	18:15-17	303	124	TWO REQUIREMENTS TO ENTER THE KINGDOM
LUKE	18:18-27	304-305	124	TWO REQUIREMENTS TO ENTER THE KINGDOM
LUKE	18:28-30	306	125	WHAT'S IN IT FOR ME?
LUKE	18:31-34	307-308	126	THE 5TH ANNOUNCEMENT OF SUFFERINGS
LUKE	18:35-43	309	129	APPROACHING JERICHO "A CERTAIN BLIND MAN" IS HEALED
LUKE	19:1-10	309-310	130	JESUS AND ZACCHÆUS
LUKE	19:11-28	311	132	THE BRUTALITY OF WORLDLY RULERSHIP

LUKE	19:29-44	314-315	136	THE SECOND OR TRIUMPHAL ENTRY INTO JERUSALEM
LUKE	19:45-46	316	138	THE THIRD TEMPLE CLEANSING
LUKE	19:47 *to* 1st.	316	139	PREACHING IN THE TEMPLE GROUNDS
LUKE	19:47-48 *But*	318	139	PREACHING IN THE TEMPLE GROUNDS
LUKE	20:1-8	319-320	141	DISPUTING WITH THE PRIESTS, SCRIBES, AND ELDERS
LUKE	20:9-18	320-321	141	DISPUTING WITH THE PRIESTS, SCRIBES, AND ELDERS
LUKE	20:19	321	141	DISPUTING WITH THE PRIESTS, SCRIBES, AND ELDERS
LUKE	20:20-26	323	143	FAILED ATTEMPTS TO ENTRAP JESUS
LUKE	20:27-38	324-325	143	FAILED ATTEMPTS TO ENTRAP JESUS
LUKE	20:39-40	326	143	FAILED ATTEMPTS TO ENTRAP JESUS
LUKE	20:41-44	326-327	144	THE DIVINITY OF THE CHRIST
LUKE	20:45-47	327	145	BEWARE OF THE SCRIBES
LUKE	21:1-4	327	146	A CERTAIN POOR WIDOW A PROPHECY
LUKE	21:5-38	329-331	148	THE FIRST PORTION OF JESUS' PROPHECY
LUKE	22:1-2	337	152	PLOTTING TO KILL JESUS WITHOUT CREATING AN UPROAR
LUKE	22:3-6	339	154	JUDAS ARRANGES THE BETRAYAL OF JESUS
LUKE	22:7-13	339-340	155	PREPARATION FOR THE LAST SUPPER
LUKE	22:14	340	156	SUPPER – FOOT WASHING – THE NEW TESTAMENT
LUKE	22:15-19	340	156	SUPPER – FOOT WASHING – THE NEW TESTAMENT
LUKE	22:20-23	342	156	SUPPER – FOOT WASHING – THE NEW TESTAMENT
LUKE	22:24-34	343-344	156	SUPPER – FOOT WASHING – THE NEW TESTAMENT
LUKE	22:35-38	344	157	REVISED INSTRUCTIONS FOR CHANGED CONDITIONS
LUKE	22:39-46	351-352	163	IN THE GARDEN
LUKE	22:47-50	354	164	THE BETRAYAL AND ARREST
LUKE	22:51, 52-53	355	164	THE BETRAYAL AND ARREST
LUKE	22:54	356	165	ECCLESIASTICAL TRIALS & PETER'S DENIALS
LUKE	22:55	357	165	ECCLESIASTICAL TRIALS & PETER'S DENIALS
LUKE	22:56-57	358	165	ECCLESIASTICAL TRIALS & PETER'S DENIALS
LUKE	22:58, 59-60	359	165	ECCLESIASTICAL TRIALS & PETER'S DENIALS
LUKE	22:60-71	360	165	ECCLESIASTICAL TRIALS & PETER'S DENIALS
LUKE	23:1	360	165	ECCLESIASTICAL TRIALS & PETER'S DENIALS
LUKE	23:2	361	167	THE TRIAL BEFORE PILATE BEGINS
LUKE	23:3,4	362	167	THE TRIAL BEFORE PILATE BEGINS
LUKE	23:5	363	167	THE TRIAL BEFORE PILATE BEGINS
LUKE	23:6-12	363	168	THE MOCK TRIAL BEFORE HEROD
LUKE	23:13-15, 16-17	363-364	169	THE TRIAL BEFORE PILATE RESUMES
LUKE	23:18-23	365	169	THE TRIAL BEFORE PILATE RESUMES
LUKE	23:24-25	365-366	170	SENTENCING
LUKE	23:26-28	368	172	THE WALK TO GOLGOTHA
LUKE	23:29-32	369	172	THE WALK TO GOLGOTHA
LUKE	23:33-34	369	173	THE CRUCIFIXION
LUKE	23:35-38	370	173	THE CRUCIFIXION
LUKE	23:39-43	371	173	THE CRUCIFIXION
LUKE	23:44-45, 46	372	173	THE CRUCIFIXION
LUKE	23:47-48	373	174	EVENTS IMMEDIATELY FOLLOWING
LUKE	23:49, 50-56	374-375	174	EVENTS IMMEDIATELY FOLLOWING
LUKE	24:1, 2	376	176	RESURRECTION DAY
LUKE	24:3-4	377	176	RESURRECTION DAY
LUKE	24:5-8	378	176	RESURRECTION DAY
LUKE	24:9-12, 13	379	176	RESURRECTION DAY
LUKE	24:14-34	380	176	RESURRECTION DAY
LUKE	24:235	381	176	RESURRECTION DAY
LUKE	34:36-49	381-382	176	RESURRECTION DAY
LUKE	34:50-51, 52-53	385	179	FINAL INSTRUCTIONS, THE RETURN TO GLORY AND THE FIRST FRUITS

7.4 - VERSE LOCATOR FOR THE GOSPEL ACCORDING TO JOHN

Book	Chapter: Verse(s)	Page No.	Chapter No.	Chapter Title
JOHN	1:1-5	175	1	THE ETERNAL ORDER OF BEING
JOHN	1:6-13	175	3	THE MISSION OF JOHN THE BAPTIST
JOHN	1:14	177	5	MARY CONCEIVES CHRIST JESUS
JOHN	1:15-28	186-187	15	THE BAPTISM OF JESUS THE CHRIST
JOHN	1:29-51	188-189	17	THE FIRST SIX DISCIPLES
JOHN	2:1-12	189-190	18	WATER INTO WINE
JOHN	2:13-25	190-191	19	THE FIRST TEMPLE CLEANSING

JOHN	3:1-21	191-192	20	THE NEED FOR SPIRITUAL REBIRTH
JOHN	3:22-36	194-195	22	QUESTIONS ABOUT BAPTISM
JOHN	4:1-4	195	22	QUESTIONS ABOUT BAPTISM
JOHN	4:5-44	195-197	23	TRUE WORSHIP OF THE TRUE GOD
JOHN	4:45-54	198	25	JESUS DEPARTS NAZARETH TO DWELL IN CAPERNAUM
JOHN	5:1-47	217-219	44	PARALYSIS HEALED AT THE POOL OF BETHESADA
JOHN	6:1-13	246	67	THE LOAVES AND FISHES MULTIPLIED (1ST OCCASION)
JOHN	6:14-15	246-247	68	JESUS ESCAPES BEING MADE A KING
JOHN	6:16-21	247	69	LAWS OF NATURE AND PHYSICS NULLIFIED
JOHN	6:22-71	249-251	71	SPIRITUAL TEACHING REJECTED BY MANY
JOHN	7:1-10	268-269	90	TREACHEROUS ADVICE REJECTED
JOHN	7:11-53	272-274	97	JESUS AT THE FEAST OF TABERNACLES
JOHN	8:1	274	97	JESUS AT THE FEAST OF TABERNACLES
JOHN	8:2-11	274-275	98	A CRUEL AND HEARTLESS STRATEGY TO ENTRAP JESUS
JOHN	8:12-30	275-276	99	THE LIGHT OF THE WORLD
JOHN	8:31-59	276-277	100	JESUS CONFUTES THE HOSTILE DISCIPLES AT JERUSALEM
JOHN	9:1-41	277-279	101	HEALING A MAN BORN BLIND
JOHN	10:1-21	279-280	101	HEALING A MAN BORN BLIND
JOHN	10:22-39	289-290	109	IN JERUSALEM AT THE FEAST OF DEDICATION
JOHN	10:40-42	290	110	TEACHING IN RETREAT BEYOND JORDAN
JOHN	11:1-44	300-302	122	THE RESURRECTION OF LAZARUS
JOHN	11:45-54	303	123	OPPOSING REACTIONS TO RAISING LAZARUS
JOHN	11:55-57	311-312	132	THE BRUTALITY OF WORLDLY RULERSHIP
JOHN	12:1	313	134	THE SECOND TEMPLE CLEANSING
JOHN	12:2-11	313	135	THE SECOND ANOINTING
JOHN	12:12-19	314	136	THE SECOND OR TRIUMPHAL ENTRY INTO JERUSALEM
JOHN	12:20-50	316-318	139	PREACHING IN THE TEMPLE GROUNDS
JOHN	13:1	340	156	SUPPER – FOOT WASHING – THE NEW TESTAMENT
JOHN	13:1-18	341	156	SUPPER – FOOT WASHING – THE NEW TESTAMENT
JOHN	13:19-22	341-342	156	SUPPER – FOOT WASHING – THE NEW TESTAMENT
JOHN	13:23-30	342	156	SUPPER – FOOT WASHING – THE NEW TESTAMENT
JOHN	13:31-38	343	156	SUPPER – FOOT WASHING – THE NEW TESTAMENT
JOHN	14:1-31	344-346	158	DISCOURSE ON THE COMFORTER
JOHN	15:1-27	346-347	159	DISCOURSE ON DEMONSTRATION
JOHN	16:1-33	348-349	160	THE LAST HOUR REMINDER: TAKE CARE NOT TO DESERT
JOHN	17:1-26	349-351	161	THE FAREWELL DISCOURSE
JOHN	18:1	351	162	DEPARTURE TO THE MOUNT OF OLIVES
JOHN	18:2-3	353	164	THE BETRAYAL AND ARREST
JOHN	18:4-9	354	164	THE BETRAYAL AND ARREST
JOHN	18:10-11	355	164	THE BETRAYAL AND ARREST
JOHN	18:12	356	164	THE BETRAYAL AND ARREST
JOHN	18:13-24	356	165	ECCLESIASTICAL TRIALS & PETER'S DENIALS
JOHN	18:25-27	359	165	ECCLESIASTICAL TRIALS & PETER'S DENIALS
JOHN	18:28-30	361	167	THE TRIAL BEFORE PILATE BEGINS
JOHN	18:31-32, 33-38	362-363	167	THE TRIAL BEFORE PILATE BEGINS
JOHN	18:39 *to* :	364	169	THE TRIAL BEFORE PILATE RESUMES
JOHN	18:39-40 *will*	365	169	THE TRIAL BEFORE PILATE RESUMES
JOHN	19:1	366	170	SENTENCING
JOHN	19:2-15, 16	366-368	171	MALTREATMENT AFTER SENTENCING
JOHN	19:17-22	368	172	THE WALK TO GOLGOTHA
JOHN	19:23-24	369	173	THE CRUCIFIXION
JOHN	19:25-27	371	173	THE CRUCIFIXION
JOHN	19:28-29, 30	372	173	THE CRUCIFIXION
JOHN	19:31-37	373-374	174	EVENTS IMMEDIATELY FOLLOWING
JOHN	19:38-42	375	174	EVENTS IMMEDIATELY FOLLOWING
JOHN	20:1-10	376-377	176	RESURRECTION DAY
JOHN	20:11-17	377-378	176	RESURRECTION DAY
JOHN	20:18	379	176	RESURRECTION DAY
JOHN	20:19-25	381	176	RESURRECTION DAY
JOHN	20:26-29, 30-31	382	177	DAYS OF PREPARATION
JOHN	21:1-24	383-384	178	THE MORNING MEAL
JOHN	21:25	385	179	FINAL INSTRUCTIONS, THE RETURN TO GLORY AND THE FIRST FRUITS

APPENDIX 8
QUOTATIONS TO PONDER

1 Jesus said, "Whoever finds the interpretation of these sayings will not experience death."
2 Jesus said, "Let him who seeks continue seeking until he finds. When he finds, he will become troubled. When he becomes troubled, he will be astonished, and he will rule over all."
15 Jesus said, "When you see someone who was not born of woman, prostrate ourselves on your faces and worship him. That one is your father." - The Coptic Gospel of Thomas

"What is matter? Will it last forever?"

The Teacher answered: "All that is born, all that is created, all the elements of the world are interwoven and united with each other. all that is composed shall be decomposed; *everything returns to its roots; matter returns to the origins of matter. Those who have ears, let them hear."*

"*Attachment to matter gives rise to passion against nature. Thus trouble arises in the whole body this is why I tell you: 'Be in harmony . . . '*

If you are out of balance, take inspiration from manifestations of your true nature. Those who have ears, Let them hear." The Gospel of Mary Magdalene. - Page 7:1-10 & Page 8:1-10.

There is no life, truth, intelligence, nor substance in matter. All is infinite Mind and its infinite manifestation, for God is All-in-all. Spirit is immortal Truth; matter is mortal error. Spirit is the real and eternal; matter is the unreal and temporal. Spirit is God, and man is his image and likeness. Therefore man is not material; he is spiritual. - Mary Baker Eddy – S&H 468:9-15.

"'I left the world with the aid of another world; a design was erased by virtue of a higher design. Henceforth I travel toward Repose, where time rests in Eternity of Time; I go now into Silence.'" Having said all this, Mary became silent, for it was in silence that the Teacher spoke to her.

Then Andrew began to speak, and said to his brothers: "Tell me, what do you think of these things she has been telling us? As for me, I do not believe that the Teacher would speak like this. These ideas are too different from those we have known"

And Peter added: "How is it possible that the Teacher talked in this manner with a woman about secrets of which we ourselves are ignorant? Must we change our customs, and listen to this woman? Did he really choose her, and prefer her to us?" The Gospel of Mary Magdalene. - Page 17:1-20.

Why should Andrew and Peter ask such questions when it is recorded that Jesus plainly told them:

"These things have I spoken unto you, that ye should not be offended (desert or fall away). But now I go my way to him that sent me; I have yet many things to say unto you, but ye cannot bear them now. Howbeit, when he, the Spirit of truth, is come, he will guide you into all truth: for he shall not speak of himself; but whatsoever he shall hear, *that* shall he speak: and he will show you things to come." - John 16:1, 5 (*to* ;), 12 & 13.